D0549102

Behavioral Decisions in Organizations

SECOND EDITION

About the Author

Alvar Elbing holds a Ph.D. from the University of Washington (Seattle) and an M.S. from the State University of California, Sacramento. He has taught organizational behavior and management at the State University of New York at Albany, and at the Amos Tuck School of Dartmouth College.

Currently, Dr. Elbing is active as a teacher and as a consultant for such multinational companies as Shell International, ITT Europe, and Nestle Alimentana. He is Director, The Executive and Environment Center, Chamby, Switzerland; Visiting Professor at IMEDE, Management Development Institute, as well as the University of Lausanne; and Professor-Consultant, Elbing and Elbing, Consultants, also in Lausanne.

Behavioral Decisions in Organizations

SECOND EDITION

Alvar Elbing

Scott, Foresman and Company Glenview, Ill.
Dallas, Tex. Oakland, N.J. Palo Alto, Cal. Tucker, Ga. London, England

Library of Congress Cataloging in Publication Data

Elbing, Alvar O.
Behavioral decisions in organizations.

Includes bibliographies and index.
1. Decision-making. 2. Organizational behavior.
I. Title.
HD30.23.E4 1978 658.4 77–26732
ISBN 0–673–15025–9

12345678910–RRC–86858483828180797877

Preface

Since 1970, I have worked with large international firms and with managers from every part of the world. Perhaps more than anything else, the revision of this book reflects that fact. During these years, I have taught and consulted with executives as well as with graduate and undergraduate students of business. In the classrooms at my own Executive and Environment Center, at IMEDE (an international management institute), and at the University of Lausanne in Switzerland, there have been as many as 23 nationalities represented at one time. Sometimes case discussions were carried out through simultaneous translation. This experience, following ten years of management development and university teaching in the United States, has altered my feeling about how Organizational Behavior should be taught in North America and in other parts of the world.

Perhaps the major influence on that changed view comes from an awareness of the changing balance of world population, and, therefore, of world markets. The United States is no longer the economic island it was able to be in the past. As the population grows in the developing areas, the population of the United States will continue to decline as a percentage of the world total. It will, therefore, be increasingly necessary for American business and American managers to be multinational.

To add to the internationalizing effect, the current world monetary exchange rates have made the United States attractive for foreign investment. Therefore, both at home and abroad it will be increasingly important for people in business to be sensitive to and able to deal with different cultures, with their different assumptions, traditions, and values. Since the United States has always had such a large internal market, dealing with differing views has not been necessary in the past. In the future, however, there will be no way, for many large firms, to avoid world involvement.

It is in this area of sensitivity to social and cultural *differences* that I see the biggest contrasts between European and American managers. Europeans have grown up among such differences. They have, therefore, learned to take into consideration in a decision-making situation a great variety of social and cultural variables. These variables will be more and more important to business.

I believe that it is essential in an Organizational Behavior course, therefore, to include material, not only from different functions and industries, but also from a variety of different geographical and cultural settings. This book provides for this broader outlook. Included are new cases set in many countries, e.g., Switzerland, England, France, Germany, the Netherlands, Sweden, and Argentina. There is a new chapter on the environment with a survey of attitudes which can expand the student's perspective. Throughout the text, there are international as well as American examples, plus several articles representing international developments. The content of the book should provide a framework for beginning to develop a more international sensitivity, and help to prepare the student for what is bound to be a more international future.

The book attempts to meet the needs of both university business students and managers engaged in management development. The material, which is drawn from practical work with real firms, is useful in actual business situations. It has been extensively tested with line, operating managers who have affirmed its usefulness.

The foundation of this practical relevance lies in the book's emphasis on three managerial tools: knowledge, experience, and structure. It is the manager's use of all three of these tools that makes for effectiveness on the job. The major tool any manager has is his or her *experience*. For experience to be meaningful, however, it must be balanced with knowledge and structure. Unfortunately, these last two are often confused. Knowledge is content, while structure is form or framework. Since all thinking takes place through some structure or model, it is important for the students and managers to look at their own present structures and models, as well as to learn new and more effective ones. New and more effective structures and models can help them understand present and future experiences. Knowledge can also be useful, but it must apply to the decision-making situation specifically in question. Without a clear model or structure, we do not know how to apply knowledge to our experience.

The primary emphasis in this book, therefore, is broadening our experience (through Cases) and systematizing our structure (through Models). The knowledge portion (Chapters and Readings) is set in this pragmatic structural framework.

The organization of the book is around two basic systematic models: the Decision-Making model and the Levels of Analysis model. The first is a framework for the various stages of the decision-making process. The second reflects the necessity to separate, for purposes of analysis, the different social realms which influence individual managers, and on which they, in turn, exert such dynamic influence.

Part I of the book, "Human Behavior in Organizations," sets the broad framework for looking at the subject. The title of Chapter 1, "All Problems Are Human Problems," is designed to set the basic theme. Although a play on words, the title reflects the fact that there are no "problems" in an absolute sense. There are only problems defined by someone from some vantage point. There are, therefore, no problems except for "human" ones. If our goal is to define problems or to understand how others have defined them, we must understand the processes through which the decision making took place. It is for this reason that the focus of the book is on decision making and the decision-making model. Chapter 2 provides a brief look at the environment from which the decision makers take their data for this decision-making process. Here again the recognition is that since the data units in the environment are infinite and miscellaneous, an understanding of the manager's perceptions must precede the actual decision-making process.

Part II looks systematically at the decision-making process. Following each of its five chapters, each of which focuses on a decision-making step, are three or four cases selected to be used in understanding that particular step. It should be noted that all of the cases can be used for broader analysis as well, but their location suggests a useful discussion starting point. In Part II half of the cases are new additions to the book.

Part III provides tools for behavioral diagnosis. Included in this section are chapters and readings on the various "levels of analysis" of human behavior. If you begin with the recognition that it is always the individual who acts, who behaves, the fundamental question becomes, "What social and psychological forces influence behavior?" In Part III, therefore, the attempt is to understand these various levels of influence. Perhaps the biggest difficulty in so doing rests on the fact that at any particular moment all the "levels" are operating on the individual, but for the purposes of understanding we have to look at them one at a time. It is important, therefore, if we are looking at group behavior, for example, that we recognize that the individual is at the same time being influenced by the other "levels."

In general the readings in Part III are those readings from the first edition which proved to be most useful to most of the book's users. They are organized around the various levels of analysis as an extension of the ideas in the chapters which were written for this edition. The eight cases here are also organized so that they lend themselves to analysis through the chapter concepts.

Finally, Part IV offers four chapters and six readings designed to raise various issues of importance to management. This material is not intended to be definitive but to be provocative. A variety of issues facing managers relate to *how* they manage. Some of these are at the same time exciting and challenging. The idea of a "flexible organization," for example, is not a simple one for all business to accept. At the same time developments in Europe have shown that such organizations can meet some of the expectations of the changing environment as well as of the companies. It is useful to contemplate such developments.

In total, this book is attempting to create for its readers and users an experience which will help them to better understand their own managerial experiences and to provide a structure for looking systematically at them. The book has been designed to start one thinking and discussing, not to be the definitive work on the subject. It is my hope that it will provide for a great variety of exciting adventures in the area of managerial decision making.

I would like to repeat here my thanks to many people from whom I received a great deal of assistance in preparing the first edition. A deep debt goes to John W. Hennessey, Jr., formerly Dean of The Amos Tuck School of Business Administration at Dartmouth College, and to Robert H. Guest, Professor of Organizational Behavior at The Tuck School, who for five years were my colleagues in the area of organizational behavior. The numerous insights acquired while working with them must be recognized as underlying many of the points in this book. I am also indebted to Dean Hennessey for so freely granting permission for the use of cases.

I also wish to acknowledge the help and support of Professor Albert Mossin, Chairman of the Department of Management, State University of New York at Albany, and of my colleagues in that department. Together they created an environment in which it was possible to pursue such a project to its completion.

Two other people must be recognized for the influence they have had on this volume. Professor Theodore Barnowe of the University of Washington got me started in this area both as a student of his and as a teaching colleague. Earlier, Professor Frederick Seubert, now at the University of Oregon, was of considerable influence on my thinking while I studied under him at the University of California at Berkeley. I gratefully acknowledge the influence of these men.

Also for the use of cases, I wish to thank Professors Ben Lindberg, C. B. Richards, H. F. Dobyns, Alexander Bergmann, and Harry Knudson. I also wish to thank Andrew R. Towl, Director of Case Development, and John A. Seiler, Paul Lawrence, Harold Craig, John D. Glover, Frederick V. Fortmiller, and Richard L. Balch, now or previously associated with the Harvard University Graduate School of Business Administration, for their cooperation and permission to use copyright cases.

May I also add my thanks to IMEDE for the use of so many of its cases and for the time and resources to have written many of them. I wish also to thank the numerous faculty and research associates at IMEDE during my seven years there who have been so stimulating in their interaction.

It is only fitting that the primary acknowledgement go to my "colleague" of the past 28 years, and now my partner in business, my wife Carol, who regards methods for solving human problems as the crucial issue of our children's generation. It is to her that this book is dedicated.

Although I benefited greatly from all this help, I of course absolve all these friends and colleagues of any responsibility for the final contents. That must be mine.

The Executive and Environmental Center — Alvar Elbing
Mount Cubly
1832 Chamby
Switzerland

Contents

Behavioral Decisions in Organizations

SECOND EDITION

PART ONE

Human Behavior in Organizations

Chapter

1 All Problems Are Human Problems

As humans prepare to commute to the outer planets, to convert sunshine into usable energy, to measure continental drift in inches per year, and to farm the seas, it would seem that we know a great deal about decision making. The number of individual decisions necessary to make a space probe, for example, can be estimated in the billions, most of which must necessarily have been correct decisions or the space vehicle would not have accomplished its mission. Measured by their intended results, however, not all decisions currently being made in our society are "correct" ones. The decision-making know-how which conquered space has not directly transferred to decision making in the human area of behavior.

Solving the problems of human beings is quite different from solving the problems of things. The nature of the difference between these two kinds of decision situations, and the basis of the problem of transferring guidelines from one to the other, is pointed up in the following analogy:

> If the foot of a walking man hits a pebble, energy is transferred from the foot to the stone; the latter will be displaced and will eventually come to rest again in a position which is fully determined by such factors as the amount of energy transferred, the shape and weight of the pebble, and the nature of the surface on which it rolls. If, on the other hand, the man kicks a dog instead of the pebble, the dog may jump up and bite him. In this case, the relation between the kick and the bite is of a very different order. It is obvious that the dog takes the energy for his reaction from his own metabolism and not from the kick. What is transferred, therefore, is no longer energy, but rather information (Watzlawick, *et al.*, 1967, p. 29).

The dynamics of human-to-animal action and reaction—cause and effect—are not the same as the dynamics of mass and density, speed and time. And when man "kicks" *man*, the variables become even more complex. Since man has the power to delay his reaction, he may "bite" you in two weeks, rather than now.

The purpose of this book is to pursue the peculiarities of decision making in the realm of human behavior, not only in the one-to-one situation or the small group, but also in the total social system of the large organization. It undertakes the systematic study of decision making on specifically human problems, from the vantage point of the manager who has a unique responsibility for the results of that behavior.

To those individuals coming from technical studies where problems of human behavior are not directly involved, there must be a major adjustment to human variables. For in organizations, which are inescapably social systems as well as technical systems, every technical plan, however sophisticated and rational it may be, is dependent on the human social system of the organization to carry it out. The specialist who tries to maneuver people in a social system the way he maneuvers nonhuman things—balls or ballbearings—can indeed botch up productivity. Even the productivity of the technology can be botched up since it does not function without human processes.

If a manager has focused attention on technical results—such as productivity and profits—and has been allowed to ignore the human factors in the organization, he or she may come to the study of human behavior in organizations with the attitude that it is an *obstacle* in marching toward technical goals. But this study is not intended to add obstacles. On the contrary, its purpose is to develop skills that prevent the human problems which are the obstacles to productivity.

STANDARDS OF METHOD IN THE STUDY OF BEHAVIOR AND ITS MANAGEMENT

Before going directly to a step-by-step analysis of the decision-making process, let us consider the basic question of method. This question needs clarification, particularly for persons coming from three orientations: (1) those who may have advanced technical backgrounds in some areas but little or no background in the human factors of management; (2) those who are already experienced managers but have not approached the management of people as a systematic discipline; and (3) those who, while having knowledge in the behavioral sciences, have approached human behavior in terms of research and model building rather than as a management-action concept.

Connotations of the Scientific Method

To persons coming from technical fields, and even to a majority of laymen, the concept of method tends to be synonymous with the concept of "scientific method." It connotes mathematical terminology or the methods of the physical sciences, or both. It suggests images of certain tools—laboratories, test tubes, computers, and so on. It suggests images of things or activities which can be quantified, measured, counted, charted, graphed, or weighed. Managers for whom *scientific method* carries such connotations usually react in one of two ways when faced with the questions of method in relation to the human problems of an organization.

On the one hand, such managers may wrench particular techniques or tools from mathematics or the physical sciences and try to apply them to human problems—even where they do not fit. To get around the resulting impasse, the problem may then be changed to make it fit the borrowed tools and techniques. Certain aspects of the problem may even be ignored because they do not fit the borrowed methods. One widely quoted "scientific" study of managerial work behavior took random samples of decision-making behavior between 8 and 5 o'clock as a basis for drawing conclusions on how decisions are made. The study failed to consider the non-observable hours of evening since such observation was not possible. Therefore, evening decisions were designed out of the study.

Other managers use the *criteria* of mathematics and the physical sciences to declare that human problems are not amenable to rigorous method at all, and conclude that everything in the human realm is hunch and guesswork. Depending on the manager's temperament, it may even be decided that human management requires a mystical talent, or it may be dismissed as an imprecise and inferior endeavor, in terms of a particular concept of scientific method. In this case, a manager may rely totally on past experience, which may not be relevant in the given situation.

The above approaches to human management are built into a concept of "method" that primarily encompasses the techniques and tools of the physical sciences and mathematics. But we should recognize that the essential criteria of rigorous method in the realm of human behavior do *not* necessarily involve procedures, techniques, and tools designed for the physical sciences or mathematics. Rather, the essential criterion of method is that it constitute *that method most appropriate to the nature of the given problem which best withstands the tests of critical appraisal.*

The Concept of Critical Method as a Standard

In this book the term *critical method* is used for the study of human behavior rather than *scientific method.* Since the connotations of the term *scientific method* involve concepts of quantified data and the hardware of laboratories or computers, "critical method" may be a more useful concept of a standard for the analysis and management of human behavior. Whichever term is chosen, however, training in decision making and in the management of human behavior will be meaningless unless one adheres to the most rigorous standard of method. The results of lax standards of method are no less dire in the field of analyzing and managing human behavior than they are in any other field. Therefore, the insistence on a standard of critical method, although it recognizes that not all human problems are amenable to the techniques of the physical sciences and mathematics, forestalls the conclusion that in the management of human behavior there are no objective criteria for method at all, and that any method is as good as any other.

The Specifications for Critical Method

Throughout training in the analysis and management of human behavior, one should continuously measure one's own methods against the basic criteria of critical method, which include the following minimum specifications:

1. Critical method begins with a *bona fide question*. Its point of beginning is not a fixed answer or solution, but a proposition or hypothesis which carries with it a burden of proof. In the emotion-filled realm of human problems, there is a tendency to jump to conclusions and to start with solutions. Such a process, whether it is labeled "intuition," "common sense," "statement of authority," "tradition," "human nature," or whatever, is no part of critical or scientific method. No method is a "critical method" that does not start with a question open to inquiry and investigation.
2. The end point of critical method (or scientific method) is not a fixed, absolute answer. Nothing is handed down as final dogma or declared to be above criticism. Answers are always subject to restatement as hypotheses for further investigation. An answer is acceptable only so long as no alternative answer can be offered that is supported by a stronger case.
3. Critical method is that method which best stands up under the tests of evidence, reasoning, investigation, criticism, and assessment. This means that the method is specified in words (or some other explicit form) and presented so that the method itself is readily amenable to question, replication, testing, investigation, and final assessment.
4. In a field where critical method prevails, opposing opinions on the same questions are not considered a matter of tolerance. Rather, disagreements are considered matters for investigation. The method itself provides a basis for critical choice among competing answers. To resolve a disagreement, that answer is considered preferable which, at the given time, best stands up under the severest tests of objective criticism.
5. Critical method distinguishes between symbols used for data and the data itself, and does not make generalizations or conclusions beyond those warranted by the data.

It may be noted that the above criteria fit the "scientific method" of the physical sciences, as well as any other critical method deserving the name. Critical methods, like scientific methods, are not methods which provide absolute or final answers, but merely those methods which at a given time and for a given problem best withstand the severest independent tests and severest rational criticism available (Elbing and Elbing, 1967, Ch. 12).

Critical Method and Mathematical Terminology

The use of mathematical symbols has come to be seen as the *sine qua non* of scientific methodology. The substitution of such a symbol for a relatively constant item allows for analysis more sophisticated than the subjective analysis of words. Let us be clear. The use of mathematical terminology is not to be equated with scientific or critical method *automatically*. A method may be fully stated in mathematical terminology throughout and not pass the above tests of critical method. A problem statement, a statement of method, or a statement of conclusion can be expressed in mathematical terminology and still be inadequate for the totality of the problem, or be incorrect, or be an inferior alternative among those available, or even be irrelevant to the problem. Consider, for example, a simple mathematical expression of a basic relationship:

$$2 + 2 = 4$$

This is probably the first quantitative relationship a child learns, and is seldom questioned. But what do we have when we add two cups of water to two cups of sugar? This question may also be relevant when we "add together" the behavior of two employees and two other employees. Of what do we have four? Obviously, the application of mathematical terminology is not the crucial test of critical method.

As stated earlier, one essential characteristic of critical method is its presentation in specific language so that it is amenable to criticism. In theory, of course, the most precise language is mathematical language. And in theory, it would be possible to reduce most decision situations to mathematical terminology. However, the ultimate issue of precision for the decision maker involves factors other than the precision of language alone. In fact, in the dynamics of organizational behavior, no method in whatever language is ultimately precise which is too inefficient to be workable in the problem situation for which it is designed. If the problem has changed by the time it can be symbolized in the chosen language, it can hardly be considered precise.

The superiority of mathematical terminology as ultimately more efficient, more precise, and more critical in the area of human problems has yet to be demonstrated. This book begins with the arbitrary judgment that reducing the discussion here to mathematical terminology would *not* increase the efficiency of the critical method. Obviously, there are many points in a given decision-making process where information expressed in mathematical terms might be very useful to the decision maker in a human situation, and where mathematical procedures might be usefully brought in. However, in the present state of our understanding, attempting to reduce the total decision-making process to mathematical language might consume more time in converting problems to mathematical terms that is spent dealing with urgent problems. In an action situation where time is a factor, the opportunity for effective management action may pass. There is also the danger, mentioned before, that in an attempt to reduce a problem to mathematical terms, those features least amenable to mathematical expression may be slighted.

Noncritical Method

The concept of method tends to fall into the realm of the scientists, just as the concept of action is associated with management. *Yet, every action or preparation for action rests on some method—implicit if not explicit.* Any method of decision making or of problem solving which is so vague and unspecified that it is not amenable to objective assessment is a "noncritical" method. Any method which starts with a conclusion, or immediately superimposes a solution or assumes an answer (instead of starting with a *bona fide* question, problem, or hypothesis) is a noncritical method. Similarly, any method, or solution growing out of it, which cannot stand up under objective reasoning, investigation, and assessment in comparison with alternative methods or solutions is a "noncritical" method. Finally, any method which consists merely of the application of untested dogma, or tradition, or absolute principles which are not open to inquiry is a "noncritical" method.

Unfortunately, managers, caught in the pressures of daily decision making, are frequently forced to make decisions based on their quick reactions. This approach may be necessary and even effective under certain circumstances but it must be recognized for what it is. Attempts to justify various methods because they are based on common sense or intuition, or are habitual or traditional methods that "come naturally," merely signify that these methods are noncritical. Intuition and common sense can be valuable if they produce hypotheses that can be tested by a critical method, but they are not critical methods in themselves.

As we have mentioned, there are those for whom the whole concept of method in the human realm is something alien. It can only be pointed out that one is bound to use *some* method. However inarticulate, however haphazard, however unexamined, each person's way of arriving at decisions is a "method." Even choosing to ignore a particular human problem of management is a *de facto* choice of method with reference to the problem. Ultimately the manager chooses whether to use the best critical methods possible, or to settle for some nebulous lesser standard.

CRITICAL METHOD IN THE BEHAVIORAL SCIENCES AND IN DECISION MAKING

Specifically, managers are urged to use critical method in two important areas:

1. They should use information and concepts about human behavior derived from the behavioral sciences, which, being derived from the best critical methods available and having already passed the severest tests of critical assessment available, are preferable to mere human hunches. Of course, hunches or assumptions are unavoidable in any form of management. Every choice and action with reference to other human beings is based on behavioral assumptions acquired from a lifetime of personal experience. One's assumptions may be fully recognized and clearly stated, or they may be unrecognized and implicit. In this sense, we are all psychologists and sociologists, whether we draw from the accumulated research findings of professional psychologists and sociologists or restrict ourselves to our own "findings." It is important that each of us go beyond our own set of experiences and develop our own findings—that is, our own use of critical method in the human realm.
2. Managers should use critical method in the management process of *decision making*, and specifically should test each step of the decision process against the general criteria of critical method.

Having advocated the systematic use of a critical method in the behavioral sciences and in decision making, let us now define the two basic terms *behavioral science* and *decision making*.

Behavioral Science

The term *behavioral science* is not restricted to investigations in a particular academic discipline; it refers, instead, to particular methods and purposes of investigation. In this book, the term *behavioral science* denotes any social science, such as psychology, sociology, and anthropology, insofar as it is a study of the *behavior* of human beings in their physical and social environment and utilizes experimental and observational methods. The behavioral sciences use critical method in that they start with *bona fide* questions, employ highly developed procedures that are self-critical, offer objective tests for distinguishing between opposing answers to a question, and contain no dogma regarded as above investigation.

Bradford, Gibb, and Benne (1964) point out the value to the decision maker of behavioral science methods. They begin by asking what is the value of "morality" of science, and they answer the question succinctly:

> One element (in science) is an obligation to face all of the facts involved in a problem and its solution. Frequently, human facts are not faced by

> practical decision makers—facts about feelings, motivations, personal and collective potentialities for growth, contribution potentials of persons and subgroups—as they define and attempt to solve social problems. Not only do decision makers neglect to face the facts of other people's behavioral involvements, but they also frequently neglect to face and manage their own involvements as persons. Their difficulty arises partly from lack of knowledge and skill in making sense of behavioral facts, and also from resistances toward becoming aware of the human consequences of their actions. Ideally, behavioral scientists have faced both of these difficulties in their studies and can be of help to practical men in facing their own similar difficulties (p. 8).

Even though a manager may shun knowledge of the behavioral sciences, his or her behavior is based unavoidably on some form of psychological and sociological assumptions about the nature of human beings and the nature of behavior. Also, the manager must deal with employees who themselves perceive behavior, remember past behavior, impute various motivations to behavior, and have various needs—and who may be labeled by the manager as bored, sick, unhappy, upset, lazy, and so on. The way a manager thinks about human reactions is the manager's own brand of behavioral science. And this brand of behavioral science will determine his or her methods for dealing with employees.

The issue, therefore, is not whether the manager uses or fails to use behavioral assumptions. All action must reflect some such assumptions. The issue, rather, is how sound are the manager's behavioral assumptions. The critical methods of the behavioral sciences can help the manager better understand how human beings tick, how one's own needs and emotions enter into the decision-making process, and how to arrive at more realistic, and therefore more workable, decisions about people.

Decision Making

Decision making is often considered to consist of problem solving, or planning, or organizing, and is sometimes extended to include all aspects of thinking and acting. However, the literature on organizational decision making stresses *choice making* as the key feature. Choice may be exercised in a simple situation, as in the selection of a pen from a well-stocked desk drawer, of lunch from a menu, or of a route to walk from one office to another. It may also be required in a complicated situation that involves conflicting goals and values, many minds, and much expenditure of time: a long-range plan for an entire organization, an appropriate offer to make in upcoming union negotiations, or the selection of a new company president. In any case, selection among alternatives seems to be the key concept in *decision making.*

This concept of choice is frequently expressed in the literature on decision making. The philosopher-sociologist Harald Ofstad (1961) states that "to make a decision (means) to make a judgment regarding what one *ought* to do in a certain situation after having deliberated on some alternative courses of action" (p. 15). Many writers agree on definitions similar to that of Ofstad. Irwin Bross (1953) states: "The process of selecting one action from a number of alternatives is what I shall mean by decision" (p. 1). Feldman and Kanter (1965) suggest that "the decision problem is that of selecting a path which will move the system—individual, computer program, or organization—from some initial state to some terminal state" (pp. 614–615). Claude George (1964) makes this point even more explicitly: To decide means to cut short, to cut off. However, we must frequently give it the connotation of reaching a conclusion, or of making up our minds. This, of course, implies deliberation and thought, making it a conscious act. In contrast, when a 'decision' is a natural reaction or an unconscious act, it is not truly a decision but would be more properly labeled a habit or a reflex act" (p. 21). Ofstad makes a similar distinction; he calls the unconscious process "compulsion" rather than "decision." In all of these definitions, decision making is set forth as being concerned with making conscious choices among alternatives.

Many writers, however, do not limit their definition of *decision making* to a selection or choice among alternatives. Although they may agree that choosing is the characteristic step in a decision-making process, they define *decision making* in a much broader sense. Don Taylor (1965) suggests that "decision making is that thinking which results in the choice among alternative courses of action" (p. 48), and therefore his definition includes the entire thinking process related to the problem prior to a decision choice. Herbert Simon (1960) considers *decision making* synonymous with *managing*: "In treating decision making as synonymous with managing, I shall be referring not merely to the final act of choice among alternatives, but rather to the whole process of decisions" (p. 1). Leonard Sayles (1964) also refers to a broader process when he says: "Decision making is an organizational process. It is shaped as much by the pattern of interaction of managers as it is by the contemplation and cognitive processes of the individual" (p. 207). In this view, decision making goes beyond the point of choice and includes the whole process of managerial functioning.

Since the manager must be concerned with decision making in the broader sense, this book uses the term to refer to *the total problem-solving process*: decision making includes, but is not limited to, the key act of choosing among alternatives. Specifically, the following five steps constitute a generic model of the total management decision-making process (see Figure 1):

1. Perception of the environment or situation: observing and becoming sensitive to potential problem situations.
2. Diagnosis: attempting to understand what is happening in a particular problem situation.
3. Definition of the problem to be solved: identifying and stating a problem in relation to organizational and personal goals.
4. Determination of alternative methods and solutions and choice of

Figure 1 The Decision-Making Process

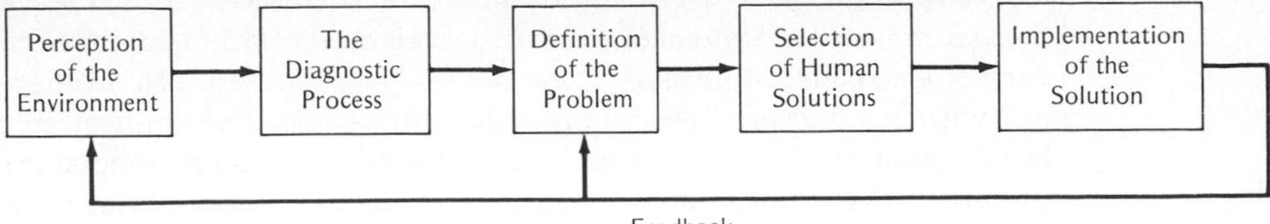

the best solution: selecting a course of action from a series of alternatives.

5. Implementation of the chosen solution: the entire process of actualizing the chosen solution.

These five steps are integral parts of the decision-making process and cannot be avoided. Whether followed consciously or unconsciously, explicitly or implicitly, they are inherent in the role of the manager in the following ways:

1. A manager inevitably experiences feelings of disequilibrium and regards some situations as problem situations, whether or not there is a clear, identifiable basis for this perception.
2. The response to the disequilibrium necessarily involves an assumption about the underlying cause, or a diagnosis of the situation, whether or not this diagnosis is conscious, systematic, and explicit.
3. The response to the disequilibrium necessarily implies definition of the problem to be solved, whether definition of the problem is ambiguous or clear, sound or unsound, explicit or implicit.
4. The response consititutes a selection of method and solution, whether by conscious design or not.
5. Finally, the response also constitutes implementation of the choice, whether or not it actually leads to the solution of the problem.

In other words, these decision-making steps are *necessarily* taken by every decision maker, whether explicitly or implicitly, critically or noncritically.

"All Problems Are Human Problems"

Thinking of decision making in this broad sense, it becomes clear that problems, as such, do not exist—they are found. That is, no situation or event exists as a problem in exactly the same way for every observer, for every organization, for every country, etc. Situations or events become problems for someone when they are defined as such. Situations and events become problems when they violate a standard or goal for someone. To be a problem at all a situation or event must be a problem for someone; therefore *all problems are human problems.* There are no problems unless they are defined as such by someone.

In thinking about decision making, therefore, it is important to focus not only on the situation or event, but on the person who identifies the situation or event and defines it as a problem. In this sense, there is a human dimension to every decision situation whether the subject is labeled "technical," "economic," or "human." In addition, every financial or economic act is also a human act. The application of behavioral sciences to decision making has the purpose of understanding the decision maker and the decision-making process as well as the problem situation. In decisions about humans, of course, our behavioral assumptions are even more important.

ORIENTATION TO DECISION MAKING AS A SYSTEMATIC DISCIPLINE

There are unique problems in approaching decision making as a systematic discipline. Let us face them at the outset. One problem is that everyone has already acquired a good deal of experience in decision making. Since early childhood we have all been developing our own personal decision method. Much of that experience has been reasonably successful—enough so to have kept us alive and brought us to our present situations.

However, past experience in decision making is no guarantee that we have learned the best possible methods of analysis, the best possible hypotheses about motivation, or the best possible methods of decision making and problem solving. Learning from experience is usually random. Furthermore, although we all *learn experiences*, there is no guarantee that we *learn from experiences*. In fact, it is possible to learn downright errors and second-rate methods from experience, as in playing golf without taking lessons from a professional. The manager who says, "We've always done it that way" is relying on an experience from the past environment. It would be better to ask, "What have I learned from doing it that way?"

A second shortcoming of learning only from experience is that it is necessarily circumscribed by the limits of the particular situations and events which happen to come our way. Thus, although all of us are "experienced" decision makers, our lifetime of decision making has been limited in scope. The management trainee has seldom been placed in an actual managerial position, and therefore has not been called upon to make managerial decisions. The marketing manager has seldom been called upon to make production decisions, nor the executive vice president to make presidential decisions. Thus, each individual's sphere of decision making is generally circumscribed by social or organizational roles.

There is a third problem in decision making based only on experience. Even if what we have learned in limited past roles is adequate as a decision method, we are all called upon from time to time to make decisions in new situations. Parents' decisions about their first child, the beginning investor's decisions in the stock market, the graduate's decisions about a first job, the vice president's decisions as acting president, the president's decisions in response to new legislation—all are new decision-making challenges. These challenges require insights and understanding not already developed from past experience. The individual today is in a world of swift change, continually facing new situations. How does one react in new situations where decisions are called for?

Decision Making in New Situations

In new situations, individual reactions vary. Some persons may assume that a new situation is identical to an old one and make a decision based on this assumption. A former vice president for marketing who has just been made president may approach a general management problem that has a marketing dimension the same way such a problem was approached in marketing. Other persons may seek the help of colleagues who appear to have had suitable, comparable experiences. New parents may seek child-rearing advice from their parents, just as a young manager facing a difficult choice might query an experienced manager. Other individuals might hire a consulting expert, seek spiritual guidance, seek the advice and emotional support of a friend, or resort to various combinations of these alternatives. Still others may *decide* to do nothing, or just do nothing without deciding.

What a manager does in a new situation—in defining and reacting to it—will reflect the manager's personal frame of reference *vis-à-vis* the situation. As Gordon Allport (1955) explains, "The way a man defines his situation constitutes for him its reality" (p. 84). A decision maker who views all human behavior as arising from chance will define reality differently, and therefore behave differently, from one who views all human behavior as motivated. A person who believes behavior is predestined will behave differently from one who views people as capable of making choices. It is in new situations that decisions will reflect the decision maker's basic understanding of human behavior.

What generally happens in new situations is that the individual tends to define the new situation in old terms. For example, an experienced manager may pigeonhole the human problems that come up into a few general "types" for which there are set solutions. Rather than attempting to analyze problems objectively, this manager is "solution-oriented" and sees the decision situations in terms of habitual solutions; e.g., "We've always hired Harvard graduates." Thus, what long experience can mean is not always more and more objective analysis and more and more systematic methods of decision making; rather it can mean the reduction of new human-decision situations to the limited frame of reference of the manager's past perceptions.

Past decision-making experience in the realm of human problems is not the same thing as past experience in, say, solving mathematical problems. In many technical fields, the same methods and even the same answers can be applied to the same problems. In the human realm, however, every decision situation is unique. A human situation is never exactly repeated. Its history of having occurred before makes it different from the first event. Similarly, a human act which is repeated has a different meaning the second time by virtue of its being a repetition. Arriving late to work for the first time is not the same as arriving late to work after having done so four days in a row. This means that in the human realm, there is no mathematical formula for decision making or problem solving which can be simply applied to "Problem A." Problem A never happens a second time. To a far greater extent than is true of technical fields, each new experience is unique. Any assumption that a particular experience is "the same as" a prior experience is, in reality, a judgment which can be made only *after* a careful diagnosis of both situations, not before it.

Thus, a further major problem in decision making as a systematic discipline is that of avoiding the temptation to classify a new situation simply as being like "that old familiar one" so that handy old decision-making formulas can be used. In the human realm, this tendency can be fatal to effective management. On his first assignment to Europe an American manager who has had freedom to fire employees finds unsatisfactory consequences if he assumes that his experiences can be the sole determinant of his action now.

To assume that two situations are even similar can be risky. The cause-and-effect relationship of some variables is more predictable than for other variables—that is, the behavior of some variables is more consistent over time. The more "technical" a situation—the more that nonhuman relationships are the primary variables—the greater the possibility that one situation may indeed be similar to another. Two mechanical problems on a production line may turn out to be virtually identical. By contrast, however, the more human, nontechnical behavior is involved in the problem situations being compared, the less similarity one can automatically count on.

Human Decisions vs. Technical Decisions

Although the distinction between human decisions and technical decisions may appear to be a simple one, the implications of the distinction are very significant. Our knowledge and skill concerning technical phenomena are increasing more rapidly than are our knowledge and skill in human management. In part, this is because it is much easier to transfer from generation to generation an understanding of the physical sciences and technology than it is to transfer an understanding of human behavior. Each new generation is able to build upon the science and technology of the previous generation simply through intellectual mastery of its content.

Factual "knowledge" *about* human behavior is similarly transferable, but the kind of full understanding of human behavior required for management skill cannot be gained through any intellectual process alone. A certain degree of personal maturity is also required. In fact, skill in the application of insights about human behavior is a variable partially independent of the intellectual knowledge itself. The required maturity of comprehension is developed through structured experiences as well as intellectual concepts. And ordinarily the individual gains the appropriate structured experiences only through systematic training.

Because "predigested" help is much more readily available in the technical realm than in the human realm, technical problems are being more easily and rapidly solved than are human problems. As a consequence, the decision maker is apt to try to find technical solutions for human problems situations. Indeed, managers often reduce human problems to their technical features, so that neat technical solutions can be applied—usually with bad results!

The disparity between our understanding of technological developments and the human problems that accompany them appears to many observers to be widening. Technological development has tended to breed progressively more technological development, but awareness of human problems has increased slowly. The widening gap has become one of the major problems of our society. For the manager of a sociotechnical organization, this phenomenon may present two problems: (1) technological advances may be thwarted by human problems which have gone unsolved, even where the technical advance could aid the persons who resist it; and (2) the technological changes initiated by an organization may have social repercussions in the organization or throughout the total community, creating as many human problems as they are intended to solve (this is certainly a factor in organizations involved in mass communication media). Hence, greater understanding of human behavior and greater skill in its management are vital goals for the development of today's managers.

CONCLUSION

Although the rapid technological developments of the twentieth century indicate modern competencies in the area of decision making, the rapid advance of social problems reveals its shortcomings. To deal with the organizational situation in which we live, our approach must be conceptually sound. We must use critical methods on the behavioral processes we manage. The study of human behavior has become the Number One priority for the managers of society's organizations.

REFERENCES

Allport, Gordon. *Becoming.* Yale University Press, 1955.

Benne, Kenneth D. "Case Methods in the Training of Administrators." In

Research Papers and Technical Notes, No. 28. Boston University Human Relations Center.
Bradford, Leland P., Jack R. Gibb, and Kenneth D. Benne. *T-Group Theory and Laboratory Method*. Wiley, 1964.
Bross, Irwin D. J. *Design for Decision*. Macmillan, 1953.
Churchman, C. West. *Challenge to Reason*. McGraw-Hill, 1968.
Elbing, Alvar O., Jr., and Carol J. Elbing. "Critical and Noncritical Methods." In *The Value Issue of Business*, Ch. 12. McGraw-Hill, 1967.
Feldman, Julian, and Herschel E. Kanter. "Organizational Decision Making." In *Handbook of Organizations*, ed. James G. March. Rand McNally, 1965.
French, Wendell. *The Personnel Management Process*. Houghton Mifflin, 1964.
George, Claude, Jr. *Management in Industry*. Prentice-Hall, 1964.
Lundberg, Craig. "Toward Understanding Behavioral Science by Administrators." *California Management Review*, Vol. 6, No. 1 (1963).
Lundberg, George. *Can Science Save Us?* London: Longmans, Green, 1947.
Newman, William H., Charles E. Summer, and E. Kirby Warren. *The Process of Management*, 2nd ed. Prentice-Hall, 1967.
Ofstad, Harald. *An Inquiry into the Freedom of Decision*. Oslo: Norwegian Universities Press, 1961.
Sayles, Leonard. *Managerial Behavior*. McGraw-Hill, 1964.
Schlaifer, Robert. *Probability and Statistics for Business Decisions*. McGraw-Hill, 1959.
Simon, Herbert. *New Science of Management Decisions*. Harper & Row, 1960.
Taylor, Donald W. "Decision Making and Problem Solving." In *Handbook of Organizations*, ed. James G. March. Rand McNally, 1965.
Taylor, Frederick W. *The Principles of Scientific Management*. Harper & Row, 1911.
Watzlawick, Paul, Janet H. Beavin, and Don D. Jackson. *Pragmatics of Human Communication*. Norton, 1967.

Chapter

2 The Environment for Decision Making

Organizational decision making, and indeed all decision making, takes place within a *perceived environment.* The individual perceives particular stimuli or clues in the environment which have meaning, and these become the basis for decision-making activity. Which stimuli or clues are perceived and the meaning given to them depend as much on the decision maker as on the environment. The purpose of this chapter is to consider the balance between the two.

THE ENVIRONMENT AS STRUCTURED

The environment contains an infinite amount of miscellaneous data. It can be thought of as the total of all the economic, social, physical, political, and technical forces or conditions around the decision maker. The decision maker does not simply mirror this complex environment. On the contrary, the individual gathers from the environment those data which he or she is prepared to perceive, based on past experiences and on expectations, models, needs, feelings, etc. (See Figure 1.)

Figure 1 Perception of the Environment

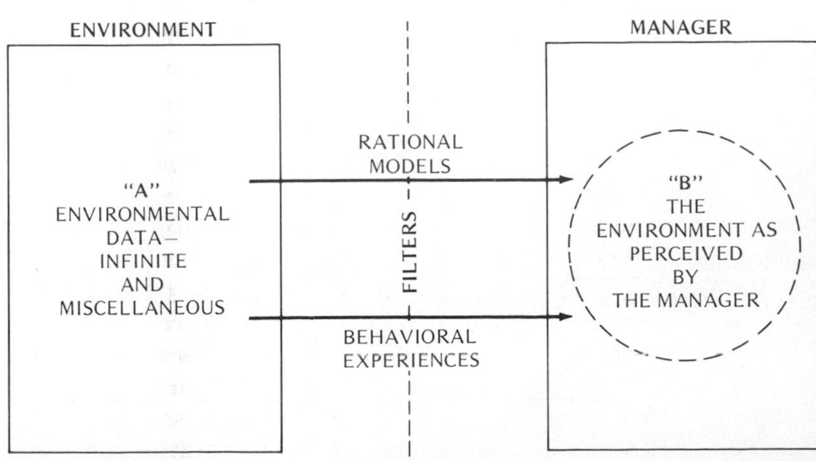

These preselected data—these perceptions—constitute the basis for the individual's psychological structuring of the environment. It is this *psychologically structured environment* which constitutes the meaningful environment for the individual and, therefore, the basis for all related decision-making activity. It should be clearly noted at this point that the psychological structuring of the environment does not necessarily reflect accurately the nature of the environment itself. It reflects a dynamic interaction between the environmental clues and the frame of reference of the decision maker.

Three points can be made about the ways in which data are structured:

1. The data in the environment are in themselves prestructured to some degree. This means that to some extent the meaning associated with certain environmental stimuli is inherent in the stimuli themselves. A table, for example, is a table because of conventional usage and terminology. In general it will be perceived as such, although someone may, of course, see it as a desk, work bench, high platform, or something else. In other cases the meaning of the stimuli may be unclear. The same "table" with steps attached, painted in stripes and holding a red waste basket may not be as clear within its own structure. To the extent that the stimulus itself lacks clarity to the observer, meaning must be projected into it from the individual observer (Figure 2).

If in an organizational situation, for example, when one enters an office and observes a desk, telephone, and chair, the structure of these objects provides reasonably clear meaning to the observer as to their nature. If, on the other hand, one observes an individual with his back to the door, an empty automobile with the door open and the motor running, or a group of people standing around the desk of a colleague, these stimuli in themselves hold little meaning. Note that the behavior of people generally is less clear than the meaning of things. In these situations the individual provides the structure and, therefore, his or her own meaning.

2. As we've seen, the structure of the environment rests partially on the traditional or conventional grouping and usage of various elements. This meaning or structuring may rest on the nature of a person's language, which groups certain stimuli together. Thus, people who look at the environment through different languages may see different

Figure 2 Perception, Processing, Projection

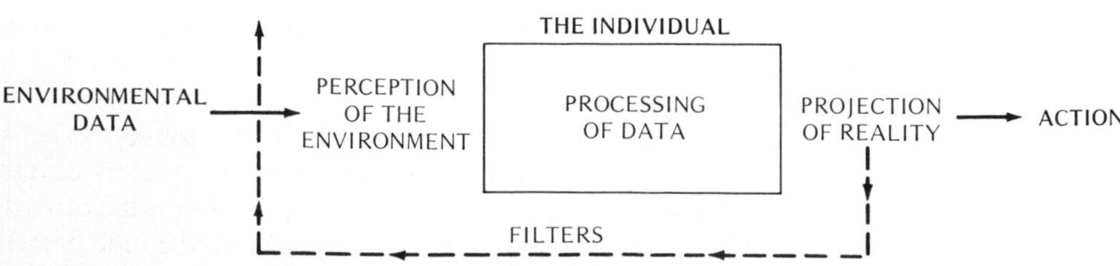

things. There is, for example, in English essentially one word for the white ice crystals that cover the ground in winter—*snow.* In Eskimo language there are purported to be many words for snow, because different kinds of snow meet different needs of the culture.

3. The meaning or structure in the environment also rests on historical, political, or social systems within which the individual is operating. Activities that tend to relate to the economic functioning of society tend to be grouped together as *economic variables.* A good deal of literature, considerable research and study, and certainly a great deal of public discussion surrounds the state of the economy, the nature of economic variables, and the economic future. It is clear, however, that economic variables and economic consequences are also *social variables.* Conversely, social variables are frequently economic ones. Furthermore, both can be considered *political.* It is useful to group environmental variables under classifications—economic, social, physical, political, technical—for the purpose of discussion and analysis. It is necessary, however, to keep in mind that the distinctions may be only in our definitions, and not necessarily in the "reality" of the environment. Figure 3 presents a detailed model of the decision-making process.

The Economic Environment

The economic environment of business is not merely the situation existing outside the business enterprise; it is *an interaction between general economic conditions and the economic activities of the firm itself.* It is this interaction which is of greatest importance to the manager. Some aspects of the general economic situation do not directly affect the industry and may not be relevant to the individual manager, at least not in the short run. As one reads economic information, however, it appears to have been gathered and presented around certain *units,* such as countries, industries, years, currencies, theories, etc. These units may or may not coincide with the needs or activities of particular decision makers. For example, persons holding stock on the New York Stock Exchange may read the daily Dow Jones averages whether or not they relate to their particular stocks.

The *internal consequences* of the economic environment—such as the cost and availability of resources and raw materials, the cost of labor, the productivity at a particular point in time, the stability of the labor force and of one's customers—are a function of the general situation but at the same time are unique to the particular organization. Even in periods of general economic decline, some sections of the economy prosper: some companies, some industries, some countries advance. In periods of boom, some sections fail.

In viewing the economic environment, therefore, managers must be aware of what system of indices, data groupings, or sources of data are readily available; and they should ask whether the data coincide with their own needs. If not, managers then must structure the data in

Figure 3 Detailed Model of the Decision-Making Process

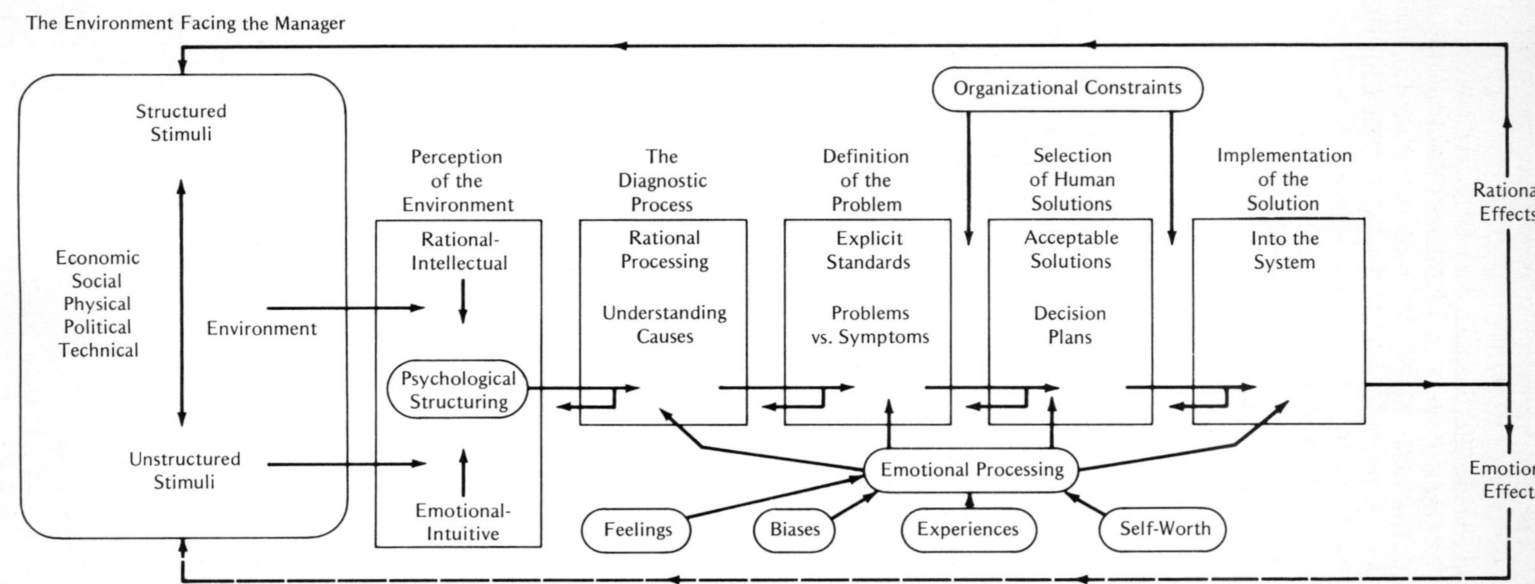

Our rational processing tends to be conscious, while our emotional processing tends to be unconscious. For effective decision making the goal is to bring the emotional processing into our conscious awareness. Otherwise, unprocessed emotions produce boundaries to our rational processes.

the environment for themselves so that the data *are* perceivable in a way relevant to their own needs.

Most conventional environmental data sources refer to present or past economic conditions. Organizational decision making refers to present or future activities of the firm. Converting data from the past to a basis for decision making in the future requires additional intervening models or structure, which again must be related to the particular situation. If, for example, the supply of a particular raw material has been declining and a price increase is forecast, the manager must determine how important the raw material is for the company, what alternative materials are available, and what influence each alternative would have on company costs before making a plan or decision for the future.

Perhaps one of the biggest difficulties in looking at the economic environment is to think of it as solely "economic." Economic data are rather the synthesis of an infinite number of social actions, each of which has had its own motivations. Whether we consider the aggregate economic data, or the individual social motivations that underlie the data, as more important for decision making depends on how the firm will use those data. An intended expansion and therefore an acquisition of funds may be a response to aggregate economic data, while a new market strategy may rest more significantly on the individual social motivations of people in the marketplace.

The Social Environment

The social environment of business must also be thought of as an *interaction between those forces predominantly external to the firm and the social behavior within the firm.* The individuals who operate within the firm are, of course, also part of its external environment. The secretary, for example, is also customer, voter, taxpayer, and citizen. The impact of the social environment on the decision maker, therefore, takes two forms: (1) the *direct* impact on the firm of economic, social, legal, and political systems and (2) the *indirect* consequences of those systems on the individuals who make up the company, and who, therefore, behave within the company in relation to many of those norms and values.

At one level, the firm interacts with the *systems* that are a part of the social environment, that is, the firm must obey the laws, relate to the political structure, and operate within the broader sociocultural framework. These systems tend to appear to be stable. They are, however, stable only in the short run, since there is always a change in balance of attitudes and values among individuals collectively.

These sociocultural systems tend to be related to political units (cities, states, and countries) and to the historic stream of thinking and action on which the systems have been built. The firm is interacting less with a given fixed system of laws, politics, or geography than with an *historic way* of thinking, acting, and organizing, which is reflected in these systems. Roman law differs from common law. Latin languages structure the world differently from Germanic or Asiatic languages. The traditions that settled North America differ from the pressures of an expanding African continent. Dealing with these traditions—these predetermined ways of organizing data—requires a sensitivity to the forces for change as much as a sensitivity to the reality of the present.

Within these systems, of course, are individuals. Individuals are influenced by the system, but also by their old fears, anxieties, hopes, and expectations. They perceive the environment in terms of themselves, whether the events or stimuli are intended to relate to them directly or not. Disasters or terrorist acts, or opposite events of joy or progress occurring in all parts of the world are transmitted to them almost instantaneously through mass communication media. Their feelings and behavior are based partly on the social system and partly on their own reactions to the constant bombardment of communication stimuli.

One consequence of these social forces, both organized and random, is an individual who uses an economic organization—perhaps a business—as the major basis for existence. This individual *perceives* the firm, *is motivated* by its policies and procedures, and *reacts* to its leadership, in terms of the personal needs created by the broader social system. If, as we have indicated, problems are defined by people, the individual is influenced in the definition of problems by all of the social variables outside as well as inside the firm.

To manage effectively, therefore, it is necessary for a manager to develop increased sensitivity to a whole set of social variables acting on the people who must make or carry out decisions in the firm. Such a sensitivity is a new dimension of business life for many managers, since the relative importance of social variables has increased dramatically in less than a generation.

The Physical Environment

The interrelationship between the external and internal physical environment is one that is traditionally well understood. The firm, in general, is nothing more than a unit that gathers together resources of various kinds and transfers them into a new form, which is then distributed in the marketplace. The relationship between the availability of these resources and products is a constant daily concern of the manager. The profitability and stability of the firm is in many ways directly related to the continued availability of necessary resources.

Historically, it was possible to identify a kind of resource, a good source for it, and a method of transportation for getting it to the processing facilities. Cost was the major determinant in the selection of resources, and the buyer was able to negotiate among suppliers. The acquisition of resources, therefore, became a technical task dependent primarily on the identification of specifications and one's ability to negotiate the suppliers' prices.

The world energy crises during the early 1970's must be seen as the dividing line between the world just described and the world of the future. Although resource shortages, transferability, and control had been evolving gradually, it was the oil or energy crises which brought the world's attention to the dramatic changes taking place. Unlimited supplies of traditional resources became, in some cases, limited. Resources always available on the marketplace disappeared and were only available through barter. Increased costs through governmental action—whether monopolistic (government ownership) or for the protection of the environment—changed the balance of attractiveness of traditional resources.

While in the past the primary function of business was to sell or distribute the goods or services produced, gradually the emphasis has shifted toward the acquiring of resources which would allow continued production. The marketing function in business more and more focuses on acquisition rather than distribution. Whatever way it moves, the relationship of productive processes in the firm to changing resources and ecological environment will not be the same. *The necessity to be able to think about the environment, to produce an appropriate structure, and, therefore, to be able to forecast the changing conditions in which the firm is operating becomes a high-priority item for all managers.*

The Political Environment

The political environment can be viewed in two parts: the actual political or governmental system or philosophy, and the "politics" or power interrelationships of a particular industry or location. If, for example, one does business with a particular government, the political system—Democrat or Republican, Conservative or Liberal, Left or Right—influences the nature of the relationship between the company and the government. Each political system sees progress in its own way, and, of course, to participate in this "progress" the company must understand its particular dynamics.

At the same time there is a political environment which consists of how things are done. It is suggested, for example, that in some countries the people who sell telecommunication equipment to the government, such as the PTT (Post, Telegraph, & Telephone), may receive a promotion in the organization at the same time as their counterparts receive one in government in order to maintain the positive relationship. This is "politics."

These political environments are particularly important for multinational companies or companies doing business in various countries. The difficulty for the manager from one country to understand the numerous "norms" of behavior which are different in each country in which the company operates leads to uncertainty, potential problems, and often embarrassment. Although the motives behind the numerous examples of bribery worldwide may be many and varied, in some cases failure to understand internal "political" relationships has led to unfortunate consequences. In one European country, for example, a bribe allegedly offered to the Queen's husband was more sadly received than other bribery attempts. You don't bribe royalty, apparently.

The political situation does not, of course, remain constant. What is or was considered appropriate may change rapidly. Certainly the "political" considerations in the United States changed dramatically after Watergrate, just as did the gift-giving norms worldwide after the "Lockheed Affair." As more and more business becomes multinational, these problems increase in magnitude and importance. It should be remembered, however, that outside the United States almost all business is "multinational." National boundaries of smaller countries cannot be considered the economic boundaries of the companies. Therefore, the experience in various political systems is much greater outside the United States. *To move comfortably within and among various nations, management must be sensitive to an ever changing political scene at both levels.*

The Technical Environment

The state of technology—of scientific discovery—moves rapidly, but innovation within a firm will be far less rapid. The difficulty tends to be in relating technological advances to the firm's methods and processes. Although most managers are sensitive to the state of development and change within their own industry, it is less possible than before to determine the industry's boundaries. As an example, the Swiss watch industry responded dramatically to the technological developments of the tuning fork and quartz as a basis for accuracy, but found itself significantly behind in the printed circuit, the digital watch, and the wrist computer. The interrelationship among technologies may be expanding as rapidly as the technologies themselves. This constitutes an added dimension of difficulty for the manager—especially one who is not technically trained.

A basic priority, then, for every organization is the monitoring of the technological environment for early clues of technological changes which might make it a "buggy whip industry." And while continual monitoring of the changing technological environment is essential, the organization must also be prepared to act decisively on the recommendations of those who are most knowledgeable. During the early 1970's one large oil company paid two economists to work full time in the planning department, doing nothing but thinking about the future price of oil and why it would move in the direction that it would. After exhaustive study they predicted with extreme accuracy what would happen to the price of oil in the near future. Their prediction, however, was given only a 5-percent probability rating by management; instead of seriously considering the implications of the specialists' work, management took what was described as a "muddling through" forecast. Essentially assuming that things would be as they had been, management was unable to change its view of the environment and could not use the analysis presented to it.

During a period of technological change and the organization's adaptation to it, the effect on the labor force may be important. However, it is not uncommon to hear managers say that they will first of all decide what the new technology will be and "afterward" they will think about the human and managerial needs of the organization. "Afterward" may be too late. *Unless the labor force—including management—is not only technically retrained, but psychologically or organizationally adjusted to the new processes and expectations, the new technology may mark the decline rather than the advance of the organization.*

THE ENVIRONMENT AND THE MANAGER

Referring again to Figure 3, the processes through which the manager structures and organizes the environment are of critical importance. Analyzing one's own psychological processes, therefore, may be the first step in understanding the decision-making process.

The organization of the environment, as indicated earlier, rests in part in the observer. Since the environmental clues are infinite and miscellaneous, we cannot observe everything but only those things that we are prepared or conditioned to observe. We view the environment through a filter based on our past experiences, our learning, and our expectations. It is as though we are looking through a prepunched IBM card and observe only those data which appear through the holes. Each of us, of course, possesses a personal, uniquely punched card for each situation. With new experiences these card patterns can change, become more open or more closed. In different situations we may substitute different cards which identify and emphasize certain aspects of the environment rather than others. Or we may acquire a particular environmental filter at one point in life, and through its repeated use reinforce a particular set of relationships; eventually we may be unable to change our "view cards."

Formal organization in the environment may in itself be simply a structure imposed by someone or some group to meet personal perception needs. Gradually this model comes to be seen as reality. Others begin to accept it as though it *were* reality. On the other hand, a particular pattern may only reflect a current theoretical model or a traditional historical view of the environment. A concept like gross national product yields figures representing "*the* economic health of the country." Providing one investigates carefully the assumptions of this index, it does indeed clarify the environment. Unfortunately, it is all too easy to assume that GNP *is* "absolute" economic health: when GNP goes up, the environment *is* "absolutely" economically "better off." This assumption can be disastrous for an individual or an organization if it makes the assumption that a particular movement of GNP has meaning apart from the numerous other environmental factors affecting the particular organization.

Environmental Boundaries

What constitutes the environment for the manager is basically a question of boundaries; it is whatever exists outside a set boundary. For example, managers might think of the environment as everything outside themselves or their roles. For some purposes, this may be a useful concept, since it focuses their thinking clearly on factors external to themselves which act as stimuli on them. A sales representative physically removed from headquarters and regularly interacting with customers and competitors may benefit from considering everyone as "the environment."

For other purposes, environmental boundaries may be drawn around the work group, the function, the organization, or a larger political unit. Each boundary serves a different purpose.

The environment of the *manager's role* differs significantly from the environment of the *company.* This difference frequently becomes the basis for psychological or organizational conflict. In the attempt to meet personal or role needs, the individual manager interacts with an "environment." This interaction may put the individual in conflict with the organization as it attempts to meet *its* needs, interacting with *its* environment.

One large Swiss chemical company, for example, decided that the Scandinavian market would take second priority in its sales efforts while the company built up its business in certain other markets. They, in effect, defined their interaction strategy with their particular environment. At the same time, they gave responsibility for Scandinavia to an aggressive, goal-oriented manager. He defined his personal priorities differently from company policy and interacted with the Scandinavian market aggressively. The more effective he was, the more he violated the company's goal to maximize other markets. Gradually the company became part of "the outside environment" for this manager, since he saw himself in conflict with it. His needs for personal advancement forced him to relate to the company as though it were a competitor rather than an ally. This led, of course, to his leaving the company.

Defining one's "environment" determines, to some degree, one's style and strategy. Once the boundaries are defined between one's own role or organization *and* the environment, one begins to differentiate in behavior between the two. Choices can be made of when to use power and when to use cooperation and participation. There is some evidence to suggest that cooperation or participation may be a more desirable approach inside one's boundaries, while the use of power may be a necessary ingredient with the environment outside one's boundaries. In any case, the boundary definition becomes critical to one's managerial style.

In the example above of the Swiss chemical company, the individual had defined the organization itself as in the outside "environment." Earlier attempts at cooperation had not led to rewards, since the manager's personal goals were in conflict with company policy. Hence he began using power in relationships within his own firm.

Managers often do not face directly the task of drawing boundaries which delimit the environment. The definition of the environment becomes vague, it is made by someone else, or it changes. Two individuals in the same organization may well draw different environmental boundaries, thereby making communication difficult.

Influencing the manager is the fact that factors in the outside environment that relate to the individual or to the organization do not remain stable. Other people and groups are constantly redefining their own boundaries. In 1975, for example, it was felt by the French government that the educational system was training too many young people to be teachers. The demand for teachers was going down, while the number of graduates was increasing. The government decreed, therefore, that a larger percentage of the young people would be enrolled to study business administration. From the companies' standpoint the environment changed. More people would be looking for work in industry at a time when the companies were attempting to reduce employment levels. Governmental pressure to support its decision would constitute an additional environmental change.

Failure to redefine the "environment" regularly and to reconsider one's strategy toward it could thus have long-term negative consequences. After the decline in the birth rate in Germany in the late 1960's, the "baby buggy" industries—those providing products for infants and babies—declined 40 percent in sales. Many of those companies were unprepared, several going into bankruptcy. Although the birth rate decline was quite predictable, they had perceived the environment as constant.

Environmental Assumptions

Since one's assumptions about the environment determine the models one applies, it is important to analyze continually one's assumptions. Conflicts in assumptions among team members, organizational colleagues, etc., can lead to conflicting plans and to arguments. A useful environmental exercise is to complete the following questionnaire and compare the results with those of colleagues. The questionnaire can be expanded; items can be added to cover any particular issue one desires to include. As presented it reflects the aspects of the environment that are currently most variable.

The purpose is, first of all, to identify where on a particular continuum you perceive the environment affecting you. In the first question, for example, you are asked to determine where on a continuum of stability/instability the political environment is. This political environment could be seen as local, state, federal, or world. Once that decision is made, the most important choice is: In what direction is that environment going? Will it become more stable or more unstable? Attempt at that point to articulate as briefly as possible—in just a few words—what you consider to be the most important forces leading to your forecast.

The completion of all twelve questions becomes a useful basis for discussion with colleagues for whom the environment holds similar importance.

Survey of the Environment

Below are twelve issues concerning the political, economic, technological, and social environment. For each issue, indicate your assumption about the present, your forecast for ten years from now, and your evaluation of this trend for business.

Instructions:

1. *The Present*: For each continuum, circle the number (1–7) which indicates your assumptions about the present situation in ________ (define the area).
2. *The Future*: For each continuum, circle the letter A, B, or C, which indicates the direction in which this area will move in the next ten years.
3. *Your explanation of the future trend*: In one or two words indicate your reason for seeing the environment more in the forecasted direction.

The Political Environment

Generally Stable ________________ Generally Unstable

1 2 3 4 5 6 7

Future: A. →
(circle one) B. ←
C. No change

Why?

Emphasis on Needs of the Individual ________________ Emphasis on Needs of Society

1 2 3 4 5 6 7

Future: A. →
(circle one) B. ←
C. No change

Why?

International in Orientation ________________ National in Orientation

1 2 3 4 5 6 7

Future: A. →
(circle one) B. ←
C. No change

Why?

The Economic Environment

Generally Stable ________________ Generally Unstable

1 2 3 4 5 6 7

Future: A. →
(circle one) B. ←
C. No change

Why?

Free Market Economy — Government Control of Market

1 2 3 4 5 6 7

Future: A. →   Why?
(circle one) B. ←
C. No change

Continued Economic Growth — Zero Economic Growth

1 2 3 4 5 6 7

Future: A. →   Why?
(circle one) B. ←
C. No change

Natural Resources and Technology

Unlimited Natural Resources — Critical Shortages of Resources

1 2 3 4 5 6 7

Future: A. →   Why?
(circle one) B. ←
C. No change

Little Concern for Physical Environment — Great Concern for Physical Environment

1 2 3 4 5 6 7

Future: A. →   Why?
(circle one) B. ←
C. No change

Unlimited Potential of Technology — Critical Limits to Potential of Technology

1 2 3 4 5 6 7

Future: A. →   Why?
(circle one) B. ←
C. No change

The Social Environment

Tight Moral Philosophies — Loose Moral Philosophies

1 2 3 4 5 6 7

Future: A. →   Why?
(circle one) B. ←
C. No change

Strong Family Units — Weak Family Units

1 2 3 4 5 6 7

Future: A. →   Why?
(circle one) B. ←
C. No change

Effective Population Control — Overpopulation

1 2 3 4 5 6 7

Future: A. →   Why?
(circle one) B. ←
C. No change

CONCLUSION

The purpose of this discussion was to focus on the interaction between the decision maker and the environment as an active dynamic changing process. It is extremely dangerous to think of the environment as a constant, or even as perceived similarly by all observers. The environment does not remain constant, nor does the basis of individual perception.

Of primary importance is the recognition that decision making is based on one's *psychological structuring of the environment*—on the models of reality which one applies—rather than on "the" environment in some *absolute* sense. Examination of one's own structuring of the environment may be of more importance than analysis of the environment itself.

Gray Drake Airlines Case

Tim Botz was a student at Eastern State University in Dover, New Hampshire. He was 21 years of age and a native of Kellte, Maine, a small town right across the New Hampshire state line.

Tim's major was business administration. During the fall quarter of his senior year at Eastern State, he signed up for a nine-credit transportation course, which was to continue over the remainder of his senior year. As a part of this course, he was assigned to do research for Gray Drake Airlines, a small independent company that operated scheduled flights linking the main cities of the New England states. Gray Drake had flights connecting New York; Boston; Portland, Maine; Dover and Portsmouth, New Hampshire; Derby and New Haven, Connecticut; Middlebury, Vermont; Lexington, Massachusetts; and Concord, New Hampshire. They had 20 planes in use. The crews consisted of flight attendants and pilots. There were 50 of the former working for the company and 30 pilots (see Figure 1). The company's home office was in Dover.

The directors of Gray Drake Airlines interviewed Tim at a board meeting and expressed pleasure at having a student from the University do research for them. Consequently, they created a nonsalaried position, director of research, for Tim. He was to be given full access to company files, office space, telephone, mimeograph work, etc. The board of directors recommended that Tim work on the problems of publicity and passenger comfort.

In September, when Tim started to work for the company, he was taken around by Mr. N. S. Roake, his immediate superior (see Figure 1), and introduced to the department heads. It was made clear at this time that anything that Tim suggested, if it had the approval of Mr. Roake, was to be followed. An interoffice memo was also sent around explaining Tim's position and asking that cooperation be accorded him. By October, Tim had decided that the best way to gain the information he needed would be to distribute questionnaires to the passengers. Tim felt that the speediest way to do this would entail having the chief flight attendant distribute the questionnaires on his periodic rounds of checks on the flight attendants.[1] The flight attendants would distribute the questionnaires to the passengers as they embarked on their trip and collect them at the end of the flight. The flight attendant could then either mail the completed questionnaires to Dover or give them to the chief flight attendant on his next trip. This plan was approved of by Mr. Roake, as were the questionnaires. Tim then personally made a pretesting by going on several flights and administering the questionnaires. By the middle of November, he felt that he was actually ready to begin work.

Tim then went to the chief flight attendant to explain the procedure to him. He was surprised to find that he had had previous contact with the chief flight attendant, Sam Green. Tim had first met Mr. Green in the summer of 1953 when, in connection with a sociology class at Eastern State, he had done

[1] On Gray Drake Airlines, because the flights were so short, there were no stewardesses. The flight attendant undertook the necessary duties concerning the passengers, baggage, mail, etc.

Figure 1 Gray Drake Airlines Organization Chart

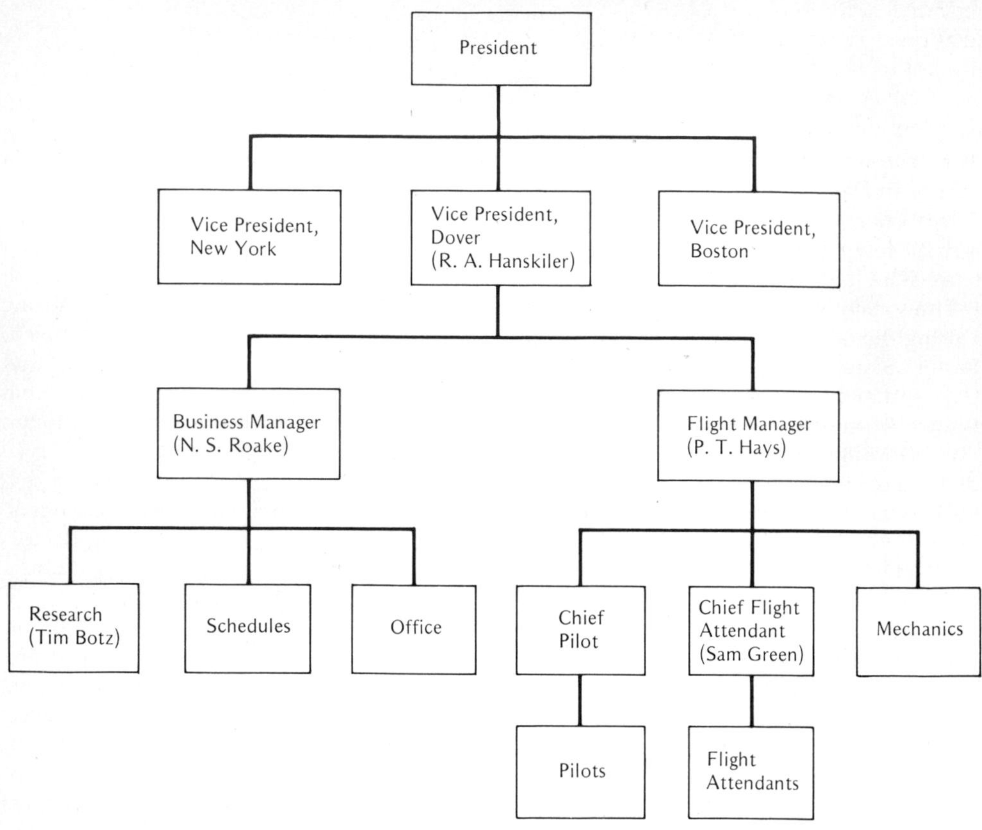

a project on personality research. Among those on his list to interview—a list of names of volunteers furnished by the instructor—Green's name occurred. Consequently, Tim had two personal interviews with Green during that summer. During the interviews, Sam was quite agreeable and furnished Tim with much helpful information about himself and his background.

Sam Green was 26 years old. In 1945 when he graduated from a Maine high school, he entered the service for three years. Upon returning, he started at Eastern State University. He majored in architecture and also pledged a fraternity. After three years of college, during which he received many low grades, he went to work as a flight attendant for Gray Drake Airlines. Two years later, because of his leadership ability, he was offered the job of chief flight attendant. He had held this job about six months when Tim first started doing survey work for the company.

When Tim entered Green's office to discuss his current research for the airlines, Tim felt that Green was distant or cool compared with what Tim expected, and he decided that perhaps, for some reason, Green did not wish to remember their previous encounter. Hence Tim did not mention it but merely presented his plan concerning the distribution and collection of the questionnaires. Tim was aware of the interoffice letter sent out to all the men explaining his position with the airlines and the fact that all the personnel were to cooperate with him. He mentioned this to Green and received only a grunt of recognition. During the interview, Green talked very little and seemed to focus his attention elsewhere. Tim left the interview without a feeling of accomplishment but did feel that he had tried his best.

At the beginning of the first week in December, Tim left 1000 questionnaires[2] with the secretary in Green's office (Green was not in then). Tim attached a memo reminding Green of the procedure to be followed. Tim felt that this was a good time to start distribution, as the Christmas rush was nearing. He mentioned this in his note to Green. The following day Tim checked with the secretary and learned that she had personally given the materials to Green the previous afternoon. She commented that Green had read the memo and shrugged his shoulders. But she did see that when he left for his weekly trip he stuffed over half of the questionnaires into his brief case. This seemed like a good omen to Tim. During the two weeks that followed, Tim expected to receive some of the completed questionnaires either by mail or personally from Green; but none came in. As Green did not return to home base, Tim concluded that everything was tied up by the Christmas rush. As the end of the school quarter neared and he was busy with tests, Tim decided to let things rest until January.

The second week of January, Tim returned to his office at Gray Drake Airlines expecting to find many completed questionnaires. However, none were there; and, in checking with the secretary, he learned that Green had left no message for him. Tim then went to see Mr. Roake and explained what had happened. Roake was busy gathering material to take to an airlines convention the following day in New York. His only suggestion was that Tim see Green and get to the bottom of the situation. Tim returned to the office, picked up another batch of questionnaires, and went into Green's office. After an exchange of pleasantries, the following discussion took place:

Tim: Well, Sam, I've been waiting for a report on my questionnaires, but as yet have received no information, nor have I received any completed questionnaires. So, I concluded that you brought them back with you. Do you have them?

Sam: Yes, some were completed. I stuck them somewhere. Let's see now. [He rummaged through several desk drawers and finally pulled out about seventy-five and handed them to Tim.]

Tim: [Tim glanced over them for a moment and noted that they were correctly filled out.] But Sam, what about the rest? You know during the Christmas rush, both Mr. Roake and I agreed, was an ideal time to query our passengers. And you were fully indoctrinated with the policies of distribution and the importance of this survey. What happened?

Sam: Well, we were pretty busy. I did what I could. [Pause.] Excuse me, but I have a luncheon date and must be going.

Tim: Before you go, here are some more questionnaires. Please try to get them completed and back by your next trip. You'll be back in about two weeks, won't you?

Sam: Sure, sure, kid, I'll see you in a couple of weeks.

Tim felt discouraged, but he felt that a start could be made with the seventy-five completed ones he had. He could begin coding them at any rate.

During the next two weeks, no questionnaires were returned, and Tim began to worry. He personally contacted seven flight attendants who came into Dover during his hours at the office. From four of the seven he learned that they had not received any questionnaires to distribute from Green, and three said they had been handed a few by Green who mumbled something about

[2] A copy of this questionnaire appears at the end of this case.

"some college kid's scheme." As a result, Tim felt they were completely ignorant of the whole research project. Tim explained fully to each of them what the project was aimed at, his part in it, what their share of the job was, and also showed them a copy of the interoffice memo written by Roake authorizing utmost cooperation for the project. The men all seemed interested and Tim left fifty questionnaires with each of them to distribute that day. They promised to return them promptly.

Within the next week all but 100 of these were returned completed and with requests for more. However, as yet there was no word from Green. Tim felt that the project was definitely under way. He concluded that perhaps he had been wrong in giving the job to Green to take care of. But as Tim had only been able to contact ten flight attendants personally at Dover, he saw no other way to distribute the questionnaires except through the fieldman, Green. In repeated attempts to see Green during his next few days at the home office, Tim met with no success. Green was either too busy to be disturbed or he was out. As Tim felt that he had almost exhausted the supply of new passengers coming to and going from Dover (most of the planes flying from Dover carried the same passengers on business trips to and from New York, Boston, and Portland), he felt that in order to get a well-rounded and unbiased survey it was mandatory that he reach the opinion of passengers in the six other outlying cities where Gray Drake planes flew. Consequently, he wrote an interoffice memo (which is reproduced below on the facing page) to Green and also sent copies to Mr. Roake, Mr. Hays (Green's boss), and Mr. Hanskiler, the vice president in charge of the Dover port. Eight days passed and Tim received neither an answer from Green nor any completed questionnaires. He wondered what to do.

Gray Drake Airlines Survey Questionnaire

To improve Gray Drake Airlines' service to you, we would appreciate your completing the following questionnaire (sealing it if you wish) and returning it to your flight attendant. You may omit any question that you do not wish to answer.

At what town did you board? ____________________

At what town will you get off? ____________________

About how many times have you flown by commercial, scheduled airlines in the past year? ________

About how many times have you flown by Gray Drake Airlines in the past year? ________

Please rate the ground personnel that served you before this flight:

	Below average	*Average*	*Excellent*
Courtesy			
Appearance			
Efficiency			
Willingness to cooperate			
Comments:			

Please rate the flight attendant now on duty regarding:

	Below average	*Average*	*Excellent*
Courtesy			
Appearance			
Efficiency			
Willingness to cooperate			
Comments:			

What is the purpose of your trip today?

______Business only ______Recreation only ______Business and recreation ______Vacation ______I live there ______Visit to my family ______Other ____

If the purpose of your trip is business, what type of business are you engaged in?

____

What has influenced you most in choosing to fly Gray Drake Airlines?
______Newspaper advertising ______Radio advertising ______Friends ______Mail addressed to me
______News item ______Other ____

If Gray Drake Airlines' service had not been available, how would you have made this trip?
______Automobile ______Train ______Bus ______Another airline ______Uncertain

If Gray Drake Airlines' service were discontinued:
Would you, as an individual, be inconvenienced? ______Yes ______No
Would it impair the efficiency of your business? ______Yes ______No
Would it place your organization at a disadvantage? ______Yes ______No

Do you have any comments regarding this aircraft?

____

Is your annual income under $5000 ________ over $5000? ________

Would you mind giving us your name and home address?
Name: Mr. ______Mrs. ______Miss ____
Address ____

Would you mind giving us your approximate age? ____

Additional remarks regarding service, schedules, personnel, etc.

____

Thank you very much,

TIMOTHY JONAS BOTZ, *Director*
Gray Drake Airlines Research
Eastern State University

Interoffice Memorandum

February 10, 1954

To: Sam Green
From: Tim Botz
Subject: Questionnaire distribution

I have found it extremely difficult to work out a method whereby the inflight questionnaires can be distributed to flight attendant personnel. My many attempts to discuss this project with you have met with disinterest and abruptness, which I am at a loss to comprehend. I do lack the necessary instructions from your office in order to execute this portion of the project.

As it is my understanding that you were to cooperate with me in this endeavor, I am therefore making this final attempt to solicit your help. I naturally desire to get this work under way as soon as possible, and my memorandum of the eleventh[3] sufficiently covered the implements necessary to the project.

Your response at the earliest possible date will be greatly appreciated.

Respectfully,

TIMOTHY JONAS BOTZ

cc: N. S. Roake
P. T. Hays
R. A. Hanskiler

[3] This refers to the first memo Tim sent to Green, accompanying the first group of questionnaires left in Green's office.

Redmond Manufacturing Company Case

The Redmond Manufacturing Company produced machinery in the suburbs of a large Eastern city. In the inspection department were 60 men and women. A rush job of inspecting 2000 spindles with attachments assembled had been brought into the department. It was a two-day job and there were two inspections to be made. The woman who had been assigned to the job had finished the first inspection when she found that her children had scarlet fever, and she had to leave the job to nurse them.

Some of the other inspectors discovered that the children had been sick a week before the mother knew that they had scarlet fever. The foreman turned the job over to another woman to complete. She refused, stating that she was afraid of catching the disease. Her stand became known to the rest of the workers, and they all backed her up. Although the foreman tried to get someone else to do the job, the others were all ready to walk out if forced to touch the spindles. The boxes lay on the floor a full day after the woman left.

On the morning of the second day the foreman told the personnel director of the problem. The personnel director called in the production manager to see whether the spindles could be disinfected. The production manager said that before any disinfecting could be done each piece would have to be disassembled, a process which involved taking out three screws and two springs on each of the 2000 spindles. Otherwise, the disinfecting solution would rust the polished portions of the piece. Besides being expensive, this operation would cause a long delay on a rush job that was scheduled for shipment that very afternoon.

Both men wanted to meet the shipping promise.

Joyería La Perla Case (A)

George Stauffer, owner/manager of Joyería La Perla, a small chain of jewelry stores in Córdoba, Argentina, pondered the dilemma he faced. "A kidnap victim," he cursed; "why me, of all people?" He glanced around him at the small windowless room in which he found himself prisoner, and went over again in his mind the events of the past three hours.

At 6:30 P.M., as usual on Saturday evenings, he had locked the door of his shop, located on one of the main streets in Córdoba, and started his short walk home. As he crossed one of the major intersections in town, a black limousine pulled up in front of him, blocking his way. Three armed men jumped out of the car and tried to jostle him into the back seat. As he struggled to free himself, one of the bandits pulled out a gun and fired a shot, which grazed his chest. Wounded, Mr. Stauffer was soon forced into the car, tied, and blindfolded. He lost consciousness thereafter . . . and awoke to find himself lying on a hard bed in a small but clean room, his chest bandaged, and some food on a tray beside him. He had no idea where he was.

At that moment, one of his kidnappers suddenly opened the door of the room, and seeing that Mr. Stauffer was awake, asked him how he felt.

"A little bruised," he replied, "but listen, who *are* you?"

"We're members of the ERP," he answered. "You know what we're after. We're not out to hurt you as long as you cooperate. Now, I'll bring you some hot food, and would you like a newspaper to read?"

"Yes, please," said Mr. Stauffer quietly. With that, the fellow left and promptly returned with a bowl of hot stew and a paper. He then turned and left Mr. Stauffer alone again.

The ERP (Ejército Revolucionario del Pueblo) was a well-known guerilla group in Argentina. About 2000 of its members lived in Córdoba, a city of over 1,000,000 people. It was widely known that the group's primary objectives were to take from the pockets of the rich in order to give financial aid to the poverty-stricken Argentine farmers. By means of terrorist activities, the group claimed to lend support to over one third of the Argentine people, and in this way to be restoring justice to the country.

Mr. Stauffer realized that the ERP members normally demanded several million pesos[1] in ransom money. For this reason he could not understand why they had decided to choose a small jewelry chain owner, such as himself. George Stauffer owned two jewelry shops in Córdoba, both specializing in the sale of Swiss watches and other fine imported jewelry. Sales for the two stores reached 10 million pesos in 1975, while after-tax income amounted to 1.5 million pesos. Although Joyería La Perla had enjoyed quite a successful business record over the past twenty years, Mr. Stauffer did not consider himself to be a wealthy individual. He felt that in the city of Córdoba, there must be hundreds of businessmen more wealthy than himself.

At the age of 20, he had been sent to Argentina by a Swiss firm of jewellers with whom he had been working in Geneva. His first assignment was to learn the Argentine gem market. After one year in Argentina he was so impressed with the country that he decided to renew his contract for another three years. Then in 1930, at the age of 24, he left the firm to open his own jewelry store in Córdoba. After several difficult years, the business eventually began to run smoothly, becoming so successful that Mr. Stauffer was able to open a second store in 1970. Together the two retail outlets employed ten Argentinians.

Mr. Stauffer could not help but wonder how much the ERP would ask for his release. He remembered that it was the ERP's policy to set a ransom price which reflected their view of the kidnap victim's business ethics. They usually managed to procure a copy of their hostage's personal income tax return, from which they would establish a feasible base ransom price. Then if the group con-

[1] In June 1975, $1.00 = 32.15 pesos.

sidered the individual to be a "crook" in the business world, the ransom fee would be increased accordingly. If he was judged to be an honest person, the end price would differ very little from the original figure.

George Stauffer felt that over the past 35 years he had been an honest, socially conscious businessman. He had had no skirmishes with the local authorities nor with the Argentine businessmen in the area. In fact, he tended to keep very much to himself whenever possible. Friends in Córdoba had told him that as a foreigner, he was generally well respected in the community (Mr. Stauffer still retained his Swiss nationality); although, outside his immediate circle of friends and business colleagues, he felt that he was not well known.

As he reflected over what negotiating strategy he might develop in dealing with his kidnappers and what arguments he could use to lower the ransom price, he overheard a heated argument brewing among his three captors in the next room. It was obvious that the young man who had shot him was being thoroughly reprimanded by the other two. As Mr. Stauffer moved closer to the door to listen, he heard one of the kidnappers shout: "You fool, we cannot afford mistakes!" Suddenly the sharp crack of a gunshot rang out.

Mr. Stauffer could only guess what had happened. As he thought about it, he felt certain that the shooting in fact represented the disciplinary action of a well-organized group against one of its members. The young man had evidently panicked in a crisis situation, shot and wounded Mr. Stauffer, and now had had to pay for this lack of judgment.

. . . .

At the hotel in Córdoba where Mr. Stauffer had been staying (with his family living in Europe, he preferred to stay in a hotel), the phone had been ringing constantly. He had been expected to dine with friends on the evening of the kidnapping; and they, alarmed by his absence, called the hotel. When no one there seemed to know of his whereabouts, they checked with other friends and work associates, but to no avail. Word eventually reached the hotel Sunday evening that a man of Mr. Stauffer's height and build had been seen abducted the night before near a major intersection in central Córdoba.

After verifying the story, the hotel management contacted the Swiss Consulate in Córdoba—which, in turn, notified Mr. Stauffer's family in Geneva, explaining the few facts that were known. Mr. Stauffer's son, Hans, age 30, made immediate plans to fly to Argentina. He arrived early Tuesday afternoon in Córdoba, and decided to stay in his father's room at the hotel to await word from the kidnappers, and hopefully from his father. Since the night of the kidnapping, no message had been received.

. . . .

The next day, George Stauffer was told by the kidnappers of his son's arrival. He immediately asked them to deliver a message to Hans, explaining that he was alive and well. The note was dropped in one of the shop mailboxes on Wednesday morning, and delivered to Hans Stauffer that afternoon.

On that same afternoon, the kidnappers informed George Stauffer of their asking price for his freedom. He was stunned by their demand. "Seven million pesos," he exclaimed. "You're out of your mind. It's an impossible amount. The most I could possibly afford is 2 million."

The other two laughed. "Don't play around with us or you'll be sorry," said one, wielding his gun. It's 7 million, and we want the funds delivered in Swiss Francs."

Mr. Stauffer gasped. "But . . . " and he stopped short. He remembered some words of advice he'd heard before: act quickly and negotiate as rapidly as possible.

"We'll leave you alone to think it over," said the gun-wielder.

Mr. Stauffer was exasperated. "Surely they must realize that I have nothing close to 7 million pesos. He wondered how much the ERP really knew about his personal financial position. Perhaps they did not know that he had a family to support in Switzerland. His wife had decided to move back to Geneva when their three children were old enough to go to school, as she had wanted them to be educated in Europe. He returned to Switzerland twice a year to visit with them.

Now he wondered if he would ever see them again. "I must get out of here" he winced. "But how?" For a moment, he toyed with the idea of trying to escape or even of attacking his abductors. After all, he was still physically able for his age. But gradually he turned his mind back to the problem of negotiating a better ransom price. "If they really put the pressure on," he thought, "I could probably scrape together 3 million pesos by the end of the week, but they must understand that I have no funds in Switzerland."

He realized that he would have to be extremely cautious in dealing with his banks. In Argentina, banks were often forbidden by the government to release funds for the payment of ransoms. He therefore hoped that Hans had not notified the police of the kidnapping. They were known to be inefficient and unreliable, and Mr. Stauffer was sure that they would only complicate matters and make them worse. With these thoughts, he decided to write Hans another note, explaining what action should be taken.

Joyería La Perla Case (B)

George Stauffer, owner/manager of Joyería La Perla, a small chain of jewelry stores in Córdoba, Argentina, had spent the past two days negotiating the price of his freedom with two members of the ERP (Ejército Revolucionario del Pueblo). The guerilla group members had kidnapped him one week earlier. (See Joyería La Perla [A] case). After many long hours spent arguing, explaining, and bargaining, Mr. Stauffer eventually agreed, with much reluctance, that he would meet the kidnappers' demands for 4 million pesos. He had managed to convince his abductors to lower the ransom fee from their original price of 7 million pesos. The kidnappers had also agreed to drop the condition that the payment be made in Swiss francs.

It was arranged that Mr. Stauffer would be released upon receipt of the first 3 million pesos in cash; the balance would be due two weeks later. In order to obtain the first 3 million pesos, Mr. Stauffer wrote a series of checks to his son. These were to be dropped in the store mailboxes, and subsequently delivered to Hans at the hotel.

Mr. Stauffer, exhausted, then dropped down on the hard bed in his cubicle, to rest after the long negotiating ordeal. "I feel

---

"Joyería La Perla Case (B)" was prepared by Candis Descent and Deborah Henderson, Research Associates, under the supervision of Professor Alvar O. Elbing.

completely ruined," he muttered to himself. "Every last penny of my retirement savings has gone towards this cursed ransom." He shuddered at the idea that another 1 million pesos still had to be raised, and wondered how he'd ever be able to pay back the loans.

When Hans Stauffer received the checks from his father, he gasped at the total amount, but he understood immediately what had to be done. He visited several banks in the city and discreetly cashed a check in each one of them. Although he knew that his father did not have 3 million pesos available in cash, he felt he could rely on the good banking relationships which his father had developed, in order to obtain the majority of the funds. By the time he had completed his bank visits, he had 2 million pesos. He then decided to see some of his father's friends. Many of them had heard of the kidnapping and were prepared to help out, so that towards the end of the afternoon, Hans had managed to raise the remaining required funds.

Thursday morning he received a note from the ERP kidnappers, telling him where to leave the ransom money. As soon as the 3 million pesos had been claimed, his father would be released. At 5 P.M. Hans left the box of bills in the designated room of an empty office building and drove back to the hotel to wait.

At 8:30 P.M. he received a call from his father, who was waiting in a restaurant just outside Córdoba. It was a happy moment for both of them when Hans finally reached the restaurant. Although Mr. Stauffer was tired, he had not been badly treated. His captors had even bought him a smart new jacket to replace the blood-stained one that he had been wearing Saturday evening.

On the drive back to the hotel, George Stauffer was very quiet.

"What is it, Dad? You should be overjoyed to be free! We'll manage somehow without the 3 million pesos," gestured Hans sincerely.

"I'm not yet free in reality, Hans," explained Mr. Stauffer. "In the deal I reached with the ERP I agreed to raise another million pesos within the next two weeks."

"You're crazy! Now that you're out, you can forget about paying the rest. We'll leave Córdoba tonight and fly back to Switzerland. They'll never catch you there."

"It's not that simple. Don't you see, I've got my lifetime investment here. I can't just get up and leave it."

"Why not? Think of your family, yourself. You'll never be able to pay the money back."

George Stauffer was silent. He had heard that the rules of the ERP were very strict. In previous kidnapping cases, when businessmen had held out on further payments, other family members had been abducted. Some had been killed, others held for indefinite periods of time, and the ransom fees were usually higher still.

"Could we not inform the police now?" suggested Hans. "They could protect you while they searched for the culprits."

"No, I don't think so. It's too risky with the police here."

When they reached the hotel, George Stauffer did not want to listen to any more arguments. "I'll sleep on it, Hans," he said quietly. "I've got a lot of thinking to do. Good night."

Joyería La Perla Case (C)

Hans Stauffer had spent hours trying to convince his father, George Stauffer (owner/manager of a small chain of jewelry stores in Córdoba, Argentina), that he ought to leave Argentina once and for all; but his words fell on deaf ears. His father was determined to stay in Córdoba to raise the remaining 1 million pesos which the ERP guerilla group had demanded as ransom money. Mr. Stauffer spent the next two weeks meeting with his bank managers, selling stocks and securities, paying back the funds borrowed from friends, and convincing his store personnel that all was well. When Hans recognized that his arguments were futile, he left Córdoba to return to his work and family in Switzerland.

Exactly two weeks after Mr. Stauffer's release, a visibly disguised man suddenly stopped him in the street and inquired about the 1 million pesos. Mr. Stauffer assured him that the money was available, and wondered where he should deposit it. "I'll book in as a tourist at your hotel, taking the room next to yours," explained the young man. "Then at 8:30 tonight, I want you to deliver the funds personally to me."

"Isn't that method a bit dangerous?" suggested Mr. Stauffer. "The police may easily be watching the hotel. I'm sure that they know of the kidnapping by now, and I have a strong suspicion that they've been watching me." It was not unusual for kidnappers to demand further ransom money after the release of their hostages, as they had done in George Stauffer's case. If the police suspected that further contact would be made between a released hostage and the guerilla group, a detective was often assigned to follow the freed kidnapped victim.

But the ERP representative ignored the warning and disappeared.

At exactly 8:30 P.M., Mr. Stauffer delivered the remaining million pesos, as instructed. He watched closely as the young man counted the bills, nodded an approval, and transferred the cash to a suitcase. Mr. Stauffer then picked up the empty box which had contained the bills, turned, and left the man alone.

About an hour later, from his hotel room, Mr. Stauffer suddenly heard three gunshots ring out in the street below. He leaned out of his window, but could only see three or four men scrambling away in the darkness. Then all was silent.

The next morning he was shocked to read in the newspaper that one ERP member had been killed outside the hotel, another injured, and one had escaped unharmed. The police had also recovered a small amount of money in the incident. "Oh, my God," muttered Mr. Stauffer to himself. "I warned the fellow; but he didn't listen to me." Later that morning he received a telephone call from the Swiss Consulate. They had read about the events of the night before, and were adamant that he should return to Europe for at least six months, to avoid any possible reprisals.

But George Stauffer was not so ready to take a quick decision. After all, he had so many debts to pay back that he wondered how he could justifiably leave the country.

"Joyería La Perla Case (C)" was prepared by Candis Descent and Deborah Henderson, Research Associates, under the supervision of Professor Alvar O. Elbing.

PART TWO

A Framework for Decision Making

Chapter

3 Step 1: Perception of the Environment

The first step in decision making seems so obvious that it is commonly glossed over. This first step is the manager's perception that a situation or organizational process is in a state of *disequilibrium*—that it is not as it ought to be. The situation is perceived as requiring a solution.

This step of the decision process is likely to be taken for granted. Ordinarily, little attention is given to *why* certain situations are perceived as being in disequilibrium. Instead, it is the situation itself which grips attention—it is the solution process that begins to usurp the manager's energies. The perception that "a problem situation exists," however, is the key starting point to the entire decision process of organizational management.

The crux of the matter is this: No solution can be effective if it solves the wrong problem. And no problem can even begin to be solved if the manager does not recognize its existence. The only problems that can be dealt with by decision makers are those they *perceive* as problems. And for something to be perceived as a "problem," it must be perceived as falling within the manager's scope of responsibility or interest. Problems that are not perceived as such pass managers by and nothing is done to correct them.

Yet managers usually spend much more time solving problems, or attempting to solve them, than they spend considering the important questions involved in this step: On what basis do I decide *what* to solve? How am I alerted to those things I call *problems*? What signals give me clues to human disequilibria in human situations and processes?

THE MANAGER'S SOURCES OF STIMULI

Since the environment contains an infinite amount of "data," that is, an infinite number of sensory clues that could be perceived, obviously the decision maker cannot perceive all of them. Some are irrelevant to the manager's interests or role; some are outside the scope of familiar experience and go unnoticed; some are misinterpreted; and some are not recognized as "data." Nonetheless, in each decision the manager is responding to selected bits of data. The data perceived as relevant to the job can be thought of, from the manager's point of view, as information. *Information*, then, may be defined as that part of the available data that is viewed as meaningful by the decision maker.

The source of the clues or information that may initiate the decision-making process—that produce awareness of disequilibria—are, of course, many and varied. They may relate directly to the manager or to the organization. The process may be caused by the manager's personality or expectations, or by organizational standards or criteria. The source may be historic or current. It may be internal or external to the organization, chronic or acute. For the purposes of this analysis, stimuli that arouse feelings of disequilibria in the decision maker will be grouped into two kinds: those that are *structured* in themselves and those that are *unstructured*. For the decision-making process, the distinction is significant.

Structured Stimuli

Part of the manager's job is to give structure to the information that pertains to organizational management. The activities for which the manager is responsible are monitored through the formal routes set up by the manager for the flow of crucial information. A personnel manager, for example, may set up an index to monitor turnover, accident rates, or grievances. A production manager may monitor scrap rates, down time, and inventory levels. A marketing manager may be watching the ratio of this year's sales to last year's. A financial manager may regularly scrutinize the level of accounts receivable. Out of potential chaos, selected information is rationally structured to meet a manager's functional needs.

The particular structure applied to the information may be created by the manager as, for example, in setting up a procedure for the systematic reporting of organizational turnover rates, production figures, or tolerance levels on controlled processes. Or the manager may merely monitor a structure that was created elsewhere, such as gross national product figures, the delivery schedules of suppliers, official readings of the levels of water pollution, or daily stock market averages. These are all examples of structured stimuli in the manager's environment.

Structured stimuli, then, are signal systems set up in advance to warn the decision maker when certain important states of disequilibrium may warrant decision making. *The disequilibrium point is identified by the signal system itself, so that in effect, the first step of the decision-making process is initiated by the signal system.* Specified "crisis points" can often be determined rationally ahead of time. Even crisis points which are not constant, but change in relation to specific variables, can be a predetermined part of the system. A turnover rate of 5 percent may be prestructured as "normal," where 10 percent automatically initiates a review of causal factors.

It might be said that the major task of a good manager is to structure as much of the necessary information in the environment as possible so as to be free for other activities. However, the danger in placing total reliance on structured clues is that monitoring may pick up only the information selected by the system and overlook other meaningful information. This may delay one's reaction to change.

Unstructured Stimuli

Regardless of how well a manager structures the environment, not all the clues to the possible existence of a problem can be structured in advance. Unplanned-for stimuli often arouse a feeling of disequilibrium. An offhand comment by a superior or a subordinate, an unexpected piece of news, conflicting reports from different sources, or even an indefinable feeling of the decision maker that something in the organization is "not right" may be perceived as signaling problems even though they do not fall into a structured category.

The principal source of unstructured stimuli is the social system of the organization. It is primarily in the behavior of this social system that the aware manager discovers clues to the existence of problems. It is in responding to these unstructured stimuli that a manager most clearly demonstrates managerial skill and sensitivity.

Although the consequences of the collective behavior of employees can generally be structured and monitored in terms of output, turnover, absenteeism, wage levels, union membership figures, and so on, other factors, such as the satisfactions and dissatisfactions that result in high or low morale among workers, are less easily structured. In such instances, *it is sensitivity to unstructured "messages" and knowledge about behavior that enables the manager to initiate a decision-making process at the appropriate time.*

Thus a major concern of the manager must be the perception of unstructured stimuli in the area of human behavior—stimuli that may indicate potential problems.

SELF-AWARENESS AND UNSTRUCTURED STIMULI

One of the most important determinants of the perception of unstructured stimuli is the perception process itself. As noted in Chapter 2, psychological findings on the perception process indicate that human beings do not simply "mirror" reality; perception of any situation is a complex behavioral process—influenced as significantly by internal psychological factors as by external stimuli. All of our perceptions are a psychological "structuring" of the given stimuli. By such processes as the selection, addition, omission, and interpretation of data, based on numerous factors in our past experience, we actually shape what we

Table 1 Individual Frame of Reference in Decision Making

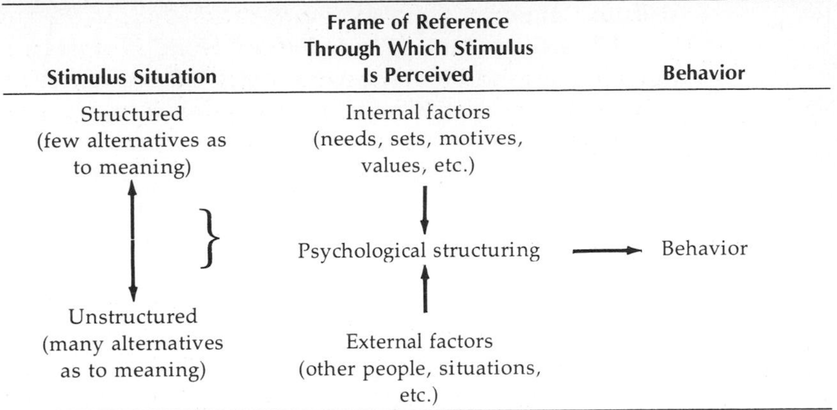

Stimulus Situation	Frame of Reference Through Which Stimulus Is Perceived		Behavior
Structured (few alternatives as to meaning)	Internal factors (needs, sets, motives, values, etc.)		
↕ }	↓ Psychological structuring ↑	→	Behavior
Unstructured (many alternatives as to meaning)	External factors (other people, situations, etc.)		

Source: Sherif and Sherif (1956), p. 79 (adapted).

see. Hence it can be said that the organization and labeling of information is as much a function of the observer as of the data observed.

Everyone has a personal *frame of reference,* a unique "system of functional relations among factors operative at a given time which determine psychological structuring and hence behavior" (Sherif and Sherif, 1956, p. 80). That frame of reference includes all the internal factors that are important to the individual—attitudes, norms, values, beliefs, fears, goals, etc.—as well as all the external stimuli which supplement the original stimulus situation, such as other people, the location, the physical environment, the sequence of acts, and the social context. All of these internal and external factors operate psychologically to structure the otherwise unstructured stimuli; and new information tends to be organized so as to maintain preexisting views. Table 1 illustrates the psychological structuring process.

In order for the individual to process data psychologically, it must have some form or structure; no one can exist in a totally amorphous or ambiguous situation. The structure of the data may be external to the individual—that is, it may exist in the stimulus or the environment—or it may be imposed by the individual. The relationship between the amount of structure inherent in a stimulus (or assigned to it beforehand) and the amount of psychological structuring necessarily imposed by the decision maker is generally inverse. That is, the greater its external organization, the clearer it will seem to the manager, offering less opportunity to structure it from one's own frame of reference. On the other hand, the less structured the stimulus, the greater the need for internal structuring to make it "make sense" so that the decision maker can respond to it. In any case, a stimulus must have structure of one form or another before a decision maker can respond to it. And the less clear the stimulus, the greater the role the individual's own structuring will play in perception.

Thus the organization of the real world is to a large extent determined by the individual decision maker's frame of reference. *To understand that world successfully—its infinite number of data—the manager must first have an accurate insight into his or her own frame of reference, how that frame of reference structures the world.* Such self-awareness must rank high on the decision maker's priority list. But how can one go about increasing it?

Identification and Acceptance of Feelings

A first step in gaining a better sense of self-awareness is developing the ability *to identify* and *to accept* one's own feelings, which is not so simple or easy as might be supposed. Feelings of discomfort, guilt, envy, joy, anger, fear, satisfaction, or whatever, are generally vague experiences unless we make a special effort to identify them in words. However, unless we can emotionally *accept* our true feelings rather than disapprove of them, we are very likely unwilling to identify them honestly. We actually cannot be clear about the nature of our feelings if we do not accept them. Ultimately, unless we accept and identify our real feelings, our emotional energy may be expended in guilt rather than in the all-important process of deciding what to do about them. The first requirement then in managing is to *know one's own feelings*. Only then is it possible to begin to understand one's own frame of reference.

But feelings are not always easy to define. How often do we feel uncomfortable for no apparent reason? How often are some feelings confused with other, conflicting feelings? How often is their *referent* (object toward which they are directed) not recognized? Inability to define feelings may result in behavior that is highly inappropriate. (How many of us get nasty with a secretary or the switchboard operator after being criticized by our boss?)

It is understandable, then, that our feelings in a particular situation or our general emotional state at a particular time have a great deal to do with how we structure external stimuli. Unstable feelings in themselves may cause us to view the behavior of others as constituting a problem. Unidentified feelings in ourselves may cause us to sense a disequilibrium in a distorted way. We may view the behavior of others as a problem when it is our own feelings which are the problem. We may label a particular stimulus as a symptom of a disequilibrium solely because of our own psychological structuring. We may perceive a situation in a way that has little to do with the true meaning of the stimulus situation. The greater the awareness we have of our own state of feelings, the greater will be our ability to differentiate between the inherent structure of *external* stimuli and the structure our own *internal* feelings impose upon those stimuli.

Guidelines for Self-Management

To develop self-management, which begins with self-awareness, we should train ourselves to follow these guidelines habitually in response to our own emotions:

1. *Know what we are feeling.* It is necessary that we allow ourselves to fully experience our true feelings and to identify exactly how we are feeling at any given time, rather than to seal off our feelings as being inappropriate or wrong even before they are recognized. Feelings not faced may eventually express themselves in ways we would rather not have happen.

2. *Identify the probable cause and referent of our feelings.* Relating our feelings to their cause can assist us in accepting them as legitimate, and assist us in understanding whether or not the feeling is appropriate to the situation at issue, or only to some prior experience of our own. Understanding our feelings can assist us in more clearly differentiating external stimuli from our subjective frame of reference, and can prepare us for doing something constructive about our feelings.

3. *Express feelings at the appropriate time.* Feelings should be expressed, not suppressed. Rather than letting feelings build up and influence our life in a general way, we should express them in an *appropriate* way. If, for example, the behavior of a subordinate makes us angry, it is one thing to express that feeling by saying to ourselves—or even aloud—"I'm mad!" It is another to fire the subordinate summarily. As managers, we must train ourselves to express our feelings in a nondestructive manner. The point is that *we* must decide the manner and place for expressing feelings, rather than letting the feelings manage us.

4. *Separate feelings from situations.* The next stage in developing self-awareness and self-management is development of the ability to distinguish feelings from the situations that give rise to them. This means that we train ourselves to perceive, not vague, uncomfortable situations, but ourselves as uncomfortable and the situations as separate. Further, we learn to distinguish between our own feelings and those of others, rather than color others' behavior with feelings we impute to them.

5. *Examine our behavior.* Finally, we can develop self-awareness and self-management through the habit of reflecting upon and questioning our own responses. When confronted by a particular stimulus, *why* did we behave as we did? Did we perceive it as similar to some prior stimulus? Did we behave in a manner which suggests that we applied a ready-made structure to it?

Perhaps the most important step in the decision-making process, and the most difficult step to understand, is discovering how or why we identify certain stimuli as reflecting a problem—an organization out of equilibrium—while we ignore other stimuli. This is an important matter for analytical reflection, for the only problems we can eventually solve, or even attempt to solve, are those we can identify.

In interpreting our behavior we will find it useful to compare it with the behavior of others in a common or similar situation. Did we react differently from others in the situation? Why? Why did others see it differently? This is not a question of whose behavior is "right" or "wrong," but an attempt to understand, by reflecting on our responses, how we structured the stimuli in that situation. Discussing a situation with someone who behaved differently may furnish useful insights into how and why each person structured it differently. Indeed, a major purpose of case discussions in the classroom is that individuals can respond differently to a stimulus situation and examine the reasons for their different responses.

Once we understand that our own perceptual processes tend to structure our experiences, we can watch for the ways by which we habitually structure situations that interfere with objective observation. Lombard (1950) has usefully defined *observation* as "the capacity to discriminate between reality as it actually is and reality as any one of us sees it" (p. 291). Any roadblock to objective observation of organizational disequilibria impairs the entire decision-making process.

ROADBLOCKS IN THE DECISION-MAKING PROCESS

Since the objective recognition of a "disequilibrium" initiates the decision process, it is important to recognize those factors that hamper decision-making effectiveness. There are a number of potential roadblocks to this first step in decision making. The following are the most common.

1. *The tendency to evaluate.* When first confronted with decision-making situations, most people have a tendency to evaluate rather than investigate. Clyde Kluckhohn (1951), the noted anthropologist, sees this tendency to evaluate as a basic human characteristic. A tardy worker is "bad"; someone else's way of doing something is "wrong"; our own way is "right." This tendency to respond with an immediate evaluation must be retrained. Evaluation precludes inquiry into a fuller understanding of the situation—*why* the worker was late, or *why* someone approached a situation differently from how we did. Always, the keynote to the beginning of the decision-making process is to *substitute inquiry for evaluation.*

2. *The tendency to equate new and old experiences.* Because our own experiences seem so clear to us, they usually become the basis of our approach to future situations. As we have noted, however, relying on past experiences tends to make us search for similarities between a current and a prior experience and to reduce a new situation to the terms of an old one. Even in truly similar situations, the second will differ from the first—if only because the two occurred at different points in time. An American professor returning to a European management institute ten years after his first visit was extremely unhappy when he tried to

recreate the prior experience. Both he and the institute had changed.

Experience can be useful, but in general people merely *learn an experience* rather than learning *from* that experience. Those who work in an authoritarian environment, for example, tend to learn behavior that is appropriate to such an environment; they are less likely to learn from the experience about the *effects* of authoritarianism as compared with other leadership styles. To learn *from* an experience, one must make a conscious inquiry, which begins by viewing each situation as basically unique, not simply a reflection of an old experience.

3. *The tendency to use available solutions.* The ready availability of an apparent solution may make an administrator more or less indifferent to the precise nature of a problem. Thus, overemphasis on solutions may block progress in decision making. Having taken an advanced course in modern marketing methods, for example, a student may see all problems in terms of marketing solutions. Similarly, having acquired a new computer, a manager may define all administrative problems in terms of computer solutions. This factor is even built into specific professional disciplines. Certain professionals may have spent so much time preparing themselves to see certain variables that they see all situations in terms of their particular specialties. When we focus on an available solution, we may also inadvertently define the disequilibrium to fit that preconceived solution. When hiring a consultant or expert, in fact, one may have defined the solution when selecting the expert. An engineer is not likely to define a problem as psychological.

4. *The tendency to deal with problems at face value.* When we are presented with information about a problem, our reaction may be to deal with it in the terms in which it is presented. Then, once the situation has been defined, further inquiry may be blocked. Managers should take their cue from physicians, who begin with the symptoms their patients define. But they do not stop there. They also make firsthand investigations.

5. *The tendency to direct decisions toward a single goal.* Behavior is usually goal-oriented. Certainly organizational behavior is oriented toward organizational goals, but sometimes organizational goals are reduced to a single goal in the mind of a manager. Tending to view all situations in terms of this one goal, the manager may overlook other goals more relevant in a specific situation. For example, a sales manager attempting to increase sales volume in a territory may emphasize fast-moving products and neglect the company's policy of maintaining a diversified line. A clear picture of goals, both individual and organizational, and of the hierarchical relationships among goals, is essential for a balanced view of disequilibria.

6. *The tendency to confuse symptoms and problems.* A stimulus that tells us something is wrong may indeed constitute the problem. On the other hand, a stimulus may be a symptom of a wholly different problem. Or a stimulus may constitute one problem and also be a symptom of other problems in the organization. It is always important to investigate

beyond symptoms to find out what cause may be at the bottom of the problem situation.

Consider the case of an employee who initiates a large number of grievances: the washroom is dirty, the cafeteria's lunches are cold, the stockroom workers are uncooperative. If we respond to these stimuli without further examination, we might accept the grievances as the only problems. Indeed, the grievances, the disequilibria, *may* be the only problems, but on the other hand they may be evidence that the individual is having difficulty adjusting to the job and needs help. Or further investigation might reveal that the complaints are only a symptom of unrest in an entire unit of the organization. The complainer may be the person who has the least tolerance for such unrest and therefore is the first to express grievances. A better understanding of the situation may be required to determine whether these grievances result from the problems of one employee or from a problem situation, or both.

7. *The tendency to overlook "unsolvable" problems*. Situations that have been long endured as problem situations may eventually be labeled unsolvable. For example, a long-time employee who is difficult to get along with may come to be viewed as being "that way," and everyone adjusts to his or her behavior. After a time, the employee's behavior is regarded as an "unsolvable" problem and taken for granted, and eventually the problem behavior ceases being defined as a problem. As a result, when a crisis occurs, the personality of the long-time employee may be overlooked among the factors that caused the crisis. The manager should make a special effort not to overlook long-term "unsolvable" problems as part of the overall disequilibrium picture.

8. *The tendency to look at the referent.* Value judgments may reveal more about the evaluator than about their object. If, for example, we are told that water is hot, we have been told very little about the temperature of the water. For this evaluation to be clear, we must understand its context—the evaluator's expectations, experience with water under these circumstances, and so on. Hot water is a different thing to a person making tea than to a barber preparing lather, to a mother bathing an infant, to a summertime swimmer, or to an Arctic explorer. Despite the fact that such an evaluation is relative, we nevertheless tend to inspect the referent, the water, to confirm its "hotness." Similarly, if in a human situation we are told that an employee is irresponsible, we are apt to look first for signs of irresponsibility. A more appropriate first step in such a case is to consider the evaluator: we should attempt to understand why this evaluation was made, what evidence supports it, and what the circumstances were. In this context, we can determine whether we agree with the evaluation.

9. *The tendency to respond automatically.* All the foregoing tendencies add up to a tendency to preconceive the nature of a disequilibrium, and preconception has a strong effect on the structure of decision making. It leads to premature, automatic responses, rather than to the systematic inquiry which constitutes effective decision making.

CONCLUSION

It is vital to distinguish between a disequilibrium that calls our attention to the fact that something is wrong, and the problem itself. Although these phenomena may be identical, more often they will be different and distinct. In human management, the decision-making process is usually initiated by the perception that something is wrong, that there is a problem, that something is out of equilibrium, that a situation requires a decision. Generally, managers tend to focus on the situation rather than on their perception of it, but both require analysis if the problem's definition is to be objective and lead to appropriate decision making.

REFERENCES

Dearborn, D. C., and H. Simon. "Selective Perception: A Note on the Departmental Identification of Executives." *Sociometry*, June 1958.

Elbing, Alvar O., Jr. "Perception, Motivation, and Business Behavior." In *Interdisciplinary Studies in Business Behavior*, ed. Joseph McGuire. South-Western, 1962.

Kluckhohn, Clyde, et al. "Values and Value-Orientation in the Theory of Action." In *Toward a General Theory of Action*, ed. Talcott Parsons and Edward Shils. Harvard University Press, 1951.

Lombard, George F. F. "Self-Awareness and the Scientific Method." *Science*, September 15, 1960.

Sherif, Muzafer, and Carolyn Sherif. *An Outline of Social Psychology*, rev. ed. Harper & Row, 1956.

Wittreich, W. J. "Visual Perception and Personality." *Scientific American*, April 1959.

The Case of Norrköping-Beta

In October 1970, the stockholders of Norrköping Electronics, Sweden's second largest producer of communications equipment, approved its merger with Svenska-Beta, a developer of highly specialized telecommunication installations. Although the two companies had been in competition for only about 25 percent of their sales, their general areas of technical expertise, as well as their production capabilities, were somewhat overlapping. The merger had the potential for both the rationalization of manufacturing and for more effective channels of distribution.

The approval of the merger followed one and a half years of careful negotiation and planning by an Integration Committee, consisting of the Executive Committees of the two firms and a specially selected integration staff. Well aware of the potential problems facing the new organization, the committee and staff were attentive to every detail of the proposed merger. The merger's overwhelming acceptance was a tribute to their work.

The newly merged organization—Norrköping-Beta—became the largest Swedish producer in the telecommunications industry. Prior to the merger the two firms had had quite different styles of operation and quite different managerial philosophies. These differences appeared to be successfully resolved. From most points of view the merger was judged successful. Within two years the new organization had successfully integrated, worldwide, 40,000 employees, 32 production facilities, and total assets of over 5 billion Swedish Kroners. From a marketing point of view, the new organization was quickly recognized and accepted by the public.

Although the merger was successful overall, the effects on individual managers varied. Some managers benefited and some felt no change at all, while for some it caused a major disruption of their careers. Although both organizations insisted that no one would lose his job because of the merger, not everyone, of course, was placed where he wished to be.

Some three years after the merger Norrköping-Beta asked an outside consultant to investigate what the merger had meant to the careers of various managers. A brief description of four of those cases is presented here.

Rolf Jensen

At the time of the merger, both organizations had, within their components divisions, departments responsible for manufacturing semiconductors. Rolf Jensen had started the department at Norrköping several years before, and from the standpoint of financial results, had been very successful. He was a good salesman, developed the German and Scandinavian markets outside Sweden, and ran a profitable department. As a manager, however, he was felt to have several shortcomings. Complaints were frequently heard from his subordinates that he remained aloof in the office, developed an unnecessary status difference between himself and other members of his staff, and was dictatorial. Since the department was profitable, the Norrköping Executive Committee had always rewarded him for his performance, however.

Ulf Landin was head of semiconductors at Beta. A slightly younger man than Rolf, Ulf had been identified as having a strong potential in that organization. As a result of their investigations, the integration staff felt Landin had a greater potential for the long run, primarily because of his more modern managerial style. On their recommendation Landin was chosen to head the semiconductor department of the components division of the newly merged organization.

Rolf Jensen was then offered the position of head of marketing under Landin, to be responsible for semiconductor marketing worldwide. During the discussion of this offer, when Landin proposed his future plans to Jensen, it was obvious that the two were in total disagreement at every point. Jensen was unwilling to work under Landin and refused to accept the position. He demanded that some other, more appropriate place be found for him in the organization. The position of head of marketing was then offered to a former subordinate of Rolf Jensen, who accepted it.

Rolf Jensen's case went to the Executive Committee with the clear notation that he had turned down the offer made to him by the Merger Committee. This was not a point in his favor. Although the Committee attempted to fulfill its mandate to find a position for everyone, for some time there seemed to be no place for Jensen. Several months later, however, a small joint venture was being formed in Denmark with an American company. The marketing operation fell within the general area of Jensen's past experience. He was asked if he would be willing to become its managing director. It was felt that Jensen's marketing skills could be used in this organization and since the new unit was smaller, his managerial skills might be adequate. Jensen accepted the position.

He remained in the position for one and half years, during which time the operation lost money. His leadership style again plagued him, although it was not altogether clear that the organization's lack of success was his fault: there were some cost problems associated with the manufacture of the product. Nonetheless, the Executive Committee was unwilling to leave Jensen in the position any longer. The director of corporate development was willing to add Jensen to his headquarters staff for a short period while they looked for another position for him. Jensen's usefulness there decreased rapidly and after a few months he pleaded with the Executive Committee to give him something to do—"anything to do."

Although the request was not well received by the Committee, one committee member had been Jensen's former superior at Norrköping and remembered him as a successful manager. He came to Jensen's defense. From his standpoint Jensen had been a "results"-oriented manager in the old Norrköping company and he didn't see why Jensen couldn't be effective now.

The Executive Committee decided to intervene with the manager of printed circuits, who finally agreed to offer Jensen a staff position in marketing. Jensen has been on that job now for six months and it is too early to tell if he is working out.

To problems still facing the organization are that Jensen is relatively young—probably 50—so that if he does not work out he is too young for retirement; the second problem is that his salary is considerably higher than the level at which he is working, and this salary is being charged to the printed-circuits department.

Jon Jaeger

At the time Norrköping Electronics and Svenska-Beta merged, both companies had sales and marketing organizations in Latin

America. They were virtually identical. Therefore, two people existed for each job. Jon Jaeger was Norrköping's sales manager for Peru, Colombia, Venezuela, and Panama. He had been quite successful in this position. He had worked hard, sacrificing time from his family and his own leisure, and believed that he would be appropriately rewarded by the organization.

To cope with the duplication of staff after the merger, however, it was necessary for each territory to be cut in half. Instead of four countries, Jaeger was offered responsibility only for Venezuela and Panama. In addition, to accommodate to the new organizational structure, his immediate superior was moved down one level in the organization, causing Jon to move down as well.

Along with the merger, a new organizational system was being introduced. Decision making was being passed down to the local countries, making the area manager's position more advisory than authoritative. Under the former organization, Jaeger had been the final authority on decision making in all four countries. He was "Mr. Norrköping," and no important decision was made without him. Now, however, in place of having power he had merely influence. What's more, the Latin American operation now was responsible for planning, control, and information systems. For Jaeger, the merger amounted to a smaller territory, a lower position in the organization, less power, and new functions about which he felt uncomfortable. He refused to take the new position.

Division management was not unhappy with Jaeger's decision since they had too many people anyway. At that point, Jaeger took home leave in order to discuss his situation with management in Sweden. Although Jaeger was given unfavorable reports by some of his subordinates, his performance had been excellent and his future looked good. The Executive Committee, therefore, suggested he return to the division and wait for things to settle down. The Committee advised him to apologize, saying that he had been rash, and to accept whatever position he was offered. By this time, however, a month had passed and all positions had been allocated. Now, desperate for a position, Jaeger visited the director of management development and said, "My whole world has collapsed. I gave everything to that job. My son told me last night that I wasn't even a good father. I did everything for the company, and now you want to get rid of me."

It was not easy to deal with Jaeger's problem. Latin America was overstaffed, decisions had been made, and Jaeger had refused the organization's wishes. At the same time his situation was compelling. Fortunately, a new consumer products division was being formed to distribute some newly developed consumer products in Latin America. Jaeger's qualifications were presented to that division's management, and they were pleased with his Latin American experience. He eventually returned to Latin America as a salesman for consumer products, a job less important than the one he had been offered, but in the area of his expertise.

Alf Ericcson

During the period 1962 to 1968 Svenska-Beta had developed rapidly, especially in North America. At that time a large number of new managers were brought into the organization from outside. Alf Ericcson was brought in at that time. He was a Swedish national who had been hired in the United States but had returned to the parent organization to take a staff job coordinating the marketing of various products. His record in the States had been very good and he proved very clever in this coordinating position.

At the time of the merger discussions,

Ericcson was given the assignment of coordinating several areas of production in the new division. This moved him to the level of the Divisional Integration Committee—a dramatic jump for a man of his age. While serving on the Divisional Committee, the head of the division was promoted to the Executive Committee and, at 42, Ericcson was made division manager. This made him the youngest division manager in the new company.

The position of division manager at Norrköping-Beta is only one step from the top—from the Executive Committee. It is assumed that Ericcson will some day be promoted to that Committee, but he has 23 years remaining before retirement, with only that one promotion available. Owing to the merger, openings occurred rapidly for Ericcson, so that now he is out of line with the normal promotion schedule. In his present position, Ericcson is a strong manager, generally well received by his subordinates. He is also very interested in community social problems. He has recently announced that he would not accept as a manager in his division any man who was not *committed* to the resolution of social problems in the community external to the organization. It is Ericcson's view that organizations like Norrköping-Beta have a significant responsibility in the solution of community problems.

Bo Hanson

From early in his life, Bo Hanson wanted an executive position. As a boy he had reached top levels of the Boy Scouts, and at the present time is a top-ranking Swedish army officer. When he entered Norrköping Electronics at the age of 40 (it was six years before the merger), he was seen as a bright young man who should do well in the organization. His legal training and experience seemed well suited to the position eventually assigned to him—secretary to the Executive Committee. When the discussions for the merger began, it was noted by the Norrköping Executive Committee that the secretary to Beta's Executive Committee was one level higher in the organization than was Hanson. For strategic bargaining purposes, therefore, Hanson's position was moved one level higher.

Because Hanson's counterpart at Beta was older, more experienced, and more capable in that position, Hanson did not survive the competition for secretary to the new Executive Committee, and was moved to the staff of the Integration Committee, where he served for two years. When the Integration Committee was dissolved at the time of the merger, it became necessary to find a position for Hanson at the same level to which he had been moved. He was, therefore, given division head responsibilities at age 46.

The Aircraft Brake Scandal

The B. F. Goodrich Company is what business magazines like to refer to as "a major American corporation." It has operations in a dozen states and as many foreign countries; and of these far-flung facilities, the Goodrich plant at Troy, Ohio, is not the most imposing. It is a small, one-story building, once used to manufacture airplanes. Set in the grassy flatlands of west-central Ohio, it employs only about six hundred people. Nevertheless, it is one of the three largest manufacturers of aircraft wheels and brakes, a leader in a most profitable industry. Goodrich wheels and brakes support such well-known planes as the F111, the C5A, the Boeing 727, the XB70, and many others.

Contracts for aircraft wheels and brakes often run into millions of dollars, and ordinarily a contract with a total value of less than $70,000, though welcome, would not create any special stir of joy in the hearts of Goodrich sales personnel. But purchase order P-237138—issued on June 18, 1967, by the LTV Aerospace Corporation, ordering 202 brake assemblies for a new Air Force plane at a total price of $69,417—was received by Goodrich with considerable glee. And there was good reason. Some ten years previously, Goodrich had built a brake for LTV that was, to say the least, considerably less than a rousing success. The brake had not lived up to Goodrich's promises, and after experiencing considerable difficulty, LTV had written off Goodrich as a source of brakes. Since that time, Goodrich salesmen had been unable to sell so much as a shot of brake fluid to LTV. So in 1967, when LTV requested bids on wheels and brakes for the new A7D light attack aircraft it proposed to build for the Air Force, Goodrich submitted a bid that was absurdly low, so low that LTV could not, in all prudence, turn it down.

Goodrich had, in industry parlance, "bought into the business." The company did not expect to make a profit on the initial deal; it was prepared, if necessary, to lose money. But aircraft brakes are not something that can be ordered off the shelf. They are designed for a particular aircraft, and once an aircraft manufacturer buys a brake, he is forced to purchase all replacement parts from the brake manufacturer. The $70,000 that Goodrich would get for making the brake would be a drop in the bucket when compared with the cost of the linings and other parts the Air Force would have to buy from Goodrich during the lifetime of the aircraft.

There was another factor, besides the low bid, that had undoubtedly influenced LTV. All aircraft brakes made today are of the disk type, and the bid submitted by Goodrich called for a relatively small brake, one containing four disks and weighing only 106 pounds. The weight of any aircraft part is extremely important: the lighter a part is, the heavier the plane's payload can be.

The brake was designed by one of Goodrich's most capable engineers, John Warren. A tall, lanky, blond graduate of Purdue, Warren had come from the Chrysler Corporation seven years before and had become adept at aircraft brake design. The happy-go-lucky manner he usually maintained belied a temper that exploded whenever anyone ventured to offer criticism of his work, no matter how small. On these occasions,

Warren would turn red in the face, often throwing or slamming something and then stalking from the scene. As his coworkers learned the consequences of criticizing him, they did so less and less readily, and when he submitted his preliminary design for the A7D brake, it was accepted without question.

Warren was named project engineer for the A7D, and he, in turn, assigned the task of producing the final production design to a newcomer to the Goodrich engineering stable, Searle Lawson. Just turned 26, Lawson had been out of the Northrop Institute of Technology only one year when he came to Goodrich in January 1967. He had been assigned to various "paper projects" to break him in, and after several months spent reviewing statistics and old brake designs, he was beginning to fret at the lack of challenge. When told he was being assigned to his first "real" project, he was elated and immediately plunged into his work.

The major portion of the design had already been completed by Warren, and major subassemblies for the brake had already been ordered from Goodrich suppliers. Naturally, however, before Goodrich could start making the brakes on a production basis, much testing would have to be done. Lawson would have to determine the best materials to use for the linings and discover what minor adjustments in the design would have to be made.

Then, after the preliminary testing and after the brake was judged ready for production, one whole brake assembly would undergo a series of grueling, simulated braking stops and other severe trials called qualification tests. These tests are required by the military, which gives very detailed specifications on how they are to be conducted, the criteria for failure, and so on. They are performed in the Goodrich plant's test laboratory, where huge machines called dynamometers can simulate the weight and speed of almost any aircraft.

A Dismal Beginning

Searle Lawson was well aware that much work had to be done before the A7D brake could go into production, and he knew that LTV had set the last two weeks in June 1968 as the starting dates for flight tests. So he decided to begin testing immediately. Goodrich's suppliers had not yet delivered the brake housing and other parts, but the brake disks had arrived, and using the housing from a brake similar in size and weight to the A7D brake, Lawson built a prototype. The prototype was installed in a test wheel and placed on one of the big dynamometers in the plant's test laboratory. Lawson began a series of tests, "landing" the wheel and brake at the A7D's landing speed and braking it to a stop. The main purpose of these preliminary tests was to learn what temperatures would develop within the brake during the simulated stops and to evaluate lining materials tentatively selected for use.

During a normal aircraft landing the temperatures inside the brake may reach 1000 degrees, and occasionally a bit higher. During Lawson's first simulated landings, the temperature of his prototype brake reached 1500 degrees. The brake glowed a bright cherry-red and threw off incandescent particles of metal and lining material as the temperature reached its peak. After a few such stops, the brake was dismantled and the linings were found to be almost completely disintegrated. Lawson chalked this first failure up to chance and, ordering new lining materials, tried again.

The second attempt was a repeat of the first. The brake became extremely hot, causing the lining materials to crumble into dust.

After the third such failure, Lawson, inexperienced though he was, knew that the fault lay not in defective parts or unsuitable lining material but in the basic design of the brake itself. Ignoring Warren's original computations, Lawson made his own, and it didn't take him long to discover where the trouble lay—the brake was too small. There simply was not enough surface area on the disks to stop the aircraft without generating the excessive heat that caused the linings to fail.

The answer to the problem was obvious, but far from simple—the four-disk brake would have to be scrapped, and a new design, using five disks, would have to be developed. The implications were not lost on Lawson. Such a step would require junking the four-disk-brake subassemblies, many of which had now begun to arrive from the various suppliers. It would also mean several weeks of preliminary design and testing and many more weeks of waiting while the suppliers made and delivered the new subassemblies.

Yet, several weeks had already gone by since LTV's order had arrived, and the date for delivery of the first production brakes for flight testing was only a few months away.

Although John Warren had more or less turned the A7D over to Lawson, he knew of the difficulties Lawson had been experiencing. He had assured the young engineer that the problem revolved around getting the right kind of lining material. Once that was found, he said, the difficulties would end.

Despite the evidence of the abortive tests and Lawson's careful computations, Warren rejected the suggestion that the four-disk brake was too light for the job. He knew that his superior had already told LTV, in rather glowing terms, that the preliminary tests on the A7D brake were very successful. Indeed, Warren's superiors weren't aware at this time of the troubles on the brake. It would have been difficult for Warren to admit not only that he had made a serious error in his calculations and original design but that his mistakes had been caught by a green kid, barely out of college.

Warren's reaction to a five-disk brake was not unexpected by Lawson, and, seeing that the four-disk brake was not to be abandoned so easily, he took his calculations and dismal test results one step up the corporate ladder.

At Goodrich, the man who supervises the engineers working on projects slated for production is called, predictably, the projects manager. The job was held by a short, chubby, bald man named Robert Sink. Some fifteen years before, Sink had begun working at Goodrich as a lowly draftsman. Slowly, he worked his way up. Despite his geniality, Sink was neither respected nor liked by the majority of the engineers, and his appointment as their supervisor did not improve their feelings toward him. He possessed only a high-school diploma, and it quite naturally rankled those who had gone through years of college to be commanded by a man whom they considered their intellectual inferior. But, though Sink had no college training, he had something even more useful: a fine working knowledge of company politics.

Puffing on a Meerschaum pipe, Sink listened gravely as young Lawson confided his fears about the four-disk brake. Then he examined Lawson's calculations and the results of the abortive tests. Despite the fact that he was not a qualified engineer, in the strictest sense of the word, it must certainly have been obvious to Sink that Lawson's calculations were correct and that a four-disk brake would never work on the A7D.

But other things of equal importance were also obvious. First, to concede that Lawson's calculations were correct would also mean conceding that Warren's calculations were incorrect. As projects manager, not only was he responsible for Warren's activities, but, in admitting that Warren had erred, he would have to admit that he had erred in trusting Warren's judgment. It also meant that, as projects manager, it would be he who would have to explain the whole messy situation to the Goodrich hierarchy, not only at Troy but possibly on the corporate level at Goodrich's Akron offices. And having taken

Warren's judgment of the four-disk brake at face value, he had assured LTV, not once but several times, that about all there was left to do on the brake was pack it in a crate and ship it out the door.

There's really no problem at all, he told Lawson. After all, Warren was an experienced engineer, and if he said the brake would work, it would work. Just keep on testing and probably, maybe even on the very next try, it'll work out just fine.

Lawson was far from convinced, but without the support of his superiors there was little he could do except keep on testing. By now, housings for the four-disk brake had begun to arrive at the plant, and Lawson was able to build a production model of the brake and begin the formal qualification tests demanded by the military.

The first qualification attempts went exactly as the tests on the prototype had. Terrific heat developed within the brakes, and after a few short, simulated stops the linings crumbled. A new type of lining material was ordered and once again an attempt to qualify the brake was made. Again, failure.

Experts were called in from lining manufacturers, and new lining "mixes" were tried, always with the same result. Failure.

It was now the last week in March 1968, and flight tests were scheduled to begin in seventy days. Twelve separate attempts had been made to qualify the brake, and all had failed. It was no longer possible for anyone to ignore the glaring truth that the brake was a dismal failure and that nothing short of a major design change could ever make it work.

On April 4, the thirteenth attempt at qualification was begun. This time no attempt was made to conduct the tests by the methods and techniques spelled out in the military specifications. Regardless of how it had to be done, the brake was to be "nursed" through the required fifty simulated stops.

Fans were set up to provide special cooling. Instead of maintaining pressure on the brake until the test wheel had come to a complete stop, the pressure was reduced when the wheel had decelerated to around 15 mph, allowing it to "coast" to a stop. After each stop, the brake was disassembled and carefully cleaned, and after some of the stops, internal brake parts were machined in order to remove warp and other disfigurations caused by the high heat.

By these and other methods, all clearly contrary to the techniques established by the military specifications, the brake was coaxed through the fifty stops. But even using these methods, the brake could not meet all the requirements. On one stop the wheel rolled for a distance of 16,000 feet, or over three miles, before the brake could bring it to a stop. The normal distance required for such a stop was around 3500 feet.

Nursing It Through

On April 11, the day the thirteenth test was completed, I became personally involved in the A7D situation.

I had worked in the Goodrich test laboratory for five years, starting first as an instrumentation engineer, then later becoming a data analyst and technical writer. As part of my duties, I analyzed the reams and reams of instrumentation data that came from the many testing machines in the lab, then transcribed all of it to a more usable form for the engineering department. When a new-type brake had successfully completed the required qualification tests, I would issue a formal qualification report.

Qualification reports are an accumulation of all the data and test logs compiled during the qualification tests and are documentary proof that a brake has met all the requirements established by the military specifications and is therefore presumed safe for flight testing. Before actual flight tests are conducted on a brake, qualification reports have to be delivered to the customer and to various government officials.

On April 11, I was looking over the data from the latest A7D test, and I noticed that many irregularities in testing methods had been noted on the test logs.

Technically, of course, there was nothing wrong with conducting tests in any manner desired, so long as the test was for research purposes only. But qualification test methods are clearly delineated by the military, and I knew that this test had been a formal qualification attempt. One particular notation on the test logs caught my eye. For some of the stops, the instrument that recorded the brake pressure had been deliberately miscalibrated so that, while the brake pressure used during the stops was recorded as 1000 psi (pounds per square inch)—the maximum pressure that would be available on the A7D aircraft—the pressure had actually been 1100 psi.

I showed the test logs to the test lab supervisor, Ralph Gretzinger, who said he had learned from the technician who had miscalibrated the instrument that he had been asked to do so by Lawson. Lawson, said Gretzinger, readily admitted asking for the miscalibration, saying he had been told to do so by Sink.

I asked Gretzinger why anyone would want to miscalibrate the data-recording instruments.

"Why? I'll tell you why," he snorted. "That brake is a failure. It's way too small for the job, and they're not ever going to get it to work. They're getting desperate, and instead of scrapping the damned thing and starting over, they figure they can horse around down here in the lab and qualify it that way."

An expert engineer, Gretzinger had been responsible for several innovations in brake design. It was he who had invented the unique brake system used on the famous XB70. "If you want to find out what's going on," said Gretzinger, "ask Lawson; he'll tell you."

Curious, I did ask Lawson the next time he came into the lab. He seemed eager to discuss the A7D and gave me the history of his months of frustrating efforts to get Warren and Sink to change the brake design. "I just can't believe this is really happening," said Lawson, shaking his head slowly. "This isn't engineering, at least not what I thought it would be. Back in school, I thought that when you were an engineer, you tried to do your best, no matter what it cost. But this is something else."

He sat across the desk from me, his chin propped in his hand. "Just wait," he warned. "You'll get a chance to see what I'm talking about. You're going to get in the act too, because I've already had the word that we're going to make one more attempt to qualify the brake, and that's it. Win or lose, we're going to issue a qualification report!"

I reminded him that a qualification report could be issued only after a brake had successfully met all military requirements, and therefore, unless the next qualification attempt was a success, no report would be issued.

"You'll find out," retorted Lawson. "I was already told that regardless of what the brake does on test, it's going to be qualified." He said he had been told in those exact words at a conference with Sink and Russell Van Horn.

This was the first indication that Sink had brought his boss, Van Horn, into the mess. Although Van Horn, as manager of the design engineering section, was responsible for the entire department, he was not necessarily familiar with all phases of every project, and it was not uncommon for those under him to exercise the what-he-doesn't-know-won't-hurt-him philosophy. If he was aware of the full extent of the A7D situation, it meant that Sink had decided not only to call for help but to look toward that moment when blame must be borne and, if possible, shared.

Also, if Van Horn had said, "regardless of what the brake does on test, it's going to be qualified," then it could only mean that, if necessary, a false qualification report would be issued. I discussed this possibility with Gretzinger, and he assured me that under no circumstances would such a report ever be issued.

"If they want a qualification report, we'll write them one, but we'll tell it just like it is," he declared emphatically. "No false data or false reports are going to come out of this lab."

On May 2, 1968, the fourteenth and final attempt to qualify the brake was begun. Although the same improper methods used to nurse the brake through the previous tests were employed, it soon became obvious that this too would end in failure.

When the tests were about half completed, Lawson asked if I would start preparing the various engineering curves and graphic displays that were normally incorporated in a qualification report. I flatly refused to have anything to do with the matter and immediately told Gretzinger what I had been asked to do. He was furious and repeated his previous declaration that under no circumstances would any false data or other matter be issued from the lab.

"I'm going to get this settled right now, once and for all," he declared. "I'm going to see Line [Russell Line, manager of the Goodrich Technical Services Section, of which the test lab was a part] and find out just how far this thing is going to go!" He stormed out of the room.

In about an hour, he returned and called me to his desk. He sat silently for a few moments, then muttered, half to himself, "I wonder what the hell they'd do if I just quit?" I didn't answer and I didn't ask him what he meant. I knew. He had been beaten down. He had reached the point when the decision had to be made. Defy them now while there was still time—or knuckle under, sell out.

"You know," he went on uncertainly, looking down at his desk, "I've been an engineer for a long time, and I've always believed that ethics and integrity were every bit as important as theorems and formulas, and never once has anything happened to change my beliefs. Now this . . . Hell, I've got two sons I've got to put through school and I just . . . " His voice trailed off.

He sat for a few more minutes, then, looking over the top of his glasses, said hoarsely, "Well, it looks like we're licked. The way it stands now, we're to go ahead and prepare the data and other things for the graphic presentation in the report, and when we're finished, someone upstairs will actually write the report.

"After all," he continued, "we're just drawing some curves, and what happens to them after they leave here—well, we're not responsible for that."

I wasn't at all satisfied with the situation and decided that I too would discuss the matter with Russell Line, the senior executive in our section.

Tall, powerfully built, his teeth flashing white, his face tanned to a coffee-brown by a daily stint with a sunlamp, Line looked and acted every inch the executive. He had been transferred from the Akron offices some two years previously, and he commanded great respect and had come to be well liked by those of us who worked under him.

He listened sympathetically while I explained how I felt about the A7D situation, and when I had finished, he asked me what I wanted him to do about it. I said that as employees of the Goodrich Company we had a responsibility to protect the company and its reputation if at all possible. I said I was certain that officers on the corporate level would never knowingly allow such tactics as had been employed on the A7D.

"I agree with you," he remarked, "but I still want to know what you want me to do about it."

I suggested that in all probability the chief engineer at the Troy plant, H. C. "Bud" Sunderman, was unaware of the A7D problem and that he, Line, could tell him what was going on.

Line laughed, good-humoredly. "Sure, I could, but I'm not going to. Bud probably already knows about this thing anyway, and if he doesn't, I'm sure not going to be the one to tell him."

"But why?"

"Because it's none of my business, and it's none of yours. I learned a long time ago not to worry about things over which I had no control. I have no control over this."

I wasn't satisfied with his answer, and I asked him if his conscience wouldn't bother him if, say, during flight tests on the brake, something should happen resulting in death or injury to the test pilot.

"Look," he said, becoming somewhat exasperated, "I just told you I have no control over this. Why should my conscience bother me?"

His voice took on a quiet, soothing tone as he continued, "You're just getting all upset over this thing for nothing. I just do as I'm told, and I'd advise you to do the same."

I made no attempt to rationalize what I had been asked to do. It made no difference who would falsify which part of the report or whether the actual falsification would be by misleading numbers or misleading words. Whether by acts of commission or omission, all of us who contributed to the fraud would be guilty. The only question left for me to decide was whether or not I would become a part to the fraud.

Before coming to Goodrich in 1963, I had held a variety of jobs, each a little more pleasant, a little more rewarding than the last. At 42, with seven children, I had decided that the Goodrich Company would probably be my "home" for the rest of my working life. The job paid well, it was pleasant and challenging, and the future looked reasonably bright. My wife and I had bought a home and we were ready to settle down into a comfortable, middle-age, middle-class rut. If I refused to take part in the A7D fraud, I would have either to resign or be fired. The report would be written by someone anyway, but I would have the satisfaction of knowing I had had no part in the matter. But bills aren't paid with personal satisfaction, nor house payments with ethical principles. I made my decision. The next morning, I telephoned Lawson and told him I was ready to begin on the qualification report.

I had written dozens of qualification reports, and I knew what a "good" one looked like. Resorting to the actual test data only on occasion, Lawson and I proceeded to prepare page after page of elaborate, detailed engineering curves, charts, and test logs, which purported to show what had happened during the formal qualification tests. Where temperatures were too high, we deliberately chopped them down a few hundred degrees, and where they were too low, we raised them to a value that would appear reasonable to the LTV and military engineers. Brake pressure, torque values, distances, times—everything of consequence was tailored to fit.

Occasionally, we would find that some test either hadn't been performed at all or had been conducted improperly. On those occasions, we "conducted" the test—successfully, of course—on paper.

For nearly a month we worked on the graphic presentation that would be a part of the report. Meanwhile, the final qualification attempt had been completed, and the brake, not unexpectedly, had failed again.

We finished our work on the graphic portion of the report around the first of June. Altogether, we had prepared nearly two hundred pages of data, containing dozens of deliberate falsifications and misrepresentations. I delivered the data to Gretzinger, who said he had been instructed to deliver it personally to the chief engineer, Bud Sunderman, who in turn would assign someone in the engineering department to complete the written portion of the report. He gathered the bundle of data and left the office. Within minutes, he was back with the data, his face white with anger.

"That damned Sink's beat me to it," he said furiously. "He's already talked to Bud about this, and now Sunderman says no one in the engineering department has time to write the report. He wants us to do it, and I told him we couldn't."

The words had barely left his mouth when Russell Line burst in the door. "What the hell's all the fuss about this damned report?" he demanded.

Patiently, Gretzinger explained. "There's no fuss. Sunderman just told me that we'd have to write the report down here, and I said we couldn't. Russ," he went on, "I've told you before that we weren't going to write the report. I made my position clear on that a long time ago."

Line shut him up with a wave of his hand and, turning to me, bellowed, "I'm getting sick and tired of hearing about this damned report. Now, write the goddamn thing and shut up about it!" He slammed out of the office.

Gretzinger and I just sat for a few seconds looking at each other. Then he spoke.

"Well, I guess he's made it pretty clear, hasn't he? We can either write the thing or quit. You know, what we should have done was quit a long time ago. Now, it's too late."

Somehow, I wasn't at all surprised at this turn of events, and it didn't really make that much difference. As far as I was concerned, we were all up to our necks in the thing anyway, and writing the narrative portion of the report couldn't make me more guilty than I already felt myself to be.

Within two days, I had completed the narrative, or written portion, of the report. As a final sop to my own self-respect, in the conclusion of the report I wrote, "The B. F. Goodrich P/N2-1162-3 brake assembly does not meet the intent or the requirement of the applicable specification documents and therefore is not qualified."

This was a meaningless gesture, since I knew that this would certainly be changed when the report went through the final typing process. Sure enough, when the report was published, the negative conclusion had been made positive.

One final and significant incident occurred just before publication.

Qualification reports always bear the signature of the person who has prepared them. I refused to sign the report, as did Lawson. Warren was later asked to sign the report. He replied that he would "when I receive a signed statement from Bob Sink ordering me to sign it."

The engineering secretary who was delegated the responsibility of "dogging" the report through publication told me later that after I, Lawson, and Warren had all refused to sign the report, she had asked Sink if he would sign. He replied. "On something of this nature, I don't think a signature is really needed."

Near Crashes

On June 5, 1968, the report was officially published and copies were delivered by hand to the Air Force and LTV. Within a week flight tests were begun at Edwards Air Force Base in California. Searle Lawson was sent to California as Goodrich's representative. Within approximately two weeks, he returned because some rather unusual incidents during the tests had caused them to be canceled.

His face was grim as he related stories of several near crashes during landings—caused by brake troubles. He told me about one incident in which, upon landing, one brake was literally welded together by the intense heat developed during the test stop. The wheel locked, and the plane skidded for nearly 1500 feet before coming to a halt. The plane was jacked up and the wheel removed. The fused parts within the brake had to be pried apart.

That evening I left work early and went to see my attorney. After I told him the story, he advised that, while I was probably not actually guilty of fraud, I was certainly part of a conspiracy to defraud. He advised me to go to the Federal Bureau of Investigation and offered to arrange an appointment. The following week he took me to the Dayton office of the FBI and after I had been warned that I would not be immune from prosecution, I disclosed the A7D matter to one of the agents. The agent told me to say nothing about the episode to anyone and to report any further incidents to him. He said he would forward the story to his superiors in Washington.

A few days later, Lawson returned from a conference with LTV in Dallas and said that the Air Force, which had previously approved the qualification report, had suddenly rescinded that approval and was demanding to see some of the raw test data. I gathered that the FBI had passed the word.

Omitting any reference to the FBI, I told Lawson I had been to an attorney and that we were probably guilty of conspiracy.

"Can you get me an appointment with your attorney?" he asked. Within a week, he had been to the FBI and told them of his part in the mess. He too was advised to say nothing but to keep on the job reporting any new development.

Naturally, with the rescinding of Air Force approval and the demand to see raw test data, Goodrich officials were in a panic. A conference was called for July 27, a Saturday morning affair at which Lawson, Sink, Warren, and I were present. We met in a tiny conference room in the deserted engineering department. Lawson and I, by now openly hostile to Warren and Sink, arranged ourselves on one side of the conference table while Warren sat on the other side. Sink, chairing the meeting, paced slowly in front of a blackboard, puffing furiously on a pipe.

The meeting was called, Sink began, "to see where we stand on the A7D." What we were going to do, he said, was to "level" with LTV and tell them the "whole truth" about the A7D. "After all," he said, "they're in this thing with us, and they have the right to know how matters stand."

"In other words," I asked, "we're going to tell them the truth?"

"That's right," he replied. "We're going to level with them and let them handle the ball from there."

"There's one thing I don't quite understand," I interjected. "Isn't it going to be pretty hard for us to admit to them that we've lied?"

"Now, wait a minute," he said angrily. "Let's don't go off half-cocked on this thing. It's not a matter of lying. We've just interpreted the information the way we felt it should be."

"I don't know what you call it," I replied, "but to me it's lying, and it's going to be damned hard to confess to them that we've been lying all along."

He became very agitated at this and repeated, "We're not lying," adding, "I don't like this sort of talk."

I dropped the matter at this point, and he began discussing the various discrepancies in the report.

We broke for lunch, and afterward, I came back to the plant to find Sink sitting alone at his desk, waiting to resume the meeting. He called me over and said he wanted to apologize for his outburst that morning. "This thing has kind of gotten me down," he confessed, "and I think you've got the wrong picture. I don't think you really understand everything about this."

Perhaps so, I conceded, but it seemed to me that if we had already told LTV one thing and then had to tell them another, changing our story completely, we would have to admit we were lying.

"No," he explained patiently, "we're not really lying. All we were doing was interpreting the figures the way we knew they should be. We were just exercising engineering license."

During the afternoon session, we marked some forty-three discrepant points in the report: forty-three points that LTV would surely spot as occasions where we had exercised "engineering license."

After Sink listed those points on the blackboard, we discussed each one individually. As each point came up, Sink would explain that it was probably "too minor to bother about," or that perhaps it "wouldn't be wise to open that can of worms," or that maybe this was a point that "LTV just wouldn't understand." When the meeting was over, it had been decided that only three points were "worth mentioning."

Similar conferences were held during August and September, and the summer was punctuated with frequent treks between Dallas and Troy and demands by the Air Force to see the raw test data. Tempers were short, and matters seemed to grow worse.

Finally, early in October 1968, Lawson submitted his resignation, to take effect on October 25. On October 18, I submitted my own resignation, to take effect on November 1. In my resignation, addressed to Russell Line, I cited the A7D report and stated: "As you are aware, this report contained numerous deliberate and willful misrepresentations which, according to legal counsel, constitute fraud and expose both myself and others to criminal charges of conspiracy to defraud. . . . The events of the past seven months have created an atmosphere of deceit and distrust in which it is impossible to work. . . . "

On October 25, I received a sharp summons to the office of Bud Sunderman. Tall and graying, impeccably dressed at all times, he was capable of producing a dazzling smile or a hearty chuckle or immobilizing his face into marble hardness, as the occasion required.

I faced the marble hardness when I reached his office. He motioned me to a chair. "I have your resignation here," he snapped, "and I must say you have made some rather shocking, I might even say irresponsible, charges. This is very serious."

Before I could reply, he was demanding an explanation. "I want to know exactly what the fraud is in connection with the A7D and how you can dare accuse this company of such a thing!"

I started to tell some of the things that had happened during the testing, but he shut me off, saying, "There's nothing wrong with anything we've done here. You aren't aware of all the things that have been going on behind the scenes. If you had known the true situation, you would never have made these charges." He said that in view of my apparent "disloyalty" he had decided to accept my resignation "right now," and said it would be better for all concerned if I left the plant immediately. As I got up to leave he asked me if I intended to "carry this thing further."

I answered simply, "Yes," to which he replied, "Suit yourself." Within twenty minutes, I had cleaned out my desk and left. Forty-eight hours later, the B. F. Goodrich Company recalled the qualification report and the four-disk brake, announcing that it would replace the brake with a new, improved, five-disk brake at no cost to LTV.

Ten months later, on August 13, 1969, I was the chief government witness at a hearing conducted before Senator William Proxmire's Economy in Government Subcommittee. I related the A7D story to the committee, and my testimony was supported by Searle Lawson, who followed me to the witness stand. Air Force officers also testified, as well as a four-man team from the General Accounting Office, which had conducted an investigation of the A7D brake at the request of Senator Proxmire. Both Air Force and GAO investigators declared that the brake was dangerous and had not been tested properly.

Testifying for Goodrich was R. G. Jeter, vice-president and general counsel of the company, from the Akron headquarters. Representing the Troy plant was Robert Sink. These two denied any wrongdoing on the part of the Goodrich Company, despite the expert testimony to the contrary by Air Force and GAO officials. Sink was quick to deny any connection with the writing of the report or directing of any falsifications, claiming to have been on the West Coast at the time. John Warren was the man who had supervised its writing, said Sink.

As for me, I was dismissed as a high-school graduate with no technical training, while Sink testified that Lawson was a young, inexperienced engineer. "We tried to give him guidance," Sink testified, "but he preferred to have his own convictions."

About changing the data and figures in the report, Sink said: "When you take data from several different sources, you have to rationalize among those data what is the true story. This is part of your engineering know-how." He admitted that changes had been made in the data, "but only to make them more consistent with the overall picture of the data that is available."

Jeter pooh-poohed the suggestion that anything improper occurred, saying: "We have thirty-odd engineers at this plant . . . and I say to you that it is incredible that these men would stand idly by and see reports changed or falsified. . . . I mean you just do not have to do that working for anybody. . . . Just nobody does that."

The four-hour hearing adjourned with no real conclusion reached by the subcommittee. But the following day the Department of Defense made sweeping changes in its inspection, testing, and reporting procedures. A spokesman for the DOD said the changes were a result of the Goodrich episode.

The A7D is now in service, sporting a Goodrich-made five-disk brake, a brake that works very well, I'm told. Business at the Goodrich plant is good. Lawson is now an engineer for LTV and has been assigned to the A7D project, possibly explaining why the A7D's new brakes work so well. And I am now a newspaper reporter.

At this writing, those remaining at Goodrich—including Warren—are still secure in the same positions, all except Russell Line and Robert Sink. Line has been rewarded with a promotion to production superintendent, a large step upward on the corporate ladder. As for Sink, he moved up into Line's old job.

California Paper Company Case

The toughest immediate decision facing Wes Palmer, general manager of the hardboard division of the California Paper Company, when he returned from a three weeks' vacation was what to do about George Sherman, the general superintendent. Sherman, a few days after Wes left on vacation, had gotten the company into serious trouble with the state pollution commission. The manufacturing vice president had immediately reported this to Wes by long-distance telephone. He said: "I don't want to fire Sherman in your absence. You will have to decide what to do yourself when you get back. It's your problem. But if you keep him and he gets us into another jam, I'll fire you."

George Sherman had been associated with Wes Palmer and the California Paper Company for six years, in one capacity or another. He was currently about 50 years old, of less than medium height, thin and wiry. He was a mechanical engineer, with a bachelor's degree from the University of Illinois. During the four years preceding the entry of the United States into World War II, he had owned and managed a small plastics plant in the Midwest. When materials became hard to obtain because of wartime shortages and restrictions, he had sold this business, coming out pretty well financially on the sale. He then had headed for the Pacific Coast, where he spent the remaining war years as a shipyard superintendent. At war's end he had purchased a machine shop, obtained some profitable subcontracts, and done very well. When he sold this a couple of years later, he had accumulated a total capital in excess of $50,000. He had reinvested this in a lime quarry. This had failed, partly because it was unfavorably located from the standpoint of freight rates, and partly because bad weather for two successive years had resulted in a poor agricultural market for fertilizers. The bank from which he had borrowed heavily had finally instituted foreclosure proceedings and he had ended up broke. For a short time thereafter he had worked as inspector on a power dam.

Wes Palmer first met George Sherman while he was employed at the dam. George read in a newspaper that the California Paper Company was building a highly mechanized hardboard mill and that Wes Palmer had been named to manage it. He went to see Wes and asked him for a job. Wes then was dividing his time about equally between his old job as head of California Paper Company's research laboratories and an interim post as company liaison man with the contractor building the new hardboard mill.[1] Wes told George that he might be able to fit him into the mechanical end of the mill operation when it started up but that for the time being, at least, nothing was available.

When the hardboard mill was about 50 percent finished, Wes hired George to check on the contractor's compliance with specifications and to calculate periodically, as a basis for payments to the contractor, the percent of contract currently completed. George also helped in the laboratory on problems involved in making hardboard from the waste wood, including bark, resulting from lumbering and sawmill operations. He proved to be a pretty good lab man and got along well personally with the small staff of technicians employed there.

When the mill was nearly ready for operation, Wes announced four major appointments to his staff:

1. Jay Miller as general superintendent. Miller had many years of experience in Celotex and softboard manufacture but none in hardboard. The two processes were very different.

2. Paul Wilding as quality control manager.

3. George Sherman as plant engineer, in charge of plant maintenance. In this capacity

[1] Wes Palmer had a master's degree in chemistry, with a major in chemistry and a minor in chemical engineering. He had over a dozen years of research laboratory experience, during which he had worked on problems of synthetic rubber, turpentine, and hardboard development.

George would have a foreman with a crew of 12 under him.

4. Lloyd Hayes as master mechanic, in charge of equipment maintenance.

During the first five years of operation, production of the hardboard mill increased tremendously, as know-how increased, manufacturing problems were solved one by one, and the selling organization developed new customers:

1st year	6 million	sq.	ft.	produced
2nd	12 "	"	"	"
3rd	20 "	"	"	"
4th	30 "	"	"	"
5th	39 "	"	"	"

This more-than-sixfold increase was accomplished with the original equipment and with an expansion in work force from the original sixty to only eighty.

As with any new mill, there were many mechanical headaches, many process changes to make. Production secrets and know-how were carefully guarded by competing hardboard manufacturers and each newcomer to the field had to learn by trial and error. Wes Palmer and his staff had to feel their way along in spite of the fact that the mill and processes had been very well engineered in advance in California Paper Company's research laboratory, which had installed a small-scale pilot plant. The research and pilot plant production, unfortunately, had been done on one-quarter-inch board, whereas sales turned out to be 70 percent one-eighth-inch board.

At frequent intervals throughout the five years of operation, Wes wryly recalled, George Sherman had shown a positive talent for getting into trouble himself or causing trouble for others. As he looked back, Wes could remember at least one unpleasant incident each year in which George had been involved. He particularly remembered the following ones.

First year. Jay Miller, the first general superintendent, proved to be very excitable. When anything went wrong he acted like a wild man. George made a point of recounting to Wes many of Jay's difficulties, slanted in a manner calculated to make Jay appear incompetent and slightly ridiculous. Wes realized that George was trying to undercut Jay and suspected that Jay knew this also.

Wes was acutely aware, from his own observations, that Jay was not working out as general superintendent. He had decided, however, to give Jay a six months' trial, in the hope that he would gradually get on top of the situation. The situation and Jay's morale deteriorated steadily, however, and at the end of six months Wes had to let him go. The hard facts, not George's snide remarks, led him to this decision.

When he heard about Jay's dismissal, Jack Ross, a shop committeeman, said to Wes: "You fired the wrong man. It should have been Sherman." Wes interpreted this remark at the time as an expression of loyalty toward Jay. When he finally made up his mind that Jay must go, Wes also decided to give George a shot at the general superintendent's job. Lloyd Hayes moved up to plant engineer, taking over responsibility for both plant maintenance and equipment maintenance. The position of master mechanic was abolished.

Within a few weeks, George started a campaign to undermine the shipping superintendent, one of his subordinates. Wes, tired of George's constant carping, removed the shipping superintendent from George's jurisdiction. Thereafter he reported directly to Wes, handling scheduling as well as shipping.

Second year. During the first half of this year George did a good job of solving mechanical problems as they came along. On the human side he did not do nearly as well. He got into trouble several times with members of the work force and with the union. The situation, however, did not at any time get out of control.

Then came a six weeks' strike, called by the local and confined to the hardboard mill. Several customers cancelled their orders and sought new sources of supply during this period. As a result, when the mill started up again it operated on a four-day-a-week basis until markets were reestablished.

A month after the men came back, one of the workers made a serious mistake. George dressed him down on the spot, swearing at him several times. The worker started to take a punch at George, thought better of it in time, and took his grievance to the union instead.

This incident occurred on a Friday afternoon. On the following Monday morning the men gathered at the gate but didn't come into the mill. When Wes arrived, he asked what the trouble was. The men told him their side of the story, which varied somewhat from the sweetened-up version George had fed Wes over the weekend. Wes listened a few minutes, then said: "You've got a contract which says you work, pending settlement of grievances through the regular grievance procedure. You're violating it." He then called the union business agent, who persuaded the men to go back to work.

On Monday afternoon Wes and George met with the business agent and the grievance committee. The union position was that, because of his actions on Friday, the crews would refuse in the future to take orders directly from George. They would have to be transmitted instead through the foremen. The crews would, however, continue as in the past to take orders direct from Wes. Wes said: "O.K. George will give his orders via the foreman. And so will I."

George blamed Jack Ross, the shop committeeman who had told Wes nearly two years earlier that he had fired the wrong man, for stirring up this trouble. He said: "I'll get that ____." Wes replied: "Leave him alone or he'll get you instead."

George was pretty subdued for a month or so. Then he gradually began chatting with the men again. He got along particularly well with the skilled mechanics, except for an occasional man he didn't like and managed to get rid of.

Third year. For seven weeks, early in this year, the mill was shut down by an industry-wide strike. While the strike was on, George was upset because he had no work to do. He had no outside interests and therefore had developed a bad habit of working nine or ten hours a day. Idleness bored him.

During the startup period following the strike, George complained to Wes on several occasions about Paul Wilding, the quality-control manager. Finally the two men got into a big wrangle, which Wes had to settle himself. George said that Paul was too critical about quality and was interrupting production too often, without cause. Wes backed Paul, then said: "You two get along, or else; if you don't, one of you is going." Thereafter the two men ignored each other completely.

Later in the third year, headquarters executives of the California Paper Company instructed Wes to begin direct distribution of hardboard to industrial customers on a nationwide basis. Prior to this change, the industrial market had been served through a single distributor. During the transition period Wes had to spend more time than usual on sales, less on production. He was at first away from the mill for three weeks at a time, every four months, traveling with his newly appointed sales manager. During his absences, George was in charge at the mill.

On one occasion, while Wes was away on a trip, George refused to alter the mill schedule to accommodate a wholesale customer. He had been asked to do so by Wallace Goodyear, the mill's sales liaison man with the distributor, who had continued on as the mill's exclusive outlet to the wholesale and retail trade. Wes, reviewing this dispute on his return, came to the following conclusions:

1. George was correct in deciding not to alter the schedule.

2. Wallace had been a little arrogant in demanding that the schedule be changed.

3. George, knowing he was in the right, had in refusing Wallace's demand gone out of his way to antagonize him, deliberately needled him.

George and Wallace did not engage in any further infighting. Instead they maintained a quiet truce and kept away from each other thereafter as much as possible.

Fourth year. Upon his return from a sales trip, Wes found waiting on his desk a formal grievance from the union. This stated that George Sherman had, in violation of the seniority clause on promotion in the contract, ignored a man with a long and satisfactory service record and filled a vacancy at higher hourly pay by assigning it instead to a man with substantially less seniority. The union demanded enforcement of the seniority provision in favor of the man passed over.

Wes did a little checking of the facts on his own, then called George and the union representatives in. He said to George: "Why didn't you make this promotion in accordance with the contract?"

George first claimed that the man with most seniority had not applied for the job. When the union representatives produced evidence that this was definitely not true, George shifted his ground, stating that the complainant did not have the necessary skills to hold down the job. During the ensuing conversation it became clear that George had passed the man by because he did not like him personally.

Wes reversed George's decision and awarded the complainant the disputed job on a trial basis.[2] Then, when the union representative had left his office, he gave George a real going over. He told George that the manufacturing vice president had gotten wind of the incident through the union while he was away and had recommended to Wes that he fire George out of hand. This was by no means the first time, Wes told George, that the manufacturing vice president had discussed George with him in uncomplimentary terms.

Soon after this episode, Wes was informed from several sources that George was backbiting him. He called George in, quoted several of his more sarcastic remarks, and said to him: "Let's have no more of this behind-my-back stuff. When you've got something to criticize me about, tell me to my face."

Toward the end of this year, George got the company into really serious trouble with the state pollution commission, which had been uneasy for some time about pulp discharge from the hardboard mill. Their commission's engineers frequently set up test screens in the rivers below the mill to determine whether the pulp content was so high as to endanger fish life therein. The commission had served notice on the company during the third year of mill operation that they would require it to put in a pulp impounding pond if the existing pollution level was exceeded in the future by any substantial amount.

One day while George was walking through the mill, he suddenly decided that he wanted a chest containing waste pulp cleaned. He immediately told a workman to dump the whole chest of waste pulp directly into the river, without putting it through the effluent screen as usual. This was in definite violation of explicit instructions which Wes had given him and which he in turn had passed on to his foremen and their crews.

[2] The man worked out fine, easily qualifying for the job on a permanent basis.

The concentrated discharge of pulp from the emptied chest rammed into a test screen which the state fisheries department had recently set up to keep fish out of a series of irrigation ditches fed by the river. The screen broke, the fisheries department protested by telephone to the pollution commission, and the latter's resident engineer in turn invited Wes and the manufacturing vice president to inspect the damage. They narrowly averted issuance of a shut-down order by promising, on their word of honor, that pulp would never be dumped directly into the river again. A few weeks later, nevertheless, the commission instructed the company to start work immediately on a pulp impounding pond. This cost $200,000. While it probably would have been necessary to build this facility a year or so later anyhow, as hardboard output continued to increase, the investment of $200,000 was financially embarrassing at the moment.

When Wes got back from his inspection of the fish screen he was boiling mad. He said to George: "Why in _ did you do it?"

George first denied having anything to do with the dumping. It was news to him, he said. He had just heard about it himself. Wes then confronted him with the man who had actually performed the dumping operation, at George's specific order. George then said: "O.K. I told him to."

Wes was so angry that he didn't trust himself to speak. Instead he walked away, just to cool off.

Fifth year. While Wes was on vacation, as described in the first paragraph of this case, a waste pulp chest was dumped directly into the river again, intead of being discharged through the screen into the new impounding pond. George was not directly responsible on this occasion, in the sense that he had specifically ordered this done. As general superintendent he could be held responsible, however, for not making certain that direct dumping never happened again.

The fish screen was smashed for the second time. The pollution commission's resident engineer immediately called on the manufacturing vice president and told him that his solemn promise had been broken. The vice president called in George, who said: "I just heard about the dumping myself a few minutes ago." The state engineer, the vice president, and George then went down to the fish screen to look at the damage.

When they returned to the mill, George told the vice president that he would get the facts from the shift foreman and report back immediately. In a few minutes he reported back, saying that the shift foreman had gone off duty and no one seemed to know anything about the incident.

The manufacturing vice president then conducted his own investigation. He found the employee who had dumped the chest. This man told him that he had washed out the chest's contents through the screen into the impounding pond. When he thought the chest was empty, he had pulled the plug. It was not completely empty, however, and the residue had gone directly into the river.

In response to further questioning by the vice president, the employee said that George had told him: "You needn't bother to keep the gate from the chests to the river locked when you're emptying chests into the impounding pond." The gate had been unlocked for the past several weeks.

The vice president confronted George with the facts he had just unearthed. George admitted telling the employee that he didn't have to make sure the gate was locked before beginning the chest-dumping operation. The vice president, as related in the first paragraph of the case, didn't want to fire George while Wes was away. Instead, he left this decision to Wes on his return.

Chapter 4

Step 2: The Diagnostic Process

The second step of the decision-making process is *diagnosis*. Here, in order to determine the exact problem that needs solution, the decision maker carefully inquires into all the information relevant to the situation that is perceived to be in disequilibrium. The central purpose of this chapter is to demonstrate the importance of diagnosis in the decision process, to examine common difficulties in its execution, and to establish criteria for effective diagnosis.

THE IMPORTANCE OF DIAGNOSIS

A diagnosis is an attempt to explain what happened in some period in the past, and why. Something did indeed happen, but of course no exact record is available for our examination. An instant slow-motion replay, so effective for televised sports, is essentially what we attempt to replicate with a diagnosis. In some kinds of situations it is obvious that an explicit diagnosis is required. If a machine breaks down, we do not attempt to fix it without determining precisely how the mechanism works and the source of difficulty. However, when we are confronted by interpersonal problems, problems in the human rather than the technical realm, we tend to bypass systematic diagnosis and act on the basis of rather sketchy diagnostic assumptions.

For example, when we are confronted with the worker who submits numerous grievances, it is easy to apply value judgments about workers who file grievances, or about workers in general, or about this worker in particular. Thus we can forego a systematic diagnosis and summarize the problem in a handy prejudgment: "People who file grievances are troublemakers"; "All workers are lazy; that's the problem"; or "This guy is a malingerer." In Britain an employee who threw a wrench into expensive equipment was charged with malicious wrongdoing. The court, however, looking at the routine, repetitive job that the man had been required to do during the prior ten years, ruled that his action was justifiable. By evaluating the original stimuli as presented to us, it is easy to categorize the problem in terms of preestablished stereotypes: employees who damage equipment are bad. This may or may not bear upon a particular situation. Thus we make an *implicit* diagnosis, based only on our first perceptions rather than on an investigation of the situation.

The consequences of weak or faulty diagnosis in some situations can be very serious: an innocent person may be convicted of a crime; a costly government program may fail to achieve its goal; a merger between two corporations may collapse; a valuable employee may be fired. Many a poor diagnosis has led to costly wrong decisions.

No solution is better than the quality of the diagnosis on which it is built. If, for example, we decide that a formerly productive worker, who is not now producing his quota, is slackening his effort with the purpose of cheating the company, we may have only one course of action: to fire him. But a sophisticated diagnosis would first inquire into other explanations for his behavior: Why has the worker's behavior changed? Why *now*? What needs does he feel he is satisfying by behaving this way at this time? How do other workers respond to the same stimuli? It may well be that, through sound diagnosis, the worker's misbehavior can be rectified in such a way that he will return to his former state of productivity.

Decision making should never be based on hasty, implicit diagnoses; it should be based on explicit, conscious, systematic, diagnostic investigation. In other words, a decision maker should use a critical rather than a noncritical method in the diagnostic process (see Ch. 1). Specifically, a sound diagnosis must meet the following criteria:

1. A sound diagnosis differentiates between events and the language used to describe events.
2. A sound diagnosis specifies the degree of precision of available information.
3. A sound diagnosis specifies underlying causes, not just fixes blame.
4. A sound diagnosis specifies multiple causality, rather than a single cause.
5. In its final working form, a sound diagnosis is explicitly formulated, not vague.

CRITERION 1: DIFFERENTIATING BETWEEN LANGUAGE AND EVENTS

The words people use to explain "what happened" are a manager's best source of clues to the nature of the problem. It is of primary importance that the manager, in weighing this information, be keenly aware of the effect of the language employees use when describing a problem. The difficulty with language is that words do not automatically mirror facts. As S. I. Hayakawa (1949) observes, "The map is not the territory" (p. 31). Just as a map is not the actual land mass of a state or country, the language we use to explain a situation is not the situation itself. Language is only an abstraction of a real situation.

Most importantly, the decision maker must be aware that the

language a person chooses for representing a particular event reflects the perceptions of that person. The observer's perception is necessarily imprecise, and the language used to present it is a further imprecise abstraction of that perception. In making diagnoses, therefore, *the decision maker must be wary of taking at face value the language in which information is presented.* Language can alter and distort the perception of past situations. It may reflect more about the reporter than about the situation reported. Therefore if a union leader, for example, in a particular plant describes all problems in terms of management exploitation, and a manager in the same plant brands the same problems as union harassment, it is necessary to go beyond these stereotyped accusations to understand a given situation.

The importance of language in the definition of problems is dramatically demonstrated by Orvis Collins' (1946) study of ethnic relationships in a small New England factory. Because the workers regarded some jobs as properly assigned to the "Yankees" and some as properly assigned to the Irish, the latter threatened a walkout when a Yankee was hired as a janitor, a job perceived as "belonging" to the Irish. The dispute was ended, according to Collins, when the job title was changed to "sanitary engineer," a "Yankee"-sounding title. In this case, the differentiation of language from the real situation was the chief factor in solving the problem.

A similar problem involving the disparity of language and event can occur when a job description differs from the way the job is performed. A managerial incumbent, for example, may tend to concentrate on personally satisfying aspects of the job and ignore or delegate disliked aspects. The new manager may take on "temporary" duties that are gradually made permanent. In effect, the job will become tailored, probably in an evolutionary way, to the particular skills, abilities, and temperament of the particular person.

After a few years, what the incumbent does may come to vary substantially from the formal job description on file in the personnel office. If the manager is then promoted or leaves the company, the personnel officer charged with making a replacement is well advised to verify the accuracy of the job description before specifying the skills and experience required of applicants for that job. If personnel officers rely only on the language of the job description, they may hire an ineffective replacement.

A sound diagnosis, therefore, differentiates between language and actual events, but the ambiguity of language is not the only problem; the decision maker must also know how accurate information is.

CRITERION 2: SPECIFYING THE DEGREE OF PRECISION OF AVAILABLE INFORMATION

Partly because language is imprecise, an important phase of diagnosis is the examination of information to determine its degree of precision.

Just as we must differentiate between language and events, we must also differentiate between two *scales* of precision: (1), whether a specific bit of information is a *fact or only an opinion*; and (2), the degree of *certainty* with which it has been verified as one or the other.

Distinguishing Fact and Opinion

Although it may be a *fact* that a person holds a particular *opinion*, the substance of the opinion itself is not necessarily factual. A manager who complains that every new subordinate is uncooperative (opinion), may be failing to recognize that he has not made his expectations explicit to them (fact). In discussing the Thomas Motor Company case, we attempt to understand Ralph Turner's feelings or opinions about the other workers in the garage. We could say it is his opinion that they leave the radio playing when they go on their coffee break just to annoy him. One of our diagnostic tasks is to determine if in fact this is Turner's opinion. If it is, it is important to our understanding of his behavior. Opinions are always important factors in diagnosis, whether they are factual or not. A second task is to determine whether the content of the opinion is factual—if, indeed, the other workers' intent is to annoy Turner. This also is important to our reconstruction of the situation. The differentiation of factual from nonfactual opinion is a crucial step in the decision process, but a difficult one.

One difficulty in making the distinction between fact and opinion is that opinions are usually stated as though they were facts: "This job was well done"; "He is our best foreman"; "The competition uses illegal procedures." Such opinions include the speaker's judgment of the event. It is part of the diagnostician's job to sort out facts from opinions. A job might be judged well done by one manager because it met his tolerance standards; it might be only adequate to another manager. The "best" foreman may be the one who lets the workers quit early, or it may be the one who gets the greatest productivity from them; it all depends on the vantage point of the speaker. Opinions, then, are useful sources of information in the diagnostic process, but not until an implicit value standard has been identified and their degree of factual precision clarified.

Verifying the Judgment

Once we have judged whether or not an important opinion is in the realm of fact, we must determine the extent to which that judgment can be verified and therefore considered certain. For example, in the Thomas Motor case let us suppose the manager has formed a judgment: (1) Turner's opinion (the radio is left on to spite him) is important to the diagnosis, but (2) the fact is, it was *not* done for that reason.

The process of verification involves differentiating facts, inferences, speculations, and assumptions. Using the information available to us in the case, we cannot verify, in an absolute sense, either Turner's motivation or that of the other workers. We do have some verifiable clues, however. We know that Turner was not bothered by the radio when the men were there, that the radio played all the time, and that no behavioral evidence exists to suggest that the other workers were antagonistic to Turner. Given these *facts*, we can say that the manager's judgment is probably correct: Turner's opinion does not conform to the facts. Such a judgment, made with a strong degree of supporting evidence, is called an *inference*.

The stronger the evidence (the facts) supporting a diagnostic judgment, the stronger the inference and the more reliable the diagnosis. If supporting evidence is very strong, an inference can be as reliable and useful as a fact. If, however, the evidence for an inference is not strong, the inference is weak.

Judgments further down the scale of certainty, where lines of reasoning arise from clues in the situation but where verification is not possible, are labeled *speculation*. For example, when the inspectors in the Redmond Manufacturing case refused to examine the spindles, they were judging the spindles to be contaminated with scarlet fever germs. The fact of the case is that a woman whose children had scarlet fever performed the first inspection of the spindles. However, because the inspectors' conviction that she had therefore contaminated the spindles is not verifiable, their judgment must be labeled a speculation, not an inference.

Further down the hierarchy of certainty are *assumptions*, lines of reasoning that arise entirely from a subjective frame of reference or from personal theories, and that are independent of verifiable clues in a real situation. Suppose that, in attempting to diagnose the reasons for the inspectors' behavior, we judged that their response was motivated by their membership in a union attempting to organize the company. This judgment is an assumption, rather than an inference or speculation, because there is no factual evidence in the real situation to support it. An important point about speculations and assumptions must be kept in mind, however; despite their lack of verification, they *may*, nonetheless, be facts. Moreover, speculations and assumptions may offer the best available explanation for a situation. However, they cannot be equated with facts; their degree of certainty is relatively much lower.

It is apparent that speculations and assumptions are considerably less reliable than facts and inferences, and therefore must be approached warily in the process of trying to determine what has actually occurred in a situation. A good diagnosis will rely most on facts and inferences, holding speculations and assumptions in reserve as tentative hypotheses, always open to question.

In making a diagnosis it is helpful explicitly to label units of information as facts, opinions, inferences, speculations, or assumptions, as the case may be, as an aid in the important process of clarifying the soundness of evidence. Making such distinctions among levels of certainty points up where information is only weakly supported by evidence, and keeps us searching for the strongest evidence available. Our diagnostic process does not stop with superficial speculation; we always attempt to improve the level of certainty of the evidence we are using.

The continuum of certainty shown below is offered simply as an aid to conceptualizing the idea that some information has a higher probability than other information of reflecting what actually did happen:

Continuum of Certainty

	100%
Certainty	Facts
of	Inferences
our	Speculations
judgments	Assumptions
	0%

To sum up, verified *facts* are our surest form of information (so long as they are not deceiving or misleading). *Inferences* are strong or weak in direct relation to the strength or weakness of their supporting evidence. *Speculations* are only hypotheses, based on clues found in external situations; and *assumptions* are hypotheses we apply to a situation primarily from our personal frame of reference.

CRITERION 3: SPECIFYING UNDERLYING CAUSE RATHER THAN BLAME

A good diagnostic process is guided by the attempt to understand rather than judge. Its purpose is to investigate the dynamics of a situation and to determine the causes of difficulty. The trained diagnostician withholds judgment, and asks, "What makes this situation tick? What are the sources of trouble?"

This criterion is vital because, when problems irritate us, our human tendency is to seek culprits and fix blame. This tendency to evaluate is antithetical to the diagnostic process because it impedes objectivity. At the diagnostic stage, it is of no practical help to make value judgments. Instead, we must try to understand what is going on and put together a sound explanation of why particular events occurred. We are trying to understand, not looking for "sins"; we are looking for causes; not culprits. Our goal is to maintain what the psychologist Alexander Leighton (1949) described as the "functional point of view."

Looking for causal relationships is very different from attempting to fix blame on someone. The attempt to fix blame is based on the assumption of a deliberate attempt to disrupt an organization. This assumption (of deliberate malicious intent) was implicit in a conflict between the marketing vice president and the manager of research and development in a large textile company. Each blamed the other for the company's failure to develop new products. Marketing accused R & D of ignoring customer tastes in its new designs, and R & D accused marketing of not trying to sell its innovations. The real problem was that each group was only attempting to protect itself, and refused to fully consider new product ideas from the other group. Although they continued to blame each other, neither group attempted to discover the real cause of the conflict.

Attempting to fix blame may also rest on the assumption that one person's contrary view is the *fault* of a different person. One manager, for example, with whom another disagrees may lay the disagreement to the other's being a negative sort of person, and think that the real blame rests with the organizational superiors who tolerate such persons. Such a "chain of blame" can take us through the various levels of an organization—and all the way back to Adam and Eve—without ever providing a useful diagnosis.

Another difficulty with premature value judgment is that its primary function may be to serve the evaluator's immediate emotional needs. Rather than contributing to an understanding of the human needs that gave rise to a problem situation, such value judgments shift decision makers' focus to themselves, to their own needs and values. If, for example, an accident occurs in a plant that results in a slowdown of production, the plant managers no doubt will be upset, and might either deplore the "carelessness" of workers (fix blame), or inquire into the conditions that caused the accident. Calling workers careless (a value judgment) tells us more about the managers who labeled workers than about the cause of the accident. It is one thing to judge a situation *after* we understand its causes and are ready to make a decision; it is quite a different thing to do this before we have attempted to understand precisely why certain events occurred.

Although seeking to fix blame is not a useful diagnosis, it does give the illusion that the problem has been alleviated: "It's *your* fault!" But of course placing blame does nothing to remedy the conditions that have caused a problem. A person who has been blamed may well attempt to minimize his own involvement and counter with, "No, it's not; it's *your* fault!" At that point, the decision maker has added nothing to his diagnosis.

It is by no means easy to suppress the tendency to prematurely evaluate. Clyde Kluckhohn (1951), the anthropologist, believes that the evaluating tendency is a strong force in human behavior: "Surely one of the broadest generalizations to be made by a natural historian observing the human species is that man is an evaluating animal" (p. 403).

One major difficulty in attempting to suppress premature evaluation is that problem situations are called to our attention by a value judgment—by the feeling that something is "not right." We consider a situation to be in a state of disequilibrium if it is beyond the tolerance limits of our values, goals, standards, policies, expectations, or some other value reference. Difficult though it may be, however, the value judgment involved in defining a state of disequilibrium must be followed by a conscious attempt to avoid the use of the value judgment that made us interested in the first place. Managers who oppose everything a union stands for must understand the union's rationale before they can resolve problems in the union-management relationship. Only by suspending value judgments can we develop an understanding of causes and make a sound diagnosis.

To avoid the use of value judgments in the diagnostic step, we must form the habit of explicitly asking the fundamental diagnostic question: *Why*? (Why did they behave as they did? Why did they respond as they did?) Then, to get at the interaction patterns involved, we must ask the second major diagnostic question: *How*? (How does this situation motivate X? How do X and Y motivate each other's behavior?)

A salesman, for example, who meets or does not meet his quota is generally praised or criticized. Focusing on the "why" and "how" may be far more important than the praise or criticism. For example, he may have made his quota for reasons undesirable to the total organization—he may have overstocked certain large customers rather than develop new business. His failure may be as much a result of competitor's activity as of his own.

In addition to asking *why* and *how* as a basis for analysis and investigation, the decision maker should learn to draw out the views of the other persons involved in the situation being studied. Much information necessary to a sound diagnosis can be gained only through skill in eliciting full and accurate information from others. The difficulty of acquiring this skill should not be underestimated, however. Even though we might consciously attempt to avoid value judgments in our diagnoses, they are a subtle part of our reactions to other people.

To avoid the pitfalls of being evaluative as we attempt to draw out full and accurate information from another person is a skill that requires training and practice, but it is essential in understanding the causes of a problem situation. Every manager should have training in nonevaluative interview techniques.

CRITERION 4: SPECIFYING MULTIPLE CAUSALITY

The tendency to evaluate is generally coupled with a tendency to search for a single cause in a problem situation. Such an effort is usually fruitless. A human problem situation generally involves at least two persons and a variety of organizational events, and this is especially true in our modern-day, complicated organizations. Disequilibrium is less often the result of a single event or scapegoat than the product of a variety of interacting events.

In the Thomas Motor case, for example, the changed work environment and Ralph Turner's new workplace come into direct conflict with his foreman's rules on coffee breaks. Finding himself left out of this daily social get-together, he returns to finding satisfaction in tinkering with his father's trucks. But this solution is not satisfactory for his helper, Dexter, who complains about being left out of the coffee breaks when he works with Turner. Turner then begins to make serious mistakes in his work. The foreman makes the hasty assumptive diagnosis of a single cause for Turner's mistakes: that he is working too fast. As a consequence, the foreman's "solution" is to tell Turner to slow down.

A systematic diagnosis would reveal that Turner's behavior results, not from one cause, too much speed, but from a combination of factors: his expectations of the job, the pressures of the new environment, the new work procedures, the response of his helper, the leadership approach of his foreman, and the reactions of the other workers. This example points up the importance of our fourth criterion of a sound diagnostic process, that the decision maker should not assume a single cause for a problem but, instead, should search for multiple factors.

CRITERION 5: EXPLICITLY FORMULATING THE FINAL WORKING DIAGNOSIS

The end goal of the diagnostic process is to formulate a working diagnosis on which to base problem-solving procedures. To accomplish this, the decision maker must assess the available information, not all of which is of equal value. As discussed earlier, the environment contains an infinite number of data, and the manager must determine which data are relevant information. Then this information must be weighed to determine the soundest explanation for what has occurred. Finally, the manager must settle on a stated working diagnosis as a basis for the procedure of problem solving.

It is important that this working diagnosis be explicitly stated, for two reasons: (1) an explicit diagnostic statement facilitates checking the relevance of the diagnosis to the statement of the problem; and (2) it facilitates assessing the relevance and importance of any new information which may be discovered.

Managers may check their statements of the working diagnosis against the following questions: (1) Does the diagnosis take into account all the available relevant information? (Or is it based on incomplete information?) (2) Does the diagnosis specify the degree of certainty of information and the relative importance of information? (Or is it merely a collection of unassessed data?) (3) Does the diagnosis *specify* problems, causes, events, persons, interactions, facts, evidence, and so on? (Or is it merely a vague generalization about human nature or psychological principles which provide little guidance for specific problems?) (4) Does the diagnosis include an examination of the relationships among points of view? (Or does it describe factors in the situation as if they were independent?) (5) Is the diagnosis organized in such a way that it facilitates identification of the central problem to be solved? (Or is it organized merely to facilitate such irrelevant goals as fixing blame, abstract theorizing, self-justification, etc.?)

SUMMARY OF CRITERIA

The entire diagnostic process, if it is to be soundly based and eventually helpful in the process of solving problems, should meet the following criteria:

1. It should differentiate between the actual events in the problem situation and the language used to describe these events.
2. It should specify the degree of precision of the available information by differentiating between facts and opinions, and by clearly labeling bits of information as facts, inferences, speculations or assumptions.
3. It should specify and explain the factors which have caused the given situation, rather than merely fixing blame.
4. It should examine the multiple causes and their relationships, rather than claim a single cause.
5. It should result in a clear and explicit statement of a final working diagnosis.

REFERENCES

Allport, Gordon W. "What Units Shall We Employ?" In *Assessment of Human Motives*, ed. Gardner Lindzey. Holt, 1958.

Collins, Orvis. "Ethnic Behavior in Industry: Sponsorship and Rejection in a New England Factory." *American Journal of Sociology*, January 1946.

Chase, Stuart, *Power of Words*. Harcourt, 1954.

Gragg, Charles I. "Whose Fault Is It?" *Harvard Business Review*, January–February 1964.

Hayakawa, S. I. *Language in Thought and Action*. Harcourt, 1949.

Kelly, George A. "Man's Construction of His Alternatives." In *Assessment of Human Motives*, ed. Gardner Lindzey. Holt, 1958.

Kluckhohn, Clyde, et al. "Values and Value-Orientation in the Theory of Action." In *Toward a General Theory of Action*, ed. Talcott Parsons and Edward Shils. Harvard University Press, 1951.

Leighton, Alexander. *Human Relations in a Changing World*. Dutton, 1949.

Likert, Rensis. *The Human Organization*. McGraw-Hill, 1967.

Ready, R. K. *The Administrator's Job*. McGraw-Hill, 1967.

Electronic Systems Company Case

The Electronic Systems Company was a growing concern in 1966, having experienced continuous, comfortable growth in its first ten years of operation. Its founder and owner, Francis Walker, was a classic success-story entrepreneur. He conceived an idea for a new electronic component, invented and initially developed it in the basement of his home, and sold it on the basis of quality, price, and quick delivery service. It was an exciting company, created from scratch in Walker's image. It employed around 250 people and its sales approached $4 million. Although the company was molded by him in every significant detail, he had gathered around him associates who shared his passions and his enthusiasms and who expressed outstanding commitments to the goals of the organization.

One such enthusiastic employee was Barry Welch, who came to work at Electronic Systems after having completed his tour of duty with the Air Force in the latter part of the 1950s. Later, around 1962 or 1963, Barry expressed a desire for a college education. The company offered to finance part of the expense, so Barry enrolled in the evening division of a local college, majoring in physics and minoring in math. (When I arrived at the company in 1968, Welch was in the second semester of his junior year.)

It was not uncommon in this young organization to find that several employees wore various departmental "hats." For example, after several years as a process engineer in the research and development laboratory. Barry was the prime organizer and supervisor of the raw-material and finished-goods stockrooms and the production control department. These three areas were managed by Welch until 1967, when Mr. Walker, seeing a need for a new and improved information system and professing great faith in Welch's ability as an organizer and manager, decided to send Welch to one of IBM's data processing schools. Before leaving for school, Welch agreed that when he returned he would devote his full time to the management of the data processing department, relinquishing his responsibilities in the other three areas. (It should be noted here that, in each of the three areas, Welch had developed capable managerial personnel prior to his departure.)

It was at this time that Mr. Walker sensed his business was growing too big for a one-man operation. Numerous new contracts from both government and commercial sources made the future look optimistic, but the workload for one man was difficult. Mr. Walker decided to seek outside help. Therefore, in response to various offers, he sold his company to a Wall Street investment firm that was very much impressed with Electronic Systems' great potential for sales growth. Mr. Walker was retained as a member of the board of directors, and also served in a consultative capacity as vice president for planning and development.

The investment firm hired Mr. Daniel Wilson as the new president of Electronic Systems. He, too, quickly saw the need for an improved information system as a tool for decision making. Therefore, Welch's initial project for the new president was to expedite plans for the proposed IBM equipment by training key punchers and machine operators and designing the initial systems. Organizationally, the new data processing department was to be managed by Welch,

"Electronic Systems Company Case" was written by Craig T. Galipeau under the supervision of Alvar O. Elbing. Names of people and places have been disguised.

who would report directly to the controller, Thomas Haley. Haley had worked for a leading optical company before Wilson asked him to join Electronic Systems in the latter half of 1967.

Although Haley had little knowledge of data processing operations, the organization established by Electronic Systems reflected the organization used by the majority of new companies in the data processing field. Mr. Haley, however, was quite familiar with the application of a total accounting system, which could be generated by the hardware in Barry's department. Even so, the main objective and top priority of the new equipment was to be its use for logistic purposes—production control, production, and inventory control—with the marketing system given second priority and the accounting system given least priority.

In June of 1968 I was hired for the summer to assist Barry in the design and implementation of the management information system. During my second week of work with Barry, I discovered what I thought to be a redundant system in one of the early systems applications. Barry confirmed my finding and showed no particular surprise. He then related how he had argued this particular point with Mr. Haley early in its application.

Barry: I explained to Haley earlier that this type of a thing would happen. And now this proves me correct.

Author: Well, couldn't he see that eventually we would run into this problem?

Barry: No. He didn't buy my argument that this would happen in the first place. Besides, it appears to me that as long as we get a system going as fast as possible, he doesn't care if it is right or wrong.

The president, Mr. Wilson, would usually pay a visit to Barry's office several times a week, complimenting Barry on what a fine job he was doing. Since very little application was made of the machines at this time, Mr. Wilson always expressed interest in the proposed overall system that Barry and I were working on. He was very pleased to see some of the ideas we had arrived at already, commenting that we seemed to be in good shape to meet the target date for our oral presentation in August. (Mr. Wilson gave us the go-ahead for implementing logistics subsystems before our August target date, however.)

At the same time, Mr. Haley did not find Barry's work satisfactory. As mentioned previously, the top priority for machine and design time was given to the logistics systems. However, Mr. Haley was continually putting pressure on Barry to get the complete accounting system established on the machines. This irritated Barry, and our conversations at coffee breaks and lunch continually centered around Haley and his accounting system.

Pressured by Haley, Barry devoted many hours in the evenings and on Saturdays and even Sundays in attempting to please him. These overtime hours were always devoted to such things as the budgets, payroll, accounts receivables, etc. Yet no appreciable recognition came from Haley—just complaints about the "bugs" that are found in any new system.

The rest of the workers in the firm, of course, had knowledge of Barry's overtime duties and would good-naturedly kid him about his department. Coffee and lunch breaks were always filled with laughter, with Barry bearing the brunt of all the jokes and harassment. All the men at the table (production men, industrial engineers, accountants, salesmen) were well liked by each other, and the majority would spend much of their social time together outside the plant. Since they all knew the trouble Barry was having with Haley, they, too, began to criticize Barry's work.

Production man: Hey, "punch-card," those reports your girls passed out this morning were useless garbage.

Barry: Look, you give me garbage, my machines will give you garbage back. [Laughter.]

Salesman: Who are you kidding? I give you good, accurate data, and the reports I get, too, are completely useless. Are you sure you know what you are doing over there, Barry? Maybe Tom will help you get straightened out. [Laughter.]

Barry: Yeah, by the way "Little Haley" [referring to Jim, the head of the accounting department], did Tom see that memo I left on his desk this morning?

Jim: Oh yeah, he told me to take care of it as usual, and then went back to reading his *Wall Street Journal* so he could have some free time later on this afternoon to play golf with his kid.

Barry: Beautiful! That's par for the course.

Production man: Well Barry, you better get back over there and get those budgets out so Tom won't have so much work during the day. When are you guys going to relieve me of some paperwork?

All this kidding, however, developed into a hassle between the vice president for manufacturing and Mr. Haley. At one of our meetings, the vice president said he felt the data processing department was not living up to its expectations of relieving some of the paperwork from the foremen while at the same time yielding reliable information. He asserted that too much time was being spent on the accounting system and not enough time in the production area. Mr. Haley disagreed vehemently. The vice president then requested that a report be submitted showing the actual time Barry spent in each area. (Although the report showed less actual running time for accounting reports, the production people were not getting the various reports which were promised them in the beginning, nor was their system as completely "debugged" as Haley's system.)

One morning in late July, Mr. Haley called Barry into his office. It was the time of the annual review at Electronic Systems, and I knew of Barry's expectations for a raise in salary. After two hours or so, Barry was back in the data processing department, looking very unhappy.

Author: Well, how'd it go?

Barry: I'm sending out résumés starting tonight. I can't hack that bald jerk much longer.

Author: You mean he didn't give you a raise?

Barry: Oh sure. I got a raise all right. But even with the raise I'll be making less than I did this year. You see, the raise puts me into another salary bracket where you don't collect any overtime pay on anything less than sixteen hours in a month. Right now, he's got me working about fifteen hours or so, but I get compensated for it. I'm getting the hell out of this joint as soon as I can. By the way, he wants me to get that lousy payroll on the machines soon, and you know what a tough job that will be.

Author: Yeah, the men from IBM told me it would be a long time getting that baby to work.

Barry just sat in his office the rest of the day, staring at the walls. The next morning he came in with his résumé to get my opinion of it. It looked impressive; and I realized how serious he was about leaving Electronic Systems.

During the first week in August, Barry worked almost exclusively with card design and programming for the new payroll system. Mr. Haley asked Barry to work Saturday to try to iron out some of the problems with the payroll system. Since our presentation of the proposed system was due in a few weeks, I also received the go-ahead to work Saturdays. That Saturday Barry was preparing the cards for all salaried personnel at Electronic Systems from a classified file, and my work was interrupted several times that morning with either Barry's laughter or his cries of disbelief.

Barry: Boy! You wouldn't believe what this guy is making. You should see the raise he got—and for what? He sure has got the wool pulled over someone's eyes.

Back to work for a few minutes. Then laughter from Barry's corner.

Barry: Hey, Craig. Here's another guy with a lousy deal. Gee, the job he has done here has been fantastic. Do you know when he's on vacation, he still spends his time in here? Boy, this place doesn't appreciate him. And what a lousy salary.

It was from this time on that Barry felt he was not the only employee of Electronic Systems who was being shortchanged. Of course, this made him sulk even more, and he sat staring at the walls and pondering his future. During the following week and up until the time I left, a steady stream of people came to Barry's office to discuss their common predicament—their dislike of Haley, who handled the majority of reviews and salary allotments. The air was filled with talk of résumés and new employer contacts.

In the weeks before our proposed presentation was to be made, two men from IBM were brought in to consult with Barry and me on the system. They presented some helpful suggestions for our system and were of useful support in many of our departmental meetings. However, they showed great concern that Barry had not yet written any standard operating procedures which would be of use to the company in times of Barry's absence. Barry always countered by saying he would begin writing them and developing a manual that week. However, Barry and I knew better. Barry had always told me that this knowledge would be kept in his head until he thought it was appropriate to record it. It was, as Barry said, his "job security," for as long as he held that knowledge in his head, they needed him. Besides, he also felt it would be a good way to get back at Mr. Haley if and when Barry left.

It was at this time that Mr. Haley again came under attack from the vice president of manufacturing and the plant manager over the monthly work-in-process inventory. Earlier in 1968, Haley had promised that this would be taken out of the hands of the foremen and handled by the data processing machines. This, of course, would save many man-hours by the production-line workers, and the foremen were pleased to hear they would be spared the task. However, by August (although this system was running in June when I arrived), Electronic Systems was still running parallel systems. One was done monthly by the machines, the other was done monthly by the workers on the line. To top it all off, neither system ever came close to the other in reporting the work-in-process inventory.

This was a great thorn in Haley's side, as he was constantly kept aware of the speech he made promising elimination of the monthly physical inventory by production workers. Again, he was under attack for devoting too much time to the accounting system. Finally, Haley cornered Barry in his office and told him to solve the problem. Barry told Haley what the problem was from the data processing angle. However, this problem could easily have been solved by correcting just one of the daily reporting procedures incurred on the production line. Barry knew how to solve this problem quite simply. Haley did not, and neither would the foremen whom Haley went to question. It was Barry's secret, and he gave me a little smile as Haley left his office.

During the end of the week prior to our week-long proposal presentation, Mr. Haley called Barry into his office and told him he was not to attend the first few meetings but was to continue working on the payroll system. Electronic Systems was experiencing great difficulty with this system—so much that a team from IBM, which specialized in payroll installations, agreed to assist Barry later in the month of August.

Barry missed the first day of meetings, but pressure was put on Haley by the various people attending the meeting to allow Barry to be present at the rest of them. Since Barry was to run the operation, many were very much interested in his views. At the end of the week, we had won over the majority, and Mr. Wilson gave his OK to that part of the system that had not already been implemented.

When I was making my rounds of goodbyes to the various personnel, the most common piece of advice given to me was not to come back to work at Electronic Systems full time. Most of the workers told me that if I came back next summer, there was a good chance they would be gone. They were starting to get responses from the résumés they, too, had sent out during the summer.

The Foster Creek Post Office Case

The United States Post Office in Foster Creek, New York, is a small, first-class office serving a suburban community of 11,000. Normally, the post office employs eleven people—a postmaster, an assistant postmaster, six carriers (including one parcel-post truck driver), and three clerks.

Each postal employee's job requirements are minutely subdivided and explicitly prescribed by the *Post Office Manual*—a large, two-volume publication of the U.S. Post Office Department in Washington, D.C. There is a "suggested" rate per minute and/or day for sorting and delivering letters, of which every postal employee is well aware. The work is highly prescribed, routine, and repetitive, with little basis for the development of individual initiative. Although each man contrives a few little tricks (which he may or may not pass along to his fellow workers) for easing his *own* work load, there is little incentive for a postal employee to attempt to improve any part of the mail delivery system *as a whole*. Each man performs pretty much as he is expected to perform (nothing more or less). Roger, the assistant postmaster, clearly verbalized this attitude, "The inspectors can't get us if we go by the book [manual]."

The irregular, unannounced visits by the district postal inspectors arouse a strange fear in *all* the employees at the Foster Creek Post Office. Although each of the eleven employees is fairly well acquainted with the inspectors, there is something disturbing about the presence of a man whose recommendations may mean the loss of your job. The security of their position in the post office is highly valued by employees of Foster Creek, some of whom are no longer young and must provide for their families. It is customary, therefore, to see an entire post office staff snap to attention and work harder at the arrival, or possibility of arrival, of a postal inspector.

Larry, the Foster Creek postmaster, had a philosophy regarding the affairs of his office which was: "Keep the patrons and the inspectors happy." Outside of this requirement and an additional one which made it imperative that each employee punch in and off the time clock at the exact appointed time (this requirement was primarily for the ease of bookkeeping), each man could do his job

"The Foster Creek Post Office Case" was written under the supervision of Alvar O. Elbing. Names of people and places have been disguised.

Figure 1 Foster Creek Post Office Formal Organization

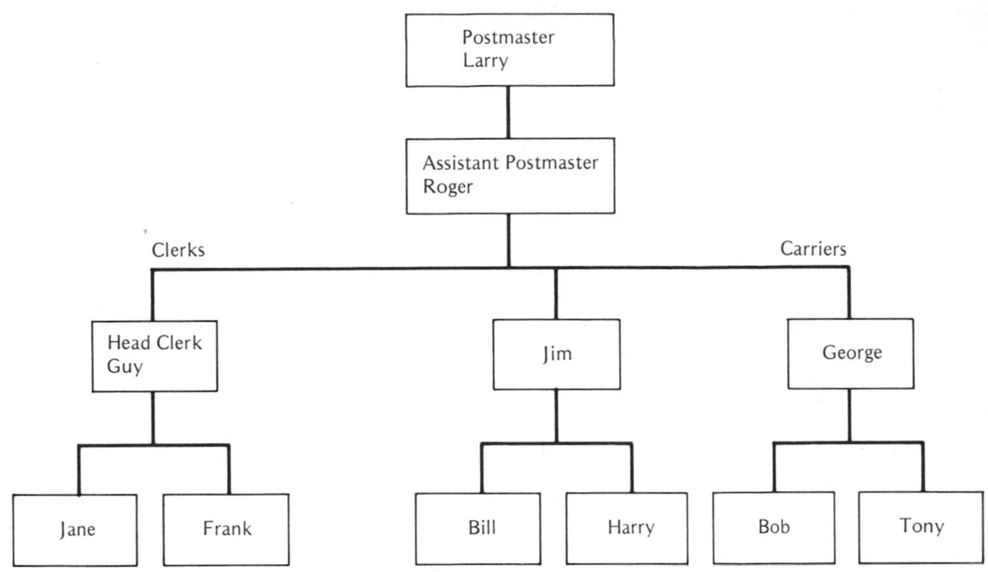

pretty much as he wished. The clerks reported at 6 A.M. to sort the day's mail into different stacks for the carriers who arrived at 7 A.M. The carriers then "cased" (further sorting according to street and number) their letters and usually were "on the road" by 9 A.M. They were required to be back in the office at 3:30 P.M., if possible, for further casing, and at 5 P.M. all the carriers went home.

In the summer months when the mail is relatively light and the weather is clear, each carrier easily finishes his route (including time allowed for a half-hour lunch break) by 1:30 P.M. It is standard procedure for the men to relax at home for two hours before reporting back in at 3:30 P.M. In the winter, on the other hand, with snow piled high in the yards, each carrier can no longer take the shorter route across the yards, and the men often finish long after 3:30 P.M. Larry is well aware of this procedure and says: "It all balances out, and in the hot summer they can use the extra hours to take it easy."

At 3:30 P.M. (or so) the day's big social event takes place at the post office. With the cry of "Flip for Cokes," all the employees except Jane, the one female clerk, match dimes to see who will be the day's loser and provide cokes for the others. This daily gaming is one of the many examples of the free and frequent sociability which exists among the ten male employees. Although the office's formal organization is detailed by postal regulations (see Figure 1), owing to the similar socioeconomic status and interests of the employees, the post office atmosphere is very relaxed and informal (see Figure 2). Many of the men bowl together; they go to the same church; and they often attend high school graduations and funerals affecting the families of their coworkers.

On payday (every Friday), each of the ten male employees contributes 50 cents of his paycheck to "the fund." This fund is used for coffee and donuts, to provide sick employees with flowers and "get-well" cards, and to purchase a ham to be shared at work during Christmas time.

Other important parts of each day are the

Figure 2 Foster Creek Post Office Informal Organization

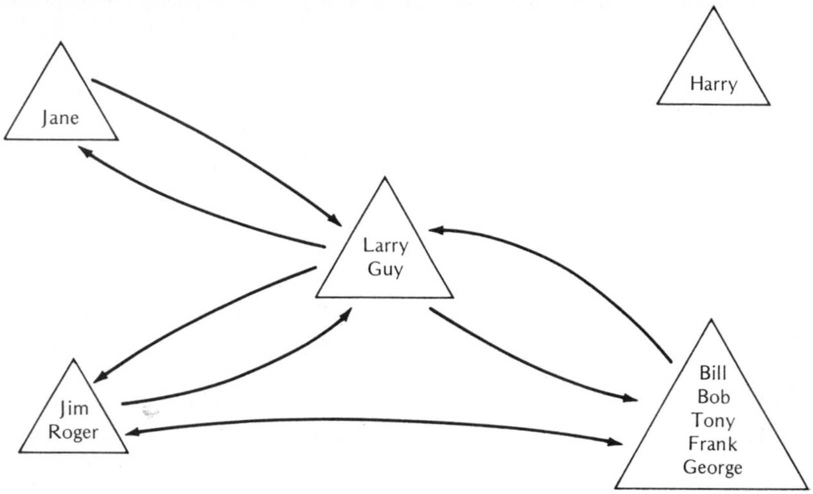

regular morning and afternoon conversations. In the morning, the talk invariably turns to news items in the morning's paper. In addition, the men often talk about "those politicians in Washington" and the possibility of a postal pay raise. In the afternoons, the men relate any interesting experiences from the day's rounds. These experiences range from dog bites to coffee with an attractive female patron.

In general the eleven employees of the Foster Creek Post Office enjoyed their work. They comprised a close-knit team doing similar and somewhat distasteful work, but, as George, a senior carrier, put it, "We get good, steady pay; and it's a lot easier than digging ditches."

In mid-June 1968, Larry filed a request for a carrier to replace a regular Foster Creek carrier who had died suddenly. At 7 A.M. on Monday, July 8th, Harry reported for work as a permanent replacement.

Harry was a tall, skinny man with thinning hair, long fingers, and wire-rimmed eye glasses. He appeared to be in his fifties. He seemed nervous and shy, and when Larry introduced him to the Foster Creek regulars, Harry stared at the floor and said only "Hi!" Initial opinions of this new carrier were mixed. Jim, another senior carrier, probably best expressed the employees' sentiments when he said: "He's not too friendly—yet—he's probably a little nervous here—but *man* can he case mail!"

Harry was an excellent caser. For 27 years he had been a clerk in the main post office. The attitudes and work environment in big city post offices differ markedly from those in smaller offices (as Larry was quick to point out when any of Foster Creek's employees complained). In the city post offices, where competition for the few available positions is extremely keen, a man must not only be very competent but must follow the postal regulations *to the letter.* As Harry said quietly to Roger upon his arrival at Foster Creek, "Things were just too pushy in the city. And besides, my wife and I wanted to move out here in the country to have a house and garden of our own to take care of."

Harry had a well-kept and attractive house and garden. It was apparent that Harry loved to take care of his lawn and garden, because he spent all day Sunday working on it. As a

Figure 3 Foster Creek Post Office Layout

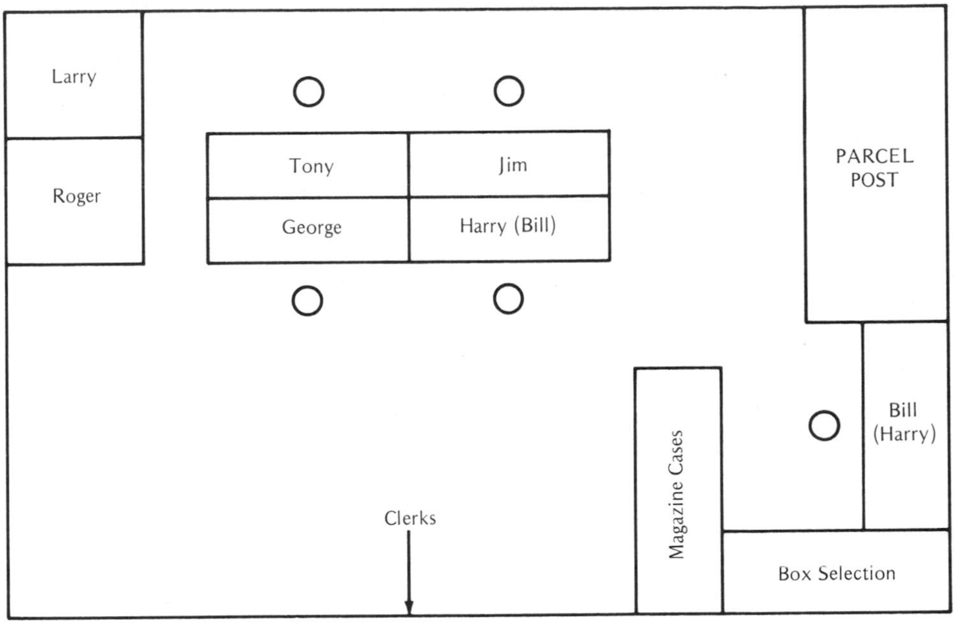

member of the Foster Creek Building and Loan Association, Larry knew that Harry had purchased the property with cash.

On Wednesday, Harry's third day at work, the opinions regarding Harry had become more concrete. As Jim said: "Harry's strange. He thinks he's better than all of us, coming from that city office. He never talks to us or says anything about himself. All he does is stand there and case mail, but *man* is he fast at that!"

The first real problem arose on the fourth day. Harry had learned his route well enough so that he, too, was able to finish by 1:30 P.M. His ability to case and "tie out" (gathering the mail in leather straps) his mail so quickly put him on the road by 8:30 in the morning—ahead of the other four carriers.

On this Thursday afternoon Harry reported back to the post office at 1:15, having finished his entire route. Upon seeing this, Roger's first reaction was to say, "Go home and have some lunch, Harry. Relax at home for a little while."

Harry replied, "I've had my lunch. There are letters on my case. I've got to do them now. I've got to do my job." Having said this, he began to case the several hundred letters which had piled up since the morning. He finished these quickly, and then went on and cased all the mail which was lying on the other four carriers' cases. When the four regular carriers returned at 3:30 P.M., they were, to say the least, surprised.

Bill, the youngest and least energetic of the carriers, thanked Harry. However, Jim and George in particular were very angry. They grumbled about having a "newcomer" interfere, with his "city tricks" and "fancy casing." They were especially angry that Harry had violated the 3:30 rule. They were determined that he would not be the one who would make them lose their precious privileges, and they complained to Larry about Harry. The postmaster told Harry to case only his own mail, and to take it easy when walking his route in the future.

The next day, Friday, was payday. Each man contributed his share to "the fund." Harry refused. "I don't drink colas," was his only answer. No one pushed the matter further, although discontent over Harry had developed among all the employees.

As the next week passed by, Harry appeared to sink into an even deeper shell. He punched in at 7 A.M. and punched out at 5 P.M. In between, he neither looked at nor spoke to any of the other employees. He continued to report back into the office before 3:30, case all his own mail, and then sit on the stool in front of his case reading magazines. Larry was worried primarily about Harry's exposure to the public as he sat at his case reading, and so on Friday of Harry's second week, Harry's and Bill's cases were switched (see Figure 3).

When each of the carriers reported in on Friday afternoon, Bill was told that his case was moved so as to give him more room to handle his quickly growing route (which, in part, was true). Harry said nothing about the switch, but went straight to work in his new location.

During Harry's third week at the post office, Larry began to worry even more about his behavior. Although the carrier was hidden from the public now, a postal inspector could catch Harry reading at his case very easily.

On Thursday, July 18th, Larry's worst fears were realized. An inspector came to the Foster Creek Post Office. As he walked in, Harry was sitting quietly at his case, reading as usual. The inspector looked at Harry, then at Larry.

Larry explained that Harry had an easier route than the other carriers. Because of this and his ability as a caser, Harry was able to finish his route more easily. Larry pointed out that he did not know what to say to the carrier, for he had finished all his *required* work. The inspector suggested that Larry readjust the routes to give Harry more houses to deliver and more mail to case. This was attempted, but Jim, George, and Tony reacted unfavorably.

Nestlé U.K. Case (A)

"You have a difficult task ahead of you, Miss Thomson, but we're behind you all the way," said Jack Dobson, plant manager of Nestlé U.K., Ltd., as he introduced Ruth Thomson to her new job as manager of the Order Processing Department.

"We've had nothing but problems with the department recently. The keypunch operators are slow and often make mistakes, so that delays occur in filling customers' orders. Yet rapid and accurate order processing is of crucial importance in our organization. We have, in fact, guaranteed that goods will be delivered to customers within three days from the time the order is received at Nestlé. We're relying on you to solve the problems associated with the departmental inefficiency. Good luck in your new job!"

Company Background

In Great Britain, the Nestlé Company is involved with the production and distribution of food products. The company can be divided into four major product groups:

- Nescafé and other powdered drinks
- Confectionery and other sweets
- Frozen foods
- Other products (e.g., canned food, sauces, spices).

Although the production of quality products is an essential aspect of Nestlé's marketing strategy, good customer service is considered to be of primary importance in determining the company's overall success. Therefore, all departments in direct connection with customers must operate efficiently and without delay. The Order Processing Department is one of the most critical departments in this regard.

Ruth Thomson joined the Nestlé Company when she accepted the position as manager of the Order Processing Department. She had previously been working as a supervisor in the Outpatient Department of a children's hospital near London. Although she had never operated a keypunch machine herself, she was anxious to take up the challenge of solving the inefficiencies in the Order Processing Department.

Time Constraints for the Order Processing Department

From the moment a customer's mail order is received at the Nestlé plant in Croydon, England, 12 hours are required to prepare and process the order. It then requires 1½ to 2 days to deliver the goods to the retail stores. Timing is especially important in the preparation and processing stage, as any small delay during the first 12 hours can result in a delivery delay of more than 24 hours.

The Order Processing Procedure

Mail orders arrive twice daily—at 7:00 A.M. and 10:30 A.M.—at Nestlé. The order forms from retail stores are recognizable by their green-framed envelopes. These forms are assigned high priority status and are sent directly to the Data Preparation Department. The envelopes are opened and a sequential number is stamped on each order form. See Exhibits 1a and 1b for samples of an order form. The orders are then scrutinized to ensure that all the necessary information has been correctly recorded, after which batches (of 50 forms each) are bound together with an appropriate batch slip (as shown in Exhibit 2). By 8:30 A.M. the first delivery of these batches is made to the keypunch room; the second delivery is made at 12 o'clock noon. In the keypunch room the batches are allocated to keypunch operators, who transfer the information to computer cards. Exhibits 3, 3a, and 3b present examples of computer cards.

It is the punch room supervisor's responsibility to allocate the order batches among 20 keypunch operators. Although at one time the operators were allowed to choose their own workloads, this "self-selection" process was discontinued when all the unpopular, complicated orders were left untouched. Each batch consists of 50 orders, regardless of the order's length or difficulty in processing. In order to guarantee an equitable distribution of unpopular work, the punch room supervisor takes the batches to each operator at the operator's workplace.

On average, each order requires nearly

"Nestlé U.K. Case (A)" was prepared by Deborah Henderson and George Möller-Racke, Research Associates, under the supervision of Professor Alvar O. Elbing as a basis for class discussion.

Exhibit 1a Nestlé U.K. Order Form (for Order Less Than Ten Items)

CUSTOMER NUMBER	THE NESTLÉ CO. LTD.	DATE OF ENTRY	ENTER IN CAPITALS
8416842	REP'S REMARKS	11 / 11 / 74	GARDNER FOODS
		CAR SALES SIG.	LINCOLN

ENTER CHOCOLATE ONLY

Item	Size	Code	Qty
Milky Bar	Sm.	96 2767	
Milky Bar	F.P.	20 2733	
Milky Bar	Med.	60 2768	
Milky Bar	Lge.	36 2701	
Tom & Jerry (shape)		60 2236	
Animal Bar	Std.	60 2291	
Animal Bar	F.P.	15 2124	
Robin Hood	Std.	60 2231	
Robin Hood	F.P.	15 2267	
Noah & Nelly		60 2289	
Noah & Nelly	F.P.	15 2257	
Rupert (choc.)	Std.	96 2089	
Rupert (choc.)	F.P.	20 2095	
Pink Panther	Sm.	96 1960	
Pink Panther	Std.	60 2064	
Pink Panther	F.P.	15 2069	
Fruity Family Banana		48 2249	
Fruity Family Orange		48 2250	
Fruity Family Raspb.		48 2251	
Milk Block	F.P.	24 2905	
Milk Block	Std.	36 2030	
Milk Block	Med.	24 2026	
Milk Block	Lge.	24 2902	
Dairy Crunch	F.P.	24 2183	
Dairy Crunch	Std.	36 2181	
Dairy Crunch	Med.	24 2098	6
Peanut Extra	Med.	24 2010	
Coff.& Biscuit Snack		36 2048	
Feast	Med.	24 2085	
Raisin	Lge.	24 2043	
Feast	Lge.	24 2995	12
Hazel Nut	Lge.	24 2015	
Frt.& Alm. Pin.	Lg.	24 2014	
Peanut Extra	Lge.	24 2008	
Brazil Nut	Lge.	24 2016	
Gala Peter	Lge.	18 2302	
Airline	Std.	30 2927	
Airline	Lge.	10 2926	
VENDING BLOCKS			
Milk Block	10p	24 2032	
Dairy Crunch	10p	24 2189	
Peanut Extra	10p	24 2046	
Feast	10p	24 2982	
Superfine	10p	24 2415	
Fruit & Nut	10p	24 2323	

Item	Size	Code	Qty
W. Irish Coffee Bar		12 1243	
W. Bitterswt. Bar		12 7892	
W. Irish Mint Crisp		12 7995	
Coffee Crm. Bar		36 1518	
Peppermint Crm.		36 1519	
Jellimallo		36 2985	
Toffimallo		36 2963	
Milk Crosqs.		18 1182	
½ lb. Home Asst.		6 3309	
1 lb. Home Asst.		3 3310	
Gala Chocs.		12 3160	
Pep. Crm. Drums		5 3120	
K. Ches. Fudge		12 3124	
K. Choc. Caramel		12 3125	
K. Choc. Hum Truf.		12 3126	
K. Choc. Pep. Crms.		12 3127	
K. Choc. Frt. Crms.		12 3148	
K. Choc. T. Delight		12 3149	
K. Choc. Asst.	5 lb	1 8720	
K. Choc. Caram.	5 lb	1 6722	
K. Choc.Pep.Crm.	5 lb	1 6724	
K. Choc. Ginger	½ lb	6 8139	
GROUP SYMBOL –1 CASE RATE c/s 2			
Butterscotch	¼ lb	20 9081	
Butterscotch	½ lb	10 6880	
Buttermints		20 6219	
Clearfruits		20 6218	
Bttd. Choc.		20 6217	
Sherb. Frts.		20 8216	
Frt. BonBons		20 6215	
Dev. Toffees		20 6214	
Butterscotch		20 6213	
Choc. Eclairs		20 6212	
Clearmints		20 6211	
Lem. Honeys		20 6210	
Barley Sugar		20 9209	
Mint Lumps		20 8208	
Buttd. Ginger		20 6207	
Apples		20 6937	
Blkc. Honeys		20 5689	
Liquorice Mints		20 6693	
Strawb. Eclairs	20p	20 6624	
Coffee Eclairs	20p	20 6623	
Blkcurr. Eclairs	20p	20 6622	
Oranges & Lemons		20 6740	
Real Frt. Jellios		20 6744	
VENDING PACKS	10p		
Buttermints		20 6895	4
Clearfruits		20 6896	4
Sherb. Frts.		20 6897	4
Barley Sugar		20 6898	
Clearmints		20 6899	4

ENTER SUGAR ONLY

Item	Size	Code	Qty
Tom & Jerry/Toff.		96 2235	
Dennis the Menace		72 2810	
W. Silvermints		36 1032	4
W. Freshers		36 1031	2
Butterscotch	5½ lb	J 8237	
Apples	5.2 lb	J 8114	
Or. & Lemons	5 lb	J 8260	
Buttd. Choc.	5 lb	J 8234	
Buttd. Ginger	5 lb	J 8236	
Buttermints	5 lb	J 8271	
Clearfruits	5 lb	J 8112	
Clearmints	5 lb	J 8113	
Barley Sugar	5 lb	J 8223	
Lemon Honeys	5 lb	J 8233	
Frt. BonBons	5 lb	J 8242	
Liquorice Mints	5 lb	J 8263	
Blk. Honeys	5 lb	J 8272	
Choc. Eclairs	4½ lb	J 8038	
Dev. Toffees	4¼ lb	J 8270	
Sherb. B/Bons	4½ lb	J 8259	
Sherb. Frts.	4 lb	J 8259	
Mint Lumps	4 lb	J 8210	
POLYBAGS			
Butterscotch	7 lb	PB 8190	
Apples	7 lb	PB 8036	
order in multiples of 4 on a separate order			
Buttd. Ginger	7 lb	PB 8195	
Frt. BonBons	7 lb	PB 8030	
Choc. Eclairs	7 lb	PB 8104	
Sherb. Frts.	7 lb	PB 8144	
Clearfruits	7 lb	PB 8177	
Buttd. Choc.	7 lb	PB 8193	
Barley Sugar	7 lb	PB 8297	
Buttermints	7 lb	PB 8287	
Lemon Honeys	7 lb	PB 8290	
Clearmints	7 lb	PB 8103	
Devon Toffees	7 lb	PB 8069	
Or. & Lemons	7 lb	PB 8029	
Sherb. B/Bons	7 lb	PB 8152	
GROUP SYMBOL –2 CASE RATE c/s			
LIBBY'S PRODUCTS			
FOILPACK DRINKS			
Orange "C"	6.5 fl.oz.	60 5700	
Apple Barrel	6.5 fl.oz.	60 5701	
4½ fl. oz. CANS			
Or.Jce. (swt)	4¼ fl.oz.	72 5709	
Or.Jce. (swt)	4¼ fl.oz.	60 5710	
G'fr.Jce.(swt)	4¼fl.oz.	72 5711	
" (unswt)	4¼fl.oz.	72 5712	
P'apple Juice	4¼ fl.oz.	72 5713	
Tom. Juice	4¼ fl.oz.	72 5714	
Tom.Jce.Ckt.	4¼fl.oz.	72 5715	
GROUP SYMBOL –8 CASE RATE c/s			

BONUSES	£	Customer's Order No.	Delivery Date	Entered and checked by	Rep. No.
			Any Other Delivery Instructions	A. Wright	2352

Exhibit 1b Nestlé U.K. Order Form (Order More Than Ten Items)

CUSTOMER NUMBER	THE NESTLÉ CO. LTD.	DATE OF ENTRY	ENTER IN CAPITALS
8416117	REP'S REMARKS	11 11 74	GARDNER FOODS
		CAR SALES SIG.	LINCOLN

ENTER CHOCOLATE ONLY

Item		Code	Qty
Milky Bar	Sm.	96 2767	
Milky Bar	F.P.	20 2733	
Milky Bar	Med.	60 2768	/
Milky Bar	Lge.	36 2701	
Tom & Jerry (shape)		60 2236	
Animal Bar	Std.	60 2291	
Animal Bar	F.P.	15 2124	
Robin Hood	Std.	60 2231	
Robin Hood	F.P.	15 2267	
Noah & Nelly		60 2289	
Noah & Nelly	F.P.	15 2257	
Rupert (choc.)	Std.	96 2089	
Rupert (choc.)	F.P.	20 2095	
Pink Panther	Sm.	96 1960	
Pink Panther	Std.	60 2064	
Pink Panther	F.P.	15 2069	
Fruity Family Banana		48 2249	
Fruity Family Orange		48 2250	
Fruity Family Raspb.		48 2251	
Milk Block	F.P.	24 2905	/
Milk Block	Std.	36 2030	
Milk Block	Med.	24 2026	
Milk Block	Lge.	24 2902	
Dairy Crunch	F.P.	24 2183	
Dairy Crunch	Std.	36 2181	
Dairy Crunch	Med.	24 2098	/
Peanut Extra	Med.	24 2010	
Coff.& Biscuit Snack		36 2048	
Feast	Med.	24 2085	
Raisin	Lge.	24 2043	
Feast	Lge.	24 2995	
Hazel Nut	Lge.	24 2015	
Frt.& Alm. Pin.	Lg.	24 2014	
Peanut Extra	Lge.	24 2008	
Brazil Nut	Lge.	24 2016	
Gala Peter	Lge.	18 2302	
Airline	Std.	30 2927	
Airline	Lge.	10 2926	
VENDING BLOCKS			
Milk Block	10p	24 2032	
Dairy Crunch	10p	24 2189	
Peanut Extra	10p	24 2046	
Feast	10p	24 2982	
Superfine	10p	24 2415	
Fruit & Nut	10p	24 2323	

Item		Code	Qty
W. Irish Coffee Bar		12 1243	
W. Bitterswt. Bar		12 7892	
W. Irish Mint Crisp		12 7995	
Coffee Crm. Bar		36 1518	
Peppermint Crm.		36 1519	
Jellimallo		36 2985	
Toffimallo		36 2963	
Milk Crosqs.		18 1182	
½ lb. Home Asst.		6 3309	
1 lb. Home Asst.		3 3310	
Gala Chocs.		12 3160	
Pep. Crm. Drums		5 3120	
K. Ches. Fudge		12 3124	
K. Choc. Caramel		12 3125	
K. Choc. Hum Truf.		12 3126	
K. Choc. Pep. Crms.		12 3127	
K. Choc. Frt. Crms.		12 3148	
K. Choc. T. Delight		12 3149	
K. Choc. Asst.	5 lb	1 8720	
K. Choc. Caram.	5 lb	1 6722	
K. Choc.Pep.Crm.	5 lb	1 6724	
K. Choc. Ginger	½ lb	6 8139	
GROUP SYMBOL –1			
CASE RATE c/s 2			
Butterscotch	¼ lb	20 9081	
Butterscotch	½ lb	10 6880	
Buttermints		20 6219	
Clearfruits		20 6218	
Bttd. Choc.		20 6217	/
Sherb. Frts.		20 8216	
Frt. BonBons		20 6215	
Dev. Toffees		20 6214	/
Butterscotch		20 6213	
Choc. Eclairs		20 6212	3
Clearmints		20 6211	
Lem. Honeys		20 6210	/
Barley Sugar		20 9209	
Mint Lumps		20 8208	
Buttd. Ginger		20 6207	
Apples		20 6937	
Blkc. Honeys		20 5689	
Liquorice Mints		20 6693	
Strawb. Eclairs	20p	20 6624	
Coffee Eclairs	20p	20 6623	
Blkcurr. Eclairs	20p	20 6622	
Oranges & Lemons		20 6740	/
Real Frt. Jellios		20 6744	
VENDING PACKS 10p			
Buttermints		20 6895	2
Clearfruits		20 6896	2
Sherb. Frts.		20 6897	1
Barley Sugar		20 6898	2
Clearmints		20 6899	2

ENTER SUGAR ONLY

Item		Code	Qty
Tom & Jerry/Toff.		96 2235	
Dennis the Menace		72 2810	
W. Silvermints		36 1032	
W. Freshers		36 1031	
Butterscotch	5½ lb	J 8237	
Apples	5.2 lb	J 8114	
Or. & Lemons	5 lb	J 8260	
Buttd. Choc.	5 lb	J 8234	
Buttd. Ginger	5 lb	J 8236	
Buttermints	5 lb	J 8271	
Clearfruits	5 lb	J 8112	
Clearmints	5 lb	J 8113	
Barley Sugar	5 lb	J 8223	
Lemon Honeys	5 lb	J 8233	
Frt. BonBons	5 lb	J 8242	
Liquorice Mints	5 lb	J 8263	
Blk. Honeys	5 lb	J 8272	
Choc. Eclairs	4½ lb	J 8038	
Dev. Toffees	4¼ lb	J 8270	
Sherb. B/Bons	4½ lb	J 8259	
Sherb. Frts.	4 lb	J 8259	
Mint Lumps	4 lb	J 8210	
POLYBAGS			
Butterscotch	7 lb	PB 8190	
Apples	7 lb	PB 8036	
order in multiples of 4 on a separate order			
Buttd. Ginger	7 lb	PB 8195	
Frt. BonBons	7 lb	PB 8030	
Choc. Eclairs	7 lb	PB 8104	
Sherb. Frts.	7 lb	PB 8144	
Clearfruits	7 lb	PB 8177	
Buttd. Choc.	7 lb	PB 8193	
Barley Sugar	7 lb	PB 8297	
Buttermints	7 lb	PB 8287	
Lemon Honeys	7 lb	PB 8290	
Clearmints	7 lb	PB 8103	
Devon Toffees	7 lb	PB 8069	
Or. & Lemons	7 lb	PB 8029	
Sherb. B/Bons	7 lb	PB 8152	
GROUP SYMBOL –2			
CASE RATE c/s			
LIBBY'S PRODUCTS			
FOILPACK DRINKS			
Orange "C"	6.5 fl.oz.	60 5700	
Apple Barrel	6.5 fl.oz.	60 5701	
4½ fl. oz. CANS			
Or.Jce. (swt)	4¼ fl.oz.	72 5709	
Or.Jce. (swt)	4¼ fl.oz.	60 5710	
G'fr.Jce.(swt)	4¼fl.oz.	72 5711	
" (unswt)	4¼fl.oz.	72 5712	
P'apple Juice	4¼ fl.oz.	72 5713	
Tom. Juice	4¼ fl.oz.	72 5714	
Tom.Jce.Ckt.	4¼fl.oz.	72 5715	
GROUP SYMBOL –8			
CASE RATE c/s			

BONUSES	Customer's Order No.	Delivery Date	Entered and checked by	Rep. No.
£		Any Other Delivery Instructions	U. Wright	2352

Exhibit 2 Nestlé U.K. Batch Slip

BATCH CONTROL SLIP

Field		Columns	Entry
CLASS OF CARD COLUMN ONE		1	☒
COMPANY NUMBER COLUMN TWO		2	5
BATCH NUMBER COLUMNS 3-4		3 4	5 7
DEPOT (IF DIFFERENT) COLUMNS 5-6	SKIP	5 6	
NUMBER OF ORDERS COLUMNS 7-8		7 8	0 2
DATE COLUMNS 9-13		YEAR 9 10 / DAY 11 12 13	7 4 3 1 6

PUNCHED BY:-	VERIFIED BY:-
3	22

ORDERS EXTRACTED

ORDER NO.	SIGNATURE

IBM No. 3449B

Exhibit 3

Nestlé U.K. Batch Card As Transferred from Batch Slip

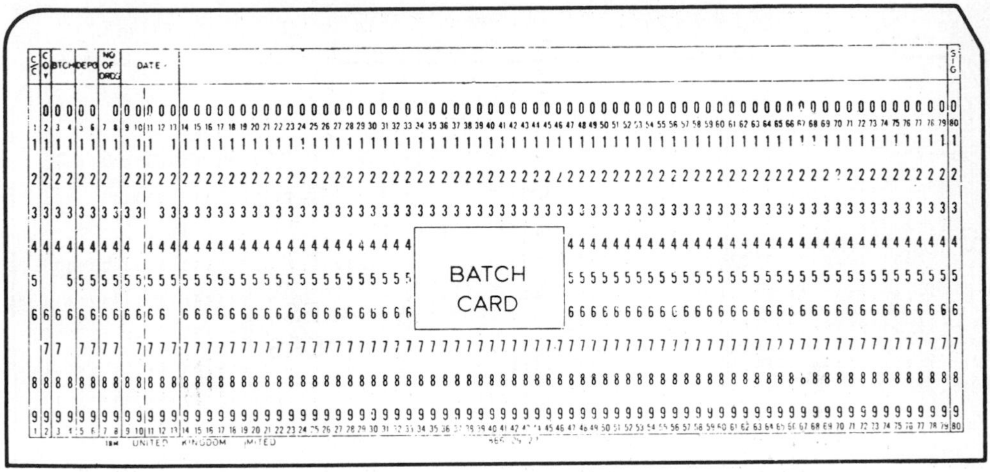

CC | BTCH | DEPO | NO OF ORDS | DATE | SIG

BATCH CARD

IBM UNITED KINGDOM LIMITED

Exhibit 3a

Nestlé U.K. Computer Card (Order of Less Than Ten Items)

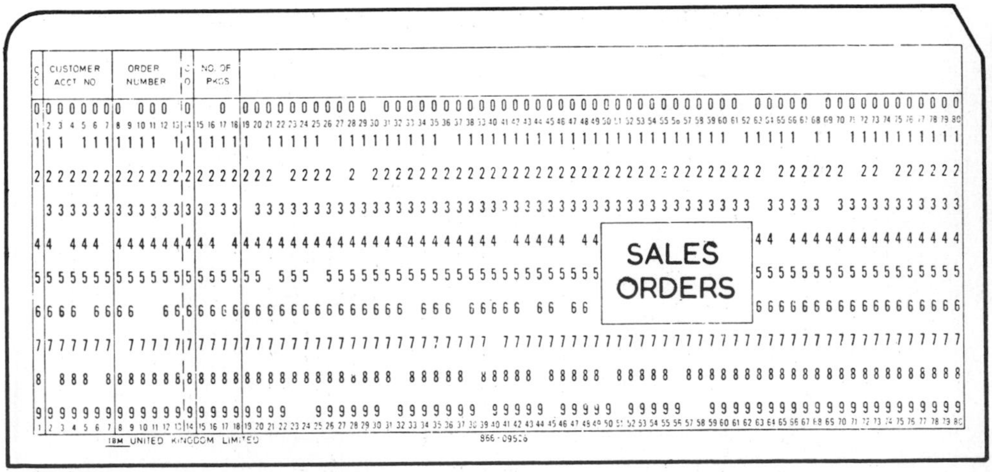

CC | CUSTOMER ACCT NO | ORDER NUMBER | CO | NO. OF PKGS

SALES ORDERS

IBM UNITED KINGDOM LIMITED 866-09526

Exhibit 3b
Nestlé U.K. Computer Cards (Order of More Than Ten Items)

1)

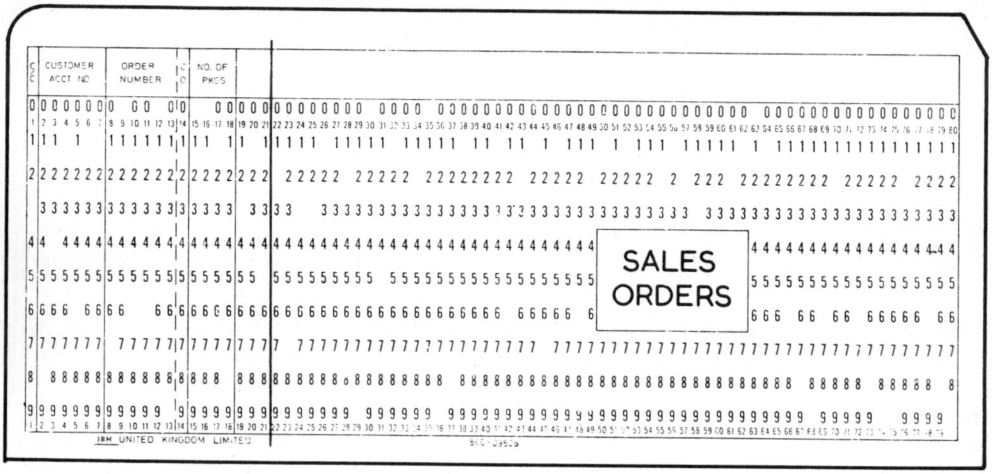

CC | CUSTOMER ACCT. NO. | ORDER NUMBER | CO | NO. OF PKGS

SALES ORDERS

IBM UNITED KINGDOM LIMITED

2) order continued

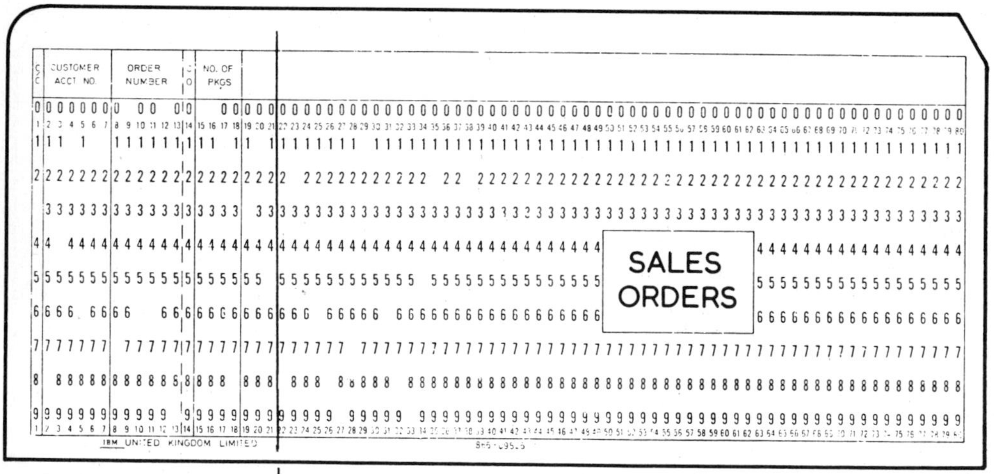

CC | CUSTOMER ACCT. NO. | ORDER NUMBER | CO | NO. OF PKGS

SALES ORDERS

IBM UNITED KINGDOM LIMITED

Fixed Info > | < **Variable Info**

200 key punches. The number of key depressions per order can be broken down as follows:

Fixed Information	*No. of Digits*
• Customer number	7
• Date of entry	6
• Order number	6
• Selling division number	2
• Product classification number	1
Total number of digits:	22

Variable Information (based on average of 20 items per order)	*Average No. of Digits*
• Six digits per item ordered	120
• Delivery instructions (varies from 0–35)	20
• Repetition of fixed information (if more than ten items, a new card must be punched)	22
Total number of digits:	184

During a normal working day, approximately 3500 orders are received at Nestlé, yet in peak periods (at the beginning of the week, at Christmas time, etc.), the average number of orders received climbs to 5000 per day—calling for possibly 1 million key depressions.

After a batch of 50 orders has been keypunched, it is given to one of 20 verifiers, who compares the order forms with the punched cards. If a mistake is detected, the order is handed back to the keypunch operator concerned for correction. See Exhibit 4 for an illustration of the punch room floor plan.

The punched, verified, and corrected computer card orders are assembled in card boxes and forwarded to the computer room. Three hours are required for computer processing. The computer produces two forms of output: (1) an invoice (see Exhibits 5a and 5b); and (2) a consignment note (see Exhibits 6a and 6b).

Both the invoices and the consignment notes are prepared for mailing in the guillotine room. Here, the two types of forms are cut to size and packed in envelopes. Approximately two hours are needed for mail preparation. In order to meet the evening mail pick-up deadline, all orders must leave the keypunch room by 2:00 P.M.

Invoices are mailed directly to customers and must be prepared for pick-up at 8:00 P.M. Consignment notes are sent to various distribution points in England. At 7:00 P.M., a truck driver collects the notes and drives them to various London train stations, from where they are transported overnight to the depots. According to the instructions on the notes, the depots then prepare the goods for delivery, and truck them to the customers.

Working Hours in the Order Processing Department

The keypunch operators come in to work at approximately 8:00 A.M. At 10:30, half of the employees are permitted to take a tea break of 15 minutes. The supervisor determines which half of the verifiers and the operators may take their break, so that a continuous work flow is guaranteed for at least part of the department. The remainder may take their break from 10:45 to 11:00 A.M. One hour is allowed for lunch, which takes place between 12:00 and 2:00 P.M. The supervisor again determines who can take lunch at what time. The employees are discouraged from taking breaks during the rest of the day. Often the supervisor will ask for an explanation if an employee leaves her desk more than twice a day.

As a result of the 2:00 P.M. deadline for the

Exhibit 4 Nestlé U.K. Punch Room Floor Plan

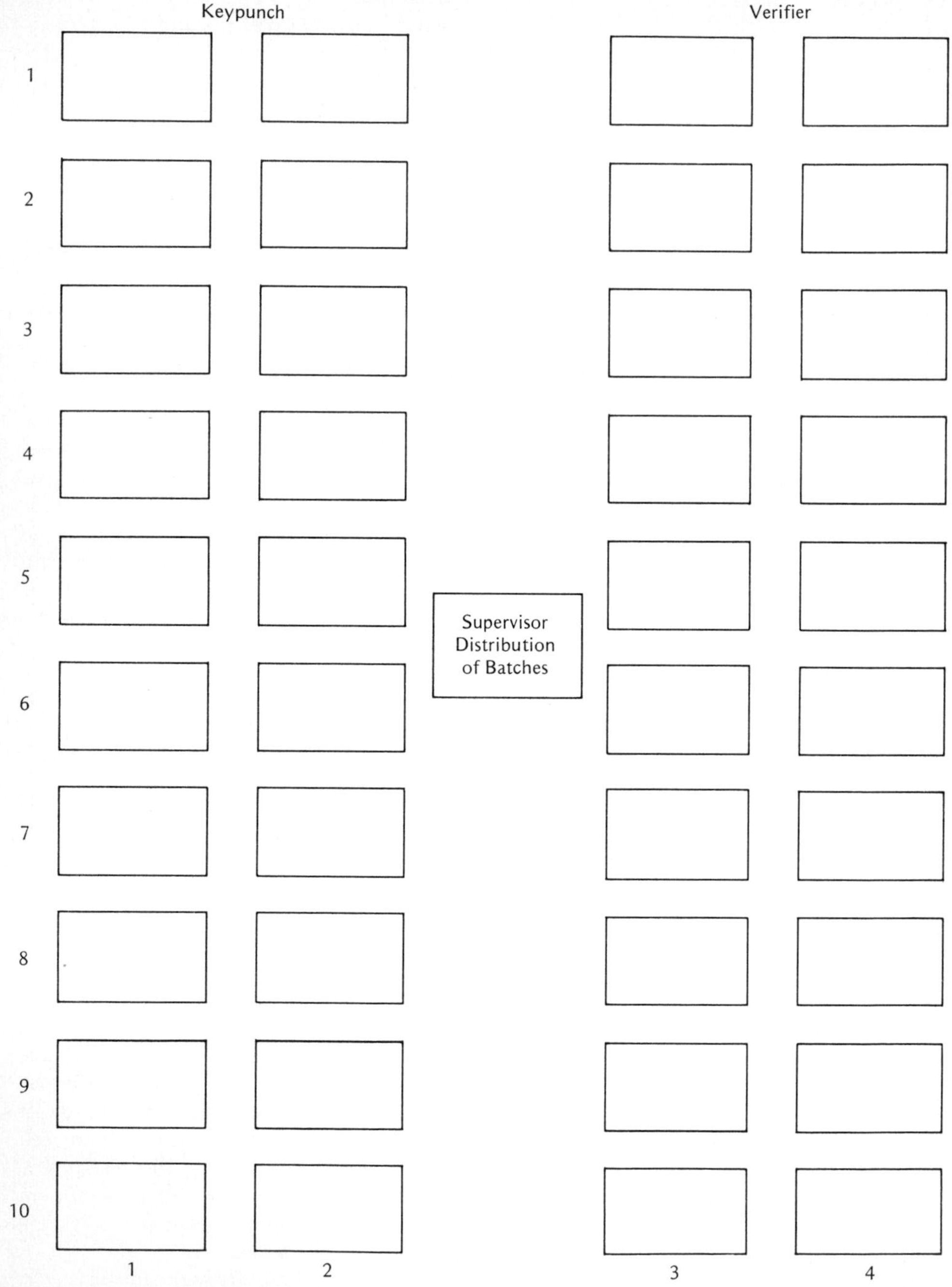

Exhibit 5a
Nestlé U.K. Invoice (Order of Less Than Ten Items)

THE NESTLÉ COMPANY LTD
REGD. OFFICE: ST. GEORGE'S HOUSE, CROYDON, SURREY

PAYMENT TO: THE NESTLÉ COMPANY LTD
ST. GEORGE'S HOUSE
CROYDON, SURREY, CR9 1NR

Nestlé
INVOICE

REMITTANCE ADVICE
THE NESTLÉ COMPANY LTD
REGD. OFFICE: ST. GEORGE'S HOUSE, CROYDON, SURREY

CUSTOMER No.	INVOICE No.	INVOICE DATE (TAX POINT)	IMPORTANT PLEASE QUOTE CUSTOMER No., INVOICE No. AND INVOICE DATE ON ALL COMMUNICATIONS	ANY ACCOUNT QUERIES TO:	FULL OFFICE ADDRESS & TELEPHONE NUMBER OVERLEAF.	GROUND	T	DATE ORDER TAKEN	INVOICE DATE	INVOICE No.	GROUND
841684	53706610	13 11 74				2352	1	11 11 74			

SOLD TO

Gardner Merchant Food
Services Ltd.
c/o Swift Poultry Co. Ltd.
Tritton Road, Lincoln LN6 7QY

GOODS TO

THIS ACCOUNT IS DUE AND PAYABLE WITHIN 30 DAYS OF THE INVOICE DATE.

NO STATEMENT RENDERED UNLESS REQUESTED

REC. CONSUMER PRICE INCL. V.A.T. EXTENSION	UNIT	DESCRIPTION		PACK	LINE CODE	% V.A.T. RATE	QUANTITY	PRICE (EXCL. V.A.T.)	NETT PRICE (EXCL. V.A.T.)	EXTENSION (EXCL. V.A.T.)
2.88	0,04	Willwood Freshers	4P	36	1031	8.000	2	0.98	0.98	1,96
5.76	0,04	Willwood Silvermints	4P	36	1032	8.000	4	0.98	0.98	3.92
11.52	0,04	Dairy Crunch N/D		48	2098	8.000	6	1.36½	1.36½	3.10
21.60	0,05	Feast	5P	36	2995	8.000	12	1.27	1.27	15.24
8.00	0,10	Buttermints Vending	10P	20	6895	8.000	4	1.33	1.33	5.32
8.00	0,10	Clearfruits Vending	10P	20	6896	8.000	4	1.33	1.33	5.32
8.00	0,10	Sherbet Fruits Vending	10P	20	6897	8.000	4	1.33	1.33	5.32
8.00	0.10	Clearmints Vending	10P	20	6899	8.000	4	1.33	1.33	5.32
		Cash discount for	8.000	VAT	ITEMS					0.63

Please note - the new consumer prices include vat

```
*****************SUMMARY OF TOTALS *************************
*Percent     * Value     *  PROM ALLCES ETC SHEWN  *  NET VALUE *
*VAT RATE    * Excl Vat  *  BELOW INVOICED ITEMS   *  EXCL VAT
*            *           *                         *
*  8,000     * 50.59     *  LESS    0.63           *  49.96   PLUS INPUT VAT      4.00
```

CUSTOMER No.	COY	DOCUMENT No.
AMOUNT REMITTED		

NO DEDUCTIONS PERMISSIBLE
NOTE: Chocolate and Confectionery trade prices are STRICTLY NET.

DETACH THIS ADVICE AND SEND WITH YOUR REMITTANCE TO THE PAYMENT ADDRESS **OR** USE THE CREDIT TRANSFER OVERLEAF.

RECEIPTS WILL NOT BE ISSUED FOR PAYMENTS MADE BY CHEQUE UNLESS REQUESTED.

CUSTOMER'S OWN INFORMATION — OUR V.A.T. REGISTRATION No. IS 217 8567 37

ORDER No.	BRANCH	REF	SERIAL No.	TOTAL PKGS	TYPE OF SUPPLY	THIS INVOICE INCLUDES
	14684		55720318	40	SALE	£ 4.00 FOR V.A.T.

£ 53.96

AMOUNT DUE AND PAYABLE

CONDITIONS OF SALE AND CLAIMS PROCEDURE ARE DETAILED OVERLEAF

STRICTLY NET

Exhibit 5b

Nestlé U.K. Invoice (Order of More Than Ten Items)

THE NESTLÉ COMPANY LTD
REGD. OFFICE: ST. GEORGE'S HOUSE, CROYDON, SURREY

PAYMENT TO: THE NESTLÉ COMPANY LTD
ST. GEORGE'S HOUSE
CROYDON, SURREY, CR9 1NR

Nestlé
INVOICE

REMITTANCE ADVICE
THE NESTLÉ COMPANY LTD
REGD. OFFICE: ST. GEORGE'S HOUSE, CROYDON, SURREY

CUSTOMER No.	INVOICE No.	INVOICE DATE (TAX POINT)	IMPORTANT PLEASE QUOTE CUSTOMER No., INVOICE No. AND INVOICE DATE ON ALL COMMUNICATIONS
841611	53706609	13 11 74	

ANY ACCOUNT QUERIES TO: FULL OFFICE ADDRESS & TELEPHONE NUMBER OVERLEAF.

GROUND	T	DATE ORDER TAKEN
2352	I	11 11 74

INVOICE DATE	INVOICE No.	GROUND

SOLD TO

Gardners Merchant Food
Services Ltd.
C/O Leys Casting Co. Ltd.
Statton Road
North Hyklam Lincoln

GOODS TO

THIS ACCOUNT IS DUE AND PAYABLE WITHIN 30 DAYS OF THE INVOICE DATE.

NO STATEMENT RENDERED UNLESS REQUESTED

REC. CONSUMER PRICE INCL. V.A.T. EXTENSION	UNIT	DESCRIPTION		PACK	LINE CODE	% V.A.T. RATE	QUANTITY	PRICE (EXCL. V.A.T.)	NETT PRICE (EXCL. V.A.T.)	EXTENSION (EXCL. V.A.T.)
1.92	0,04	Dairy Crunch N/D	4P	48	2098	8.000	1	1.36½	1.36½	1.36
2.52	0,07	Milky Bar	7P	36	2733	8.000	1	1.78½	1.78½	1.78
1.92	0,04	Milk Block	4P	48	2905	8.000	1	1.36½	1.36½	1.36
2.40	0,12	Keiller Lemon Honeys		20	6210	8.000	1	1.59½	1.59½	1.59
7.20	0,12	Keiller Chocolate Eclairs		20	6212	8.000	3	1.59½	1.59½	4.78
2.40	0.12	Keiller Devon Toffee		20	6214	8.000	1	CANCELLED		
2.40	0,12	Keiller Buttered Chocolate		20	6217	8.000	1	CANCELLED		
4.00	0,10	Buttermints Vending	10P	20	6895	8.000	2	1.33	1.33	2.80
4.00	0,10	Clearfruits Vending	10P	20	6896	8.000	2	1.33	1.33	2.66
2.00	0,10	Sherbet Fruits Vending	10P	20	6897	8.000	1	1.33	1.33	1.33
4.00	0,10	Vending Barley Sugar	10P	20	6898	8.000	2	1.33	1.33	2.60
4.00	0,10	Clearmints Vending	10P	20	6899	8.000	2	1.33	1.33	2.68
		CASH DISCOUNT FOR 8.000 VAT ITEMS								0.29
		PLEASE NOTE - THE NEW CONSUMER PRICES INCLUDE VAT								

CUSTOMER No.	COY		DOCUMENT No.
AMOUNT REMITTED			

NO DEDUCTIONS PERMISSIBLE
NOTE: Chocolate and Confectionery trade prices are STRICTLY NET.

DETACH THIS ADVICE AND SEND WITH YOUR REMITTANCE TO THE PAYMENT ADDRESS **OR** USE THE CREDIT TRANSFER OVERLEAF.

RECEIPTS WILL NOT BE ISSUED FOR PAYMENTS MADE BY CHEQUE UNLESS REQUESTED.

CUSTOMER'S OWN INFORMATION

ORDER No.	BRANCH	REF	SERIAL No.	TOTAL PKGS.	TYPE OF SUPPLY	THIS INVOICE INCLUDES
						£ FOR V.A.T.

OUR V.A.T. REGISTRATION No. IS 217 8567 37

£

AMOUNT DUE AND PAYABLE

CONDITIONS OF SALE AND CLAIMS PROCEDURE ARE DETAILED OVERLEAF

STRICTLY NET

Exhibit 5b (cont'd)

THE NESTLÉ COMPANY LTD
REGD. OFFICE: ST. GEORGE'S HOUSE, CROYDON, SURREY

PAYMENT TO: THE NESTLÉ COMPANY LTD
ST. GEORGE'S HOUSE
CROYDON, SURREY, CR9 1NR

Nestlé
INVOICE

REMITTANCE ADVICE
THE NESTLÉ COMPANY LTD
REGD. OFFICE: ST. GEORGE'S HOUSE, CROYDON, SURREY

CUSTOMER No.	INVOICE No.	INVOICE DATE (TAX POINT)	IMPORTANT PLEASE QUOTE CUSTOMER No., INVOICE No. AND INVOICE DATE ON ALL COMMUNICATIONS
841611	53706609	13 11 74	

ANY ACCOUNT QUERIES TO: FULL OFFICE ADDRESS & TELEPHONE NUMBER OVERLEAF

GROUND	T	DATE ORDER TAKEN
2352	I	11 11 74

INVOICE DATE	INVOICE No.	GROUND

SOLD TO

GARDNER MERCHANT FOOD

GOODS TO

THIS ACCOUNT IS DUE AND PAYABLE WITHIN 30 DAYS OF THE INVOICE DATE.

NO STATEMENT RENDERED UNLESS REQUESTED

REC. CONSUMER PRICE INCL. V.A.T. EXTENSION	UNIT	DESCRIPTION	PACK	LINE CODE	% V.A.T. RATE	QUANTITY	PRICE (EXCL. V.A.T.)	NETT PRICE (EXCL. V.A.T.)	EXTENSION (EXCL. V.A.T.)
		** CONTINUATION **							

```
*************************  S U M M A R Y   O F   T O T A L S  **************
* PERCENT    *    VALUE     *  PROM ALLCES ETC SHEWN  *  NET VALUE    *
* VAT RATE   *    EXCL VAT  *  BELOW INVOICED ITEMS   *  EXCL VAT     *
*            *              *                         *               *
*  8.000     *    22.84     *  LESS          0.29     *  22.55   PLUS INPUT VAT      1.20
```

CUSTOMER No.	COY		DOCUMENT No.

AMOUNT REMITTED

NO DEDUCTIONS PERMISSIBLE
NOTE: Chocolate and Confectionery trade prices are STRICTLY NET.

DETACH THIS ADVICE AND SEND WITH YOUR REMITTANCE TO THE PAYMENT ADDRESS **OR** USE THE CREDIT TRANSFER OVERLEAF.

RECEIPTS WILL NOT BE ISSUED FOR PAYMENTS MADE BY CHEQUE UNLESS REQUESTED.

CUSTOMER'S OWN INFORMATION

OUR V.A.T. REGISTRATION No. IS 217 8567 37

ORDER No.	BRANCH	REF	SERIAL No.	TOTAL PKGS.	TYPE OF SUPPLY	THIS INVOICE INCLUDES
	14611		55720317	16	SALE	£ 1.80 FOR V.A.T.

£ 24.35

AMOUNT DUE AND PAYABLE

STRICTLY NET

CONDITIONS OF SALE AND CLAIMS PROCEDURE ARE DETAILED OVERLEAF

Exhibit 6a

Nestlé U.K. Consignment Note (Order of Less Than Ten Items)

GOODS TO

GARDNER MERCHANT FOOD
SERVICES LTD
C/O SWIFT POULTRY CO LTD
TRITTON ROAD
LINCOLN LN6 7QY 2352

THE NESTLÉ COMPANY LTD.
Head Office: ST. GEORGE'S HOUSE, CROYDON, CR9 1NR
Telephone: 01-686 3333 Telex: 23117

Nestlé
CONSIGNMENT NOTE

PAGE No.

CARRIER (UNLESS DELIVERED BY OWN VAN)			CUSTOMER'S ORDER No.

PLEASE QUOTE THESE DETAILS ON ALL COMMUNICATIONS	CUSTOMER No.	INVOICE No.	SERIAL No.	INVOICE DATE
	841684	53706610	557 20318	13 11 74

	DESCRIPTION AND SIZE		PACK	LINE CODE	QUANTITY	CHECKED	GOODS UNDELIVERED QUANTITY	GOODS UNDELIVERED REASON
0.04	WILLWOOD FRESHERS	4P	36	1031	2			
0.04	WILLWOOD SILVERMINTS	4P	36	1032	4			
0.04	DAILY CRUNCH N/D	4P	48	2098	6			
0.05	FEAST	5P	36	2995	12			
0.10	BUTTERMINTS VENDING	10P	20	6895	4			
0.10	CLEARFRUITS VENDING	10P	20	6896	4			
0.10	SHERBET FRUITS VENDING	10P	20	6897	4			
0.10	CLEARMINTS VENDING	10P	20	6899	4			

CONFECTIONERY JARS — Collected

JAR CREDIT REF. No. 8

CONSIGNMENT REFUSED

Reason..........

Redeliver on..........

PCVs ATTACHED Serial Numbers		OUT	BACK
	TOTAL PALLET QTY. ON PCVs +		
	CHEP PALLETS		
	TOTAL	=	
PCV Received (Serial No.)	NESTLÉ PALLETS		
	PLASTIC JAR CRATES		

Customer Receipt No.

QUANTITY RECEIVED IN GOOD CONDITION

TOTAL PKGS.

CUSTOMER'S SIGNATURE

CANCELLATIONS

Cancellation Ref. No. 2

Reason Code

Complete/Part Delivery Code

Line Code	Quantity

DEPOT BALANCE ORDER/S

Date	Serial No.

DESPATCH DATE

DO NOT DELIVER AS INDICATED	MON		TUE		WED		THU		FRI		DELIVERY INSTRUCTIONS
	am	pm	am	pm	am	pm	am	pm	am	pm	

WEIGHT KGS.	DEC. CWTS.
90	1,77

Exhibit 6b

Nestlé U.K. Consignment Note (Order of More Than Ten Items)

GOODS TO

GARDNER MERCHANT FOOD
SERVICES LTD.
C/O LEYS CASTING CO LTD
STATTON ROAD
NORTH HYKEHAM LINCOLN 2352

THE NESTLÉ COMPANY LTD.
Head Office: ST. GEORGE'S HOUSE, CROYDON, CR9 1NR
Telephone: 01-686 3333 Telex: 23117

Nestlé
CONSIGNMENT NOTE

PAGE No.

CARRIER (UNLESS DELIVERED BY OWN VAN)

CUSTOMER'S ORDER No.

PLEASE QUOTE THESE DETAILS ON ALL COMMUNICATIONS	CUSTOMER No.	INVOICE No.	SERIAL No.	INVOICE DATE
	841611	53706609	557 20317	13 11 74

	DESCRIPTION AND SIZE		PACK	LINE CODE	QUANTITY	CHECKED	GOODS UNDELIVERED QUANTITY	GOODS UNDELIVERED REASON
0.04	DAIRY CRUNCH N/D	4P	48	2098	1			
0.07	MILKY BAR	7P	36	2733	1			
0,04	MILK BLOCK	4P	48	2905	1			
0.12	KEILLER LEMON HONEYS		20	6210	1			
0.12	KEILLER CHOCOLATE ECLAIRS		20	6212	3			
0.10	BUTTERMINTS VENDING	10P	20	6895	2			
0.10	CLEARFRUITS VENDING	10P	20	6896	2			
0.10	SHERBET FRUITS VENDING	10P	20	6897	1			
0.10	VENDING BARLEY SUGAR	10P	20	6898	2			
0.10	CLEARMINT VENDING	10P	20	6899	2			
	KEILLER DEVON TOFFEE		20		ICANCELLO			
	KEILLER BUTTERED CHOCOLATE		20		ICANCELLO			

CONFECTIONERY JARS — Collected

JAR CREDIT REF. No. 8

CONSIGNMENT REFUSED

Reason........

Redeliver on........

PCVs ATTACHED Serial Numbers		OUT	BACK
	TOTAL PALLET QTY. ON PCVs +		
	CHEP PALLETS		
	TOTAL	=	
PCV Received (Serial No.)	NESTLÉ PALLETS		
	PLASTIC JAR CRATES		

Customer Receipt No.

TOTAL PKGS.

QUANTITY RECEIVED IN GOOD CONDITION

CUSTOMER'S SIGNATURE

CANCELLATIONS

Cancellation Ref. No. 2

Reason Code

Complete/Part Delivery Code

Line Code | Quantity

DEPOT BALANCE ORDER/S

Date | Serial No.

DESPATCH DATE

DO NOT DELIVER AS INDICATED	MON	TUE	WED	THU	FRI
	am pm	am pm	am pm	am pm	am pm

DELIVERY INSTRUCTIONS

WEIGHT KGS.	DEC. CWTS.
46	0.99

Exhibit 7 Nestlé U.K.
Sequence of Events in Order Processing

If day x is date on order form:

DAY	*TIME*		*ACTIVITY*
x + 1	7:00	10:30	mail received
	8:30	12:00	orders are batched
			keypunching
			verification
		14:00	correction
		17:00	sorting
		18:00	mail preparation
		19:00	pick-up of consignment notes
		20:00	mail pick-up
x + 2		7:00	delivery of consignment notes
	8:30–17:00		preparation of goods ordered
		19:00	pick-up of goods
x + 3		8:00	delivery of goods

punch room, all keypunching for the day must be completed within a 4¾-hour time span. Exhibit 7 summarizes the total time schedule for the processing of an order. Frequently the deadline was not being met. Operators were averaging about 8000 key depressions per hour—although the IBM standard for a similar setting is 12,000 punches per hour.

The Problem Facing Nestlé Management

Jack Dobson, the plant manager, was becoming more and more concerned with the delays in the Order Processing Department. The delays were causing a substantial increase in computer costs. Also, errors made by the keypunch operators had increased to 6 percent of total output. Finally, the delays in the delivery of merchandise were beginning to affect Nestlé's reputation as a quick, efficient supplier.

When delays in the department first became serious, management took steps to tighten up the work pace. As described above, the strict rules for tea breaks and lunch breaks were instilled, and the order batches were distributed to the operators on a pre-selected basis. In order to improve the working conditions in the department, the older noisy keypunch machines were replaced with new ones which operated more quietly. Yet in spite of these changes, the delays still continued.

Ruth Thomson recognized the importance of her new assignment and wondered where to begin.

Nestlé U.K. Case (B)

The main task facing Ruth Thomson as she took over as manager of the Order Processing Department was to understand the reason behind the inefficiencies in the department. She had recently been hired by the plant manager of Nestlé U.K. to solve the problems associated with the tardiness of the keypunch operators.

Ruth Thomson's Appraisal

Ruth set out to interview each employee individually in order to determine the general job attitudes and human needs prevailing in the department. She soon realized that the real problem in the department was neither the equipment nor the work preparation, but the fact that the employees were painfully bored and depressed with their work. For most of them, it was difficult to work intensively for a long uninterrupted time.

She discovered that after a half hour of working, nearly every keypuncher took a "natural break." Even the more conscientious employees who did not stop after half an hour, slowed down their productivity rate considerably at the end of the second hour of uninterrupted work. Ruth felt that the employees would perform better if they were allowed to leave their machines when they needed to, instead of being restricted to the official break periods.

Changes Needed in the Department

1. *Environmental changes.* Ruth was convinced that the new keypunch machines, in fact, added to the monotony of the punching job. She therefore decided that the older noisier machines should be reintroduced into the department. The noise, she felt, would be more stimulating for the keypunchers, as it would prove to them that the punch cards were actually making progress as they were handled. In addition, she felt that the machines in the office should be relocated, and the girls given new seats to provide more individual workplaces. Green plants would be put in the office and a carpet put on the floor. She decided the changes should be made with the consultation and consent of each employee.

2. *Work redesign.* Ruth recognized that a main complaint among the employees was the unequal distribution of orders. Some batches were much more complicated and difficult to process than others. She therefore decided to rate the orders according to their length and complexity. The next step would be to develop a productivity guideline which listed the theoretical amount of time that each rated order should require for completion. The orders would be grouped in batches of similar difficulty, so that each batch would take approximately half an hour to complete. Ruth felt that this batch length would coincide with the "natural break" which most employees took after 30 minutes of concentrated keypunching.

3. *Wage and bonus plan.* With the new rating system, it would be possible to rank each employee according to rate of productivity. Ruth decided that after an initial trial period of two months, each keypuncher should be classified into one of the following productivity groups:

- between 8000 and 10,000 key depressions/hour
- between 10,000 and 12,000 key depressions/hour
- between 12,000 and 14,000 key depressions/hour
- 14,000 or more key depressions/hour

After a second two-month working period, the employees would be tested again and their salaries or bonuses determined on the basis of their achievements or gains in productivity.

Employees would be encouraged to set their own targets of work for the day and be allowed to choose their own batches for keypunching. These targets and individual performances in turn, would determine each

---

"Nestlé U.K. Case (B)" was prepared by Deborah Henderson and George Möller-Racke, Research Associates, under the supervision of Professor Alvar O. Elbing as a basis for class discussion.

employee's daily pay. Ruth also intended to set up an incentive plan whereby exceptionally high productivity would be rewarded with a financial bonus.

4. *Regulation for breaks.* Ruth felt that the keypunchers should be allowed to take a break at any point after the first half hour of straight working, provided they didn't leave the building. They would be allowed to knit or read at their leisure. Since an exact working target would be set for each day, the employees would be able to allocate their working time in accordance with the percentage of work they had achieved. They could leave the office when their daily target was met.

5. *Group competition.* Ruth decided that if the keypunchers were divided into four separate groups or work units with four group leaders, the groups would develop competition among themselves, whereby each would try to be first to finish a job in the correct manner. She would design a chart to record each group's work outputs, as well as each individual's daily productivity. Additional financial incentives could be assigned to each group for outstanding performance.

Ruth hoped that, when implemented, these changes would improve the work conditions and work productivity among the keypunch operators in the Order Processing Department.

Nestlé U.K. Case (C)

Ruth Thomson, new manager of the Order Processing Department, decided to present her proposal of changes to the company's plant manager, Jack Dobson. After receiving his approval, she proceeded to carry out the changes as outlined in the Nestlé U.K. (B) case.

"Nestle U.K. Case (C)" was prepared by Deborah Henderson and George Möller-Racke, Research Associates, under the supervision of Professor Alvar O. Elbing as a basis for class discussion.

Three months later, productivity among the keypunch operators in the department had nearly doubled—from 8000 to over 14,500 key depressions per hour. The error ratio in key punching was reduced from 6 percent to less than 1 percent; delays in processing the orders were eliminated; and the morale of the employees had improved immensely. Output had increased to such an extent that Jack Dobson was able to reduce the staff size in the department from 40 to 30. Most of the ten extra employees were absorbed by other departments at Nestlé, but some resigned voluntarily.

Chapter 5

Step 3: Definition of the Problem

After diagnosis, the next step in sound decision making is selection and definition of the problem to be solved. This chapter will present the criteria for defining the problem in a manner conducive to systematic solution. First, however, let us consider the significance of problem definition to the decision process.

THE SIGNIFICANCE OF PROBLEM DEFINITION

Definition of the problem, like the diagnostic step, is generally glossed over when the human problems of organizational management are considered. Frequently, the definition of the problem is assumed to be obvious and is taken for granted. The worker is "uncooperative," in need of "shaping up," etc. Solving the problem is assumed to present the real difficulty, and usually claims most of our attention and our best efforts. Psychologically, it is uncomfortable to focus attention on a problem. This discomfort is relieved when instead we consider solutions.

In the formal study of decision making, the learning process itself prolongs each step, hence the discomfort of postponing solutions is aggravated. As a result, some analysts of the decision process begin with a consideration of alternative management solutions or courses of action. Case studies, for example, often end with the question "What would you do?" directing the reader first to a solution and only afterward to its justification. Quantitative approaches, such as decision theory, tend to emphasize the manipulation of the variables related to solutions rather than inquiry into the problem itself. These are gratifying exercises, but often miss the mark.

Any consideration of alternative solutions before the problem is well defined may sabotage the effectiveness of the entire decision process. Actual management experience indicates that inadequate definition of a problem is a far more common cause of failure in the decision process than an inadequate weighing of alternative solutions. This is true because the original formulation of a problem structures the kinds of solutions that appear for consideration in the first place. No proposed solution can be better than the formulation of the problem it is designed to solve. If a problem has been inadequately defined, the "solution" cannot be adequate. Hence a key management skill is skill in defining problems, which includes concommitant development of the emotional capacity to tolerate the impatience and discomfort involved in focusing on the problem long enough to define it adequately, before indulging in the relief of considering solutions.

There are certain definite guidelines or criteria against which problem formulation should be assessed before an attempt is made to consider solutions. The following criteria, essential to sound problem formulation, are those which experience has shown to be most often neglected in the management decision process:

1. The problem should be stated explicitly.
2. The problem statement should include a working diagnosis.
3. The problem statement should specify the standard violated.
4. The problem should be stated in specific behavioral terms.
5. The problem statement should not be expressed merely as an implied solution.
6. The problem statement should specify whose problem it is.
7. The problem statement should differentiate the short run and the long run in a problem situation.
8. The problem should not be stated as a dilemma.

CRITERION 1: STATING THE PROBLEM EXPLICITLY

Unbelievable as it may seem, the application of decision making to human problems rarely includes an explicit statement of the problem to be solved. There is a tendency to assume that, because a disequilibrium has been felt and/or a problem situation has been diagnosed and understood, the specific problem is too obvious to require explicit statement. Nevertheless, all our thinking may not alter our preliminary view of a problem unless the various relationships have been spelled out. Vague, general complaints about communication problems or low morale, for example, are less easily solved than explicit statements of the particular actions that resulted in those conditions. The more explicitly the problem can be stated, the more explicit can be the consideration of solutions.

Training in the decision process should include training in the writing of explicit problem statements. An excellent decision-making habit, which is especially valuable in the face of complex human problems, is to thrash out a problem statement on paper before attempting to tackle the problem. This process forces the manager to clarify and sharpen the formulation of the problem in a way that "thinking through" alone does not. The manager is then less apt to base actions on shifting impressions about a vaguely defined "problem cloud." In a very real sense, a well-defined problem is already half solved.

CRITERION 2: INCLUDING A WORKING DIAGNOSIS IN THE PROBLEM STATEMENT

The formulation of a problem statement should include, as an integral part, the manager's final working diagnosis, which is an important key for considering alternative courses of action. As has been indicated, a working diagnosis is always subject to change on the basis of further information, but it nevertheless should be explicitly stated. An explicit working diagnosis helps the manager focus on causes rather than mere symptoms in choosing and defining the precise problem to be solved.

A problem statement should *not* be a mere description of a symptom or symptoms. In the Nestlé U.K. (A) case, it would not have been helpful to have said that the problem was that the keypunch operators did not meet the company's deadlines. This reaction on their part is really a symptom that something more fundamental is wrong in the relationship between management and the work force. As we have said, symptoms may constitute problems in themselves, but a problem statement that is confined to symptoms, and contains no diagnosis of causes, is inadequate. Most often the critical problem—the problem to be solved—will be related to underlying causes.

CRITERION 3: SPECIFYING THE STANDARD VIOLATED

Effective problem definition should specify the standard according to which a situation is considered to be a problem. The object of the diagnostic stage of the decision process is to understand what is happening in a particular situation. But understanding a situation is not the same as determining whether a problem exists that needs solution. Two factors must be present before we can identify a situation as a problem: (1) the situation must be relevant to an accepted standard or set of standards, and (2) the situation must involve behavior that violates such standards.

One of the most common failings in decision making is to omit conscious consideration of the standards by which one situation is judged as a problem and another as not a problem. This omission can be wasteful. Ambivalence or vagueness about standards on the part of the manager means ambivalence and vagueness about methods and goals in the later stages of decision making.

Further, the degree of importance assigned to various standards is often taken for granted rather than made explicit. However, when we consciously make explicit the standards by which we define problems, we sometimes become aware that a particular standard is more important or less important in the total picture than we had unconsciously assumed. Thus, a part of solving the problem may be actually altering the priority we give certain standards.

As the manager attempts to specify which standards are relevant to a given situation, what possible standards are considered? What are the sources of the standards to be applied? Standards have their roots in different "levels" of the decision maker's frame of reference, ranging from rather specific individual habits or personality traits to high-level abstractions concerning human rights. These levels are not mutually exclusive; several may be functioning as standards at the same time. A given situation may well violate different levels and therefore give rise to the identification of more than one problem to be solved. The following hierarchy of standards is offered as an aid to the manager in specifying which standards may be relevant to the assessment of a particular situation.

The Hierarchy of Standards Governing Problem Identification

Personality factors. Our habits, tastes, preferences, style or way of life, and self-image together constitute a standard that we apply to the world around us. Conflicting personal standards present conflicts in problem definition.[1]

Group norms. Our identification with the norms of a reference group—be it informal friendship group, formal club group, or assigned work group—and our perceptions of violations of these norms together constitute a second level of standards we apply to our environment. Conflicting norms among the reference groups of an individual may lead to inner conflicts about problem definition.[2]

Individual values. Although some individual values change when an individual changes reference groups, others reflect deeper, longer lasting convictions that can withstand and supersede group norms. Many major individual values are set in childhood and resist rapid change. Such values originate in a reference group (the family, for example) and thus can determine which groups become new reference groups for the individual. Group norms which differ from deep-seated values may produce psychological conflict and hence difficulty in identifying problems. Conflicts also arise when values considered desirable differ from what is immediately desired in a particular situation.[3]

Rationalized organizational goals. Our role in an organization is associated with standards and goals that we perceive as applicable to situations that arise in that organization. In a business, for example, our views on such factors as profitability, reduced costs, general economic conditions, corporate goals, physical property, success, corporate im-

[1] For a discussion of personality factors that can influence decision making, see Leavitt (1964), especially Chs. 1–7.

[2] For a discussion of the effects of group norms on individual decision making, see Sherif and Sherif (1956).

[3] For a discussion of individual values and decision making, see Ofstad (1961), especially Ch. 7.

age, the marketplace, responsibility to stockholders, and the assumptions of the economic model are standards against which we measure behavior.[4]

Rationalized national goals. Judgments about the nation's position in the world are also standards of behavior. Views on world leadership, peace and war, poverty and wealth, and the proper international role of the nation are standards often applied in organizational situations.[5]

Concepts of ultimate human values. Justice, equality, opportunity, freedom, the pursuit of happiness, and the nature and purpose of human beings are some of the broader concepts we incorporate in our standards of behavior. Abstract though they may be, they can be decisive standards when they are applied to specific situations.[6]

Conflicting Standards

It is easy to see that a particular event might cause some individuals to refer to one level of the hierarchy, and others to a different level. For example, a person who identifies work problems solely in terms of rationalizing organizational goals might perceive an increased number of grievances solely in terms of workers' unwillingness to do the jobs assigned them in the manner determined by management. Another person might perceive the situation in broad terms of human rights and its effects on the personalities of the workers. *The decision maker must recognize that situations do not present themselves as prelabeled and predefined problems. A problem is in part defined by the standards each observer applies.*

Two types of problems can arise for a decision maker as a result of a conflict of standards. On the one hand, a person may be in a position where various standards conflict with each other. The sales manager of a medium-sized manufacturing company, for example, was charged with *de facto* racial discrimination because of the small number of employees from racial minorities in his division. His difficulty in resolving the situation was complicated by two factors: he had feelings of discomfort when people of any racial minority applied for jobs, owing to a lack of experience in dealing with them; and furthermore, his peer group (other managers on the same level in the community) tended to resist the pressures of civil rights organizations for a proportionate share of the jobs for minorities. However, this manager did not see himself as a racist or as a person who discriminated against others, and he believed

[4] For a discussion of the rationalized goals of economics and decision making, see Elbing and Elbing (1967), especially Sec. 1.

[5] For a discussion of the relationship between national goals and organizational decision making, see McClelland (1962).

[6] For a discussion of ultimate values and decision making, see John Galbraith (1958 and 1964).

that everyone should help eliminate discrimination. Moreover, on the highest level of abstraction, he believed that every individual has the right to equal job opportunities. Because this manager was able to verbalize his value conflicts, he was able to distinguish among them, place them in a hierarchy of personal importance, and make specific decisions as to which values took precedence in various situations.

Verbalizing and choosing among our own values may not seem to be a crucial managerial skill. However, unless we can verbalize internal value conflicts, we cannot separate their personal and their external aspects. Many problems therefore will remain enigmas to us, needlessly and perhaps unsolvably structured as dilemmas. Approaching problems as dilemmas because of unspecified internal conflicts always erodes a manager's skill in solving them.

The second type of conflict-of-standards problem which can arise is a conflict between the decision maker's own standards and those of others in the organization with whom he or she has direct contact. Let us suppose that the sales manager resolved his internal conflict about hiring blacks in terms of the national interest and the equal rights of all people, but that his immediate superior resisted the idea. The sales manager (or any other subordinate) is then faced with the necessity of either "going along" with or resisting the boss and endangering his own organizational position and economic security. The gravest temptation in such a value conflict is to take a "short cut," that is, to avoid confronting and articulating the problem and making a decision, and instead, merely to act in each situation upon the line of least resistance. This habit, however, is extremely corrosive of the managerial role and mitigates the development of a high level of managerial skill. The essence of improving managerial skill lies in perceiving disequilibria, diagnosing and defining problems (including value conflicts), specifying alternatives, and making decisions—rather than allowing events to develop by default.

Three managers, two in business and one in government, whose superiors held discriminatory policies, made three different decisions. One, after trying but failing to change his superior's policy and after consultation with his family, found another job. The second manager kept his job and became active in community programs outside the firm, hoping that a change in community norms would gradually alter his superior's policies. The third, who was a member of a racial minority and who had been completely independent since the age of fourteen, said in effect: "Let those people who feel discriminated against make it on their own the way I did." Although each solution is too complex for easy labeling as right or wrong, a notable factor in all three cases was that each manager actually made a value decision, rather than merely ignoring the issue.

It can be shown that, over time, as individuals live in a similar environment and become able to satisfy their needs, they tend to develop and to apply similar norms, values, and standards. Executives in the same office, mechanics in the same shop, or teachers in the same school tend to define a particular problem in the same way as a result of their close relationships over time. Under such circumstances a problem may appear to be absolute and clear-cut. In reality, it may not be that the problem is clear-cut but that the application of standards is consistent and unquestioned. Outsiders viewing the situation might define the problem quite differently.

The more explicit we can be about the hierarchy of standards being applied to a situation, the more explicit can be our definition of the problem, and therefore, the more appropriate our solutions. If conflicts over standards exist but go unrecognized, solutions may be blocked. In many hospitals, for example, where the problems associated with the shortages of nurses are frequently defined in organizational terms—work assignments, shifts, and supervisory relationships—the standards implicitly applied by the nurses often relate to the maintenance of their professional status. The result is that the hospitals' solutions often overlook the nurses' professional status and are therefore resisted by the nurses.

CRITERION 4: STATING THE PROBLEM IN SPECIFIC BEHAVIORAL TERMS

It is important that the problem statement be couched in specific behavioral terms rather than vague, general terms. A common pitfall of problem identification, especially for students who are first learning about the behavioral sciences, is verbalizing a problem in broad generalizations about human behavior rather than in operational terms relevant to a specific situation. A problem merely labeled as a personality conflict, a lack of communication, a defense mechanism, a projection, a feeling of guilt, or in other general or categorical terms has not been identified adequately for solution. Although these statements can offer considerable insight into human behavior, as stated in general form they give few specific clues to the events or attitudes that have caused the problem, clues which the decision maker needs as guides to choice and action.

Another danger in using general labels as problem statements is that they suggest a fixed condition. For example, to say that a problem is a result of a personality conflict suggests that two personalities are in more or less constant conflict. Although it is conceivable that two individuals can be so generally antagonistic to one another that they are almost always in conflict, it is more often the case that two individuals tolerate one another generally but come into conflict under specific circumstances. It is much more fruitful for the decision maker to identify and understand these circumstances than to simply label the problem a conflict of personalities. The more specific and operational the problem statement, the more easily a solution can be devised that deals directly with the cause of the problem.

It is possible, of course, that a manager will encounter employees who have serious emotional problems and whose behavior might properly be defined as psychologically abnormal. These problems, however, are usually beyond the competence of the typical manager and should be fully diagnosed and dealt with by a psychiatrist or clinical psychologist who has the appropriate skills. Our discussion is limited to the typical cases that confront the organizational administrator: job-related emotional problems that arise among individuals who normally function satisfactorily within the organization. In these cases, the manager will find it much more useful to state the problem in specific behavioral terms, rather than giving the problem some psychological label. It is less useful, for example, to point out that two people have a *personality* conflict than to note the specific behavior that led to the application of that label.

Not only should the problem be stated in specific behavioral terms, the standard by which something is judged to be a problem should also be so stated. Otherwise, the standard is too vague to facilitate a clear definition of the problem. Furthermore, a standard for behavior constitutes part of the goal of the decision process, which means that it, too, must be stated in specific behavioral terms or it will not provide a clear guideline for choice and action. Thus the manager should attempt to answer explicitly three closely related questions: What specific behavioral standards are being violated? What specific behavioral change is wanted? What behavior would constitute a solution to the problem?

CRITERION 5: AVOIDING STATEMENT OF THE PROBLEM AS MERELY AN IMPLIED SOLUTION

Because there is such a strong tendency to think in terms of solutions, problems are often framed in terms of solutions available or popular. A problem laid out in solution terms tends to block adequate analysis and adequate consideration of alternative choices. For example, when asked for a problem statement for the case of the employee who submitted an excessive number of grievances, a student offered: "The problem is how to arrange time for more social contact." Because this statement is a disguised solution, it tends to preclude consideration of such alternative solutions as rotating, tranferring, promoting, or even discharging the employee. The built-in restriction of an implied solution allows a manager little flexibility. Although the tendency to be solution-oriented is a critical problem for businessmen, it is in no sense unique to them (a cartoon that appeared during an international crisis showed former President Charles de Gaulle of France sitting behind his desk and saying: "Find me some problems to fit my solutions").

Once committed to a particular course of action—whether it be the centralization of purchasing, the introduction of a new computer, the need to reduce the number of employees, the application of decision theory, or whatever—the decision maker may tend to define future problems in terms of preconceived and available solutions. Allowing solutions to shape problems can be costly. For example, during the early days of introducing electronic data processing to government, a large eastern state wished to fully utilize its new equipment and decided that the cost of preparing its payroll could be reduced by automating the process. However, because EDP was not appropriate to the particular payroll problems of that organization, automating the process more than tripled the cost. The problem had been defined in terms of the new "solution," and it was months before the problem was redefined.

A subtle variation of solution orientation arises from the tendency (also discussed earlier) to learn experiences themselves rather than to learn *from* them. For example, an executive who progresses up the organizational hierarchy learns ways of solving problems that are related to experiences in a particular organizational role. As the executive moves into organizational levels where new types of problems occur, he or she may define them in terms of solutions learned in the past. Focusing on formerly useful solutions, the executive may err in defining new problems.

Another difficulty in stating problems in terms of solutions is that it may lead to ignoring problems that have no obvious solutions. For example, problems arising from summer heat in the workplace, poor commuter train schedules, or the disruptive personality of a firm's owner-manager might be written off as unsolvable. Since these kinds of problems have no obvious solutions, they may never be explicitly identified as problems. They may then be ignored, even though they might be very real contributing factors which ought to be taken into account in the decision process.

Specifying a problem apart from a consideration of solutions can help us maintain awareness of the role of problem factors in the total picture, and help us more realistically and comprehensively evaluate situations in which they are involved. Furthermore, many an "unsolvable" problem, when clearly identified as a problem, has turned out to be solvable after all.

CRITERION 6: SPECIFYING WHOSE PROBLEM IT IS

It is extremely helpful in sorting out a particular problem situation to define *whose* problem it is—in several senses. First, the manager should answer the question, "*Who* is experiencing disequilibrium or discomfort?" Part of a problem's solution may be simply the reduction of personal discomfort.

There is no such thing as "a problem," by itself. Such an assumption implies that a particular situation will be perceived by everyone in the same terms, or indeed even as a problem at all. Obviously, everyone will apply his own hierarchy of standards to identifying problems. (This is one reason why it is so difficult for groups to define problems quickly.) It is vital that a problem statement specify how each of the key persons involved views "the problem." An individual who is aware of the history of a certain set of events may, for example, define a situation differently from one who does not have this historical awareness. The manager, concerned that a subordinate does not respond to a situation the same way as the manager, might well consider whether the incident *could* be perceived as a problem at all by the subordinate. Each view will be different.

It is important at this point to distinguish among (1) an organizational problem, (2) the discomfort of a manager, and (3) the discomfort of others involved in the situation. The discomfort of either the manager or other participants may be solved without necessarily solving the organizational problem. Conversely, an organizational problem may be solved without resolving the human discomfort involved. By distinguishing *who* has what problem, we can differentiate between organizational problems and personal problems, and have a better basis for considering solutions.

Another important distinction to make concerns who has the responsibility for solving the problem. Wherever possible, the person who has responsibility in the organizational structure for dealing with a particular type of problem should be the one to solve it. If a problem is clearly the responsibility of a particular individual, it is vital not to let it be solved by a less appropriate person, or by inaction.

Internal situations are not the only sources of problems for an organization. Rapid changes in technology, racial conflict, hard-core unemployment, activist political behavior, student unrest, labor demands, and community demands for "law and order" produce an environment, at least partly external to the organization, which may result in problems for which no one in the organization is assigned responsibility, and which past generations of managers did not even think of as organizational problems. Failure to clearly identify responsibility within the organization for the identification of new problem areas impinging on the organization from the outside may result in the organization's failure to perceive a problem before it is too late for choice or action. A striking example occurred during the 1968–69 academic year, when many American universities found themselves facing problems with which they were totally unprepared to deal. The standards which governed problem definition by students (and other groups in society) changed quickly, without a coincident change of standards within university administrations, and without adequate recognition by the administrations of the new forces building up to challenge them. In most cases no one had been thinking in terms of "new" problem areas external to the established framework of organizational operation, because those problems were seen to be outside each one's sphere of responsibility.

This kind of crisis points up the necessity for making explicit in any problem statement just whose responsibility it is to come to grips with the problem, particularly in cases where the problem in question falls outside the established organizational chart.

CRITERION 7: DIFFERENTIATING LONG-RUN AND SHORT-RUN PROBLEMS REQUIRING SOLUTION

A situation that has fallen into disequilibrium may be a problem in both the short run and the long run. For example, when a worker quits in anger, the problem may have been caused by an immediate crisis in the work situation. At the same time, it may be symptomatic of a basic or long-run problem situation in the work group or in the entire organization. In such a case, a short-run solution for the immediate problem alone would not be an adequate solution. Long-run plans need to be made for building, over time, the kind of social system in the organization that handles problems before they become crises. When faced with a problem in the short run, it is always necessary to consider the relationship of that problem and its solution to the long-run picture.

The opposite is also true, of course. When confronted with what might be considered long-run problems, it is important not to overlook the immediate short-run crisis. In the Norrköping-Beta case, for example, it is clear that the company at the time of the merger was concerned with the longer run, overall relationships with employees but was not aware or concerned with the immediate crises that were developing for certain managers. These crises developed into difficult and costly problems for the company.

CRITERION 8: AVOIDING STATEMENT OF THE PROBLEM AS A DILEMMA

Some managers in effect circumvent the entire decision process by never seeing or stating problems, but only dilemmas. Every problem is somehow structured as an unsolvable predicament. Usually underlying such habitual structuring of dilemmas is a desire for some satisfaction other than solving the problem—possibly a desire for ego building, sympathy, or attention; or a desire to vent anger or gain vengeance; or a desire to avoid the effort, responsibility, or risk involved in problem solving. If the decision maker's primary desire is for something other than the solution of the problem, the decision-making effort is bound to be sabotaged.

In one large manufacturing firm, for example, the managers of two departments, although ostensibly engaged in mutual decision making on a corporate problem, were in reality engaged in competitive infighting to reduce the other's sphere of influence. Both came up with problem statements structured as dilemmas. Each of them avoided defining the problem in solvable terms, lest the solution of the problem bring some success for the other manager.

On occasions when our own ego is deeply at stake, all of us may resort to structuring problems as dilemmas. However, for the manager who wishes effectively to manage his or her own feelings, explicit definition of the problem to be solved and the goal for change, both stated in behavioral terms, can help bring awareness of the real problem, separate from personal motivations. If personal motivations are allowed to continue to structure problem statements and goals, however, problems may remain mere dilemmas, subverting a constructive decision process.

SUMMARY OF CRITERIA

Definition of the problem is presented as a separate step in the decision-making process because it is a crucial act by which all following acts of the decision process are determined. There is a temptation to bypass an explicit problem statement, but this step requires explicit formulation through systematic critical method if subsequent steps of the decision process are to be sound. Indeed, the formulation of the problem structures the kinds of solutions subsequently considered. Therefore, the problem definition should meet eight important criteria:

1. The problem should be stated explicitly.
2. The problem statement should include a working diagnosis.
3. The problem statement should specify the standard violated.
4. The problem should be stated in specific behavioral terms.
5. The problem statement should not be expressed merely as an implied solution.
6. The problem statement should specify whom the problem affects (that is, who is suffering discomfort and who is responsible for a solution).
7. The problem statement should differentiate the short run and the long run in a problem situation.
8. The problem should be stated as a problem, not as a dilemma.

REFERENCES

Elbing, Alvar O., Jr., and Carol J. Elbing. *The Value Issue of Business.* McGraw-Hill, 1967.

Galbraith, John K. "Economics and the Quality of Life." *Science*, July 1964.

——. *The Affluent Society.* Houghton Mifflin, 1958.

Leavitt, Harold. *Managerial Psychology*, rev. ed. University of Chicago Press, 1964.

McClelland, David C. "Business Decisions and National Achievement." *Harvard Business Review*, July–August 1962.

Ofstad, Harold. *An Inquiry into the Freedom of Decision.* Norwegian Universities Press, 1961.

Sherif, Muzafer, and Carolyn Sherif. *An Outline of Social Psychology*, rev. ed. Harper & Row, 1956.

Case of the Changing Cage

I

The voucher–check filing unit was a work unit in the home office of the Atlantic Insurance Company. The assigned task of the unit was to file checks and vouchers written by the company as they were cashed and returned. This filing was the necessary foundation for the main function of the unit: locating any particular check for examination upon demand. There were usually eight to ten requests for specific checks from as many different departments during the day. One of the most frequent reasons checks were requested from the unit was to determine whether checks in payment of claims against the company had been cashed. Thus efficiency in the unit directly affected customer satisfaction with the company. Complaints or inquiries about payments could not be answered with the accuracy and speed conducive to client satisfaction unless the unit could supply the necessary document immediately.

Toward the end of 1952, nine workers manned this unit. There was an assistant (a position equivalent to a foreman in a factory) named Miss Dunn, five other fulltime employees, and three parttime workers.

The work area of the unit was well defined. Walls bounded the unit on three sides. The one exterior wall was pierced by light-admitting north windows. The west interior partition was blank. A door opening into a corridor pierced the south interior partition. The east side of the work area was enclosed by a steel mesh reaching from wall to wall and floor to ceiling. This open metal barrier gave rise to the customary name of the unit—"the voucher cage." A sliding door through this mesh gave access from the unit's territory to the work area of the rest of the company's agency audit division, of which it was a part, located on the same floor.

The unit's territory was kept inviolate by locks on both doors, fastened at all times. No one not working within the cage was permitted inside unless his name appeared on a special list in the custody of Miss Dunn. The door through the steel mesh was used generally for departmental business. Messengers and runners from other departments usually came to the corridor door and pressed a buzzer for service.

The steel mesh front was reinforced by a bank of metal filing cases where checks were filed. Lined up just inside the barrier, they hid the unit's workers from the view of workers outside their territory, including the section head responsible for overall supervision of this unit according to the company's formal plan of operation.

II

On top of the cabinets which were backed against the steel mesh, one of the male employees in the unit neatly stacked pasteboard boxes in which checks were transported to the cage. They were later reused to hold older checks sent into storage. His intention was less getting these boxes out of the way than increasing the effective height of the sight barrier so the section head could not see into the cage "even when he stood up."

"Topography and Culture: The Case of the Changing Cage" by Cara E. Richards and Henry F. Dobyns. Reproduced by permission of the Society for Applied Anthropology from *Human Organization*, Vol. 16, No. 1, 1957.

The girls stood at the door of the cage which led into the corridor and talked to the messenger boys. Out this door also the workers slipped unnoticed to bring in their customary afternoon snack. Inside the cage, the workers sometimes engaged in a good-natured game of rubber-band "sniping."

Workers in the cage possessed good capacity to work together consistently and workers outside the cage often expressed envy of those in it because of the "nice people" and friendly atmosphere there. The unit had no apparent difficulty keeping up with its work load.

III

For some time prior to 1952 the controller's department of the company had not been able to meet its own standards of efficient service to clients. Company officials felt the primary cause to be spatial. Various divisions of the controller's department were scattered over the entire 22-story company building. Communication between them required phone calls, messengers, or personal visits, all costing time. The spatial separation had not seemed very important when the company's business volume was smaller prior to World War II. But business had grown tremendously since then and spatial separation appeared increasingly inefficient.

Finally, in November of 1952, company officials began to consolidate the controller's department by relocating two divisions together on one floor. One was the agency audit division, which included the voucher–check filing unit. As soon as the decision to move was made, lower–level supervisors were called in to help with planning. Line workers were not consulted, but were kept informed by assistants of the planning progress. Company officials were concerned about the problem of transporting many tons of equipment and some 200 workers from two locations to another single location without disrupting work flow. So the move was planned to occur over a single weekend, by means of the most efficient resources available. Assistants were kept busy planning positions for files and desks in the new location.

Desks, files, chairs and even wastebaskets were numbered prior to the move, and relocated according to a master chart checked on the spot by the assistant. Employees were briefed as to where the new location was, and which elevators they should take to reach it. The company successfully transported the paraphernalia of the voucher–check filing unit from one floor to another over one weekend. Workers in the cage quit Friday afternoon at the old stand, and reported back Monday at the new.

The exterior boundaries of the new cage were still three building walls and the steel mesh, but the new cage possessed only one door—the sliding door through the steel mesh into the work area of the rest of the agency–audit division. The territory of the cage had also been reduced in size. An entire bank of filing cabinets had to be left behind in the old location, to be taken over by the unit moving there. The new cage was arranged so that there was no longer a row of metal filing cabinets lined up inside the steel mesh and obstructing the view into the cage.

IV

When the workers in the cage inquired about the removal of the filing cabinets from along the steel-mesh fencing, they found that Mr. Burke had insisted that these cabinets be rearranged so his view into the cage would not be obstructed by them. Miss Dunn had tried to retain the cabinets in their prior position, but her efforts had been overridden.

Mr. Burke disapproved of conversation. Since he could see workers conversing in the new cage, he "requested" Miss Dunn to put a stop to all unnecessary talk. Attempts by female clerks to talk to messenger boys brought the wrath of her superior down on Miss Dunn, who was then forced to reprimand the girls.

Mr. Burke also disapproved of an untidy working area, and any boxes or papers which were in sight were a source of annoyance to him. He did not exert supervision directly, but would "request" Miss Dunn to "do something about those boxes." In the new cage, desks had to be completely cleared at the end of the day, in contrast to the work-in-progress piles left out in the old cage. Boxes could not accumulate on top of filing cases.

The custom of afternoon snacking also ran into trouble. Lacking a corridor door, the food bringers had to venture forth and pack their snack tray back through the work area of the rest of their section, bringing this hitherto unique custom to the attention of workers outside the cage. The latter promptly recognized the desirability of afternoon snacks and began agitation for the same privilege. This annoyed the section head, who forbade workers in the cage from continuing this custom.

V

Mr. Burke later made a rule which permitted one worker to leave the cage at a set time every afternoon to bring up food for the rest. This rigidity irked the cage personnel, accustomed to a snack when the mood struck, or none at all. Having made his concession to the cage force, Mr. Burke was unable to prevent workers outside the cage from doing the same thing. What had once been unique to the workers in the cage was now common practice in the section.

Although Miss Dunn never outwardly expressed anything but compliance to and approval of superiors' directives, she exhibited definite signs of anxiety. All cage workers reacted against Burke's increased domination. When he imposed his decisions upon the voucher–check filing unit, he became "Old Grandma" to its personnel. The cage workers sneered at him and ridiculed him behind his back. Workers who formerly had obeyed company policy as a matter of course began to find reasons for loafing and obstructing work in the new cage. One of the changes that took place in the behavior of the workers had to do with their game of rubber-band sniping. All knew Mr. Burke would disapprove of this game. It became highly clandestine and fraught with dangers. Yet shooting rubber bands *increased.*

Newly arrived checks were put out of sight as soon as possible, filed or not. Workers hid unfiled checks, generally stuffing them into desk drawers or unused file drawers. Since boxes were forbidden, there were fewer unused file drawers than there had been in the old cage. So the day's work was sometimes undone when several clerks hastily shoved vouchers and checks indiscriminately into the same file drawer at the end of the day.

Before a worker in the cage filed incoming checks, she measured with her ruler the thickness in inches of each bundle she filed. At the end of each day she totaled her input and reported it to Miss Dunn. All incoming checks were measured upon arrival. Thus Miss Dunn had a rough estimate of unit intake compared with file input. Theoretically, she was able to tell at any time how much unfiled material she had on hand and how well the unit was keeping up with its task. Despite this running check, when the annual inventory of unfiled checks on hand in the cage was taken at the beginning of the calendar year 1953, a seriously large backlog of unfiled checks was found. To the surprise and dismay of Miss Dunn, the inventory showed the unit to be far behind schedule, filing much more slowly than before the relocation of the cage.

Electrical Manufacturing Company Case

Electrical Manufacturing Company is a large international company that manufactures many types of electrical machinery, appliances, and military hardware. The company was organized late in the 19th century to capitalize on anticipated rapid development in the electrical industry. There was, indeed, rapid development, especially during the period 1915 to 1930 and after World War II. During the years 1945 to 1950, the company had a period of accelerated growth. By that time the various divisions of the company overlapped and were only loosely coordinated. The company was organized primarily along geographical lines.

In 1950, under new management, the company was completely restructured into a large number of autonomous departments, collected into divisions appropriate to the market or industry served. Each department was responsible for its own business welfare, supposedly having direct control over all the inputs of financial and human resources needed for success. Each general manager, in theory at least, was made completely responsible for the welfare and success of his department. If the department did not meet the goals set by the corporate headquarters, the general manager was usually replaced.

While this decentralization had many useful aspects, it led to a short-range view of departmental success. Few general managers survived to savor long-range successes if immediate profit goals were not realized. This emphasis on short-run profits led to the use of high-cost "emergency" expedients in certain areas of manufacturing, to reduced emphasis on quality control, to only marginal investment in new facilities, and occasionally to doubtful personnel policies.

At the same time, the sharp profit-and-loss perspective provided for many significant improvements in operating efficiency, including improved channels for communication and better cost control.

One large factory in the Midwest was totally engaged in the design and manufacture of heavy naval machinery. In 1965 this plant employed about 6,000 people, including a large number of technicians and engineers who worked in engineering, manufacturing, and sales. Many of these individuals had spent their entire careers, ranging up to 50 years, with the company.

One of the engineers, Mr. Frank Johnson, had very great influence on the character of the organization and its product between 1945 and 1950. He was an enthusiastic and persuasive leader, filled with imaginative ideas and the ability to sell them to management and to the consumer. He was also an innovator and possessed many patents. His technical decisions tended to be impulsive, and were frequently inaccurate, but he was equally quick to reverse his direction when this proved to be true. His decisiveness was a major asset. His vast experience more than offset his shortcomings and enabled him to make major contributions and receive significant recognition for them.

Jack Stover "grew up" under Johnson, and reported to him in various capacities for 25 years. Jack's personal characteristics complemented those of his boss; he was steady, conscientious, and reliable, and he served as legman, "interpreter," fact collector, and stabilizer. In this environment, Jack grew

"Electrical Manufacturing Company Case" was written under the supervision of Alvar O. Elbing. Names of people and places have been disguised.

steadily in his level of contribution and influence. By 1960 he had acquired managerial responsibilities for a large number of other people and was widely recognized for his contributions to the business.

Jack was a small man physically, but this was generally unnoticed. He lived on a conservative scale, well within his income and status. He seemed relatively happy and cheerful and was regarded as a good superior by those who reported to him.

In 1955 the old section manager retired and a new one, from another organization, replaced him. The new manager, Mr. Ray Latimer, was Frank Johnson's direct superior and was an entirely different type of engineer. Technically brilliant, he possessed a cold, analytical mind which responded only to "the facts." His phenomenal ability to digest, qualify, and analyze data continually amazed his colleagues, but his cold, calculating mind seemed to be impervious to emotion.

His instinctive behavior was to turn the entire organization into data gatherers, who collected facts for him to analyze, and to make the important decisions himself. Latimer's tendency to question subordinates in great detail generally affected morale, resulting in a loss of self-confidence for many of them.

Mr. Johnson found this atmosphere stifling. He frequently rebelled, with characteristic impatience. His impetuous though often sound decisions were difficult to justify to Latimer, and the relationship developed an ever-increasing strain. Finally, Johnson retired, becoming a consultant at age 58 and taking a pension at 60.

Latimer promptly replaced Johnson with an individual more like himself—cool, unemotional, and logical. This new manager assumed direct control over the activities of Jack Stover.

Stover began to age visibly after the departure of Johnson. It became apparent that his natural pessimism, as well as his ego, had been helped or bolstered by his association with the ebullient Johnson. He developed new outlooks, often predicting grim happenings at the hands of the Russians, the competitors, the unions, and the minorities. He continually prophesied a 1932-type depression, which he thought was sure to occur within three months.

His technical contributions became fewer as he tried to satisfy his new bosses, who demanded that he know more and more details about an ever increasing variety of problems. His natural tendency to depend on and develop his subordinates was continually questioned, and it became apparent that he could never please those who were over him.

When walking with him, his taller associates would often see him stride out and urge them to walk faster. He developed a taste for expensive things. He bought a new car every year and a second home on the lake. He joined numerous exclusive organizations. He often exaggerated or misquoted others in defense of his points. He began taking personal credit for the ideas of associates and subordinates. Throughout these years, however, he seemed to retain a warm personality. He was usually available for discussion, although he was frequently defensive and pessimistic.

Five years after Johnson retired, a general reorganization occurred and Stover lost his managerial position. He became a "consultant" with loosely defined responsibilities "befitting his broad experience." His trend toward pessimistic outlooks accelerated after this harsh experience. His contemporaries and former subordinates agreed that Stover had been reduced to a fraction of his old effectiveness.

Merdon State College Athletic Authority Case

In January, 1951, the Board of Athletic Authority of Merdon State College met for the first time to consider the desirability of increased emphasis on intercollegiate sports and on upgrading athletic competition.

Merdon State College was located in a large midwestern city and, under the leadership of its president, Philip Kirkman, had developed from a state teachers' college with an enrollment of 1000 students in 1945 to a state-supported liberal arts college of 3500 students in 1951. Kirkman had been one of the first midwestern advocates of general education, and the college had gained considerable academic status since he assumed the presidency. After the war, he had greatly increased the quality of teaching by bringing capable young men to Merdon State College, offering them higher faculty rank than they might have received elsewhere. Kirkman was very well thought of in academic circles and was the chairman of the state association of college presidents.

In the fall of 1950, Kirkman appointed Tilden Langston as dean of students at a salary of $8500 a year. Dean Langston was well known and highly regarded by other student personnel administrators and had recently received attractive job offers from three universities. Langston accepted the position at Merdon State College in part because of the challenge he saw there and in part because of his regard for Kirkman. He had approached his new job cautiously and had, according to Kirkman, built up an excellent relationship with his coworkers, the faculty, and many student leaders.

On coming to Merdon State College, Langston bought a house near the campus for his wife and three children, a boy of 18 and two girls, 14 and 10. Langston was sending his son, who had been a star basketball player in high school, to a small eastern college which had only an intramural athletic program.

At Merdon State College, Langston was immediately involved in several problems. The system of student government was being reorganized. As dean of students, he was one of twelve voting members of the student senate, the new student governing body, and the only faculty member. A new student advisory system needed to be developed because the rapid and extensive growth of the student body had made the previous advising practices inadequate. He believed all of the other functions of the dean of student's office also required reorganizing to meet the changed conditions. He also discovered that, athletically, the school was in a period of transition.

Merdon State College fielded teams in virtually every sport, with competition at about a class D level. The school had, for fifteen years, been a member of the Middle States Conference, which was made up of seven small teachers' colleges in addition to Merdon State College. Football competition was limited to the conference membership and to other comparable small schools. The bas-

---

"Merdon State College Athletic Authority Case" 9-454-013, was prepared by Frederick V. Fortmiller under the direction of Richard L. Balch of the Harvard University Graduate School of Business Administration as a basis for classroom discussion rather than to illustrate either effective or ineffective handling of administrative situations.

ketball and track teams scheduled stronger regional opponents, but the fundamental emphasis was on conference competition. In other sports, opponents were chosen largely on a local basis. Athletics had long been under the sole jurisdiction of the physical education department, and there had been little or no consultation with the college administration, general faculty, or student body. All the coaches were regular members of the physical education staff, holding faculty rank and having regular teaching responsibilities.

Athletic facilities and funds for major items of athletic equipment were provided by the college in the physical education budget. The student body, through its student activities board, provided funds for all direct items of expense attributable to the intercollegiate athletics program (game officials, traveling expenses, game uniforms, etc.) and received all gate receipts. The student activities board managed ticket sales, provided ushers, leased space to vendors, printed and sold game programs, paid guarantees for visiting teams, and administered all other similar activities. Game receipts were insufficient to cover even these direct items, and the deficit was supported by an allocation from study-activity dues.

A few months before Kirkman appointed Langston as dean, he had brought Cal Salvio to Merdon State College to be the new head football coach and had given him the rank of full professor. The president had selected Salvio without consulting the physical education department; consequently, Salvio felt responsible only to Kirkman. Salvio was a vigorous, dynamic man of small stature, who had turned out state championship football teams for ten years at Merdon High School. Later, he was head football coach at a small eastern college, which scheduled strong nationally rated opponents. Unsuccessful in the postwar years in building a winning team for the eastern school, and under heavy alumni pressure, he was pleased to resign and to accept the position at Merdon State College in his old home town.

Kirkman remarked to Salvio after the first rally of the season: "Cal, I hope the team does fairly well this year. Merdon has got to grow up to meet its new responsibilities. These include athletics. A college of our size ought to be known and supported in our area, both academically and on the athletic field. I don't want to see us in the 'big time,' but I would like to see us grow up a little."

The 1950 football season, Salvio's first as head football coach, was the most successful in the school's history. The team won the Middle States Conference championship and went on to a regional post-season bowl game. By the end of the season, in November, 1950, intense interest among the students, supported by the first athletic gate receipts of any consequence, led Kirkman to seek a stronger student and college administration voice in the conduct of athletics. He felt a need for greater central control and for formally established operating policies. Also, he wanted the students to have a voice in these policies because of their importance to the athletic program. Therefore, he appointed a joint student-faculty committee to study the intercollegiate athletic program. This committee was made up of two student leaders, Salvio, Langston, and two faculty members (including Mr. Morton, chairman of the physical education department).

The two student members of the committee, Charles Romano and Ken O'Shea, were both veterans, and each had great influence in the student body. Romano was student body president; while O'Shea, as treasurer of the student senate, was chairman of the student activities board, which administered the funds for the conduct of all student activities. O'Shea headed the fraternity faction, and Romano was the first nonfraternity man ever elected to a major student office.

The committee members decided to establish a permanent administrative body, the

Board of Athletic Authority, and a charter was drawn up outlining its responsibilities. The charter specified that the board was to establish and approve all policies dealing with athletics and designated a director of intercollegiate athletics as the board's chief administrative officer.

The new board was to consist of six voting members: Dean Langston, representing President Kirkman; Mr. Hooper, the college business manager; Lang Gilman, the track coach, representing the physical education department; Ken O'Shea, the senate treasurer and chairman of the student activities board; Lee Downs, the president of the varsity letter society; and John Dickson, a student member at large, appointed by the student body president, Charles Romano, and approved by the student senate.

There were also to be ex-officio members: Cal Salvio, the football coach; Bill Ives, the student body graduate manager; Professor Pierce, the college representative to the Middle States Conference; and Frank Cutler, vice president of the student body.

A simple majority of the voting members was required to approve a motion.

Immediately after the charter of the Board of Athletic Authority was drawn up, Kirkman appointed Salvio to the newly created post of director of intercollegiate athletics. As such, Salvio was to administer all functions of the intercollegiate program. This responsibility had formerly been vested in Morton, chairman of the physical education department. Morton had been at Merdon State College for over twenty years and was a strong advocate of the kind of "low-pressure" athletics the school had been conducting in the past. Some of the faculty saw Salvio's appointment as tacit approval by Kirkman of a more vigorous intercollegiate program.

After the winning football season, there was strong feeling on the campus that more emphasis should be placed on athletics. Many of the students and a few members of the faculty were clamoring for a higher level of competition, in the hope that this would gain more recognition for the school. Located in the downtown area of a large midwestern city, Merdon State College was not very well known to the people of the community, and was frequently confused with the more renowned Merdon University, which, although only a third the size of Merdon State College, consistently fielded a football team which competed successfully against the strongest teams in the nation.

All but a handful of students at Merdon State College were commuters. Many had made a considerable financial sacrifice to attend. Tuition was nominal, but most of the students came from low-income families, and little scholarship aid was available. Over two thirds of the student body worked part time, averaging 16 hours per week. Some students worked 40 and even 60 hours per week in addition to going to classes.

The alumni had little influence in the affairs of the school. The total group was small, and most were teachers scattered over the country. However, as the successful football season progressed, a number of members of the larger postwar classes, which had seen Merdon State College change to a liberal arts school, became interested and vocal in its development.

The newly constituted Board of Athletic Authority met in January 1951. The first item considered was a suggestion by Dickson that Merdon State College withdraw from the Middle States Conference and make exploratory contacts with the Upper West Athletic Association. The UWAA did not represent "big-time" athletics, but was a league of schools, of comparable size and academic standards to Merdon State College, which fielded substantially stronger teams than were represented in the Middle States Conference.

Langston opposed this action from the beginning. At the first meeting of the board, he stated his view.

"This action is contrary to the aims of Merdon State, as I see them. This is an institution of learning with high standards. We should pride ourselves on this fact and not on the ability of our football team to beat XYZ University. Anyone can watch our team play on Saturdays and enjoy the game when the team plays as it did this fall.

"But is further emphasis on athletics the true end and purpose of Merdon State? Gentlemen, when President Kirkman led this school from a small teachers' college to an institution of liberal arts, the choice was made for us. Merdon is no longer primarily a place to train people to do a specific job like teaching. Neither should we become an institution primarily to train healthy males in athletic prowess and to provide a number of other young people to watch the athletics.

"You'll say this is old-fashioned, I know. But I am not saying we should cut out football or *any* sports; I *am* saying that an overemphasis on sports defeats the purposes of this college by inducing a false sense of values among the students which is incompatible with what we are trying to build here. [He grips the table, his knuckles white.]

"I feel very strongly about this. Merdon State today is a young institution. Most of us have been here but a few years. My own association has been even shorter. For Merdon's sake, we should move more slowly and avoid a hasty judgment. Let's not let one successful season go to our heads."

Heated debate followed, and the meeting was adjourned without a vote being taken, to allow the members to report back to their respective groups.

The day after this meeting, Langston went to see Kirkman. Toward the end of the conversation, in which Langston reiterated his views, Kirkman said:

"Tilden, I see your point, and it's a good one. But aren't you visualizing an extreme situation? Academically, our objectives are much more similar to the schools in the UWAA than to any one of the teachers' colleges in the Middle States Conference. This doesn't seem to me to be an overemphasis on athletics, but merely a readjustment to our new size and curriculum. Be realistic, Tilden, and don't let this take on an importance all out of proportion to its significance. Let's show our confidence in the board and let them decide without any pressure from us."

The faculty was sharply split over the question of athletic emphasis, and many were wary of expressing an opinion. Student sentiment was more obvious. Following the first board meeting, the student newspaper carried articles under two headlines:

DEAN LANGSTON SAYS "GO SLOW" ON ENTRANCE INTO UWAA

SALVIO SAYS "TEAM CAN DO IT": STUDENT SENATE PASSES ATHLETIC RESOLUTION

The following editorial appeared under the headlines:

"The Student Senate resolved today that O'Shea, Downs, and Dickson, members of the Board of Athletic Authority, should vote in favor of a stronger football schedule. Charles Romano, president of the senate, submitted the resolution, which stated that since the football team has shown itself capable, it is now feasible to enter the Upper West Athletic Association. Ken O'Shea stated that student-activity dues could be lowered if the football team had the type of competition which would attract spectators and increase gate receipts.

"The whole policy of an increased pace in athletics is consistent with the growth of Merdon State. We are proud of our college, and a successful football team would bring more spirit to the whole student body. The editors of this paper, who have been critical of much that the senate has done in the past, feel that this is one of the most constructive moves it has made. A true student government should be active in forming policy and not just approving college administration policy.

"Cal Salvio has brought confidence and a fighting spirit to the football team. The student senate has shown the way. We say: 'Hats off to the senate.'"

On February 20, 1951, the board voted 4 to 2 (Langston and Gilman against) to approve a tentative football schedule for 1951, submitted by Salvio, which included most of the members of the UWAA, and which was substantially stronger than previous schedules had ever been. By the same margin (and with the same men voting against the issue), the board empowered Salvio to apply for formal admission to the UWAA as soon as possible.

The next meeting of the Board of Athletic Authority was held on March 19, 1951. The minutes of the last meeting were read, and Professor Pierce reported on the completion of the 1951 football schedule.

The next speaker to be recognized was Cal Salvio, who said:

"Men, I have a problem, I think I went over this with you, Bill [nodding to Ives across the table]. Anyway, I was talking with President Kirkman the other day, and he thought something could be worked out. As you know, we have strong opponents next season. This board has gone on record in favor of the schedule and entering the UWAA, and I think it's great that you're all behind us. The problem I have is twofold, and I'll try to explain the situation to you.

"You may not know this, but last season the 'M' Club, a recently organized alumni booster group, pledged to give books and part-time work to one of the sophomores on the squad and to pay the tuition of another boy. Well, this raised a stink on the squad, not only because two of the boys were getting help and others weren't, but because the 'M' club didn't fulfill all its pledges to the boys. We all know that the big guns of the alumni aren't too big and aren't well organized. They are mostly recent graduates of the college and not too well-heeled as far as money goes. But they wanted to do something, and they tried. Well, that's one part of the problem. The 'M' Club wants to help the squad in some way. The club is bound to do something, even if it's not effective or supervised by the college.

"The second part of my problem is this: Most of the boys on the football squad have to work part-time to come to State, just like most of the other students who come here. They aren't privileged characters. Most of the boys have a tough time being on the football squad, working, and getting their studies done. I might add that the academic average of the squad was damn good. With the heavier schedule coming up, we have to have all the men in there pitching all the time. And we have to attract good men to carry out the policy which this board approved when it voted for a heaver schedule—as good as any of the teams we play attract. President Kirkman and I talked this over, and I talked with Bill Ives also. They agree with me when I say that we must have some form of subsidy for the boys on the squad who need it. Why penalize a man just because he wants to play football?

"As I said before, the problem is twofold. The men on the squad should have some sort of help and we should be able to attract the kind of fellow to Merdon who will enable us to compete successfully. If we don't, the 'M' club is going to try to do it, anyway. This will be worse than if the thing is well organized and run by the college. OK, that's my speech. What do you say?"

Considerable confusion and hubbub followed. Downs finally got the floor and said:

"I talked with some members of the squad after the last varsity letter club meeting, and I agree with Mr. Salvio. If we don't take a hand in this, we'll be in the soup. As Mr.

Salvio said, we have to have the men to compete, and we might as well not have a team at all if the men of the squad don't know where they stand with the college or the 'M' Club. Besides, I understand that all the UWAA teams give help of one kind or another to their players. We're going to have to do the same thing to keep up with them."

After the other two student members had expressed similar opinions, Langston got up to speak. He reiterated what he had said at the previous meeting, and ended by saying:

"Gentlemen, I was afraid this was going to happen. Are sports going to become a *part* of the educational process at Merdon State, or are we going to make football an end in itself? It has always been my belief that playing the game is more important than playing because one gets paid for it. I think subsidies are a very dangerous thing. In effect, we would be sponsoring a professional team and not just a group of boys who are interested in playing because they like the game. It seems to me that we should set up rules that would control the 'M' Club or any other group that wants to pay our boys. I don't like this any more than our new schedule."

It was finally decided that each member of the board would talk with the people he represented and sound out their opinions before voting on the issue.

After the meeting, Langston left immediately for Kirkman's office, where he told the president what had taken place and continued: "This has gotten way out of hand. I didn't know that the 'M' Club had given help to two of the boys on the squad. We can't allow this subsidization to continue!"

Kirkman put down his papers and interrupted Langston:

"Look, Tilden, I know how you feel. I don't like the subsidy idea, either. But as Salvio pointed out to me, all of the schools in the UWAA are doing it, and we've got to do something to get boys good enough to compete. I'm so convinced that we've got to upgrade our competition that I'm willing to go along—to a point. I think the board must clearly spell out, and put definite limits on, what it is going to do for the players. We can't allow a frenzied bidding and counterbidding to 'break' the student body. Nor can we allow the 'M' Club to handle this sub rosa. You know how I feel. Now, you do what you think best. I'll leave it in your hands."

For the next week, in various formal and informal gatherings, feelings ran high. The student newspaper printed interviews with the president of the "M" Club and members of the football squad. Having turned the issue over to Langston, Kirkman did not publicly express himself. The student senate did not consider the question; but some of its members, in newspaper interviews, appeared sympathetic to giving the boys on the football squad some kind of financial aid. They also indicated preference for a subsidy administered by the student body or the college, rather than by the alumni. Several other student leaders and a few of the more outspoken faculty members took forthright stands, in interviews, against "letting athletics get out of hand."

On March 30, 1951, the Board of Athletic Authority was to reconvene to consider the subsidy question. Langston, feeling himself to be in a very difficult position, was considering what he should do.

Chapter

6 Step 4: Selection of Human Solutions

The early stages of the decision-making process—identifying a disequilibrium, diagnosing the situation, and stating the problem—lead to the fourth step: selection of a particular course of action designed either to return the organization to a previous state of equilibrium or to bring it to a new state of equilibrium. Skill in creating an operational solution to a stated problem is the test of all the preceding steps in the decision-making process and is therefore the test of the manager's decision-making ability. It is essential therefore that this stage of the process be approached just as systematically and just as critically as the earlier stages.

Fortunately, a considerable body of literature is available on solution choice. Most of the literature on decision making, in fact, centers on this particular step, ranging from generalized normative models of behavior to proposed solutions for the most specific problems.[1] This chapter presents a framework for the development of knowledge and skill in choosing a solution.

Although the literature on decision making stresses the choice of a solution as the key step of the decision process, experience with both managers and students shows that they have a tendency to overemphasize this step in the total process. In most cases, if the diagnosis has been accurate and thorough and the problem has been accurately and clearly defined, alternative solutions often stand out with corresponding clarity, and the choice of a course of action is not difficult. The choice step more often fails because of errors in diagnosis and problem definition than from any other cause.

THE SOLUTION CRITERIA

The process of choosing a solution begins when the decision maker, alone or in discussion with others, compiles as many ideas for alternative solutions as possible. The process of creating ideas for alternative

[1] For a bibliography of this material, see Taylor (1965), pp. 82–86.

solutions is one more process in decision making where evaluation must be postponed if the process is to be effective. Studies have shown that ideas are more prolific and come more rapidly in a nonevaluative atmosphere. At this early stage, therefore, the decision maker should minimize analysis and evaluation of the solutions that occur to him or to others. If the problem has been clearly stated, "brainstorming" is much more productive than immediately scrutinizing each tentative offering.[2] However, once a list of solutions has been compiled, they should be assessed in terms of the following essential criteria:

1. A solution should be of a *quality* satisfactory to meet organizational goals.
2. A solution must be *acceptable* to those affected by it and to those who must implement it.
3. A solution should be evaluated in terms of the *anticipated responses* to it.
4. The choice of a solution should focus on *present* alternatives, not past possibilities.
5. The *risks* of each alternative solution should be considered.
6. Multiple solutions should be arranged in a proper *sequence*.

The first two criteria are often confused with each other, but are quite distinct. Neither one can be omitted in the assessment of solutions for human problems in organizations.

In some technical decision situations which have only a minimal influence on the lives of a work force, the acceptability of a solution may be of little concern in choosing an alternative, and only the technical quality of the solution need be assessed. In human situations, however, even the highest quality alternative may be a poor choice if no one involved finds it acceptable enough to be motivated to implement it. Some managers, because of their personalities or their experiences, may place entire emphasis on one dimension or the other, unaware of the important distinctions between the two. In choosing a solution, however, neither quality nor acceptability should be taken for granted. Both should be explicitly applied as criteria when assessing alternative solutions.

CRITERION 1: DETERMINING THAT A SOLUTION IS OF A QUALITY TO MEET ORGANIZATIONAL GOALS

The solution ultimately chosen should be the best one available to solve the problem and meet organizational goals. That is, it should be the one which will most fully accomplish the desired short-run and long-run

[2] In general, there is controversy over the effectiveness of brainstorming. See Osborn (1963) for an affirmative treatment; see Taylor, Berry, and Block (1958), pp. 23–47, for qualification. The important point, however, is that if we have a clear statement of a problem, brainstorming can be useful in considering a wide range of solutions, even though they may not seem appropriate at first glance. The rather interesting solutions that are sometimes generated by this method require the participation of several individuals, all of whom thoroughly understand the problem.

goals quickly, efficiently, and economically. It is this quality dimension of solution choice that most of the decision-making literature treats; and each functional area of business—marketing, finance, accounting, personnel, and so on—has developed its own body of knowledge about decision quality. The manager who must make decisions in any of these areas is, of course, expected to be technically qualified.

To facilitate the process of selecting the optimum course of action, the decision maker may use many types of decision tools. These tools, about which a great deal has been written, tend to stress techniques that are suitable for use with the rapidly developing computer technology. They include such varied techniques as decision theory, operations research, heuristic programming, linear programming, simulation, and game theory, all of which can offer insights into complicated multidimensional problems. They are designed to increase the manager's information, help structure choices, provide alternative courses of action, or provide a decision matrix that can assist in weighting these choices.

In general, the usefulness of these specialized tools depends on the feasibility of quantifying important variables,[3] more appropriate to some types of situations than to others. Because at the present time the applicability of most quantitative tools to the problems of human relationships is at best indirect, they are of little day-to-day usefulness as methods of decision making on problems of organizational behavior, and therefore are not discussed here.[4] However, the criteria that are given here will assist the manager in deciding where and when such approaches can be useful.

Each manager will choose the tools most appropriate to the situation. Whatever tools are chosen, it is clear that the goal is to make the best decision possible—but quality alone does not necessarily make for the best decision.

CRITERION 2: DETERMINING THAT A SOLUTION IS ACCEPTABLE

The second criterion for choosing a solution is that it be acceptable to those who are affected by it, and particularly by those who must implement it. When decisions are made relative to behavior, it is obvious that their acceptability is almost always a crucial factor. Of all the resources used by managers, the human resource is the only one that *cares* how it is used. A piece of steel does not care how it is processed; a Swiss franc or a dollar bill does not care how it is spent. Workers, on the other hand, may have passionate preferences; they cannot be manipulated in the

[3] See Alexis and Wilson (1967), Chs. 4–6.

[4] It is not the intent here to minimize in any way the contributions of quantitative techniques to decision making. The point, instead, is that a business manager is in day-by-day confrontation with problem situations in which the first responsibility is to understand the situation and define the nature of the problem; and at any stage of the process he may choose to quantify the information that is available. The important point is that a choice be made rather than a particular technique be applied automatically.

same arbitrary manner as other resources. Thus the manager must attempt to understand motivations, and assess solutions in terms of the cooperation that can be elicited to implement them. Recognizing this, the decision maker is always aware that the best decision technically may not be workable or acceptable in a given situation.

In a sense, acceptability can be thought of as another dimension of quality, but the distinction aids the task of assessment in two ways. First, it helps the manager clarify the reasons for the strengths and weaknesses of the alternatives. Second, it is a reminder that a good solution should allow for minimizing resistance and developing acceptance.

Observers' Reactions to Decisions

Although the criterion of acceptability should be considered primarily in relation to employees who are directly affected by the decision in question, a manager should also consider the reactions of those who merely observe the situation. Depending upon the nature of the situation, these observers may be inside or outside the firm; they may be other work groups or managers; they may be customers, suppliers, representatives of government agencies; or they may be stockholders. In any case, the reactions of such observers may be one of the overall consequences of a decision. In one experimental study, for example, observers of a role-playing situation, who were committed to a position on the subject under discussion, experienced as dramatic a change in attitude as did the participants (Elbing, 1967).

If, therefore, the potential reaction of observers is important, this factor should be included in the assessment of a proposed solution. In choosing a solution, a manager is not merely solving a particular problem, but is setting the policy, precedent, and expectations for this type of problem in the eyes of observers. The handling of rioters by police, for example, affects not only the rioters and the police but the public's attitude on rioting (especially when they see the rioting on television). If managers can identify and predict the attitudes and reactions of observers, they can avoid creating new problems in relationships that are important to the functions of the firm.

EMPLOYEE PARTICIPATION IN DECISION MAKING

One way of creating or increasing the acceptability of a solution is to allow the key persons involved in the problem situation to participate in choosing among the alternative solutions available. Employee participation in management decision making has been frequently discussed in the literature on management and has generated considerable pro-and-con comment (see Marrow, *et al.*, 1967). To some writers, participation is *the* answer to most human difficulties in decision making. They argue that employees who feel they are part of the process of making a decision will accept it more readily and will be motivated to implement it more effectively. The imposition of an apparently arbitrary decision, it is claimed, may invite a passive or even a negative reaction (See McGregor, 1960, and Likert, 1961).

Other writers just as strongly oppose participation in decision making and stress its potential pitfalls. It must be recognized, they argue, that if the solutions chosen by employees turn out to be inadequate and are ultimately not used, more resistance will result than if the employees had not participated in the first place. In addition, they say, because a manager must forego some of his own prerogatives and managerial flexibility, further problems may appear, even in other situations. Finally, they argue that employee participation in decision making is a time-consuming, cumbersome, and costly process (see Jaques, 1951, and Sofer, 1961).

In considering the use of participation as a part of decision strategy, it is helpful to assess it in terms of the criteria of quality and acceptability. In a decision situation where the quality of the decision is considered to be paramount, participation by employees other than the specialists who determine this quality may be of questionable value. Its worth is particularly questionable if a decision's direct effect on the work group is minor and the factor of acceptability is therefore relatively unimportant. However, if all the alternatives are of equal or similar quality but employee response is crucial, participation may be a very useful method of winning acceptance.

Participation is not advisable when the manager has already made a decision, or when the employee's feelings of personal or job security are at stake. Consider the reaction of the employee in the following instance to his superior's attempt to involve him in performance appraisal:

> Salary administration policy in my company requires an annual performance appraisal, tied directly to salary increases, which consists of a preprinted form with such questions as "What are this man's strengths?" and "What factors are most likely to hinder this man's future development?"
>
> The intent of this appraisal is to get the employee to improve his performance. However, I found that after each appraisal I was in a disturbed state of mind. Although my appraisals themselves were all above average, I found that each time my manager criticized my communication techniques I became defensive. I tried to refute each instance he cited of poor communication.
>
> Another criticism of his was that I did not pay sufficient attention to detail. Again, I defensively attempted to show him that his examples were less than one-tenth of one percent of my output. I finally stopped objecting and told him that I couldn't help getting defensive but did agree he had a point.
>
> I tried to analyze why I was so defensive and nonaccepting of criticism. The answer, I feel, was that the appraisal was tied directly to a salary increase. This meant a great deal to me, both financially and in showing that my work was appreciated.

My manager later stated that he felt a little bad about the discussion we had but that he had to justify the budgeted raise already accorded to me.

In this situation the company's appraisal system, which was ostensibly designed to be participative, was actually used, at least in part, to justify an already existing salary decision. Rather than gaining the support of the employee, which might have been the result of a mutual search for areas of improvement, this use of "participation" produced a defensive employee who became skeptical of management's purposes.

A full assessment of participation for a specific decision process should include a predictive diagnosis of the capability of the particular group or individual to participate in the process. Such a prediction is more likely to be accurate and effective if it is based on an initial, systematic trial of the participative method. The potential rewards of the method make such a trial worth the effort. Potentially, participation can increase worker identification with organizational goals, motivate greater effort toward attaining those goals, and promote cooperation among the members of the participating group. It is a method of choosing a solution worth consideration whenever acceptability is crucial to implementation.

CRITERION 3: EVALUATING A SOLUTION IN TERMS OF ANTICIPATED RESPONSES TO IT

In a problem situation involving behavior, the ultimate goal of the decision maker is to create a specific change in the behavior that is at the root of the problem. If a solution is to be effective, it must produce that change. If it does not produce the desired behavioral change, the chosen alternative (by definition) was the wrong one.

Although the manager may to some extent be oriented to his or her own behavior (What shall *I* do?) or to the behavior of other managers who will attempt to solve the problem (What should *they* do?), the behavior of greatest importance is that in which change is desired. The critical questions, therefore, are "*What* will the responses be?" and "*How* will the proposed solution bring about the desired behavior?"

In order to answer these questions, the decision maker must necessarily forecast behavior. In part, this forecast derives from specific information about the people and the situation in question; however, it also necessarily derives from the manager's framework of assumptions about behavior in general. The more accurate the behavioral assumptions, the greater the probability that a decision will succeed as forecasted.

In the Nestlé U.K. case, the importance of underlying behavioral assumptions is quite apparent. The behavioral assumptions made by management under the original work arrangement were obviously inappropriate. The conditions provided did not coincide with the needs of the employees in the keypunch department. The success of the new supervisor related at least to some degree to her perception of employee needs, together with her more appropriate behavioral assumptions. The original decision to put in new silent machines, for example, was most likely based on some assumptions about the relationship between noise and productivity. Although some forms of noise at some volume levels would indeed negatively influence productivity, in this case the typing noise was an important sign of productivity to the employees and its absence was distracting.

After her experience in the keypunch department at Nestlé (U.K.), the supervisor was transferred to the accounts receivable department where there was also a problem of productivity. She was again faced with the question of appropriate assumptions in the new situation. Whatever she decides to do, her reaction will reflect her general assumptions about behavior as well as her understanding of the new situation at hand. The accuracy of these assumptions and the corresponding level of understanding about the situation at hand will determine whether she can solve the next problem, or whether she will merely treat a symptom, leaving the fundamental aspects of the problem unsolved.

While a basic knowledge of human behavior is important in all stages of the decision-making process, it is crucial in the diagnosis and in the selection of a solution, which involves a forecast of behavior. Sound forecasting, like sound diagnosis, relies on sound behavioral concepts. Various behavioral models can provide a framework that will help the manager prepare a realistic forecast:

1. The *individual behavior model* is an aid in structuring information around one basic question which must be answered by a good forecast: How will the particular worker's frame of reference structure the proposed solution?
2. The *interpersonal behavior model* aids the forecaster in structuring information around a second major question basic to good forecasting: How will the proposed solution affect and be affected by the existing interaction patterns?
3. The *group behavior model* structures information around a third vital question: How will the proposed solution fit in with group norms, values, and attitudes?

One final note concerning the forecasting of behavior. The expected behavioral response to a solution must be compared with the existing solution goal of that problem situation. In order to assess a proposed solution, the desired objective or goal must be clear. To be clear, the goal—the desired equilibrium—should also be stated in specific behavioral terms, rather than in vague generalizations.

CRITERION 4: FOCUSING ON PRESENT SOLUTIONS AND NOT PAST POSSIBILITIES

In choosing a solution, it is important for a decision maker to distinguish between what should have been done in the past to have avoided a current problem, and what can be done now to solve it. In some cases these solutions will be the same. If, for example, a manager finds that a machine is out of fuel, he realizes that he should have filled the tank, and filling the tank now will solve the problem. If a manager should have hired a replacement for a foreman who was promoted six weeks ago, hiring one now will fill the vacancy.

In most situations, however, what should have been done earlier and what should be done now are *not* the same. If the absent-minded manager failed to add oil to a machine's engine, he may now have to overhaul or replace it. Failure on the part of the manager to hire a replacement for the foreman may have brought about a new set of social relationships and organizational expectations, creating new problems of wider scope. If management has failed to explain changes in a production process via regular communication channels and employees have responded with a wildcat strike, a standard communication may no longer be enough to put them back on the job.

There is a tendency to assume that, had we done something differently at an earlier time, the situation would be different now. This is, of course, in the realm of speculation; all we can really know about a situation is what did happen. To assume how matters might have developed had a different course of action been taken may only distract the decision maker from considering the existing effects of the course of action that was taken, and thereby distract from dealing with the problem that currently has to be solved. Although it is useful to search during the diagnostic stage of the decision process for the causes of the problem situations that face us, it is wasteful to dwell on lost opportunities during the solution-choice stage.

CRITERION 5: CONSIDERING THE RISKS OF EACH ALTERNATIVE SOLUTION

Not only should alternative solutions be examined in terms of their probability of success, they should also be examined in terms of associated risks. Implicit in any solution, of course, is the risk that it will fail, and analysis of this risk should be coincident with analysis of a solution's potential success. If the failure cost of a particular solution is great, it may not be feasible to try it. Risks can also be personal as well as organizational; that is, the choice of a solution may risk the reputation of the employees involved, as in the electrical industry price-fixing cases of 1961 (see Walton and Cleveland, 1964) and the numerous bribery cases of the mid 1970's.

A top-level manager should be aware that placing the members of the organization under great personal risk for failure and defining failure in rigid terms may induce misleading solutions from subordinates. Consider the consequences of the decision made in the following instance, as reported by a middle manager:

> At our shop, a foreman whose unit doesn't maintain an 80-percent production time/total time ratio is in trouble. If his group misses consistently,

> he loses his foreman's job. Therefore, foremen turn in false crane waiting time, machine down time, engineering time, and so on, all of which does not count against production time. By doing this, they can cover low productitivy and get their 80 percent. No one is ever reprimanded for turning in too much waiting time—even though the written policy specifies that time should be reported accurately. The few "fanatics" who have played it straight and reported actual time lost their jobs.
>
> On occasion this conflict of written and implicit policy backfires. One example of this occurred this month. A cracked $50,000 casting came through. Castings can be ground to remove surface defects, but if a casting has a deep crack, it must be scrapped. However, scrapping a casting this expensive can cause a major disruption in production. So the foreman said to the machinist, "Grind around the edge to remove that defect. If this one is scrapped the department will miss the schedule." The worker saw that the defect was too deep to correct by grinding, so he welded the area to disguise the crack. The crack was in a critical area and the welding was ineffective. The unit failed in testing, and a new casting had to be substituted, at great expense and loss of time. The worker thought he was doing what the foreman wanted. The foreman had communicated the message, "Get the casting processed at all costs."

At this company, top management had set a framework designed to insure the success of its solutions to production problems which, in actual practice, merely led to the concealment of problems and the creation of additional problems. The lower-level decision makers (managers, foremen, and workers) could not afford to consider any risks involved in solutions except the risks to their job security.

CRITERION 6: ARRANGING MULTIPLE SOLUTIONS IN PROPER SEQUENCE

A common assumption of decision makers is that alternative solutions must be mutually exclusive and independent of one another and, therefore, that decisions must be limited to one alternative. In certain situations, however, various courses of action thought of as alternatives can be arranged in a hierarchical order and performed in sequence. Some of the alternatives—or steps in the decision sequence—may be so easy to implement, entail so little risk, and even provide substantial additional information, that they are worth trying before proceeding to other courses of action that may be more complicated, time-consuming, or risky. It is worth exploring whether alternatives can be placed in a sequence of steps.

In the Merdon State College case, Dean Langston is faced with a committee meeting which, in his best estimate, will reject his position on athletic scholarships by a 4 to 2 vote. He has four days in which to decide what he should do. The following possible courses of action were proposed by one group of students who discussed the case. He could:

1. Resign his job.

2. Seek the support of President Kirkman, who has remained outside the controversy.
3. Appeal to the student body for support.
4. Seek support among the other committee members.
5. Propose a modified scholarship program to the committee.
6. Discuss the problem with Salvio, the coach, to discover his position.
7. Ascertain the practice of other schools in the conference.
8. Accept the committee's decision.

At least seven different actions are available to Langston. On examination, it is obvious that they are not all mutually exclusive. They could be ordered and arranged to form a *critical path*, or a sequential strategy for solving his problem.

Step 1: First, he can inquire into the practices of other conference schools on the matter of athletic scholarships. This would help him in deciding whether the existing pattern of athletic scholarships is acceptable to him—a critical point. If it is, he can prepare a proposal that reflects the pattern of these programs and argue for a comparable Merdon program. If, on the other hand, he finds the existing pattern unacceptable, he can develop his own proposal.

Step 2: He can talk to Salvio to discover the coach's ideas for the scholarship program—another critical point. Salvio's ideas and Langston's might be compatible. In this case, a majority of the board would probably vote for a proposal Langston could accept. If, however, Salvio desires a program that is unacceptable to Langston, or if he refuses to disclose his recommendation, Langston will at least have learned something about his opposition.

Step 3: He can discuss the alternatives with Kirkman and seek the president's support—a third critical point. If Kirkman supports Langston's position, he will do so actively or passively. If his support is active, pressure can be applied to other committee members. This is another critical point, and the proper steps can be worked out for this eventuality. If Kirkman's support is passive, alternative steps can be developed with the assurance that the president is at least behind Langston. On the other hand, if Kirkman refuses to take a position, as before, Langston could talk with the other committee members.

Step 4: Knowing the probable position of the student members of the committee, he could attempt to determine the positions of the other two voting members—another critical point. He can present his case to them and attempt to gain a commitment from them, or at least an insight into how they will vote. If they choose to vote with him, he may have a tie vote at the meeting, which could delay the decision and give him more time. If, on the other hand, he cannot get assurance of their support, Langston would be faced with three final alternatives: (1) continuing to seek support, (2) accepting the committee's decision, or (3) resigning. Inasmuch as neither (2) nor (3) is necessary as yet, and depending upon the importance attached to the issue, Langston could take step 5.

Step 5: He could approach the student body for support. This alternative has long-term risks, but if Langston has strong convictions, he may wish to make this approach despite the risks. Again, he will face a critical juncture: either he will gain student support or he will not. If he does, this support can be channeled toward changing the vote of the student members of the committee. If he does not get student support, he is again faced with alternatives (2) and (3): accepting the committee's decision, or resigning. (This, of course, is the ultimate pair of alternatives for all decision makers; at one point or another they must accept a decision of others in the organization and live with it, or leave the organization.)

This case-example points up the fact that *a decision maker need not consider all alternatives as being of equal value or as mutually exclusive*. The decision maker can prepare a planned sequence of acts which includes alternative moves at various critical junctures. Such a "decision tree" is an aid in preparing creative strategies in advance for various eventualities. Furthermore, it uses several good solution ideas instead of risking success on one strategy.

One alternative has been left out so far: Langston could simply do nothing—which in effect would be to accept the decision of the committee. However, *it is important to distinguish between deciding to do nothing, and failing to define or face a problem*. Although both may have the same outcome, they do have considerably different meanings. A manager who performs the decision process, considers all alternatives, and then decides that the best alternative is to do nothing, has emotionally mastered the situation and has fulfilled responsibility as a manager. Doing nothing because of failure to define the problem or to decide what to do is an entirely different matter.

The implications of the distinction between deciding to do nothing and failing to decide can be very significant. A manager who is unskilled in the processes of observing disequilibria, diagnosing problem situations, stating problems, and assessing solutions will regularly fail to decide. Some of these failures will turn out well. Ultimately, however, *an organization is weakened by the absence of managerial decision making*. And in missing opportunities for exercising decision skills, the manager will have foregone the process of professional growth and abdicated decision-making responsibilities.

SUMMARY OF CRITERIA

Many techniques are available to the decision maker for choosing a course of action as the solution of a problem. But no matter what resources are chosen to be used, the solutions will be sounder if they are assessed in terms of certain criteria. Thus an important step in the decision-making process is choosing among alternative solutions. This choice is facilitated by testing each proposed solution against the following criteria:

1. A solution should be of a quality satisfactory to meet organizational goals.
2. A solution must be acceptable to those affected by it and to those who must implement it.
3. A solution should be evaluated in terms of the anticipated responses to it.
4. The choice of a solution should focus on present alternatives, not past possibilities.
5. The risks of each alternative solution should be considered.
6. Multiple solutions should be arranged in a proper sequence.

REFERENCES

Alexis, Marcus, and Charles Z. Wilson. *Organizational Decision Making.* Prentice-Hall, 1967.

Elbing, Alvar O., Jr. "The Influence of Prior Attitudes on Role Playing Results." *Personnel Psychology,* Autumn 1967.

Jaques, Elliott. *The Changing Culture of the Factory.* Tavistock, 1951.

Likert, Rensis. *New Patterns of Management.* McGraw-Hill, 1961.

McGregor, Douglas. *The Human Side of Enterprise.* McGraw-Hill, 1960.

Marrow, Alfred J., David G. Bowers, and Stanley E. Seashore. *Management by Participation.* Harper & Row, 1967.

Osborn, Alexander. *Applied Imagination: Principles and Procedures of Creative Problem Solving,* 3rd ed. Scribners, 1963.

Sofer, Cyril. *The Organization from Within.* Quadrangle, 1961.

Taylor, Donald W. "Decision Making and Problem Solving." In *Handbook of Organizations,* ed. James G. March. Rand McNally, 1965.

——, Paul C. Berry, and Clifford H. Block. "Does Group Participation When Using Brainstorming Facilitate or Inhibit Creative Thinking?" *Administrative Science Quarterly,* Vol. 3, 1958.

Walton, Clarence C., and Frederick W. Cleveland, Jr. *Corporations on Trial: The Electric Case.* Wadsworth, 1964.

A Shade of Gray (A)

Calvin McGruder was the union shop steward at Tinytogland, a children's clothing manufacturing firm in a midwestern state.

The company-union contract between the Amalgamated Clothing Workers' Union and Tinytogland stipulated that the union steward had the right to work overtime if any of his union subordinates worked, and if he were qualified for the work being performed.

Due to heavy snow predictions and an accumulation of almost five inches by midnight, Tuesday, the plowing crew was scheduled to report for early overtime assignment to start at 4 A.M. Wednesday to plow out roads and the parking lot. This crew consisted of one driver and three shovel men. Plowing was done by a large plow attached to the front of a heavy truck. When McGruder was notified of the overtime, he exercised his right to the assignment and was scheduled in as a shovel man.

Upon arrival at the garage where the plowing operation would start, he found that the regular driver was late. Since there was no truck key, rather than reporting to the foreman McGruder obtained an emergency key from the plant protection man. He then returned to the garage and stated that he would do the plowing. Though he initially had trouble backing the truck out of the garage, he drove to the front parking lot and started to plow. However, during his first swipe he hit a manhole cover and bent one of the plow braces. He then backed up but lost control and ran unto a parked car belonging to a fellow employee, causing considerable damage to the car (later determined to be $217). The truck was not damaged other than the plow brace.

At this point the regular driver appeared and took over the remainder of the job.

The following information was obtained by the labor relations supervisor after his arrival at 7 A.M. Wednesday morning.

1. McGruder had been told only to help out the plow crew as a shovel man. He was not then classified and had never held the company classification "truck driver," nor had he ever driven the truck before. Truck driving required a chauffeur's license, and his act was strictly on his own.

2. McGruder had only within the past month regained his driving license for a pleasure car, which had been revoked for the prior year due to an accident in which he had been found at fault.

3. McGruder had already made arrangements with the owner of the car he struck to pay for repairs. He had asked the owner not to report the accident because, if it were reported, he could lose his license again. The owner had assured him he would not report the accident if his car was properly repaired.

4. McGruder readily admitted he had driven the truck and had hit the car. He was not questioned regarding the damage to the plow.

5. State law required that accidents involving damage over $150 be reported.

At 1 P.M. the labor relations supervisor reported to the industrial relations manager of the plant to ask for advice as to how to proceed. The two of them discussed the following items.

"A Shade of Gray (A)" was written under the supervision of Alvar O. Elbing. Names of people and places have been disguised.

1. In trying to determine what prompted McGruder to drive the plow truck, they decided that probably the best explanation was that he was trying to become qualified on the plow so he could exercise overtime rights against the operator in future overtime assignments.

2. The facts would undoubtedly substantiate discipline of McGruder, either on a charge of "unauthorized operation of company equipment" or "careless use of company equipment." The maximum discipline that could probably be justified would be "one day off." If disciplinary action were taken, it should be in accordance with company policy that discipline be "corrective" rather than punitive.

3. McGruder had been a very troublesome committeeman and had filed many grievances almost on whim. If disciplinary action were taken, it was anticipated that he would probably file 10 to 20 additional grievances.

4. At the staff meeting that day, the plant manager remarked offhandedly that "we will probably have 30 to 40 grievances before the day is over." This indicated that he expected a disciplinary investigation to be held.

5. During the day many facetious inquiries had been made of both the industrial relations manager and the labor relations supervisor as to what would happen to "our new truck driver."

6. On the bottom of the state accident reporting form is the following notation: "An accident causing death, personal injury, or damage over $150 to the property of any one person must be reported within 10 days. Failure to report within 10 days is a misdemeanor, and subjects license and/or registration to suspension until report is filed."

If disciplinary action were to be taken, it should be done as quickly as possible, and no later than the following day.

A Shade of Gray (B)

Two questions had to be decided initially in the incident involving Calvin McGruder:

1. Should he be disciplined on one or both charges?

2. What should be done about reporting the accident?

The following statement was made by the personnel manager of Tinytogland after the incident was closed:

"Concerning the first, we decided nothing could be gained by discipline. First, the man was very obviously deeply worried that he would lose his license, and this should prove as effectively 'corrective' as further discipline. Further, it would probably appear that we were on a vendetta because he had filed past grievances. Third, since no extensive damage was done to the truck, we lost nothing and perhaps would gain in our future relations with McGruder. The plant manager concurred with our decision in this regard.

"The question of reporting the accident was more complicated. The first consideration was the legal question. If in fact we were legally responsible to report the accident, we had no choice, for otherwise not only would we knowingly be violating the law, but in addition we would be subjecting the company to possible blackmail by both McGruder and the employee whose car he hit. However, if we reported the accident, McGruder would unquestionably lose his driver's license, probably permanently. Not only would this result in extremely hard feelings, poor company-union relationships and a resultant increase in grievances, but from a personal standpoint we were sympathetic to his plight.

"Initially I was doubtful that the company or owner would be held legally responsible under these conditions for reporting an accident. I became more so after contacting both my personal insurance firm and the firm handling the company truck. In both instances they assured me they were *almost* certain the company had to report the accident. I finally called the local Motor Vehicle Office and was told by an employee that the company was *not* responsible under these circumstances.

"Not only was the legal situation unclear but the industrial relations manager wondered if the company could, with the knowledge possessed, completely overlook the matter? To avoid any possibility of criticism I decided to pass the problem to McGruder, since it was really his anyway. I asked him to come to my office, and upon his arrival let him read the law concerning reporting. (And here, I admit, I resorted to chicanery in that I did not disclose the interpretation of the Motor Vehicle Office.) I then said 'Cal, this has got to be reported,' and pointed out that he was setting himself up for blackmail and a possible misdemeanor. Things then went from bad to worse. He explained that he could not report the accident because he had just obtained his license renewal; that it had been done by an undertable payment and that reporting could bring this all to light. He then produced a waiver, signed by the owner of the damaged car, indicating that damage of $217 had been paid in full for the accident. I pointed out that this was clear evidence he had been involved in an accident and would hardly be to his benefit. He stated he would see his attorney that night.

"Two days later he came to my office to show me a supposedly valid estimate of damage for $146.50. I accepted it at face value and marked the case closed."

The Case of Savemore Food Store 5116

The Savemore Corporation is a chain of 400 retail supermarkets located primarily in the northeastern section of the United States. Store 5116 employs over 50 persons, all of whom live within suburban Portage, New York, where the store is located.

Wally Shultz served as general manager of store 5116 for six years. Last April he was transferred to another store in the chain. At that time the employees were told by the district manager, Mr. Finnie, that Wally Shultz was being promoted to manage a larger store in another township.

Most of the employees seemed unhappy

to lose their old manager. Nearly everyone agreed with the opinion that Shultz was a "good guy to work for." As examples of his desirability as a boss the employees told how Wally had frequently helped the arthritic Negro porter with his floor mopping, how he had shut the store five minutes early each night so that certain employees might catch their busses, of a Christmas party held each year for employees at his own expense, and his general willingness to pitch in. All employees had been on a first-name basis with the manager. About half of them had begun work with the Savemore Corporation when the Portage store was opened.

Wally Shultz was replaced by Clark Raymond. Raymond, about 25 years old, was a graduate of an ivy league college and had been with Savemore a little over one year. After completion of his six-month training program, he served as manager of one of the chain's smaller stores, before being advanced to store 5116. In introducing Raymond to the employees, Mr. Finnie stressed his rapid advancement and the profit increase that occurred while Raymond had charge of his last store.

I began my employment in store 5116 early in June. Mr. Raymond was the first person I met in the store, and he impressed me as being more intelligent and efficient than the managers I had worked for in previous summers at other stores. After a brief conversation concerning our respective colleges, he assigned me to a cash register, and I began my duties as a checker and bagger.

In the course of the next month I began to sense that relationships between Raymond and his employees were somewhat strained.

"The Case of Savemore Food Store 5116" from *Organizational Behavior: Cases and Readings*, by Austin Grimshaw and John W. Hennessey. Copyright © 1960 by McGraw-Hill, Inc. Used with the permission of McGraw-Hill Book Company and John W. Hennessey.

At the time of this case, the author, a college student, was employed for the summer as a checker and stockboy in store 5116.

This attitude was particularly evident among the older employees of the store, who had worked in store 5116 since its opening. As we all ate our sandwiches together in the cage (an area about 20 feet square in the cellar fenced in by chicken wire, to be used during coffee breaks and lunch hours), I began to question some of the older employees as to why they disliked Mr. Raymond. Laura Morgan, a fellow checker about 40 years of age and the mother of two grade-school boys, gave the most specific answers. Her complaints were:

1. Raymond had fired the arthritic Negro porter on the grounds that a porter who "can't mop is no good to the company."

2. Raymond had not employed new help to make up for normal attrition. Because of this, everybody's work load was much heavier than it ever had been before.

3. The new manager made everyone call him "mister. . . . He's unfriendly."

4. Raymond didn't pitch in. Wally Shultz had, according to Laura, helped people when they were behind in their work. She said that Shultz had helped her bag on rushed Friday nights when a long line waited at her checkout booth, but "Raymond wouldn't lift a finger if you were dying."

5. Employees were no longer let out early to catch busses. Because of the relative infrequency of this means of transportation, some employees now arrived home up to an hour later.

6. "Young Mr. Know-it-all with his fancy degree . . . takes all the fun out of this place."

Other employees had similar complaints. Gloria, another checker, claimed that "he sends the company nurse to your home every time you call in sick." Margo, a meat wrapper, remarked: "Everyone knows how he's having an affair with that new bookkeeper he hired to replace Carol when she quit." Pops Devery, the head checker, who had been with the chain for over ten years, was perhaps the most vehement of the group. He expressed his views in the following manner: "That new guy's a real louse . . . got a mean streak a mile long. Always trying to cut corners. First it's not enough help, then no overtime, and now, come Saturday mornings, we have to use boxes for the orders 'til the truck arrives.[1] If it wasn't just a year 'til retirement, I'd leave. Things just aren't what they used to be when Wally was around." The last statement was repeated in different forms by many of the other employees. Hearing all this praise of Wally, I was rather surprised when Mr. Finnie dropped the comment to me one morning that Wally had been demoted for inefficiency, and that no one at store 5116 had been told this. It was important that Mr. Schultz save face, Mr. Finnie told me.

A few days later, on Saturday of the busy weekend preceding the July 4 holiday, store 5116 again ran out of paper bags. However, the delivery truck did not arrive at ten o'clock, and by 10:30 the supply of cardboard cartons was also low. Mr. Raymond put in a hurried call to the warehouse. The men there did not know the whereabouts of the truck but promised to get an emergency supply of bags to us around noon. By eleven o'clock, there were no more containers of any type available, and Mr. Raymond reluctantly locked the doors to all further customers. The 20 checkers and packers remained in their respective booths, chatting among themselves. After a few minutes, Mr. Raymond requested that they all retire to the cellar cage because he had a few words for them. As soon as the group was seated on the wooden benches in the chicken-wire enclosed area, Mr. Raymond began to speak, his back to the cellar stairs. In what appeared to be an angered tone, he began, "I'm out for myself first, Savemore second, the customer third, and you last. The inefficiency in this store has amazed me from the moment I arrived here. . . . "

At about this time I noticed Mr. Finnie, the district manager, standing at the head of the cellar stairs. It was not surprising to see him at this time because he usually made three or four unannounced visits to the store each week as part of his regular supervisory procedure. Mr. Raymond, his back turned, had not observed Finnie's entrance.

Mr. Raymond continued, "Contrary to what seems to be the opinion of many of you, the Savemore Corporation is not running a social club here. We're in business for just one thing . . . to make money. One way that we lose money is by closing the store on Saturday morning at eleven o'clock. Another way that we lose money is by using a 60-pound paper bag to do the job of a 20-pound bag. A 60-pound bag costs us over 2 cents apiece; a 20-pound bag costs less than a penny. So when you sell a couple of quarts of milk or a loaf of bread, don't use the big bags. Why do you think we have four different sizes anyway? There's no great intelligence or effort required to pick the right size. So do it. This store wouldn't be closed right now if you'd used your common sense. We started out this week with enough bags to last 'til Monday . . . and they would have lasted 'til Monday if you'd only used your brains. This kind of thing doesn't look good for the store, and it doesn't look good for me. Some of you have been bagging for over five years . . . you oughta be able to do it right by now. . . ." Mr. Raymond paused and then said, "I trust I've made myself clear on this point."

The cage was silent for a moment, and then Pops Devery, the head checker, spoke

[1] The truck from the company warehouse bringing merchandise for sale and store supplies normally arrived at ten o'clock on Saturday morning. Frequently, the stock of large paper bags would be temporarily depleted. It was then necessary to pack orders in cardboard cartons until the truck was unloaded.

up: "Just one thing, Mis-tuh Raymond. Things were running pretty well before you came around. When Wally was here we never ran outa bags. The customers never complained about overloaded bags or the bottoms falling out before you got here. What're you gonna tell somebody when they ask for a couple extra bags to use in garbage cans? What're you gonna tell somebody when they want their groceries in a bag, an' not a box? You gonna tell them the manager's too damn cheap to give 'em bags? Is that what you're gonna tell 'em? No sir, things were never like this when Wally Shultz was around. We never had to apologize for a cheap manager who didn't order enough then. Whatta you got to say to that, Mis-tuh Raymond?"

Mr. Raymond, his tone more emphatic, began again. "I've got just one thing to say to that, Mr. Devery, and that's this: store 5116 never did much better than break even when Shultz was in charge here. I've shown a profit better than the best he ever hit in six years every week since I've been here. You can check that fact in the book upstairs any time you want. If you don't like the way I'm running things around here, there's nobody begging you to stay. . . ."

At this point, Pops Devery interrupted and, looking up the stairs at the district manager, asked, "What about that, Mr. Finnie? You've been around here as long as I have. You told us how Wally got promoted 'cause he was such a good boss. Supposin' you tell this young feller here what a good manager is really like? How about that, Mr. Finnie?"

A rather surprised Mr. Raymond turned around to look up the stairs at Mr. Finnie. The manager of store 5116 and his checkers and packers waited for Mr. Finnie's answer.

The Jim Baxter Case

During the early 1930s, Jim Baxter pumped gas and worked as a mechanic's helper in order to support his wife and recently adopted son, Jon. The job was new to him, quite different from the plant job he had before the Depression. After a few years of experience in the garage, however, he found a real interest in it and exhibited considerable ability in repairing automobile and truck engines. By 1938 Jim was in charge of all the engine repair work for the garage. The owner Gus, at age 60, was glad to have Jim take care of the heavy work and manage the two boy helpers.

In the spring of 1940, Gus suffered a stroke and was unable to continue working. At the insistence of Gus's wife, Jim, although reluctant to do so, took over total responsibility of the service station. However, the long hours and constant problems with Gus's nephew

This case was written under the supervision of Alvar O. Elbing. Names of people and places have been disguised.

(hired by Gus's wife as assistant mechanic), led Jim to leave the garage and set up an engine machine shop on the other side of town.

Jim had saved enough to rent a small one-room shop in a building which housed two other businesses—a radiator shop and a general automobile repair and maintenance garage. Since little paperwork or customer contact was required in any of these businesses, the small office in the front of the building was shared by all.

Much of Jim's business came from service-station owners with whom he had made contact through Gus. Since most gas stations are not equipped to do overhaul work, they send the engine blocks out to shops such as Jim's for replacement or grinding of valves, reboring the head, replacing rings, etc. Delivery and pickup of the finished block is done by the customer—whether service station, car dealer, or industrial plant.

With the great increase in sales of automobiles after World War II, Jim was flooded with business. But rather than expand, he decided to accept just as much as he and a boy helper could do. Excess business was turned away.

In 1945 Jim's only son Jon entered junior high school. On the way home from school Jon passed his father's shop and often went in to help for a couple of hours before dinner. Jon enjoyed the work. By the time he was 16 he was able to completely overhaul an engine himself, with his father's instruction. Thereafter during summers and on Saturday mornings, Jim paid Jon mechanic's wages for his work. Although the Baxters wanted Jon to go to college, when he graduated from high school he immediately began working full time at the shop.

Both Jon and his father were meticulous workmen and highly regarded for their friendly service and craftsmanship. Jon was especially conscious of doing a good job. He usually rechecked micrometer readings several times, always cleaned burrs from ground or drilled materials, double-checked fittings—in general he was very cautious and clean. Jon felt that his work was an extension of himself. Poor craftsmanship would be a reflection on his integrity.

In many ways Jon was like his father. He was interested in working hard and earning a fair day's wage. He was seldom known to raise his voice and his social life was limited to his family and a weekly evening at the local rifleman's club for archery practice and a few beers. Both their lives centered around the shop.

About 1960, Jim began to seriously think of the future of the business after he passed away. An accountant friend suggested that heavy inheritance taxes could be avoided if he sold the business to Jon for a reasonable price. His son in turn would hire his father, while paying for the shop over a period of five years or more. Confronted with these ideas, which could only be of benefit to him, Jon graciously accepted the offer.

The plan was carried out during the early 1960s. Official ownership passed to Jon in 1967. Although Jim was nearly 70, he continued to work every day. Any suggestion that he slow down or retire was laughed off. If pressed, he took it as an insult and countered with a stern face and silence. Mrs. Baxter died in 1965 after a short illness, leaving the shop Jim's only source of pleasure and contact with the world.

For a man his age Jim was very healthy. In the two years after Mrs. Baxter's death, however, his thinking ability and sight definitely began to show signs of deterioration. Jon had suspected this for several years but largely ignored the occasional side remarks to this effect made by the mechanics in the radiator shop or garage. During the next year things were different, however. Early in the spring, several engines were returned because of poor workmanship. Rechecking the records, Jon determined that in each case it was work his father had done. Although it was not an extreme burden, the additional cost and labor needed to fix the engines wiped out the original profit on the job. Unfortunately, two of the engines were from the same dealer, who began taking his work elsewhere.

After considerable pressure from his son, Jim agreed to take a short vacation early in June to visit his only surviving brother. In five days he was back on the job, claiming he couldn't stand the boredom. Two weeks later, a marine engine was returned that had been in the shop a week earlier for an overhaul. The local marine owner was furious. The engine was for one of his ferry boats, which was now inoperative during the height of the season.

Jon was very concerned about the loss of another good customer. His father had worked on the engine, grinding the valve seats unevenly. This caused one valve to crack and two others to be badly burned after the engine had been replaced in the ferry. Jim claimed that the probable cause of the mishap was defective values, something Jon found impossible to believe.

Increasingly Jon spent time checking his father's work before it was sent out. He worried so much about losing customers that he wouldn't leave his father alone in the shop. Late in August another customer was lost due to Jim's work. Shortly thereafter a very frustrated Jon wondered what could be done about the situation.

The Case of Old Piet

On a Monday morning in the beginning of June at 8 o'clock sharp, the intercom buzzed in Jan Smith's office.

Jan, who was in his middle thirties, had just returned to his company after completing a one-year management training program at an international business school. He had worked with the company for 15 years and had gradually advanced from youngest invoice clerk to become personal assistant to the chief executive officer, Mr. Boom.

The company was one of the twenty-five largest business enterprises in the country, and the biggest in its industry group. The head office was located in the capital city and several factories and distribution depots were spread across the country. Some 1500 people were on the payroll. The company was well known in the community, it took an active part in the running of industrial organizations, and it was often asked to appoint members of its staff to governmental committees.

The chief executive officer was a hardworking, dedicated, and self-sufficient type of administrator who maintained close control over all aspects of the company's affairs. He expected high integrity and complete loyalty from his employees and he was particularly insistent on punctuality.

Jan knew Mr. Boom's habits and always

"The Case of Old Piet" was prepared by "Jan Smith" under the supervision of Professor Alvar O. Elbing.

arrived at the office on time, especially on Monday mornings. He was not surprised when he pressed the reply button on the intercom and heard Mr. Boom asking him if he could spare a few minutes.

Mr. Boom's office was next door and Jan went straight in.

Mr. Boom looked up and said, "Jan, I have thought carefully over the whole weekend about a certain personnel problem that the company faces. I want you to keep the matter to yourself but think it over for a couple of days and then let me hear your opinion. You remember old Piet. You worked together in the same office many years ago. Actually, when I started myself 30-odd years ago, Piet had already done more than 10 years with the company. Within the last year when you were away he celebrated 45 years with the company, as well as his sixtieth birthday. Well, Piet has not been in for a couple of months. He is in jail."

"In jail," exclaimed Jan.

"Yes, he got 20 months for grand larceny. He was cashier for more than a decade in a little local savings society in his area, and over the last three years he has embezzled about $5000. An unannounced audit unveiled the case."

"But nearly two years for $5000! How come?" asked Jan.

"It seems hard, I agree, but you know the savers were people of little means. Probably they have never seen a bank from the inside and in such cases the law tends to be applied with the maximum of severity. Now, it all started when Hans (the company's personnel manager) came into my office a couple of months ago, deeply shaken. He told me that Piet's wife had phoned him a few hours before and in tearful voice had informed him that Piet was being held by the police. Hans is, as you know, something of a little missionary, and he, too, has known Piet for years. He tried to do his best to calm Piet's wife down and promised to call her back later. Hans immediately started an inquiry with the authorities, and within half an hour we had the whole story. Piet had stolen the money over a period of several years in small weekly sums and had clumsily adjusted the books. Piet does not drink or gamble, and it seems that he has used the money to buy old coins. He is known as a keen numismatist. Piet pleaded guilty and was convicted shortly after the disclosure of the crime.

"You know our policy. We do not accept dishonesty, and in principle Piet should have been kicked out immediately, but I just could not do it. I do not like letting my personal feelings enter into a company decision in this way and I think that company policy will have to be upheld. However, I told Hans to phone Piet's wife and tell her that we will consider our position and, in the meantime, will treat Piet's absence as sick leave. At the same time, a similar message was given to his department head.

"I have asked our legal advisor for his opinion on whether Piet could be allowed to continue in our employment after he is released from jail. He has told me that, as we have had no previous problems with Piet and he has no possibility whatever to come near cash or books here, I have no responsibility toward the board in this regard and am free to make whatever decision I wish.

"Now, you realize that we are only three in this house who know the truth, and I want it kept that way. You have just been through the newest in personnel policy thinking at your management course, and since you are also one of our old hands and have known Piet for years, I would appreciate your opinion on the problem. I do not promise to follow your suggestions, though."

Jan went back to his office and sat for a long time thinking over the problem.

He wondered what responsibility, if any, the company had towards Piet. If the company dismissed him, he could probably not get a job elsewhere. Jan pondered over whether the company had paid Piet reasonably during the last years. Looking at the pension tables, he realized that Piet would only get half of his expected pension if he was dismissed now instead of continuing to age 65. Jan asked himself whether an employer had special responsibilities toward a man who had served the company well for 45 years but made one mistake outside his job. Does a company finding itself in a situation like this have any responsibility towards society to help rehabilitate Piet? Does Piet wish to come back at all? If he comes back, how do we treat him? Do we or do we not inform his colleagues of the circumstances? Do we leave it to Piet to tell his colleagues whatever he chooses? His name was not disclosed at court, so concealment of the facts would be possible. Can we expect his colleagues to accept to work with him again if he does come back and they know what has happened? Could we perhaps transfer him to one of our factories?

Jan remembered Piet as a good solid office clerk who took upon himself any routine job which ambitious youngsters refused to do. He was the image of the self-effacing office worker with a slightly nervous attitude toward his superiors.

How about the economics side? Do we pay his salary during the time he will be away? Are Piet's dependents any of our concern while he is in jail?

These and many more thoughts flew through Jan's head.

What should Jan suggest?

Chapter 7

Step 5: Implementation of the Solution

The final step in the decision process is implementation of the selected solution. In this chapter we discuss its importance as a unique decision step, and the major considerations or guidelines by which it may be continuously assessed. Finally, we discuss the concept of problem prevention (as contrasted with problem solving) as one aspect of effective decision making.

THE IMPORTANCE OF CONSIDERING IMPLEMENTATION AS A SEPARATE DECISION STEP

In many technical decision situations it is not necessary to give special consideration to implementation; once a solution has been decided upon, implementation may be a simple and obvious matter of course. For example, if a decision has been made for new landscaping, air conditioning, or a new accounting system, a manager may implement the decision simply by having someone install it. However, in decision making related to behavioral problems, and indeed for most technical problems, implementation may be a crucial factor in decision effectiveness.

The *choice* of a solution may not be the end of a problem. It often happens that the more difficult and crucial step in the management process, at least in situations where people are involved, is *effecting* this solution. If, for example, we decide to change a malfunctioning work group by rearranging work assignments, or by changing its work standards, or by hiring or firing a group member, the success of the decision may well hinge on the plan for implementation and how skillfully it is carried out. Even the success of a purely technical decision, such as installing new machinery or adjusting a lighting system,[1] may depend on the strategic psychological adjustments made during the process of

[1] The lighting studies in Western Electric's Hawthorne plant are credited with arousing interest in human reactions to the implementation process; see Roethlisberger and Dickson (1947).

implementation. In the end, a decision is worthless unless it can be implemented in the organizational situation.

The ultimate test of the soundness of all decisions involving human factors is their realization in changed behavior. No solution is so astute or mathematically precise that it cannot be undermined by inept motivation of employee response. In all human situations, therefore, the question of what solution to choose must always be followed by another question, *How*? That is, by what *method* is the solution to be brought about? To omit this question from a concept of decision making is to divorce the decision process from the practical realities of the dynamic social system of the organization.

SOME BASIC CONSIDERATIONS FOR SOUND IMPLEMENTATION

In its broadest sense, good implementation is good management. This chapter is not an attempt to catalog good management principles, but it does offer some basic guidelines to help avoid common pitfalls in planning and managing the implementation of a solution. (In keeping with our overall purpose, these guidelines deal with the social or human aspects of implementation, rather than with the technical.)

The general guidelines offered here are factors which should be considered throughout the implementation process, until a solution is finally achieved. They apply to the assessment of implementation, whether assessment takes a few minutes while the manager is preparing for a meeting, or whether it involves elaborate procedures to achieve major organizational change over a period of years. These guidelines include considerations of (1) assessment of solution workability, (2) the specification of each step in motivating and activating behavior, (3) provision for feedback as an integral part of the implementation plan and procedure, (4) the planning and carrying out of leadership functions.

Assessment of Workability

Before hastily initiating implementation to get a problem out of the way, the manager should assess the chosen solution in terms of its potential workability. Not every "solution" can be implemented, although if the solution has been properly chosen in the first place, workability has already been taken into consideration. (Specifically, if, as discussed earlier, the solution was chosen on the basis of acceptability as well as quality, and if it was designed in terms of a realistic forecast of behavioral responses, there is a sound basis for proceeding with implementation plans.) However, if the manager did not participate in the solution choice, the question of workability should be explicitly raised before going ahead. Better an early confrontation on this point than failure after a costly attempt.

In the Foster Creek Post Office case there is an example of a situation where the workability of a proposed solution should be assessed before it is implemented. If Larry, the postmaster, makes a thorough diagnosis of the situation, he will be aware of the importance of the social system in the work situation. If he has some understanding of group processes he will recognize that the employees of the post office are a group, in the technical sense of that word, and that their norms and values are an important part of their work environment. If he is to deal with the arrival of Harry, the new postman, he must take into consideration these group norms. In short, he will have to be aware that the success of his solution to invite Harry to work in the post office depends on Harry fitting into these norms. If he does not consider these norms, there is little chance that Harry will last on the job.

Motivating and Activating Each Change in Behavior

The implementation plan should specify how each step of behavioral change is to be motivated and activated. This point is first considered when a solution is chosen; in implementation, it takes the form of preparing plans. If these plans are to be realistic, they must *specify* in concrete terms how behavioral change is to be brought about.

The first step in implementation planning, whether implementation time is a matter of minutes or months, *must begin with the existing situation*. This point is stressed because of the strong tendency in decision making to assume that the people who are involved in a problem situation can, as it were, erase the past and start from scratch. In real situations, unfortunately, people do not behave that way. It is impossible for them to ignore their immediate social situation, to forget the past, and to transform relationships instantly.

In the Foster Creek Post Office case, Larry must face the existing conditions that certain norms of behavior exist, that these norms meet the needs of the employees to deal with the seasonal work load, and that this situation is real and important. Merely wishing they did not exist will not suffice. Any change will have to begin where the work is at the time. Larry has no choice but to base his thinking and remedial planning on the situation as it is. It is a waste of time to begin implementation with a fantasy of the situation as it ought to be.

All implementation planning, therefore, should begin with explicit, detailed answers to these questions: Where are we now in relation to the problem? What is the situation in which we now find ourselves? How will the members of the work group react to the proposed changes? What will motivate and activate each desired behavioral change from this point to the desired goal?

No step in the implementation plan should assume abrupt changes in behavior. Rather, the steps should develop a strategy which clearly shows what motivates and activates behavior from point A to point B, from point B to point C, and so on, until the behavioral goal is reached. Finally, implementation plans should never assume magical changes in attitudes or behavior for which a motivation force neither exists nor has been provided.

Provision for Feedback

Each step of an implementation plan should be performed on the basis of a continuing assessment of feedback or responses from the preceding step. The feedback from step A should be assessed before proceeding to step B, and so on. Thus every good plan has built-in feedback flexibility.

The importance of feedback is perhaps best illustrated by instances that reveal what can happen when feedback is ignored. A large electronics company decided to change the name of one of its subsidiaries to that of the parent company—shortly after it had replaced the subsidiary's popular general manager with a man from the home office. Although the replaced manager became a corporation director, the move was abrupt and unexplained. Announcement of the name change was equally abrupt. It was made in a full-page advertisement in a trade newspaper, the first indication of the name change for the employees of the subsidiary company!

Because the parent company did not provide for feedback on these changes, it was unaware of the fact that, for many employees, the old name carried status not associated with the parent-company name. In fact, some employees had chosen to work for the subsidiary rather than other divisions of the parent company at the time they were recruited, because they preferred to be identified with its prestigious name.

Feedback of employee reaction to the changes did not reach the parent company until a state of open conflict had developed between the new manager and the employees, cooperation and productivity had fallen to an all-time low, and several valued employees had quit their jobs. The employees' anger at the impersonal announcement of the name change and the sudden change of general managers had precipitated a series of resistant attitudes to all subsequent executive acts, culminating in the crisis. Although more or less aware of an atmosphere of unrest, the new manager had uncritically appraised what informal feedback had come to him and had continued "implementation" by merely issuing orders.

Resistance to what was perceived as a takeover increased to the point that the manager's ability to implement further organizational changes was critically impaired. Ultimately, the parent company had no alternative but to undertake another, costly replacement of the general manager and a much more elaborate problem-solving procedure than would have been necessary if provisions for feedback had been built into the original decision processes. The assumption that a decision to make a change is tantamount to its success is not viable where human behavior is concerned; in such instances, plans for feedback are a critical part of the overall implementation plan.

As feedback comes in, its relevance to each of the decision steps must be assessed: (1) to determine changes in disequilibria; (2) to appraise the diagnosis in terms of new information; (3) to determine whether the problem requires redefinition or whether an entirely new problem may have arisen; (4) to monitor the effectiveness of the chosen solution; and (5) to monitor the effectiveness of the method of implementation.

It is in the process of assessing feedback that a decision maker becomes fully aware of the usefulness of having made explicit diagnoses, explicit problem statements, and explicit solution plans. If these steps have *not* been explicit, there is little clear basis for the assessment of feedback. The meaning of incoming information can be clear-cut to the extent that its context has been structured in a clear-cut way.

As we as managers continue to assess feedback, it is important that we recognize the point at which we face a distinct new problem. New stimuli—even the particular "solution" being implemented—may create a new and different problem. If the new problem is recognized, the decision-making process begins anew, focusing on the new disequilibrium, a fresh diagnosis, a new problem statement, and so on.

One pitfall in decision making is the tendency to assess feedback in terms of a previously defined problem. We as managers should be aware of the probability that every implementation step may in some way alter a problem situation. It is therefore vital that the decision maker, in assessing feedback, continually distinguishes between the original definition of a problem and the existing problem situation.

Planning and Carrying Out Leadership Functions

While it may be feasible to take for granted the exercise of leadership in certain limited technical decisions—for example, with respect to using wood or brick in building a partition—in situations that involve behavioral problems, managerial leadership may largely determine the successful implementation of a decision. Such leadership functions include motivating, activating, coordinating, supervising, and selectively reinforcing employees' actions. Active, participative leadership is particularly necessary when marked changes in attitudes or relationships among people are required. In such cases, "implementation" that consists merely of making announcements and issuing orders is likely to fail.

Part of a manager's effect on a situation derives not only from leadership skills but from the very role of leader, which subordinates often view as "larger than life." In their eyes a manager is, in a very real sense, an "authority figure." A male manager may be viewed, unconsciously, as a "father figure"; a female manager may be reacted to as a "mother figure." Some company executives are seen as benevolent grandfathers, whom everyone tries to please; some as top sergeants, whom everyone tries to outwit; some as absentee, impersonal executives, the center of rumors and fears; and so on. Thus the leadership role can be a very important variable in the implementation of a plan—in either a negative or a positive sense. Each style of leadership influences the style of implementation.

One consequence of a manager's leadership style is the particular "tone" or emotional atmosphere it creates. A manager's style is created by attitudes toward self, toward other people in the organization, and toward the subject at issue. This cluster of attitudes tends to call forth reciprocal attitudes. Poor attitudes can elicit poor attitudes in response.

For example, one executive was unconsciously secretive about the total picture of company operations when he was with his division managers. The managers developed the uneasy suspicion that something in the hidden picture of the company must be disadvantageous to them personally. Also, because they were insulted by the executive's lack of trust in them, they developed subtly competitive rather than cooperative attitudes toward him.

Another executive, who was genuinely interested in new ideas, unconsciously frowned at each new idea presented to him and immediately bombarded it with analytical, scrutinizing questions, responses that his subordinates interpreted as hostile. Gradually, as he came to recognize that no new ideas were being presented to him, he learned to give new ideas strong positive reinforcement before subjecting them to analysis, and to end discussions with further positive reinforcement. In the two foregoing instances the managerial "tone" affected employee behavior.

It is particularly important that the manager does not impute hostile or malicious motives to others in advance of valid feedback, and thereby elicit hostility. Imputing any attitude to others tends to elicit the very attitude imputed. For example, in a particular office, many beginning managers, because of their own insecurity in giving orders for the first time, imputed hostility to a secretary who was merely impersonal. She tended to give them hostility in return. On the other hand, secure managers, who did not impute hostility to her and therefore approached her openly and in good humor, received her ready cooperation.

To employees, the tone created by the manager's leadership style colors all his attempts at implementing decisions. However, a manager's tone cannot be transformed overnight in an attempt to manipulate behavior. For example, a manager who habitually approaches subordinates in an autocratic, impersonal manner will lack credibility if he or she suddenly begins to employ a folksy, personal manner in an attempt to maneuver a particular change. A "tone" conducive to effective leadership must of necessity be developed over time. Consider the following brief example:

> The management of the general manufacturing division in my company has developed a reputation for being inconsiderate and generally not

telling the truth. They are working hard to overcome this reputation, but it is very difficult. Any benefits or genuine interest shown by the company are suspected of involving ulterior motives. Because of this, the stock purchase plan developed to provide employee security has had little success among hourly workers. The plan calls for matching company payments on stock purchase and is a definite benefit to the employee. However, participation in the manufacturing division is less than 5 percent. The hourly workers do not believe the company would give them something for nothing.

Because the tone of this organization created a credibility gap, its attempts to implement a program actually designed to benefit workers were largely negated.

The importance of managerial tone in implementation is one more indication of the need for self-awareness on the part of the manager. It is hardly possible for us as managers to develop a positive tone, which is a reflection of our attitudes, without first being aware of our attitudes. This is one of the reasons why management-development programs should include experiences that build self-awareness and skill in leadership functions, as well as inculcating knowledge from the behavioral and managerial sciences.

PREVENTIVE DECISION MAKING

Preventive problem solving is best discussed in conjunction with implementation because it is when the manager attempts to implement solutions to difficult problems that he or she becomes most keenly aware of the importance of prevention. At that point, whatever the manager has done, or has not done, to forestall problems directly affects the resources available for use. Implementation is an acid test of preventive decision making.

Preventive decision making is the constructive process of building good relationships among members of the social system of an organization. This entails the creation of an atmosphere in which the work force can relieve its tensions, find answers to its questions, receive the emotional support it needs, and freely communicate about problems as they arise. The more that a work force is able to do these things, the greater the likelihood that a manager can avoid the problem situations that are the most difficult to solve.

In preventive decision making, our efforts as managers in building good relationships should include building positive support for ourselves. The building of such support has been aptly compared to building a bank account: we as managers build up "funds" in the management-employee relationship that we can draw upon when we need them. If, over time, our "deposits" to this relationship have accumulated a balance in our favor, we can expect cooperation in implementing quality decisions which otherwise might be resisted. On the other hand, if we have not built up a leadership "bank account" within our organization, we have no capital on which to draw when we need organizational support in implementing a difficult solution. Furthermore, if our relationship with subordinates has been psychologically "overdrawn" for an extended period, a small problem can precipitate a crisis.

An example of this "bank account" concept can be seen in the electronics company subsidiary case discussed earlier in this chapter. The former general manager of the subsidiary had built such reserves of good will that the employees anticipated problems and discussed them freely. When the parent company removed him and changed the name of the subsidiary, however, such a hostile environment began to build up around his replacement that the new manager found himself with no "bank account" in the organization: he was "overdrawn" before he started. Resistance to his directives reached the point that he was unable to implement effectively even the smallest organizational changes, and he had to be replaced.

A program of prevention not only facilitates implementation but every other step of decision making as well. When the relationships within an organization are positive and communication is good, it is relatively easy for the manager to identify a disequilibrium at an early stage, when it is most easily corrected. (It is deep-felt frustrations, which fester in a hostile environment, that are most difficult to uncover.) Diagnosis is also facilitated because the causes behind problems are more willingly exposed in a positive atmosphere. (In an environment that is perceived as hostile, on the other hand, workers are reluctant to reveal the underlying reasons for difficulties.) Therefore, because a better diagnosis is possible, a more complete and accurate definition of a problem is possible and, in turn, a more appropriate solution may be developed. Furthermore, managers have a greater choice of alternative solutions because they can count on a greater degree of cooperation from their work force.

Thus, although discussions of decision making generally presume that the process begins with a problem, it is a fitting culmination for our discussion to emphasize the fact that decision making need not—and should not—begin with problems and thus be restricted to "firefighting." There will be fewer fires to put out if decision making is conceived as a process of creating optimal organizational conditions rather than as a process of merely combatting problems as they erupt. Obviously, the best way of "solving" a problem is to prevent its occurrence. It is difficult, of course, to anticipate and avoid all problems. Nevertheless, the overall relationship that develops between a manager and work groups will, to a large extent, determine the nature and number of problems that occur.

SUMMARY

The final step in the decision-making process—the implementation of a chosen solution—is a step of significantly greater importance in the realm of problem solving related to behavior than in the technical realm. Human beings, as vehicles through which decisions are implemented, react not only to the quality of the decision, but to the total sociotechnical environment associated with the decision. They cannot be manipulated in the same sense that other resources can be. Therefore, the manager's job is not limited to the exercise of knowledge and skill in choosing desirable solutions; it also includes the knowledge and skill required to transform those solutions into the dynamics of behavior in a particular organizational social system.

In the process of implementation, the manager will be aided by careful consideration of several guidelines appropriate to the process: (1) the assessment of solution workability; (2) the specification of each step in motivating and activating behavior; (3) provision for feedback as an integral part of implementation; and (4) the planning and carrying out of leadership functions.

The best groundwork for good implementation, however, is preventive decision making. Problems prevented are problems solved. The decision steps presented in this book can serve as a basic framework for an ongoing observation of an organization for the purpose of anticipating and preventing problem situations, and for building the kind of organization in which the potential for human crisis is reduced.

A FINAL NOTE ON DECISION MAKING

Although we have reached the end of the model, in reality the decision-making process in large-scale organizations has no beginning and no end. The decision maker, who must be constantly alert to clues of disequilibria in the organization, is always engaged in a process of diagnosis to determine whether or not there is a problem to be solved. And once implemented, solutions are constantly under scrutiny to determine their effectiveness. When approached systematically, this decision-feedback cycle can be developed over time to the point where the skilled decision maker has become so sensitive to the processes operating in the environment that he or she can truly engage in "preventive decision making." In this sense, then, decision making and managing are synonymous.

Breaking down this process into its various steps serves primarily to clarify the decision maker's stage in the process. Obviously, there is frequently not time during the active process of day-to-day decision making for a full examination of each stituation in terms of all the criteria presented. Nevertheless, when we as managers become fully experienced in identifying where we are in the process, and hence what is our next step, decision-making time can be significantly reduced by the elimination of wasted effort.

Decision making, therefore, is an entire approach to management rather than simply one task. The effective decision maker is one who understands the environmental structure, who approaches situations systematically, and who uses the best methods available in investigating and solving problems.

REFERENCES

Argyris, Chris, *Interpersonal Competence and Organizational Effectiveness*. Irwin (Dorsey), 1962.

Berelson, Bernard, and Gary A. Steiner. *Human Behavior: An Inventory of Scientific Findings*. Harcourt, 1964.

Bennis, Warren G. *Changing Organizations*. McGraw-Hill, 1966.

Bradford, Leland P., Jack R. Gibb, and Kenneth D. Benne. *T-Group Theory and Laboratory Method*. Wiley, 1964.

Guest, Robert H. *Organizational Change: The Effect of Successful Leadership*. Irwin, 1962.

Krech, David, Richard S. Crutchfield, and Egerton L. Ballachey. *Individual in Society*. McGraw-Hill, 1962.

Roethlisberger, Fritz, and William Dickson. *Management and the Worker*. Harvard University Press, 1947.

Dilemma . . . and Decision

Dilemma

Managing director George Saunders' secretary had just said "goodnight," when sales director Frank Wallace brushed past her into his office. "For the past three years, I've been trying to do a good job here," Wallace exploded. "I think my record shows that I've been quite successful. But I just don't have to put up with the stupidity and obstruction from within our own company."

Saunders stopped stuffing papers in his briefcase. "What do you mean, Frank?" he asked.

Wallace continued in a hard, even voice. "One of our salesmen finally cracked the Atlas account. They are having trouble getting deliveries from one of their regular suppliers. They told us that if we can fill the order by next Wednesday, they'll become regular customers."

"That's great news, Frank," Saunders said. "What's the problem?"

"The problem is that the salesman phoned in the order to our production department. They couldn't possibly get around to it for three weeks. The salesman called me, and I went to see our stalwart production director, Elroy Travers.

"I kept as calm as I could and explained the importance of the Atlas order. His first response was that this was great for my bonus, but it would wreck his budget to interrupt a long production run to process a rush order. Then he tells me he thinks maybe Atlas is in a tight spot now and even if we do get the order, they'll go back to their old suppliers as soon as the emergency is over. Yet he knows nothing of the Atlas situation. I reminded him that last time we went through this battle, he worked a weekend shift and we got the Consolidated business.

"Then he tells me the overtime costs on such a rush job would wipe out any profit—before he even sat down to look at the order specification. Five minutes later he's telling me they couldn't possibly deliver it by next Wednesday even if they wanted to. Damn it, I'm not a production man, but I know *I* could get that order out."

Saunders had listened thoughtfully, and at last he interrupted. "Look, I agree with you. I'm late for a party right now, but Elroy usually works late. I'll see if he's still around."

Saunders scooped up the telephone and after a number of rings Travers answered. A short conversation ensued. Finally Saunders said: "Elroy, I know you can do it. This order means a lot to the company, and we're counting on you." He hung up the telephone and turned to Wallace. "You'll have the work out on Wednesday. You just have to humor Elroy a little—make him feel important."

Wallace's reaction surprised him: "Maybe *you* have to humor him; I don't. I knew he could get that order out. What if you'd been out of town? Besides, why should I have to put up with a lot of obstruction from an incompetent like him?"

Saunders' tone hardened. "Look, Frank, you've got your order coming. Why not let it go at that? As I've said before, you aren't really in a position to judge Elroy's abilities."

"Maybe not," Wallace replied. "But I de-

"Dilemma . . . and Decision" reprinted by special permission from the April 1973 issue of *International Management*. "Decision" is by Alvar Elbing.

cided this afternoon that no matter what happened to this Atlas order, I'm not going to work in the same company with Travers any longer."

Saunders was angry about the ultimatum as he drove home. He felt that to capitulate to Wallace would undermine his authority. Yet, he felt, Wallace was partly right. Of the two men, he would much prefer to keep Wallace. Saunders had risen through the marketing department, and he recognized that Wallace was definitely the best sales director the company had ever had. In the three years since Saunders had hired him from a competitor, Wallace had boosted sales by 20 percent a year.

Travers was in his early fifties and had been with the company for 23 years. He had a reputation for being uncooperative, but Saunders relied on his technical expertise, since he knew or cared little about production details himself. Also he owed Travers something for his years of loyalty to both him and the firm.

Saunders recalled a similar confrontation two years ealier. He had intervened on Wallace's behalf then too. But when Wallace continued to complain about every production delay, Saunders showed his annoyance. Wallace had stopped complaining, ending a tense situation. Saunders resolved to say nothing more and hope the storm would blow out again.

Three days later, however, Wallace came into his office, asking whether a decision had been made. "I'm going to talk firmly to Travers," Saunders assured him. But Wallace pulled two envelopes from his pocket and handed one to Saunders. It was his resignation, outlining all his complaints against Travers. The other was a carbon copy for the chairman. "I'm sorry I have to do this," Wallace said. Now what should Saunders do?

• • •

Decision

The question, "What to do?" about an organizational problem has two dimensions: what to do in the immediate crisis facing the manager, and what to do about the larger organizational problem which caused the crisis. In this case, the larger organizational problem is the more important and I shall deal with it first.

Marketing and production should be closely linked in purpose since a company's success depends upon their mutual cooperation. All too frequently, however, the formal systems of evaluation for the two functions put them at odds with each other. In this case, for example, marketing is rewarded with a bonus on sales; production, by contrast, seems to be evaluated on the basis of cost minimization. Marketing is rewarded for additional sales at almost any cost, while production is rewarded for resisting the increased costs of fulfilling the rush sales order.

Inevitably, these conflicting evaluation systems produce conflicts between the two departments. The behavior of both Travers and Wallace is quite rational, given the systems. When a quick decision is needed (such as in the Atlas order in this case), the evaluation systems serve to reduce organizational flexibility.

George Saunders' personal relationship with department heads only exacerbates the difficulties. As a marketing man he admits little interest in production and has left such decisions to Travers in the past, left them, that is, until the sales manager needs help. Then, Saunders identifies with sales, intervenes and "wins" the conflict for marketing.

Such problems often occur because the managing director has risen through one functional specialty in the organization—in this case, marketing—and continues to define all problems in terms of his own specialty, rather than the total organization.

From the organization's point of view, a case like this can be extremely delicate since there usually is no one to tell the managing director about the effects of his own behavior. Travers, for example, must feel that Saunders only trusts him with production decisions when there are no difficulties. When conflicts arise, Saunders countermands him. What else can Travers do in the relationship but complain and resist in order to defend his own needs?

What has actually occurred is that Saunders has "taught" the organization to respond as it does. Both his personal responses and the evaluation systems have reinforced the behavior that led to this problem. Saunders, furthermore, provides no leadership outside of crises. Then he undermines the relationship between the two department heads, a relationship which he should have been helping to develop. Travers and Wallace have learned that they do not need to resolve their conflicts, because Saunders will do it for them.

The organization will continue to respond in the same way unless Saunders changes his behavior. He must start a system of evaluation which allows marketing and production to see their interests as mutual and which gives them a framework for settling their differences without having to refer to him. Then Saunders must support both production and sales directors. After all, if sales increased 20 percent each year, production must have increased too. Travers deserves some credit for this increase just as Wallace does and he, too, needs some incentive for rush orders.

Now what about the immediate situation? Saunders is confronted by his enraged sales manager who has just tossed his written resignation on the desk. Since the relationship with Wallace has deteriorated to the point that ultimatums and written attacks are the mode of communication, so little trust seems to be left that there is not much point in preventing his departure. Saunders should accept the resignation on the spot.

At the same time, however, recognizing his own contribution to the crisis, Saunders should see if a new relationship with Wallace is possible. He can attempt to provide the psychological climate necessary for them to cancel the resignation and attempt to work together. This may not be possible but, given Wallace's success as sales manager, it is worth a try. More likely, however, a new sales manager will have to be the starting point from which a more aware Saunders begins a new approach to the organization. Saunders must attempt to develop trust by opening up organization communication. At the outset he should propose three-way discussions about marketing and production problems.

The important point is this: when the immediate crisis situation has been decided, the basic problem still remains. Whether or not Wallace leaves, the fundamental problem is the underlying organizational one. It is this one that Saunders must attack head on.

Bon Passage Case

"But, Monsieur, if you fire my lover, he'll commit suicide. He even tried to take his life last night. He was so upset yesterday after you spoke with him about his chances of staying with the company. Please do what you can to keep him."

Hans Hoffman, personnel manager at Bon Passage, S.A., a large department store in Geneva, hung up the phone and pondered the dilemma he faced. Yesterday he had explained to Albert Dupuis, a television installer for Bon Passage, that it was company policy to fire any employee who was caught stealing merchandise from the store. As he

Figure 1 Organizational Structure of Bon Passage and the Television and Radio Appliance Department

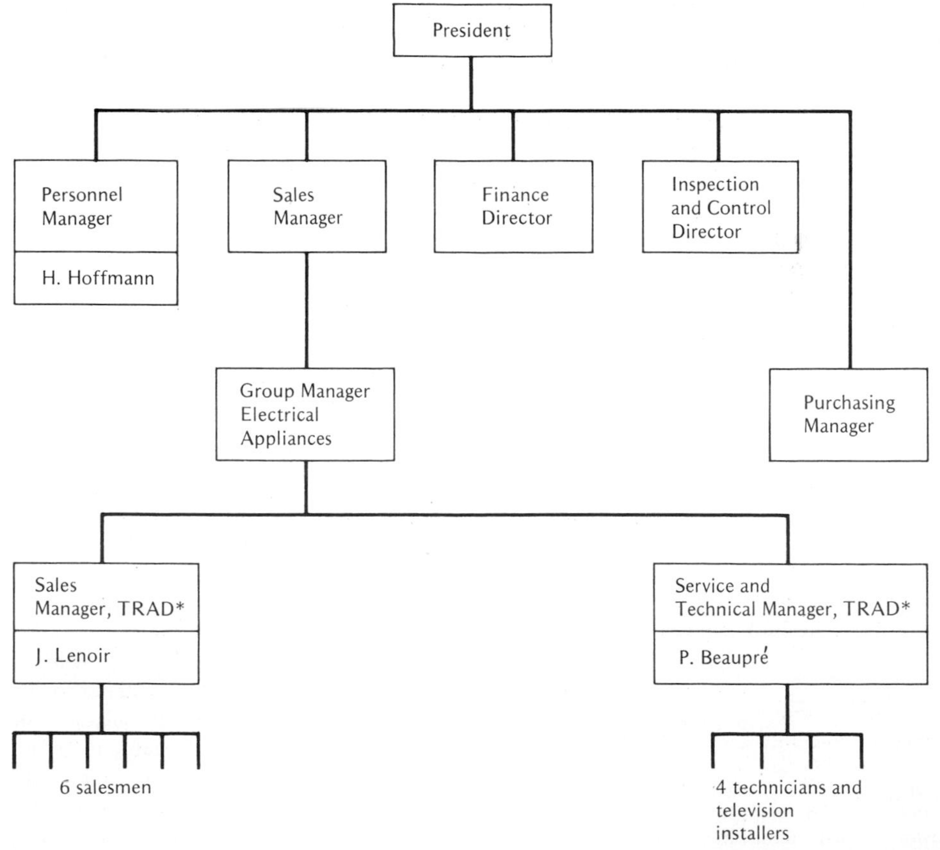

*TRAD—Television and Radio Appliance Department

Exhibit 1 Bon Passage Performance Evaluation and Salary Report

Name: Albert Dupuis

Evaluation Criteria	**Remarks**	**Marks** 1	2	3	4	5*
1. Professional knowledge and aptitudes	good knowledge of area; conscientious		x			
2. Skill; speed; efficiency			x			
3. Working methods; adaptability			x			
4. Enthusiasm; effectiveness		x				
5. Professional attitude	improving		x			
6. Cleanliness			x			
7. Character; behavior with colleagues; team spirit	lacks teams spirit		x			
	AVERAGE MARK:		1.87			

Monthly Salary: SwF 1750 + SwF 150 (bonus) = SwF 1900

Signed: Paul Beaupré

* Marks range from Excellent (1) to Poor (5)

turned to study the personnel file in front of him, Mr. Hoffman recalled that three days ago he had known nothing about Albert Dupuis. It was not normally his responsibility to hire and fire nonmanagerial employees. Theft of company merchandise, however, was considered a serious matter which warranted the attention of the personnel manager. (A brief organizational chart of Bon Passage is presented in Figure 1.)

Hans Hoffman had been working as personnel manager for Bon Passage, a store with 2500 employees, for over three years. Prior to that he had worked as a chemical engineer and as a product manager in the heavy equipment industry in Switzerland. His decision to accept the personnel position at Bon Passage reflected his desire for a change in both the content and pace of his work. Since his move, he had strived to create a managerial climate at Bon Passage Company that was progressive, positive, and employee-conscious.

The Case Against Albert Dupuis

According to performance evaluation records, Albert Dupuis was a competent, hard-working, and honest employee. He had worked as a television installer for Bon Passage for over ten years. His salary, which was determined by the annual performance reports, had reached SwF 1900 per month, almost double his starting salary of ten years ago. Exhibit 1 presents a copy of Mr. Dupuis' most recent evaluation report and salary rec-

Exhibit 2 Bon Passage Information on Employee

Name: Albert Dupuis

A. Identity

1. Birthdate:	January 3, 1923
2. Civil status:	Divorced (1970)
3. Married to:	Thérèse Deznez
4. Children:	1–Henri–born 02.08.49
5. Nationality:	Swiss (Vaud)

B. General Information

1. Occupation:	Television installer
2. Employer:	Bon Passage
3. Period with company:	more than 10 years
4. Previous employer and comments:	—Rauber S. A. in Lausanne. We were not able to contact them, as the company has gone bankrupt. —Radio-Materiels in Lausanne. Nothing unfavorable reported. Overall, considered to be a serious and honest person.

C. Education

Type of Schools	*No. of years*
1. Primary	9
2. Secondary	–
3. Commerce	–

D. Previous Work Experience

Name of Company	*No. of years*	*Position*
1. Bucheron Meubles, Geneva	9	Chauffeur
2. Television-Suisse, Geneva	6	Driver and antenna installer
3. Radio-Materiels, Lausanne	2	Television installer
4. Rauber, Lausanne	1	Television installer

ord. Exhibit 2 provides general background information on the employee.

Two days ago, however, Albert Dupuis signed a declaration admitting his guilt in the theft of some electrical equipment from the Bon Passage television department. It was estimated that the value of the stolen goods was about SwF 400. A copy of Mr. Dupuis' full confession is presented in Exhibit 3. In addition to the theft of electrical equipment, management had reason to suspect that Mr. Dupuis might have been involved in earlier, larger thefts of television sets from the department.

The Problem of Missing Inventories

During the annual audit of the Television and Radio Appliance Department (TRAD) two years previously, it was discovered that the accounting inventory figures in the department differed from the actual physical inventory count by SwF 150,000. These missing inventories of television sets could not be accounted for. At first, management attributed the inventory differences to errors in the store's accounting system.

Over the ensuing year the inventory discrepancies continued, and substantial evi-

Exhibit 3 Bon Passage Confession Made by Albert Dupuis

I, the undersigned, Albert Dupuis, admit that I purposefully lost the following invoices: Nos. 7365, 7368, and 7377 and that I kept the money which I had received, for myself. I cannot remember the exact amount of the money that I kept, but I recognize that it did not belong to me. I am aware that the act of keeping this money is extremely serious; and that it could have serious consequences for me.

Also, I sold, on my own, some second-hand televisions which customers had given me; and I kept the money.

I was aware also that some of the televisions which I delivered, left the store without their papers; and that there was no control over televisions leaving the store.

I returned two booklets of invoices: Nos. 4551 to 4600 and Nos. 7351 to 7400, to the Inspector. I recognize, as well, that one of the booklets of invoices which I had, has disappeared.

Geneva, June 21

Signed: Albert Dupuis

dence that some television sales were not being recorded was accumulated. In other words, some invoices and payments from COD (cash-on-delivery) deliveries were not being returned to the store. The company inspectors suspected that the majority of these thefts represented the work of a team or group of employees within the department. After further investigations by the Inspection and Control Division of Bon Passage, Albert Dupuis was accused of stealing electrical equipment from the store.

His theft had been traced from several missing invoice slips, which represented the only conclusive proof of stealing in the department. When presented with the evidence, Mr. Dupuis admitted the truth of the accusations and signed a confession.

Action Taken with Regard to Thefts

After receiving the findings of the Inspection Division, Hans Hoffman immediately gave Jacques Lenoir, the sales manager, his notice of dismissal on grounds of poor performance and poor control over his subordinates. As sales manager, Mr. Lenoir was responsible for the supervision of six salesmen (see Figure 1) and for the overall profitability of the department. Although Mr. Lenoir was considered an excellent technician, it was felt that he had failed to implement adequate financial control in the department. He was, however, allowed to continue working for four more months at Bon Passage while he looked for new employment.

Mr. Hoffman also fired one of the salesmen, Thierry Pache, who was suspected of stealing television sets. A second salesman in the department resigned voluntarily.

Prior to receiving the recent telephone call, the personnel manager had decided to present Albert Dupuis with his notice. Now, in light of this new event, he felt compelled to rethink his decision. He had spent an hour with Mr. Dupuis the previous day, explaining the company's policy with regard to theft. The employee had been visibly upset and in tears, and had pleaded to be allowed to remain at Bon Passage. Mr. Dupuis explained that he did not consider himself a dishonest person, that he very much regretted his actions and that he was already over 50 and would have trouble finding another job. Hans Hoffman wondered, too, if a fair amount of the blame for the thefts should be placed on the sales manager; through lack of adequate controls, he had permitted a climate to develop in which stealing could take place.

Mr. Hoffman also remembered that Paul Beaupré, the technical manager, had begged him to keep Mr. Dupuis on the payroll for at least another two weeks, as the Technical Department was very short-staffed. Mr. Beaupré had explained that it would be extremely difficult to find a replacement as experienced as Mr. Dupuis on such short notice.

As Hans Hoffman deliberated over what action he should take, he recalled that the president of Bon Passage had expressed disapproval at one of his earlier decisions to fire an employee. He therefore wanted to consider this case carefully.

Northeastern Electric Light and Power Corporation Case

Introduction

The material presented in this case study was gathered from the observations made by Bill Peterson during the summer of 1967. Peterson, a newly graduated engineer, had accepted summer employment with the Northeastern Electric Light and Power Corporation in order to earn money to finance a graduate education in personnel management.

Bill, along with another college student, Fred Greene, had been hired as an engineering aid for the company's land surveying department. This was one of the smallest departments in the company, which was one of the largest utilities in the country. There were 14 people in this department: seven aids, three instrument operators, three crew chiefs, and a chief surveyor.

"Northeastern Electric Light and Power Corporation Case" was written by Andrew P. Krueger under the supervision of Alvar O. Elbing. Names of people and places have been disguised.

The duties of the crew chief were to plan the work assignments that were given to him by the chief surveyor every week. He was to make sure that the work was finished during the week, take care of the crew's expense account money, make out the daily time sheets, and generally oversee the three or four men on his crew.

The instrument man on each crew had one major function; this was operating and maintaining the surveyor's transit that each crew had. In addition, he was to take charge of the crew in the crew chief's absence and also to assist him in the preparation of charts, maps, and other engineering paperwork.

The aids were responsible for the upkeep of the truck supplies and were required to take turns driving to the sites of various company projects. They were also supposed to help the chief with surface measuring (done with steel and cloth measuring tapes) and to hold range poles and measuring rods for the instrument man. Other duties ranged from washing the trucks each week to sharpening the axes and brush hooks that were needed for cutting foliage in some areas.

The chief surveyor, Don Williams, was the overall boss of the three crews. A large part of his time was spent in the drafting department. Don and the drafting foreman passed information and drawings back and forth between the two departments. Williams was relatively new to the job, having previously been a licensed surveyor in Illinois until Northeastern hired him in May, 1967. At the beginning of the summer, according to the older employees in the department, he did not seem to know his job very well. Up until the end of June, Don Williams spent most of his time working with Mr. James, the company's chief engineer. Mr. James was in charge of the engineering section, of which the drafting and surveying departments were part. The chief engineer had his own office adjacent to the drafting room—located on the third floor of the large building, which also housed administrative offices and a garage for company vehicles—and he was rarely seen by any of the surveying crew. His orders and assignments were usually passed to Don, the drafting foreman, and two other foremen in different departments of the engineering section.

Organization of the Surveying Crews

The thirteen employees—other than Don—were organized into three crews. Each consisted of a crew chief, an instrument man, and two or three aids. One group had three aids and the other two groups had two aids. There was also a panel truck with a complete set of surveying equipment for each crew. The trucks had been specially outfitted with drawers, compartments, and a foldout desk. Thus in most cases, the three groups were completely independent of one another.

In practice, the personnel were switched between crews every week. There were several reasons for this. The aids, some of whom carried quite a bit of seniority, were changed almost every week. Those with seniority were entitled to have the first chance to work on the projects that were more than 40 miles away from the plant. These projects carried more pay than did the "in-town" jobs. The company paid $10.50 per day on "out-of-town work" for board and lodging and only $1.50 per day on in-town work for lunch money. The instrument men were also changed, but with much less regularity than the aids. All three of them had equal seniority, but they possessed slightly different skills with the "gun," which made it desirable to have them working on certain projects. They were usually rotated between in-town and out-of-town very regularly, as were the crew chiefs, because of union rules regarding employees having equal seniority. Most of the time everyone—except Peterson and Greene, who were nonunion and had no seniority—was satisfied that he was getting his share of out-of-town work. Table 1 gives more explicit data on the personal background, seniority, and work status of the individual members of the surveying department.

Relations Between the Employees

Table 1 shows that there was quite a difference in personal background among several of the men in the surveying department. Bill noticed, however, that these disparities actually made little difference in the status of each group member.

There was only one striking exception to this. That was Herb, the oldest aid. During the very first week that Bill was with the group, Herb had remarked privately: "This is a pretty good job. The work's not bad—most of the guys have a good time out here. But you got to watch out for guys like Pat.

Table 1
Background Data of the Survey Crew Members

Name and Job	Age	Seniority (in years)	Education	Marital Status
Pat (chief)	50	21	gs	m
Doug (chief)	59	22	hs	m
Jack (chief)	48	20	hs	m
Jim ("gunman")	48	20	2 yrs hs	s
"Stick" ("gunman")	44	21	hs	m
Hank ("gunman")	48	18	hs	m
Fred (aid)	20	0	3 yrs coll	s
Bill (aid)	21	0	coll	s
Ralph (aid)	23	1	hs	m
Dave (aid)	23	1	hs	m
Alan (aid)	19	5 mos	1½ yrs coll	m
Gerry (aid)	24	2	hs	m
Herb (aid)	42	20	gs	m

He'll go out of his way to make you look bad if you let him—he's always trying to cut somebody's throat. Some of the others will too, but not as much as Pat."

Pat, a crew chief and the union steward for the surveyors, was generally agreed by most to be a tough but fair boss. He had no great liking for Herb, though, as was evidenced by his constant complaining about Herb's "stupidity." At Pat's request, however, Herb was usually put on his crew because he was the most experienced of the aids. This made quite a difference to Pat, who had, on occasion, remeasured some of the younger aids' work because he did not trust them.

Pat was noted for getting work done on schedule. On one occasion, Jim (an instrument man) had said: "If that damn Pat wasn't the steward, he'd probably work everyone to death. No matter what else, he always gets his work done. They see that upstairs and they like it. That's why Pat gets most of the good jobs."

Jim, "Stick" (a contraction of his last name), and Hank were the instrument men. It was generally agreed that they did their jobs well and were good men to work with. Pat was the only one to criticize them, but he was the "complainer" in the group and the instrument men (many of whom had been here as long as Pat) paid little attention to him.

The remaining two crew chiefs were Doug and Jack, both of whom were amiable and easygoing and were highly regarded by the aids and instrument men. Neither of them was noted for being particularly industrious, however, and this was the reason Pat was usually put on the important projects. Don had quickly recognized this and had gone so far as to nickname Doug, the oldest member of the group, "the old speedball."

The remaining four aids were about the same age and had about the same experience. Ralph and Dave had been in military service together before coming to work for the company in 1966. They had gone to high school together, and now lived quite near each other. Alan had started to work for the company in February 1967, after dropping out of an engineering program in college halfway through his sophomore year. Gerry had come to the department from another one of the company's largest generating plants in the middle of May, just before Bill and Fred started their summer work. Thus there were three new men in the department—Bill, Fred, and Gerry.

Company Organization

The Northeastern Electric Light and Power Corporation, which served portions of three large states, was broken into nine divisions. There were three divisions per state: the eastern, western, and central divisions. Each division had its own survey crews that were responsible for, among other things, the layout of new and relocated transmission and distribution lines, the layout of natural-gas pipelines, and the site engineering of new substation facilities.

The area of the crews that Bill Peterson worked with was approximately 6000 square miles. It was frequently a long distance from the main plant to the projects that they were working on. Some jobs were within a mile or two of the plant, while others were as far as 170 miles away. When the employees had to travel more than 40 miles to their jobs, as mentioned above, the company paid extra for board and room if the job lasted more than one day. With this extra pay, the men were expected to stay near the job until it was finished.

Work started at 8 A.M. and was to progress until 5 P.M., with an hour out for lunch between 12 and 1 P.M. In actual practice, however, none of the crews ever operated this way. (The work behavior of the crews is discussed in the next section.)

During the summer months, the crews worked a six-day week. Rarely did anyone complain about this; but if somebody wanted a Saturday off, he only had to tell Don a few days in advance.

Activities of the Group

The work routine of the survey crews started at 8 A.M. on Monday. At this time, everyone checked the crew schedule to find out what crew he was to be with for the coming week. Since Don and Mr. James came in around 8:30, there was a little time for the crew chiefs to make out the time sheets and expense-account reports for the previous week. Usually the instrument men helped the chiefs with this work, while the aids were busy cleaning the trucks and restocking them with supplies. At 8:30 the crew chiefs would go up to Don's office to get the assignment sheets and be briefed on the week's projects. These briefings ran anywhere from one-half hour and sometimes as long as two hours.

As soon as the aids and instrument men were finished taking care of the trucks, tool sharpening, and resupplying, they usually went off to other parts of the garage to talk to friends in different departments. Monday morning was the only time that the members of the surveying department had to get together with others in different groups. Bill eventually became good friends with Pete, a young man who worked in the supply cage. Pete always gave Bill a good supply of pens, pencils, and paper, which Bill felt would come in handy during school the following fall. During this time, Fred, Ralph, and Dave could be found talking to Dave's uncle, who was a "hot wire" line foreman. His truck was always parked down at the far end of the garage. During this time, all the men in the department (except the crew chiefs) were spread out all over the plant. Consequently, each crew chief had to walk around and find his crew members when he was ready to leave.

After leaving the plant, the crews usually met at a prearranged place for coffee and to talk over the upcoming work. (Only if a crew had to travel a great distance for a one-day job did they fail to have coffee with the group.) Then each crew would go its own way to the job. After working until about 11:30, the crew would load the equipment back into the truck and go to lunch. Most of the chiefs knew all of the good places to eat, no matter where the crew was.

The lunch period lasted as long as the crew chief desired. Pat usually took about half an hour; Jack about an hour or an hour and a quarter; Doug sometimes as much as two hours, depending on the job and the weather. After lunch, the crews would drive back to the job and work until between 3:30 and 5:00 or until they finished, depending on the crew chief.

Pat usually worked until at least 4:30; Doug and Jack were known to quit as early as 3:00 on days when they were doing out-of-town work. After work, the crews with Doug and Jack would almost always adjourn to a favorite bar and have a beer or two before starting for home. Occasionally, the two crews would meet, but this was not the usual case.

The trip home was another story. Everyone always went home at night, even if they had been working hundreds of miles away. This was easy enough to do because, on out-of-town jobs, one member of the crew always brought his car. The truck was left in a company-approved service station near the job. The individuals on each crew would take turns during the week driving to the service station in a car pool which met near the members' homes in the morning. The drawback to this was the fact that in order to get anything at all accomplished during the day, it was often necessary to meet as early as 5:30 in the morning. However, the company's $10.50 a day "handout" more than made up for this inconvenience. Except for the aid whose turn it was to drive, everyone usually slept on the way out to the job, so that no sleep was lost.

Because Don never came down to the garage until he left at 5:30 P.M., it was possible for the "in-town" crews to bring their trucks in as early as 4:00 and quietly leave in their own cars, which were parked in the company's parking lot on the side of the plant away from Don's window.

On two successive Wednesdays in the latter part of July, Bill Peterson made the following observations on the operation of two of the crews:

Jack's Crew ("Out")

7:15 Meet at car pool
8:00 Finish having coffee; drive to the job.
9:30 Arrive at project site.
10:00 Set up equipment and start work.
11:30 Stop work, repack equipment, go to lunch.
1:15 Leave lunch, return to work.
1:45 Set up equipment and start work.
3:15 Pack up and leave work.
4:45 Arrive at service station.

Doug's Crew ("In")

8:00 Report to plant.
8:20 Leave plant (just in time to miss Don coming in).
8:50 Arrive at diner, have coffee, talk about day's work.
10:00 Leave diner, drive to work.
10:15 Arrive at project site.
10:30 Unpack equipment, begin work.
11:30 Pack up, go to lunch
1:15 Leave lunch, return to work.
1:30 Unpack equipment, start work.
3:30 Stop work, pack up equipment.
3:45 Leave project site.
4:10 Arrive at plant, put truck away, leave for home.

Foreman's Reactions and Conclusion

It is obvious from the above schedules that the self-imposed work day of the crews was quite different from the standards which the company had set up. According to Doug, however, it had always been that way, from the time that Clyde Daniels (Don's predecessor) was the chief surveyor. Jack's reaction to Bill's questions on the subject were the same.

"What's the difference?" Jack had said. "We always get our weekly assignments done. You've seen that on some Saturdays, when we're getting time and a half, that we don't have a damn thing to do after lunchtime." To be sure, this was true. The crews always had their weekly work completed by quitting time Saturday. Bill had observed, however, that some projects had to be redone by another crew right after the first crew had supposedly finished them. On one occasion a certain substation layout was done three times in three successive weeks by three different crews before the engineering section was satisfied with the work.

Around the middle of August, Don started to get out of the plant more often than he had when he first came to work for the company. On several occasions he personally visited the project sites where the crews were working. Most of the time he either visited Pat's crew, who put in a pretty full day, or else he dropped by after lunch when the other two crews were working as they were supposed to.

After a while Don began to visit every crew at least three times a week and started to find out how the different crew chiefs went about their work. Now he started to realize that perhaps they were not getting as much work to do as they were capable of doing. In the next few weeks, the weekly work assignments became longer. All assignments were completed, but the quality of the work took a drastic dip. The previously mentioned substation project was a prime example of the problem that Don now realized he was facing. Because of company policies and union contract clauses, it was almost impossible to lay off help that was not needed. There were three crews to watch, plus the fact that he had his own office work to do. The company also advised him that he should not consider laying off the two students because they were personnel the company was trying to attract for full-time employment after their studies were completed.

At the end of Bill's summer employment (the middle of September), the situation was still the same. At this time there had developed a considerable amount of animosity on the part of the workers towards Don. Part of this was due to the lectures on efficiency that the crew chiefs were constantly getting from him, and part of it was caused by the fact that the employees regarded Don's visits to the sites as "spy trips." At the end of the summer, Don Williams was faced with a very real problem.

PART THREE

Levels of Analysis for Human Behavior in Organizations

Chapter

8 The Individual: Basic Unit of Behavior

Human behavior can be examined from a variety of points of view—focusing, for example, on the individual, on relationships between individuals, on relationships between and among groups, on organizational and cultural patterns, and so on. Each point of view—each level of analysis—deals with a particular kind of influence on individual behavior. In reality, a particular kind of human behavior never has a single cause; it is always a consequence of the interaction of forces small and large, individual and collective, past and present. For the purposes of analysis, however, it is possible—even necessary—to isolate these various influences.

For the purpose of understanding, then, we can think about the *individual* as one level for analysis. In any kind of organizational management, this is the most basic level, since it is ultimately individuals who work, act, and react. It is the individual who puts into motion the processes of change, and who resists them. Indeed, when thinking of any other level of influence, the ultimate issue is: How does it affect the individual? Many important behavioral questions hinge upon this one, such as: Does the particular management method allow the individual to retain initiative, or is initiative subordinated to the behavior of another person or group? When thinking about the individual, we are thinking about motivation, influencing or being influenced.

The individual responds to inner pressures as well as to environmental ones. Each kind affects the other. The individual can be thought of as a "black box," programmed with the experiences of childhood, adolescence, and maturity. This black box is filled with a total record of past experiences, yet the record is virtually unavailable to the outside observer attempting to understand the person. It even is ordinarily little

Figure 1 Individual Behavior

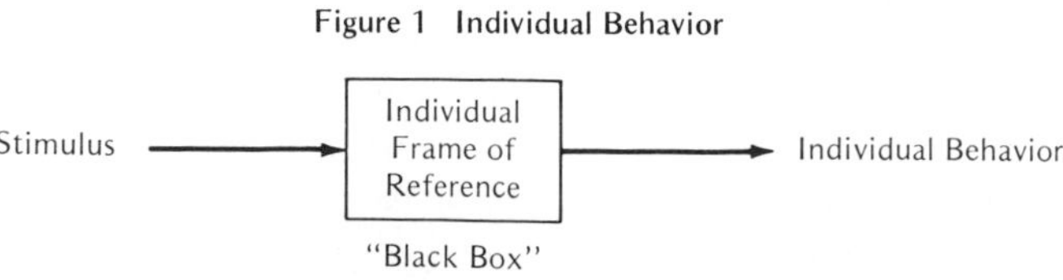

understood by the person in question. In ways that are frequently unnoticed, present feelings and behavior are influenced by experiences long forgotten by the conscious mind, but reinforced in the past by consistent behavior on the part of others—mother, father, siblings.

THE INDIVIDUAL BEHAVIOR MODEL

The particular way an individual views the world can be thought of as his or her personal "frame of reference." Because each person's past is different, each individual's frame of reference is, of course, different from every other frame of reference. Since we are blind to another's frame of reference and view from our own, we must begin making "inferences" based on observable data. We can observe the stimuli which act on the individual's frame of reference. We can observe the behavior which emerges from the individual. From these data—stimuli and behavior—we can infer certain processes operating in the frame of reference of the individual (see Figure 1).

In using this model, we must remind ourselves that we can never *fully* understand another's frame of reference, his or her "black box." We have only the observed behavior (output) as primary evidence for inferences about another person's motives, goals, and values. The inference may be supported by evidence of the stimuli to which the person is responding (input). For example, an incident or event that coincided with a change in behavior may have provided the stimulus for the reaction.

In attempting to relate stimulus to behavior, we must use caution, because we and the person we are observing may not perceive the stimulus in the same way. Indeed, that person may be responding to an entirely different stimulus not apparent to us. Pressures within the subject that relate to earlier events or to situations outside the organization may be the actual stimuli.

Thus it is obvious that, as we make inferences in our attempts to explain the behavior of others, we come face to face again with our own frame of reference—another reason why it is essential to a good diagnosis that we have insight into our own frame of reference (see Ch. 3).

In addition to understanding the effect of our frame of reference on what we perceive, it is necessary that, as decision makers, we understand the various forces that operate within an individual whose behavior we are observing. Here it is helpful to attempt to *empathize*; that is, to put ourselves in the other person's place and attempt to experience how that person sees and feels a given situation. It is also important to ask: What forces determine how the person psychologically processes the given data? It is here that the manager's knowledge about human behavior is put to direct use. A general awareness of basic psychological processes aids immeasurably in making logical inferences about the causes of behavior. It can aid inquiry, shift the focus from one's own frame of reference to that of the subject, and help the decision maker understand behavior that might otherwise appear irrational or illogical.

Stimuli are not left to chance in a managerial or organizational situation. The manager creates stimuli, acting in such a way as to attempt to get a particular behavioral result. Whatever is wanted—higher sales, greater productivity, creativity—the manager does something, either systematic or unsystematic, to try to create the necessary behavior. The stimulus is interpreted within the individual and responded to; and the response may, of course, be the desired one or not. Stimuli are motivating, but they must be well managed to achieve the kind of motivation desired.

An example of mismanaged stimuli occurred in the sales organization of a large multinational company. The motivational design was to offer prizes for outstanding performance in a variety of categories. The prize, however, was delivered by the immediate sales manager with his own personal problems. This sales manager delivered the prize (motivational stimulus) by throwing it in the back seat of the salesman's car and saying: "Don't let this go to your head!" What was the actual stimulus on the individual? The prize, or the denigrating managerial behavior? Unless we have some insight into the psychological processes going on inside the individual, it becomes difficult to determine the effect of one stimulus or the other. In this particular case, the salesman quit one month after he had been thrown his "prize."

THE INDIVIDUAL'S FRAME OF REFERENCE

The individual's frame of reference can be "structured" in a variety of ways. Psychologically, one may hypothesize certain categories of influence within the frame of reference. From the point of view of the manager, however, it is useful to view the individual's frame of reference as being made up of several operational categories that can be understood and influenced in a managerial situation. These are the individual's: (1) accumulated knowledge base, (2) decision-making processes, (3) assumptions about cause and effect, (4) human needs, (5) past experiences, (6) expectations, and (7) culture and values (Figure 2).

Accumulated Knowledge Base

Each individual acquires a knowledge base, both formally and informally. This knowledge base may be theoretical or practical, simple or complicated, specialized or general, systematic or random, modern or ancient, etc. The importance of the knowledge base is that it influences the way in which one can look at the world and the emphasis one puts on the observation. One's sense of reality may be significantly determined by the manner in which the knowledge base is acquired and the particular set of assumptions it includes. In Europe, for example, there is a tendency for education to be rather specialized at an early age. This

Figure 2 Categories Within the Individual's Frame of Reference

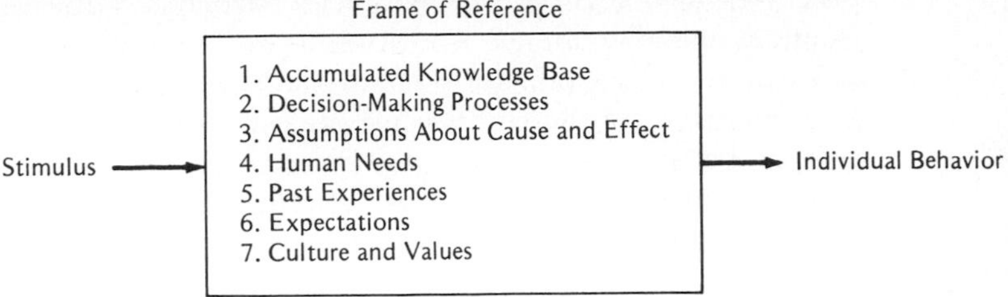

is a relatively new phenomenon, since the historic educational pattern was classical. In Switzerland, at the present, the child may be forced to choose a career path area as early as ten years old. At that point, an examination determines whether or not the child enters advanced education. At twelve, the child may have to choose a specialty of classic languages, modern languages, science and mathematics, commercial subjects, or general subjects. If, for example, the child chooses sciences and mathematics at twelve, this determines what streams can be followed in the gymnasium and the university or polytechnique. It is unlikely that a child choosing languages at twelve would be allowed to enter the study of science at sixteen or nineteen.

The model of the world that the student learns becomes the reality of the world, since the student knows no other models. At each stage of knowledge development, this model of the world is reinforced. In one research study, art and engineering students were tested on creativity and rationality at the university. After the four years of education, the art students scored significantly higher on creativity, and the engineering students on rationality, than before their education. The acquisition of a knowledge base, therefore, is an extremely important aspect of the frame of reference.

The importance of this knowledge base may explain the difficulties certain managers have as they shift from one area of speciality to another or from one level of management to another. The importance of technical knowledge diminishes and the importance of behavioral knowledge increases as the individual rises on the management ladder. New knowledge about social conditions is also important to deal with the changing social situations in the firm's environment.

When trying to diagnose or understand a person's frame of reference, it is important to understand how and where that person acquired knowledge and what system of thinking he or she may be using.

Decision-Making Processes

The processes that an individual uses for decision making may be closely interrelated to his or her knowledge base. A person trained in the sciences, for example, may attempt to use more rational decision-making processes than one trained in the humanities. Decision-making processes also tend to be related to particular subject matters. For example, we may not use as rational a process in choosing an assistant as we do in buying office equipment. How decisions are made may also be influenced by the culture and organization of the company. New employees, new managers, new companies may learn to make decisions based on the model of past company decision processes. The company decision-making model may be based on a strong individual, or it may be group-based. It may be based on a philosophy of standing out in the crowd, or being a member of the team. As managers, we need to understand not only the decision-making processes but our role in creating them in the organization.

Assumptions About Cause and Effect

Obviously an individual's assumptions about cause-and-effect relationships are related both to his or her knowledge base and decision-making processes. It is identified here as a special topic because it is so fundamental to managerial thinking. In the area of human behavior, most people are not trained to think about social factors which cause certain consequences. It is not uncommon, in fact, for individuals to reverse the cause-and-effect relationship, based on some assumptions that they hold.

This subject is of particular importance when an individual changes from one level of management to another. If, for example, a man is a technical specialist dealing with technical substances, his concern for cause and effect may directly relate to his system of knowledge and thinking. If he then becomes a manager, he will find the concept of cause and effect too limited for human situations. It is useful, therefore, for each of us to attempt to understand our own assumptions about cause and effect.

Human Needs

It is probably clear and without question that every human being has fundamental needs, some of which are unique to the individual, and some of which are common to everyone. Of particular importance when attempting to understand an individual is the fact that there is a high degree of probability that *the individual's behavior is for him or her need-satisfying behavior.* That is, psychologically a person will attempt to meet a felt need. There are times, of course, when our behavior does not operate as we had intended; nonetheless, the *motivation* for behavior is basically need-meeting. Some of the most fundamental work on needs was done by Abraham Maslow (see "A Theory of Human Motivation" in the readings following this chapter). Maslow's major contribution

Figure 3 Maslow's Need Hierarchy

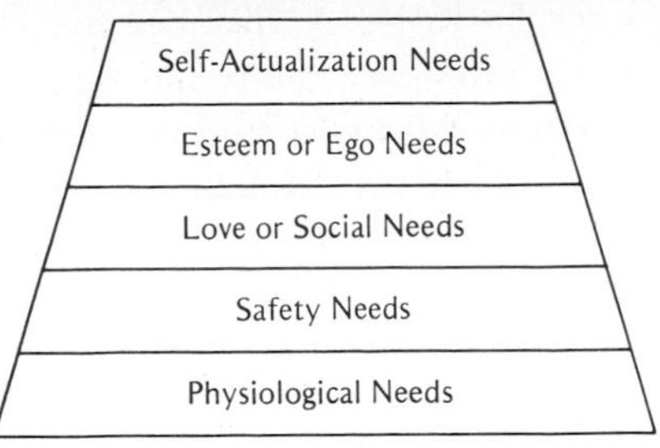

Source: Abraham Maslow, "A Theory of Motivation," *Psychological Review*, Vol. 50, 1943.

was to order needs into a hierarchy and to indicate that as lower-level needs are met, higher-order needs become dominant (Figure 3).

In Maslow's need hierarchy the basic needs are physiological and safety needs. He argues that if these needs are not being met, a person will attempt to meet them before meeting any other needs. Someone who is starving may forego all other need-meeting behavior to acquire food or drink. At the same time, in Western society most people are meeting physiological and safety needs at some level, and to that extent, employees in most multinational companies are attempting to meet higher-order needs—social, ego, and self-actualization needs. As we establish systems of motivation, systems of reward and punishment, and expectations for performance, it is essential that we understand the kind of need structure that exists in our employees and the kind of needs that commonly derive from particular situations.

Maslow's way of looking at needs is simply a set of categories into which we can begin to place behavior. It also can be the basis for assumptions about managerial attitudes. Douglas McGregor, for example, argues that some managers assumed that people were basically "lazy," "unwilling to take responsibility," "only interested in money," etc. He labeled this set of assumptions Theory X (see "The Human Side of Enterprise" in the readings following this chapter). Theory Y was the opposite assumption: that people were basically motivated to work, contribute, take responsibility, and be in control of their behavior. They had to be managerially trained to lose such a motivation. The importance of McGregor's work is that it focuses attention on the managerial assumptions about the kind of needs people are meeting. The terms "Theory X" and "Theory Y" are really different managerial philosophies about the need patterns of individual workers.

In summary, there are numerous ways of looking at human needs, none of which necessarily reflects the exact need pattern of any one individual. As managers, it is important, however, that we attempt to understand what needs are operating at a particular time in a particular individual and to understand our own basic assumptions about people's needs.

Past Experiences

Although some basic needs may be inherent in the individual, higher-level needs tend to be learned in a person's experiences. Fundamentally, each of us is the accumulation of our life experiences. In early childhood, experiences tend to be repeated, since most childhood experiences are acquired in relationship to the same individuals—family members. The repeated reinforcement of these experiences makes them a basic part of our personality. The problem, as we saw earlier, is that through reinforcement we tend to learn the *experience*—rather than to learn *from* it. A person undergoing a certain set of vivid experiences may not be aware that there are other experiential possibilities for those situations.

In an organization, too, the kind of experiences we create for people are learned by them. The process of learning insight *from* those experiences must be an additional intellectual process. Managers do not automatically learn accurate behavioral insights from long experience. They may simply relearn misinterpretations. This is why behavioral training is important.

Reference to the law of effect (see Mason Haire's "The Problem of Learning and The Law of Effect" in the readings following this chapter) suggests that "behavior which seems to lead to reward will tend to be repeated; while behavior which seems to lead to punishment tends not to be repeated." This is the basis of the learning process. As managers, therefore, we must understand the experience and learning environment we are creating, so that we can understand the experiences that people are having and learning.

Expectations

Experiences lead toward expectations. Every situation, then, is evaluated in terms of one's expectations for it. If expectations are higher than what comes, our evaluation tends to be that of dissatisfaction. If, on the other hand, we have lower expectations than what comes, we may be delighted. For example, the same noise level in a new office may be disappointing or pleasing to two different people, depending on their differing expectations. As managers, we create many of the expectations in our employees. Frequently we create expectations which cannot be met in the environment in which we are working. Sensitivity to the expectations we are creating and ability to fulfill expectations we create should be a high-priority item for consideration.

The role of expectations can be clearly seen in an experiment where elementary school teachers were given fictitious aptitude test scores for their students. The scores were randomly distributed, so that the test result assigned to each child had no necessary relationship to actual aptitude. Those children that the teacher thought had the highest aptitudes, however, actually did learn more and had the highest results at the end of the year. They definitely outperformed other children. Somehow, the expectation on the part of the teacher that certain children should learn more influenced those children's behavior—consciously or unconsciously—in such a way that they did learn more. Correspondingly, our expectations in the managerial situation may determine exactly how much a particular individual can do. For example, if we hold a Theory X assumption—that someone does not want to accept responsibility—and therefore never give that person the opportunity to exhibit responsibility, there is no way the person can demonstrate that quality. Our expectation can determine performance. This phenomenon is known as a self-fulfilling prophecy (see Robert Merton's "The Self-Fulfilling Prophecy" in the readings following this chapter).

It is extremely important, therefore, to try to understand our own expectations and the expectations others have of us when we are concerned with understanding a worker's frame of reference.

Culture and Values

A fundamental part of our frame of reference is the culture and language in which we grew up and developed. During early life we take on our culture as our own sense of reality. From it and from the relationship with our family, we learn some very basic values. These values often are the dominant base for a frame of reference in the future. Our native language can structure how we see the world and therefore be an important variable in our frame of reference.

In one classroom, which included both native English and native French students, language variation played an important role for the instructor. The instructor asked the students to meet in small groups and arrive at their *alternative* solutions to a problem. After the small-group sessions, the English-speaking groups were asked to identify their alternatives and did so, producing seven or eight. The French group, however, produced only one alternative. After some confusion, it was identified that the word "alternative" in English signifies any number of options, while "alternative" in French means only one—"the other." Each group saw the assignment based on its language and this influenced its behavior.

To understand the person's frame of reference—a task necessary for every manager—one has to learn how to infer what factors are most important in the other individual at a particular time. This process is not innate, but can be systematically learned.

CONCLUSION

In conclusion, then, as managers we must be particularly sensitive to the concept of the individual's frame of reference since each one's is different, including our own. The danger is that because our own frame of reference is dominant to us, we will assume others' are like ours. Pausing a moment to consider various frame of reference categories can give us a sounder basis for decision making.

ALVAR O. ELBING

Perception, Motivation, and Business Behavior

Traditional explanations of firm behavior have tended to be based on the premise that the primary if not the single motivation of the businessman is profit maximization. Implicit in this premise is the assumption that to achieve this goal, the profit-maximizing individual rationally chooses the best of all possible courses of action, based on his omniscient analysis of all the available alternatives. Investigations in the social and behavioral sciences, however, have opened a number of roads of inquiry into human behavior which bring this assumption into question and which offer considerable insight into the issues which must be faced in building a generally applicable theory of firm behavior.

It is our purpose here to examine certain current concepts in theories of perception and motivation which offer insight into the processes of human behavior and which, therefore, must be considered in the building of any theory of firm behavior. There will be no attempt to develop a general theory of firm behavior based on these concepts nor to answer all of the many unanswered questions about firm behavior. Rather, our purpose will be to identify appropriate questions raised by current concepts of perception and motivation which must be faced in any eventual construction of a general theory of firm behavior.

Traditional economic theory has considered the firm to be an abstract unit separate from the individuals who are a part of it. Actions of the firm have been explained in terms of rational goals of a business enterprise, e.g., maximization of profit; these goals were then assumed to be those of the individuals who made up the firm. Can we, however, consider an organization apart from the individuals who form that organization? E. Wight Bakke of Yale University suggests that we cannot. He states (1952, p. 7):

"Perception, Motivation, and Business Behavior" from *Interdisciplinary Studies in Business Behavior,* Joseph W. McGuire, ed., South-Western Publishing Co., 1962. Reprinted by permission of the publisher.

> When we observe an "organization" we are observing people organized, and when we observe "organizational activity" we are observing the behavior of people acting as agents of the organizations. When, therefore, we refer to an organization and its activities, we are referring to agents of the organization and their behavior. The substance of an organization is human behavior; the structure of an organization is defined simply as human behavior which is systematized and stabilized.

If we accept Bakke's assumption, then, that firm behavior is the composite of the behavior of individuals who make up the firm, it is appropriate that we examine the current concepts of individual perception and motivation as essential considerations in any theory of firm behavior.

PERCEPTION

What are some of the currently advanced key concepts of human perception that must be applied to behavior in a firm? The assumption that human beings simply perceive precisely "what is there" is no longer considered a safe assumption. It is no longer generally accepted that there is a necessary, obvious, and inevitable correlation between objective factors in the environment and human perception of them. According to Mason Haire (1956, p. 40):

> If we make a separation between the physical world outside of us, on the one hand, and the psychological environment, or the world that we see, on the other, we come to see that the order and organization is not in the physical stimulus but in the observer.

Psychologists today, in advancing the theory that there is no fixed correlation between data in the environment and perceived data, describe perception as a process. Any data perceived might be described appropriately as "processed data." The processing of data through perception operates in certain general ways. First, we know that persons tend to selectively perceive data in ways that enable them to cope most readily with it. On the visual level of perception, for example, we tend to take in primarily that visual data which enables us to judge distance quickly for the immediate purpose of reaching an object or taking a step down a stair or otherwise carrying out an immediate practical purpose. Thus we do not register all sense data on an equal basis; we tend to focus on those factors in the environment which enable us to make a ready adjustment. The individual, in fact, never perceives an entire situation, nor does he construct what he does see in the same way on different occasions.

Further, our perceptions tend to have fixity. If a certain perceptual framework for coping with a repeated problem has worked before, that perception tends to become fixed. We then tend to think of the perceptual judgments as existing in the reality "out there," rather than recognizing that we are merely using a portion of what is out there to pick up certain clues which will enable us to maintain stable behavior. If we accept these two concepts—that perceptions do not necessarily have direct correlation with "reality" and that perceptions, whether corresponding to reality or not, have fixity—we must call into question a basic assumption of traditional economic theory: that the businessman is able to perceive and take into account all factors objectively in making a business decision.

Organization of Perception

Another concept of perception is that individuals tend to perceive data as organized wholes. This perceiving of data as organized wholes is one of the ways we "process" data. We do not register data as an audiometer might record units of sound; rather, we tend to organize what we perceive automatically. Numerous illustrations of this human tendency have been provided through psychological experiments. As just one example, the following group of dots in parentheses (::) is normally perceived as forming a square; i.e., as forming an organized whole. This organizing tendency obviously could affect firm behavior in numerous ways. A businessman in hiring employees may fail to "see" certain aspects of individuals under consideration because he may perceive each as an "organized whole" personality type. As Haire states, "in putting together items of information, we tend to make organized wholes which may distort the meaning of some of the parts which are included. This is particularly true when the items are aspects of a personality" (1956, p. 161).

It should be pointed out that this tendency to perceive things as organized wholes involves certain very important processes that affect the data perceived. (1) In perceiving things as organized wholes, we tend to leave out certain factors which spoil the neatness of our organization. For example, a businessman may be unable to notice certain data which indicate his product is becoming obsolete because such an observation would spoil the neatly organized picture he has of his firm. (2) In perceiving data in terms of an organized whole, we tend to add to the data to make our "organized wholes" more reasonable. For example, a sales manager, in preparing a market analysis that gives some sort of organized picture, may unconsciously add to the data, overemphasizing certain factors to make for a more organized report. (3) In perceiving data in terms of organized wholes, we tend to structure the data; i.e., to perceive it in some kind of intelligible pattern. An executive may see an authoritarian personnel manager as highly effective because he has always perceived authoritarian behavior as part of the role pattern of any managerial position. Or an executive may assume that his competitors will move in a certain direction on the assumption, or projection, that they will act as he would act if in their situation, a situation which he may see as an organized whole different from that "whole" which his competitor sees. It is apparent, then, that an individual constantly distorts data in a number of ways to fit in with the organizing tendency of his perception.

Another concept of perception is that an individual tends to perceive data in terms of his already existing picture of reality. Each person has his own unique frame of reference through which he perceives data, based on his own particular past experiences, biases, sets, attitudes, goals, etc. Herbert Simon expresses a variation of this "picture of reality" concept when he states that people are constantly engaged in mentally building organized "models" of the world. He states that people never see the real world as it "is," but continually perceive that "model" of the world which they themselves have built (1957, p. 199). They are engaged in a continuous process of perceiving miscellaneous data in terms of their model, again leaving out that which cannot fit within the framework of the model, adding to it in order to make the model complete, and structuring it to keep the pattern of the model safe from disturbances. The concept that there is a certain set of objective data which all executives or managers would perceive in the same way and from which any two of them would make the same decision with regard to maximizing profit would not stand up under current analysis with regard to perception theory.

Perception as Factual and Rational

Even the supposed "factuality" of certain data may be a relative matter. Research in the social sciences has suggested that we tend to perceive only those data as "factual" which society generally agrees upon as being "factual." It has been pointed out that the only way an individual can adjust to other human beings is by checking his own impressions and observations against others' opinions. Only when his perceptions are adjusted to correspond sufficiently with the perceptions of others can he relate to others and communicate with them at all. Thus, perceptions of everyone in a society or social group tend to conform to one another. Persons actually tend to perceive only those things which fit in with an agreed-upon picture of things. As a result of this conformance to socially accepted actuality, it may be difficult for a manager not only to raise as a problem something which he feels his superiors will not see as a problem, but it may be difficult for him even to perceive such a problem in the first place.

The two opposing processes—that of building our own unique perceptual framework from our own individual experiences, and that of trimming and supplementing our perceptual framework to conform with others' perceptions (others' opinions being part of our individual experience)—go on continuously. However, it should be clear that neither of these perceptual processes results necessarily in objective perception of data. When a part of a person's unique perceptual processes conforms to society, this does not mean it conforms to "reality."

Another factor affecting human perception in our culture is that persons want to perceive data as having a rational basis and want to give rational explanations for data. This concept suggests the possibility that the entire theory of firm behavior proposed by traditional economists may have been created in an effort to perceive firm behavior as having an objective, rational basis. Once such a rational theory is created, most people would be more willing to hold onto that rationality than to begin investigation again in a realm of nonrational flux.

Despite the fact that we may view the perceived data as rational, emotion and many other nonrational factors may strongly affect perception (see Wittreich, 1959, pp. 56–60). Karen Horney stresses particularly the distorting effect of anxiety upon perception. Horney has pointed out that states of anxiety or perceived threat cause the perceiving individual to narrow significantly his perceptual framework (Horney, 1937, Ch. 3). An anxious person, a person who perceives himself under threat, actually does not observe as much as he does when not threatened. Individuals in a firm who are operating more or less continually under threat will have correspondingly limited perceptual behavior. Surely this is a factor of importance in any theory which attempts to account for the behavior of firms when dealing with crucial problems under threatening conditions.

Persistence of Perceptual Framework

The great attachment man has for his perceptual framework can scarcely be overemphasized. He is highly reluctant to give up any of his perceptions, his organized whole, his models which seem to work. If a frame of reference for perception allows the individual to operate without too much stress and without blocking him with too many problems, he will cling vigorously to that perceptual frame. One of man's strongest desires is for the security of an ordered environment. According to Haire, "man is reluctant to give up any organizations that seem to work, because of the danger that is involved in being lost in a disorganized environment" (*op. cit.*, p. 41). Man does not wish to upset areas of order except when forced to do so, even though such order may be only illusional. Since a man's own self-concept is involved in that perceptual frame, giving up his perceptual frame may mean giving up his sense of his own identity and meaningfulness. Thus, in many businesses, we observe that outmoded techniques continue to be retained longer than the concept of "maximization of profit" and other traditional concepts of firm behavior would suggest.

MOTIVATION

In the search for a theory of firm behavior, it is also important to be aware of certain assumptions about human "motivation." It no longer appears possible to assume that executives and managers are simply embodiments of the motivation for profit maximization and that their behavior can be explained merely in terms of this single motive. In order to attempt to understand the behavior of businessmen, we must take into account other concepts of motivation.

It should be noted at the outset, however, that concepts of motivation cannot be separated from related concepts of perception. The separation of these two aspects of behavior for the purposes of this discussion should be considered as a method which, although useful in analysis, is somewhat unrealistic, in that behavior is "seamless."

Definition of "Motive"

The idea of a "motive" is so common in lay conversation and thinking that it might be well to outline briefly the concept of motivation as it is used here. Motivation may be meaningfully discussed from two angles. First, it may be discussed in terms of its internal aspect, its reference to a state of inner dissatisfaction, a state of needs, wants, or desires, a state in which bodily energy is mobilized, a state of a drive which the organism is impelled to relieve. Secondly, motivation may be discussed from its outer aspect, as a sequence of behavior selectively directed in terms of a goal. Goal, then, refers to the outer directional aspect of behavior in a given situation. Thus, we may define motivation as characterized both by a state of drive and by the direction of behavior toward some goal selected in preference to other possible goals. Since all theories do not give equal emphasis to these two aspects of motivation, let us begin by considering the two approaches separately.

"Inner Motivation": Emphasis on the Individual

One widely accepted concept is that all persons are motivated by certain needs. Various lists of such needs have been advanced by a number of investigators, and though we find differences among the lists, they are generally similar. Perhaps most investigators would agree upon this basic list of needs: physiological needs (need for air, food, water, etc.), social needs (need to belong to a group and to have social relations with others), and ego or individual needs (need for approval, acceptance, mastery, etc.). There are certainly many longer lists which include such items as need for security, need for wider experience, need for a sense of meaningfulness, etc. Theodore Brammeld, however, considers a list of even three needs too long, since it implies that man is somehow composed of separate compartments. Brammeld points out that there is no sense of ego separate from the socially perceived ego; and therefore the self is a social self. Further, the physical components of the organism cannot be separated from the mental or psychological components. Brammeld therefore suggests that man has but one basic drive or motivating force: "social self-realization" (1956, p. 119).

The assumption that businessmen are motivated for maximization of profit is very different from the assumption that men have certain basic needs or drives seeking fulfillment. Maximization of profit certainly may serve in some ways several of these physiological, social and ego needs, but it is evident that other channels as well present themselves as means for serving these drives in the atmosphere of the business organization. Some of the opportunities for serving man's needs may be in actual conflict with the firm's maximization of profit.

"Outer Motivation": Emphasis on the Situation

On the other end of the continuum there are those theorists who see motivation as having its roots primarily in the situation or in environment. Karl Mannheim, a representative of this view, states that "both motives and actions very often originate not from within but from the situation in which individuals find themselves" (1940, p. 249). Allport suggests that "situational variability has led many social scientists to the conviction that any search for a consistent personality with specifiable motives and traits is doomed to failure" (1956, p. 243). He goes on to quote William James to the effect that each situation has different motives: "A man has as many selves as there are distinct groups about whose opinion he cares" (p. 244). When considering the motives of businessmen, one must be aware of the influence of the business situation. At the same time, it is a dangerous generalization to assume that any two situations are ever the same or that any two individual businessmen will perceive any situation in exactly the same way, or even that one businessman will perceive the same situation the same way on two different occasions. Further, it may be readily seen that the business environment may provide many motives for the individual in addition to that of profit maximization. The businessman may be motivated by titles, large offices, or personal friendships as well as by his personal or family security. Such motives may have no direct connection with the goals of the firm.

Role Theory in Relation to Motivation

This emphasis on the situation borders on the concept of "role theory," which assumes that individuals take on certain motives as they assume different roles. A "role" is defined by Sargent as "a pattern or type of social behavior which seems situationally appropriate to the individual in terms of the demands and expectations of those in his group" (1950, p. 279). Role theory suggests that as the individual's position in the group changes, his motivations may also change. Mannheim, for example, posits that businessmen change their motives as they assume different roles on the way up the business ladder. "There is normally a graduated scale of motives by which men from different social classes are driven to work. . . . Whenever a man rises to a higher class . . . he switches over from one set of motives to another" (Mannheim, *op. cit.*, p. 316). It should be noted however that not all writers on role theory place this much emphasis on role as a motivating factor. The sociologist Nelson Foote, for example, states that "roles as such do not provide their own motives" (1951, p. 14). Mason Haire suggests that the "social definition" of a role is not specific enough to completely govern the behavior of an individual (*op. cit.*, p. 184). According to Herbert Simon: "Any particular concrete behavior is a resultant of a large number of premises, only some of which are prescribed by the role" (1959, p. 274). Although role theory does not appear to give a total explanation to individual motivation in a particular setting, it does suggest one additional source of motivation. If we can become aware of how individuals perceive their role at a particular time, we may be able to gain insight into behavior at that time.

Middle of the Continuum

A number of writers stress the importance of understanding both the "inner" individual and the "outer" situation in order to understand the motivation of the individual. George Kelly, while stating that a knowledge of the situation is essential to understanding psychological motives involved (1958, p. 63), indicates the reciprocal relationship between the two. Allport is another who gives both factors weight: "The perceiver himself may . . . be the principal source of variance; the situation in which the object-person acts may be the second source of variance; and the fixed traits and motives of the object-person may be only a minor factor" (*op. cit.*, p. 243).

Complexity and Multiplicity of Motivations

Traditional economists suggest a single business motivation, that of profit maximization. Recent psychological and sociological research, however, seems to indicate the interrelatedness of motives. Maslow, as a result of his investigations, concludes: "Most behavior is multimotivated. Within the sphere of motivational determinants, any behavior tends to be determined by several or all the basic needs simultaneously rather than by any one of them" (1954, p. 102). According to Allport, "It seems clear that the units we seek in personality and in motivation are relatively complex structures, not molecular" (*op. cit.*, p. 242). An attempt to explain business behavior based on a single overriding motive appears unrealistic in view of current research. A businessman's personal goals probably are not the same as those of the "organization," and, in fact, as Festinger points out, the satisfaction of either the goals of the business or of the individual may prohibit the satisfaction of the other's goals (1958, pp. 65–86). However, Festinger also suggests that in a situation in which the goals of the individual conflict with the goals of the firm, "there will be some tendency for the person to attempt to change one of them so that they do fit together, thus reducing or eliminating the dissonance" (p. 70). Yet it may be the organizational goals he attempts to change in favor of his own.

Aspiration Level

One aspect of motivation which has received some attention recently and which proponents feel offers considerable insight into understanding and predicting human behavior is the concept of "level of aspiration." J. D. Frank, an early writer on this concept, defines "level of aspiration" as "the level of future performance in a familiar task which an individual, knowing his level of past performance in that task, explicitly undertakes to reach" (1935, p. 119). Kurt Lewin found from his experiments that "success and failure influence deeply the emotional staus of the person, his goals, and his social relations. . . . After success, a person generally sets himself a higher goal. After failure, his level of aspiration generally goes down" (1936, p. 926). Lewin states: "The stronger the success the greater will be the percentage of raising the level of aspiration, and the stronger the failure the greater the percent of lowering the level of aspiration" (1944, p. 338). Simon stresses the correspondence of the two from his findings, stating: "In the long run the level of aspiration and attainable maximum will be very close together" (*op. cit.*, p. 272). Such findings suggest that if we know the level of aspiration of a particular businessman we could begin to predict his behavior in certain situations. For example, if the owner of a construction firm had aspirations of a future large job, such an individual might retain his employees in relation to such aspirations rather than let workers go when work is slack. In such a case, prediction of behavior in terms of aspiration levels might be considerably different from a prediction in terms of maximization of profit.

The concept of "aspiration level," however, is not without criticism. John Gardner suggests that there may be a "region" of aspiration or a "direction" of aspiration, but that a "level" does not appear to be a realistic term. He views the concept of a "level of aspiration" as an attempt to quantify something which is qualitative. He also suggests that there may be two or more aspiration levels operating in an individual at a particular time (1958, pp. 229–34). Katona questions the concept of individual "levels of aspirations" in that "aspirations are influenced by the performance of the members of the group to which one belongs" (1953, p. 316). Here again we are confronted with those internal-external factors of motivation discussed earlier. Nevertheless, the concept of "level of aspiration" with regard to motivation is a concept which must be faced by businessmen and economists in attempting to develop a general theory of firm behavior.

In summary, it may be said that modern psychological concepts of motivation do not support the traditional economic theory that firm behavior may be explained by the single motivation of maximization of profit. Human motivation is not single but complex, and even conflicting. Further, human motives based on a number of needs or drives may well be satisfied through the firm in ways other than through maximization of profit.

COMMENTS

Having presented some general concepts in the theories of perception and motivation, we must point out that although the two subjects were separated for the purposes of analysis, they are inherently interrelated, and their contributions toward an understanding of firm behavior are of the same nature. There are, however, certain limitations to the usefulness of the concepts of perception and motivation.

Problems in Ascertaining Motivations and Perceptions

Probably the most serious limitations of these theories involve the difficulty of ascertaining perceptions and motivations. Two methods for determining perceptions and motivations are (1) to have the individual state what his motivations are and how he sees or perceives the world, or (2) to observe overt actions and draw assumptions from these actions.

A problem in the first method is that we are faced with the task of interpreting the individual's statement about his motivations. Even though he desired to communicate his perceptions and motivations accurately, we find that his word symbols for his subjective experiences may be difficult to interpret with assurance. The problem is further complicated because of the fact that an individual's verbal behavior is not necessarily indicative of his attitudes. Behavior which is visible to others may be "edited" so that it appears acceptable to others. A number of writers have asked businessmen what their motives are, yet the results may be no more valuable than the original concept of profit maximization (see Hickman and Kuhn, 1956, Ch. 2).

The second alternative for ascertaining perceptions and motivations—that of observing behavior—adds the problem of the projection of the motivations and perceptions of the observer on to the observed and the fact that the observations are recorded in the vocabulary of the observer rather than that of the observed. As noted above, the observer may influence the data with his own specific, individualized meaning.

Other Criticisms of Motivation and Perception Theory

Certain aspects of motivation theory have been criticized on several grounds other than the difficulty of ascertainment. Maslow has stated that "too many of the findings that have been made in animals have been proven to be true only for animals and not for human beings. There is no reason whatsoever why we should start with animals in order to study human motivation" (*op. cit.*, pp. 103–4). This criticism seems to suggest that much of the investigation about theories of motivation has been "zoo-morphic." Maslow also points out that many of the findings in motivation theory have come from the study of seriously disturbed people and that these generalizations may not hold true for individuals who appear to be able to cope with society, e.g., businessmen. Further, motivation theory has been criticized as being static, i.e., based on a premise of static properties in individuals. Finally, as has been suggested previously, motivation theory has been criticized as being highly prone to the dangers of projection. It has been suggested that possibly we can tell more about the person who attributes certain motives to another than we can about the person to whom the motives were attributed. Methods of investigating motivations must involve specific means of offsetting the dangers presented above.

Despite certain specific criticism of motivation theory, however, it seems to be well established that human motivation is so complex that no single explanation of motivation, such as that of profit maximization, can be applied to all businessmen or to all business behavior. It may be difficult to accommodate ourselves to this conclusion, however, because it makes the building of a "tight" business model very difficult.

CONCLUSION

The problem of building a theory of firm behavior *today* can readily be seen to be highly complex. It is possible that, in a previous era, motivation of the individual in the firm could have been conceived in more singular terms than it is today. Indeed, Schumpeter points out that during the late nineteenth century a primary emphasis of the businessman appeared to be the acquisition of a large home, a large family, and a large estate to leave to his descendants (1950, pp. 156–63). Thus, perhaps it is possible that during the late nineteenth century the motivations of businessmen could be explained in more single terms, for example, by the motive of profit maximization, than they may be today. However, the problem of constructing a theory of firm behavior, in view of recent investigations into individual perception and behavior, can no longer be resolved by the simple positing of a single and rational profit motive.

Nevertheless, while the explanation of business motivation in terms of a single primary motivation of profit maximization appears to be an unwarranted oversimplification of business behavior, we cannot altogether reject the profit motive as an important factor in business behavior. As Katona stated: "There can be no doubt that in present-day American business thinking the function and role of profits is substantial" (1951, p. 194). What must be thrown open to question and further investigation is the extent to which actions of businessmen can be explained by the profit motive as well as by the many other motives that propel human behavior.

This article has presented some of the current investigations into motivation and perception which must be considered in constructing a new theory of firm behavior. It may be seen that perception and motivation theories do not in themselves provide a ready-made general theory of firm behavior applicable to all situations. It may be, in fact, that such an all-encompassing theory is not feasible. Katona suggests that "the proximate aim of scientific research is a body of empirically validatable generalizations and not a theory that is validated under any and all circumstances" (1953, p. 317). Yet, in the search for a variety of such generalizations capable of explaining behavior under given circumstances, motivation and perception theory will offer considerable insight into firm behavior.

REFERENCES

Allport, Gordon W. "What Units Shall We Employ?" In *Assessment of Human Motives*, ed. Gardner Lindzey. Holt, 1958.

Bakke, E. Wight. *Organization and the Individual*. Yale University Labor and Management Center, 1952.

Brammeld, Theodore. *Toward a Reconstructed Philosophy of Education*. Dryden, 1956.

Festinger, Leon. "The Motivating Effect of Cognitive Dissonance." In *Assessment of Human Motives*, ed. Gardner Lindzey, Holt, 1958.

Foote, Nelson N. "Identification as the Basis for a Theory of Motivation." *American Sociological Review*, Vol. 16, No. 1, February 1951.
Frank, J. D. "Individual Differences in Certain Aspects of the Level of Aspiration." *American Journal of Psychology*, Vol. 45, 1935.
Gardner, John W. "The Use of the Term 'Level of Aspiration.'" In *Understanding Human Motivation*, eds. C. L. Stacey and M. F. Martino. Howard Allen, 1958.
Haire, Mason. *Psychology in Management*. McGraw-Hill, 1956.
Hickman, C. A., and M. H. Kuhn. *Individuals, Groups, and Economic Behavior*. Dryden, 1956.
Horney, Karen. *The Neurotic Personality of Our Time*. Norton, 1937.
Katona, George. "Rational Behavior and Economic Behavior." *Psychological Review*, July 1953.
——. *Psychological Analysis of Economic Behavior*. McGraw-Hill, 1951.
Kelly, George A. "Man's Construction of His Alternatives." In *Assessment of Human Motives*, ed. Gardner Lindzey. Holt, 1958.
Lewin, Kurt. "Psychology of Success and Failure." *Occupations*, Vol. 14, No. 9, June 1936.
Lewin, Kurt, Tamara Dembo, Leon Festinger, and Pauline Sears. "Level of Aspiration." In *Personality and the Behavior Disorders*, ed. J. McV. Hunt. Howard Allen, 1958 (2 vols).
Mannheim, Karl. *Man and Society in an Age of Reconstruction*. Harcourt, 1940.
Maslow, A. H. *Motivation and Personality*. Harper, 1954.
Sargent, S. Stansfeld. *Social Psychology: An Integrative Interpretation*. Ronald, 1950.
Schumpeter, Joseph A. *Capitalism, Socialism, and Democracy*, 3rd ed. Harper & Row, 1950.
Simon, Herbert A. "Decision Making in Economics." *American Economic Review*, June 1959.
——. *Models of Man: Social and Rational*. Wiley, 1957.
Wittreich, Warren J. "Visual Perception and Personality" *Scientific American*, April 1959.

ABRAHAM MASLOW

A Theory of Human Motivation

DYNAMICS OF THE BASIC NEEDS

The "Physiological" Needs

The needs that are usually taken as the starting point for motivation theory are the so-called physiological drives. Two recent lines of research make it necessary to revise our customary notions about these needs: first, the development of the concept of homeostasis, and, second, the finding that appetites (preferential choices among foods) are a fairly efficient indication of actual needs or lacks in the body.

Homeostasis refers to the body's automatic efforts to maintain a constant, normal state of the blood stream. Cannon (1932) has described this process for (1) the water content of the blood, (2) salt content, (3) sugar content, (4) protein content, (5) fat content, (6) calcium content, (7) oxygen content, (8) constant hydrogen-ion level (acid-base balance) and (9) constant temperature of the blood. Obviously this list can be extended to include other minerals, the hormones, vitamins, etc.

Young, in a recent article (1941, pp. 129–64), has summarized the work on appetite in its relation to body needs. If the body lacks some chemical, the individual will tend to develop a specific appetite or partial hunger for that food element.

Thus it seems impossible as well as useless to make any list of fundamental physiological needs for they can come to almost any number one might wish, depending on the degree of specificity of description. We cannot identify all physiological needs as homeostatic. That sexual desire, sleepiness, sheer activity, and maternal behavior in animals are homeostatic has not yet been demonstrated. Furthermore, this list would not include the various sensory pleasures (tastes, smells, tickling, stroking) which are probably physiological and which may become the goals of motivated behavior.

In a previous paper (Maslow, 1943, pp. 85–92) it has been pointed out that these physiological drives or needs are to be considered unusual rather than typical because they are isolable and because they are localizable somatically. That is to say, they are relatively independent of each other, of other motivations and of the organism as a whole, and, in many cases, it is possible to demonstrate a localized, underlying somatic base for the drive. This is true less generally than has been thought (exceptions are fatigue, sleepiness, maternal responses), but it is still true in the classic instances of hunger, sex, and thirst.

It should be pointed out again that any of the physiological needs and the consummatory behavior involved with them serve as channels for all sorts of other needs as well. The person who thinks he is hungry may actually be seeking more for comfort or dependence than for vitamins or proteins. Conversely, it is possible to satisfy the hunger need in part by other activities, such as drinking water or smoking cigarettes. In other words, these physiological needs are only relatively isolable.

Undoubtedly these physiological needs are the most prepotent of all needs. What this means specifically is that, in the human being who is missing everything in life in an extreme fashion, it is most likely that the major motivation would be the physiological needs rather than any others. A person who is lacking food, safety, love, and esteem would most probably hunger for food more strongly than for anything else.

If all the needs are unsatisfied, and the organism is then dominated by the physiological needs, all other needs may become simply non-existent or be pushed into the background. It is then fair to characterize the whole organism by saying simply that it is hungry, for consciousness is almost completely pre-empted by hunger. All capacities are put into the service of hunger-satisfaction, and the organization of these capacities is almost entirely deter-

---

mined by the one purpose of satisying hunger. The receptors and effectors, the intelligence, memory, habits, all may now be defined simply as hunger-gratifying tools. Capacities that are not useful for this purpose lie dormant or are pushed into the background. The urge to write poetry, the desire to acquire an automobile, the interest in American history, the desire for a new pair of shoes are, in the extreme case, forgotten or become of secondary importance. For the man who is extremely and dangerously hungry, no other interests exist but food. He dreams food, he remembers food, he thinks about food, he emotes only about food, he perceives only food, and he wants only food. The more subtle determinants that ordinarily fuse with the physiological drives in organizing even feeding, drinking, or sexual behavior may now be so completely overwhelmed as to allow us to speak at this time (but *only* at this time) of pure hunger drive and behavior, with the one unqualified aim of relief.

Another peculiar characteristic of the human organism when it is dominated by a certain need is that the whole philosophy of the future tends also to change. For our chronically and extremely hungry man, utopia can be defined very simply as a place where there is plenty of food. He tends to think that, if only he is guaranteed food for the rest of his life, he will be perfectly happy and will never want anything more. Life itself tends to be defined in terms of eating. Anything else will be defined as unimportant. Freedom, love, community feeling, respect, philosophy, may all be waved aside as fripperies which are useless, since they fail to fill the stomach. Such a man may fairly be said to live by bread alone.

It cannot possibly be denied that such things are true, but their *generality* can be denied. Emergency conditions are, almost by definition, rare in the normally functioning peaceful society. That this truism can be forgotten is due mainly to two reasons. First, rats have few motivations other than physiological ones, and since so much of the research upon motivation has been made with these animals, it is easy to carry the rat-picture over to the human being. Second, it is too often not realized that culture itself is an adaptive tool, one of whose main functions is to make the physiological emergencies come less and less often. In most of the known societies, chronic extreme hunger of the emergency type is rare rather than common. In any case, this is still true in the United States. The average American citizen is experiencing appetite rather than hunger when he says, "I am hungry." He is apt to experience sheer life-and-death hunger only by accident and then only a few times through his entire life.

Obviously a good way to obscure the "higher" motivations, and to get a lopsided view of human capacities and human nature, is to make the organism extremely and chronically hungry or thirsty. Anyone who attempts to make an emergency picture into a typical one and who will measure all of man's goals and desires by his behavior during extreme physiological deprivation is certainly being blind to many things. It is quite true that man lives by bread alone—when there is no bread. But what happens to man's desires when there *is* plenty of bread and when his belly is chronically filled?

At once other (and "higher") needs emerge and these, rather than physiological hungers, dominate the organism. And when these in turn are satisfied, again new (and still "higher") needs emerge, and so on. This is what we mean by saying that the basic human needs are organized into a hierarchy of relative prepotency.

One main implication of this phrasing is that gratification becomes as important a concept as deprivation in motivation theory, for it releases the organism from the domination of a relatively more physiological need, permitting thereby the emergence of other, more social goals. The physiological needs, along with their partial goals, when chronically gratified cease to exist only in a potential fashion in the sense that they may emerge again to dominate the organism if they are thwarted. But a want that is satisfied is no longer a want. The organism is dominated and its behavior organized only by unsatisfied needs. If hunger is satisfied, it becomes unimportant in the current dynamics of the individual.

This statement is somewhat qualified by a hypothesis to be discussed more fully later, namely, that it is precisely those individuals in whom a certain need has always been satisifed who are best equipped to tolerate deprivation of that need in the future; furthermore, those who have been deprived in the past will react to current satisfactions differently from the one who has never been deprived.

The Safety Needs

If the physiological needs are relatively well gratified, there then emerges a new set of needs, which we may categorize roughly as the safety needs. All that has been said of the physiological needs is equally true, although in lesser degree, of these desires. The organism may equally well be wholly dominated by them. They may serve as the almost exclusive organizers of behavior, recruiting all the capacities of the organism in their service, and we may then fairly describe the whole organism as a safety-seeking mechanism. Again we may say of the receptors, the effectors, of the intellect and the other capacities that they are primarily safety-seeking tools. Again, as in the hungry man, we find that the dominating goal is a strong determinant not only of his current world-outlook and philosophy but also of his philosophy of the future. Practically everything looks less important than safety (even sometimes the physiological needs, which, being satisfied, are now underestimated). A man in this state, if it is extreme enough and chronic enough, may be characterized as living almost for safety alone.

Although in this paper we are interested primarily in the needs of the adult, we can approach an understanding of his safety needs perhaps more efficiently by observation of infants and children, in whom these needs are much more simple and obvious. One reason for the clearer appearance of the threat or danger reaction in infants is that they do not inhibit this reaction at all, whereas adults in our society have been taught to inhibit it at all costs. Thus even when adults do feel their safety to be threatened, we may not be able to see this on the surface. Infants will react in a total fashion, and as if they were endangered, if they are disturbed or dropped suddenly, startled by loud noises, flashing light, or other sensory stimulation, by rough handling, by general loss of support in the mother's arms, or by inadequate support.[1]

In infants we can also see a much more direct reaction to bodily illnesses of various kinds. Sometimes these illnesses seem to be immediately and per se threatening and seem to make the child feel unsafe. For instance, vomiting, colic, or other sharp pains seem to make the child look at the whole world in a

---

[1] As the child grows up, sheer knowledge and familiarity as well as better motor development make these "dangers" less and less dangerous and more and more manageable. Throughout life it may be said that one of the main conative functions of education is this neutralizing of apparent dangers through knowledge, e.g., I am not afraid of thunder because I know something about it.

different way At such a moment of pain, it may be postulated that, for the child, the appearance of the whole world suddenly changes from sunniness to darkness, so to speak, and becomes a place in which anything at all might happen, in which previously stable things have suddenly become unstable. Thus a child who because of some bad food is taken ill may, for a day or two, develop fear, nightmares, and a need for protection and reassurance never seen in him before his illness.

Another indication of the child's need for safety is his preference for some kind of undisrupted routine or rhythm. He seems to want a predictable, orderly world. For instance, injustice, unfairness, or inconsistency in the parents seems to make a child feel anxious and unsafe. This attitude may be not so much because of the injustice per se or any particular pains involved, but rather because this treatment threatens to make the world look unreliable or unsafe or unpredictable. Young children seem to thrive better under a system which has at least a skeletal outline of rigidity, in which there is a schedule of a kind, some sort of routine, something that can be counted upon, not only for the present, but also far into the future. Perhaps one could express this more accurately by saying that the child needs an organized world rather than an unorganized or unstructured one.

The central role of the parents and the normal family setup are indisputable. Quarreling, physical assault, separation, divorce, or death within the family may be particularly terrifying. Also parental outbursts of rage or threats of punishment directed to the child, calling him names, speaking to him harshly, shaking him, handling him roughly, or actual physical punishment sometimes elicit such total panic and terror in the child that we must assume more is involved than the physical pain alone. While it is true that in some children this terror may represent also a fear of loss of parental love, it can also occur in completely rejected children, who seem to cling to the hating parents more for sheer safety and protection than because of hope of love.

Confronting the average child with new, unfamiliar, strange, unmanageable stimuli or situations will too frequently elicit the danger or terror reaction, as, for example, getting lost or even being separated from the parents for a short time, being confronted with new faces, new situations, or new tasks, the sight of strange, unfamiliar or uncontrollable objects, illness, or death. Particularly at such times, the child's frantic clinging to his parents is eloquent testimony to their role as protectors (quite apart from their roles as food-givers and love-givers).

From these and similar observations, we may generalize and say that the average child in our society usually prefers a safe, orderly, predictable, organized world which he can count on and in which unexpected, unmanageable, or other dangerous things do not happen and in which, in any case, he has all-powerful parents who protect and shield him from harm.

That these reactions may so easily be observed in children is in a way a proof of the fact that children in our society feel too unsafe (or, in a word, are badly brought up). Children who are reared in an unthreatening, loving family do *not* ordinarily react as we have described above (see Shirley, 1942, pp. 201–17). In such children the danger reactions are apt to come mostly to objects or situations that adults too would consider dangerous.[2]

[2] A "test battery" for safety might be confronting the child with a small exploding firecracker or with a bewhiskered face, having the mother leave the room, putting him upon a high ladder, giving him a hypodermic injection, having a mouse crawl up to him,

The healthy, normal, fortunate adult in our culture is largely satisfied in his safety needs. The peaceful, smoothly running, "good" society ordinarily makes its members feel safe enough from wild animals, extremes of temperature, criminals, assault and murder, tyranny, etc. Therefore, in a very real sense, they no longer have any safety needs as active motivators. Just as a sated man no longer feels hungry, a safe man no longer feels endangered. If we wish to see these needs directly and clearly, we must turn to neurotic or near-neurotic individuals, and to the economic and social underdogs. In between these extremes, we can perceive the expressions of safety needs only in such phenomena as, for instance, the common preference for a job with tenure and protection, the desire for a savings account, and for insurance of various kinds (medical, dental, unemployment, disability, old age).

Other broader aspects of the attempt to seek safety and stability in the world are seen in the very common preference for familiar rather than unfamiliar things, or for the known rather than the unknown. The tendency to have some religion or world-philosophy that organizes the universe and the men in it into some sort of satisfactorily coherent, meaningful whole is also in part motivated by safety-seeking. Here too we may list science and philosophy in general as partially motivated by the safety needs (we shall see later that there are also other motivations to scientific, philosophical, or religious endeavor).

Otherwise the need for safety is seen as an active and dominant mobilizer of the organism's resources only in emergencies, e.g., war, disease, natural catastrophes, crime waves, societal disorganization, neurosis, brain injury—chronically bad situations.

Some neurotic adults in our society are, in many ways, like the unsafe child in their desire for safety, although in the former it takes on a somewhat special appearance. They often react to unknown, psychological dangers in a world that is perceived to be hostile, overwhelming and threatening. Such a person behaves as if a great catastrophe were almost always impending, i.e., he is usually responding as if to an emergency. His safety needs often find specific expression in a search for a protector, or a stronger person on whom he may depend, or perhaps a *Führer*.

The neurotic individual may be described in a slightly different way, with some usefulness, as a grown-up person who retains his childish attitudes toward the world. That is to say, a neurotic adult may be said to behave "as if" he were actually afraid of a spanking or of his mother's disapproval or of being abandoned by his parents or of having his food taken away from him. It is as if his childish attitudes of fear and threat reaction to a dangerous world had gone underground and, untouched by the growing up and learning processes, were now ready to be called out by any stimulus that would make a child feel endangered and threatened.[3]

The neurosis in which the search for safety takes its clearest form is the compulsive-obsessive neurosis. Compulsive-obsessives try frantically to order and stabilize the world so that no unmanageable, unexpected, or unfamiliar dangers will ever appear (see Maslow and Mittelmann, 1941). They hedge themselves about with all sorts of ceremonials, rules, and formulas so that every

---

etc. Of course I cannot seriously recommend the deliberate use of such "tests," for they might very well harm the child being tested. But these and similar situations come up by the score in the child's ordinary day-to-day living and may be observed. There is no reason why these stimuli should not be used with, for example, young chimpanzees.

[3] Not all neurotic individuals feel unsafe. Neurosis may have at its core a thwarting of the affection and esteem needs in a person who is generally safe.

possible contingency may be provided for and so that no new contingencies may appear. They are much like the brain-injured cases, described by Goldstein (1939), who manage to maintain their equilibrium by avoiding everything unfamiliar and strange and by ordering their restricted world in such a neat, disciplined, orderly fashion that everything in the world can be counted upon. They try to arrange the world so that anything unexpected (dangers) cannot possibly occur. If, through no fault of their own, something unexpected does occur, they go into a panic reaction as if this unexpected occurrence constituted a grave danger. What we can see only as a none-too-strong preference in the healthy person, e.g., preference for the familiar, becomes a life-and-death necessity in abnormal cases.

The Love Needs

If both the physiological and the safety needs are fairly well gratified, then there will emerge the love and affection and belongingness needs, and the whole cycle already described will repeat itself with this new center. Now the person will feel keenly, as never before, the absence of friends or a sweetheart or a wife or children. He will hunger for affectionate relations with people in general, namely, for a place in his group, and he will strive with great intensity to achieve this goal. He will want to attain such a place more than anything else in the world and may even forget that once, when he was hungry, he sneered at love.

In our society the thwarting of these needs is the most commonly found core in cases of maladjustment and more severe psychopathology. Love and affection, as well as their possible expression in sexuality, are generally looked upon with ambivalence and are customarily hedged about with many restrictions and inhibitions. Practically all theorists of psychopathology have stressed thwarting of the love needs as basic in the picture of maladjustment. Many clinical studies have therefore been made of this need and we know more about it, perhaps, than any of the other needs except the physiological ones (see Maslow and Mittelmann, *op. cit.*).

One thing that must be stressed at this point is that love is not synonymous with sex. Sex may be studied as a purely physiological need. Ordinarily sexual behavior is multi-determined, that is to say, determined not only by sexual but also by other needs, chief among which are the love and affection needs. Also not to be overlooked is the fact that the love needs involve both giving *and* receiving love (see Maslow, 1942, pp. 331–44; and Plant, 1937, Ch. 5).

The Esteem Needs

All people in our society (with a few pathological exceptions) have a need or desire for a stable, firmly based (usually) high evaluation of themselves, for self-respect, or self-esteem, and for the esteem of others. By firmly based self-esteem, we mean that which is soundly based upon real capacity, achievement, and respect from others. These needs may be classified into two subsidiary sets. These are, first, the desire for strength, for achievement, for adequacy, for confidence in the face of the world, and for independence and freedom.[4] Second, we have what we may call the desire for reputation or prestige (defining it as respect or esteem from other people), recognition,

[4] Whether or not this particular desire is universal we do not know. The crucial question, especially important today, is "Will men who are enslaved and dominated

attention, importance, or appreciation.[5] These needs have been relatively stressed by Alfred Adler and his followers, and have been relatively neglected by Freud and the psychoanalysts. More and more today, however, there is appearing widespread appreciation of their central importance.

Satisfaction of the self-esteem need leads to feelings of self-confidence, worth, strength, capability, and adequacy, of being useful and necessary in the world. But thwarting of these needs produces feelings of inferiority, of weakness, and of helplessness. These feelings in turn give rise to either basic discouragement or else compensatory or neurotic trends. An appreciation of the necessity of basic self-confidence and an understanding of how helpless people are without it can be easily gained from a study of severe traumatic neurosis (Kardiner, 1941).[6]

The Need for Self-Actualization

Even if all these needs are satisfied, we may still often (if not always) expect that a new discontent and restlessness will soon develop, unless the individual is doing what he is fitted for. A musician must make music, an artist must paint, a poet must write, if he is to be ultimately happy. What a man *can* be, he *must* be. This need we may call self-actualization.

This term, first coined by Kurt Goldstein, is being used in this paper in a much more specific and limited fashion. It refers to the desire for self-fulfilment, namely, to the tendency for one to become actualized in what one is potentially. This tendency might be phrased as the desire to become more and more what one is, to become everything that one is capable of becoming.

The specific form that these needs take will of course vary greatly from person to person. In one individual it may be expressed maternally, as the desire to be an ideal mother, in another athletically, in still another aesthetically, in the painting of pictures, and in another inventively in the creation of new contrivances. It is not necessarily a creative urge, although in people who have any capabilities for creation it will take this form.

The clear emergence of these needs rests upon prior satisfaction of the physiological, safety, love and esteem needs. We shall call people who are satisfied in these needs basically satisfied people, and it is from these that we may expect the fullest (and healthiest) creativeness.[7] Since, in our society,

---

inevitably feel dissatisfied and rebellious?" We may assume on the basis of commonly known clinical data that a man who has known true freedom (not paid for by giving up safety and security but rather built on the basis of adequate safety and security) will not willingly or easily allow his freedom to be taken away from him. But we do not know that this is true for the person born into slavery. The events of the next decade should give us our answer. See the discussion of this problem in Fromm (1941), Ch. 5.

[5] Perhaps the desire for prestige and respect from others is subsidiary to the desire for self-esteem or confidence in one's self. Observation of children seems to indicate that this is so, but clinical data give no clear support of such a conclusion.

[6] For more extensive discussion of normal self-esteem, as well as for reports of various researches, see Maslow (1939), pp. 3–39.

[7] Clearly creative behavior, like painting, is like any other behavior in having multiple determinants. It may be seen in "innately creative" people whether they are satisfied or not, happy or unhappy, hungry or sated. Also, it is clear that creative activity may be compensatory, ameliorative, or purely economic. It is my impression (as yet unconfirmed) that it is possible to distinguish the artistic and intellectual products of basically satisfied people from those of basically unsatisfied people by inspection alone. In any case, here too we must distinguish, in a dynamic fashion, the overt behavior itself from its various motivations or purposes.

basically satisfied people are the exception, we do not know much about self-actualization, either experimentally or clinically. It remains a challenging problem for research.

There are certain conditions which are immediate prerequisites for the basic need satisfactions. Danger to these is reacted to almost as if it were a direct danger to the basic needs themselves. Such conditions as freedom to speak, freedom to do what one wishes so long as no harm is done to others, freedom to express one's self, freedom to investigate and seek for information, freedom to defend one's self, justice, fairness, honesty, orderliness in the group are examples of such preconditions for basic need satisfactions. Thwarting of these freedoms will be reacted to with a threat or emergency response. These conditions are not ends in themselves but they are *almost* so, since they are so closely related to the basic needs, which are apparently the only ends in themselves. These conditions are defended because without them the basic satisfactions are quite impossible, or at least, very severely endangered.

If we remember that the cognitive capacities (perceptual, intellectual, learning) are a set of adjustive tools, which have, among other functions, that of satisfaction of our basic needs, then it is clear that any danger to them, any deprivation or blocking of their free use, must also be indirectly threatening to the basic needs themselves. Such a statement is a partial solution to the general problems of curiosity, the search for knowledge, truth, and wisdom, and the ever persistent urge to solve the cosmic mysteries.

We must therefore introduce another hypothesis and speak of degrees of closeness to the basic needs, for we have already pointed out that *any* conscious desires (partial goals) are more or less important as they are more or less close to the basic needs. The same statement may be made for various behavior acts. An act is psychologically important if it contributes directly to satisfaction of basic needs. The less directly it so contributes, or the weaker this contribution is, the less important this act must be conceived to be from the point of view of dynamic psychology. A similar statement may be made for the various defense or coping mechanisms. Some are very directly related to the protection or attainment of the basic needs, others are only weakly and distantly related. Indeed, if we wished, we could speak of more basic and less basic defense mechanisms and then affirm that danger to the more basic defenses is more threatening than danger to less basic defenses (always remembering that this is so only because of their relationship to the basic needs).

So far, we have mentioned the cognitive needs only in passing. Acquiring knowledge and systematizing the universe have been considered as, in part, techniques for the achievement of basic safety in the world, or, for the intelligent man, expressions of self-actualization. Also freedom of inquiry and expression have been discussed as preconditions of satisfactions of the basic needs. True though these formulations may be, they do not constitute definitive answers to the question as to the motivation role of curiosity, learning, philosophizing, experimenting, etc. They are, at best, no more than partial answers.

This question is especially difficult because we know so little about the facts. Curiosity, exploration, desire for the facts, desire to know may certainly be observed easily enough. The fact that they often are pursued even at great cost to the individual's safety is an earnest of the partial character of our previous discussion. In addition, the writer must admit that, though he has sufficient clinical evidence to postulate the desire to know as a very strong drive in intelligent people, no data are available for unintelligent people. It may then be largely a function of relatively high intelligence. Rather tentatively, then, and largely in the hope of stimulating discussion and research, we shall postulate a basic desire to know, to be aware of reality, to get the facts, to satisfy curiosity, or as Wertheimer phrases it, to see rather than to be blind.

This postulation, however, is not enough. Even after we know, we are impelled to know more and more minutely and microscopically, on the one hand, and, on the other, more and more extensively in the direction of a world philosophy, religion, etc. The facts that we acquire, if they are isolated or atomistic, inevitably get theorized about, and either analyzed or organized or both. This process has been phrased by some as the search for "meaning." We shall then postulate a desire to understand, to systematize, or organize, or analyze, to look for relations and meanings.

Once these desires are accepted for discussion, we see that they too form themselves into a small hierarchy in which the desire to know is prepotent over the desire to understand. All the characteristics of a hierarchy of prepotency that we have described above seem to hold for this one as well.

We must guard ourselves against the too easy tendency to separate these desires from the basic needs we have discussed above, i.e., to make a sharp dichotomy between "cognitive" and "conative" needs. The desire to know and to understand are themselves conative, i.e., have a striving character, and are as much personality needs as the "basic needs" we have already discussed (Wertheimer, unpublished lectures).

FURTHER CHARACTERISTICS OF THE BASIC NEEDS

The Degree of Fixity of the Hierarchy of Basic Needs

We have spoken so far as if this hierarchy were a fixed order but actually it is not nearly as rigid as we may have implied. It is true that most of the people with whom we have worked have seemed to have these basic needs in about the order that has been indicated. However, there have been a number of exceptions.

1. There are some people in whom, for instance, self-esteem seems to be more important than love. This most common reversal in the hierarchy is usually due to the development of the notion that the person who is most likely to be loved is a strong or powerful person, one who inspires respect or fear and who is self-confident or aggressive. Therefore, such people who lack love and seek it may try hard to put on a front of aggressive, confident behavior. But essentially they seek high self-esteem and its behavior expressions more as a means-to-an-end than for its own sake; they seek self-assertion for the sake of love rather than for self-esteem itself.

2. There are other, apparently innately creative people in whom the drive to creativeness seems to be more important than any other counterdeterminant. Their creativeness might appear as self-actualization released not by basic satisfaction but in spite of their lack of basic satisfaction.

3. In certain people the level of aspiration may be permanently deadened or lowered. That is to say, the less prepotent goals may simply be lost and may disappear forever, so that the person who has experienced life at a very low level, i.e., chronic unemployment, may continue to be satisfied for the rest of his life if only he can get enough food.

4. The so-called "psychopathic personality" is another example of permanent loss of the love needs. These are people who, according to the best data available

(see Levy 1937, pp. 643–52), have been starved for love in the earliest months of their lives and have simply lost forever the desire and the ability to give and to receive affection (as animals lose sucking or pecking reflexes that are not exercised soon enough after birth).

5. Another cause of reversal of the hierarchy is that when a need has been satisfied for a long time, this need may be underevaluated. People who have never experienced chronic hunger are apt to underestimate its effects and to look upon food as a rather unimportant thing. If they are dominated by a higher need, this higher need will seem to be the most important of all. It then becomes possible, and indeed does actually happen, that they may, for the sake of this higher need, put themselves into the position of being deprived in a more basic need. We may expect that after a long-time deprivation of the more basic need there will be a tendency to re-evaluate both needs so that the more prepotent need will actually become consciously prepotent for the individual who may have given it up very lightly. Thus, a man who has given up his job rather than lose his self-respect, and who then starves for six months or so, may be willing to take his job back even at the price of losing his self-respect.

6. Another partial explanation of *apparent* reversals is seen in the fact that we have been talking about the hierarchy of prepotency in terms of consciously felt wants or desires rather than of behavior. Looking at behavior itself may give us the wrong impression. What we have claimed is that the person will *want* the more basic of two needs when deprived in both. There is no necessary implication here that he will act upon his desires. Let us say again that there are many determinants of behavior other than needs and desires.

7. Perhaps more important than all these exceptions are the ones that involve ideals, high social standards, high values, and the like. With such values people become martyrs; they will give up everything for the sake of a particular ideal, or value. These people may be understood, at least in part, by reference to one basic concept (or hypothesis) which may be called "increased frustration-tolerance through early gratification." People who have been satisfied in their basic needs throughout their lives, particularly in their earlier years, seem to develop exceptional power to withstand present or future thwarting of these needs simply because they have strong, healthy character structure as a result of basic satisfaction. They are the "strong" people who can easily weather disagreement or opposition, who can swim against the stream of public opinion, and who can stand up for the truth at great personal cost. It is those who have loved and been well loved and who have had many deep friendships who can hold out against hatred, rejection or persecution.

I say all this in spite of the fact that there is a certain amount of sheer habituation which is also involved in any full discussion of frustration-tolerance. For instance, it is likely that those persons who have been accustomed to relative starvation for a long time are partially enabled thereby to withstand food deprivation. What sort of balance must be made between these two tendencies, of habituation on the one hand, and of past satisfaction breeding present frustration-tolerance on the other hand, remains to be worked out by further research. Meanwhile we may assume that they are both operative, side by side, since they do not contradict each other. In respect to this phenomenon of increased frustration-tolerance, it seems probable that the most important gratifications come in the first two years of life. That is to say, people who have been made secure and strong in the earliest years tend to remain secure and strong thereafter in the face of whatever threatens.

Degrees of Relative Satisfaction

So far, our theoretical discussion may have given the impression that these five sets of needs are somehow in a stepwise, all-or-none relationship to one another. We have spoken in such terms as the following: "If one need is satisfied, then another emerges." This statement might give the false impression that a need must be satisfied 100 percent before the next need emerges. In actual fact, most members of our society who are normal are partially satisfied in all their basic needs and partially unsatisfied in all their basic needs at the same time. A more realistic description of the hierarchy would be in terms of decreasing percentages of satisfaction as we go up the hierarchy of prepotency. For instance, if I may assign arbitrary figures for the sake of illustration, it is as if the average citizen is satisfied perhaps 85 percent in his physiological needs, 70 percent in his safety needs, 50 percent in his love needs, 40 percent in his self-esteem needs, and 10 percent in his self-actualization needs.

As for the concept of emergence of a new need after satisfaction of the prepotent needs, this emergence is not a sudden, saltatory phenomenon but rather a gradual emergence by slow degrees from nothingness. For instance, if prepotent need A is satisfied only 10 percent, then need B may not be visible at all. However, as this need A becomes satisfied 25 percent, need B may emerge 5 percent; as need A becomes satisfied 75 percent, need B may emerge 90 percent; and so on.

Unconscious Character of Needs

These needs are neither necessarily conscious nor unconscious. On the whole, however, in the average person, they are more often unconscious. It is not necessary at this point to overhaul the tremendous mass of evidence which indicates the crucial importance of unconscious motivation. It would by now be expected, on a priori grounds alone, that unconscious motivations would on the whole be rather more important than the conscious motivations. What we have called the basic needs are very often largely unconscious, although they may, with suitable techniques and with sophisticated people, become conscious.

The Role of Gratified Needs

It has been pointed out above several times that our higher needs usually emerge only when more prepotent needs have been gratified. Thus gratification has an important role in motivation theory. Apart from this, however, needs cease to play an active determining or organizing role as soon as they are gratified.

What this means, for example, is that a basically satisfied person no longer has the needs for esteem, love, safety, etc. The only sense in which he might be said to have them is in the almost metaphysical sense that a sated man has hunger or a filled bottle has emptiness. If we are interested in what *actually* motivates us and not in what has, will, or might motivate us, then a satisfied need is not a motivator. It must be considered, for all practical purposes, simply not to exist, to have disappeared. This point should be emphasized because it has been either overlooked or contradicted in every theory of motivation I know.[8] The

[8] Note that acceptance of this theory necessitates basic revision of the Freudian theory.

perfectly healthy, normal, fortunate man has no sex needs or hunger needs, or needs for safety or for love or for prestige or for self-esteem, except in stray moments of quickly passing threat. If we were to say otherwise, we should also have to aver that every man had all the pathological reflexes (e.g., Babinski, etc.), because if his nervous system were damaged, these would appear.

It is such considerations as these that suggest the bold postulation that a man who is thwarted in any of his basic needs may fairly be envisaged simply as a sick man. This is a fair parallel to our designation as "sick" of the man who lacks vitamins or minerals. Who is to say that a lack of love is less important than a lack of vitamins? Since we know the pathogenic effects of love starvation, who is to say that we are invoking value-questions in an unscientific or illegitimate way, any more than the physician does who diagnoses and treats pellagra or scurvy? If I were permitted this usage, I should then say simply that a healthy man is primarily motivated by his needs to develop and actualize his fullest potentialities and capacities. If a man has any other basic needs in any active, chronic sense, then he is simply an unhealthy man. He is as surely sick as if he had suddenly developed a strong salt-hunger or calcium hunger.[9]

If this statement seems unusual or paradoxical the reader may be assured that this is only one among many such paradoxes that will appear as we revise our ways of looking at man's deeper motivations. When we ask what man wants of life, we deal with his very essence.

SUMMARY

1. There are at least five sets of goals which we may call basic needs. These are, briefly, physiological, safety, love, esteem, and self-actualization. In addition, we are motivated by the desire to achieve or maintain the various conditions upon which these basic satisfactions rest and by certain more intellectual desires.
2. These basic goals are related to one another, being arranged in a hierarchy of prepotency. This means that the most prepotent goal will monopolize consciousness and will tend of itself to organize the recruitment of the various capacities of the organism. The less prepotent needs are minimized, even forgotten or denied. But when a need is fairly well satisfied, the next prepotent ("higher") need emerges, in turn to dominate the conscious life and to serve as the center of organization of behavior, since gratified needs are not active motivators.

   Thus man is a perpetually wanting animal. Ordinarily the satisfaction of these wants is not altogether mutually exclusive but only tends to be. The average member of our society is most often partially satisfied and partially unsatisfied in all of his wants. The hierarchy principle is usually empirically observed in terms of increasing percentages of non-satisfaction as we go up the hierarchy. Reversals of the average order of the hierarchy are sometimes observed. Also it has been observed that an individual may permanently lose

[9] If we were to use the "sick" in this way, we should then also have to face squarely the relations of man to his society. One clear implication of our definition would be that (1) since a man is to be called sick who is basically thwarted, and (2) since such basic thwarting is made possible ultimately only by forces outside the individual, then (3) sickness in the individual must come ultimately from a sickness in the society. The "good" or healthy society would then be defined as one that permitted man's highest purposes to emerge by satisfying all his prepotent basic needs.

the higher wants in the hierarchy under special conditions. There are not only ordinarily multiple motivations for usual behavior but, in addition, many determinants other than motives.

3. Any thwarting or possibility of thwarting these basic human goals, or danger to the defenses which protect them or to the conditions upon which they rest, is considered to be a psychological threat. With a few exceptions, all psychopathology may be partially traced to such threats. A basically thwarted man may actually be defined as a "sick" man.
4. It is such basic threats which bring about the general emergency reactions.
5. Certain other basic problems have not been dealt with because of limitations of space. Among these are (*a*) the problem of values in any definitive motivation theory, (*b*) the relation between appetites, desires, needs and what is "good" for the organism, (*c*) the etiology of the basic needs and their possible derivation in early childhood, (*d*) redefinition of motivational concepts, i.e., drive, desire, wish, need, goal, (*e*) implication of our theory for hedonistic theory, (*f*) the nature of the uncompleted act, of success and failure, and of aspiration-level, (*g*) the role of association, habit, and conditioning, (*h*) relation to the theory of interpersonal relations, (*i*) implications for psychotherapy, (*j*) implication for theory of society, (*k*) the theory of selfishness, (*l*) the relation between needs and cultural patterns, (*m*) the relation between this theory and Allport's theory of functional autonomy. These as well as certain other less important questions must be considered as motivation theory attempts to become definitive.

REFERENCES

Cannon, W. B. *Wisdom of the Body*. Norton, 1932.

Fromm, Erich. *Escape from Freedom*. Holt, 1941.

Goldstein, K. *The Organism*. American Book Company, 1939.

Kardiner, K. *The Traumatic Neuroses of War*. Hoeber, 1941.

Levy, D. M. "Primary Affect Hunger." *American Journal of Psychiatry*, Vol. 94, 1937.

Maslow, A. H. "A Preface to Motivation Theory." *Psychosomatic Medicine*, Vol. 5, 1943.

——. "The Dynamics of Psychological Security-Insecurity." *Character and Personality*, Vol. 10, 1942.

——. "Dominance, Personality, and Social Behavior in Women." *Journal of Social Psychology*, Vol. 10, 1939.

——, and B. Mittelmann. *Principles of Abnormal Psychology*. Harper, 1941.

Plant, J. *Personality and the Cultural Pattern*. Commonwealth Fund, 1937.

Shirley, M. "Children's Adjustment to a Strange Situation." *Journal of Abnormal and Social Psychology*, Vol. 37, 1942.

Wertheimer, M. Unpublished lectures at the New School for Social Research, New York, N.Y.

Young, P. T. "The Experimental Analysis of Appetite." *Psychological Bulletin*, Vol. 38, 1941.

DOUGLAS M. McGREGOR

The Human Side of Enterprise

It has become trite to say that the most significant developments of the next quarter-century will take place not in the physical but in the social sciences, that industry—the economic organ of society—has the fundamental know-how to utilize physical science and technology for the material benefit of mankind, and that we must now learn how to utilize the social sciences to make our human organizations truly effective.

Many people agree in principle with such statements; but so far they represent a pious hope—and little else. Consider with me, if you will, something of what may be involved when we attempt to transform the hope into reality.

PROBLEMS AND OPPORTUNITIES FACING MANAGEMENT

Let me begin with an analogy. A quarter-century ago basic conceptions of the nature of matter and energy had changed profoundly from what they had been since Newton's time. The physical scientists were persuaded that under proper conditions new and hitherto unimagined sources of energy could be made available to mankind.

We know what has happened since then. First came the bomb. Then, during the past decade, have come many other attempts to exploit these scientific discoveries—some successful, some not.

The point of my analogy, however, is that the application of theory in this field is a slow and costly matter. We expect it always to be thus. No one is impatient with the scientist because he cannot tell industry how to build a simple, cheap, all-purpose source of atomic energy today. That it will take at least another decade and the investment of billions of dollars to achieve results which are economically competitive with present sources of power is understood and accepted.

It is transparently pretentious to suggest any *direct* similarity between the developments in the physical sciences leading to the harnessing of atomic energy and potential developments in the social sciences. Nevertheless, the analogy is not as absurd as it might appear to be at first glance.

To a lesser degree, and in a much more tentative fashion, we are in a position in the social sciences today like that of the physical sciences with respect to atomic energy in the thirties. We know that past conceptions of the nature of man are inadequate and in many ways incorrect. We are becoming quite certain that, under proper conditions, unimagined resources of creative human energy could become available within the organizational setting.

We cannot tell industrial management how to apply this new knowledge in simple, economic ways. We know it will require years of exploration, much costly development research, and a substantial amount of creative imagination

---

"The Human Side of Enterprise" reprinted from *Leadership and Motivation* by Douglas McGregor by permission of The M. I. T. Press, Cambridge, Massachusetts.

on the part of management to discover how to apply this growing knowledge to the organization of human effort in industry.

May I ask that you keep this analogy in mind—overdrawn and pretentious though it may be—as a framework for what I have to say.

Management's Task: Conventional View

The conventional conception of management's task in harnessing human energy to organizational requirements can be stated broadly in terms of three propositions. In order to avoid the complications introduced by a label, I shall call this set of propositions "Theory X":

1. Management is responsible for organizing the elements of productive enterprise—money, materials, equipment, people—in the interest of economic ends.
2. With respect to people, this is a process of directing their efforts, motivating them, controlling their actions, modifying their behavior to fit the needs of the organization.
3. Without this active intervention by management, people would be passive—even resistant—to organizational needs. They must therefore be persuaded, rewarded, punished, controlled—their activities must be directed. This is management's task—in managing subordinate managers or workers. We often sum it up by saying that management consists of getting things done through other people.

Behind this conventional theory there are several additional beliefs—less explicit, but widespread:

4. The average man is by nature indolent—he works as little as possible.
5. He lacks ambition, dislikes responsibility, prefers to be led.
6. He is inherently self-centered, indifferent to organizational needs.
7. He is by nature resistant to change.
8. He is gullible, not very bright, the ready dupe of the charlatan and the demagogue.

The human side of economic enterprise today is fashioned from propositions and beliefs such as these. Conventional organization structures, managerial policies, practices, and programs reflect these assumptions.

In accomplishing its task—with these assumptions as guides—management has conceived of a range of possibilities between two extremes.

The Hard or the Soft Approach?

At one extreme, management can be "hard" or "strong." The methods for directing behavior involve coercion and threat (usually disguised), close supervision, tight controls over behavior. At the other extreme, management can be "soft" or "weak." The methods for directing behavior involve being permissive, satisfying people's demands, achieving harmony. Then they will be tractable, accept direction.

This range has been fairly completely explored during the past half-century, and management has learned some things from the exploration. There are difficulties in the "hard" approach. Force breeds counterforces: restriction of output, antagonism, militant unionism, subtle but effective sabotage of management objectives. This approach is especially difficult during times of full employment.

There are also difficulties in the "soft" approach. It leads frequently to the abdication of management—to harmony, perhaps, but to indifferent performance. People take advantage of the soft approach. They continually expect more, but they give less and less.

Currently, the popular theme is "firm but fair." This is an attempt to gain the advantages of both the hard and the soft approaches. It is reminiscent of Teddy Roosevelt's "speak softy and carry a big stick."

Is the Conventional View Correct?

The findings which are beginning to emerge from the social sciences challenge this whole set of beliefs about man and human nature and about the task of management. The evidence is far from conclusive, certainly, but it is suggestive. It comes from the laboratory, the clinic, the schoolroom, the home, and even to a limited extent from industry itself.

The social scientist does not deny that human behavior in industrial organizations today is approximately what management perceives it to be. He has, in fact, observed it and studied it fairly extensively. But he is pretty sure that this behavior is *not* a consequence of man's inherent nature. It is a consequence, rather, of the nature of industrial organizations, of management philosophy, policy, and practice. The conventional approach of Theory X is based on mistaken notions of what is cause and what is effect.

"Well," you ask, "what then is the *true* nature of man? What evidence leads the social scientist to deny what is obvious?" And, if I am not mistaken, you are also thinking, "Tell me—simply, and without a lot of scientific verbiage—what you think you know that is so unusual. Give me—without a lot of intellectual claptrap and theoretical nonsense—some practical ideas which will enable me to improve the situation in my organization. And remember, I'm faced with increasing costs and narrowing profit margins. I want proof that such ideas won't result simply in new and costly human relations frills. I want practical results, and I want them now."

If these are your wishes, you are going to be disappointed. Such requests can no more be met by the social scientist today than could comparable ones with respect to atomic energy be met by the physicist fifteen years ago. I can, however, indicate a few of the reasons for asserting that conventional assumptions about the human side of enterprise are inadequate. And I can suggest—tentatively—some of the propositions that will comprise a more adequate theory of the management of people. The magnitude of the task that confronts us will then, I think, be apparent.

MAN AS A WANTING ANIMAL

Perhaps the best way to indicate why the conventional approach of management is inadequate is to consider the subject of motivation. In discussing this subject I will draw heavily on the work of my colleague, Abraham Maslow of Brandeis University. His is the most fruitful approach I know. Naturally, what I have to say will be overgeneralized and will ignore important qualifications. In the time at our disposal, this is inevitable.

Physiological and Safety Needs

Man is a wanting animal—as soon as one of his needs is satisfied, another appears in its place. This process is unending. It continues from birth to death.

Man's needs are organized in a series of levels—a hierarchy of importance. At the lowest level, but pre-eminent in importance when they are thwarted, are his physiological needs. Man lives by bread alone, when there is no bread. Unless the circumstances are unusual, his needs for love, for status, for recognition are inoperative when his stomach has been empty for a while. But when he eats regularly and adequately, hunger ceases to be an important need. The sated man has hunger only in the sense that a full bottle has emptiness. The same is true of the other physiological needs of man—for rest, exercise, shelter, protection from the elements.

A satisfied need is not a motivator of behavior! This is a fact of profound significance. It is a fact which is regularly ignored in the conventional approach to the management of people. I shall return to it later. For the moment, one example will make my point. Consider your own need for air. Except as you are deprived of it, it has no appreciable motivating effect upon your behavior.

When the physiological needs are reasonably satisfied, needs at the next higher level begin to dominate man's behavior—to motivate him. These are called safety needs. They are needs for protection against danger, threat, deprivation. Some people mistakenly refer to these as needs for security. However, unless man is in a dependent relationship where he fears arbitrary deprivation, he does not demand security. The need is for the "fairest possible break." When he is confident of this, he is more than willing to take risks. But when he feels threatened or dependent, his greatest need is for guarantees, for protection, for security.

The fact needs little emphasis that since every industrial employee is in a dependent relationship, safety needs may assume considerable importance. Arbitrary management actions, behavior which arouses uncertainty with respect to continued employment or which reflects favoritism or discrimination, unpredictable administration of policy—these can be powerful motivators of the safety needs in the employment relationship *at every level* from worker to vice president.

Social Needs

When man's physiological needs are satisfied and he is no longer fearful about his physical welfare, his social needs become important motivators of his behavior—for belonging, for association, for acceptance by his fellows, for giving and receiving friendship and love.

Management knows today of the existence of these needs, but it often assumes quite wrongly that they represent a threat to the organization. Many studies have demonstrated that the tightly knit, cohesive work group may, under proper conditions, be far more effective than an equal number of separate individuals in achieving organizational goals.

Yet management, fearing group hostility to its own objectives, often goes to considerable lengths to control and direct human efforts in ways that are inimical to the natural "groupiness" of human beings. When man's social needs—and perhaps his safety needs, too—are thus thwarted, he behaves in ways which tend to defeat organizational objectives. He becomes resistant, antagonistic, uncooperative. But this behavior is a consequence, not a cause.

Ego Needs

Above the social needs—in the sense that they do not become motivators until lower needs are reasonably satisfied—are the needs of greatest significance to management and to man himself. They are the egoistic needs, and they are of two kinds:

1. Those needs that relate to one's self-esteem—needs for self-confidence, for independence, for achievement, for competence, for knowledge.
2. Those needs that relate to one's reputation—needs for status, for recognition, for appreciation, for the deserved respect of one's fellows.

Unlike the lower needs, these are rarely satisfied; man seeks indefinitely for more satisfaction of these needs once they have become important to him. But they do not appear in any significant way until physiological, safety, and social needs are all reasonably satisfied.

The typical industrial organization offers few opportunities for the satisfaction of these egoistic needs to people at lower levels in the hierarchy. The conventional methods of organizing work, particularly in mass production industries, give little heed to these aspects of human motivation. If the practices of scientific management were deliberately calculated to thwart these needs—which, of course, they are not—they could hardly accomplish this purpose better than they do.

Self-Fulfillment Needs

Finally—a capstone, as it were, on the hierarchy of man's needs—there are what we may call the needs for self-fulfillment. These are the needs for realizing one's own potentialities, for continued self-development, for being creative in the broadest sense of that term.

It is clear that the conditions of modern life give only limited opportunity for these relatively weak needs to obtain expression. The deprivation most people experience with respect to other lower-level needs diverts their energies into the struggle to satisfy *those* needs, and the needs for self-fulfillment remain dormant.

THE DYNAMICS OF MOTIVATION

Now, briefly, a few general comments about motivation.

We recognize readily enough that a man suffering from a severe dietary deficiency is sick. The deprivation of physiological needs has behavioral consequences. The same is true—although less well recognized—of deprivation of higher-level needs. The man whose needs for safety, association, independence, or status are thwarted is sick just as surely as is he who has rickets. And his sickness will have behavioral consequences. We will be mistaken if we attribute his resultant passivity, his hostility, his refusal to accept responsibility to his inherent "human nature." These forms of behavior are *symptoms* of illness—of deprivation of his social and egoistic needs.

The man whose lower-level needs are satisfied is not motivated to satisfy those needs any longer. For practical purposes, they exist no longer. (Remember my point about your need for air.) Management often asks, "Why aren't people more productive? We pay good wages, provide good working conditions, have excellent fringe benefits and steady employment. Yet people do not seem to be willing to put forth more than minimum effort."

The fact that management has provided for these physiological and safety needs has shifted the motivational emphasis to the social and perhaps to the egoistic needs. Unless there are opportunities *at work* to satisfy these higher-level needs, people will be deprived; and their behavior will reflect this deprivation. Under such conditions, if management continues to focus its attention on physiological needs, its efforts are bound to be ineffective.

People *will* make insistent demands for more money under these conditions. It becomes more important than ever to buy the material goods and services which can provide limited satisfaction of the thwarted needs. Although money has only limited value in satisfying many higher-level needs, it can become the focus of interest if it is the *only* means available.

The Carrot and Stick Approach

The carrot and stick theory of motivation (like Newtonian physical theory) works reasonably well under certain circumstances. The *means* for satisfying man's physiological and (within limits) his safety needs can be provided or withheld by management. Employment itself is such a means, and so are wages, working conditions, and benefits. By these means the individual can be controlled so long as he is struggling for subsistence. Man lives for bread alone when there is no bread.

But the carrot and stick theory does not work at all once man has reached an adequate subsistence level and is motivated primarily by higher needs. Management cannot provide a man with self-respect, or with the respect of his fellows, or with the satisfaction of needs for self-fulfillment. It can create conditions such that he is encouraged and enabled to seek such satisfactions *for himself*, or it can thwart him by failing to create those conditions.

But this creation of conditions is not "control." It is not a good device for directing behavior. And so management finds itself in an odd position. The high standard of living created by our modern technological know-how provides quite adequately for the satisfaction of physiological and safety needs. The only significant exception is where management practices have not created confidence in a "fair break"—and thus where safety needs are thwarted. But by making possible the satisfaction of low-level needs, management has deprived itself of the ability to use as motivators the devices on which conventional theory has taught it to rely—rewards, promises, incentives, or threats and other coercive devices.

Neither Hard nor Soft

The philosophy of management by direction and control—*regardless of whether it is hard or soft*—is inadequate to motivate because the human needs on which this approach relies are today unimportant motivators of behavior. Direction and control are essentially useless in motivating people whose important needs are social and egoistic. Both the hard and the soft approach fail today because they are simply irrelevant to the situation.

People, deprived of opportunities to satisfy at work the needs which are now important to them, behave exactly as we might predict—with indolence, passivity, resistance to change, lack of responsibility, willingness to follow the demagogue, unreasonable demands for economic benefits. It would seem that we are caught in a web of our own weaving.

In summary, then, of these comments about motivation: Management by direction and control—whether implemented with the hard, the soft, or the firm but fair approach—fails under today's conditions to provide effective motivation of human effort toward organizational objectives. It fails because direction and control are useless methods of motivating people whose physiological and safety needs are reasonably satisfied and whose social, egoistic, and self-fulfillment needs are predominant.

A NEW PERSPECTIVE

For these and many other reasons, we require a different theory of the task of managing people based on more adequate assumptions about human nature and human motivation. I am going to be so bold as to suggest the broad dimensions of such a theory. Call it "Theory Y," if you will.

1. Management is responsible for organizing the elements of productive enterprise—money, materials, equipment, people—in the interest of economic ends.
2. People are *not* by nature passive or resistant to organizational needs. They have become so as a result of experience in organizations.
3. The motivation, the potential for development, the capacity for assuming responsibility, the readiness to direct behavior toward organizational goals are all present in people. Management does not put them there. It is a responsibility of management to make it possible for people to recognize and develop these human characteristics for themselves.
4. The essential task of management is to arrange organizational conditions and methods of operation so that people can achieve their own goals *best* by directing *their own* efforts toward organizational objectives.

This is a process primarily of creating opportunities, releasing potential, removing obstacles, encouraging growth, providing guidance. It is what Peter Drucker has called "management by objectives" in contrast to "management by control."

And I hasten to add that it does *not* involve the abdication of management, the absence of leadership, the lowering of standards, or the other characteristics usually associated with the "soft" approach under Theory X. Much to the contrary. It is no more possible to create an organization today which will be a fully effective application of this theory than it was to build an atomic power plant in 1945. There are many formidable obstacles to overcome.

Some Difficulties

The conditions imposed by conventional organization theory and by the approach of scientific management for the past half-century have tied men to limited jobs which do not utilize their capabilities, have discouraged the acceptance of responsibility, have encouraged passivity, have eliminated meaning from work. Man's habits, attitudes, expectations—his whole conception of membership in an industrial organization—have been conditioned by his experience under these circumstances. Changes in the direction of Theory Y will be slow, and it will require extensive modification of the attitudes of management and workers alike.

People today are accustomed to being directed, manipulated, controlled in industrial organizations and to finding satisfaction for their social, egoistic, and self-fulfilment needs away from the job. This is true of much of management as well as of workers. Genuine "industrial citizenship"—to borrow again a term from Drucker—is a remote and unrealistic idea, the meaning of which has not even been considered by most members of industrial organizations.

Another way of saying this is that Theory X places exclusive reliance upon external control of human behavior, while Theory Y relies heavily on self-control and self-direction. It is worth noting that this difference is the difference between treating people as children and treating them as mature adults. After generations of the former, we cannot expect to shift to the latter overnight.

APPLICATIONS OF THE THEORY

Before we are overwhelmed by the obstacles, let us remember that the application of theory is always slow. Progress is usually achieved in small steps.

Consider with me a few innovative ideas which are entirely consistent with Theory Y and which are today being applied with some success.

Decentralization and Delegation

These are ways of freeing people from the too-close control of conventional organization, giving them a degree of freedom to direct their own activities, to assume responsibility, and, importantly, to satisfy their egoistic needs. In this connection, the flat organization of Sears, Roebuck and Company provides an interesting example. It forces "management by objectives" since it enlarges the number of people reporting to a manager until he cannot direct and control them in the conventional manner.

Job Enlargement

This concept, pioneered by IBM and Detroit Edison, is quite consistent with Theory Y. It encourages the acceptance of responsibility at the bottom of the organization; it provides opportunities for satisfying social and egoistic needs. In fact, the reorganization of work at the factory level offers one of the most challenging opportunities for innovation consistent with Theory Y. The studies by A. T. M. Wilson and his associates of British coal mining and Indian textile manufacture have added appreciably to our understanding of work organization. Moreover, the economic and psychological results achieved by this work have been substantial.

Participation and Consultative Management

Under proper conditions these results provide encouragement to people to direct their creative energies toward organizational objectives, give them some voice in decisions that affect them, provide significant opportunities for the satisfaction of social and egoistic needs. I need only mention the Scanlon Plan as the outstanding embodiment of these ideas in practice.

The not infrequent failure of such ideas as these to work as well as expected is often attributable to the fact that a management has "bought the idea" but applied it within the framework of Theory X and its assumptions.

Delegation is not an effective way of exercising management by control. Participation becomes a farce when it is applied as a sales gimmick or a device for kidding people into thinking they are important. Only the management that has confidence in human capacities and is itself directed toward organizational objectives rather than toward the preservation of personal power can grasp the implications of this emerging theory. Such management will find and apply successfully other innovative ideas as we move slowly toward the full implementation of a theory like Y.

Performance Appraisal

Before I stop, let me mention one other practical application of Theory Y which—while still highly tentative—may well have important consequences. This has to do with performance appraisal within the ranks of management. Even a cursory examination of conventional programs of performance appraisal will reveal how completely consistent they are with Theory X. In fact, most such programs tend to treat the individual as though he were a product under inspection on the assembly line.

Take the typical plan: substitute "product" for "subordinate being appraised," substitute "inspector" for "superior making the appraisal," substitute "rework" for "training or development," and, except for the attributes being judged, the human appraisal process will be virtually indistinguishable from the product inspection process.

A few companies—among them General Mills, Ansul Chemical, and General Electric—have been experimenting with approaches which involve the individual in setting "targets" or objectives *for himself* and in a *self*-evaluation of performance semi-annually or annually. Of course, the superior plays an important leadership role in this process—one, in fact, which demands substantially more competence than the conventional approach. The role is, however, considerably more congenial to many managers than the role of "judge" or "inspector" which is forced upon them by conventional performance. Above all, the individual is encouraged to take a greater responsibility for planning and appraising his own contribution to organizational objectives; and the accompanying effects on egoistic and self-fulfillment needs are substantial. This approach to performance appraisal represents one more innovative idea being explored by a few managements who are moving toward the implementation of Theory Y.

CONCLUSION

And now I am back where I began. I share the belief that we could realize substantial improvements in the effectiveness of industrial organizations during the next decade or two. Moreover, I believe the social sciences can contribute much to such developments. We are only beginning to grasp the implications of the growing body of knowledge in these fields. But if this conviction is to become a reality instead of a pious hope, we will need to view the process much as we view the process of releasing the energy of the atom for constructive human ends—as a slow, costly, sometimes discouraging approach toward a goal which would seem to many to be quite unrealistic.

The ingenuity and the perseverance of industrial management in the pursuit of economic ends have changed many scientific and technological dreams into commonplace realities. It is now becoming clear that the application of these same talents to the human side of enterprise will not only enhance substantially these materialistic achievements but will bring us one step closer to "the good society." Shall we get on with the job?

MASON HAIRE

The Problem of Learning and the Law of Effect

We are constantly faced, in industry, with the problem of making changes in behavior. The job of management is very seldom to keep people doing exactly as they are doing. Usually we either want a group of people to start doing something that they aren't doing now, or to stop doing something that they are doing. Almost always, the big problems come in changing behavior. Since a large part of human activity is involved in the process of modifying behavior patterns and shaping them so that they will be more nearly goal-oriented, it is important for us to look at the processes that occur and the principles that govern them, so that we may utilize these principles efficiently in producing changes.

Psychologists speak frequently of a principle of learning which is called "the Law of Effect." It means, simply, that behavior which seems to lead to reward tends to be repeated, while behavior which seems not to lead to reward or seems to lead to punishment tends not to be repeated. It is not a particularly complicated principle, but it is very important in shaping behavior. For some reason, we all seem to be able to keep it clearly in mind and to use it in practice when we are, for example, housebreaking a dog, but when we become involved in more complicated situations in human interactions we lose track of it. The principle is exactly the same in human behavior, and it is essential for us to see it clearly in the cases in which we want to modify behavior.

It is part of the superior's role in a hierarchical organization that he controls many, if not most, of the rewards that are available to subordinates. All people at work are looking for the satisfaction of many of their needs. We shall have to go

---

into the kinds of needs that motivate people a little later on, but the fact remains that everyone is constantly striving for need satisfactions. It is part of the nature of the situation that, at work, the superior controls many of the means to need-satisfaction. By the proper use of his control of the means for need-satisfaction, he can provide or withhold rewards at appropriate times. When we remember the principle of the Law of Effect—that behavior which seems to be rewarded tends to be repeated, while that which seems not to lead to reward or seems to lead to punishment tends to be eliminated—it is clear that the superior has a great opportunity for shaping behavior. Indeed, whether he is conscious of it or not, the superior is bound to be constantly shaping the behavior of his subordinates by the way in which he utilizes the rewards that are at his disposal, and he will inevitably modify the behavior patterns of his work group thereby. For this reason, it is important to see as clearly as possible what is going on, so that the changes can be planned and chosen in advance, rather than simply accepted after the fact.

An example may make the point clear in its application to industrial practice. It is not at all uncommon to hear members of management describe a situation in which two applicants for a promotion are nearly equal in merit. The poorer one, however, let us say, has considerably more seniority. Although there is leeway in the contract for a promotion on the basis of merit, the man with the greater seniority is promoted, in order to avoid argument. It is also not at all uncommon to hear the same people say at another time, "Our biggest problem is that people don't try hard any more, the way they used to. They used to figure that if they worked hard they'd get ahead, but now they just figure that if they wait long enough they'll be promoted, so they sweat it out rather than trying to do a good job." The members of management, in these cases, are not entitled to express surprise or dissatisfaction at their subordinates' performance. The reason the subordinates produce the kind of behavior they do is because they have been trained to behave that way. They have been shown that rewards come for seniority and not for merit. According to the principle, the behavior that seems to lead to reward tends to be repeated, while the behavior that seems not to lead to reward tends to be dropped out. The way in which the reward is administered determines the behavior.

This does not mean that rewards for seniority are bad. Long service deserves compensations. However, in order to produce the kind of behavior we want, we should not let it become confused with other kinds of reward that are properly designed to encourage other types of activity. Protection by virtue of seniority is a reward for certain kinds of behavior which we want to encourage, as well as an obligation to the senior worker. However, if we want to encourage quality in performance, in addition to simple long-term service, we should be careful that the rewards for the two do not overlap, and that they do not compete with each other. Clear-cut rewards must be retained for merit and must be clearly structured so that they are seen as such.

A similar situation develops in all kinds of small everyday administrations which do not seem, at first glance, to be rewards or punishments, but which operate that way just the same. We often hear it said, "The men in the work force don't ever give a thought to ways to do their jobs better." We think of this as a general characteristic of a group of people. But have we trained them to act this way, or have we, on the other hand, provided actual rewards in practice for just such thinking about the job? When someone approaches a foreman with a suggestion about something to do, does the foreman imply by his tone and manner, "Your job is to do the work—I'll do the planning"? This can be as effective a punishment, or at least lack of reward, as many more carefully planned acts, and these small everyday occurrences are the day-by-day administrations of reward and punishment by which the superior shapes the behavior of his subordinates. Underlying the process throughout, we have the principle of the Law of Effect: that behavior which seems not to lead to reward, or to lead to punishment, tends not to be repeated. As we go on to other problems and practices of dealing with people we shall see this principle coming into play repeatedly.

One often hears members of bank managements complain that their tellers are not sufficiently zealous in building good customer contact. They wish the teller would realize that the bank's continued success depends on the customer, and make him feel welcome and well treated. Too often, they say, when a depositor approaches the window, the teller gives the impression that he has been interrupted in an important job (if, indeed, the customer hasn't been made to wait while the teller finishes adding his column of figures) and that the customer will throw his figures out of balance by making a transaction. Why does this kind of thing happen? The members of management might well ask themselves whether they have trained the tellers to do just this and, if so, whether this is the way they should be trained. The teller has found all his rewards in the past for careful balancing of the books, and his punishments for failures in this line. He has probably never been rewarded or punished for his treatment of customers. Under these circumstances, an understanding of the Law of Effect will let us predict certainly what will happen. Those behaviors which seem to lead to reward (balancing the books) will tend to be repeated; those behaviors which seem not to lead to reward (dealing with the customers well) will tend to be eliminated. The bank will suffer. Because of the overriding nature of the problem of control within banks, they have often slipped inadvertently into a policy which they would never make explicit: balancing the books is the only important thing. From this implicit policy has flowed a daily training which has taught the teller how to behave: balance the books at all costs; anything which interrupts that task is a liability. There has never been a real decision to train the tellers this way, but the silent focusing on the problem of control has put it into the actions of every level of management, and because the subordinates are subject to the operation of the Law of Effect, it works as a training policy.

What could be done differently? No one would ask that management adopt a policy that it doesn't matter whether the books balance, as long as the customers are happy. As in the case of the example a little earlier concerning promotion on merit or seniority, both aspects of the teller's work are important. Rewards must be provided both for his balancing and for his customer contact, and they must be kept separate and distinct, so that it is possible to create a situation where both kinds of behavior tend to be repeated. In order to do this it is necessary to be clear and explicit about the aims of the business, about the things that need to be done, and about the rewards that are provided for doing these things. Otherwise we slip into the situation of inadvertently training out an essential pattern of behavior.

One further point should be made clear before we leave the Law of Effect. We must be careful to notice that it is stated that "behavior which *seems* to lead to reward tends to be repeated, and behavior which *seems* not to lead to reward or *seems* to lead to punishment tends not to be repeated." It is not always true that the behavior which in fact leads to reward, or which was the boss's reason for providing the reward, will be seen to be the path to reward by the subordinate.

If the reward occurs too long after the behavior, it may be ineffective; if the connection between the behavior and the reward is difficult to see, it may be ineffective. Moreover, in many cases the subordinate may mistakenly assume that a reward came for a particular bit of behavior which was not at all what management intended to reward. We shall see in more detail later on how this problem of the subordinate's making sense of the world and organizing things in his own mind complicates the picture. Here we need simply to realize that the effective rewards are those that he has put with a particular bit of behavior. In addition to providing reward and punishment, management must accept the responsibility for seeing that the appropriate connection between behavior and reward is appreciated by the recipient of the reward.

There is some evidence, in the laboratory, that those behaviors which are followed by reward tend to be repeated whether or not the individual is aware of the connection. Learning is probably not as effective in this situation as it is when the connection is clear, but it is not impossible, either. This means that in many cases where it is difficult to maintain a close contact in the employee's mind between behavior and reward—where the situation is too complex, or the time too long, or the like—it is still possible to rely on the operation of the Law of Effect. This kind of "silent" operation of the principle only points up the responsibility of management for the consistent provision of rewards in modifying behavior.

It would be well, at this point, to say another word about the operation of reward and punishment under the Law of Effect. We have so far spoken of them as if they operated equally, but in the opposite directions. This is not quite true. While it is true that those behaviors which seem to lead to punishment tend not to be repeated, it is also clear, in laboratory experiments, that the most important effect of punishment is to produce variability of behavior, so that it becomes possible for the superior to provide reward for the desired behavior and hence increase its likelihood of repetition. Often the response to the positive side of the Law of Effect seems to be, "It's very well to talk about rewarding the kind of behavior that you want repeated. What do you do when it occurs so seldom that you don't get any chance to reward it?" It is just here that the role of punishment is most effective. The consistent application of punishment in the face of undesirable behavior leads the person to try other kinds of behavior from his repertoire of responses, and this variability makes it possible to find and reward the desired behavior.

KURT LEWIN

The Psychology of Success and Failure

I

The great importance of success and failure is recognized by practically all psychological schools. Thorndike's law of effect,[1] as well as Adler's ideas, has close relation to this problem. Pedagogically, the importance of success is universally stressed.

Indeed, success and failure influence deeply the emotional status of the person, his goals, and his social relations. From the point of view of guidance, one can emphasize the fact that these problems are important throughout the whole age range and are as basic for the very young child as for the adult.

In spite of the common recognition of these factors, our knowledge about the psychology of success and failure is meager. The law of effect may, for instance, suggest that a person who has succeeded in a special activity will have a tendency to repeat that activity. Indeed, children of two or three years tend to repeat activities again and again. Yet experiments show, at least for older persons, that a spontaneous repetition of a successful act is not very likely and that, if it does occur, the activity is generally distinctly changed. As a matter of fact, the tendency to go back spontaneously to a special activity is, as Ovseankina has shown, about ninety times as high if the activity is not completed as if it is successfully completed. This shows, at least, that the whole problem is much more complicated than one might expect.

II

The first question one should be able to answer is: Under what conditions will a person experience success or failure? The experiments of Hoppe point to some fundamental facts which one could have learned from everyday experience; namely, it is not possible to correlate the objective achievement on the one side with the feeling of success or failure on the other. The same achievement can result once in the feeling of great success, another time in the feeling of complete failure. This is true not only for different individuals, but even for the same individual. For instance, a person may throw a discus forty yards the first time. The second time he may reach fifty, and feel very successful. After short practice, he may reach sixty-five. If he then throws fifty yards again, he will experience a definite failure in spite of the fact that he got a thrill out of the same achievement but a short time before. This means that the experience of success and failure does not depend upon the achievement as such, but rather upon the relation

"The Psychology of Success and Failure" by Kurt Lewin from *Occupations*, Vol. 14, 1936, pp. 926–930. Reprinted by permission of the American Personnel and Guidance Association.

[1] Law of effect: One learns quickly those reactions which are accompanied or followed by a satisfying state of affairs; one does not learn quickly those which result in an annoying state of affairs or learns not to make such reactions. See English (1934).

between the achievement and the person's expectation. One can speak, in this respect, about the person's "level of aspiration," and can say that the experience and the degree of success and failure depend upon whether the achievement is above or below the momentary level of aspiration.[2]

One may ask whether a person always has a definite level of aspiration in respect to a certain task. The answer is no. If one, for instance, does something for the first time, one generally does not set himself a definite goal. It is interesting additional evidence of the relation between success and the level of aspiration that in such situations no strong failure is experienced. If one wishes to avoid or diminish the feeling of failure in the child, one often says to him: "Just try." In this way a definite level of aspiration is eliminated.

Not only is the level of aspiration fundamental for the experience of success and failure, but the level of aspiration itself is changed by success and failure. After success, a person generally sets himself a higher goal. After failure, his level of aspiration generally goes down. There are some exceptions to this general trend which one should notice. In the experiments of Hoppe, success led to a rise of the level of aspiration only in 69 percent, in 7 percent it remained the same; and in 24 percent the person stopped the activity entirely. After failure, the level of aspiration was never raised, but it was lowered in only 50 percent of the cases. In 21 percent it remained the same; in 2 percent the person consoled himself by the realization of previous successes; and in 27 percent the person ceased the activity entirely. This varying behavior is due partly to the fact that there are cases which are neither clear successes nor clear failures. On the whole, the person is more ready to raise the level of aspiration after success than to lower it after failure.

It is important to note that a person, instead of lowering his level of aspiration after failure, may stop entirely. There is a significant difference between individuals in this respect. Some persons are relatively easily influenced to lower their levels of aspiration, whereas others show a stiff backbone. The latter maintain their levels of aspiration in spite of failures and may prefer to leave the field entirely rather than to lower it. Lack of persistence sometimes has to be attributed to such an unwillingness to yield. On the other hand, there are cases of apparent persistence, in which a person sticks to an activity only at the price of constantly lowering his level of aspiration. This sort of persistency may be found in the hysteric type. In problems of guidance involving unusually high or low persistency, the possible reasons behind such behavior should be carefully examined, because the advisable measures should be different in accordance with the underlying psychological facts.

Surprisingly enough, a person may leave the field of activity not only after failure but after success, too. Such abandonment of the field after success occurs generally when this success follows a series of failures. One obviously does not like to quit a task after failure. One continues, eager to find a successful termination, and uses the first occasion to stop, out of fear that further repetitions may bring new failures.

III

One has to consider quite detailed facts in order to understand the forces which govern the level of aspiration.

---

[2] The problems discussed here are treated more thoroughly in Lewin (1935). Here also may be found the references for the experimental work.

The first point to mention is that any goal has a position within a set of goals. If a child is asked, "How much is three times four?" the answer, "Twelve," determines a definite circumscribed goal he has to reach. The answer will be either right or wrong. But if the child has to write an English composition or to translate a passage of French or to build a wooden boat, there is no such absolutely determined goal but, rather, a variety of possible achievements which may differ greatly in quality. Most tasks are of this nature. It is generally technically possible to order the different possible achievements of a task according to their degree of difficulty. This allows one to compare the achievement and the level of aspiration of different persons and to determine in a given case the effect of success and failure. The range of acceptable achievement has often a "natural maximum" and a "natural minimum." In Hoppe's experiment, for instance, the subject had to solve one of a group of puzzles, each different in difficulty. A subject who was not able to solve any one of the puzzles but who was able to return the stones to their proper places in the box would certainly not have reached the natural minimum of the task. On the other hand, it would be above the natural maximum to reach a solution of the most difficult puzzle within one second. Some tasks have no natural maximum. This holds, for instance, for many sport activities—there is always the possibility of jumping higher and running faster. The lack of this natural maximum within the goal structure of many sport activities has led to a biologically unsound race without end.

The individual usually is conscious of the variety of possible goals within the task. He conceives the single action in its significance for a larger field of actions. Besides the goals for the momentary act, he has some general goal in regard to this larger field. For instance, when a person in a competition throws a discus, his goal for a certain trial might be to throw at least fifty yards; his goal for the whole group of actions would be to win! There always exists besides the goal for the next act, or, as we may say, besides the immediate goal, an ideal goal. This ideal goal may be to become the best discus thrower of the college or even to become world champion.

Such a goal can possess any degree of reality or unreality. For the student who does well in the first weeks of his sporting activities, the ideal to become world champion may be only an occasional daydream without any significance. The ideal goal, to become the best player of the university, may have considerably more reality. In a vague way, a student entering college may dream about the possibility of becoming a leading surgeon, without even confessing this goal to himself. If he progresses in college, and does well in medical school, this ideal goal may become somewhat more real. According to Hoppe, success narrows the gap between the immediate goal and the ideal goal and brings the ideal goal from the level of unreality gradually down to the level of reality. Failure has the opposite effect: a previously real goal vanishes into the world of dreams. If the ideal goal should be reached (a case more frequent in experiments than in life), generally a new ideal goal arises.

IV

If it is true that the degree of success and failure depends upon the amount of difference between the immediate goal and the achievement, it should be possible to create a very strong feeling of success by making the task so easy that the achievement will be much better than the task demands. On the other hand, it should be possible to create a very strong feeling of failure by assigning a very difficult task. Experiments show that this is not true. If the task is above a certain degree of difficulty, no feeling of failure arises, and no feeling of success arises if the task is below a certain degree of difficulty. In other words, if one represents the possible degree of difficulty of a task on a scale, this scale is infinite in direction, both to greater ease and to greater difficulty. But an individual reacts with success and failure only to a small region within this scale. In fact, the tasks which an individual considers "very easy," "easy," "medium," "difficult," and "very difficult" circumscribe only a small region in the scale. Above and below this region lie a great many tasks which the individual calls "too easy" or "too difficult." The "too difficult" tasks are considered "objectively impossible," entirely out of the range of the individual's ability, and no feeling of failure is attached to such a task. Similarly, in the case of a "too easy" task, the achievement is taken so much for granted that no feeling of success is aroused. Contrary to the scale of possible difficulties, the scale of possible achievements is not infinite but has a definite upper limit for a given individual at a given time. Both success and failure occur only if the difficulty of the task lies close to the upper limit of achievement. In other words, the feeling of failure occurs only if there is a chance for success, and a feeling of success occurs only if there is a chance for failure. Behind success and failure, therefore, one can always find a conflict situation.

This conflict situation makes somewhat understandable the laws which govern the position and the change in the level of aspiration. These laws are probably among the most fundamental for all human behavior. They are quite complicated, and we are only beginning to understand them. If it were true that life is ruled by the tendency to get as much pleasure as possible, one might expect that everybody would keep his level of aspiration as low as possible, because in this case his performance would be always above his level of aspiration, and he would feel successful. As a matter of fact, there is a marked tendency to keep the level of aspiration down out of fear of failure. Yet there is at the same time a strong tendency to raise the level of aspiration as high as possible. The experiments of J. D. Frank (1935a, pp. 119–28, 1935b, pp. 285–93, and 1935c) show that both tendencies are of different strength in different individuals and that a third tendency may have to be distinguished, namely, the tendency to keep one's expectation about one's future performance as close as possible to reality. A cautious person usually starts with a relatively low level of aspiration and, after succeeding, he raises the level only by short steps. Other persons tend to maintain their levels of aspiration well above their achievements. The rigidity of the level of aspiration, i.e, the tendency to keep the level constant rather than to shift it, shows marked differences among individuals. Frank found that these differences are highly reliable and largely independent of the special nature of the task.

It is important to know whether success and failure change the level of aspiration only in the particular activity in question, or whether success and failure in one task influence the level of aspiration in another task too. This is important for problems of guidance, where the effects of achievement or failure in different fields of activity on each other are of great significance, as, for instance, in the realm of school motivation and of delinquency. Frank found a marked relationship between success and failure in one task and the level of aspiration in another, if the tasks concerned had sufficient psychological relations. Mr. Jacknat's experiments verified this result but showed that this influence is weak or negligible if past experience has rigidly fixed the level of aspiration within a task.

V

These studies point to a relation between the level of aspiration for a specific task and something that one may call self-esteem, which means the feeling of the person about his own status and general standards. All experiments indicate that this relation is very fundamental. There is, for instance, a marked tendency, in the case of failure, to blame an inadequate tool or an accident for the lack of achievement. To experience success or failure the person has to attribute the result of an action to himself in a very specific way. In case of inadequate performance, the person often tries to get rid of the feeling of failure by cutting the tie of belongingness between him and the result, and by rejecting his responsibility for the outcome. Also the tendency to raise the level of aspiration as high as possible seems to be closely related to self-esteem, particularly to the feeling of the person about his status in the social group. The level of aspiration is determined first by the upper limit of the person's achievement—in other words, by his ability. A second fundamental factor is the level of achievement prevailing in the social group to which a person belongs—for instance, among his business friends, his comrades, his playmates. The social group can have a strong influence in keeping the level of aspiration either too high or too low for a person's ability. This is especially true for children. The expectation of his parents, or the standards of his group, may keep the level of aspiration for the less able child too high and lead to continuous failure and overtension, whereas the level of aspiration for the very able child may be kept too low. (This may be the reason for Wellman's finding that children with a relatively high IQ gain less in IQ in the nursery school than children with a relatively low IQ.)

Fajans has shown that success and failure influence greatly the degree of activeness among active and passive children. Chase found an increase in achievement following success. Fajans has further determined the degree to which praise has an effect similar to real success. The effects of being successful, and of being socially recognized or being loved, resemble each other closely. This relation is important for adults, and even more so in the case of adolescents and children.

REFERENCES

English, H. B. *A Student's Dictionary of Psychological Terms.* Harper, 1934.

Frank, Jerome D. "Individual Difference in Certain Aspects of the Level of Aspiration." *American Journal of Psychology,* Vol. 47, January 1935a.

——. "Some Psychological Detriments of the Level of Aspiration." *AJP,* Vol. 47, April 1935b.

——. "The Influence of the Level of Performance in One Task on the Level of Performance in Another." *Journal of Experimental Psychology,* Vol. 18, No. 2, April 1935c.

Lewin, Kurt. *A Dynamic Theory of Personality.* McGraw-Hill, 1935.

The Case of Lift, Inc.

In 1971 the Board of Directors of Lift, Inc., Chicago, the oldest and one of the largest manufacturers of elevators in the world, nominated David Palma, 55, vice-president and head of international operations. The international division controlled about 50 companies all over the world, which together generated a sales volume roughly equal to that of the U.S. subsidiaries.

David Palma, an Italian national who had worked for Lift for twenty years, took on his new job at a moment when international operations were clearly in bad shape. During the preceding year they had netted only $50,000 profits for $300 million of sales; and although Lift was still the world leader in market share (with about 20 percent of the world market), its position was weakening.

Lift's Weakening Position

Palma assessed the reasons for the situation to be the following:

1. Competition was cutthroat. As the industry was labor intensive, and as its products were old, without patent protection, and often custom-made, there seemed to be little advantage of size against hundreds of small local competitors.

2. Lift had made no thorough analysis of its competition, nor of the different markets it served.

3. There was no product policy. Most products were developed in the U.S. and did not meet local needs nor local building code specifications; for lack of competitive products, Lift found itself excluded from a series of growing markets; there was no product diversification.

4. Management at all levels was inadequate. It was complacent (in many cases, managers of local subsidiaries were even unable to give a gross figure on the financial performance of their company; they had never been asked, either—even when a company lost money for several years, no questions were asked or actions taken). There was almost no turnover in management, and no outside recruiting; there was no management development and training.

5. Controls were inadequate. There were no performance goals and standards, no job descriptions, no performance appraisals (nor rewards for outstanding work or punishment for poor performance).

6. Coordination between and control of the different local subsidiaries was almost nonexistent, as was any organization at division headquarters (where nobody was specifically assigned to head Marketing, Production, Finance, etc., where adequate staffs were lacking, and where one had to turn to corporate staffs for the solution of every major functional problem).

Palma's Plan for Recovery

Palma, who had asserted his independence right away by moving international headquarters to Milan, decided at once to turn the situation around in a spectacular manner. He saw two major steps to be taken at once to

"The Case of Lift, Inc." was prepared by Alexander Bergmann, Professor at IMEDE.

realize any recovery and expansion: the introduction of a new product policy and a reorganization of structures and procedures.

As to products, he would revolutionize the industry by trying to apply a new concept: Lift would be building standardized models in a module system. This would allow for substantial economy through mass production of different standardized parts in different factories; it would allow centralized R&D to advance; it would lead to better service; etc. David Palma, himself an engineer, decided to focus all his attention on this strategic change in Lift's traditional operations as well as on possibilities of diversification through mergers and acquisitions.

He decided, therefore, to leave the organizational and administrative problems to somebody else, hired Joe Pfeffer as a director of human resources, and gave him carte blanche to implement his goal of introducing a new profitable product line.

Joe Pfeffer, 38, was an American with a pretty good record as a personnel administrator. He was the first manager to be hired from outside and only the third personnel administrator altogether. He described himself as a compulsive achiever who had struggled to advance in business ever since he was four years old. He had obtained his MBA in evening courses and had written two books on management (between 10 P.M. and 3 A.M., as he said). When he moved to Milan, he left his wife and child in New York, so that he could concentrate all his energy on his new job. Work is his primary hobby. He considers business an exciting adventure and tough challenge.

How Pfeffer Saw His Job

He described how he approached the challenge at Lift in the following way:

"My job was to turn this organization around from a paternalistic institution to a dynamic, successful, healthy, profitable, growing business.

"This meant, above all, to bring professionalism into the firm. Lift was at best 20, at worst 50 years behind in modern management techniques, with managers lacking discipline, drive, professional skills, the ability to work in teams, etc.

"Far-reaching changes were necessary. But you have to go slowly and not make mistakes. You have to establish a base from which to operate. You try to learn as much about the business as possible. And as a human resources manager you better be as comfortable with a financial statement as a financial VP is; otherwise, nobody will listen to you.

"The first thing I did was to ask management at the operating companies controlled by Lift International to prepare action plans to improve productivity and to reduce costs and expenses immediately. These plans were then discussed in Milan or, in the case of larger subsidiaries, at their local headquarters. If in these meetings someone came up with a watered-down budget, he was in trouble; we kicked the shit out of him. Note, however, that in a confrontation with a line man (especially one who is making money) the staff man always loses. So you have to know when to back off and wait until he makes a stupid mistake (they always do) and then sack him.

"We set the objectives at headquarters—time was short; inertia had to be removed: we knew that South Africa was performing poorly and should have improved 200 percent; so we set a target of 100 percent. You have to be reasonable and practical. You can't let these people set their own goals; they'll set them too low.

"I like to confront people one by one. We had only two staff meetings in 3½ years. But we do have individually tailored management seminars which I conducted personally. These were really MBO sessions—very simple, basic, and completely authoritarian: We gave as an assignment to the participants to state their greatest problems at the present; we then selected from the problems mentioned a few which seemed most important and discussed possible solutions. . . . We have come up with ideas which have saved the company millions, and I made sure that they were implemented. That is, I visited the companies frequently, giving them usually two months' advance notice so they could shape up before my arrival.

"We wanted the different companies to compete with each other. So we called, for instance, the Latin Americans together: the Mexicans were making $11 million with 1100 people; the Argentines $35 million with 600—very embarrassing. . . . When I went to Australia for the first time, at 4:30 P.M. everybody was gone—no competitive spirit. Now, with my new man there, everybody works until 7 P.M.

"As I met all these executives, I started to establish a worldwide manpower inventory. I interviewed systematically the 350 people in top positions. Interviews took typically about two hours. You give a guy the benefit of the doubt, but actually you know after 30 minutes what the man is like. In one case, I increased a man's salary by 20 percent on the spot (without even checking with his superior) and sometimes I started to look for a replacement the same day. Altogether we had to replace almost all of top management. Keeping them in their positions would really have been too costly. Either we kept them in an advisory function compatible with their technical expertise, or we just had to have them go.

"We hired only people from outside who had a good job; smart people . . . people who already earned $40,000 but were looking for better promotion prospects. The man on the top is decisive. I focus all the effort on him. If you have good top managers, you don't have to worry much more; they will not tolerate mediocrity down the line; you can leave them alone until they lack in performance. I have had no problems with them—I hired these guys. And none of them ever quit of his own desire.

"I'll train the new men; then they'll report directly to me during the first year; and after that I maintain a heavy dotted-line relationship to them. Some may say that this is not my business—I answer that everything involving people is my business.

"As to performance, I don't care what a man does (short of stealing from the company) as long as he gets results. That's why I like to hire locals as financial managers (while in many multinationals the finance men come from HQ). For they know the local conditions and how to circumvent the law, legally or illegally.

"It's hard to measure the long-term impact of managers on an organization. I don't worry about the uncontrollable; there is enough of what is controllable to worry about—we measure performance; that's what counts. What happens in five years is an illusion, anyway."

Pfeffer's Next Moves

After about two years of initial housecleaning, Joe Pfeffer started to (a) initiate a more formalized manpower planning system, to (b) establish standard personnel policies (although he avoids getting all policies down in writing—"often it is too dangerous to commit yourself"), and to (c) reorganize Lift headquarters operations.

More specifically, he developed position descriptions and performance standards for many key management positions; he introduced a uniform worldwide performance appraisal and review program (he established an incentive plan and formal annual salary reviews based on worldwide salary survey data); he encouraged on-the-job training of new managers away from their home country (while not supporting the attendance of training programs outside the company—"we can't afford to let our people go for two weeks' training"); and he has made it an obligation for every manager to identify and develop high-potential young executives.

Moreover, Joe Pfeffer has worked on the (re)organization of the Milan headquarters. Operations were divided into four regional divisions: Europe, Far East, Latin America, and Other. Each of these new divisions had to be provided with sizable marketing, finance, and engineering staffs which were recruited either from the cream of what was available in the operating units or from outside the company. Only for himself did Joe Pfeffer not create a big staff. He said he did not have the budget to hire first-rate people and preferred to work alone rather than with second-rate people. The constitution of a strong group in Milan had the purpose of helping the International Division gain more independence from Chicago (which was said to lack understanding for the international business) and at the same time of gaining control over the local operating units (which were believed to be drifting).

With all this, Lift International attained, in 1973, sales of $530 million and profits of $35 million, thus bypassing the North American operations for the first time, both in sales volume and profitability. Employment was down 13 percent (since 1970), to 33,000.

The Hern File Case (A)

The memoranda and letters reproduced or summarized herein are from the file of Stanley Hern, a junior in the School of Commerce and Finance at Pennel City College.

1. *February 14, 1956.* Associate Professor Leeds wrote Hern reminding him of several previous oral requests that he return to Leeds a term paper he had submitted during the fall term in Leeds' course, Personnel 357. He asked Hern to bring or mail in this paper immediately.

2. *February 21, 1956.* Professor Leeds wrote Hern that since he had not returned the term paper as requested in the February 14 letter, he (Leeds) had referred the matter to the discipline committee of the School of Commerce and Finance.

3. *February 27, 1956.* Professor Worthington, chairman of the discipline committee, wrote Hern asking him to appear at 2 P.M., March 9, in connection with "reported irregularities in Personnel 357." He asked Hern to submit in writing, prior to the committee hearing, a statement presenting the facts as he understood them; and he told Hern: "If you do not comply, you expose yourself to drastic penalties."

4. *February 29, 1956.* Hern wrote Professor Worthington to the effect that he could not prepare a written statement until he was informed, in writing, what the charges against him were and who had filed them.

"The Hern File Case (A)" from *Organizational Behavior: Cases and Readings,* by Austin Grimshaw and John W. Hennessey. Copyright © 1960 by McGraw-Hill, Inc. Used with the permission of McGraw-Hill Book Company and John W. Hennessey.

5. *March 2, 1956.* Professor Worthington sent Hern the following letter:

"Professor Leeds has written you twice, asking that you come to his office. You have ignored these, so Professor Leeds, in accordance with the regulations of Pennel City College, has referred the matter to our committee for action.

"I strongly urge you to turn in at once the written statement requested in my letter of February 27 and to try to make your peace with Professor Leeds prior to your required appearance before the discipline committee on March 9."

6. *March 6, 1956.* Hern wrote Professor Worthington that, in his opinion, the latter had evaded in his letter of March 2 Hern's February 29 request that he be informed as to the exact nature of the charges he was expected to reply to by written statement. He added: "My sin appears to be a failure to answer my mail. Is there a regulation which requires me to do so?"

7. *March 8, 1956.* Professor Leeds sent Professor Worthington the following memorandum:

"At your request I would like to submit in writing the facts of the Hern case. I will attempt to set down here the essence of my original presentation to you.

"Mr. Stanley Hern was a student in my section of Personnel 357 during the fall semester 1955–1956. There was nothing in his behavior or performance in this class until the incident in question that seems to me to have any bearing on understanding his case. He was an average student as measured by the examinations which were a part of the course, and he attended class regularly although he did not take a very active part in the discussions. Later evidence leads me to hypothesize that his mental attitude toward this course and its rather unique teaching-learning process was relatively negative.

"As a required part of the course, each student was asked at the beginning to write a personal experience as a term paper, to be submitted in the twelfth week of the semester. During the semester we discussed many times in class what this assignment involved and what would be acceptable as a personal experience. I invited the students to consult with me as they progressed on this assignment, and many students did come to see me. Mr. Hern talked with me briefly about a personal experience in the armed services that he thought might make a good term paper. My response was to encourage him to develop it.

"The papers were submitted to me at the beginning of the twelfth week of the semester, and I spent the next week reading and evaluating them. When I came upon Mr. Hern's, I discovered that it was a rather thin disguise of some material we have used many times in the course, but did not use in the fall semester, 1955–56. This is copyrighted by Grayson University. I immediately got out a copy and compared Mr. Hern's work with it. In Mr. Hern's version all of the names had been altered along with a few numbers. There was no notation of any kind that would lead the reader to believe that this was anything but an original study prepared by student Hern. Although some paragraphs had been juxtaposed, Mr. Hern's paper was word-for-word extracted from the Grayson original. There was no reasonable doubt that Mr. Hern had copied the Grayson material with the intention of submitting it to me as his own.

"I clipped Mr. Hern's paper to a mimeographed copy of the Grayson material, gave it no grade, and wrote in the upper right-hand corner that this was not an adequate fulfillment of the assignment and that I would like to see him personally to discuss this.

"When I returned the papers in class, Hern approached me at the end of the period with a question about why I had given him a copy of the Grayson material. When I explained that his paper was in fact taken from it, Mr. Hern denied that this was so. I explained to him that I had established this fact beyond any doubt. After that, Mr. Hern's response was to the effect that a situation had developed at his wife's place of employment which was so similar to the Grayson case that it seemed to him unnecessary to attempt to write it up when the authors of the Grayson material had already performed this task so adequately. My response to Mr. Hern was that this was a very serious problem, which had to be settled between us, and that I would appreciate his visiting me at his earliest convenience in my office. Mr. Hern's demeanor during this conversation surprised me with its implicit and rather aggressive communication that any indiscretion in this matter was mine rather than his.

"The following day Mr. Hern came to my office to keep an appointment we had made several days previously for the purpose of discussing the fact that he might not be able to attend our final examination because of an impending out-of-town trip. Our discussion of this problem was quite brief and routine. (As it turned out, Mr. Hern was in attendance at the examination.) When this matter had been discussed and Hern rose to leave, I again urged upon him the seriousness of his having submitted the Grayson material as his own and requested both that he come to talk about the matter and bring his paper. At this point, he put on my desk a copy of what he said was a changed version of his paper, which he said I could read or not read. I responded that I would put it in his file but that it was not in any way either a substitute for our conference or an influence upon my feeling about his original act.

"Since that time, Mr. Hern has never come to see me nor has he responded in any way to my letters requesting that he see me and that he return the paper he had originally submitted. I should add that I have never submitted a grade for Mr. Hern for Personnel 357 but have retained his grade card in my possession."

8. *March 9, 1956*. The discipline committee met with Hern. The minutes of the meeting read:

"The second case before the committee concerned Stanley Hern, a student in Professor Leeds' Personnel 357 class. Professor Leeds appeared before the committee and reported that Hern was involved in plagiarism in connection with a class assignment. Professor Leeds reported that he had written two letters to the student asking him to return the material in question and discuss the situation. The student had not responded to the letters. Professor Leeds finally informed the student by letter that the matter had been turned over to the school discipline committee. Professor Leeds outlined the circumstances for the committee as set forth in his written statement (attached). (See Leeds' memorandum of March 8.)

"Following Professor Leeds' statement, the committee called in Mr. Hern. He appeared in an Air Force Lieutenant's uniform. When Professor Worthington apologized for the few minutes' wait, Hern answered that he had until 4 P.M., when he was to report at Fort Eustis. Professor Worthington asked him about his military status and, in the following exchange, Mr. Hern replied in turn that he was (*a*) on active duty, (*b*) on active reserve duty, (*c*) on ready reserve subject to recall on two weeks' notice but not actually on active duty at present. The purpose of Professor Worthington's question was to put the student at ease, but in the course of questioning it appeared the student had no reason to be wearing the uniform. Mr. Hern was then asked to tell the committee about the problem before the committee. Mr. Hern asked to know what the charges were. Professor Connolly replied that the committee was not a trial board and was preferring no charges. It was aware that a problem had arisen between Mr. Hern and one of the school's faculty members and the committee's wish was to help solve this problem. Before attempting to go any further, the committee asked the student to give his version of the circumstances leading to the presentation of this problem to the committee. Mr. Hern replied that he had nothing to say and asked again for a statement of charges. When asked how he would account for the difficulty between him and the instructor he replied, 'Personality conflict.' In response to a request that he tell the committee what might have led to the personality conflict, he drew a memo from his briefcase in which Professor Leeds had commended him for his work on another assignment. Mr. Hern refused to elaborate on the matter of personality conflict.

"There followed efforts by each member of the committee to persuade Mr. Hern to tell his story of what had occurred between Professor Leeds and himself. Mr. Hern's reply to each plea was that he had nothing to say. The committee recessed for a few moments, asking Mr. Hern to wait in the outer office.

"It was decided to warn Mr. Hern that unless he would cooperate with the committee by furnishing information in connection with this problem he could expect that a severe penalty would be assessed. The purpose of this warning was not to penalize but to try to induce him to cooperate with the committee. He still refused to communicate his version of the situation to the committee. He was then dismissed with the statement that he would hear from the committee within a few days.

"Professor Clark moved and Professor Connolly seconded a motion that the committee recommend to the dean that Mr. Hern be suspended from the school for one year, effective June 15, 1956."

9. *March 16, 1956.* Dean Potts wrote Hern:

"You are hereby suspended from school for one year, effective June 15, 1956. Reinstatement at the end of this period will be approved only if you are then able to persuade the discipline committee that your attitude is so improved as to justify their permitting you to proceed further toward a professional degree in business.

"If the term were not already well under way, I would suspend you as of today, causing you to lose credit for this semester's work.

"If you wish to appeal to the president, you must ask him for a review within twenty days."

10. *April 17, 1956.* An *ad hoc* committee appointed by the president met to consider Hern's appeal. The minutes of this meeting follow:

"Committee members: Berry, Chairman, Jewett, Thornlee

"The Chairman made an opening statement reviewing events leading up to the present meeting:

1. That Hern had been suspended for one year by the dean of the School of Commerce and Finance upon recommendation of the discipline committee of that school.
2. That Hern apparently felt this was an injustice and had appealed to the president.
3. That the president had requested this committee to review the case and report its findings to him.
4. That the committee was open-minded about the case, had every desire to be fair and had arranged this meeting with the student before arranging any meeting with Professor Leeds or with the discipline committee.

"The Chairman then requested Hern to give his view of what had happened, step by step, leading up to the suspension.

"Hern demonstrated considerable interest in the composition of the *ad hoc* committee, leaving the impression that he believed the matter was actually being referred back to the School of Commerce and Finance since two members of the committee were from its faculty.

"Hern stated he felt two problems were involved, one being his relationship with Professor Leeds and the other his relationship with the discipline committee.

"*Problem 1.* Hern indicated that there were several possible sources of friction between himself and Leeds and that the lack of specific charges made it impossible for him to know what or which activity was being questioned. He seemed more desirous of discussing other incidents than the term paper incident. The committee asked him specifically about the incident of the paper turned in to Professor Leeds. Hern stated that he had used the Grayson material as a guide to aid him in writing up a similar case which had occurred in his wife's place of employment. When questioned why he had bothered to change the names of the people if he planned merely to use this material as a guide, he said because he liked the new names better (paper one). He then wrote up his own paper (paper two) using paper one as a guide. He stated that he inadvertently turned paper one in to Professor Leeds instead of paper two.

"When Professor Leeds returned paper one to him with a copy of the Grayson material, Hern submitted paper two. When questioned as to the present location of paper one, he said he had destroyed it. When questioned why he had destroyed it, he said he destroyed all his papers. He stated that there was no plagiarism involved at all. He stated he felt paper two satisfied Professor Leeds' requirement. He received Professor Leeds' letters of March 16 and March 23 after the end of the semester and made no reply, feeling that he was no longer a student of Professor Leeds and that his problem with Leeds had been solved when he turned in paper two.

"The committee expressed to Hern its feeling that he used very poor judgment in making no response to Professor Leeds' letters and that, since he had received no grade for the course, he was still very much a student of Leeds, had to satisfy Leeds' requirements for the course, and was injudicious in not complying with Leeds' request for him to come in.

"*Problem 2.* Speaking of his relationship with the discipline committee, Hern said that the discipline committee did not state the reason why he was called before it and that he did not know why he was there; that the discipline committee did not mention the question of the term paper but asked merely if he had anything to say about Professor Leeds. He said he had taken the term paper with him to the discipline committee meeting and was prepared to discuss it and would have done so, if a question concerning it had been asked.

"The *ad hoc* committee expressed its feeling that Hern was extremely technical and legalistic in his relation with the discipline committee, that he undoubtedly knew why he was there, and that, if he had opened up to the discipline committee, the present penalty against him might not have been imposed.

"The committee asked Hern if he would be willing to discuss this matter now with the discipline committee if given an opportunity. He made no definite answer to this question but left the impression that he would be willing to talk about any specific matters brought up to him.

"Hern expressed concern over the penciled notation on his record to the effect that he would not be allowed to reregister and that a transcript of his record could not be issued. He stated if this meant he could not transfer to another school and finish his last year of college, the penalty was more severe than that imposed by the dean.

"The committee felt Hern was not completely frank and cooperative but was somewhat reluctant to discuss the obvious problem freely. He was probably more cooperative with this committee than he had been with the discipline committee but only because the specific issue was presented to him directly."

11. *April 24, 1956.* The *ad hoc* committee held a second meeting. The chairman's notes on this read:

"The *ad hoc* committee met April 24, 1956, to discuss the Hern case. One question which arose during the discussion was, 'Had the discipline committee at any time specifically stated to Hern that they wished to discuss the term paper incident with him?' (The minutes of the meeting of the discipline committee with Hern had not mentioned this specific incident.) It appeared advisable to ask the discipline committee this question before proceeding further.

"The chairman of the *ad hoc* committee then telephoned Professors Worthington, Connolly, and Clark and asked them if they would possibly be able to meet with the *ad hoc* committee, then in session. They were all willing to come, as was Mrs. Culver, ex-officio member and secretary of the committee.

"It was established in the ensuing discussion that the discipline committee had made no specific mention of the term paper incident in their meeting with Hern.

"The approach of the discipline committee, which has been successful in all other cases, is simply to state to the student that 'certain irregularities appeared in such and such a course; the committee would like to understand what occurred and would like the student to recite his version.' The committee has wished to be an aid to the student in getting any irregularities straightened out. It has not looked upon itself as a trial board supposed to prefer formal charges against the student, dig out fact, weigh evidence from student and faculty, and hand down a decision.

"The *ad hoc* committee expressed the view that Hern had some basis for complaint, if he wished to be technical and legalistic, since the discipline committee had not specifically brought to his attention the term paper incident that started the chain of events leading to his appearance before the committee. Most members of the discipline committee agreed they would be willing to invite Hern to appear before it again and to make specific mention of the term paper incident, hoping that Hern then would open up as he had with the *ad hoc* committee.

"One member of the discipline committee felt this would be making a trial board out of the discipline committee and would encourage students like Hern to feel they could force a faculty committee trying to be informal and friendly to fit a student's preconceived notions of what such a committee should be. This member of the committee was willing to give Hern another opportunity to meet with the committee but preferred to conduct such a meeting along the lines of the previous one, without making specific mention of the term paper incident. This member, however, did say he would yield on this point if there were a chance of Hern's bringing unfavorable publicity upon the college.

"There was some discussion then of the title 'discipline committee' and whether this should not be changed to something which does not sound punitive. There was also some discussion regarding the function of the committee and whether it should be a fact-finding board, prefer charges, etc.

"Most members of the discipline committee felt that they would like to continue asking any student to tell his side of the story, and if this did not elicit any information, to then specifically mention the incident which had brought the student before the committee."

12. *May 10, 1956.* The *ad hoc* committee reported its findings to the president. These were:

1. The discipline committee of the School of Commerce and Finance has always tried to be informal and friendly; it does not believe it should operate as a trial board and prefer charges. It has always heretofore been successful in getting a student's cooperation simply by asking him to state his version of the difficulty he was in. Following this customary procedure in the Hern case, the discipline committee made no specific mention to Hern of the term paper incident which precipitated the chain of events leading to his appearance before the committee.
2. Hern has viewed the situation as a legalistic one in which definite charges should be placed against a student, or at least the specific incident or incidents which bring the student before the committee should be stated by the committee. The fact that this was not done is, in our opinion, the crux of this case, because it is viewed by Hern as a loophole in his hearing.
3. There is a great deal of evidence that Hern's attitude has been poor and his judgment questionable. This committee certainly does not condone his behavior in many respects. Yet he has been suspended for a year for noncooperation with the discipline committee. We feel this penalty is so serious that the discipline committee should have another meeting with Hern, bring up specific matters it wishes to discuss, and try again to get him to state his version.
4. We believe Hern, if given another opportunity to meet with the discipline committee and if asked directly about the term paper incident, will tell the committee his version.
5. The discipline committee has expressed a willingness to give Hern another hearing and direct specific questions to him about the term paper incident.
6. Dean Potts had no intention of preventing Hern from attending another university by withholding a transcript. The dean has written the registrar a letter requesting that the penciled notation to that effect on Hern's record be deleted. A copy of this letter has been sent to Hern. (This finding is in connection with the next to the last paragraph in the minutes of the *ad hoc* committee meeting of April 17, 1956.)

13. *May 21, 1956*. Professor Worthington informed Hern that as a result of his appeal, the discipline committee had agreed to grant him another hearing. He asked Hern to present himself, for this purpose, at 2:30 P.M., May 28.

14. *June 7, 1956*. The president sent Hern a brief note:

"Professor Worthington informs me that you did not take advantage of the offer of his committee to grant you a rehearing. I therefore have no recourse other than to confirm the terms of your suspension as outlined in Dean Potts' letter of March 16."

15. *June 7, 1956*. The president instructed the dean of students to study existing regulations on student discipline with possible revision in mind, "in light of the Hern case." Excerpts from the new sections on student conduct and discipline, drafted by the dean of students under the presidential directive and adopted officially by the faculty of Pennel City College in June, 1957, follow:

Section I. Student Conduct

Standards. Attendance at the college presupposes that students will observe the laws and deport themselves according to accepted standards of personal and group conduct. It presupposes further that they will abide by such rules, regulations, and procedures as are or may be established by the college for all students or by the various schools and departments for their own students. Failure to observe such laws, standards, rules, regulations, or procedures shall render students subject to penalties, which may include dismissal from the college.

Section II. Discipline

Schools. (a) The dean and faculty of each school are responsible for the administration of discipline for infractions of rules and regulations of the school or for unacceptable conduct by students in matters relating to their academic or professional progress. *(b)* The instructor is responsible for the maintenance of order and proper conduct in the classroom, and he is authorized to take such steps as are necessary to preserve order and to maintain the effective cooperation of the class in fulfilling the objectives of the course.

Section III. Interpretations, Procedures, and Records

A. *Interpretations.* The procedures set forth below shall be interpreted and administered in such a way as to assure the student charged with a breach of conduct of a fair hearing. Formalities are not required in initial disciplinary proceedings, but, in the case of reviews and rehearings, more formal procedures are desirable. Conduct disciplinary proceedings are not to be construed as adversary proceedings or judicial trials.

B. *Procedures and Records in Initial Disciplinary Proceedings.* The officer, committee, faculty members, or student organization responsible for maintaining discipline (hereinafter called "disciplinary authority") shall be guided by the following principles:

1. The student involved shall be informed by the disciplinary authority, orally or in writing, of the charge against him at the earliest reasonable time;
2. The student shall be given an opportunity to be heard by the disciplinary authority and to present evidence, testimonial or documentary, in his own behalf;
3. Every effort shall be made by the disciplinary authority to bring the matter to a speedy conclusion;
4. *(a)* In all instances of disciplinary action by a faculty member, the report shall be filed with the executive officer of the department in which the course is offered. The executive officer shall notify his dean. The dean shall notify the dean of any other school in which the student may be enrolled. Either dean may initiate such additional disciplinary action as the circumstances warrant. *(b)* In all instances of disciplinary action by officers, faculty committees, or student organizations, the report shall be filed with the dean to whom they are responsible, or, if a presidential committee, with the president;
5. The officer with whom the report is filed, within five days thereafter, shall notify the student in writing, and, if possible, orally, of the action taken and of his right to request a review. The written notification shall point out that the request for review must be in writing and must be filed with the officer sending the notice not more than twenty days from the day upon which the oral notice was given or the written notice would be received in the normal course of events.

C. *Review.* (1) In all cases where disciplinary action is taken, the student involved shall be advised that he has the right to request one review of the case, such review to be accorded by the next immediate superior of the officer or agency taking the action, except as hereinafter provided (see paragraph C2 below). Such requests for review must be made in writing within the twenty-day period provided above. Action taken by faculty members or school disciplinary committees shall be subject to review by the dean of the school in which the case arose. Actions of the Dean of Men and/or the Dean of Women shall be subject to review by the Dean of Students. Actions taken by the dean of a school or the Dean of Students shall be subject to review by the president. (2) In cases involving expulsion or suspension, the record of the case shall be forwarded to the president for review before the decision is announced. In these cases, the president, after reviewing the record, should indicate (*a*) his approval of the action, or (*b*) his suggestions as to additional steps which should be taken on the matter. No further review will be provided in such cases.

Section IV. Delegation

Authority to Delegate. Responsibility for taking disciplinary action may in certain cases be delegated by the Dean of Students or by the dean of a school to a committee of the college faculty, to a committee of the faculty of the school concerned, to student organizations, or to a student-faculty committee, subject to such terms and conditions, not in conflict with this part, as may be necessary to assure a sound disciplinary program.

[Sections I, II (*b*), and IV above had been in effect since 1954. Section III, however, was new except for B4 (*a*), which was also carried over from the 1954 action. Section III C replaced section III of the 1954 rules, which had said only:]

Review. Disciplinary decisions of the Dean of Students, or of the school, or of the instructor are final, subject to such review as the president may establish, except that any disciplinary action resulting in the permanent dismissal of a student from the college must have the approval of the president.

16. *July 16, 1956.* Hern wrote Dean Potts to inquire whether the registrar would honor requests from other universities for copies of his transcript.

17. *July 23, 1956.* Dean Potts replied that he had already instructed the registrar, as of June 25, to delete its "hold" notation on Hern's transcript and that it was now available to other universities. Dean Potts wrote: "Without such release, it would have been difficult or impossible for you to obtain admission to another university. This was not our intention."

18. *October 15, 1956.* Professor Leeds sent a memorandum to the registrar:

"Mr. Stanley Hern has been the central party in a discipline case which grew out of his behavior in Personnel 357. This case involved protracted problems. It is now closed, and I am free to submit the enclosed grade card (E), withheld until now with the knowledge of your office."

19. *August 23, 1957.* The registrar's office wrote a routine letter to Hern suggesting that he make an attempt to clear his record of the still-in-force suspension before his transcript was requested by any other university to which he might wish to apply for admission.

20. *September 16, 1957.* The admissions committee of Darberry State University wrote to the registrar of Pennel City College:

"We have received a transcript from your office for Stanley Hern, who last attended Pennel City College in the spring semester, 1956. On this transcript there is a notation: '3/16/56, suspended from the School of Commerce and Finance for one year, effective 6/15/56. Reinstatement not automatic. Must be allowed by school's discipline committee.'

"We would appreciate it if you would let us know the reason for this student's suspension and if he would be accepted again by your school."

This letter was referred to Dean Potts for disposition.

21. *September 20, 1957.* Dean Potts replied:

"This is in answer to your request to the registrar concerning Mr. Stanley Hern.

"Mr. Hern became subject to disciplinary action when one of his professors reported that he had turned in a term paper that was supposed to be original but was instead a direct copy from a standard text with the names of individuals changed. It is entirely probable that Mr. Hern would not have been suspended had he pleaded a misunderstanding as to the assignment or admitted that he had committed an improper action. Mr. Hern, however, preferred to take a legalistic attitude, refused to answer questions from the committee members, and regarded our whole investigation as a trial procedure subject to the laws of evidence, which it definitely was not.

"Mr. Hern was suspended more for his attitude than for his indiscretion as regards the term paper."

22. *January 8, 1958*. Hern wrote Dean Potts that he wished to appeal his "E" grade in Personnel 357.

23. *January 13, 1958*. Dean Potts wrote Hern that the grade in Personnel 357 was not subject to change and that he had no right to appeal.

24. *January 28, 1958*. Hern wrote Dean Potts again, asking why his "E" grade could not be appealed. Dean Potts made a notation on Hern's letter:

"Not to be answered. Useless to keep this matter going, in view of Hern's attitude."

25. *February 18, 1958*. Hern wrote Dean Potts a third letter along the lines of the previous two and asked for a citation of "the regulation which prohibits appeal." He also requested an itemized listing of all his week-to-week grades in Personnel 357.

26. *July 8, 1958*. Hern wrote Dean Potts asking the latter to arrange for him to appear before the discipline committee during the week of July 21.

27. *July 10, 1958*. Dean Potts sent a memorandum to Professors Lowery, Berry, Connolly, and Clark, and Mrs. Culver. This read:

"Mr. Stanley Hern, who was suspended for one year in 1956 for plagiarism in Professor Leeds' class, has asked for a hearing before the discipline committee for the purpose of lifting his suspension. Are you free to meet with him on Monday, July 21, at 3:30 P.M.? If not, when during that week? When I have all your replies, I will write Mr. Hern as to the exact time.

"Professor Lowery is the only present member of the discipline committee on campus this summer, and I am therefore asking him to be chairman. Professors Berry, Connolly, and Clark, and Mrs. Culver were all involved in the Hern case at the time of suspension. The five of you would seem to be, with Mrs. Culver acting as secretary ex officio, a reasonable interim committee to hear the case."

28. *July 21, 1958*. The minutes of the *ad hoc* discipline committee to hear the Hern appeal, prepared by Mrs. Culver, were approved as follows:

"Present: Professor Lowery, Chairman, Professors Berry, Connolly, Clark, and Mrs. Culver, secretary ex officio.

"The committee asked Mr. Hern to state his reasons for asking for a meeting at this time. It was pointed out that this could have been done a year earlier, and the committee was interested in what he had been doing since his suspension as well as his present purpose in asking for the lifting of the suspension.

"Mr. Hern replied that his letter of suspension had given him the the right to a meeting with the committee at any time after one year and that he was exercising that right at this time. He said it was up to the committee to decide whether he would be allowed to finish his education since he is prevented from being admitted to other schools because of his suspension from this college.

"The committee asked him why he thought the suspension should be lifted, to which Mr. Hern replied that he had done no harm to the school, but the school had definitely damaged him by suspending him. He repeated that it was up to the committee to take action to clear his record and permit him to complete his education. When asked where he planned to continue his education if the suspension were lifted, he replied he could not say at this time.

"Mr. Hern replied to questions about his activities the past two years that he felt they had no bearing on the case. Through further questioning, the committee learned that Hern had taken some night school courses at Darberry State University but had been denied admission as a degree candidate because of his suspension. He said he had been told he could appeal to their admissions board, but he had not done so because he felt it was up to this school to clear his record.

"The committee then excused Mr. Hern in order to discuss possible action with regard to this situation. It was generally agreed that Hern's attitude had not changed appreciably, but the committee was also in agreement that continuance of the suspension could accomplish nothing of benefit either to him or the school.

"The committee's decision was to recommend to the dean that the suspension of Stanley Hern be lifted at this time."

29. *July 23, 1958*. Dean Potts wrote to Hern:

"On the recommendation of the discipline committee which heard your appeal on July 21, I am lifting your suspension, effective immediately. You are therefore free to register for the fall or any subsequent semester, at your option."

30. *July 25, 1958*. At Dean Potts's request, Mrs. Culver wrote up from her notes an informal digest of the sequence of events at the July 21 hearing. This read:

"The committee had asked Hern to wait in the foyer for a few minutes while they discussed the procedure to be followed. (This was where I came in, a little late because of a 3:30 appointment.) I gathered from the discussion that Professor Connolly had greeted Hern cordially as he entered the outer office and that his efforts to be pleasant had been repulsed by Hern.

"The committee agreed upon a plan of action and called Hern in. After asking him if he knew all the members present, Professor Lowery asked him to tell the committee why he had decided to ask that his suspension be lifted now, almost a year after it could have been removed from his record. He replied, 'You people have taken the authority upon yourselves to decide the future of my education.' He said that he had a letter (here he consulted a sheet of paper he had brought with him which looked to me like a list of names and dates) from the Dean dated April 17, 1956, stating that he could call a meeting of the committee at any time after one year. 'So now I am calling it,' he said, 'and it's up to you to decide.' He added he had been told that the college would not deny him a release to enter another school, but that it had, and he felt he had been deceived since he had been refused admission to another school because of his suspension.

"When asked for more details, he repeated that such information had nothing to do with the question before the committee. 'I feel that I did the college no damage,' he said, 'but the college has caused me damage. I believe this could be proved in court.'

"Here Professor Connolly interposed a remark that he was reasonably certain no legal recourse would be possible in these circumstances. Hern replied that it might take a long time, but he had been told that compensation for damages was possible in his situation. (I felt there was implied a threat to sue if the committee did not lift the suspension.) I asked him if his purpose in calling the meeting was to build a case, but he did not answer the question.

"Hern continued to refuse to give information on his activities since his suspension or to state his reasons for feeling the suspension should be lifted at this time. 'It is up to you to decide,' he repeated.

"Intermittently, during the early part of the meeting, Professor Lowery attempted to explain at length and to no avail the committee's desire to reach a reasonable decision on the basis of information concerning Hern's activities since his suspension and his plans for the future. Little information was obtained as a result of these explanations and questions.

"Eventually, Professor Connolly burst out with the statement, 'Hern, I'm sorry for you. You're scared, and you are hurting yourself by your attitude that the college is a den of wolves out to get you. Why don't you try us and see if we are really so bad, after all. Come on, tell us about yourself, your experiences in the past two years, and your plans for the future. Give us a chance to show you that we can be fair and reasonable, that we are your friends.'

"To this, Hern replied, 'Professor Connolly, I did not come here to get my knees dirty.'

"Whereupon Professor Connolly rose from his chair and said, 'Hern, I will have no more to do with you since you apparently have no intention of cooperating in this discussion.' Turning to Professor Lowery, he asked to be excused, and started for the door. But as he neared the door, he stopped and said, 'Oh, hell, I'll stay,' and returned to his seat. At this Hern laughed derisively, watching Professor Connolly as he resumed his place at the table.

"Professor Berry then asked Hern if he remembered him from the appeal committee of two years ago. When Hern replied, 'Yes,' Professor Berry asked him if he was correct in his remembrance that Hern had said he would be willing to give information to the committee if he could have another hearing at that time. When Hern agreed this was correct, Professor Berry asked him why, then, he refused to answer the questions of this committee. Hern replied that what he had been doing or what he was going to do had no bearing on this committee's decision. 'Besides,' he said, 'I can't *prophesize* what I will be doing in the future.'

"In the following few minutes, the committee, by asking specific questions as to the school to which he had applied for admission and his understanding of the reason for its disapproval, was able to garner some facts about Hern's activities in this connection. Hern admitted he had been told he could appeal the denial of admission by appearing before the admissions board of the other school. He said he did not do so because he felt it was up to this college to release him.

"Members of the committee then continued their pleading with Hern for cooperation and a change of attitude, to no avail.

"(About this time, I scribbled a note to Professor Lowery asking if we could have a recess, because I felt this pleading was getting us nowhere.)

"Professor Lowery then asked if the committee would agree to a recess for a few moments. Other members of the committee seemed rather taken aback but made no objection, so Professor Lowery asked Hern to step out into the outer office and wait.

"I then told the committee I had asked for the recess because it seemed obvious to me that exhorting Hern to cooperate was getting us nowhere. I asked if they did not feel that we made better progress when we asked specific questions and pieced together the information.

"The consensus was that we could not get much in any case, and perhaps we should decide what to do without further questions to Hern.

"It was agreed that there seemed to be little change in Hern's attitude. Although the committee was aware of the dean's statement of the conditions under which the suspension would be lifted, i.e., that Hern's attitude change, all members seemed to feel that nothing could be gained by continuing the suspension. The original offense in the class was not so serious that it should be punished further, they believed.

"There was some concern as to whether the dean would agree to the recommendation, but the committee decided to recommend that the suspension be lifted.

"The question of what to tell Hern was discussed, first with the idea of telling him that the committee deplored his continued resistant attitude but would reluctantly recommend lifting his suspension. Further discussion, however, led to the decision to tell him he would be informed by letter from the dean as to the result of this meeting.

"Hern was then called back into the room and was asked if he had anything in particular he wanted the committee to know. He had nothing to add, so he was told he would be notified by letter of the decision.

"Meeting then adjourned."

The Hern File Case (B)

On Monday, March 20, 1956, Professor Leeds presented what he knew of the Hern case to his class in Personnel 357, as discussion material. He disguised the names of people and some of the other facts in the case to protect the identity of Stanley Hern. After this class session, Mr. Leeds reported to a colleague that the students had found the Hern affair an excellent vehicle for discussing various key issues in organizational behavior.

The next day, March 21, one of Mr. Leeds's students, Thomas Marklin, came to his office to confer with him. Mr. Marklin, who had taken part in the Personnel 357 discussion the day before, said he had personal knowledge about Mr. Hern that might have a bearing on the case. He assented to Mr. Leeds's suggestion that they should tape-record his testimony.

The rest of this report is a transcription of Mr. Marklin's discussion of Stanley Hern.

Mr. Marklin: You will be surprised to know that this morning I found out that my lab partner in Geology is none other than Stanley Hern. Boy, was I surprised! After yesterday's discussion I couldn't believe my ears when Stan began talking. This Geology lab, we have it once a week. It's a two-hour lab every Tuesday, 10–12. You come into the lab, and you have these long tables to work at. You sit down, two fellows together, and work together each day. Each man has a sheet of paper on which he puts down what he thinks the rocks are. But you work together on it. Usually they turn out the same paper because actually you're working together. So, Stan Hern is in my lab course.

Mr. Leeds: How would you describe him? Can you remember back over the course?

Mr. Marklin: Well, the first day in there, there were three of us working on the same rocks, and so right off the bat we disagreed on a rock and the other fellow and I thought it was one thing and so Hern thought it was something else and so he and the other fellow got into a big argument over it. So I put it down on my paper and forgot about the whole thing. The next week the fellow dropped the course, so that just left the two of us. Stan seemed pretty happy about it. He said the other fellow thinks he knows everything, it's good to be rid of him.

So we identified rocks together. I didn't argue with him or have any trouble with him. He seemed pretty positive. I wouldn't argue. I would put down what I wanted to. He did well. He had the top grade average in the class.

So everything went along that way, OK, until today. Usually he's a pretty talkative kind of guy. He comes into the classroom and he's always talking about something. But I could turn it off like a radio. But today he was really quiet. I began drawing pictures of rocks. He just sat there. So I made some remark about the college. He said, "Oh, this is a lousy school. I'm going to change schools next year. Yeah, they run things so shoddily. I don't want any part of it." Suddenly he added, "Yeah, they suspended me." I said, "What did you do, slug a prof or something?" "No," he said, "they said it was my attitude." I said, "Is that right?" "Yes, someone around here has it in for me." I said, "That sounds like a phony deal, suspending you just for your attitude."

He said, "Once they get it in for you, you've had it.

"I had this course and I took a test. I knew I did well. I got it back with a bad grade. So I bided my time and he came to class and read off the way the exam should have been. I had it almost word for word. So I took it up after class and showed it to the prof.

"I had it word for word. I made a fool out of him. He said he'd mixed me up with someone else. He finally gave me my A, after I put him on the spot. It made me pretty mad because the other kid he got me mixed up with, he didn't take his A away.

"I was supposed to have a meeting with him, but I knew how he felt so I didn't go.

"I wanted to take the final exam early. The final was on a Monday. I wanted to go to New York. I had made plans to go. He said it was all right. Then a few days later he told me one day after class that college regulations wouldn't allow him to give exams early. I told him I wanted to see the regulation. So he showed it to me. And he said, 'Well, Mr. Hern, if it were anybody else I might overlook it. But seeing as how it's you we'll have to go by college regulations.'

"He thought he had outfoxed me. But I postponed my trip for a few days. Monday, at the exam, I showed up. He couldn't fox me out like that.

"I came in and took the exam. I really did a good job. I really knew the stuff. I got an A on it, I think. I haven't seen the exam. But I was really sarcastic. I put down, 'This is a fact,' 'This is an opinion.' I really showed him. He had it in for me. But I wasn't taking any chances; I knew it anyway."

Then—I'm not too clear exactly what happened. Anyway, somehow Stan got a letter. He said, "I didn't want anything to do with that guy. When I got my grade sheet, there was Personnel 357 with a big 'X.' That means you don't get any grade, you know. And," he said, "the instructor was Leeds; maybe you've heard of him."

I didn't know what to say, so I said, "Yes, a fraternity brother of mine had him in a class last semester."

Stan went on, "So I got this grade sheet. I knew he had it in for me then." All the way through he kept saying, "He had it in for me, but I made a fool of him on that test."

Then—I don't know exactly what happened. He said Leeds turned it over to the Disciplinary Committee. "He had it in for me. It was probably about the test. I had made a fool of him, you see, and he had it in for me."

But anyway he got a letter asking him to come before the Disciplinary Committee. So he appeared the day he was supposed to. He said, "It was in a closed room and they were just a bunch of sharp academic lawyers, and I knew they were just trying to get me to say something. I went in. I've been around enough with court-martials to know if you say anything you're liable to hang yourself.

"They wanted to finish it off right there. I wasn't about to finish it. I just wanted to know what the charges against me were. They wouldn't do it. They tried to get me to say something about the instructor. They obviously wanted me to say something against him so they'd have something concrete to kick me out of school on. I didn't say anything. I wouldn't open my mouth and commit myself. They tried for quite a while to get me to say something, but I wouldn't do it. I really fooled them. Finally they gave up."

He got a letter from the dean to come to see him. He did. The dean said, "This looks like a very simple case to me. Why don't you talk it over with your instructor and get it fixed up?" Hern said, "I made it plain there that I wanted nothing to do with the instructor, the way I felt about him. He admitted this was the first case like this they'd had. That proves they were out to get me. I made them admit that.

"I kept asking the dean what the charges were. He kept asking me to be more specific about what I wanted to know. That really made me mad. I really showed him up too. I told him: 'You want me to be specific. Why, in the letter you sent me asking me to come to see you, you didn't even put the building name and the room number. How can you expect me to be specific, when you aren't even specific at all?' He admitted that, that the information was left out. And I made a fool of him too. I showed him what was going on. He wanted me to say something against the instructor, but I didn't do that.

"Then I got a letter Saturday saying they were suspending me for one year, and giving me twenty days to appeal to the President."

He pulled out his notebook. He had the letter there. The first paragraph he read, relating his suspension. He didn't read the last part, but closed his notebook.

Then: "I'm going to appeal. Not that it will do any good. All these college people stick together, you know. I'll appeal it, even if it won't do any good. After the President turns it down, I'm going to take it to the VA. When they find out what kind of deal I'm getting, they can make it pretty hard on the college. They get a lot of money from these veterans."

Then he went back over it. He felt strongly that you and the committee had it in for him and were trying to get him. I think he really believed it. He thought it was really unfair. He had convinced himself. He was as sincere as could be about it.

Two or three times he said, by the way, "They don't know who they're dealing with. They're not dealing with just some young college kid. I've been around. I know the ropes. I'm smarter than most of those guys anyway." He said that about three times.

Mr. Leeds: Any other general impressions?

Mr. Marklin: Well, yes. One thing: while he talked he kept playing with the rings of his notebook. I couldn't help thinking about Capt. Queeg in *The 'Caine' Mutiny*, you know. He was nervous. He would play with his pencil too. We were hunched over in a confidential way. About fifteen minutes before the end of the period our geology instructor gave back a test and Stan was shaking, like this. He was very nervous. I think he wanted to talk with someone. He wanted to tell me and he wanted to get my reactions. Every once in a while he'd stop, and I'd say "That sounds like a rotten deal." If I had disagreed with him I think he would have stopped talking about it.

Chapter

9 Interpersonal Behavior

As we have seen, human behavior can be examined from a variety of "levels of analysis." We began by taking the individual as the basic level because the individual is the basic unit of action. Yet, the individual is never independent: significant influence is exerted by the other party in any two-person or interpersonal situation. Therefore, as our second level of analysis it will be useful to look at the *interpersonal* dimension. Like other levels of analysis, it is an abstraction from the total data, but it does yield insights into the reciprocal nature of social behavior.

THE INTERPERSONAL BEHAVIOR MODEL

In order to better understand the interpersonal behavior situation, it is useful to refer to the model presented in Figure 1. The purpose of the model is to aid the examination of a situation in which the behavior of one individual acts as a stimulus to another.

Response as Stimulus

When one person behaves in a certain way toward another, the response received, to a small or large degree, determines the first person's own future behavior. If the response is rewarding, the behavior is likely to be repeated. Conversely, if the behavior is positive, the response is likely to be favorable. Indeed, if an individual's responses do not correspond to the approaches received, this is a clue to the manager that a specially strong internal motivation is operating that may require investigation. If, for example, an individual is anxious or angry, even a

Figure 1 Two-Person Interaction

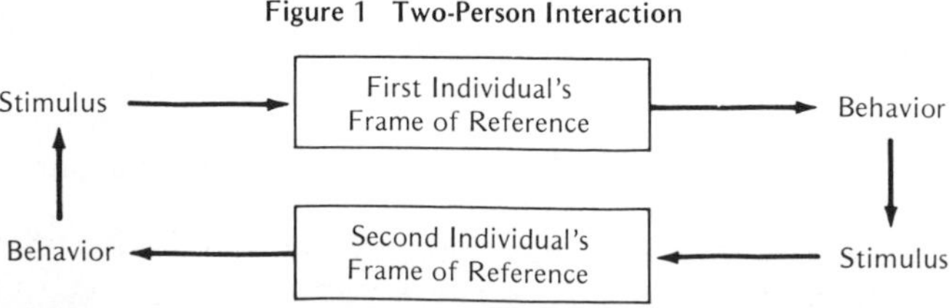

polite overture from another person may be perceived as an attack and can receive a hostile response. Such a response is not independent of variables internal to the individual because some stimulus from the second person was required to achieve it. However, in this case, the internal forces are stronger than the external forces in shaping the character of the response.

Role as Stimulus

The role or position of the other person is also a determinant in the reaction. One is not likely to respond the same way to a policeman, one's spouse, the doctor, a stranger on the street, a waiter, etc. Society has certain customs for how one responds in certain kinds of situations. Therefore, the individual is influenced not only by his or her own feelings and motivations and by the approach and personality of the other person, but also by the role and position of the other person with its incumbent social expectations.

The Thomas Motor case is an interesting example of two-person interaction over time. In each situation where Ralph Turner was having trouble, the foreman responded by telling him to slow down. The foreman avoided giving hostile criticism or exerting external pressure, merely suggesting that Turner work more slowly so as to avoid making similar mistakes. If part of Turner's basic problem originated from internal stimuli (his frustration at his inability to join in the coffee breaks, for example) the foreman's suggestions (which omit consideration of internal variables) really add external pressures which further frustrate Turner. Indeed, we see that each time Turner is told to slow down, he responds by attacking someone in the shop. This case provides a good example of how external and internal variables interact to set a pattern of apparently "illogical" behavior.

Past Behavior as Stimulus

In this connection it is useful to know that an individual's behavior can serve as a stimulus for his or her own future behavior. A lie, for example, may stimulate continued lying. A choice of clothing may be the stimulus for an individual's demeanor and the roles he or she will play. A point of view, once expressed, may be perceived as requiring self-consistent expression of the same point of view. All of these stimuli may result principally from the behavior of the individual, without much influence from the outside world.

DYNAMICS OF THE INTERACTION SITUATION

We must look beyond personalities and examine *the interaction situation* if we want to understand fully the causes for the behavior we see. In

Figure 2 The Johari Window

	Not known to self	Known to self
Known to others	2 Blind	1 Open
Not known to others	4 Unknown	3 Hidden

Known to self	Not known to self	
1 Open	2 Blind	Known to others
3 Hidden	4 Unknown	Not known to others

Source: Joseph Luft, *Group Processes: An Introduction to Group Dynamics*, 2nd ed., p. 11. Reprinted by permission of Mayfield Publishing Company (formerly National Press Books). Copyright © 1963, 1970 by Joseph Luft.

most situations, individuals are not motivated by "innate character traits." Ralph Turner, for example, does not behave "badly" because he is innately "irritable," "clumsy," "lazy," or "unskilled." Defining behavior in terms of "innate traits" is not an aid to understanding a problem, nor does it constitute diagnosis. Generally, people's responses are viewed by them as appropriate responses to environmental stimuli that have importance for them. Thus, Ralph Turner's behavior was related, not only to internal factors, but also to the foreman's acts. The interpersonal behavior model is useful for reminding the diagnostician that behavior is determined by, among other factors, the two-person interaction process in a dynamic situation.

A Model for Analyzing Interpersonal Situations

As we discussed earlier, what we perceive and what others perceive are not the same. This is the problem in interpersonal situations. A model known as the Johari window helps us think about this phenomenon, and understand how interpersonal communication is influenced differently by different patterns of awareness in one person and another (see Figure 2).

Square 1, marked "Open," refers to information that is known to the person and also to others. This would include such things as the person's size, age, job, name, etc. The relative size of square 1 is a function of the relative openness of the individual in interpersonal communication situations. Depending on the extent to which people disclose themselves to others, square 1 can increase or decrease in size.

Square 2, marked "Blind," refers to data about the individual that others know but the individual does not know—the effect of his or her behavior or communication style on others, or perhaps some physical detail of which the individual is unaware, such as a grease spot on the face or clothing. Unless the situation provides the opportunity for feedback, the individual will not be aware of these factors influencing the other person's behavior. Learning to give and receive feedback in an organization is a precondition to people understanding their "blind" areas and possibly behaving differently.

Square 3, marked "Hidden," is that information which the person does not disclose to others. It is known to the individual but not known to others. The reasons for the secret areas are as varied as past conditioning is varied. However, if the manager wishes to decrease the size of another person's "hidden" area, the manager must enable the individual to feel trust in the given situation or relationship, to feel that it is possible to share hidden feelings without negative consequences.

Finally, square 4, marked "Unknown," consists of those factors within a person of which neither the individual nor others are aware. For example, the individual may be anemic, or may be undergoing physical effects of psychological pressure.

The first person looks at the world through squares 1 and 3, while the world (the second person) sees the first person through squares 1 and 2. The interaction between them therefore will be based on different information. Ordinarily the goal of an interaction situation—especially when the individual must work regularly with a superior, family member, etc.—would be to increase the size of the open area. This would increase the shared information which could be used for problem solving and decision making. As noted above, this open area can be increased in size only by developing effective feedback mechanisms and building trust in the relationship.

This particular model becomes a useful mechanism for looking at any interpersonal situation. It can be extremely useful in diagnosis. As one gathers clues, one can place hypotheses in the appropriate squares.

Communication and Projection as Analytic Concepts

One of the most useful ways to analyze interpersonal behavior is in terms of communication. Each communication transaction is a dynamic unit of interpersonal behavior and yields good basic data for the analysis of a problem relationship in an organization. Furthermore, from a practical standpoint, a manager's insight into interpersonal dynamics must be translated into communication skills for solving management problems.

The subject of projection takes on new significance in the interpersonal model. We have seen that the first person's self-perception and perception of the other differs markedly from the second person's self-perception and perception of the other. Two-person interaction is further complicated by the fact that people, viewing themselves in a unique way, *project* that others view them in that particular way also. They then distort others' responses in terms of their own projections. The concept of projection, then, complicates the interpersonal relationship—introducing a sometimes subconscious variable which affects relationships. The better we can understand ourselves, the better we can be aware of the kinds of projections we make, and the better we can differentiate between another's behavior and our projection of what that behavior means.

CONCLUSION

The interpersonal "level of analysis" may well be the most fruitful one for inquiry in the work situation. The supervisor-subordinate relationship, the customer-client relationship, the manager-union representative relationship, can to a large extent be understood through an interpersonal model. And using the Johari window in diagnosis can be an effective way of increasing the knowledge available to both parties and for identifying the need for trust and feedback in two-person relationships.

CHRIS ARGYRIS

Interpersonal Barriers to Decision Making

The actual behavior of top executives during decision-making meetings often does not jibe with their attitudes and prescriptions about effective executive action.

The gap that often exists between what executives say and how they behave helps create barriers to openness and trust, to the effective search for alternatives, to innovation, and to flexibility in the organization.

These barriers are more destructive in important decision-making meetings than in routine meetings, and they upset effective managers more than ineffective ones.

The barriers cannot be broken down simply by intellectual exercises. Rather, executives need feedback concerning their behavior and opportunities to develop self-awareness in action. To this end, certain kinds of questioning are valuable; playing back and analyzing tape recordings of meetings has proved to be a helpful step; and laboratory education programs are valuable.

These are a few of the major findings of a study of executive decision making in six representative companies. The findings have vital implications for management groups everywhere; for while some organizations are less subject to the weaknesses described than are others, *all* groups have them in some degree. In this article I shall discuss the findings in detail and examine the implications for executives up and down the line. (For information on the company sample and research methods used in the study, see "Nature of the Study" at the end of this article.)

"Interpersonal Barriers to Decision Making" by Chris Argyris from *Harvard Business Review*, March–April 1966.

Words Versus Actions

According to top management, the effectiveness of decision-making activities depends on the degree of innovation, risk taking, flexibility, and trust in the executive system. (Risk taking is defined here as any act where the executive risks his self-esteem. This could be a moment, for example, when he goes against the group view; when he tells someone, especially the person with the highest power, something negative about his impact on the organization; or when he seeks to put millions of dollars in a new investment.)

Nearly 95 percent of the executives in our study emphasize that an organization is only as good as its top people. They constantly repeat the importance of their responsibility to help themselves and others to develop their abilities. Almost as often they report that the qualities just mentioned—motivation, risk taking, and so on—are key characteristics of any successful executive system. "People problems" head the list as the most difficult, perplexing, and crucial.

In short, the executives vote overwhelmingly for executive systems where the contributions of each executive can be maximized and where innovation, risk taking, flexibility, and trust reign supreme. Nevertheless, the *behavior* of these same executives tends to create decision-making processes that are *not* very effective. Their behavior can be fitted into two basic patterns:

Pattern A: Thoughtful, Rational, and Mildly Competitive

This is the behavior most frequently observed during the decision-making meetings. Executives following this pattern own up to their ideas in a style that emphasizes a serious concern for ideas. As they constantly battle for scarce resources and "sell" their views, their openness to others' ideas is relatively high, not because of a sincere interest in learning about the point of view of others, but so they can engage in a form of "oneupmanship"—that is, gain information about the others' points of view in order to politely discredit them.

Pattern B: Competitive First, Thoughtful and Rational Second

In this pattern, conformity to ideas replaces concern for ideas as the strongest norms. Also, antagonism to ideas is higher—in many cases higher than openness to ideas. The relatively high antagonism scores usually indicate, in addition to high competitiveness, a high degree of conflict and pent-up feelings.

Exhibit 1 summarizes data for four illustrative groups of managers—two groups with pattern A characteristics and two with pattern B characteristics.

Practical Consequences

In both patterns executives are rarely observed: taking risks or experimenting with new ideas or feelings; helping others to own up, be open, and take risks; using a style of behavior that supports the norm of individuality and trust as well as mistrust; expressing feelings, positive or negative.

These results should not be interpreted as implying that the executives do not have feelings. We know from the interviews that many of the executives have strong feelings indeed. However, the overwhelming majority (84 percent) feel

Exhibit 1 Management Groups with Pattern A and Pattern B Characteristics

	Pattern A				Pattern B			
	Group 1		Group 2		Group 3		Group 4	
Total No. of Units Analyzed[1]	**198**		**143**		**201**		**131**	
Units Characterized by:	**No.**	**%**	**No.**	**%**	**No.**	**%**	**No.**	**%**
Owning Up to Own Ideas	146	74	105	74	156	78	102	78
Concern for Others' Ideas	122	62	89	62	52	26	56	43
Conformity to Others' Ideas	54	27	38	26	87	43	62	47
Openness to Others' Ideas	46	23	34	24	31	15	25	19
Individuality	4	2	12	8	30	15	8	6
Antagonism to Others' Ideas	18	9	4	3	32	16	5	4
Unwillingness to Help Others Own Up to Their Ideas	5	2	3	2	14	7	4	3

[1] A unit is an instance of a manager speaking on a topic. If during the course of speaking he changes to a new topic, another unit is created.

that it is a sign of immaturity to express feelings openly *during decision-making meetings*. Nor should the results be interpreted to mean that the executives do not enjoy risk taking. The data permit us to conclude only that few risk-taking actions were *observed* during the meetings. (Also, we have to keep in mind that the executives were always observed in groups; it may be that their behavior in groups varies significantly from their behavior as individuals.)

Before I attempt to give my views about the reasons for the discrepancy between executives' words and actions, I should like to point out that these results are not unique to business organizations. I have obtained similar behavior patterns from leaders in education, research, the ministry, trade unions, and government. Indeed, one of the fascinating questions for me is why so many different people in so many different kinds of organizations tend to manifest similar problems.

WHY THE DISCREPANCY?

The more I observe such problems in different organizations possessing different technologies and varying greatly in size, the more I become impressed with the importance of the role played by the values or assumptions top people hold on the nature of effective human relationships and the best ways to run an organization.

Basic Values

In the studies so far I have isolated three basic values that seem to be very important:

1. *The significant human relationships are the ones which have to do with achieving the organization's objective.* My studies of over 265 different types and sizes of meetings indicate that executives almost always tend to focus their behavior on "getting the job done." In literally thousands of units of behavior, almost none are observed where the men spend some time in analyzing and maintaining their group's effectiveness. This is true even though in many meetings the group's effectiveness "bogged down" and the objectives were not being reached because of interpersonal factors. When the executives are interviewed and asked why they did not spend some time in examining the group operations or processes, they reply that they were there to get a job done. They add: "If the group isn't effective, it is up to the leader to get it back on the track by directing it."

2. *Cognitive rationality is to be emphasized; feelings and emotions are to be played down.* This value influences executives to see cognitive, intellectual discussions as "relevant," "good," "work," and so on. Emotional and interpersonal discussions tend to be viewed as "irrelevant," "immature," "not work," and so on.

As a result, when emotions and interpersonal variables become blocks to group effectiveness, all the executives report feeling that they should *not* deal with them. For example, in the event of an emotional disagreement, they would tell the members to "get back to facts" or "keep personalities out of this."

3. *Human relationships are most effectively influenced through unilateral direction, coercion, and control, as well as by rewards and penalties that sanction all three values.* This third value of direction and control is implicit in the chain of command and also in the elaborate managerial controls that have been developed within organizations.

Influence on Operations

The impact of these values can be considerable. For example, to the extent that individuals dedicate themselves to the value of intellectual rationality and "getting the job done," they will tend to be aware of and emphasize the intellectual aspects of issues in an organization and (consciously or unconsciously) to suppress the interpersonal and emotional aspects, especially those which do not seem relevant to achieving the task.

As the interpersonal and emotional aspects of behavior become suppressed, organizational norms that coerce individuals to hide their feelings or to disguise them and bring them up as technical, intellectual problems will tend to arise.

Under these conditions the individual may tend to find it very difficult to develop competence in dealing with feelings and interpersonal relationships. Also, in a world where the expression of feelings is not valued, individuals may build personal and organizational defenses to help them suppress their own feelings or inhibit others in such expression. Or they may refuse to consider ideas which, if exploded, could expose suppressed feelings.

Such a defensive reaction in an organization could eventually inhibit creativity and innovation during decision making. The participants might learn to limit themselves to those ideas and values that were not threatening. They might also decrease their openness to new ideas and values. And as the degree of openness decreased, the capacity to experiment would also decrease, and fear of taking risks would increase. This would reduce the *probability* of experimentation, thus decreasing openness to new ideas still further and constricting risk taking even more than formerly. We would thereby have a closed circuit which could become an important cause of loss of vitality in an organization.

SOME CONSEQUENCES

Aside from the impact of values on vitality, what are some other consequences of the executive behavior patterns earlier described on top-management decision making and on the effective functioning of the organization? For the sake of brevity, I shall include only examples of those consequences that were found to exist in one form or another in all organizations studied.

Restricted Commitment

One of the most frequent findings is that in major decisions that are introduced by the president, there tends to be less than open discussion of the issues, and the commitment of the officers tends to be less than complete (although they may assure the president to the contrary). For instance, consider what happened in one organization where a major administrative decision made during the period of the research was the establishment of several top-management committees to explore basic long-range problems:

As is customary with major decisions, the president discussed it in advance at a meeting of the executive committee. He began the meeting by circulating, as a basis for discussion, a draft of the announcement of the committees. Most of the members' discussion was concerned with raising questions about the wording of the proposal:

> Is the word "action" too strong?
>
> I recommend that we change "steps can be taken" to "recommendations can be made."
>
> We'd better change the word "lead" to "maintain."

As the discussion seemed to come to an end, one executive said he was worried that the announcement of the committees might be interpreted by the people below as an implication "that the executive committee believes the organization is in trouble. Let's get the idea in that all is well."

There was spontaneous agreement by all executives: "Hear, hear!"

A brief silence was broken by another executive who apparently was not satisfied with the concept of the committees. He raised a series of questions. The manner in which it was done was interesting. As he raised each issue, he kept assuring the president and the group that he was not against the concept. He just wanted to be certain that the executive committee was clear on what it was doing. For example, he assured them:

> I'm not clear. Just asking.
>
> I'm trying to get a better picture.
>
> I'm just trying to get clarification.
>
> Just so that we understand what the words mean.

The president nodded in agreement, but he seemed to become slightly impatient. He remarked that many of these problems would not arise if the members of these new committees took an overall company point of view. An executive commented (laughingly), "Oh, I'm for motherhood too!"

The proposal was tabled in order for the written statement to be revised and discussed further during the next meeting. It appeared that the proposal was the president's personal "baby," and the executive committee members would naturally go along with it. The most responsibility some felt was that they should raise questions so the president would be clear about *his* (not *their*) decision.

At the next meeting the decision-making process was the same as at the first. The president circulated copies of the revised proposal. During this session a smaller number of executives asked questions. Two pushed (with appropriate care) the notion that the duties of one of the committees were defined too broadly.

The president began to defend his proposal by citing an extremely long list of examples, indicating that in his mind "reasonable" people should find the duties clear. This comment and the long list of examples may have communicated to others a feeling that the president was becoming impatient. When he finished, there was a lengthy silence. The president then turned to one of the executives and asked directly, "Why are you worried about this?" The executive explained; then quickly added that as far as he could see the differences were not major ones and his point of view could be integrated with the president's by "changing some words."

The president agreed to the changes, looked up, and asked, "I take it now there is common agreement?" All executives replied "Yes" or nodded their heads affirmatively.

As I listened, I had begun to wonder about the commitment of the executive committee members to the idea. In subsequent interviews I asked each about his view of the proposal. Half felt that it was a good proposal. The other half had reservations ranging from moderate to serious. However, being loyal members, they would certainly do their best to make it work, they said.

Subordinate Gamesmanship

I can best illustrate the second consequence by citing from a study of the effectiveness of product planning and program review activities in another of the organizations studied:

It was company policy that peers at any given level should make the decisions. Whenever they could not agree or whenever a decision went beyond their authority, the problem was supposed to be sent to the next higher level. The buck passing stopped at the highest level. A meeting with the president became a great event. Beforehand a group would "dry run" its presentation until all were satisfied that they could present their view effectively.

Few difficulties were observed when the meeting was held to present a recommendation agreed to by all at the lower levels. The difficulties arose when "negative" information had to be fed upward. For example, a major error in the program, a major delay, or a major disagreement among the members was likely to cause such trouble.

The dynamics of these meetings was very interesting. In one case the problem to present was a major delay in a development project. In the dry run the subordinates planned to begin the session with information that "updated" the president. The information was usually presented in such a way that slowly and carefully the president was alerted to the fact that a major problem was about to be announced. One could hear such key phrases as:

> We are a bit later than expected.
>
> We're not on plan.
>
> We have had greater difficulties than expected.

It is now clear that no one should have promised what we did.

These phrases were usually followed by some reassuring statement such as:

However, we're on top of this.

Things are really looking better now.

Although we are late, we have advanced the state of the art.

If you give us another three months, we are certain that we can solve this problem.

To the observer's eyes, it is difficult to see how the president could deny the request. Apparently he felt the same way because he granted it. However, he took nearly 20 minutes to say that this shocked him; he was wondering if everyone was *really* doing everything they could; this was a serious program; this was not the way he wanted to see things run; he was sure they would agree with him; and he wanted their assurances that this would be the final delay.

A careful listening to the tape after the meeting brought out the fact that no subordinate gave such assurances. They simply kept saying that they were doing their best; they had poured a lot into this; or they had the best technical know-how working on it.

Another interesting observation is that most subordinates in this company, especially in presentations to the president, tended to go along with certain unwritten rules:

1. Before you give any bad news, give good news. Especially emphasize the capacity of the department to work hard and to rebound from a failure.

2. Play down the impact of a failure by emphasizing how close you came to achieving the target or how soon the target can be reached. If neither seems reasonable, emphasize how difficult it is to define such targets, and point out that because the state of the art is so primitive, the original commitment was not a wise one.

3. In a meeting with the president it is unfair to take advantage of another department that is in trouble, even if it is a "natural enemy." The sporting thing to do is say something nice about the other department and offer to help it in any way possible. (The offer is usually not made in concrete form, nor does the department in difficulty respond with the famous phrase, "What do you have in mind?")

The subordinates also were in agreement that too much time was spent in long presentations in order to make the president happy. The president, however, confided to the researcher that he did not enjoy listening to long and, at times, dry presentations (especially when he had seen most of the key data anyway). However, he felt that it was important to go through this because it might give the subordinates a greater sense of commitment to the problem!

Lack of Awareness

One of our most common observations in company studies is that executives lack awareness of their own behavioral patterns as well as of the negative impact of their behavior on others. This is not to imply that they are completely unaware; each individual usually senses some aspects of a problem. However, we rarely find an individual or group of individuals who is aware of enough of the scope and depth of a problem so that the need for effective action can be fully understood.

For example, during the study of the decision-making processes of the president and the nine vice presidents of a firm with nearly 3000 employees, I concluded that the members unknowingly behaved in such a way as *not* to encourage risk taking, openness, expression of feelings, and cohesive, trusting relationships. But subsequent interviews with the ten top executives showed that they held a completely different point of view from mine. They admitted that negative feelings were not expressed, but said the reason was that "we trust each other and respect each other." According to six of the men, individuality was high and conformity low; where conformity was agreed to be high, the reason given was the necessity of agreeing with the man who is boss. According to eight of the men, "We help each other all the time." Issues loaded with conflict were not handled during meetings, it was reported, for these reasons:

> We should not discuss emotional disagreements before the executive committee because when people are emotional, they are not rational.
>
> We should not air our dirty linen in front of the people who may come in to make a presentation.
>
> Why take up people's time with subjective debates?
>
> Most members are not acquainted with all the details. Under our system the person who presents the issues has really thought them through.
>
> Pre-discussion of issues helps to prevent anyone from sandbagging the executive committee.
>
> Rarely emotional; when it does happen, you can pardon it.

The executive committee climate or emotional tone was characterized by such words as "Friendly." "Not critical of each other." "Not tense." "Frank and no tensions because we've known each other for years."

How was I to fit the executives' views with mine? I went back and listened to all the interviews again. As I analyzed the tapes, I began to realize that an interesting set of contradictions arose during many of the interviews. In the early stages of the interviews the executives tended to say things that they contradicted later; Exhibit 2 contains examples of contradictions repeated by six or more of the ten top executives.

What accounts for these contradictions? My explanation is that over time the executives had come to mirror, in their behavior, the values of their culture (e.g., be rational, nonemotional, diplomatically open, and so on). They had created a culture that reinforced their own leadership styles. If an executive wanted to behave differently, he probably ran the risk of being considered a deviant. In most of the cases the executives decided to forgo this risk, and they behaved like the majority. These men, in order to live with themselves, probably had to develop various defenses and blinders about their acquiescence to an executive culture that may not have been the one they personally preferred and valued.

Incidentally, in this group there were two men who had decided to take the other route. Both men were viewed by the others as "a bit rough at the edges" or "a little too aggressive."

To check the validity of some of the findings reported, we interviewed the top 25 executives below the executive committee. If our analysis was correct, we knew, then they should tend to report that the members of the executive committee were low in openness to uncomfortable information, risk taking,

Exhibit 2 Contradictory Statements

During One Part of the Interview an Executive Said:	Yet Later in the Same Interview He Said:
The relationship among the executive committee members is "close," "friendly," and based on years of working together.	"I do not know how [my peers] feel about me. That's a tough question to answer."
"The strength of this company lies in its top people. They are a dedicated, friendly group. We never have the kinds of disagreements and fights that I hear others do."	"Yes, the more I think of it, the more I feel this is a major weakness of the company. Management is afraid to hold someone accountable, to say, 'You said you would do it. What happened?'"
"I have an open relationship with my superior."	"I have no direct idea how my superior evaluates my work and feels about me."
"The group discussions are warm, friendly, not critical."	"We trust each other not to upset one another."
"We say pretty much what we think."	"We are careful not to say anything that will antagonize anyone."
"We respect and have faith in each other."	"People do not knowingly upset each other, so they are careful in what they say."
"The executive committee tackles all issues."	"The executive committee tends to spend too much time talking about relatively unimportant issues."
"The executive committee makes decisions quickly and effectively."	"A big problem of the executive committee is that it takes forever and a day to make important decisions."
"The members trust each other."	"The members are careful not to say something that may make another member look bad. It may be misinterpreted."
"The executive committee makes the major policy decision."	"On many major issues, decisions are really made outside the executive committee meetings. The executive committee convenes to approve a decision and have 'holy water' placed on it."

trust, and capacity to deal with conflicts openly, and high in conformity. The results were as predicted (see Exhibit 3).

Blind Spots

Another result found in all organizations studied is the tendency for executives to be unaware of the negative feelings that their subordinates have about them. This finding is not startling in view of the fact that the executive problem-solving processes do not tend to reward the upward communication of information about interpersonal issues that is emotionally laden and risky to communicate. To illustrate:

In one organization, all but one of the top executive committee members reported that their relationships with their subordinates were "relatively good to excellent." When asked how they judged their relationships, most of the executives responded with such statements as: "They do everything that I ask for willingly," and "We talk together frequently and openly."

The picture from the middle management men who were the immediate

Exhibit 3 How the Executive Committee Was Rated by 25 Executives Below It

Characteristic Rated	Number of Managers Rating the Committee as:		
	Low	Moderate	High
"Openness" to "uncomfortable" information[1]	12	6	4
Risk taking	20	4	1
Trust	14	9	2
Conformity	0	2	23
Ability to deal with conflicts	19	6	0

[1] Three executives gave a "don't know" response.

subordinates was different. Apparently, top management was unaware that:

71 percent of the middle managers did not know where they stood with their superiors; they considered their relationships as ambiguous, and they were not aware of such important facts as how they were being evaluated.

65 percent of the middle managers did not know what qualities led to success in their organizations.

87 percent felt that conflicts were very seldom coped with; and that when they were, the attempts tended to be inadequate.

65 percent thought that the most important unsolved problem of the organization was that the top management was unable to help them overcome the intergroup rivalries, lack of cooperation, and poor communications; 53 percent said that if they could alter one aspect of their superior's behavior, it would be to help him see the "dog eat dog" communication problems that existed in middle management.

59 percent evaluated top management effectiveness as not too good or about average; and 62 percent reported that the development of a cohesive management team was the second most important unsolved problem.

82 percent of the middle managers wished that the status of their function and job could be increased but doubted if they could communicate this openly to the top management.

Interestingly, in all the cases that I have observed where the president asked for a discussion of any problems that the top and middle management men present thought important, the problems mentioned above were never raised.

Rather, the most frequently mentioned problem (74 percent of the cases) was the overload problem. The executives and managers reported that they were overloaded and that the situation was getting worse. The president's usual reply was that he appreciated their predicament, but "That is life." The few times he asked if the men had any suggestions, he received such replies as "More help," "Fewer meetings," "Fewer reports," "Delay of schedules," and so on. As we will see, few of these suggestions made sense, since the men were asking either for increases in costs or for a decrease in the very controls that the top management used to administer the organization.

Distrust and Antagonism

Another result of the behavior patterns earlier described is that management tends to keep promotions semisecret and most of the actual reasons for executive changes completely secret. Here is an example from an organization whose board we studied in some detail over a period of two years:

The executives complained of three practices of the board about which the board members were apparently unaware: (1) the constant alteration of organizational positions and charts, and keeping the most up-to-date versions semi-confidential; (2) shifting top executives without adequate discussion with all executives involved and without clearly communicating the real reasons for the move; and (3) developing new departments with product goals that overlapped and competed with the goals of already existing departments.

The board members admitted these practices but tended not to see them as being incompatible with the interests of the organization. For example, to take the first complaint, they defended their practice with such statements as: "If you tell them everything, all they do is worry, and we get a flood of rumors"; "The changes do not *really* affect them"; and "It will only cut in on their busy schedule and interrupt their productivity."

The void of clear-cut information from the board was, however, filled in by the executives. Their explanations ranged from such statements as "They must be changing things because they are not happy with the way things are going" to "The unhappiness is so strong they do not tell us." Even the executives who profited from some of these moves reported some concern and bewilderment. For example, three reported instances where they had been promoted over some "old-timers." In all cases they were told to "soft-pedal the promotion aspect" until the old-timers were diplomatically informed. Unfortunately, it took months to inform the latter men, and in some cases it was never done.

There was another practice of the board that produced difficulties in the organization:

Department heads cited the board's increasing intervention into the detailed administration of a department when its profit picture looked shaky. This practice was, from these subordinates' view, in violation of the stated philosophy of decentralization.

When asked, board members tended to explain this practice by saying that it was done only when they had doubts about the department head's competence, and when it was always in the interests of efficiency. When they were alerted about a department that was not doing well, they believed that the best reaction was to tighten controls, "take a closer and more frequent look," and "make sure the department head is on top of things." They quickly added that they did not tell the man in question they were beginning to doubt his competence for fear of upsetting him. Thus, again we see how the values of de-emphasizing the expression of negative feelings and the emphasizing of controls influenced the board's behavior.

The department heads, on the other hand, reported different reactions. "Why are they bothered with details? Don't they trust me? If not, why don't they say so?" Such reactions tended to produce more conformity, antagonism, mistrust, and fear of experimenting.

Still another board practice was the "diplomatic" rejection of an executive's idea that was, in the eyes of the board, offbeat, a bit too wild, or not in keeping with the corporate mission. The reasons given by the board for not being open about the evaluation again reflected adherence to the pyramidal values. For example, a board member would say, "We do not want to embarrass them," or "If you really tell them, you might restrict creativity."

This practice tended to have precisely the impact that the superiors wished to *avoid*. The subordinates reacted by asking, "Why don't they give me an opportunity to really explain it?" or "What do they mean when they suggest that the 'timing is not right' or 'funds are not currently available'?"

Processes Damaged

It is significant that defensive activities like those described are rarely observed during group meetings dealing with minor or relatively routine decisions. These activities become most noticeable when the decision is an important one in terms of dollars or in terms of the impact on the various departments in the organization. *The forces toward ineffectiveness operate most strongly during the important decision-making meetings*. The group and organizational defenses operate most frequently when they can do the most harm to decision-making effectiveness.

Another interesting finding is that the more effective and more committed executives tend to be upset about these facts, whereas the less effective, less committed people tend simply to lament them. They also tend to take on an "I told them so" attitude—one of resignation and noninvolvement in correcting the situation. In short, it is the better executives who are negatively affected.

WHAT CAN BE DONE?

What can the executive do to change this situation?

I wish that I could answer this question as fully as I should like to. Unfortunately, I cannot. Nevertheless, there are some suggestions I can make.

Blind Alleys

First, let me state what I believe will *not* work.

Learning about these problems by listening to lectures, reading about them, or exploring them through cases is not adequate; an article or book can pose some issues and get thinking started, but—in this area, at least—it cannot change behavior. Thus, in one study with 60 top executives:

Lectures were given and cases discussed on this subject for nearly a week. A test at the end of the week showed that the executives rated the lecturers very high, liked the cases, and accepted the diagnoses. Yet when they attempted to apply their newfound knowledge outside the learning situation, most were unable to do so. The major problem was that they had not learned how to make these new ideas come to life in their behavior.

As one executive stated, pointing to his head: "I know up here what I should do, but when it comes to a real meeting, I behave in the same old way. It sure is frustrating." (See Argyris, 1965a, p. 255.)

Learning about these problems through a detailed diagnosis of executives' behavior is also not enough. For example:

I studied a top-management group for nearly four months through interviews and tape recordings of their decision-making meetings. Eventually, I fed back the analysis. The executives agreed with the diagnosis as well as with the statement by one executive that he found it depressing. Another executive, however, said he now felt that he had a clearer and more coherent picture of some of the causes of their problems, and he was going to change his behavior. I predicted that he would probably find that he would be unable to change his behavior—and even if he did change, his subordinates, peers, and superiors might resist dealing with him in the new way.

The executive asked, "How can you be so sure that we can't change?" I responded that I knew of no case where managers were able successfully to alter their behavior, their group dynamics, and so forth by simply realizing intellectually that such a change was necessary. The key to success was for them to be able to show these new strategies in their behavior. To my knowledge, behavior of this type, groups with these dynamics, and organizational cultures endowed with these characteristics were very difficult to change. What kind of thin-skinned individuals would they be, and how brittle would their groups and their organizations be if they could be altered that easily?

Three of the executives decided that they were going to prove the prediction to be incorrect. They took my report and studied it carefully. In one case the executive asked his subordinates to do the same. Then they tried to alter their behavior. According to their own accounts, they were unable to do so. The only changes they reported were (1) a softening of the selling activities, (2) a reduction of their aggressive persuasion, and (3) a genuine increase in their asking for the subordinates' views.

My subsequent observations and interviews uncovered the fact that the first two changes were mistrusted by the subordinates, who had by now adapted to the old behavior of their superiors. They tended to play it carefully and to be guarded. This hesitation aggravated the executives, who felt that their subordinates were not responding to their new behavior with the enthusiasm that they (the superiors) had expected.

However, *the executives did not deal with this issue openly*. They kept working at trying to be rational, patient, and rewarding. The more irritated they became and the more they showed this irritation in their behavior, the more the subordinates felt that the superiors' "new" behavior was a gimmick.

Eventually, the process of influencing subordinates slowed down so much that the senior men returned to their more controlling styles. The irony was that in most cases the top executives interpreted the subordinates' behavior as proof that they needed to be needled and pushed, while the subordinates interpreted the top managers' behavior as proof that they did not trust their assistants and would never change.

The reason I doubt that these approaches will provide anything but temporary cures is that they do not go far enough. If changes are going to be made in the behavior of an executive, if trust is to be developed, if risk taking is to flourish, he must be placed in a different situation. He should be helped to (*a*) expose his leadership style so that he and others can take a look at its true impact; (*b*) deepen his awareness of himself and the dynamics of effective leadership; and (*c*) strive for these goals under conditions where he is in control of the amount, pace, and depth of learning.

These conditions for learning are difficult to achieve. Ideally, they require the help of a professional consultant. Also, it would be important to get away from the organization—its interruptions, pressures, and daily administrative tensions.

Value of Questions

The executive can strive to be aware that he is probably programmed with a set of values which cause him to behave in ways that are not always helpful to others and which his subordinates will not discuss frankly even when they believe he is not being helpful. He can also strive to find time to uncover, through careful questioning, his impact on others. Once in a while a session that is focused on the "How am I doing?" question can enlighten the executive and make his colleagues more flexible in dealing with him.

One simple question I have heard several presidents ask their vice presidents with success is: "Tell me what, if anything, I do that tends to prevent (or help) your being the kind of vice president you wish to be?" These presidents are careful to ask these questions during a time when they seem natural (e.g., performance review sessions), or they work hard ahead of time to create a climate so that such a discussion will not take the subordinate by surprise.

Some presidents feel uncomfortable in raising these questions, and others point out that the vice presidents are also uncomfortable. I can see how both would have such feelings. A chief executive officer may feel that he is showing weakness by asking his subordinates about his impact. The subordinate may or may not feel this way, but he may sense that his chief does, and that is enough to make him uncomfortable.

Yet in two companies I have studied where such questions were asked, superiors and subordinates soon learned that authority which gained strength by a lack of openness was weak and brittle, whereas authority resting on open feedback from below was truly strong and viable.

Working with the Group

Another step that an executive can take is to vow not to accept group ineffectiveness as part of life. Often I have heard people say, "Groups are no damned good; strong leadership is what is necessary." I agree that many groups are ineffective. I doubt, however, if either of the two leadership patterns described earlier will help the situation. As we have seen, both patterns tend to make the executive group increasingly less effective.

If my data are valid, the search process in executive decision making has become so complicated that group participation is essential. No one man seems to be able to have all the knowledge necessary to make an effective decision. If individual contributions are necessary in group meetings, it is important that a climate be created that does not discourage innovation, risk taking, and honest leveling between managers in their conversations with one another. The value of a group is to maximize individual contributions.

Interestingly, the chief executive officers in these studies are rarely observed making policy decisions in the classic sense, viz., critical selections from several alternatives and determination of future directions to be taken. This does not mean that they shy away from taking responsibility. Quite the contrary. Many report that they enjoy making decisions by themselves. Their big frustration comes from realizing that most of the major decisions they face are extremely complex and require the coordinated, honest inputs of many different executives. They are impatient at the slowness of meetings, the increasingly quantitative nature of the inputs, and, in many cases, their ignorance of what the staff groups did to the decision inputs long before they received them.

The more management deals with complexity by the use of computers and quantitative approaches, the more it will be forced to work with inputs of many different people, and the more important will be the group dynamics of decision-making meetings. If anyone doubts this, let him observe the dry runs subordinates go through to get a presentation ready for the top. He will observe,

I believe, that many data are included and excluded by subordinates on the basis of what they believe those at the top can hear.

In short, *one of the main tasks of the chief executive is to build and maintain an effective decision-making network*. I doubt that he has much choice *except* to spend time in exploring how well his group functions.

Such explorations could occur during the regular workday. For example, in one organization the president began by periodically asking members of his top group, immediately after a decision was made, to think back during the meeting and describe when they felt that the group was not being as effective as they wished. How could these conditions be altered?

As trust and openness increased, the members began to level with each other as to when they were inhibited, irritated, suppressed, confused, and withholding information. The president tried to be as encouraging as he could, and he especially rewarded people who truly leveled. Soon the executives began to think of mechanisms they could build into their group functioning so they would be alerted to these group problems and correct them early. As one man said, "We have not eliminated all our problems, but we are building a competence in our group to deal with them effectively if and when they arise."

Utilizing Feedback

Another useful exercise is for the superior and his group members to tape-record a decision-making meeting, especially one which is expected to be difficult. At a later date, the group members can gather and listen to the tape. I believe it is safe to say that simply listening to the tape is an education in itself. If one can draw from skilled company or outside help, then useful analyses can be made of group or individual behavior.

Recently, I experimented with this procedure with an "inside" board of directors of a company The directors met once a month and listened to tape recordings of their monthly board meetings. With my help they analyzed their behavior, trying to find how they could improve their individual and group effectiveness. Listening to tapes became a very involving experience for them. They spent nearly four hours in the first meeting discussing less than ten minutes of the tape.

"Binds" created. One of the major gains of these sessions was that the board members became aware of the "binds" they were creating for each other and of the impact they each had on the group's functioning. Thus Executive A was frequently heard antagonizing Executive B by saying something that B perceived as "needling." For example, A might seem to be questioning B's competence. "Look here," he would say, "anyone who can do simple arithmetic should realize that. . . . "

Executive B responded by fighting. B's way of fighting back was to utilize his extremely high capacity to verbalize and intellectualize. B's favorite tactic was to show A where he missed five important points and where his logic was faulty.

Executive A became increasingly upset as the "barrage of logic" found its mark. He tended to counteract by (*a*) remaining silent but manifesting a sense of being flustered and becoming red-faced; and/or (*b*) insisting that his logic *was* sound even though he did not express it in "highfalutin' language" as did B.

Executive B pushed harder (presumably to make A admit he was wrong) by continuing his "barrage of logic" or implying that A could not see his errors because he was upset.

Executive A would respond to this by insisting that he was not upset. "The point you are making is so simple, why, anyone can see it. Why should I be upset?"

Executive B responded by pushing harder and doing more intellectualizing. When Executive A eventually reached his breaking point, he too began to shout and fight.

At this point, Executives C, D, and E could be observed withdrawing, until A and B wore each other out.

Progress achieved. As a result of the meetings, the executives reported in interviews, board members experienced fewer binds, less hostility, less frustration, and did more constructive work. One member wondered if the group had lost some of its "zip," but the others disagreed. Here is an excerpt from the transcript of one discussion on this point:

Executive A: My feeling is, as I have said, that we have just opened this thing up, and I for one feel that we have benefited a great deal from it. I think I have improved; maybe I am merely reflecting the fact that you [Executive B] have improved. But at least I think there has been improvement in our relationship. I also see signs of not as good a relationship in other places as there might be.

I think on the whole we are much better off today than we were a year ago. I think there is a whole lot less friction today than there was a year ago, but there's still enough of it.

Now we have a much clearer organization setup; if we were to sit down here and name the people, we would probably all name exactly the same people. I don't think there is much question about who should be included and who should not be included; we've got a pretty clean organization.

Executive B: You're talking now about asking the consultant about going on with this week's session?

Executive A: It would be very nice to have the consultant if he can do it; then we should see how we can do it without him, but it'd be better with him.

Executive B: But that's the step, as I understand it, that should be taken at this stage. Is that right?

Executive A: Well, I would certainly favor doing something; I don't know what. I'm not making a specific recommendation; I just don't like to let go of it.

Executive C: What do you think?

Executive D: I'm not as optimistic as A. I wonder if anybody here agrees with me that maybe we haven't made as much progress as we think. I've personally enjoyed these experiences, and I'd like to see them continued.

Executive A: Would you like to venture to say why I think we have made progress and why I might be fooled?

Executive D: Well, I think maybe you are in the worst position to evaluate progress because if the worst possible thing that can happen is for people to no longer fight and struggle, but to say, "Yes, sir," you might call that progress. That might be the worst thing that could happen, and I sort of sense some degree of resignation—I don't think it's progress. I don't know. I might be all alone in this. What do you think?

Executive C: On one level it is progress. Whether it is institutional progress and whether it produces commensurate institutional benefits is a debatable question. It may in fact do so. I think it's very clear that there is in our meetings and in individual contact less heat, less overt friction, petulance, tension, than certainly was consistently the case. Do you agree?

Executive D: Yes, I think so.

Executive C: It has made us a great deal more aware of the extent and nature of the friction and clearly has made all of us intent on fighting less. There's some benefit to it; but there are some drawbacks.

Executive A: Well, if you and D are right, I would say for that reason we need more of the program.

Laboratory Training

Another possibility is for the executive to attend a program designed to help increase competence in this area, such as laboratory education and its various offshoots ("T-groups," the "managerial grid," "conflict management labs," and so on).[1] These learning experiences are available at various university and National Training Laboratory executive programs. They can also be tailor-made for the individual organization.

I believe outside programs offer the better way of becoming acquainted with this type of learning. Bear in mind, though, that since typically only one or two executives attend from the same organization, the biggest payoff is for the individual. The inside program provides greater possibilities for payoff to the organization.

At the same time, however, it should also be kept in mind that in-house programs *can* be dangerous to the organization. I would recommend that a thorough study be made ahead of time to ascertain whether or not a laboratory educational experience would be helpful to company executives individually and to the organization.

Open Discussion

I have never observed a group whose members wanted it to decay. I have never studied a group or an organization that was decaying where there were not some members who were aware that decay was occurring. Accordingly, one key to group and organizational effectiveness is to get this knowledge out into the open and to discuss it thoroughly. The human "motors" of the group and the organization have to be checked periodically, just as does the motor of an automobile. Without proper maintenance, all will fail.

NATURE OF THE STUDY

The six companies studied include: (1) an electronics firm with 40,000 employees, (2) a manufacturer and marketer of a new innovative product with 4000 employees, (3) a large research and development company with 3000 employees, (4) a small research and development organization with 150 employees, (5) a consulting-research firm with 400 employees, and (6) a producer of heavy equipment with 4,000 employees.

The main focus of the investigation reported here was on the behavior of 165 top executives in these companies. The executives were board members, executive committee members, upper-level managers, and (in a few cases) middle-level managers.

---

[1] For detailed discussions of such variations, see Argyris (1964), p. 60; Blake, et al. (1964), p. 135; and Schein and Bennis (1965).

Approximately 265 decision-making meetings were studied and nearly 10,000 units of behavior analyzed. The topics of the meetings ranged widely, covering investment decisions, new products, manufacturing problems, marketing strategies, new pricing policies, administrative changes, and personnel issues. An observer took notes during all but ten of the meetings; for research purposes, these ten meetings were analyzed "blind" from tapes (i.e., without ever meeting the executives). All other meetings were taped also, but analyzed at a later time.

The major device for analyzing the tapes was a new system of categories for scoring decision-making meetings.[2] Briefly, the executives' behavior was scored according to how often they: owned up to and accepted responsibility for their ideas or feelings; opened up to receive others' ideas or feelings; experimented and took risks with ideas or feelings; helped others to own up, be open, and take risks; did not own up; were not open; did not take risks; and did not help others in any of these activities.

A second scoring system was developed to produce a quantitative index of the *norms* of the executive culture. There were both positive and negative norms. The positive norms were:

1. *Individuality*, especially rewarding behavior that focused on and valued the uniqueness of each individual's ideas and feelings.
2. *Concern* for others' ideas and feelings.
3. *Trust* in others' ideas and feelings.

The negative norms were:

1. *Conformity* to others' ideas and feelings.
2. *Antagonism* toward these ideas and feelings.
3. *Mistrust* of these ideas and feelings.

In addition to our observations of the men at work, at least one semistructured interview was conducted with each executive. All of these interviews were likewise taped, and the typewritten protocols served as the basis for further analysis.

REFERENCES

Argyris, Chris. "Explorations in Interpersonal Competence, II." *Applied Behavioral Science*, Vol. 1, No. 3, 1965a.

——. *Organization and Innovation*. Irwin, 1965b.

——. "T-Groups for Organizational Effectiveness." *Harvard Business Review*, March–April 1964.

Blake, R. R., J. S. Mouton, L. B. Barnes, and L. E. Greiner. "Breakthrough in Organization Development." *Harvard Business Review*, November–December 1964.

Schein, Edgar, and Warren Bennis. *Organizational Change through Laboratory Methods*. Wiley, 1965.

[2] For a detailed discussion of the system of categories and other aspects of methodology, see Argyris (1965b).

CARL ROGERS AND FRITZ ROETHLISBERGER

Barriers and Gateways to Communication

Communication among human beings has always been a problem. But it is only fairly recently that management and management advisers have become so concerned about it and the way it works or does not work in industry. Now, as the result of endless discussion, speculation, and plans of action, a whole cloud of catchwords and catchthoughts has sprung up and surrounded it.

It is hoped that the following two descriptions of barriers and gateways to communication may help to bring the problem down to earth and show what it means in terms of simple fundamentals. First Carl R. Rogers analyzes it from the standpoint of human behavior generally (part I); then F. J. Roethlisberger illustrates it in an industrial context (part II).

I

It may seem curious that a person like myself, whose whole professional effort is devoted to psychotherapy, should be interested in problems of communication. What relationship is there between obstacles to communication and providing therapeutic help to individuals with emotional maladjustments?

Actually, the relationship is very close indeed. The whole task of psychotherapy is the task of dealing with a failure in communication. The emotionally maladjusted person, the "neurotic," is in difficulty, first, because communication within himself has broken down and, secondly, because—as a result of this—his communication with others has been damaged. To put it another way, the "neurotic" individual parts of himself which have been termed unconscious, or repressed, or denied to awareness, become blocked off so that they no longer communicate themselves to the conscious or managing part of himself. As long as this is true, there are distortions in the way he communicates himself to others, and so he suffers both within himself and in his interpersonal relations.

The task of psychotherapy is to help the person achieve, through a special relationship with a therapist, good communication within himself. Once this is achieved, he can communicate more freely and more effectively with others. We may say then that psychotherapy is good communication, within and between men. We may also turn that statement around and it will still be true. Good communication, free communication, within or between men, is always therapeutic.

It is, then, from a background of experience with communication in counseling and psychotherapy that I want to present two ideas: (1) I wish to state what I believe is one of the major factors in blocking or impeding communication, and then (2) I wish to present what in our experience has proved to be a very important way of improving or facilitating communication.

BARRIER: THE TENDENCY TO EVALUATE

I should like to propose, as a hypothesis for consideration, that the major barrier to mutual interpersonal communication is our very natural tendency to judge, to evaluate, to approve (or disapprove) the statement of the other person or the other group. Let me illustrate my meaning with some very simple examples. Suppose someone, commenting on this discussion, makes the statement, "I didn't like what that man said." What will you respond? Almost invariably your reply will be either approval or disapproval of the attitude expressed. Either you respond, "I didn't either; I thought it was terrible," or else you tend to reply, "Oh, I thought it was really good." In other words, your primary reaction is to evaluate it from your point of view, your own frame of reference.

Or take another example. Suppose I say with some feeling, "I think the Republicans are behaving in ways that show a lot of good sound sense these days." What is the response that arises in your mind? The overwhelming likelihood is that it will be evaluative. In other words, you will find yourself agreeing or disagreeing, or making some judgment about me such as "He must be conservative," or "He seems solid in his thinking." Or let us take an illustration from the international scene. Russia says vehemently, "The treaty with Japan is a war plot on the part of the United States." We rise as one person to say, "That's a lie!"

This last illustration brings in another element connected with my hypothesis. Although the tendency to make evaluations is common in almost all interchange of language, it is very much heightened in those situations where feelings and emotions are deeply involved. So the stronger our feelings, the more likely it is that there will be no mutual element in the communication. There will be just two ideas, two feelings, two judgments, missing each other in psychological space.

I am sure you recognize this from your own experience. When you have not been emotionally involved yourself and have listened to a heated discussion, you often go away thinking, "Well, they actually weren't talking about the same thing." And they were not. Each was making a judgment, an evaluation, from his own frame of reference. There was really nothing which could be called communication in any genuine sense. This tendency to react to any emotionally meaningful statement by forming an evaluation of it from our point of view is, I repeat, the major barrier to interpersonal communication.

GATEWAY: LISTENING WITH UNDERSTANDING

Is there any way of solving this problem, of avoiding this barrier? I feel that we are making exciting progress toward this goal, and I should like to present it as simply as I can. Real communication occurs, and this evaluative tendency is avoided, when we listen with understanding. What does that mean? It means to see the expressed idea and attitude from the other person's point of view, to sense how it feels to him, to achieve his frame of reference in regard to the thing he is talking about.

Stated so briefly, this may sound absurdly simple, but it is not. It is an approach which we have found extremely potent in the field of psychotherapy. It is the most effective agent we know for altering the basic personality structure of an individual and for improving his relationships and his communications with others. If I can listen to what he can tell me, if I can understand how it seems to him, if I can see its personal meaning for him, if I can sense the emotional flavor which it has for him, then I will be releasing potent forces of change in him.

Again, if I can really understand how he hates his father, or hates the company, or hates Communists—if I can catch the flavor of his fear of insanity, or his fear of atom bombs, or of Russia—it will be of the greatest help to him in altering those hatreds and fears and in establishing realistic and harmonious relationships with the very people and situations toward which he has felt hatred and fear. We know from our research that such empathic understanding—understanding with a person, not about him—is such an effective approach that it can bring about major changes in personality.

Some of you may be feeling that you listen well to people and yet you have never seen such results. The chances are great indeed that your listening has not been of the type I have described. Fortunately, I can suggest a little laboratory experiment which you can try to test the quality of your understanding. The next time you get into an argument with your wife, or your friend, or with a small group of friends, just stop the discussion for a moment and, for an experiment, institute this rule: "Each person can speak up for himself only after he has first restated the ideas and feelings of the previous speaker accurately and to that speaker's satisfaction."

You see what this would mean. It would simply mean that before presenting your own point of view, it would be necessary for you to achieve the other speaker's frame of reference—to understand his thoughts and feelings so well that you could summarize them for him. Sounds simple, doesn't it? But if you try it, you will discover that it is one of the most difficult things you have ever tried to do. However, once you have been able to see the other's point of view, your own comments will have to be drastically revised. You will also find the emotion going out of the discussion, the differences being reduced, and those differences which remain being of a rational and understandable sort.

Can you imagine what this kind of an approach would mean if it were projected into larger areas? What would happen to a labor-management dispute if it were conducted in such a way that labor, without necessarily agreeing, could accurately state management's point of view in a way that management could accept; and management, without approving labor's stand, could state labor's case in a way that labor agreed was accurate? It would mean that real communication was established, and one could practically guarantee that some reasonable solution would be reached.

If, then, this way of approach is an effective avenue to good communication and good relationships, as I am quite sure you will agree if you try the experiment I have mentioned, why is it not more widely tried and used? I will try to list the difficulties which keep it from being utilized.

Need for Courage

In the first place it takes courage, a quality which is not too widespread. I am indebted to Dr. S. I. Hayakawa, the semanticist, for pointing out that to carry on psychotherapy in this fashion is to take a very real risk, and that courage is required. If you really understand another person in this way, if you are willing to enter his private world and see the way life appears to him, without any attempt to make evaluative judgments, you run the risk of being changed yourself. You might see it his way; you might find yourself influenced in your attitudes or your personality.

This risk of being changed is one of the most frightening prospects many of us can face. If I enter, as fully as I am able, into the private world of a neurotic or psychotic individual, isn't there a risk that I might become lost in that world? Most of us are afraid to take that risk. Or if we were listening to a Russian Communist, or Senator Joe McCarthy, how many of us would dare to see the world from each of their points of view? The great majority of us could not listen; we would find ourselves compelled to evaluate, because listening would seem too dangerous. So the first requirement is courage, and we do not always have it.

Heightened Emotions

But there is a second obstacle. It is just when emotions are strongest that it is most difficult to achieve the frame of reference of the other person or group. Yet it is then that the attitude is most needed if communication is to be established. We have not found this to be an insuperable obstacle in our experience in psychotherapy. A third party, who is able to lay aside his own feelings and evaluations, can assist greatly by listening with understanding to each person or group and clarifying the views and attitudes each holds.

We have found this effective in small groups in which contradictory or antagonistic attitudes exist. When the parties to a dispute realize that they are being understood, that someone sees how the situation seems to them, the statements grow less exaggerated and less defensive, and it is no longer necessary to maintain the attitude, "I am 100 percent right and you are 100 percent wrong." The influence of such an understanding catalyst in the group permits the members to come closer and closer to the objective truth involved in the relationship. In this way mutual communication is established, and some type of agreement becomes much more possible.

So we may say that though heightened emotions make it much more difficult to understand an opponent, our experience makes it clear that a neutral, understanding, catalyst type of leader or therapist can overcome this obstacle in a small group.

Size of Group

That last phrase, however, suggests another obstacle to utilizing the approach I have described. Thus far all our experience has been with small face-to-face groups—groups exhibiting industrial tensions, religious tensions, racial tensions, and therapy groups in which many personal tensions are present. In these small groups our experience, confirmed by a limited amount of research, shows that this basic approach leads to improved communication, to greater acceptance of others and by others, and to attitudes which are most positive and more problem-solving in nature. There is a decrease in defensiveness, in exaggerated statements, in evaluative and critical behavior.

But these findings are from small groups. What about trying to achieve understanding between larger groups that are geographically remote, or between face-to-face groups that are not speaking for themselves but simply as representatives of others, like the delegates at Kaesong? Frankly, we do not know the answers to these questions. I believe the situation might be put this way: As social scientists we have a tentative test-tube solution of the problem of breakdown in communication. But to confirm the validity of this test-tube solution and to adapt it to the enormous problems of communication breakdown between classes, groups, and nations would involve additional funds, much more research, and creative thinking of a high order.

Yet with our present limited knowledge, we can see some steps which might be taken, even in large groups, to increase the amount of listening with, and decrease the amount of evaluation about. To be imaginative for a moment, let us suppose that a therapeutically oriented international group went to the Russian leaders and said, "We want to achieve a genuine understanding of your views and, even more important, of your attitudes and feelings toward the United States. We will summarize and resummarize these views and feelings if necessary, until you agree that our description represents the situation as it seems to you."

Then suppose they did the same thing with the leaders in our own country. If they then gave the widest possible distribution to these views, with the feelings clearly described but not expressed in name-calling, might not the effect be very great? It would not guarantee the type of understanding I have been describing, but it would make it much more possible. We can understand the feelings of a person who hates us much more readily when his attitudes are accurately described to us by a neutral third party than we can when he is shaking his fist at us.

Faith in Social Sciences

But even to describe such a first step is to suggest another obstacle to this approach of understanding. Our civilization does not yet have enough faith in the social sciences to utilize their findings. The opposite is true of the physical sciences. During the war, when a test-tube solution was found to the problem of synthetic rubber, millions of dollars and an army of talent were turned loose on the problem of using that finding. If synthetic rubber could be made in milligrams, it could and would be made in the thousands of tons. And it was. But in the social science realm, if a way is found of facilitating communications and mutual understanding in small groups, there is no guarantee that the finding will be utilized. It may be a generation or more before the money and the brains will be turned loose to exploit that finding.

SUMMARY

In closing, I should like to summarize this small-scale solution to the problem of barriers in communication, and to point out certain of its characteristics.

I have said that our research and experience to date would make it appear that breakdown in communication, and the evaluative tendency which is the major barrier to communication, can be avoided. The solution is provided by creating a situation in which each of the different parties comes to understand the other from the *other's* point of view. This has been achieved, in practice, even when feelings run high, by the influence of a person who is willing to understand each point of view empathically, and who thus acts as a catalyst to precipitate further understanding.

This procedure has important characteristics. It can be initiated by one party, without waiting for the other to be ready. It can even be initiated by a neutral third person, provided he can gain a minimum of cooperation from one of the parties.

This procedure can deal with the insincerities, the defensive exaggerations, the lies, the "false fronts" which characterize almost every failure in communications. These defensive distortions drop away with atonishing speed as people find that the only intent is to understand, not to judge.

This approach leads steadily and rapidly toward the discovery of the truth, toward a realistic appraisal of the objective barriers to communication. The dropping of some defensiveness by one party leads to further dropping of defensiveness by the other party, and truth is thus approached.

This procedure gradually achieves mutual communication. Mutual communication tends to be pointed toward solving a problem rather than toward attacking a person or group. It leads to a situation in which I see how the problem appears to you as well as to me, and you see how it appears to me as well as to you. Thus accurately and realistically defined, the problem is almost certain to yield to intelligent attack; or if it is in part insoluble, it will be comfortably accepted as such.

This then appears to be a test-tube solution to the breakdown of communication as it occurs in small groups. Can we take this small-scale answer, investigate it further, refine it, develop it, and apply it to the tragic and well-nigh fatal failures of communication which threaten the very existence of our modern world? It seems to me that this is a possibility and a challenge which we should explore.

II

In thinking about the many barriers to personal communication, particularly those that are due to differences of background, experience, and motivation, it seems to me extraordinary that any two persons can ever understand each other. Such reflections provoke the question of how communication is possible when people do not see and assume the same things and share the same values.

On this question there are two schools of thought. One school assumes that communication between A and B, for example, has failed when B does not accept what A has to say as being fact, true, or valid; and that the goal of communication is to get B to agree with A's opinions, ideas, facts, or information.

The position of the other school of thought is quite different. It assumes that communication has failed when B does not feel free to express his feelings to A because B fears they will not be accepted by A. Communication is facilitated when, on the part of A or B or both, there is a willingness to express and accept differences.

As these are quite divergent conceptions, let us explore them further with an example. Bill, an employee, is talking with his boss in the boss's office. The boss says, "I think, Bill, that this is the best way to do your job." Bill says, "Oh yeah!" According to the first school of thought, this reply would be a sign of poor communication. Bill does not understand the best way of doing his work. To improve communication, therefore, it is up to the boss to explain to Bill why his way is the best.

From the point of view of the second school of thought, Bill's reply is a sign neither of good nor of bad communication. Bill's response is indeterminate. But the boss has an opportunity to find out what Bill means if he so desires. Let us assume that this is what he chooses to do, i.e., to find out what Bill means. So the boss tries to get Bill to talk more about his job while he (the boss) listens.

For purposes of simplification, I shall call the boss representing the first school of thought "Smith" and the boss representing the second school of thought "Jones." In the presence of the so-called same stimulus each behaves differently. Smith chooses to explain; Jones chooses to listen. In my experience Jones's response works better than Smith's. It works better because Jones is making a more proper evaluation of what is taking place between him and Bill than Smith is. Let us test this hypothesis by continuing with our example.

WHAT SMITH ASSUMES, SEES, AND FEELS

Smith assumes that he understands what Bill means when Bill says, "Oh yeah!" so there is no need to find out. Smith is sure that Bill does not understand why this is the the best way to do his job, so Smith has to tell him. In this process let us assume Smith is logical, lucid, and clear. He presents his facts and evidence well. But, alas, Bill remains unconvinced. What does Smith do? Operating under the assumption that what is taking place between him and Bill is something essentially logical, Smith can draw only one of two conclusions: either (1) he has not been clear enough, or (2) Bill is too damned stupid to understand. So he either has to "spell out" his case in words of fewer and fewer syllables or give up. Smith is reluctant to do the latter, so he continues to explain. What happens?

If Bill still does not accept Smith's explanation of why this is the best way for him to do his job, a pattern of interacting feelings is produced of which Smith is often unaware. The more Smith cannot get Bill to understand him, the more frustrated Smith becomes and the more Bill becomes a threat to his logical capacity. Since Smith sees himself as a fairly reasonable and logical chap, this is a difficult feeling to accept. It is much easier for him to perceive Bill as uncooperative or stupid. This perception, however, will affect what Smith says and does. Under these pressures Bill comes to be evaluated more and more in terms of Smith's values. By this process Smith tends to treat Bill's values as unimportant. He tends to deny Bill's uniqueness and difference. He treats Bill as if he had little capacity for self-direction.

Let us be clear. Smith does not see that he is doing these things. When he is feverishly scratching hieroglyphics on the back of an envelope, trying to explain to Bill why this is the best way to do his job, Smith is trying to be helpful. He is a man of goodwill, and he wants to set Bill straight. This is the way Smith sees himself and his behavior. But it is for this very reason that Bill's "Oh yeah!" is getting under Smith's skin.

"How dumb can a guy be?" is Smith's attitude, and unfortunately Bill will hear that more than Smith's good intentions. Bill will feel misunderstood. He will not see Smith as a man of goodwill trying to be helpful. Rather he will perceive him as a threat to his self-esteem and personal integrity. Against this threat Bill will feel the need to defend himself at all cost. Not being so logically articulate as Smith, Bill expresses this need, again, by saying, "Oh yeah!"

WHAT JONES ASSUMES, SEES, AND FEELS

Let us leave this sad scene between Smith and Bill, which I fear is going to terminate by Bill's either leaving in a huff or being kicked out of Smith's office. Let us turn for a moment to Jones and see what he is assuming, seeing, hearing, feeling, doing, and saying when he interacts with Bill.

Jones, it will be remembered, does not assume that he knows what Bill means when he says, "Oh yeah!" so he has to find out. Moreover, he assumes that when Bill said this, he had not exhausted his vocabulary or his feelings. Bill may not necessarily mean one thing; he may mean several different things. So Jones decides to listen.

In this process Jones is not under any illusion that what will take place will be eventually logical. Rather he is assuming that what will take place will be primarily an interaction of feelings. Therefore, he cannot ignore the feelings of Bill, the effect of Bill's feelings on him, or the effect of his feelings on Bill. In other words, he cannot ignore his relationship to Bill; he cannot assume that it will make no difference to what Bill will hear or accept.

Therefore, Jones will be paying strict attention to all of the things Smith has ignored. He will be addressing himself to Bill's feelings, his own feelings, and the interactions between them.

Jones will therefore realize that he has ruffled Bill's feelings with his comment, "I think, Bill, this is the best way to do your job." So instead of trying to get Bill to understand him he decides to try to understand Bill. He does this by encouraging Bill to speak. Instead of telling Bill how he should feel or think, he asks Bill such questions as, "Is this what you feel?" "Is this what you see?" "Is this what you assume?" Instead of ignoring Bill's evaluations as irrelevant, not valid, or inconsequential, or false, he tries to understand Bill's reality as he feels it, perceives it, and assumes it to be. As Bill begins to open up, Jones's curiosity is piqued by this process.

"Bill isn't so dumb; he's quite an interesting guy" becomes Jones's attitude. And that is what Bill hears. Therefore Bill feels understood and accepted as a person. He becomes less defensive. He is in a better frame of mind to explore and re-examine his own perceptions, feelings, and assumptions. In this process he perceives Jones as a source of help. Bill feels free to express his differences. He feels that Jones has some respect for his capacity for self-direction. These positive feelings toward Jones make Bill more inclined to say, "Well, Jones, I don't quite agree with you that this is the best way to do my job, but I'll tell you what I'll do. I'll try to do it that way for a few days, and then I'll tell you what I think."

CONCLUSION

I grant that my two orientations do not work themselves out in practice in quite so simple or neat a fashion as I have been able to work them out on paper. There are many other ways in which Bill could have responded to Smith in the first place. He might even have said, "O.K., boss, I agree that your way of doing my job is better." But Smith still would not have known how Bill felt when he made this statement or whether Bill was actually going to do his job differently. Likewise, Bill could have responded to Jones in a way different from my example. In spite of Jones's attitude, Bill might still be reluctant to express himself freely to his boss.

The purpose of my examples has not been to demonstrate the right or wrong way of communicating. My purpose has been simply to provide something concrete to point to when I make the following generalizations:

1. Smith represents to me a very common pattern of misunderstanding. The misunderstanding does not arise because Smith is not clear enough in expressing himself. It arises because of Smith's misevaluation of what is taking place when two people are talking together.

2. Smith's misevaluation of the process of personal communication consists of certain very common assumptions, e.g. (*a*) that what is taking place is something essentially logical, (*b*) that words in themselves, apart from the people involved, mean something, and (*c*) that the purpose of the interaction is to get Bill to see things from Smith's point of view.

3. Because of these assumptions, a chain reaction of perceptions and negative feelings is engendered which blocks communication. By ignoring Bill's feelings and by rationalizing his own, Smith ignores his relationship to Bill as one of the most important determinants of the communication. As a result, Bill hears Smith's attitude more clearly than the logical content of Smith's words. Bill feels that his individual uniqueness is being denied. His personal integrity being at stake, he becomes defensive and belligerent. As a result, Smith feels frustrated. He perceives Bill as Stupid. So he says and does things which only provoke more defensiveness on the part of Bill.

4. In the case of Jones, I have tried to show what might possibly happen if we made a different evaluation of what is taking place when two people are talking together. Jones makes a different set of assumptions. He assumes (*a*) that what is taking place between him and Bill is an interaction of sentiments; (*b*) that Bill—not his words in themselves—means something; (*c*) that the object of the interaction is to give Bill an opportunity to express his differences freely.

5. Because of these assumptions, a psychological chain reaction of reinforcing feelings and perceptions is set up which facilitates communication between Bill and Smith. When Jones addresses himself to Bill's feelings and perceptions from Bill's point of view, Bill feels understood and accepted as a person; he feels free to express his differences. Bill sees Jones as a source of help; Jones sees Bill as an interesting person. Bill in turn becomes more cooperative.

6. If I have identified correctly these very common patterns of personal communication, then some interesting hypotheses can be stated:

a) Jones's method works better than Smith's, not because of any magic but because Jones has a better map than Smith of the process of personal communication.

b) The practice of Jones's method, however, is not merely an intellectual exercise. It depends on Jones's capacity and willingness to see and accept points of view different from his own, and to practice this orientation in a face-to-face relationship. This practice involves an emotional as well as an intellectual achievement. It depends in part on Jones's awareness of himself, in part on the practice of a skill.

c) Although our colleges and universities try to get students to intellectually appreciate points of view different from their own, very little is done to help them to implement this general intellectual appreciation in a simple face-to-face relationship—at the level of a skill. Most educational institutions train their students to be logical, lucid, and clear. Very little is done to help them to listen more skillfully. As a result, our educated world contains too many Smiths and too few Joneses.

d) The biggest block to personal communication is man's inability to listen intelligently, understandingly, and skillfully to another person. This deficiency in the modern world is widespread and appalling. In our universities, as well as elsewhere, too little is being done about it.

7. In conclusion, let me apologize for acting toward you the way Smith did. But who am I to violate a long-standing academic tradition!

JACK R. GIBB

Defensive Communication

One way to understand communication is to view it as a people process rather than as a language process. If one is to make fundamental improvement in communication, he must make changes in interpersonal relationships. One possible type of alteration—and the one with which this paper is concerned—is that of reducing the degree of defensiveness.

DEFINITION AND SIGNIFICANCE

"Defensive behavior" is behavior which occurs when an individual perceives threat or anticipates threat in the group. The person who behaves defensively, even though he also gives some attention to the common task, devotes an appreciable portion of his energy to defending himself. Besides talking about the topic, he thinks about how he appears to others, how he may be seen more favorably, how he may win, dominate, impress, or escape punishment, and/or how he may avoid or mitigate a perceived or an anticipated attack.

Such inner feelings and outward acts tend to create similarly defensive postures in others; and, if unchecked, the ensuing circular response becomes increasingly destructive. Defensive behavior, in short, engenders defensive listening, and this in turn produces postural, facial, and verbal cues which raise the defense level of the original communicator.

Defensive arousal prevents the listener from concentrating upon the message. Not only do defensive communicators send off multiple value, motive, and affect cues, but also defensive recipients distort what they receive. As a person becomes more and more defensive, he becomes less and less able to perceive

"Defensive Communication" by Jack R. Gibb from the *Journal of Communication*, Vol. 11(3), September 1961, pp. 141–148. Reprinted by permission of the author and the *Journal of Communication*.

accurately the motives, the values, and the emotions of the sender. The writer's analyses of tape-recorded discussions revealed that increases in defensive behavior were correlated positively with losses in efficiency in communication (Gibb, 1961, pp. 61–81). Specifically, distortions became greater when defensive states existed in the groups.

The converse also is true. The more "supportive" or defense-reductive the climate the less the receiver reads into the communication distorted loadings which arise from projections of his own anxieties, motives, and concerns. As defenses are reduced, the receivers become better able to concentrate upon the structure, the content, and the cognitive meanings of the message.

CATEGORIES OF DEFENSIVE AND SUPPORTIVE COMMUNICATION

In working over an eight-year period with recordings of discussions occurring in varied settings, the writer developed the six pairs of defensive and supportive categories presented in Table 1. Behavior which a listener perceives as possessing any of the characteristics listed in the left-hand column arouses defensiveness, whereas that which he interprets as having any of the qualities designated as supportive reduces defensive feelings. The degree to which these reactions occur depends upon the personal level of defensiveness and upon the general climate in the group at the time (Gibb, 1960, pp. 115–35).

Table 1 Categories of Behavior Characteristic of Supportive and Defensive Climates in Small Groups

Defensive Climates	Supportive Climates
1. Evaluation	1. Description
2. Control	2. Problem orientation
3. Strategy	3. Spontaneity
4. Neutrality	4. Empathy
5. Superiority	5. Equality
6. Certainty	6. Provisionalism

Evaluation and Description

Speech or other behavior which appears evaluative increases defensiveness. If by expression, manner of speech, tone of voice, or verbal content the sender seems to be evaluating or judging the listener, then the receiver goes on guard. Of course, other factors may inhibit the reaction. If the listener thinks that the speaker regards him as an equal and is being open and spontaneous, for example, the evaluativeness in a message will be neutralized and perhaps not even perceived. This same principle applies equally to the other five categories of potentially defense-producing climates. The six sets are interactive.

Because our attitudes toward other persons are frequently, and often necessarily, evaluative, expressions which the defensive person will regard as non-judgmental are hard to frame. Even the simplest question usually conveys the answer that the sender wishes or implies the response that would fit into his value system. A mother, for example, immediately following an earth tremor that shook the house, sought for her small son with the question: "Bobby, where are you?" The timid and plaintive "Mommy, I didn't do it" indicated how Bobby's chronic mild defensiveness predisposed him to react with a projection of his own guilt and in the context of his chronic assumption that questions are full of accusation.

Anyone who has attempted to train professionals to use information-seeking speech with neutral affect appreciates how difficult it is to teach a person to say even the simple "Who did that?" without being seen as accusing. Speech is so frequently judgmental that there is a reality base for the defensive interpretations which are so common.

When insecure, group members are particularly likely to place blame, to see others as fitting into categories of good or bad, to make moral judgments of their colleagues, and to question the value, motive, and affect loadings of the speech which they hear. Since value loadings imply a judgment of others, a belief that the standards of the speaker differ from his own causes the listener to become defensive.

Descriptive speech, in contrast to that which is evaluative, tends to arouse a minimum of uneasiness. Speech acts which the listener perceives as genuine requests for information or as material with neutral loadings are descriptive. Specifically, presentations of feelings, events, perceptions, or processes which do not ask or imply that the receiver change behavior or attitude are minimally defense-producing. The difficulty in avoiding overtone is illustrated by the problems of news reporters in writing stories about unions, Communists, Negroes, and religious activities without tipping off the "party" line of the newspaper. One can often tell from the opening words in a news article which side the newspaper's editorial policy favors.

Control and Problem Orientation

Speech which is used to control the listener evokes resistance. In most of our social intercourse someone is trying to do something to someone else—to change an attitude, to influence behavior, or to restrict the field of activity. The degree to which attempts to control produce defensiveness depends upon the openness of the effort, for a suspicion that hidden motives exist heightens resistance. For this reason attempts of non-directive therapists and progressive educators to refrain from imposing a set of values, a point of view, or a problem solution upon the receivers meet with many barriers. Since the norm is control, non-controllers must earn the perceptions that their efforts have no hidden motives. A bombardment of persuasive "messages" in the fields of politics, education, special causes, advertising, religion, medicine, industrial relations, and guidance has bred cynical and paranoidal responses in listeners.

Implicit in all attempts to alter another person is the assumption by the change agent that the person to be altered is inadequate. That the speaker secretly views the listener as ignorant, unable to make his own decisions, uninformed, immature, unwise, or possessed of wrong or inadequate attitudes is a subconscious perception which gives the latter a valid base for defensive reactions.

Methods of control are many and varied. Legalistic insistence on detail, restrictive regulations and policies, conformity norms, and all laws are among the methods. Gestures, facial expressions, other forms of non-verbal communication, and even such simple acts as holding a door open in a particular manner, are means of imposing one's will upon another and hence are potential sources of resistance.

Problem orientation, on the other hand, is the antithesis of persuasion. When the sender communicates a desire to collaborate in defining a mutual problem and in seeking its solution, he tends to create the same problem orientation in the listener; and, of greater importance, he implies that he has no predetermined solution, attitude, or method to impose. Such behavior is permissive in that it allows the receiver to set his own goals, make his own decisions, and evaluate his own progress—or to share with the sender in doing so. The exact methods of attaining permissiveness are not known, but they must involve a constellation of cues, and they certainly go beyond mere verbal assurances that the communicator has no hidden desires to exercise control.

Strategy and Spontaneity

When the sender is perceived as engaged in a stratagem involving ambiguous and multiple motivations, the receiver becomes defensive. No one wishes to be a guinea pig, a role player, or an impressed actor, and no one likes to be the victim of some hidden motivation. That which is concealed, also, may appear larger than it really is, with the degree of defensiveness of the listener determining the perceived size of the suppressed element. The intense reaction of the reading audience to the material in the *Hidden Persuaders* indicates the prevalence of defensive reactions to multiple motivations behind strategy. Group members who are seen as "taking a role," as feigning emotion, as toying with their colleagues, as withholding information, or as having special sources of data are especially resented. One participant once complained that another was "using a listening technique" on him!

A large part of the adverse reaction to much of the so-called human relations training is a feeling against what are perceived as gimmicks and tricks to fool or to "involve" people, to make a person think he is making his own decision, or to make the listener feel that the sender is genuinely interested in him as a person. Particularly violent reactions occur when it appears that someone is trying to make a stratagem appear spontaneous. One person has reported a boss who incurred resentment by habitually using the gimmick of "spontaneously" looking at his watch and saying, "My gosh, look at the time—I must run to an appointment." The belief was that the boss would create less irritation by honestly asking to be excused.

Similarly, the deliberate assumption of guilelessness and natural simplicity is especially resented. Monitoring the tapes of feedback and evaluation sessions in training groups indicates the surprising extent to which members perceive the strategies of their colleagues. This perceptual clarity may be quite shocking to the strategist, who usually feels that he has cleverly hidden the motivational aura around the gimmick.

This aversion to deceit may account for one's resistance to politicians who are suspected of behind-the-scenes planning to get his vote; to psychologists whose listening apparently is motivated by more than the manifest or content-level interest in his behavior; or to the sophisticated, smooth, or clever person whose "oneupmanship" is marked with guile. In training groups the role-flexible person frequently is resented because his changes in behavior are perceived as strategic maneuvers.

Conversely, behavior which appears to be spontaneous and free of deception is defensive-reductive. If the communicator is seen as having a clean id, as having uncomplicated motivations, as being straightforward and honest, and as behaving spontaneously in response to the situation, he is likely to arouse minimal defense.

Neutrality and Empathy

When neutrality in speech appears to the listener to indicate a lack of concern for his welfare, he becomes defensive. Group members usually desire to be perceived as valued persons, as individuals of special worth, and as objects of concern and affection. The clinical, detached, person-is-an-object-of-study attitude on the part of many psychologist-trainers is resented by group members. Speech with low affect that communicates little warmth or caring is in such contrast with the affect-laden speech in social situations that it sometimes communicates rejection.

Communication that conveys empathy for the feelings and respect for the worth of the listener, however, is particularly supportive and defense-reductive. Reassurance results when a message indicates that the speaker identifies himself with the listener's problems, shares his feelings, and accepts his emotional reactions at face value. Abortive efforts to deny the legitimacy of the receiver's emotions by assuring the receiver that he need not feel bad, that he should not feel rejected, or that he is overly anxious, though often intended as support-giving, may impress the listener as lack of acceptance. The combination of understanding and empathizing with the other person's emotions with no accompanying effort to change him apparently is supportive at a high level.

The importance of gestural behavioral cues in communicating empathy should be mentioned. Apparently spontaneous facial and bodily evidences of concern are often interpreted as especially valid evidence of deep-level acceptance.

Superiority and Equality

When a person communicates to another that he feels superior in position, power, wealth, intellectual ability, physical characteristics, or other ways, he arouses defensiveness. Here, as with the other sources of disturbance, whatever arouses feelings of inadequacy causes the listener to center upon the affect loading of the statement rather than upon the cognitive elements. The receiver then reacts by not hearing the message, by forgetting it, by competing with the sender, or by becoming jealous of him.

The person who is perceived as feeling superior communicates that he is not willing to enter into a shared problem-solving relationship, that he probably does not desire feedback, that he does not require help, and/or that he will be likely to try to reduce the power, the status, or the worth of the receiver.

Many ways exist for creating the atmosphere that the sender feels himself equal to the listener. Defenses are reduced when one perceives the sender as being willing to enter into participative planning with mutual trust and respect. Differences in talent, ability, worth, appearance, status, and power often exist, but the low-defense communicator seems to attach little importance to these distinctions.

Certainty and Provisionalism

The effects of dogmatism in producing defensiveness are well known. Those who seem to know the answers, to require no additional data, and to regard themselves as teachers rather than as co-workers tend to put others on guard. Moreover, in the writer's experiment, listeners often perceived manifest expressions of certainty as connoting inward feelings of inferiority. They saw the dogmatic individual as needing to be right, as wanting to win an argument rather than solve a problem, and as seeing his ideas as truths to be defended. This kind of behavior often was associated with acts which others regarded as attempts to exercise control. People who were right seemed to have low tolerance for members who were "wrong"—i.e., who did not agree with the sender.

One reduces the defensiveness of the listener when he communicates that he is willing to experiment with his own behavior, attitudes, and ideas. The person who appears to be taking provisional attitudes, to be investigating issues rather than taking sides on them, to be problem solving rather than debating, and to be willing to experiment and explore tends to communicate that the listener may have some control over the shared quest or the investigation of the ideas. If a person is genuinely searching for information and data, he does not resent help or company along the way.

CONCLUSION

The implications of the above material for the parent, the teacher, the manager, the administrator, or the therapist are fairly obvious. Arousing defensiveness interferes with communication and thus makes it difficult—and sometimes impossible—for anyone to convey ideas clearly and to move effectively toward the solution of therapeutic, educational, or managerial problems.

REFERENCES

Gibb, Jack R. "Defense Level and Influence in Small Groups." In *Leadership and Interpersonal Behavior,* eds. L. Petrullo and B. M. Bass. Holt, 1961.

——. "Sociophysiological Processes of Work Instruction." In *The Dynamics of Instructional Groups*, ed. N. B. Henry (59th yearbook of the National Society for the Study of Education, part 2, 1960).

The Crown Fastener Company Case

During the summer between his junior and senior years at Dartmouth College, Edgar Hagan took a job as a student trainee with the Crown Fastener Company, a medium-sized manufacturer and distributor of nuts and bolts. The training program Hagan was placed in consisted of four weeks in the company warehouse, four weeks in the company factory, and two weeks in the company offices. There were five students in the program, all of whom had the understanding that they would receive jobs as salesmen with the company after two summers in the program.

On the first day of work all five of the trainees met in the office of John Cusick, the superintendent of the warehouse. Cusick was a man in his middle thirties, a former decorated Navy veteran, and a graduate of Dartmouth College. After outlining the work program for the next four weeks and assigning each of the trainees to a specific department for the first two weeks, he offered this advice to them: "Fellows, I would be very careful in my relationships with the employees here if I were you. The majority of the people here are a pretty crude bunch. Their work is pretty much physical and routine in nature, and as a result, we can afford to hire men of generally low intelligence. They're all either Italians, Poles, or Negroes from the slums, and they're tough customers. So watch out for your valuables, and don't start any trouble with them."

For the first two weeks, Hagan was assigned to the sixth floor, hexagon nut department, under the supervision of Guildo Bovanni, a man who had been with the company since its inception twenty-two years before. Bovanni, a short but extremely powerful man, spoke in broken English and had quite a difficult time reading any material with which he was not previously familiar. When Cusick introduced Hagan to Bovanni he said: "Guildo, this is Edgar Hagan, a college trainee who'll be with us for the summer. I've decided to have him work here for the first two weeks, and I'd like you to teach him all you know about nuts. Give him all the odd jobs you have so he'll get experience with as many different types of nuts as possible. Well, good luck, Hagan. We'll get together again soon."

After Cusick had left, Bovanni said to Hagan, "A college boy, eh! I'll learn ya about nuts, but I'll do it my way. I guess Cusick there thinks I can learn ya in two weeks what I've learned in twenty years. Christ! Don't pay no attention to him. We'll start ya helping the packers so ya can work with the nuts we ship most of. You'll be lucky if ya can learn them in two weeks. Then each day I'll try to learn ya a few of the nuts we don't see very often."

Hagan was amazed that each of the nine employees in the hexagon nut department quickly told him almost the same thing as soon as he was alone with them. Typical of these comments was this statement by Ted Grant, an elderly Negro packer: "If I were you, I'd stay on the good side of Guildo. He's

"The Crown Fastener Company Case," EAA 265, 1955, was prepared by R. L. Katz under the direction of Paul Lawrence of the Harvard University Graduate School of Business Administration as a basis for classroom discussion rather than to illustrate either effective or ineffective handling of administrative situations.

one hell of a good foreman and really knows his stuff. He can teach you more about nuts and bolts than any guy in this place. Work hard for him and you'll get along swell here."

Hagan did his best to follow this advice and soon found that Bovanni was spending more and more time with him. He was very surprised when on Friday, Bovanni said: "Grab your lunch and let's go eat across the street." Bovanni regularly ate his lunch in a little bar across from the warehouse with a group of about seven other foremen. The conversation ranged from families to sports but soon settled on Cusick. Hagan was amazed at this because he, a newcomer, was there, and interpreted this to mean that Bovanni must have spoken to the men, saying that he was "OK." It was quickly obvious that Bovanni was the leader among this group, and when he summed up the conversation in the following manner everyone seemed in complete agreement with him:

"Cusick tries hard. He's tried to improve things here but he hasn't had the experience. He must be able to handle Charley Crown[1] though, look at the money he's got us for new equipment. But, Christ, then he screws up and buys the wrong stuff. He just don't know what to do and won't listen when we tell him."

On Friday of Hagan's first week, Cusick issued a bulletin stating that all forms used in the routing of materials in the warehouse would be changed to a slightly more complicated type on which material locations could be designated more concisely. The bulletin was handed out to all warehouse employees with their pay envelopes at the close of work Friday. Included was a group of the new forms. The bulletin simply stated that the change was to be made and requested that each man familiarize himself with the new forms over the weekend so that he could use them correctly on Monday. The men just took the material and stuffed it into their pockets in their haste to catch their streetcars home.

On Monday morning everyone in the hexagon nut department quickly went to work distributing the backlog of materials that had been delivered on Saturday, making a note of each shipment's ultimate location. As was the practice in this department, all of the department personnel met at Bovanni's desk at 10:30 A.M. to give this information to Bovanni so that he could copy it onto the formal forms which went to the office for inventory control. Bovanni claimed he used this procedure so that all the forms would be uniformly filled out and not mutilated by the men carrying them around as they worked. It was quite obvious, however, that his main purpose for insisting on this procedure was that he wanted to know where every shipment on his floor was located, so that when orders came through from the office he could tell the men exactly where the material ordered was located, from memory. Hagan had been constantly amazed by Bovanni's ability to remember exactly where, within each tier and row, a certain shipment was located. This ability had been built up over a period of years, and Bovanni was obviously quite proud of it.

At the Monday morning meeting there was a considerable difference of opinion among the various department personnel as to how the locations should be entered on the new forms. Bovanni insisted that it should be done in the same manner as before, where the aisle and tier of each shipment was recorded, while most of the other men protested that additional information as to the exact location within each aisle and tier should be noted. Bovanni argued that this would provide unnecessary detail and would only confuse things. He was quite adamant about this, and the other men quickly acceded to his point of view.

The next morning Cusick came up to the sixth floor and walked directly to Bovanni's

[1] The president of Crown Fastener Company.

desk. He said in quite a loud voice, "Guildo, you're filling out the forms all wrong. Didn't you read the notice? You're still doing it the old way, and that's just what we're trying to get away from. Do you think we would go to all this trouble only to have things done in the same old way? Now you've really got the office all fouled up. We need new forms on all the materials you received yesterday. You'd better get at it right away so they can make orders out on some of that material."

Guildo was sitting at his desk, looking up a catalogue number, while Cusick was talking to him. He was obviously getting madder and madder as Cusick spoke. Finally he broke in: "Look, Mr. Cusick, this department never had no trouble with its locations before. We've been getting alone fine. Why do you have to foul us up by making us change everything? I've been running this department for one hell of a long time, and I guess to Christ I know as much about it as you do. Why don't you handle the top brass and let me handle my department? As long as I get the work done, what do you care how I do it? When those orders come through, I'll be able to find those kegs just like I always have."

Cusick: "That's the trouble with you, Guildo, you only think of yourself. I've made this change in the entire warehouse. You're the only one bitching about it. From now on the office wants a complete record of exactly where everything is. Now, dammit, as long as I'm running this warehouse we're going to do it my way!"

Bovanni was getting madder all the time: "Listen, Cusick, you may run this warehouse, but I run this floor. Nobody really needs to know those locations except me, and you know it. The way we're doing things here works fine, and you know it. Why pick on me? Why don't you go climb on some of the other boys that don't get their work done? Why come nosing around here telling me how to do my job?"

Cusick moved around next to Bovanni and put his hand on Bovanni's shoulder: "Calm down, Guildo, remember who's boss here. I won't stand for your talking to me that way. Now just calm down and quit shouting."

Bovanni: "Wait a second. Who started the shouting? You come up here and broadcast to everybody that I don't know what I'm doing. I've run this floor for ten years, and you can't tell me how to do my job. Don't tell me to calm down, and take your Goddamn hand off me!"

Cusick, patting Bovanni's shoulder: "There's no sense in your getting all steamed up about this. You know damn well you're going to end up doing it my way."

Bovanni: "Get your hand off my shoulder!"

Cusick: "Let's not argue about it, you're wrong and you know it!"

Bovanni: "Take your hand off my shoulder before I slug you!"

Cusick, leaving his hand on Bovanni's shoulder: "Listen, no one talks to me that way. I won't stand for any punk telling me what to do. You'd better learn your place around here!"

Bovanni: "You heard me! Get your hand off me!"

Cusick, with his hand still on Bovanni's shoulder: "Hold on, Mac—."

Bovanni then whirled and hit Cusick squarely on the shoulder, knocking him back into a stack of kegs. Cusick recovered his balance and walked away, saying: "Okay, Buster, if that's the way you want it. . . ."

Thomas Motor Company Case

The Thomas Motor Company was a Plymouth-Dodge agency in Brownville, Michigan. The company was founded in 1927 by Mr. Edward P. Thomas. Until his unexpected death in September 1954, Mr. Thomas had been an active, respected citizen of the community and a successful businessman. Mr. Thomas's eldest son, John, succeeded to the presidency of the company.

John Thomas graduated in engineering from Mid-State University in 1947 and went to work as a salesman for Industrial Chemical Company in a nearby region. It had always been understood that he would take over the reins of the Thomas Motor Company when his father retired. John and his family returned to Brownville immediately after the elder Thomas's fatal heart attack.

John Thomas learned much about the business in a short time. In the first 13 months, he made very few administrative changes and he was guided chiefly by the recommendations of the experienced men who had worked for his father.

The Thomas Motor Company had two major divisions: sales and service. The service division had an auto-service center located downtown with the showrooms and main office. The truck-service center had its shop on the outskirts of town, about ten blocks from the main office.

The truck-repair shop regularly employed a service manager, four mechanics, a cashier-bookkeeper, and a parts man (although in late 1955 the latter was scheduled to be drafted into the service in six weeks and no replacement had yet been obtained).

The foreman and service manager of the truck center was Mr. Titus Nolan. He had been with the company since it was organized in 1927. His job included talking with customers regarding the cost and time of each job and assigning the work to the mechanics. Nolan also worked on the trucks himself when time allowed, although he had worked more closely with the men in the past than he now had time to. His ability as a foreman and a first-rate mechanic was widely respected; also Nolan was known as a quiet, unassuming man who, in the other mechanics' words, "takes things as they come and doesn't easily get excited."

The other truck mechanics were Bob, Jim, Ralph, and Dexter, an apprentice. (Their ages were 34, 32, 36, and 24, respectively.) In late 1955, Bob and Jim had been working in the shop about ten years. Ralph Turner had been employed by the Thomas Motor Company for the past 15 months. Dexter had been there for one year.

Ralph had previously worked in his father's trucking company, doing maintenance work on the trucks in their own shop. However, they did not have enough work to use their own shop profitably all of the time, as it developed, and so its use was discontinued. As a result, Mr. Turner and Ralph decided that Ralph would go to work for Mr. Thomas, and his father would send all of his truck repair and maintenance work there. This was quite a large account, and one the Thomas Company was happy to obtain.

When Ralph first came to work he asked to do the repairs on his father's trucks. Mr. Nolan said that Ralph could do this as much as was practicable. About two months later,

Mr. Nolan had an opportunity to talk to the senior Turner about his agreement. Nolan explained that the usual method of working in the shop involved each man's becoming more or less of a specialist on certain kinds of jobs and being assigned to these kinds of repairs as much as possible. Nolan felt that this led to increased efficiency and better workmanship. Also, he explained that since Mr. Turner's trucks were serviced at uneven intervals—sometimes two or three trucks at a time, sometimes none—he felt that Mr. Turner could be better served if the repairs were handled in the usual way by different men. Mr. Turner accepted this proposal.

Mr. Nolan passed the word on to Ralph. Ralph said he could see the logic of this and would accept "anything you decide upon." Nolan said at a later time that he expected this reaction from Ralph, because Ralph seemed to be getting along so well with the job and with the other men in the shop. He was "a very cooperative employee," in Nolan's words.

The mechanics were paid the going union-scale wage for their craft, and the only pay differentials were based on seniority. Dexter, new to the trade, was paid considerably less than the others.

Mr. Nolan considered Bob, Jim, and Ralph about equal in overall skill as mechanics, but Bob was the fastest man in the shop, with Jim a close second. Ralph was somewhat slower, and of course Dexter was a good deal slower because of lack of experience.

When a job was taken into the truck shop, the customer was usually told what the labor cost would be when he left the truck. From past experience the mechanic could usually judge fairly well whether he was losing too much time in the job, or whether he was going to finish on schedule or ahead of time. He tried to get ahead of the job he was doing so he could go across the street for coffee about 10 A.M. and again at 2:30 P.M. It was also an unwritten law that if a mechanic was not ahead on his job, he would not be able to go for coffee. Bob and Jim were almost always able to go, and Ralph was rarely able to go.

Dexter was almost always assigned to help one of the other mechanics. He would go for coffee if the man he was working with was able to go. Mr. Nolan, the parts man, and the cashier almost always went. These coffee sessions were looked upon as pleasant social occasions.

About August 1955, Ralph Turner began to make mistakes in his work, which Nolan attributed to haste on Ralph's part. Nolan checked the men's work carefully, and he was usually able to catch errors in the shop. However, several of Ralph's mistakes were not caught and proved to be quite serious. The first incident involved his not allowing enough clearance on a valve job. This customer returned about a week later very angry; and, although the garage did the work again free of charge, it lost a very good account.

At this time, Nolan talked to Ralph and told him to slow down and take his time even if he ran over the time that the job usually took. Ralph complained that the shop was too dirty and that this was the reason he made mistakes. He had been able to keep his own shop very clean and free from dirt when he worked for his father. Nolan replied that it wasn't possible to keep this shop as clean as Ralph's previous one because there wasn't sufficient spare time but that he felt the shop was as clean as most shops of this type. Ralph was a good deal more careful and worked at a slower rate for a couple of weeks. During this time he was never able to take a coffee break.

Nolan also noticed that Ralph had gradually shown, since he stopped working exclusively on his father's trucks, an increasing tendency to be interested in what other mechanics were doing on his father's vehicles when they were in the shop for repair. Several times Nolan had spoken to Ralph when the latter was found, during the lunch hour, tampering with a Turner truck on which one of the other mechanics was assigned to work. Nolan did not take this very seriously nor did he speak to Ralph, except mildly, because he felt it showed simply that Ralph was "eager and just solicitous about those old Dodge friends of his."

About two months later, in October 1955, Ralph failed to replace the rubber retainer in a set of hydraulic brakes he was repairing. The mistake very nearly caused a serious accident, and another account was lost. Nolan again appealed to Ralph to slow down. Ralph said that he was finding it very difficult to work with Dexter. (Nolan had been assigning Dexter to help Ralph for the previous three weeks.) Ralph said that Dexter seemed only bent on getting out for coffee. He felt that Dexter was not skillful enough to be working as fast as he tried to. He stated, "Dexter only wants to push me, not to learn from me."

Nolan replied he would have Dexter work with Bob or Jim but that he had wanted him to learn from all the men. Ralph agreed to be as careful as possible and to work more slowly.

About this same time, Ralph told his father that he had come to feel that the other mechanics had a prejudice against him. He said he could hardly work with the roar of the radio they had going at all times, either baseball or music. He had asked Bob to turn it off when Bob went out for coffee. Bob had given him a blank look and a grunt and turned it off for a couple of days.

Ralph continued, "The radio seems to be on louder than ever now. They never even think about me enough to turn it down when they go out for coffee. Furthermore, I think they are the kind that would talk about me behind my back, especially Dexter."

Nolan kept a close watch on Ralph's work. He recounted the whole problem to John Thomas when he came by one day in December 1955.

Nolan concluded by saying, "Ralph certainly is a changed man since we first hired him. In fact, if I weren't concerned about our losing the Turner account, I'd fire Ralph right now. We just can't afford his attitude and his errors. As it is, I'm afraid he's going to quit, and we'll lose the account anyway."

Chapter
10 Group Formation

MUZAFER SHERIF

Groups are composed of individuals. But when and how does a collection of individuals become a group? The phrase "group formation" suggests that something is formed. The task here is to trace the appearance of essential properties, or characteristics, which distinguish a human group.

Both for theory and research, it is instructive to adopt the strategy of tracing the formation of informal groups, rather than those instituted formally through blueprints handed down by outside authority (such as a committee or board). Despite the limitation in considering groups formed through the interaction of the membership, the implications are broad. Many social institutions and formal organizations (including governments) had informal beginnings if one goes into their histories. Informal groups are found almost invariably within stable formal structures, such as industrial, commercial, political, educational, religious, military, and recreational organizations. Finally, informal groups possess the minimum of the essential characteristics of any organized association, whether large or small.

BACKGROUND

The properties characterizing the formation of a group were treated by the 19th-century social philosophers for various reasons and with varying emphasis, each using illustrative examples known to him. But the topic was doomed to controversy until data were collected through scientific methods.

In the 1920s, Robert E. Park of the University of Chicago inspired and directed a series of investigations on human groups and their relationships to their settings (for example, Thrasher, 1927; Landesco, 1929; Shaw, 1929; Zorbaugh, 1929). Initiated to deal with the dire

---

Reprinted with permission of the publisher from the *International Encyclopedia of the Social Sciences*, David L. Sills, ed., Vol. 6, pp. 276–284.

problem of homeless and antisocial children, the work of the Soviet educator Makarenko included concrete data on the formation of group properties, which he gradually come to regard as crucial conditions for the effectiveness of his educational efforts (Makarenko, 1955; Bowen, 1962).

In the thirties, under the impetus of Elton Mayo of the Harvard Business School, studies in Western Electric's Hawthorne plant revealed the rise of groups and their impact upon the behavior of workers who had been placed together in observation rooms initially for the purpose of studying the effects of varying illumination and rest periods (Roethlisberger and Dickson, 1939). J. L. Moreno (1934) and his co-workers began the systematic sociometric mapping of friendship choices among girls in reformatory cottages and children in classrooms. Using the methods of laboratory psychology, Sherif (1939) tested sociological theories on the formation of social norms in situations of ambiguity and instability, demonstrating their subsequent retention as personal standards when individuals were alone. Lewin and his students (1939) initiated experiments varying the manner of adult supervisors of children's clubs. Meanwhile, the failure of "personality" or "intelligence" tests for selecting military leaders led the military in several countries to sponsor studies of what came to be called "leaderless groups" (Gibb, 1954; OSS, 1948).

DEFINING THE PROPERTIES OF WHAT IS FORMED

The definition presented here includes only the minimum properties found essential through extensive surveys of empirical and theoretical literature on groups of all kinds (Sherif, 1948; Sherif and Cantril, 1947; Sherif and Sherif, 1956).

Definition

A group is a social unit consisting of a number of individuals who stand in status and role relationships to one another, stabilized in some degree at a given time, and who possess a set of values or norms regulating their behavior, at least in matters of consequence to the group.

By this definition, the "groupness" of a group is a matter of degree. A collection of persons forms into a group proportional to (*a*) the degree of the stability of its organization (consisting of roles and status relations) and (*b*) the degree to which its particular set of norms for behavior are shared and binding for the participants. The undefined terms in the definition (role, status, norms) will be specified through research operations with conceptual relationship to the process of group formation.

It should be noted that this definition includes the properties covered in many modern works, while excluding others. Similar specifications are found in Bales (1949); Blau and Scott (1962); Bonner (1959); Cartwright and Zander (1960); Golembiewski (1962); and Hare (1962). The following characteristics, included by some investigators, were omitted here for the following reasons:

Interaction and *communication* are not distinctive to group formation but are essential to any kind of human association of consequence. *Shared sentiments, attitudes* and *behavior patterns* of group members are implied in the normative property; in fact the extent of sharing is one of the research measures for the degree of group formation at a given time. Many properties of existing groups (for example, *morale, solidarity* or *cohesiveness, loyalty* of members) are dependent upon the conditions of group formation, especially the degree of stability attained.

The properties essential in group formation will aid the reader in evaluating the large body of experimental research on small groups conducted both in the United States and in Europe since World War II. In summarizing this literature, Golembiewski (1962, p. 47) found that the great majority consisted of unknown persons in the laboratory briefly exposed to tasks or instructions creating temporary interdependence among individuals in their performance. Very few studies have allowed a sufficient time span for group properties to form.

Generality of Group Formation

Beneath the organized forms and routines of societies, the formation and disintegration of groups occurs in all walks of life, frequently with important consequences. Informal group formation is well documented within industrial, military, school, prison, and neighborhood settings (see Hare, 1962; Sherif and Sherif, 1956). In studying the Near North Side of Chicago, Zorbaugh (1929, p. 192) reported group formations in neighborhoods of all socioeconomic ranks with "an enormously important role in the lives of their members": exclusive clubs in the fashionable "Gold Coast," intimate groups of "nonconformists" in artists' studios, mutual benefit societies in foreign colonies, "gangs" in slum areas, cults and sects in the rooming house district.

The extensive documentation on the generality of group formation also shows the striking dependence of the process on other groups, on the material and ideational features and facilities of the environment. The process of group formation is not insulated by the bounds of the membership. The formation which results is not a closed system. The circumstances bringing individuals together initially, their motives in continuing to interact, the particular organization and norms that develop, and the degree of their stability are inevitably dependent upon the environmental circumstances and their stability or change. Included in the environmental circumstances are other groups whose activities and aims impinge favorably or unfavorably upon those of the group in formation.

FOUR ESSENTIALS IN THE PROCESS OF GROUP FORMATION

Starting with the initial conditions for interaction among individuals, the essentials of group formation can now be traced. The encounter with another person is the most elementary social situation. Even the mere presence of other persons has consequential effects on behavior and task performance. From the time when individuals are merely together to the time when the properties of a group begin to appear, we see that the consequential effects on behavior begin to assume regularities. As time goes on, these regularities reflect patterns which are the organizational and normative properties of the group. Accordingly, the essentials in the process of group formation are the following:

1. A motivational base conducive to repeated interaction.
2. Formation of an organization (structure), consisting of roles and statuses.
3. Formation of rules, traditions, values or norms.
4. Differential effects of the group properties on the attitude and behavior of participants over time.

Motivational Base

Any human motive, frustration, problem or desired goal which an individual cannot handle effectively alone is conducive to his interaction with others who are seen in the same plight. The prerequisite for group formation is that persons with motives conducive to initial interaction have the opportunity over time to recognize the concerns they share, or reciprocate, and to attempt to deal with them in concert.

The common motive faced in initial stages of interaction may be one or several of those found in any society, for example, hunger, sexual desire, desire for recognition or power in some respect, fear or anxiety in the face of threat. They may be culturally defined, for example, desire for material possessions, prestige through particular activities, or pursuit of political goals. Here only a few points can be considered.

The common problem, motive, or goal conducive to repeated interactions is necessarily dependent on environmental circumstances, both in its occurrence and in attempts to deal with it. Whatever its nature, the motivational base for group formation invariably affects the activities and tasks engaged in by members, and the kinds of personal qualities which become prized by them. When a set of norms forms, those most binding are typically related to the motives or problems which initially brought the persons together. One reason why many controversies over problems of conformity-nonconformity are inconclusive is that many theorists pay scant attention to the relationship between the particular norms of a group and the initial motivational base underlying them.

However, to the degree that group formation achieves a degree of stabilitity over time, new sources of motivation and new goals are generated among the members. They may even take precedence over those bringing the members together. Thus, the hungry person may refrain from eating until he can share with his starving fellows; the politician may spurn an advantageous political bargain out of loyalty to his supporters; the member of a group struggling for equal opportunity and freedom from fear may undergo great deprivation and bodily injury to secure recognition of his group.

Formation of Organization or Structure

Over a period of time as individuals interact in activities related to the common problems which brought them together, their behavior and their expectations for each other's behavior assume regularities from which a pattern can be constructed. Here we shall define certain features of these regularities which appear to be crucial in any group formation. Heavy reliance will be placed upon findings from three experiments on group formation and relations between groups, each lasting several weeks (summarized in Sherif and Sherif, 1956, Chs. 6 and 9, and in Sherif, 1966), and from more recent studies of naturally formed groups (Sherif and Sherif, 1964). The experiments started in each case with unacquainted persons divided into collections of ten to twelve as similar as possible in composition. All of these studies were conducted under naturalistic conditions, and data were collected with the constant awareness by the individuals that they were being investigated.

The development of organization has been defined in terms of role and status relationships among a number of individuals. *Role* denotes reciprocities in the treatments and expectations of individuals, each for the others. Unlike well-defined occupational or sex roles, definite prescriptions for behavior are lacking when unacquainted persons first meet. Reciprocities among them must be built on the basis of performance in the activities engaged in, the reactions of others to the person, and his reactions to them. The typical finding at early stages of interaction is that individual contributions to task performance differ from one activity to the next (OSS, 1948; Gibb, 1954). Thus, observers rating behavior in the different situations find that the degree of participation and prominence of the individuals differs from one task to the next, according to the individual differences in skills, abilities, temperament, or physical resources and tools, relative to the activities in question.

The single, most salient feature of group formation is that, over time, the various member roles become differentiated, not merely with regard to task performance or personal qualities, but according to the evaluation of the roles by the members. Members are accorded differing degrees of prestige and respect by their fellows. The member roles acquire differences in the relative *power* of individuals to initiate and control activities important to them all.

A member's position (rank) in a developing power structure is his *status* in the group, defined in terms of the relative effectiveness of his actions in initiating activities, making or approving decisions affecting the group, coordinating interaction, and invoking correctives for deviation.

Power, defined as effective initiative, is not identical with influence, in the limited sense that Person A affects the actions of Person B. Influence of this kind may occur with little or no relation to the effectiveness of Person A's actions in the group. Power is implemented with sanctions, while influence is not.

Status (rank in power) is not identical with popularity or the degree to which the person is liked. In fact, status and popularity may be poorly correlated (see Hare, 1962, p. 115; Sherif and Sherif, 1964, Ch. 6). Nor should status be confused with the use of force or aggression. As Whyte (1943) showed, even in a street corner group whose members valued masculine toughness, the best potential fighter was not necessarily highest in status. Status was rooted in "mutual obligations" incurred among them over time and the reliability with which a member lived up to his obligations.

Since it is defined as effective initiative, status in a group is necessarily hierarchical. The highest status represents the leadership role. Especially in societies or situations where social equality is em-

Figure 1 Gradations of Organization Structure

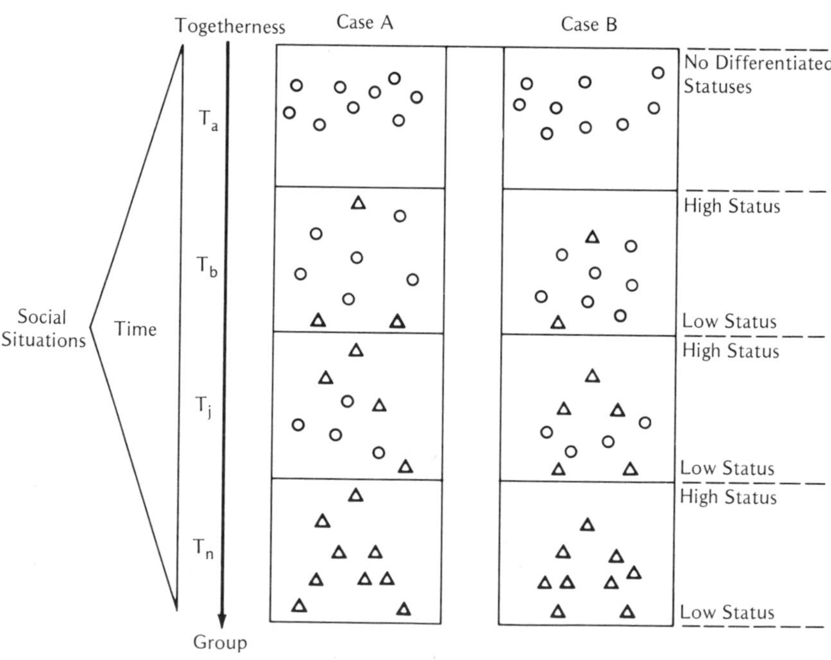

phasized, the operational leader, defined by observation of his effectiveness over time, may not be designated openly as "leader" by the members.

Figure 1 is a diagram of the stabilization of statuses, based on experimental findings for six groups. At the top (*time a*) the individuals in two collections have first encountered one another. The circles represent the individuals and indicate that, at this time, independent observers do not agree from one situation to the next on regularities in the relationships among them. Instead, their ratings of effective initiative are different in various activities.

Just below, at *time b*, the observers' ratings begin to agree (from one activity to the next and from one day to the next) that the highest and lowest positions (represented by triangles) are stabilized. Both in the experiments and in real-life groups, the leader position typically stabilizes earlier than other high positions. This does not imply that group formation consists of the "search for a leader." On the contrary, leadership is subject to change. As Hofstatter correctly pointed out (1957, esp. p. 24), tracing group organization over time is necessary to clear up many glib formulae propagated without sufficient evidence.

At *time j* in the figure, observers are able to agree on the positions most members occupy, except in the middle of the diagram. Again, this is a typical finding. In part, it reflects attempts by those in the middle to improve their standing or to align themselves with those higher in status. At *time n* in the diagram, the status relationships are stabilized, all observers agreeing on the status structure which is also revealed in a member's perceptions of it.

The diagram is intended to be representative. The different patterns of status in the two groups are intended to suggest that there is no predetermined form to the "steepness" or "flatness" of the hierarchy. Group formation represents an ideal occasion to study factors affecting the organization of groups, but little research has been done on this problem.

The rate of stabilization varies. In the experiments, the groups stabilized within about a week of continuous living together. Other investigators have reported the discernible beginnings of group structure among individuals meeting in the same location in similar activities within three to five meetings of a few hours' duration (Merei, 1949; Blake, Shepard, and Mouton, 1964). Environmental events are equally as important as internal events in affecting the speed of stabilization. The stability of the pattern is sensitive to the introduction of new members, to changes in location and facilities, and to outside threat or emergency.

In particular, the stabilization of group structure is never independent of the relationships with other groups. Prolonged competition between groups for mutually incompatible goals is particularly effective in quickly stabilizing a structure. Important intergroup confrontations, especially those resulting in defeat or humiliation, produce changes in the internal organization of a group (Sherif, 1966).

The leader of a group is, though most powerful, still a member subject to loss of status. When the group structure is stabilized in some degree for the time being, no person within it is free to ignore its regulation. It defines for its members the bounds of "we" or the in-group, as compared to others who are not members. If sufficiently stabilized, the group can continue after a leader's departure with little disruption (see Toki, 1935). This persistence of a group structure and the effects of the group even on the leader are clearer in terms of the normative property of group formation.

Formation of Group Norms

As a group structure takes shape, members come to prefer certain ways of going about their important activities. They may adopt a group name. They set up standards for the ways members should and should not behave among themselves and with outsiders. The term "norm" is a general term to refer to such products of interaction producing regularities in attitude and behavior among members.

Unlike the norm on an examination, a group norm does not, necessarily, refer to the average of individual behaviors. It designates what is expected as proper, as moral, or even as ideal. Yet a group norm seldom denotes a single action as the only way to behave. A range for individual variations is permissible in any group. A norm denotes the range of behaviors which members come to deem as socially desirable and acceptable (latitude of acceptance) and a range of behaviors condemned as objectionable (latitude of rejection).

A norm is defined, therefore, as an evaluative scale (a measuring rod), defining for individual members a latitude of acceptance and a latitude of rejection, to regulate their behavior in matters of consequence to the group (Sherif, Sherif, and Nebergall, 1965). Not all social behavior is regulated by clear-cut norms, particularly when groups are in formation.

How can a group norm be detected? There are at least three objective ways:

1. By observing similarities and regularities in the behaviors (words and deeds) which are found among one set of persons but not another set in a similar situation.
2. By observing correctives (sanctions) for certain behaviors and praise or reward for others. Reactions to deviations are among the best evidence of the bounds of acceptable behavior. These may range from disapproval and frown correctives to threats and actual punishment.
3. By noting the increasing similarity or convergence over time in the behaviors of individuals who initially behaved differently. For example, the entrance of a new member into a group provides an opportunity to detect the existence of its norms.

When groups are in the process of formation, as in the experiments, one of the best indicators of their stability is the degree of consensus among members on the correctness of their norms, and the degree to which the latitude of acceptance is binding without direct social pressure or threat of sanctions. Stabilization of the set of norms is indicated when members privately regulate their own behavior within the latitude of acceptance. The person's own conception of how he should behave and how others should act comes to fall within bounds defined by the norms. Especially when the individual has had a part in creating the norms as a group member, they become aspects of his self-concept relative to others. He experiences personal guilt or shame if he violates them.

The personal acceptance of group norms during group formation accounts in large measure for the tenacity of tradition once established. Merei (1949) demonstrated this tenacity by permitting play groups to develop procedures and rules, then introducing a new child who was older and had evidenced leadership skills in other situations.

Sherif and Sherif (1964) present evidence that the stringency of norms and resistance to their change varies according to the importance of the norm for the group. Violations in major activities, in dealings with outsiders, exposure of group secrets, or otherwise jeopardizing the maintenance of the group were unerringly responded to by strong sanctions, such as expulsion, threat, or physical punishment. Even leaders whose actions exposed the group or its members to humiliation, embarrassment, or danger were chastised.

In less important activities, the range of tolerance for individual differences was much wider, particularly for the leader and higher-status members. In matters of daily routine or amusement strictly within the group, leaders were free to innovate and sometimes engaged in behavior which would not have been tolerated from lesser members. In these fairly stable groups, the great bulk of conforming behavior occurred without direct social pressure or threat of sanctions, particularly behavior by members of moderate or high status.

Differential Effects of Group Formation on Member Attitude and Behavior

The formation of a group structure and norms has consequences for the attitude and behavior of individuals within its fold. These consequences may be referred to as the differential effects of group formation.

Any social situation provides a context for behavior which differs from a solitary situation. The context includes other people present, the activities and tasks undertaken, the physical site and its facilities, and the person's relationship to all of these. Experiments have repeatedly shown the differential effects of different aspects of the social context on behavior, compared to behavior alone.

The formation of a role system and norms during interaction among persons, over time, brings about alterations in the relative contribution of the task, activity, setting, and individual reactions. When the persons without stabilized reciprocities are at first simply *together*, their personal characteristics and skills relative to the tasks and those of other people are important determinants of behavior (Gibb, 1954; Hare, 1962). As the process of group formation starts taking shape, the developing organizational and normative schemes become more and more binding for members. As a result, over time, characteristics of the task, and the location—in short, immediate situational factors—recede in relative importance and behavior increasingly reflects the person's role in the group, the roles of others, and the emerging norms.

The group formation experiments (Sherif and Sherif, 1956, Chs. 6 and 9) traced the development of a "we-feeling," such that sociometric friendship choices became almost exclusively concentrated within the group, even though initial choices before group formation had been given predominantly to persons placed (deliberately) in another group. In one experiment, it was shown that estimates made by members of each other's performance became significantly related to the member's status, the relationship being closer when the structure was more stable. Performance by high-status members was over-estimated, that of low status persons was minimized.

In another experiment, the groups formed separately, then competed for a series of mutually exclusive goals. As predicted, norms developed in each group justifying hostility to the other group. The performance by members of the other group in a novel task was estimated to be significantly lower than performance by members of the in-group, revealing the prejudicial norm in the judgments of individual members (Sherif, *et al.*, 1961).

Proportional to the significance of a particular group in a person's life, the impact of his membership in determining his attitude and behavior increases. As the group formation stabilizes, his sense of identity becomes tied to being a member of that group, proportional to its scope and importance in his daily living. For this reason, the socialization of the person is incompletely described only by reference to his acquisition of formal prescriptions from family, school, and other official institutions. From early childhood through adolescence, groups formed among age-mates exert compelling impact upon the person's conceptions of what is desirable for him, what is acceptable in others, and what is right and wrong (Campbell, 1964; Sherif and Sherif, 1964). In other words, they become aspects of his own conscience.

Recognition of the consequences for self-concepts and attitudes of participants has led to attempts in various countries to utilize group formation for corrective and therapeutic purposes. The varied outcomes reveal both the gaps in knowledge of group formation and the lack of familiarity on the part of many practitioners with the knowledge available (Rosenbaum and Berger, 1963, esp. pp. 1–32).

The emphasis earlier in this article on the motivational base of group formation and on the importance of environmental alternatives suggests fruitful lines of inquiry. The significance of the motivational base was revealed in a study of group formation among "emotionally disturbed young adolescents of poor prognosis" by Rafferty (1962, p. 263). They interacted in a wide range of activities rather freely for five hours daily, five days a week for nine months. They lacked motivation toward the institution's aim of changing their behavior, and their personal disturbances hindered any kind of stable interpersonal relationship. However, they did unite with incipient group formation in activities reflecting a motivation genuine to them: defiance of the hospital staff in forbidden activities.

This instructive finding raises the issue of predicting or controlling the character of the structure and norms during group formation. Here, the importance of the environmental setting and the behavioral alternatives it encourages or permits becomes evident. In the group experiments referred to frequently here, solidary groups were formed, devoted to constructive activities, simply by placing unacquainted persons in situations of high appeal to them, with facilities and conditions so arranged that coordination of activity was the only way to secure individual satisfaction. Subsequently, conflict and hostility between the groups were produced; then came their reduction through cooperative efforts of the groups, entirely by varying the facilities available, other persons present, and other conditions external to both groups. Future research on group formation and its applied implications might profitably focus on the effects of varying the environmental alternatives and facilities available to groups, including those established by the presence of other groups and persons, upon the character of organization and norms which develop.

CONCLUSIONS

Whenever individuals with similar concerns, similar motives, similar frustrations, similar personal concerns for acceptance, for recognition, for stabilizing their perception of themselves encounter one another; whenever these goal-directed concerns are not effectively dealt with through the established channels of custom and law and the routine of prevailing arrangements of social organization—then individuals thus caught in the same boat tend to interact among themselves.

Repeated interaction in some common striving is conducive to differentiation of roles or functions to be performed towards the common end. And differentiation of roles and functions among the participating individuals, *over a time span*, is the pattern or formation which can be designated as *the group*. Every such human formation creates its own set of rules or norms to stabilize the regulation of behavior and attitude of members within its bounds.

In a natural group, as in any other group, the rules or norms that count, that have salience in the eyes of the members, are the ones that pertain to the existence and perpetuation of the group and the spheres of activity which are related to the common motivational concerns, that were initially conducive to repeated interaction among the individuals in question.

The main properties of the group thus formed are an organization (structure) of roles and statuses and a set of rules or standards (norms) for their activities toward the common ends. The "organization" (which need not be formally recognized) and the set of norms (which need not be formally written in blueprints) define their sense of "we-ness" cherished within the group and upheld by members in their dealings with outsiders.

In time, the standards or norms shared in the feeling of "we-ness" become personally binding for individual members. The members who are worthy and true make their judgments, justify or condemn events within the sphere related to their "we-ness" in terms of their sense of identification within the group. Proportional to the importance of the group in the lives of members, the person's self-picture, his sense of personal accountability, his loyalty, and the "dos" and "don'ts" of the group become parts of his conscience. Hence, group formation has broad implications in regulating individual attitude and behavior with and without sanctions and controls.

REFERENCES

Bales, R. F. *Interaction Process Analysis: A Method for the Study of Small Groups*. Addison-Wesley, 1949.

Blake, R. R., H. Shepard, and Jane S. Mouton. *Managing Intergroup Relations in Industry*. Gulf Publishing Co., 1964.

Blau, P. M., and W. R. Scott. *Formal Organizations: A Comparative Approach*. Chandler, 1962.

Bonner, H. *Group Dynamics: Principles and Applications*. Ronald Press, 1959.

Bowen, J. *Soviet Education: Anton Makarenko and the Years of Experiment*. University of Wisconsin Press, 1962.

Campbell, J. D. "Peer Relations in Childhood." In *Review of Child Development Resumé*. Russell Sage Foundation, 1964, Vol. 1.

Cartwright, D., and A. Zander, eds. *Group Dynamics: Research and Theory*, 2nd ed. Harper & Row, 1960.

Gibb, C. A. "Leadership." In *Handbook of Social Psychology* (Vol. 2), ed. Gardner Lindzey. Addison-Wesley, 1954.

Golembiewski, R. T. *The Small Group: An Analysis of Research Concepts and Operations*. Rand McNally, 1962.

Hare, A. P. *Handbook of Small Group Research*. The Free Press, 1962.

Hofstätter, P. R. *Gruppendynamik: Kritik der Massenspychologie*. Rowolt, 1957.

Landesco, J. "Organized Crime in Chicago." In *Illinois Crime Survey*. Illinois Association for Criminal Justice, 1929.

Lewin, K., R. Lippitt, and R. K. White. "Patterns of Aggressive Behavior in Experimentally Created 'Social Climates.' " *Journal of Social Psychology*, Vol. 10, 1939.

Makarenko, A. S. *The Road to Life: An Epic of Education* (3 vols.). Foreign Languages Publishing House, 1955.

Merei, F. "Group Leadership and Institutionalism." *Human Relations*, Vol. 2, 1949.
Moreno, J. L. *Who Shall Survive?* Nervous and Mental Disease Publishing Co., 1934.
OSS (Office of Strategic Services) Assessment Staff. *The Assessment of Men*. Holt, 1948.
Rafferty, F. T. "Development of a Social Structure in Treatment Institutions." *Journal of Nervous and Mental Disease*, Vol. 134, 1962.
Roethlisberger, F. J., and W. J. Dickson. *Management and the Worker*. Harvard University Press, 1939.
Rosenbaum, M., and M. Berger, eds. *Group Psychotherapy and Group Function*. Basic Books, 1963.
Shaw, C. R. *Delinquency Areas*. University of Chicago Press, 1929.
Sherif, Carolyn W., Muzafer Sherif, and R. E. Nebergall. *Attitude and Attitude Change*. Saunders, 1965.
Sherif, Muzafer. *Friend and Foe in Common Predicament*. Houghton Mifflin, 1966.
——. *An Outline of Social Psychology*. Harper & Row, 1948.
——. *The Psychology of Social Norms*. Harper & Row, 1936.
——, and H. Cantril. *The Psychology of Ego-Involvements*. Wiley, 1947.
——, O. J. Harvey, B. J. White, W. R. Hood, and Carolyn Sherif. *Intergroup Conflict and Cooperation*. Institute of Group Relations, 1961.
——, and Carolyn W. Sherif. *Reference Groups: Exploration into Conformity and Deviation of Adolescents*. Harper & Row, 1964.
——. *Outline of Social Psychology*, rev. ed. Harper & Row, 1956.
Thrasher, F. M. *The Gang*. University of Chicago Press, 1927.
Toki, K. "The Leader-Follower Structure in the School Class." *Japanese Journal of Psychology*, Vol. 10, 1935. English summary in E. L. Hartley and Ruth E. Hartley, *Fundamentals of Social Psychology*, Knopf, 1952.
Whyte, W. F. *Street Corner Society*, 2nd ed. University of Chicago Press, 1955.
Zorbaugh, H. W. *The Gold Coast and the Slum*. University of Chicago Press, 1929.

ALVAR ELBING

A Note on "Group Formation"

George Homans (1950) offers a useful conceptualization of the emergence of group norms and values in work situations. His definition of *group* is simpler than, but compatible with, the Sherifs':

> We mean by a group a number of persons who communicate with one another often over a span of time, and who are few enough so that each person is able to communicate with all the others . . . face-to-face (p. 1).

Homans analyzes the environment of a group and finds it is made up of physical, technical, and social factors. The environment of a work group, for

"A Note on 'Group Formation'" was written expressly for this volume by Alvar Elbing.

Figure 1 Group Behavior in the Organizational Environment (Homans, 1950, adapted)

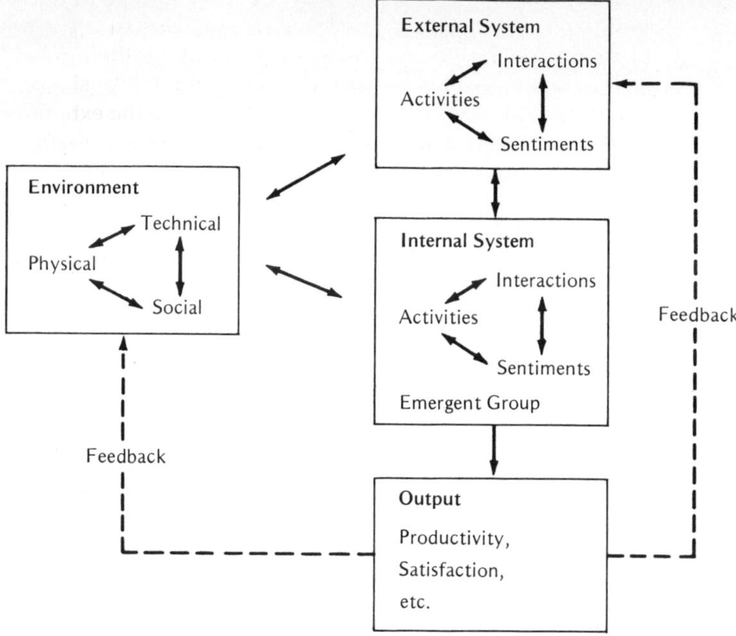

example, includes physical objects (tables, partitions, lights, etc., and their arrangement), level of technical development (craft, manned assembly line, automated assembly line, etc.), and social relationships (interactions with superiors, peers, subordinates, etc.). Furthermore, the environment of the group includes all the factors, both within the organization and in the broader community, which constitute the background of a particular job.

Conditioned by this environment, the organization identifies various tasks to be performed in order to accomplish the goals of the organization. These tasks are performed by people who have various relationships to one another and who hold various attitudes toward the tasks. Homans labels the elements of the work situation *activities*, *interactions*, and *sentiments*, and he calls their overall pattern the *external system*. These elements also become the starting point for the emergence of a group, Homans' *internal system*.

Thus, in the Homans model, three sets of systems provide the basis for analysis: the *internal* or informal system (the emergent group), which exists within and alongside the *external* or formal system (the requirements of the organization), which exists within a particular *environment*. These systems interrelate with one another and are mutually interdependent (see Figure 1). And just as the three systems are interdependent, all the elements of each system are interdependent. They are not closed systems but dynamic, interacting systems, which strongly influence each other.

The Foster Creek Post Office case (following Ch. 4) may help clarify Homans' concepts. Within the environment of the village of Foster Creek and its post office, the post office workers developed certain ways of going about their jobs.

Their basic *activities* consisted of sorting and delivering mail on various routes according to a schedule. To do this they had to *interact* with each other and with supervisors, inspectors, and community residents in a particular way. They were also expected to hold certain *sentiments* about their jobs ("Neither snow nor rain, . . ."), most of which were spelled out in the post office manual. These activities, interactions, and sentiments constituted the external system (the job requirements) within the physical, technical, and social environment of the post office.

Within the environment and paralleling the external system, an internal system or group evolved. Numerous group activities and interactions developed which were related to but not required by the external system: flipping for Cokes, contributing to the paycheck "fund," selecting topics of conversation, regulating delivery times, and so on. Group sentiments about the jobs, especially in relation to job security, are also observable. Although these group norms and values were not unrelated to the standards of the established system, the postal workers preserved their unique relationship to their group in the particular manner the members wanted it preserved. In short, the social system in the Foster Creek Post Office is an example of a strongly knit group.

The importance of understanding the interwoven fabric of activities, interactions, and sentiments is that, when a group forms in a particular situation, its emerging norms and values tend to become the norms and values of the participating individuals, for whom the group is thus a *reference* group. Frequently, these norms and values affect the work output of the members—as it did, for example, in the post office case. This factor becomes crucial for the manager who wishes to improve output.

According to Homans' work-group model, there are three possible sources for the causes of a problem: the environment, the external system, or the internal system. Of these three causal sources, a manager is *least able to bring about change in the internal system*, the characteristic structure of the group. He cannot change group norms and values in the same way he can change aspects of the environment (lights, desks, etc.) and the external system (e.g., postal route assignments). If norms and values have been internalized by workers, the effectiveness of an organizational plan for change will necessarily be in part determined by its compatibility with the group's norms. If group norms and values are not taken into consideration, even a very rational plan for change may be resisted. One problem that faces the manager, therefore, is determining how a group will react to changes in the environment or in the external system.

The output of the Foster Creek Post Office met everyone's expectations and equilibrium existed—until Harry began working there. Harry had worked in a different environment, with different organizational requirements, and his behavior reflected different norms and values. Much of Harry's behavior threatened the work group at Foster Creek since it violated the group's norms. His behavior was soon viewed as deviate by the Foster Creek work group; and the group's attitudes toward him reflected that feeling.

Not only did Harry's behavior violate group norms, it differed from the expectations of the postmaster: Harry's work broke the speed standards that had been set at Foster Creek, and he completed all his work early in the afternoon. The postmaster attempted to preserve equilibrium by changing the work stations, moving Harry's sorting cage into a corner and out of sight so he could not be seen reading magazines in his spare time. Harry's isolation preserved the group's norms, but it only temporarily relieved a symptom. When the postal inspector discovered the problem, he considered it necessary to find a solution that would meet the standards of the external system, as described in the postal manual. In the inspector's presence, the postmaster of course had to fall in line. The resulting "solution" was not a real solution of the problem, however, because it did not allay the group's distress at having its norms and established prerogatives violated.

In diagnosing work-group behavior from the vantage point of management, it is important to consider both the norms of the group and the relationship between it and the management group—that is, the *intergroup* relationship. When two individuals meet (for example, a manager and a factory worker), they create not only an interpersonal situation but also an intergroup situation (manager group–employee group). In order for managers to understand and deal with problems which involve groups, therefore, they must recognize and deal with norms and values that relate to them both as persons and as members of the management group. From the following example, written by a manager, we can draw some fairly clear inferences about the relationship between a worker group and a management group. (Proper names and designations have been disguised.)

> I was transferred [to general manufacturing] from River Glen, South Carolina, where Modern Chemical has a new fiber plant. The River Glen plant was built in 1965. The entire plant, including the shop, is air conditioned, and incorporates the latest in "daylight" lighting. The grounds are beautifully landscaped. River Glen has no union, and in general the employees seem enthusiastic about making fiber. They are paid a straight day rate. Measured against standard motion-time study (MTS) data, the plant averages 85 to 90 percent productivity.
>
> The general manufacturing plant was a shock to me. Although the hourly workers are generally paid more than those in River Glen, their productivity is only 40 to 45 percent of MTS. The shop starts at 7 A.M. but there is seldom a machine operating at 8 A.M. when the office force arrives. The machines start around 8:30 and shut down at 11 to 11:30 A.M. for an unofficial two-hour lunch. During this morning work period there is a 40-minute coffee break. The afternoon period of actual production work is from 1 to 3 P.M.
>
> I work in manufacturing engineering and have developed some communication with the shop. One day I needed a small pad milled and a hole drilled and tapped in a brass fitting for my boat. It fit in my pocket, and since it was a five-minute job I took it to a machinist to be done.
>
> He said he needed a shop order for two hours in order to do it and it would require a sketch by a union draftsman. When I told him it was for my boat, he said, "O.K." and did the operations in less than five minutes. He said he would be glad to do any personal work I brought in, since he was bored at not being able to work very much during the day. I never had another occasion to use him for personal work, but I get engineering jobs done "free" by telling him they are for my boat.

This example shows that the machinist at first responded to the engineer as an out-group member (a member of management, not of the union). However, when the engineer presented himself as an individual with a personal problem, he was able to get around existing group norms and intergroup behavior patterns. The purpose of this example is not to suggest that the engineer's method was necessarily the best one for dealing with group norms, but it does point up the role of group norms in interaction. Problems involving group norms can scarcely be solved until they are first consciously understood.

In conclusion, it should be noted that the small group is a particularly important level of analysis for understanding human behavior in organizations. The concepts of Muzafer Sherif and George Homans provide useful frameworks through which to look at the emergence of groups and for understanding their influence on individual behavior.

REFERENCES

Hickman, C. A., and M. H. Kuhn. *Individuals, Groups and Economic Behavior.* Dryden, 1956.

Homans, George. *The Human Group*. Harcourt, 1950.

Katz, Daniel, and Robert L. Kahn. "The Taking of Organizational Roles." In *The Social Psychology of Organizations*. Wiley, 1966.

Klein, Josephine. *Working with Groups*. Hutchinson University Library, 1961.

March, James, and Herbert Simon. *Organizations*. Wiley, 1958.

Maslow, Abraham. "A Theory of Motivation." *Psychological Review*, Vol. 50 (1943), 370–96. Abridged in Part Three.

Sherif, Muzafer. "Experiments in Group Conflict and Cooperation." *Scientific American*, Vol. 195 (1956), 54–58.

——. "Inter-group Relations and Leadership." In *Intergroup Relations and Leadership*, ed. M. Sherif. Wiley (1962), 3–21.

——. and Carolyn Sherif. *An Outline of Social Psychology*. Harper & Row, 1956.

Simon, Herbert. *Models of Man: Social and Rational*. Wiley, 1957.

Thelen, Herbert, and Watson Dickerman. "The Growth of Groups." *Educational Leadership*, Vol. 6, No. 5 (February 1949), 309–16.

Turner, Ralph H. "Role Taking, Role Standpoint and Reference Group Behavior." *American Journal of Sociology*, Vol. 61 (1956), 316–28. Abridged in *Role Theory*, ed. B. J. Biddle and E. J. Thomas. Wiley, 1966.

ROBERT K. MERTON

The Self-Fulfilling Prophecy

In a series of works seldom consulted outside the academic fraternity, W. I. Thomas, the dean of American sociologists, set forth a theorem basic to the social sciences: "If men define situations as real, they are real in their consequences." Were the Thomas theorem and its implications more widely known, more men would understand more of the workings of our society. Though it lacks the sweep and precision of a Newtonian theorem, it possesses the same gift of relevance, being instructively applicable to many, if indeed not most, social processes.

THE THOMAS THEOREM

"If men define situations as real, they are real in their consequences," wrote Professor Thomas. The suspicion that he was driving at a crucial point becomes all the more insistent when we note that essentially the same theorem had been repeatedly set forth by disciplined and observant minds long before Thomas.

When we find such otherwise discrepant minds as the redoubtable Bishop Bossuet in his passionate seventeenth-century defense of Catholic orthodoxy, the ironic Mandeville in his eighteenth-century allegory honeycombed with observations on the paradoxes of human society, the irascible genius Marx in his revision of Hegel's theory of historical change, the seminal Freud in works which have perhaps gone further than any others of his day toward modifying man's outlook on man, and the erudite, dogmatic, and occasionally sound Yale professor, William Graham Sumner, who lives on as the Karl Marx of the middle classes—when we find this mixed company (and I select from a longer if less distinguished list) agreeing on the truth and the pertinence of what is substantially the Thomas theorem, we may conclude that perhaps it is worth our attention as well.

To what, then, are Thomas and Bossuet, Mandeville, Marx, Freud and Sumner directing our attention?

The first part of the theorem provides an unceasing reminder that men respond not only to the objective features of a situation, but also, and at times primarily, to the meaning this situation has for them. And once they have assigned some meaning to the situation, their consequent behavior and some of the consequences of that behavior are determined by the ascribed meaning. But this is still rather abstract, and abstractions have a way of becoming unintelligible if they are not occasionally tied to concrete data. What is a case in point?

A SOCIOLOGICAL PARABLE

It is the year 1932. The Last National Bank is a flourishing institution. A large part of its resources is liquid without being watered. Cartwright Millingville has ample reason to be proud of the banking institution over which he presides. Until Black Wednesday. As he enters his bank, he notices that business is unusually brisk. A little odd that, since the men at the A.M.O.K. steel plant and the K.O.M.A. mattress factory are not usually paid until Saturday. Yet here are two dozen men, obviously from the factories, queued up in front of the tellers' cages. As he turns into his private office, the president muses rather compassionately: "Hope they haven't been laid off in midweek. They should be in the shop at this hour."

But speculations of this sort have never made for a thriving bank, and Millingville turns to the pile of documents upon his desk. His precise signature is affixed to fewer than a score of papers when he is disturbed by the absence of something familiar and the intrusion of something alien. The low, discreet hum of bank business has given way to a strange and annoying stridency of many voices. A situation has been defined as real. And that is the beginning of what ends as Black Wednesday—the last Wednesday, it might be noted, of the Last National Bank.

Cartwright Millingville had never heard of the Thomas theorem. But he had no difficulty in recognizing its workings. He knew that, despite the comparative liquidity of the bank's assets, a rumor of insolvency, once believed by enough depositors, would result in the insolvency of the bank. And by the close of Black Wednesday—and Blacker Thursday—when the long lines of anxious depositors, each frantically seeking to salvage his own, grew to longer lines of even more anxious depositors, it turned out that he was right.

The stable financial structure of the bank had depended upon one set of definitions of the situation: belief in the validity of the interlocking system of economic promises men live by. Once depositors had defined the situation otherwise, once they questioned the possibility of having these promises fulfilled, the consequences of this unreal definition were real enough.

A familiar type case this, and one doesn't need the Thomas theorem to understand how it happened—not, at least, if one is old enough to have voted for Franklin Roosevelt in 1932. But with the aid of the theorem the tragic history of Millingville's bank can perhaps be converted into a sociological parable which may help us understand not only what happened to hundreds of banks in the 1930s but also what happens to the relations between Negro and white, between Protestant and Catholic and Jew in these days.

The parable tells us that public definitions of a situation (prophecies or predictions) become an integral part of the situation and thus affect subsequent developments. This is peculiar to human affairs. It is not found in the world of nature, untouched by human hands. Predictions of the return of Halley's comet do not influence its orbit. But the rumored insolvency of Millingville's bank did affect the actual outcome. The prophecy of collapse led to its own fulfillment.

So common is the pattern of the self-fulfilling prophecy that each of us has his favored specimen. Consider the case of the examination neurosis. Convinced that he is destined to fail, the anxious student devotes more time to worry than to study and then turns in a poor examination. The initially fallacious anxiety is transformed into an entirely justified fear. Or it is believed that war between two nations is inevitable. Actuated by this conviction, representatives of the two nations become progressively alienated, apprehensively countering each "offensive" move of the other with a "defensive" move of their own. Stockpiles of armaments, raw materials, and armed men grow larger and eventually the anticipation of war helps create the actuality.

The self-fulfilling prophecy is, in the beginning, a *false* definition of the situation evoking a new behavior which makes the originally false conception come *true*. The specious validity of the self-fulfilling prophecy perpetuates a reign of error. For the prophet will cite the actual course of events as proof that he was right from the very beginning. (Yet we know that Millingville's bank was solvent, that it would have survived for many years had not the misleading rumor *created* the very conditions of its own fulfillment.) Such are the perversities of social logic. . . .

REFERENCE

Merton, R. K. "The Unanticipated Consequences of Purposive Social Action." *American Sociological Review*, Vol. 1, 1936.

EDGAR H. SCHEIN

Organizational Socialization and the Profession of Management

INTRODUCTION

I can define my topic of concern best by reviewing very briefly the kinds of issues upon which I have focused my research over the last several years. In one way or another I have been trying to understand what happens to an individual when he enters and accepts membership in an organization. My interest was originally kindled by studies of the civilian and military prisoners of the Communists during the Korean War. I thought I could discern parallels between the kind of indoctrination to which these prisoners were subjected and some of the indoctrination which goes on in American corporations when college and business school graduates first go to work for them. My research efforts came to be devoted to learning what sorts of attitudes and values students had when they left school, and what happened to these attitudes and values in the first few years of work. To this end I followed several panels of graduates of the Sloan School into their early career.

When these studies were well under way, it suddenly became quite apparent to me that if I wanted to study the impact of an organization on the attitudes and values of its members, I might as well start closer to home. We have a school through which we put some 200 men per year—undergraduates, regular master's students, Sloan fellows, and senior executives. Studies of our own students and faculty revealed that not only did the student groups differ from each other in various attitude areas, but that they also differed from the faculty.

For example, if one takes a scale builup of items which deal with the relations of government and business, one finds that the senior executives in our program are consistently against any form of government intervention, the Sloans are not as extreme, the master's students are roughly in the middle, and the faculty are in favor of such intervention. A similar line-up of attitudes can be found with respect to labor-management relations, and with respect to cynicism about how one gets ahead in industry. In case you did not guess, the senior executives are least cynical and the faculty are most cynical.

We also found that student attitudes change in many areas during school, and that they change away from business attitudes toward the faculty position. However, a recent study of Sloan fellows, conducted after their graduation, indicated that most of the changes toward the faculty had reversed themselves to a considerable degree within one year, a finding which is not unfamiliar to us in studies of training programs of all sorts.

The different positions of different groups at different stages of their manage-

"Organizational Socialization and the Profession of Management" by Edgar H. Schein from *Industrial Management Review,* Winter 1968, pp. 1–16. Reprinted by permission.

rial career and the observed changes during school clearly indicate that attitudes and values change several times during the managerial career. It is the process which brings about these changes which I would like to focus on today—a process which the sociologists would call "occupational socialization," but which I would prefer to call "organizational socialization" in order to keep our focus clearly on the setting in which the process occurs.

Organizational socialization is the process of "learning the ropes," the process of being indoctrinated and trained, the process of being taught what is important in an organization or some subunit thereof. This process occurs in school. It occurs again, and perhaps most dramatically, when the graduate enters an organization on his first job. It occurs again when he switches within the organization from one department to another, or from one rank level to another. It occurs all over again if he leaves one organization and enters another. And it occurs again when he goes back to school, and again when he returns to the organization after school.

Indeed, the process is so ubiquitous and we go through it so often during our total career that it is all too easy to overlook it. Yet it is a process which can make or break a career, and which can make or break organizational systems of manpower planning. The speed and effectiveness of socialization determine employee loyalty, commitment, productivity, and turnover. The basic stability and effectiveness of organizations therefore depend upon their ability to socialize new members.

Let us see whether we can bring the process of socialization to life by describing how it occurs. I hope to show you the power of this process, particularly as it occurs within industrial organizations. Having done this, I would like to explore a major dilemma which I see at the interface between organizations and graduate management schools. Schools socialize their students toward a concept of a profession, organizations socialize their new members to be effective members. Do the two processes of socialization supplement each other or conflict? If they conflict, what can we do about it in organizations and in the schools?

SOME BASIC ELEMENTS OF ORGANIZATIONAL SOCIALIZATION

The term socialization has a fairly clear meaning in sociology, but it has been a difficult one to assimilate in the behavioral sciences and in management. To many of my colleagues it implies unnecessary jargon, and to many of my business acquaintances it implies the teaching of socialism—a kiss of death for the concept right there. Yet the concept is most useful because it focuses clearly on the interaction between a stable social system and the new members who enter it. The concept refers to the process by which a new member learns the value system, the norms, and the required behavior patterns of the society, organization, or group which he is entering. It does not include all learning. It includes only the learning of those values, norms, and behavior patterns which, from the organization's point of view or group's point of view, it is necessary for any new member to learn. This learning is defined as the price of membership.

What are such values, norms, and behavior patterns all about? Usually they involve:

1. The basic *goals* of the organization.
2. The preferred *means* by which these goals should be attained.

3. The basic *responsibilities* of the member in the role which is being granted to him by the organization.
4. The *behavior patterns* which are required for effective performance in the role.
5. A set of rules or principles which pertain to the *maintenance of the identity and integrity* of the organization.

The new member must learn not to drive Chevrolets if he is working for Ford, not to criticize the organization in public, not to wear the wrong kind of clothes or be seen in the wrong kinds of places. If the organization is a school, beyond learning the content of what is taught, the student must accept the value of education, he must try to learn without cheating, he must accept the authority of the faculty and behave appropriately to the student role. He must not be rude in the classroom or openly disrespectful to the professor.

By what processes does the novice learn the required values and norms? The answer to this question depends in part upon the degree of prior socialization. If the novice has correctly anticipated the norms of the organization he is joining, the socialization process merely involves a reaffirmation of these norms through various communication channels, the personal example of key people in the organization, and direct instructions from supervisors, trainers, and informal coaches.

If, however, the novice comes to the organization with values and behavior patterns which are in varying degrees out of line with those expected by the organization, then the socialization process first involves a destructive or unfreezing phase. This phase serves the function of detaching the person from his former values, of proving to him that his present self is worthless from the point of view of the organization and that he must redefine himself in terms of the new roles which he is to be granted.

The extremes of this process can be seen in initiation rites or novitiates for religious orders. When the novice enters his training period, his old self is symbolically destroyed by loss of clothing, name, often his hair, titles and other self-defining equipment. These are replaced with uniforms, new names and titles, and other self-defining equipment consonant with the new role he is being trained for.

It may be comforting to think of activities like this as being characteristic only of primitive tribes or total institutions like military basic training camps, academies, and religious orders. But even a little examination of areas closer to home will reveal the same processes both in our graduate schools and in the business organizations to which our graduates go.

Perhaps the commonest version of the process in school is the imposition of a tight schedule, of an impossibly heavy reading program, and of the assignment of problems which are likely to be too difficult for the student to solve. Whether these techniques are deliberate or not, they serve effectively to remind the student that he is not as smart or capable as he may have thought he was, and, therefore, that there are still things to be learned. As our Sloan fellows tell us every year, the first summer in the program pretty well destroys many aspects of their self-image. Homework in statistics appears to enjoy a unique status comparable to having one's head shaved and clothes burned.

Studies of medical schools and our own observations of the Sloan program suggest that the work overload on students leads to the development of a peer culture, a kind of banding together of the students as a defense against the threatening faculty and as a problem-solving device to develop norms of what and how to study. If the group solutions which are developed support the organizational norms, the peer group becomes an effective instrument of socialization. However, from the school's point of view, there is the risk that peer group norms will set up counter-socializing forces and sow the seeds of sabotage, rebellion, or revolution. The positive gains of a supportive peer group generally make it worthwhile to run the risks of rebellion, however, which usually motivates the organization to encourage or actually to facilitate peer group formation.

Many of our Sloan-fellow alumni tell us that one of the most powerful features of the Sloan program is the fact that a group of some 40 men share the same fate of being put through a very tough educational regimen. The peer group ties formed during the year have proven to be one of the most durable end-results of the educational program and, of course, are one of the key supports to maintaining some of the values and attitudes learned in school. The power of this kind of socializing force can be appreciated best by pondering a further statement which many alumni have made. They stated that prior to the program they identified themselves primarily with their company. Following the program they identified themselves primarily with the other Sloan fellows, and such identification has lasted, as far as we can tell, for the rest of their career.

Let me next illustrate the industrial counterpart of these processes. Many of my panel members, when interviewed about the first six months in their new jobs, told stories of what we finally labeled as "upending experiences." Upending experiences are deliberately planned or accidentally created circumstances which dramatically and unequivocally upset or disconfirm some of the major assumptions which the new man holds about himself, his company, or his job.

One class of such experiences is to receive assignments which are so easy or so trivial that they carry the clear message that the new man is not worthy of being given anything important to do. Another class of such experiences is at the other extreme—assignments which are so difficult that failure is a certainty, thus proving unequivocally to the new man that he may not be as smart as he thought he was. Giving work which is clearly for practice only, asking for reports which are then unread or not acted upon, protracted periods of training during which the person observes others work, all have the same upending effect.

The most vivid example came from an engineering company where a supervisor had a conscious and deliberate strategy for dealing with what he considered to be unwarranted arrogance on the part of engineers whom they hired. He asked each new man to examine and diagnose a particular complex circuit, which happened to violate a number of textbook principles but actually worked very well. The new man would usually announce with confidence, even after an invitation to double-check, that the circuit could not possibly work. At this point the manager would demonstrate the circuit, tell the new man that they had been selling it for several years without customer complaint, and demand that the new man figure out why it did work. None of the men so far tested were able to do it, but all of them were thoroughly chastened and came to the manager anxious to learn where their knowledge was inadequate and needed supplementing. According to this manager, it was much easier from this point on to establish a good give-and-take relationship with his new man.

It should be noted that the success of such socializing techniques depends upon two factors which are not always under the control of the organization. The first factor is the initial motivation of the entrant to join the organization. If his motivation is high, as in the case of a fraternity pledge, he will tolerate all kinds of uncomfortable socialization experiences, even to the extremes of "hell week." If his motivation for membership is low, he may well decide to leave the organization rather than tolerate uncomfortable initiation rites. If he leaves, the socialization process has obviously failed.

The second factor is the degree to which the organization can hold the new member captive during the period of socialization. His motivation is obviously one element here, but one finds organizations using other forces as well. In the case of basic training there are legal forces to make him remain. In the case of many schools one must pay one's tuition in advance, in other words, invest one's self materially so that leaving the system becomes expensive. In the case of religious orders one must make strong initial psychological commitments in the form of vows and the severing of relationships outside the religious order. The situation is defined as one in which one will lose face or be humiliated if one leaves the organization.

In the case of business organizations the pressures are more subtle but nevertheless identifiable. New members are encouraged to get financially committed by joining pension plans, stock option plans, and/or house purchasing plans which would mean material loss if the person decided to leave. Even more subtle is the reminder by the boss that it takes a year or so to learn any new business; therefore, if you leave, you will have to start all over again. Why not suffer it out with the the hope that things will look more rosy once the initiation period is over?

Several of my panel members told me at the end of one year at work that they were quite dissatisfied, but were not sure they should leave because they had invested a year of learning in that company. Usually their boss encouraged them to think about staying. Whether or not such pressures will work depends, of course, on the labor market and other factors not under the control of the organization.

Let me summarize. Organizations socialize their new members by creating a series of events which serve the function of undoing old values so that the person will be prepared to learn the new values. This process of undoing or unfreezing is often unpleasant and therefore requires either strong motivation to endure it or strong organizational forces to make the person endure it. The formation of a peer group of novices is often a solution to the problem of defense against the powerful organization, and, at the same time, can strongly enhance the socialization process if peer group norms support organizational norms.

Let us look next at the positive side of the socialization process. Given some readiness to learn, how does the novice acquire his new learning? The answer is that he acquires it from multiple sources—the official literature of the organization; the example set by key models in the organization; the instructions given to him directly by his trainer, coach, or boss; the example of peers who have been in the organization longer and thus serve as big brothers; the rewards and punishments which result from his own efforts at problem solving and experimenting with new values and new behavior.

The instructions and guidelines given by senior members of the organization are probably one of the most potent positive sources. I can illustrate this point best by recalling several incidents from my own socialization into the Sloan School back in 1956. I came here from a research job at the invitation of Doug McGregor. I had no prior teaching experience or knowledge of organizational or managerial matters. Contrary to my expectations, I was told by Doug that knowledge of organizational psychology and management was not important, but that some interest in learning about these matters was.

The first socializing incident occurred in an initial interview with Elting Morison, who was then on our faculty. He said in a completely blunt manner that if I knew what I wanted to do and could go ahead on my own, the Sloan School would be a great place to be. If I wasn't sure and would look to others for guidance, not to bother to come.

The second incident occurred in a conversation with our then dean, Penn Brooks, a few weeks before the opening of the semester. We were discussing what and how I might teach. Penn said to me that he basically wanted each of his faculty members to find his own approach to management education. I could do whatever I wanted—so long as I did not imitate our sister school up the river. Case discussion leaders need not apply, was the clear message.

The third incident (you see I was a slow learner) occurred a few days later when I was planning my subject in social psychology for our master's students. I was quite nervous about it and unsure of how to decide what to include in the subject. I went to Doug and innocently asked him to lend me outlines of previous versions of the subject, which had been taught by Alex Bavelas, or at least to give me some advice on what to include and exclude. Doug was very nice and very patient, but also quite firm in his refusal to give me either outlines or advice. He thought there was really no need to rely on history, and expressed confidence that I could probably make up my own mind. I suffered that term but learned a good deal about the value system of the Sloan School, as well as how to organize a subject. I was, in fact, so well socialized by these early experiences that nowadays no one can get me to coordinate anything with anybody else.

Similar kinds of lessons can be learned during the course of training programs, in orientation sessions, and through company literature. But the more subtle kinds of values which the organization holds, which indeed may not even be well understood by the senior people, are often communicated through peers operating as helpful big brothers. They can communicate the subtleties of how the boss wants things done, how higher management feels about things, the kinds of things which are considered heroic in the organization, the kinds of things which are taboo.

Of course, sometimes the values of the immediate group into which a new person is hired are partially out of line with the value system of the organization as a whole. If this is the case, the new person will learn the immediate group's values much more quickly than those of the total organization, often to the chagrin of the higher levels of management. This is best exemplified at the level of hourly workers where fellow employees will have much more socializing power than the boss.

An interesting managerial example of this conflict was provided by one recent graduate who was hired into a group whose purpose was to develop cost reduction systems for a large manufacturing operation. His colleagues on the job, however, showed him how to pad his expense account whenever they traveled together. The end result of this kind of conflict was to accept neither the cost reduction values of the company nor the cost inflation values of the peer group. The man left the company in disgust to start up some businesses of his own.

One of the important functions of organizational socialization is to build commitment and loyalty to the organization. How is this accomplished? One mechanism is to invest much effort and time in the new member and thereby build up expectations of being repaid by loyalty, hard work, and rapid learning. Another mechanism is to get the new member to make a series of small behavioral commitments which can only be justified by him through the acceptance and incorporation of company values. He then becomes his own agent of socialization. Both mechanisms involve the subtle manipulation of guilt.

To illustrate the first mechanism, one of our graduates went to a public relations firm which made it clear to him that he had sufficient knowledge and skill to advance, but that his values and attitudes would have to be evaluated for a couple of years before he would be fully accepted. During the first several months he was frequently invited to join high ranking members of the organization at their luncheon meetings in order to learn more about how they thought about things. He was so flattered by the amount of time they spent on him that he worked extra hard to learn their values and became highly committed to the organization. He said that he would have felt guilty at the thought of not learning or of leaving the company. Sending people to expensive training programs, giving them extra perquisites, indeed the whole philosophy of paternalism, is built on the assumption that if you invest in the employee he will repay the company with loyalty and hard work. He would feel guilty if he did not.

The second mechanism, that of getting behavioral commitments, was most beautifully illustrated in Communist techniques of coercive persuasion. The Communists made tremendous efforts to elicit a public confession from a prisoner. One of the key functions of such a public confession, even if the prisoner knew he was making a false confession, was that it committed him publicly. Once he made this commitment, he found himself under strong internal and external pressure to justify why he had confessed. For many people it proved easier to justify the confession by coming to believe in their own crimes than to have to face the fact that they were too weak to withstand the captor's pressure.

In organizations, a similar effect can be achieved by promoting a rebellious person into a position of responsibility. The same values which the new member may have criticized and jeered at from his position at the bottom of the hierarchy suddenly look different when he has subordinates of his own whose commitment he must obtain.

Many of my panel members had very strong moral and ethical standards when they first went to work, and these stood up quite well during their first year at work, even in the face of less ethical practices by their peers and superiors. But they reported with considerable shock that some of the practices they had condemned in their bosses were quickly adopted by them once they had themselves been promoted and faced the pressures of the new position. As one man put it very poignantly—"My ethical standards changed so gradually over the first five years of work that I hardly noticed it, but it was a great shock to suddenly realize what my feelings had been five years ago and how much they had changed."

Another version of obtaining commitment is to gain the new member's acceptance of very general ideals, like "One must work for the good of the company," or "One must meet the competition." Whenever any counter-organizational behavior occurs, one can then point out that the ideal is being violated. The engineer who does not come to work on time is reminded that his behavior indicates lack of concern for the good of the company. The employee who wears the wrong kind of clothes, lives in the wrong neighborhood, or associates with the wrong people can be reminded that he is hurting the company image.

One of my panel members on a product research assignment discovered that an additive which was approved by the Food and Drug Administration might in fact be harmful to consumers. He was strongly encouraged to forget about it. His boss told him that it was the FDA's problem. If the company worried about things like that it might force prices up and thus make it tough to meet the competition.

Many of the upending experiences which new members of organizations endure are justified to them by the unarguable ideal that they should learn how the company really works before expecting a position of real responsibility. Once the new man accepts this ideal it serves to justify all kinds of training and quantities of menial work which others who have been around longer are unwilling to do themselves. This practice is known as "learning the business from the ground up," or "I had to do it when I first joined the company, now it's someone else's turn." There are clear elements of hazing involved not too different from those associated with fraternity initiations and other rites of passage.

The final mechanism to be noted in a socialization process is the transition to full-fledged member. The purpose of such transitional events is to help the new member incorporate his new values, attitudes, and norms into his identity so that they become part of him, not merely something to which he pays lip service. Initiation rites which involve severe tests of the novice serve to prove to him that he is capable of fulfilling the new role—that he now is a man, no longer merely a boy.

Organizations usually signal this transition by giving the new man some important responsibility or a position of power which, if mishandled or misused, could genuinely hurt the organization. With this transition often come titles, symbols of status, extra rights or prerogatives, sharing of confidential information or other things which in one way or another indicate that the new member has earned the trust of the organization. Although such events may not always be visible to the outside observer, they are felt strongly by the new member. He knows when he has finally "been accepted," and feels it when he becomes "identified with the company."

So much for examples of the process of socialization. Let us now look at some of the dilemmas and conflicts which arise within it.

FAILURES OF SOCIALIZATION: NONCONFORMITY AND OVERCONFORMITY

Most organizations attach differing amounts of importance to different norms and values. Some are *pivotal*. Any member of a business organization who does not believe in the value of getting a job done will not survive long. Other pivotal values in most business organizations might be belief in a reasonable profit, belief in the free enterprise system and competition, belief in a hierarchy of authority as a good way to get things done, and so on.

Other values or norms are what may be called *relevant*. These are norms which it is not absolutely necessary to accept as the price of membership, but which are considered desirable and good to accept. Many of these norms pertain to standards of dress and decorum, not being publicly disloyal to the company, living in the right neighborhood and belonging to the right political party and clubs. In some organizations some of these norms may be pivotal. Organizations vary in this regard. You all know the stereotype of IBM as a company that requires the wearing of white shirts and hats. In some parts of IBM such values are indeed pivotal; in other parts they are only relevant, and in some parts they are quite peripheral. The point is that not all norms to which the new member is exposed are equally important for the organization.

The socialization process operates across the whole range of norms, but the amount of reward and punishment for compliance or noncompliance will vary with the importance of the norm. This variation allows the new member some degrees of freedom in terms of how far to conform and allows the organization some degrees of freedom in how much conformity to demand. The new man can accept none of the values, he can accept only the pivotal values, but carefully remain independent on all those areas not seen as pivotal, or he can accept the whole range of values and norms. He can tune in so completely on what he sees to be the way others are handling themselves that he becomes a carbon copy and sometimes a caricature of them.

These basic responses to socialization can be labeled as follows:

Type 1: Rebellion–rejection of all values and norms.
Type 2: Creative individualism—acceptance only of pivotal values and norms; rejection of all others.
Type 3: Conformity—acceptance of all values and norms.

Most analyses of conformity deal only with the type 1 and 3 cases, failing to note that both can be viewed as socialization failures. The rebellious individual either is expelled from the organization or turns his energies toward defeating its goals. The conforming individual curbs his creativity and thereby moves the organization toward a sterile form of bureaucracy. The trick for most organizations is to create the type 2 response—acceptance of pivotal values and norms, but rejection of all others, a response which I would like to call "creative individualism."

To remain creatively individualistic in an organization is particularly difficult because of the constant resocialization pressures which come with promotion or lateral transfer. Every time the employee learns part of the value system of the particular group to which he is assigned, he may be laying the groundwork for conflict when he is transferred. The engineer has difficulty accepting the values of the sales department, the staff man has difficulty accepting the high pressure ways of the production department, and the line manager has difficulties accepting the service and helping ethic of a staff group. With each transfer, the forces are great toward either conforming or rebelling. It is difficult to keep focused on what is pivotal and retain one's basic individualism.

PROFESSIONAL SOCIALIZATION AND ORGANIZATIONAL SOCIALIZATION

The issue of how to maintain individualism in the face of organizational socialization pressures brings us to the final and most problematical area of concern. In the traditional professions, like medicine, law, and teaching, individualism is supported by a set of professional attitudes which serve to immunize the person against some of the forces of the organization. The questions now to be considered are (1) Is management a profession? (2) If so, do professional attitudes develop in managers? and (3) If so, do these support or conflict with organizational norms and values?

Professionalism can be defined by a number of characteristics:

1. Professional decisions are made by means of general principles, theories, or propositions which are independent of the particular case under consideration. For management this would mean that there are certain principles of how to handle people, money, information, etc., independent of any particular company. The fact that we can and do teach general subjects in these areas would support management's claim to being a profession.

2. Professional decisions imply knowledge in a specific area in which the

person is expert, not a generalized body of wisdom. The professional is an expert only in his profession, not an expert at everything. He has no license to be a "wise man." Does management fit by this criterion? I will let you decide.

3. The professional's relations with his clients are objective and independent of particular sentiments about them. The doctor or lawyer makes his decisions independently of his liking or disliking his patients or clients. On this criterion we have a real difficulty since, in the first place, it is very difficult to specify an appropriate single client for a manager, and, in the second place, it is not at all clear that decisions can or should be made independently of sentiments. What is objectively best for the stockholder may conflict with what is best for the enterprise, which, in turn may conflict with what is best for the customer.

4. A professional achieves his status by accomplishment, not by inherent qualities such as birth order, his relationship to people in power, his race, religion, or color. Industry is increasingly moving toward an acceptance of this principle for managerial selection, but in practice the process of organizational socialization may undermine it by rewarding the conformist and rejecting the individualist whose professional orientation may make him look disloyal to the organization.

5. A professional's decisions are assumed to be on behalf of the client and to be independent of self-interest. Clearly this principle is at best equivocal in manager-customer relations, though again one senses that industry is moving closer to accepting the idea.

6. The professional typically relates to a voluntary association of fellow professionals, and accepts only the authority of these colleagues as a sanction on his own behavior. The manager is least like the professional in this regard, in that he is expected to accept a principle of hierarchical authority. The dilemma is best illustrated by the previous example which I gave of our Sloan-fellow alumni who, after the program, related themselves more to other Sloans than to their company hierarchy. By this criterion they had become truly professionalized.

7. A professional has sometimes been called someone who knows better what is good for his client than the client. The professional's expertness puts the client into a very vulnerable position. This vulnerability has necessitated the development of strong professional codes and ethics which serve to protect the client. Such codes are enforced through the colleague peer group. One sees relatively few attempts to develop codes of ethics for managers or systems of enforcement.

On several bases, then, management is a profession, but on several others it is clearly not yet a profession.

This long description of what is a profession was motivated by the need to make a very crucial point. I believe that management education, particularly in a graduate school like the Sloan School, is increasingly attempting to train professionals, and in this process is socializing the students to a set of professional values which are, in fact, in severe and direct conflict with typical organizational values.

For example, I see us teaching general principles in the behavioral sciences, economics, and quantitative methods. Our applied subjects, like marketing, operations management, and finance, are also taught as bodies of knowledge governed by general principles which are applicable to a wide variety of situations. Our students are given very broad concepts which apply to the corporation as a whole, and are taught to see the relationship between the corporation, the community, and the society. They are taught to value the long-range health and survival of economic institutions, not the short-range profit of a particular company. They come to appreciate the necessary interrelationships between government, labor, and management rather than to define these as mutually warring camps. They are taught to look at organizations from the perspective of high ranking management, to solve the basic problems of the enterprise rather than the day-to-day practical problems of staff or line management. Finally, they are taught an ethic of pure rationality and emotional neutrality—analyze the problem and make the decisions independently of feelings about people, the product, the company, or the community. All of these are essentially professional values.

Organizations value many of the same things, in principle. But what is valued in principle by the higher ranking and senior people in the organization often is neither supported by their own behavior, nor even valued lower down in the organization. In fact, the value system which the graduates encounter on their first job is in many respects diametrically opposed to the professional values taught in school. The graduate is immediately expected to develop loyalty and concern for a particular company with all of its particular idiosyncrasies. He is expected to recognize the limitation of his general knowledge and to develop the sort of *ad hoc* wisdom which the school has taught him to avoid. He is expected to look to his boss for evaluation rather than to some group of colleagues outside the company.

Whereas the professional training tells him that knowledge is power, the graduate now must learn that knowledge by itself is nothing. It is the ability to "sell" knowledge to other people which is power. Only by being able to sell an application of knowledge to a highly specific, local situation can the graduate obtain respect for what he knows. Where his education has taught the graduate principles of how to manage others and to take the corporate point of view, his organizational socialization tries to teach him how to be a good subordinate, how to be influenced, and how to sell ideas from a position of lower power.

On the one hand, the organization via its recruiters and senior people tells the graduate that it is counting on him to bring fresh points of view and new techniques to bear on its problems. On the other hand, the man's first boss and peers try to socialize him into their traditional mold.

A man is hired to introduce linear programming into a production department, but once he is there he is told to lay off because if he succeeds he will make the old supervisors and engineers look bad. Another man is hired for his financial analysis skills but is not permitted access to data worth analyzing because the company does not trust him to keep them confidential. A third man is hired into a large group responsible for developing cost reduction programs in a large defense industry, and is told to ignore the fact that the group is overstaffed, inefficient, and willing to pad its expense accounts. A fourth man, hired for his energy and capability, put it this way as an explanation of why he quit to go into private consulting: "They were quite pleased with work that required only two hours per day; I wasn't."

In my panel of 1962 graduates, 73 percent have already left their first job and many are on their third or fourth. In the class of 1963, the percentage is 67, and in the class of 1964, the percentage is 50. Apparently, most of our graduates are unwilling to be socialized into organizations whose values are incompatible with the ones we teach. Yet these organizations are precisely the ones who may need creative individualists most.

What seems to happen in the early stages of the managerial career is either a kind of postponement of professional socialization while organizational socialization takes precedence, or a rebelling by the graduate against organizational socialization. The young man who submits must first learn to be a good apprentice, a good staff man, a good junior analyst, and perhaps a good low level administrator. He must prove his loyalty to the company by accepting this career path with good graces, before he is trusted enough to be given a position of power. If he has not lost his education by then, he can begin to apply some general principles when he achieves such a position of power.

The businessman wants the school to provide both the professional education and the humility which would make organizational socialization smoother. He is not aware that teaching management concepts of the future precludes justifying the practices of today. Some professional schools clearly do set out to train for the needs of the profession as it is designed today. The Sloan School appears to me to reject this concept. Instead we have a faculty which is looking at the professional manager of five, ten, or twenty years from now, and are training our graduates in management techniques which we believe are coming in the future.

Symptomatic of this approach is the fact that in many of our subjects we are highly critical of the management practices of today, and highly committed to re-educating those managers like Sloan fellows and senior executives who come back to study at MIT. We get across in a dozen different ways the belief that most organizations of today are obsolete, conservative, "constipated," and ignorant of their own problems. Furthermore, I believe that this point of view is what society and the business community demands of a good professional school.

It would be no solution to abandon our own vision of the manager of the future, and I doubt that those of you in the audience from business and industry would really want us to do this. What you probably want is to have your cake and eat it too—you want us to teach our students the management concepts of tomorrow, and you want us to teach them how to put these concepts into deep freeze while they learn the business of today. Then, when they have proven themselves worthy of advancement and have achieved a position of some influence, they should magically resurrect their education and put it to work.

Unfortunately, socialization processes are usually too powerful to permit that solution. If you succeed in socializing your young graduates to your organizations, you will probably also succeed in proving to them that their education was pretty worthless and might as well be put on a permanent rather than temporary shelf. We have research evidence that many well educated graduates do learn to be complacent and to play the organizational game. It is not at all clear whether they later ever resurrect their educational arsenal.

WHAT IS TO BE DONE ABOUT THIS SITUATION?

I think we need to accept, at the outset, the reality of organizational socialization phenomena. As my colleague, Leo Moore, so aptly put it, organizations like to put their fingerprints on people, and they have every right to do so. By the same token, graduate schools of business have a right and an obligation to pursue professional socialization to the best of their ability. We must find a way to ameliorate the conflicts at the interface, without, however, concluding that either schools or organizations are to blame and should stop what they are doing.

What the Schools Can Do

The schools, our school in particular, can do several concrete things which would help the situation. First, we can insert into our total curriculum more apprenticeship experience which would bring the realities of organizational life home to the student earlier. But such apprenticeship experiences will not become educational unless we combine them with a second idea, that of providing a practicum on how to change organizations. Such a practicum should draw on each of the course specialties and should be specifically designed to teach a student how to translate his professional knowledge into viable action programs at whatever level of the organization he is working.

Ten years ago we would not have known how to do this. Today there is no excuse for not doing it. Whether the field is operations research, sophisticated quantitative marketing, industrial dynamics, organizational psychology or whatever, we must give our students experience in trying to implement their new ideas, and we must teach them how to make the implementation effective. In effect, we must teach our students to become change agents, whatever their disciplinary specialty turns out to be. We must teach them how to influence their organizations from low positions of power without sacrificing their professional values in the process. We must teach them how to remain creative individualists in the face of strong organizational socialization pressures.

Combined with these two things, we need to do a third thing. We need to become more involved in the student's efforts at career planning and we need to coordinate our activities more closely with the company recruiters and the university placement officers. At the present I suspect that most of our faculty is quite indifferent to the student's struggles to find the right kind of a job. I suspect that this indifference leaves the door wide open to faulty selection on the part of the student, which can only lead, in the end, to an undermining of the education into which we pour so much effort. We need to work harder to insure that our graduates get jobs in which they can further the values and methods we inculcate.

What the Companies Can Do

Companies can do at least two things. First, they can make a genuine effort to become aware of and understand their own organizational socialization practices. I fear very few higher level executives know what is going on at the bottom of their organization, where all the high priced talent they call for is actually employed. At the same time, I suspect that it is their own value system which ultimately determines the socialization activities which occur throughout all segments of the organization. Greater awareness and understanding of these practices should make possible more rational choices as to which practices to encourage and which to de-emphasize. The focus should be on pivotal values only, not on peripheral or irrelevant ones.

Second, companies must come to appreciate the delicate problems which exist both for the graduate and for his first boss in the early years of the career when socialization pressures are at the maximum. If more companies appreciated the nature of this dilemma they would recognize the necessity of giving some training to the men who will be the first bosses of the graduates.

I have argued for such training for many years, but still find that most company effort goes into training the graduate rather than his boss. Yet it is the boss who really has the power to create the climate which will lead to rebellion, conformity, or creative individualism. If the companies care whether their newly hired use one or the other of these adaptation strategies, they had better start looking at the behavior of the first boss and training him for what the company wants and hopes for. Too many bosses concentrate on teaching too many peripheral values and thus undermine the possibilities for creative individualism and organization improvement.

CONCLUSION

The essence of management is to understand the forces acting in a situation and to gain control over them. It is high time that some of our managerial knowledge and skill be focused on those forces in the organizational environment which derive from the fact that organizations are social systems who do socialize their new members. If we do not learn to analyze and control the forces of organizational socialization, we are abdicating one of our primary managerial responsibilities. Let us not shrink from a little bit of social engineering and management in this most important area of the human side of the enterprise.

REFERENCES

Blau, P. M., and R. W. Scott. *Formal Organizations*. Chandler, 1962.

Goffman, E. *Asylums*. Doubleday-Anchor, 1961.

Schein, E. H. "The Wall of Misunderstanding on the First Job." *Journal of College Placement*, February–March 1967.

——. "Attitude Change During Management Education." *Administrative Science Quarterly*, Vol. 11, 1967.

——. "The Problem of Moral Education for the Business Manager." *Industrial Management Review*, Vol. 8, 1966.

——. *Organizational Psychology*. Prentice-Hall, 1965.

——. "Training in Industry: Education or Indoctrination." *Industrial Medicine and Surgery*, Vol. 33, 1964.

——. "How to Break In the College Graduate." *Harvard Business Review*, Vol. 42, 1964.

——. "Forces Which Undermine Management Development." *California Management Review*, Vol. 5, Summer 1963.

——. "Management Development as a Process of Influence." *Industrial Management Review*, Vol. 2, 1961.

——, Inge Schneier, and C. H. Barker. *Coercive Persuasion*. Norton, 1961.

The Slade Company Case

Ralph Porter, production manager of the Slade Company, was concerned by reports of dishonesty among some employees in the plating department. From reliable sources, he had learned that a few men were punching the timecards of a number of their workmates who had left early. Porter had only recently joined the Slade organization. He judged from conversations with the previous production manager and other fellow managers that they were, in general, pleased with the overall performance of the plating department.

The Slade Company was a prosperous manufacturer of metal products designed for industrial application. Its manufacturing plant, located in central Michigan, employed nearly five hundred workers, who were engaged in producing a large variety of

"The Slade Company Case," 9-406-074, was prepared by John A. Seiler under the direction of Paul Lawrence of the Harvard University Graduate School of Business Administration as a basis for classroom discussion rather than to illustrate either effective or ineffective handling of administrative situations.

Exhibit 1 The Slade Company Manufacturing Organization

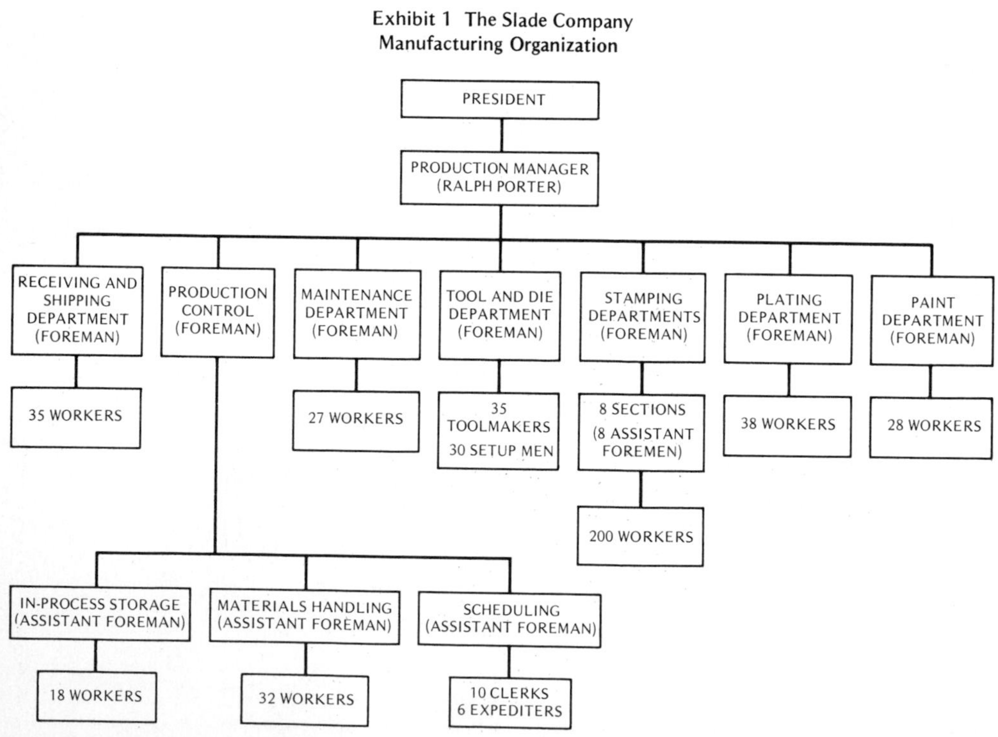

clamps, inserts, knobs, and similar items. Orders for these products were usually large and on a recurrent basis. The volume of orders fluctuated in response to business conditions in the primary industries which the company served. At the time of this case, sales volume had been high for over a year. The bases upon which the Slade Company secured orders, in rank of importance, were quality, delivery, and reasonable price.

The organization of manufacturing operations at the Slade plant is shown in Exhibit 1. The departments listed there are, from left to right, approximately in the order in which material flowed through the plant. The diemaking and setup operations required

Exhibit 2 The Slade Company
Plating Room Layout

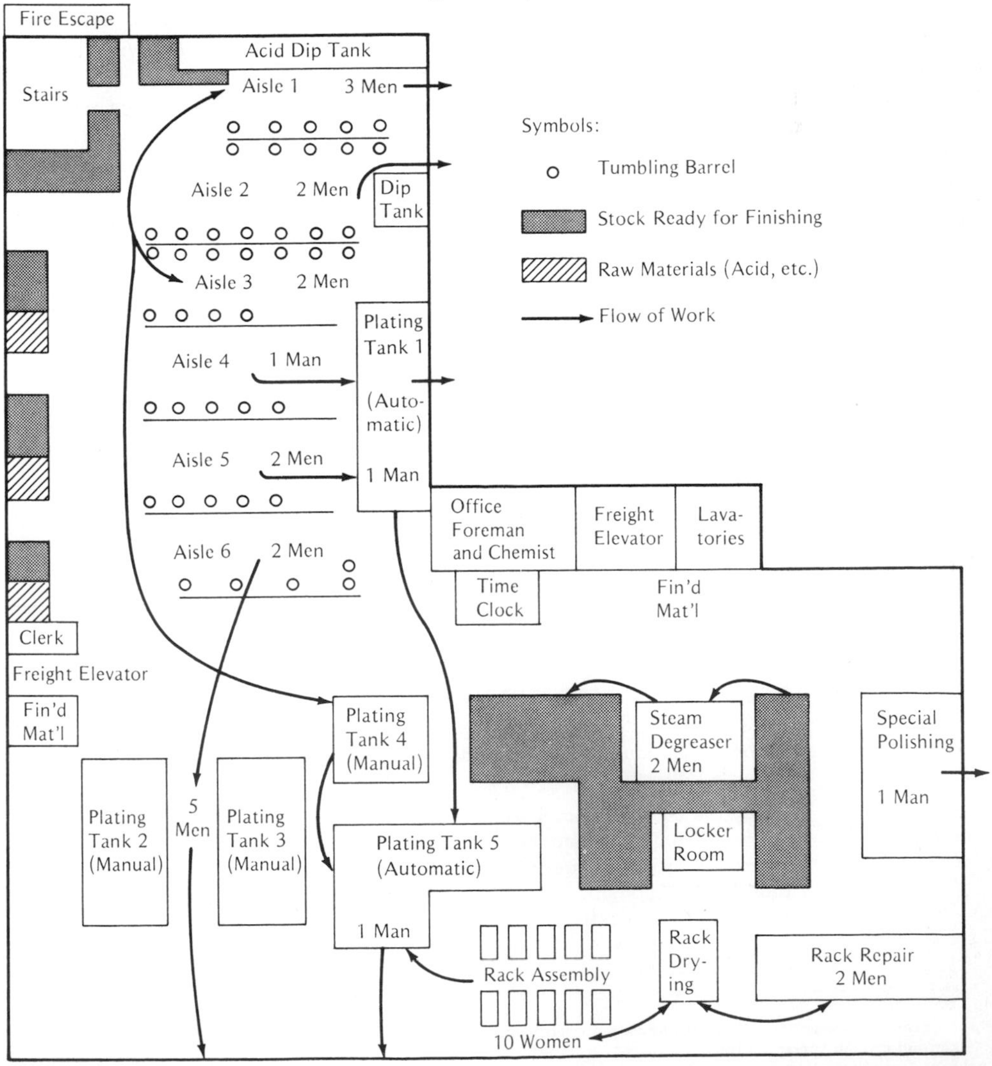

the greatest degree of skill, supplied by highly paid, long-service craftsmen. The finishing departments, divided operationally and geographically between plating and painting, attracted less highly trained but relatively skilled workers, some of whom had been employed by the company for many years. The remaining operations were largely unskilled in nature and were characterized by relatively low pay and high rate of turnover of personnel.

The plating room was the sole occupant of the top floor of the plant. Exhibit 2 shows the floor plan, the disposition of workers, and the flow of work throughout the department. Thirty-eight men and women worked in the department, plating or oxidizing the metal parts or preparing parts for the application of paint at another location in the plant. The department's work occurred in response to orders communicated by production schedules, which were revised daily. Schedule revisions, caused by last-minute order increases or rush requests from customers, resulted in short-term volume fluctuations, particularly in the plating, painting, and shipping departments. Exhibit 3 outlines the activities of the various jobs, their interrelationships, and the type of work in which each specialized. Exhibit 4 rates the various types of jobs in terms of the technical skill, physical effort, discomfort, and training time associated with their performance.

The activities which took place in the plating room were of three main types:

1. Acid dipping, in which parts were etched by being placed in baskets

Exhibit 3 The Slade Company
Outline of Plating Room Work Flow

AISLE 1:	Worked closely with Aisle 3 in preparation of parts by barrel tumbling and acid dipping for high-quality[1] plating in Tanks 4 and 5. Also did a considerable quantity of highly specialized, high-quality acid-etching work not requiring further processing.
AISLE 2:	Tumbled items of regular quality and design in preparation for painting. Less frequently, did oxidation dipping work of regular quality, but sometimes of special design, not requiring further processing.
AISLE 3:	Worked closely with Aisle 1 on high-quality tumbling work for Tanks 4 and 5.
AISLES 4 and 5:	Produced regular tumbling work for Tank 1.
AISLE 6:	Did high-quality tumbling work for special products plated in Tanks 2 and 3.
TANK 1:	Worked on standard, automated plating of regular quality not further processed in plating room, and regular work further processed in Tank 5.
TANKS 2 and 3:	Produced special, high-quality plating work not requiring further processing.
TANK 4:	Did special, high-quality plating work further plated in Tank 5.
TANK 5:	Automated production of high- and regular-quality, special- and regular-design plated parts sent directly to shipping.
RACK ASSEMBLY:	Placed parts to be plated in Tank 5 on racks.
RACK REPAIR:	Performed routine replacement and repair of racks used in Tank 5.
POLISHING:	Processed, by manual or semimanual methods, odd-lot special orders which were sent directly to shipping. Also, sorted and reclaimed parts rejected by inspectors in the shipping department.
DEGREASING:	Took incoming raw stock, processed it through caustic solution, and placed clean stock in storage ready for processing elsewhere in the plating room.

[1] Definition of terms: *High or regular quality:* The quality of finishes could broadly be distinguished by the thickness of plate and/or care in preparation. *Regular or special work:* The complexity of work depended on the routine or special character of design and finish specifications.

which were manually immersed and agitated in an acid solution.

2. Barrel tumbling, in which parts were roughened or smoothed by being loaded into machine-powered revolving drums containing abrasive, caustic, or corrosive solutions.

3. Plating—either manual, in which parts were loaded on racks and were immersed by hand through the plating sequence; or automatic, in which racks or baskets were manually loaded with parts which were then carried by a conveyor system through the plating sequence.

Within these main divisions, there were a number of variables, such as cycle times, chemical formulas, abrasive mixtures, and so forth, which distinguished particular jobs as they have been categorized in Exhibit 3.

The work of the plating room was received in batch lots whose size averaged a thousand pieces. The clerk moved each batch, which was accompanied by a routing slip, to its first operation. This routing slip indicated the operations to be performed and when each major operation on the batch was scheduled to be completed, so that the finished product could be shipped on time. From the accumulation of orders before him, each man was to organize his own work schedule so as to make optimal use of equipment, materials, and time. Upon completion of an order, each man moved the lot to its next work position or to the finished material location near the freight elevator.

The plating room was under the direct supervision of the foreman, Otto Schell, who worked a regular 8:00–to–5:00 day, five days a week. The foreman spent a good deal of his working time attending to maintenance and repair of equipment, procuring supplies, handling late schedule changes, and seeing that his people were at their proper work locations.

Working conditions in the plating room varied considerably. That part of the department containing the tumbling barrels and the plating machines was constantly awash, alternately with cold water, steaming acid, or caustic soda. Men working in this part of the room wore knee boots, long rubber aprons, and high-gauntlet rubber gloves. This uniform, consistent with the general atmosphere of the "wet" part of the room, was hot in summer, cold in winter. In contrast, the remainder of the room was dry, was relatively odor-free, and provided rea-

Exhibit 4 The Slade Company Skill Indices by Job Group[1]

Jobs	Technical Skill Required	Physical Effort Required	Degree of Discomfort Involved	Degree of Training Required[2]
Aisle 1	1	1	1	1
Tanks 2–4	3	2	1	2
Aisles 2–6	5	1	1	5
Tank 5	1	5	7	2
Tank 1	8	5	5	7
Degreasing	9	3	7	10
Polishing	6	9	9	7
Rack assembly and repair	10	10	10	10

[1] Rated on scales of 1 (the greatest) to 10 (the least) in each category.
[2] The amount of experience required to assume complete responsibility for the job.

Exhibit 5 The Slade Company Plating Room Personnel

Location	Name	Age	Marital Status	Company Seniority	Department Seniority	Pay	Education	Familial Relationships	Productivity—Skill Rating[1]
Aisle 1	Tony Sarto	30	M	13 yrs.	13 yrs.	$1.50	High school	Louis Patrici, uncle Pete Facelli, cousin	1
	Pete Facelli	26	M	8 yrs.	8 yrs.	1.30	High school	Louis Patrici, uncle Tony Sarto, cousin	2
	Joe Iambi	31	M	5 yrs.	5 yrs.	1.20	2 yrs. high school		2
Aisle 2	Herman Schell	48	S	26 yrs.	26 yrs.	1.45	Grade school	Otto Schell, brother	8
	Philip Kirk	23	M	1 yr.	1 yr.	0.90	College		2
Aisle 3	Dom Pantaleoni	31	M	10 yrs.	10 yrs.	1.30	1 yr. high school		2
	Sal Maletta	32	M	12 yrs.	12 yrs.	1.30	3 yrs. high school		3
Aisle 4	Bob Pearson	22	S	4 yrs.	4 yrs.	1.15	High school	Father in tool and die dept.	1
Aisle 5	Charlie Malone	44	M	22 yrs.	8 yrs.	1.25	Grade school		7
	John Lacey	41	S	9 yrs.	5 yrs.	1.20	1 yr. high school	Brother in paint dept.	7
Aisle 6	Jim Martin	30	S	7 yrs.	7 yrs.	1.25	High school		4
	Bill Mensch	41	M	6 yrs.	2 yrs.	1.10	Grade school		4
Tank 1	Henry La Forte	38	M	14 yrs.	6 yrs.	1.25	High school		6
Tanks 2–3	Ralph Parker	25	S	7 yrs.	7 yrs.	1.20	High school		4
	Ed Harding	27	S	8 yrs.	8 yrs.	1.20	High school		4
	George Flood	22	S	5 yrs.	5 yrs.	1.15	High school		5

Exhibit 5 The Slade Company Plating Room Personnel (cont.)

	Harry Clark	29	M	8 yrs.	8 yrs.	1.20	High school		3
	Tom Bond	25	S	6 yrs.	6 yrs.	1.20	High school		4
Tank 4	Frank Bonzani	27	M	9 yrs.	9 yrs.	1.25	High school		2
	Al Bartolo	24	M	6 yrs.	6 yrs.	1.25	High school		3
Tank 5	Louis Patrici	47	S	14 yrs.	14 yrs.	1.45	2 yrs. college	Tony Sarto, nephew Pete Facelli, nephew	1
Rack Assembly	10 women	30–40	9M, 1S	10 yrs. (av.)	10 yrs. (av.)	1.05	Grade school (av.)	6 with husbands in company	4 (av.)
Rack Maintenance	Will Partridge	57	M	14 yrs.	2 yrs.	1.20	Grade school		7
	Lloyd Swan	62	M	3 yrs.	3 yrs.	1.10	Grade school		7
Degreasing	Dave Susi	45	S	1 yr.	1 yr.	1.05	High school		5
	Mike Maher	41	M	4 yrs.	4 yrs.	1.05	Grade school		6
Polishing	Russ Perkins	49	M	12 yrs.	2 yrs.	1.20	High school		4
Foreman	Otto Schell	56	M	35 yrs.	35 yrs.	(Not available)	High school	Herman Schell, brother	3
Clerk	Bill Pierce	32	M	10 yrs.	4 yrs.	1.15	High school		4
Chemist	Frank Rutlage	24	S	2 yrs.	2 yrs.	(Not available)	2 yrs. college		6

[1] On a potential scale of 1 (top) to 10 (bottom), as evaluated by the men in the department.
[2] Kirk was the source of data for this case and, as such, was in a biased position to report accurately perceptions about himself.

Exhibit 6 The Slade Company
Informal Groupings in the Plating Room

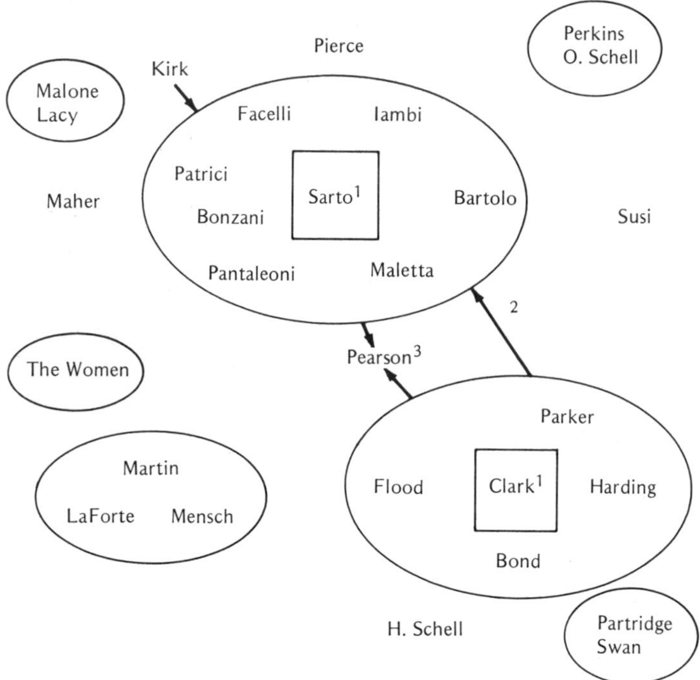

[1]The boxes indicate those men who clearly demonstrated leadership behavior (most closely personified the values shared by their groups, were most often sought for help and arbitration, and so forth).
[2]While the two- and three-man groupings had little informal contact outside their own boundaries, the five-man group did seek to join the largest group in extraplant social affairs. These were relatively infrequent.
[3]Though not an active member of any group, Bob Pearson was regarded with affection by the two large groups.

sonably stable temperature and humidity conditions for those who worked there.

The men and women employed in the plating room are listed in Exhibit 5. This exhibit provides certain personal data on each department member, including a productivity–skill rating (based on subjective and objective appraisals of potential performance), as reported by the members of the department.

The pay scale implied by Exhibit 5 was low for the central Michigan area. The average starting wage for factory work in the community was about $1.25. However, working hours for the plating room were long (from 60 hours to a possible and frequently available 76 hours per week). The first 60 hours (the normal five-day week) were paid for on straight-time rates. Saturday work was paid for at time and one half; Sunday pay was calculated on a double-time basis.

As Exhibit 5 indicates, Philip Kirk, a worker in Aisle 2, provided the data for this case. After he had been a member of the department for several months, Kirk noted that certain members of the department tended to seek each other out during free time on and off the job. He then observed that these informal associations were enduring, built upon common activities and shared ideas about what was and what was not legitimate behavior in the department. His estimate of the pattern of these associations is diagrammed in Exhibit 6.

The Sarto group, so named because Tony Sarto was its most respected member and the one who acted as arbiter between the other members, was the largest in the department. The group, except for Louis Patrici, Al Bartolo, and Frank Bonzani (who spelled each other during break periods), invariably ate lunch together on the fire escape near Aisle 1. On those Saturdays and Sundays when overtime work was required, the Sarto group operated as a team, regardless of weekday work assignments, to get overtime work completed as quickly as possible. (Few department members not affiliated with either the Sarto or the Clark groups worked on weekends.) Off the job, Sarto group members often joined in parties or weekend trips. Sarto's summer camp was a frequent rendezvous.

Sarto's group was also the most cohesive one in the department in terms of its organized punch-in and punch-out system. Since the men were regularly scheduled to work from 7:00 A.M. to 7:00 P.M. weekdays, and since all supervision was removed at 5:00 P.M., it was possible almost every day to finish a "day's work" by 5:30 and leave the plant. What is more, if one man were to stay until 7:00 P.M., he could punch the time cards of a number of men and help them gain free time without pay loss. (This system operated on weekends, also, at which times members of supervision were present, if at all, only for short periods.) In Sarto's group the duty of staying late rotated, so that no man did so more than once a week. In addition, the group members would punch a man in in the morning if he were unavoidably delayed. However, such a practice never occurred without prior notice from the man who expected to be late and never if the tardiness was expected to last beyond 8:00 A.M., the start of the day for the foreman.

Sarto explained the logic behind the system to Kirk:

"You know that our hourly pay rate is quite low, compared to other companies. What makes this the best place to work is the feeling of security you get. No one ever gets laid off in this department. With all the hours in the week, all the company ever has to do is shorten the work week when orders fall off. We have to tighten our belts, but we can all get along. When things are going well, as they are now, the company is only interested in getting out the work. It doesn't help to get it out faster than it's really needed—so we go home a little early whenever we can. Of course, some guys abuse this sort of thing—like Herman—but others work even harder, and it averages out.

"Whenever an extra order has to be pushed through, naturally I work until 7:00. So do a lot of the others. I believe that if I stay until my work is caught up and my equipment is in good shape, that's all the company wants of me. They leave us alone and expect us to produce—and we do."

When Kirk asked Sarto if he would not rather work shorter hours at higher pay in a union shop (Slade employees were not organized), he just laughed and said: "It wouldn't come close to an even trade."

The members of Sarto's group were explicit about what constituted a fair day's work. Customarily, they cited Herman Schell, Kirk's work partner and the foreman's brother, as a man who consistently produced below that level. Kirk received an informal orientation from Herman during his first days on the job. As Herman put it:

"I've worked at this job for a good many years, and I expect to stay here a good many more. You're just starting out, and you don't know which end is up yet. We spend a lot of time in here; and no matter how hard we work, the pile of work never goes down. There's always more to take its place. And I think you've found out by now that this isn't light work. You can wear yourself out fast if you're not smart. Look at Pearson up in Aisle 4. There's a kid who's just going to burn himself out. He won't last long. If he thinks he's going to get somewhere working like that, he's nuts. They'll give him all the work he can take. He makes it tough on everybody else and on himself, too."

Kirk reported further on his observations of the department:

"As nearly as I could tell, two things seemed to determine whether or not Sarto's group or any others came in for weekend work on Saturday or Sunday. It seemed usually to be caused by rush orders that were received late in the week, although I suspect it was sometimes caused by the men having spent insufficient time on the job during the previous week.

"Tony and his group couldn't understand Herman. While Herman arrived late, Tony was always half an hour early. If there was a push to get out an extra amount of work, almost everyone but Herman would work that much harder. Herman never worked overtime on weekends, while Tony's group and the men on the manual tanks almost always did. When the first, exploratory time study of the department was made, no one in the aisles slowed down, except Herman, with the possible exception, to a lesser degree, of Charlie Malone. I did hear that the men in the dry end of the room slowed down so much you could hardly see them move; but we had little to do with them, anyway. While the men I knew best seemed to find a rather full life in their work, Herman never really got involved. No wonder they couldn't understand each other.

"There was quite a different feeling about Bobby Pearson. Without the slightest doubt, Bob worked harder than anyone else in the room. Because of the tremendous variety of work produced, it was hard to make output comparisons, but I'm sure I wouldn't be far wrong in saying that Bob put out twice as much as Herman and 50 percent more than almost anyone else in the aisles. No one but Herman and a few old-timers at the dry end ever criticized Bobby for his efforts. Tony and his group seemed to feel a distant affection for Bob, but the only contact they or anyone else had with him consisted of brief greetings.

"To the men in Tony's group the most severe penalty that could be inflicted on a man was exclusion. This they did to both Pearson and Herman. Pearson, however, was tolerated; Herman was not. Evidently, Herman felt his exclusion keenly, though he answered it with derision and aggression. Herman kept up a steady stream of stories concerning his attempts to gain acceptance outside the company. He wrote popular music which was always rejected by publishers. He attempted to join several social and athletic clubs, mostly without success. His favorite pastime was fishing. He told me that fishermen were friendly, and he enjoyed meeting new people whenever he went fishing. But he was particularly quick to explain that he preferred to keep his distance from the men in the department.

"Tony's group emphasized more than just quantity in judging a man's work. Among them had grown a confidence that they could master and even improve upon any known finishing technique. Tony himself symbolized this skill. Before him, Tony's father had operated Aisle 1 and had trained Tony to take his place. Tony in his turn was training his cousin Pete. When a new finishing problem arose from a change in customer specifications, the foreman, the department chemist, or any of the men directly involved would come to Tony for help, and Tony would give it willingly. For example, when a part with a special plastic embossing was designed, Tony was the only one who could discover how to treat the metal without damaging the plastic. To a lesser degree, the other members of the group were also inventive about the problems which arose in their own sections.

"Herman, for his part, talked incessantly about his feats in design and finish creations. As far as I could tell during the year I worked in the department, the objects of these stories were obsolete or of minor importance. What's more, I never saw any department member seek Herman's help.

"Willingness to be of help was a trait Sarto's group prized. The most valued help of all was of a personal kind, though work help was also important. The members of Sarto's group were constantly lending and borrowing money, cars, clothing, and tools among themselves and, less frequently, with other members of the department. Their daily lunch bag procedure typified the "common property" feeling among them. Everyone's lunch was opened and added to a common pile, from which each member of the group chose his meal.

"On the other hand, Herman refused to help others in any way. He never left his aisle to aid those near him who were in the midst of a rush of work or a machine failure, though this was customary throughout most of the department. I can distinctly recall the picture of Herman leaning on the hot and cold water faucets which were located directly above each tumbling barrel. He would stand gazing into the tumbling pieces for hours. To the passing, casual visitor, he looked busy; and as he told me, that's just what he wanted. He, of course, expected me to act this same way, and it was this enforced boredom that I found virtually intolerable.

"More than this, Herman took no responsibility for breaking in his assigned helpers as they first entered the department, or thereafter. He had had four helpers in the space of little more than a year. Each had asked for a transfer to another department, publicly citing the work as cause, privately blaming Herman. Tony was the one who taught me the ropes when I first entered the department.

"The men who congregated around Harry Clark tended to talk like and copy the behavior of the Sarto group, though they never approached the degree of inventive skill or the amount of helping activities that Tony's group did. They sought outside social contact with the Sarto group; and several times a year, the two groups went "on the town" together. Clark's group did maintain a high level of performance in the volume of work they turned out.

"The remainder of the people in the department stayed pretty much to themselves or associated in pairs or triplets. None of these people were as inventive, as helpful, or as productive as Sarto's or Clark's groups, but most of them gave verbal support to the same values as those groups held.

"The distinction between the two organized groups and the rest of the department was clearest in the punching-out routine. The women could not work past 3:00 P.M., so they were not involved. Malone and Lacey, Partridge and Swan, and Martin, La Forte, and Mensch arranged within their small groups for punch-outs, or they remained beyond 5:00 and slept or read when they finished their work. Perkins and Pierce went home when the foreman did. Herman Schell, Susi, and Maher had no punch-out organization to rely upon. Susi and Maher invariably stayed in the department until 7:00 P.M. Herman was reported to have established an arrangement with Partridge whereby the latter punched Herman out for a fee. Such a practice was unthinkable from the point of view of Sarto's group. It evidently did not occur often because Herman usually went to sleep behind piles of work when his brother left or, particularly during the fishing season, punched himself out early. He constantly railed against the dishonesty of other men in the department, yet urged me to punch him out on several 'emergency occasions.'

"Just before I left the Slade Company to return to school after fourteen months on the job, I had a casual conversation with Mr. Porter, the production manager, in which he asked me how I had enjoyed my experience with the organization. During the conversation, I learned that he knew of the punch-out system in the plating department. What's more, he told me, he was wondering if he ought to 'blow the lid off the whole mess.'"

Pointe-SA Holland Case

"If I am going to stay with the company, there are four conditions that they will have to meet," said Alain Dubois early in 1970. "First, I will insist that I be appointed a member of the new executive committee. Second, the president will have to agree to leave the sales force alone; he cannot continue to work with them as he has in the past. Third, we will have to discharge some people, regardless of who their friends are in the company. We simply cannot afford to have anything but the most competent people with us now. And finally, I must have the authority to hire the kind of people that I need, both in terms of quality and numbers."

Alain Dubois, 33 years old, was the marketing director of the Pointe-Holland Company, a wholly owned subsidiary in Holland of a large company with headquarters in France. The Pointe-Holland Company manufactured and distributed a line of household and food products throughout Europe and was widely known and recognized because of its extensive advertising campaigns. While company headquarters were in France, the parent company had wholly owned subsidiaries in other European countries, each of which was organized as a separate company with separate presidents and administrative staff.

Each president was responsible for the operation of his organization, and each subsidiary was run as a separate profit center. While there was some centralized direction from Pointe headquarters in France, each subsidiary had wide latitude in determining the nature and extent of its activity, especially insofar as promotion and advertising of individual products or product lines were concerned. It was important for each subsidiary to have this freedom and flexibility to accommodate to national characteristics and demands.

Alain Dubois had been director of marketing of Pointe-Holland for two years. He was responsible for all sales promotion, product development, advertising, and sales management activities. He reported directly to the president of Pointe-Holland and had reporting to him all people in the organization involved with marketing activities.

Prior to joining Pointe-Holland, Alain Dubois had been an executive with an advertising agency in France, primarily responsible for preparation of advertising campaigns for organizations active in marketing consumer products. He was widely recognized in Holland for his knowledge of marketing and was considered to be one of the "bright young men." Just prior to joining Pointe-Holland he had attended two executive management programs in the U.S. and, as a result of these programs and his own study and experience, was a leader in Europe in utilizing some of the newer concepts of marketing and management. In fact, his expertise in applying new concepts was one of the primary reasons why he was highly sought after by the Pointe headquarters in France for his current job.

Background of the Current Situation

In describing the background of this current situation Alain Dubois stated, "I was really

"Pointe-SA Holland Case" was prepared by Professor Harry Knudson while at IMEDE.

put into Pointe-Holland by headquarters in France to see if something could not be done with our operations here. Up until the time I came we had been losing a great deal of money each year. We are still losing money but the amount of loss has decreased substantially; and according to my plan we should break even next year, and each year after that make a small profit.

"My relationship with the president of Pointe-Holland is unique. He is a very fine individual and he and I get along very well on a social level. However, he is not up to date in his methods of management or in his knowledge and understanding of current marketing techniques. In fact, while I report to him I really make most major decisions in the Branded-Good Division for the company in Holland, and most of what happens is done at my initiative. The president is still a figurehead but I really go ahead and do what is necessary without much regard for his opinions or feelings. I have been able to do that because I have had the support of the main office in France. I continue to have this support but some things have happened recently which make me concerned about being able to continue to make the progress that we have made here in Holland for the last two years."

Issues Bothering Alain Dubois

One of the things of concern to Alain Dubois was the formation of the new executive committee, whose purpose was to make and review major policy decisions. The two members of this committee were the president of Pointe-Holland and the vice-president for administration. Alain Dubois was not a member of this committee and thought that he should be. When asked what changes in his status would result if he were appointed a member, he replied that in effect he would be independent of the president's authority. As a member of the executive committee he would be on equal status with the president and consequently would not be subject to his control in any way.

A second issue troubling Alain Dubois recently had been the president's actions with regard to some of the sales managers. The president of Pointe-Holland had had a long career as a salesman and still had very close personal relationships with many of the sales managers who were with the company for some time. Often, perhaps every two months, the president and a few of his friends who were sales managers would meet to discuss the sales situation. Alain Dubois did not attend these meetings. According to Alain Dubois the meetings were primarily gossip sessions at which much information was exchanged, but information that had little basis in fact. For example, he described these meetings as ones in which the sales managers would report rumors from the trade; would predict how they thought people were going to react, based on information acquired during their sales activities; etc. Usually the meetings were held at rather elaborate restaurants and hotels. As the sales force reported directly to Alain Dubois, he thought that these meetings were not helpful to the overall selling effort and that they should be discontinued. He stated that he objected to the meetings on two counts: first, that they diluted his authority over the sales managers and, second, that the kind of information discussed and the results of the meetings were not at all useful to the selling effort.

Alain Dubois reported that the president had a very traditional concept of authority and would occasionally walk through the offices talking to the more junior marketing people (e.g., product managers), much in the way that a general might review an army. But Alain Dubois felt the president had no real understanding of what marketing people were now required to do. The efforts of the salesmen of Pointe-Holland could affect perhaps 40 percent of the potential market. Many of the products were sold directly to large chains of retail outlets, and the selling was done at the headquarter's level rather than in the traditional fashion of a salesman calling on an individual customer.

Alain Dubois was especially concerned, too, about one sales manager in particular—the general sales manager—who he felt was not competent to handle his job. This manager was a long-standing friend of the president, which made the matter more difficult for Alain Dubois. He stated that "I have no personal reasons for wanting to discharge this man. My reasons are entirely professional. He is just not competent to operate in the way that we have to operate now. For example, I am attempting to promote the product manager concept in which we have a great deal of flexibility in our approach for each product, depending on the situation. Unfortunately, the manager in question is very traditional in his approach and cannot adapt to this new thinking. He knows my feelings about this but the support he enjoys from the president on a friendship basis undercuts my efforts to initiate the new concepts and ideas. If we were a very large organization it might be possible to bypass this man, but we do not have enough personnel to let us do this. Each of our people has to be a good producer, and in my judgment this particular sales manager just is not adequate. Many of the people who report to him are more qualified than he—and this, of course, causes a problem of morale."

Another matter concerning Alain Dubois was that he did not have as complete freedom as he would like in hiring new people. For example, he thought that several additions to the marketing staff were very necessary, but he had not been able to secure the authority to hire additional personnel without discussing his reasons in great detail with the president of Pointe-Holland.

In summing up the current situation Alain Dubois stated: "My relationship with the president of Pointe-Holland has been fine as long as I have been able to ignore him. But with these new developments, especially the formation of the executive committee, I am going to have to get my status clarified.

"I am going to see the people in France again very soon, but rather than discuss this matter only with the top management of the parent corporation, I think that all of us should discuss it at the same time. So I plan to ask the president in France to arrange a meeting between him, the president in Holland, and myself for later this month. I will prepare a written statement of my position and give it to each man before the meeting so that each of them will know exactly how I feel. I hope that this can be resolved, for I'd like to continue the work that I have started. But I feel very strongly that I must have the freedom and the authority to do what I think is right.

"Of course, I realize that there are different ways of satisfying the conditions I have established for my own involvement, but I feel very strongly that I must have complete freedom in each of the areas I mentioned. For example, if they would agree to appoint me a member of the executive committee but not give me freedom to hire the people I need, this would not be satisfactory. Or if they would give me the authority to hire but not appoint me to the executive committee, that would not be satisfactory. In effect, I have to have all four of the conditions satisfied before I feel I can continue to make a contribution at Pointe-Holland."

Chapter 11

Fourth-Generation Organizations

STEPHEN A. ALLEN, III

An increasing number of large business and public agencies are confronting a set of environmental issues that are unique to our times. As they do, we are beginning to see the invention of a totally new set of organizational structures and systems aimed at coping with these issues. I call them *fourth-generation organizations* because I believe they represent the latest and most advanced of four basic families of organizations which have emerged since the inception of the Industrial Revolution.

My purpose is to outline the problems which have created the need for new organizational arrangements, show how these problems require a new set of performance capabilities, and describe some promising attempts to develop such capabilities. I will also touch on some of the internal problems these organizations are likely to face, some of the problems individuals may confront in working in fourth-generation organizations, and what this may mean for the future development of organizational theories.

CONTEMPORARY ORGANIZATIONAL PROBLEMS

Since the end of World War II there has been a clear trend for organizations—both private and public—to grow in size and, more importantly, in complexity. In 1946 the typical large business firm had one or a few products aimed at a single major market and frequently depended on one core technology. Today the typical firm is a diversified, multiproduct and often multinational institution which employs numerous technologies. A similar trend toward complexity can be seen in the information-gathering and -delivery systems of federal and state governments. Furthermore, these institutions face increasingly rapid shifts in client or customer expectations and in the technologies available for serving these publics.

Out of this quantum jump in environmental change and complexity have come a number of new organizational problems. Three of these are particularly important.

1. The development of a coordinated intelligence network which is linked to multiple, coordinated strategy-forming centers has emerged as an organizational problem in its own right. Traditionally, strategic information and decisions were the province of a few key people located at the apex of the organizational pyramid. Information collection was informal, and strategic decisions were reached through intuitive knowledge of a limited territory. For many contemporary organizations this is no longer a suitable approach. Sources of information have become more diverse, the stakes are much larger, and the complexity of factors which must be evaluated frequently make intuitive solutions considerably less effective.
2. Many large institutions have found that the fundamental innovations they would like to achieve lie outside of the capabilities and sometimes even conflict with the goals of existing operating units. Fundamental innovations in products or services may require major shifts in operating unit priorities, joint ventures among several units, and/or the development of entirely new operating units. Few traditional organizations have been designed to provide such a high degree of structural adaptability.
3. An increasing number of the operating units of large organizations deal with environments which require both efficiency and the ability to manage complex and shifting tasks. Examples are aerospace-electronics companies and educational and mental health institutions. While traditional organizations have been fairly successful in achieving efficiency under relatively stable conditions, few were designed to achieve both efficiency and a major capability for redeploying operating resources (people and facilities) around shifting project priorities and client needs.

What these three problems have in common is that they require organizations which are not only capable of achieving economies of scale but also of dealing in a concerted fashion with significant degrees of environmental novelty and with the need to flexibly develop and/or redeploy resources to serve shifting client needs or entirely new client groups. To understand why the basic types of organizational arrangements used up through 1960 are only partially effective in dealing with these problems it is useful to identify the first three generations of organization and examine their performance capabilities.

THE FIRST THREE GENERATIONS

At the outset I should note that this view of organizational evolution is not my invention. During the past ten years a substantial empirical and theoretical literature has developed concerning the first three generations of organization.[1] What is new is my contention that we are beginning to see the early representatives of a fourth generation.

Figure 1 summarizes the broad characteristics, performance potential, and shortcomings of each organizational family and arrays them on a rough time line. In essence we see an evolutionary trend which suggests that, as the shortcomings of each form became constraining in light of environmental requirements and opportunities, people invented fundamentally new forms. For example, as national markets and technologies began to emerge, the small, informal first-generation organizations were incapable of efficient large-scale expansion and coordination of large numbers of specialized personnel. Thus, increasing numbers of functionally organized, second-generation organizations began to appear. By 1930 the second-generation organization had become the dominant form.

By the late 1920s several large firms had developed third-generation organizations consisting of a corporate headquarters unit and separate product or geographic divisions.[2] This organizational form grew out of the inability of second-generation organizations to deal effectively with multiple product-market activities which were often geographically dispersed. It is interesting to note that at the time many economists predicted that this shortcoming of second-generation organizations would ultimately place limits on the ability of firms to grow. Obviously the predictions weren't borne out. Businessmen simply invented a new organizational form—capable of managing diversity—and went right on growing. By 1965 third-generation organizations had become the dominant form.[3]

At this point it is useful to step back and examine a few of the general features of this evolutionary scheme. First of all, as a particular organizational form becomes dominant the other forms don't simply disappear. They become the lower level building blocks of the newer generation, or they are used in their original form in environments where they are still appropriate. By dominance I mean the magnitude of economic and human resources commanded by each organizational generation. A second feature of this scheme is that it indicates a collapsing time frame. First-generation organizations were probably the dominant form for a century. It was around seventy years between the appearance of second-generation organizations and their movement to a dominant position. For third-generation organizations the comparable period was about forty-five years.

---

[1] See, for example, Ansoff, H. I., and R. D. Brandenburg. "A Language for Organizational Design." *Management Science*, August 1971; Chandler, Alfred D., Jr. *Strategy and Structure*. MIT Press, 1962; Greiner, Larry E. "Evolution and Revolution As Organizations Grow." *Harvard Business Review*, July–August 1973; and Scott, Bruce R. "The Industrial State: Old Myths and New Realities." *Harvard Business Review*, March–April 1973.

[2] For a description of the experiences of these firms see Chandler, *op. cit.*

[3] For census data in support of this contention see Scott, *op cit.*

From my earlier comments and from Figure 1 we can see some of the more significant shortcomings of the third-generation organizations. What kinds of fourth-generation organizations are emerging to deal with these shortcomings?

SOME PROMISING NEW APPROACHES

Matrix Organizations

The matrix organization is one approach which began to be used in the late 1950 s and has since found an increasing range of application. As shown in Figure 2, the basic idea is to give equal stature to a set of resource (or functional) groups on one side of the matrix and to a set of program, project, or business groups on the other side. Most people report to at least two managers simultaneously, and reporting relationships and work assignments shift frequently as business requirements change. The matrix found its first application in the electronics and aerospace industry where there was a need for frequent redeployment of expensive technical and human resources across a frequently changing group of temporary projects.[4] It has also been employed successfully by several industrial chemical companies. Most recently it has been used as a means of integrating product and geographic dimensions at top management levels of diversified multinational firms (examples are Dow Chemical and ITT).[5]

Making these organizations work is no mean task. They usually require dual planning and budgeting systems and considerable investment in organization development programs—e.g., systematic approaches to team-building, sensitivity training groups, and internal behavioral consultants. They also purposely violate many of the classical principles of organization—e.g., unity of command and "authority must equal responsibility." Nonetheless, most of these matrix approaches have proven economically viable. Many of them have several years of successful performance behind them.

New Venture Units

Another approach has been to split fundamental new developments off from existing operations until they are able to either reach a stage of successful commercialization or are deemed clearly undesirable for

[4] The following Harvard Business School cases provide examples of the use of matrix organizations: TRW Systems Group (D) and (E) and Northern Electric Company, Ltd. (A), (B), and (C) (Available through Intercollegiate Case Clearing House, Soldiers Field, Boston, Mass. 02163).

[5] For a discussion of matrix organizations in multinational firms see Stopford, John M., and Louis T. Wells, Jr. *Managing the Multinational Enterprise.* Basic Books, 1972, pp. 85–95.

Figure 1 Evolution of Three Generations of Organizations

Time Line*

1750 1st → (1860) 2nd → (1920) 3rd → 1930 2nd → 1965 3rd

*Year in box indicates approximate point of dominance. Year in parentheses indicates approximate time of invention.

First Generation		
Form	**Performance Capability**	**Shortcomings**
Entrepreneur-manager and undifferentiated work force. Coordination via individual dominance and interpersonal contact.	Flexible development of simple products in small quantities.	Low economies of scale. Limited ability to expand volume. Limited ability to develop several sophisticated products.

Second Generation		
Form	**Performance Capability**	**Shortcomings**
Single top manager and departments differentiated by function (Sales, Manufacturing, R&D). Coordination via personal contact, procedures, hierarchy, cross-functional coordinators.	Economies of scale via specialization and high volume. Operating flexibility within limited markets and technologies.	Inability to coordinate diverse products, markets, and technologies. Hampered by geographic separation and facilities.

Third Generation		
Form	**Performance Capability**	**Shortcomings**
Separate headquarters and operating divisions (product or geographic). Coordination via formal informative systems, staff, direct contact, hierarchy of general managers.	Operating flexibility across diverse product lines. Strategically responsive within existing environments.	Difficulty in coordinating corporate and division strategies. Strategically and operationally unresponsive outside of division boundaries. Loss of economies of scale in small divisions or those with shifting environments.

Figure 2 Matrix Organization Employed by Advanced Devices Center, Northern Electric Co. (1968)

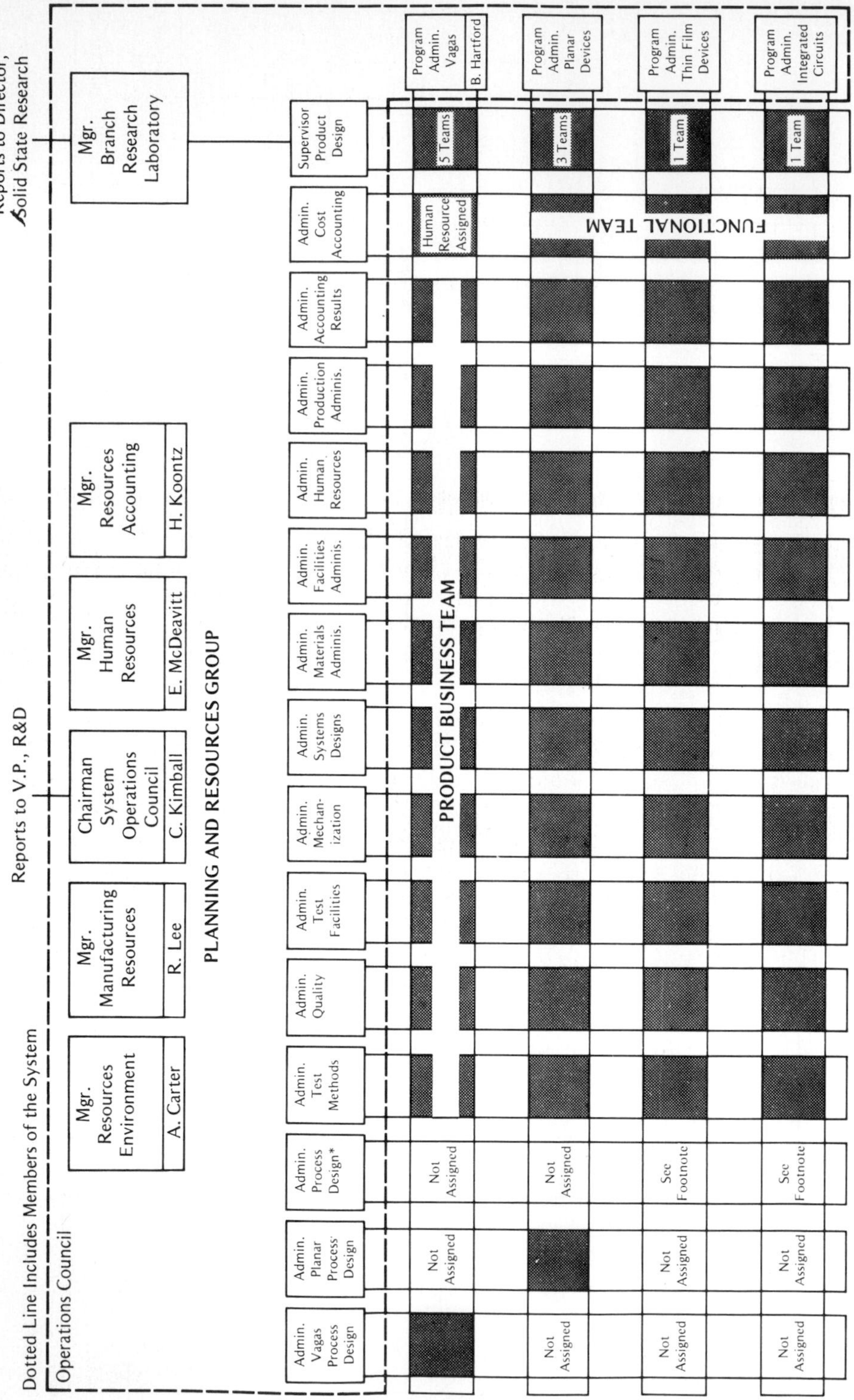

Dotted Line Includes Members of the System

Reports to V.P., R&D

Reports to Director, Solid State Research

Operations Council

Mgr. Resources Environment — A. Carter

Mgr. Manufacturing Resources — R. Lee

Chairman System Operations Council — C. Kimball

Mgr. Human Resources — E. McDeavitt

Mgr. Resources Accounting — H. Koontz

Mgr. Branch Research Laboratory

PLANNING AND RESOURCES GROUP

Admin. Vagas Process Design

Admin. Planar Process Design

Admin. Process Design*

Admin. Test Methods

Admin. Quality

Admin. Test Facilities

Admin. Mechanization

Admin. Systems Designs

Admin. Materials Adminis.

Admin. Facilities Adminis.

Admin. Human Resources

Admin. Production Adminis.

Admin. Accounting Results

Admin. Cost Accounting

Supervisor Product Design

Program Admin. Vagas — B. Hartford: Not Assigned; Not Assigned; PRODUCT BUSINESS TEAM; Human Resource Assigned; 5 Teams

Program Admin. Planar Devices: Not Assigned; Not Assigned; 3 Teams

Program Admin. Thin Film Devices: Not Assigned; Not Assigned; See Footnote; 1 Team

Program Admin. Integrated Circuits: Not Assigned; Not Assigned; See Footnote; 1 Team

FUNCTIONAL TEAM

*Program administrators for thin film and integrated circuit programs served as process design administrators for their groups.

Figure 3 Protypical Venture Unit Structure

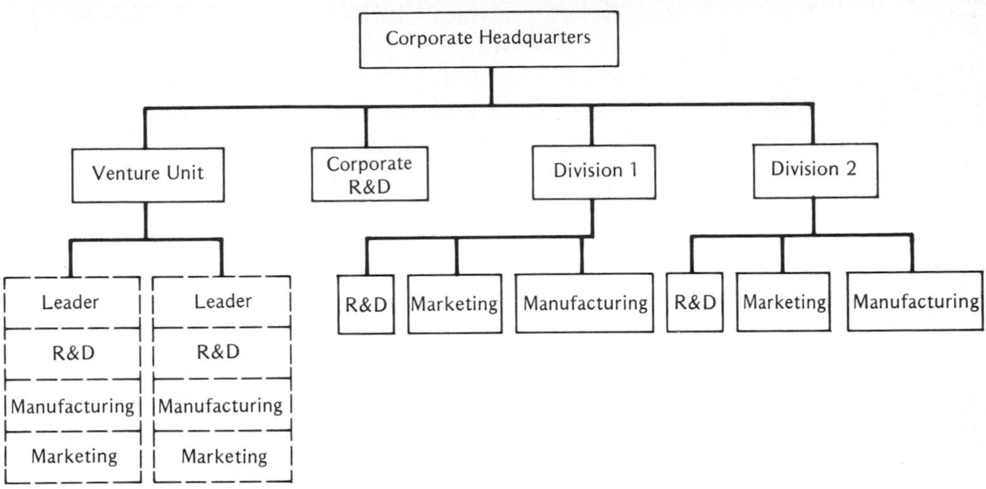

further development. One of the pioneers in this approach has been 3M Company.[6] A number of other companies have more recently begun experimenting with it. They include Borg-Warner Corporation, Monsanto, Union Carbide, and General Electric.

The typical *structure* implied by this approach is shown in Figure 3. The *process* is a good deal more complex. Usually an individual or group within central R & D or in a current division discovers an idea or technology which they believe may have fundamental new applications. They petition for the time and money necessary to develop the idea further. Funds may come from central or divisional sources. If the idea shows sufficient potential, it eventually is segregated as a venture group. The intent is to provide protection from day-to-day budgetary pressures and to release the "product champions" from regular operating duties. If all goes well, the product eventually reaches the pilot marketing and production stages. Depending on the character of the innovation, it may eventually become part of an existing division or become a division in its own right.

Clearly, these arrangements are aimed at dealing with many of the budgetary pressures and divisional parochialisms that are inherent in the structure of third-generation organizations. They represent a systematic, continuous attempt to segregate a portion of the organization's resources for fundamental innovation. The venture approach has its own implementation problems. The most notable tend to be selection and rotation of people and integrating these approaches with organization-wide rewards and career ladders. The issue of selection centers around the problem that the person who invents a product may

[6] For a description of 3M's approach see "Start More Little Businesses and More Little Businessmen," *Innovation*, No. 5, 1969, and "How Ideas Are Made into Products at 3M." *Business Week*, September 15, 1973.

not be the one most capable of carrying it to successful commercialization or efficient production (and vice versa). There can be important conflicts here between individual and organizational desires. Also, most reward systems are probably designed for lower risk situations than those faced by a venture group. How and to what degree ought the organization underwrite the psychic and career risks taken by members of the venture team? Nonethless, if companies like 3M are any indication, this approach offers considerable potential.

Information Systems Which Segregate Strategic and Operations Decisions

The final approach I shall discusss shares the same basic goals as the venture unit approach but takes a different form. Under this approach personnel in the divisional operating units are responsible for both current activities and fundamental strategic innovations. One of the early pioneers of this approach is Texas Instruments.[7] More recently General Electric has developed a similar approach.[8]

Separate planning and information systems are used for operating activities and strategic activities. Strategic planning units are identified which may or may not follow traditional organizational lines. A separate budgeting and review system is employed for each of the activities. Figure 4 is a schematic representation of the Texas Instruments reporting format.

The merit of this approach is that it can induce top and middle management to give separate attention to the more intangible strategic and more tangible operating decisions. The problems center around the complex perceptual demands this approach places on managers and whether it can be integrated into organization-wide reward systems. Suppose, for example, one manager has an excellent record on strategic decisions and a modest record on operating results while another manager has just the opposite record. How will this be treated in the organization's approach to rewards, promotion, and career development? And with what impact on future decision-making behavior?

While a considerable amount of empirical research will be required to learn about the problems and possibilities of these organizational approaches, one thing seems clear: collectively they represent an attempt to build fundamentally new types of performance potential. Today such organizations appear to be the exception rather than the rule. However, the same statement would have been true about the new third-generation organizations developed by General Motors, DuPont, and Sears Roebuck in the 1920s. My prediction is that these are protype fourth-generation organizations and that within twenty years they will

---

[7] See Harvard Business School case, "Innovation at Texas Instruments." (Intercollegiate Case Clearing House, Soldiers Field, Boston, Mass. 02163).

[8] "GE's New Strategy for Faster Growth." *Business Week*, July 8, 1972.

Figure 4 Product-Customer Center Reporting Format, Texas Instruments, Inc. (1970)

STRATEGIC ACTIVITIES	PCC PROFIT/LOSS STATEMENT		OPERATING ACTIVITIES
Corporate Development			Group
Objective			Division
Strategy	Net Sales Billed	000	PCC
	Direct Product Costs	000	
	Gross Product Margin	000	
Tactic	Operating Expense	000	
	Operating Profit	000	
	Strategic Expense	000	
	Organization Profit	000	

have emerged as the dominant form of organization. If my prediction is correct, it holds significant implications for the future development of organizational theories and for the work life of the individuals who will populate these newer organizations. I'd like to turn briefly to each of these topics.

IMPLICATIONS FOR ORGANIZATIONAL THEORY

Although the field of organizational behavior can point to theoretical roots stretching as far back as Aristotle, most of its empirical base has been developed since the end of World War II. While theory and research in this area has evolved quite rapidly, I fear that organizational practice has evolved at an equal or perhaps greater pace. Much of the basic theory which has been developed to date may prove useful in understanding fourth-generation organizations; however, there are three aspects of the current state of organizational theory which represent important gaps in knowledge and methodology.

1. Much of the study of organizations has focused on specialization and coordination around recurring sorts of situations in established activity areas—e.g., product development within existing capabilities, production scheduling, and cost control. We have relatively little systematic knowledge of the institutional aspects of fundamental invention; strategic choice; or avoidance of low-probability, high-cost events (e.g., disaster situations and nuclear safeguard systems).
2. Most studies of organizations have taken strategy as a given. The typical view has been that the role of organization is to implement a known strategy. It is more likely that organization and strategy are interdependent, that the organizational arrangements which are

adopted fundamentally affect the information gathered and the capability to act on particular information inputs.

3. The most common methodology for field studies of organizations has been point-in-time comparative analysis. It is quite unlikely that we will gain an adequate understanding of the full range of possibilities for organizational innovation or how organizations in fact can be changed using a static methodology.[9] In its place we will probably begin to see increasing use of longitudinal field studies, simulation techniques, and organizational experiments with follow-up evaluations conducted jointly by managers and researchers. Each of these approaches has been used before, but this has been the exception rather than the rule.

There are some hopeful signs that these gaps may be closed over the next few years. Several studies of the relationship between organization and policy—mainly in the public sector—have recently appeared.[10] Some researchers have begun studying the properties and uses of matrix organizations.[11] There also seems to be a growing interest in large-scale innovations in organizations—how they are conceived, nurtured, and disseminated.[12]

WORKING IN FOURTH-GENERATION ORGANIZATIONS

If the probable emergence of a fourth generation of organizations points to important shifts in the direction of organizational theory, it suggests even more profound changes in the work life of the professionals who populate these institutions.

The process of creative and adaptive role-taking (or role-making, if you like) takes on crucial significance for both the individual and the organization. Many organizations are investing much more heavily in positions and applied behavioral science techniques aimed at facilitating this process.[13] Indeed, as one watches the emergence and utilization of small group methods over the past ten years, he is left with

[9] A similar argument has been made in Argyris, Chris, *The Applicability of Organizational Sociology*. Cambridge University Press, 1972.

[10] See, for example, Ackerman, Robert W. "Influence of Integration and Diversity on the Investment Process." *Administrative Science Quarterly*, September 1970; Allison, Graham T. *The Essence of Decision: Explaining the Cuban Missile Crisis*. Little Brown, 1971; Brady, David, and Leon Rappaport. "Policy Capturing in the Field: The Nuclear Safeguards Problem." *Organizational Behavior and Human Performance*, 9, 1973; and Wilensky, Harold L. *Organizational Intelligence*. Basic Books, 1967.

[11] Galbraith, Jay, *Designing Complex Organizations*. Addision-Wesley, 1973, pp. 89–120, 142–148; and Davis, Stanley M., "Paradoxical Organizations." Working paper, Harvard Business School, 1973.

[12] Emery, F. E., and E. Thorsrud, *Form and Content of Industrial Democracy*. London: Tavistock Publications, 1969. Two such research projects in initial phases at the Harvard Business School are Gibson, Cyrus F., "The Adoption and Use of Computer Models in Organizations"; and Walton, Richard E., "Organization Innovations: Their Viability and Diffusion" (project titles, 1973).

[13] See, for example, Bennis, Warren G. *Organization Development: Its Nature, Origins, and Prospects*. Addison-Wesley, 1969; and TRW Systems Group (A) and (B) cases in Dalton,

considerable confidence that we have the wherewithal to develop the more complex role conceptions and work groups which are essential building blocks of fourth-generation organizations.

I feel somewhat less sanguine about how the individual may fare in all this. Each generation of organization seems to have supplied its own (usually negative) stereotypical man. For first-generation organizations it was the Horatio Alger figure (or the exploiter of the masses, depending on one's point of view). For the second generation it was W. H. Whyte's *Organization Man*.[14] Then there was the go-go conglomateur. Now we encounter *Future Shock*[15] and the *Temporary Society*.[16] While such stereotypes never tell the full story of the problems and the successes experienced by very different people as they work in a particular organizational climate, they do capture the concerns of a given work generation.

Toffler's *Future Shock*[17] raises a contentious problem. It appears that we are capable of building fourth-generation organizations which can successfully cope with extreme complexity and novelty. But how much novelty and complexity can an individual take—and over how long a period—without serious danger of psychic burnout? What proportion of the positions in fourth-generation organizations entail such a risk? We have no clear answers to these questions.

Some interesting trends seem to be emerging, however. In the last five years there has been increasing experimentation with and interest in employee sabbaticals,[18] early retirement from key "firing line" positions,[19] and mid-life career changes.[20] All these are potential means for individuals to back off from continuing role stress and recharge themselves.

While it is difficult to reckon the seriousness or the tractability of such problems, they certainly deserve our consideration—if for no other reason than I am talking about us. At this point my hunch is that fourth-generation organizations may well set in motion a number of forces which will fundamentally alter our perceptions and values concerning the meaning of job, career, non-work life, and how they relate to one another.

Gene W., Paul Lawrence, and Larry Greiner, *Organizational Change and Development*. Irwin, 1970.

[14] Whyte, W. H., *The Organization Man*. Simon & Schuster, 1956.

[15] Toffler, Alvin. *Future Shock*. Random House, 1970.

[16] Bennis, Warren G., and Philip E. Slater. *The Temporary Society*. Harper & Row, 1968.

[17] Toffler, *op. cit*.

[18] Goldston, Eli. "Executive Sabbaticals: About to Take Off?" *Harvard Business Review*, September–October 1973.

[19] Changes of this sort for top management employees have recently been announced by Texas Instruments, IBM, and Westinghouse Electric.

[20] See the two-article series, "The Great Escape." *Wall Street Journal*, February 19 and 22, 1971.

EDGAR H. SCHEIN

Organizational Effectiveness

Early theories of organization were content to talk of "profit maximization," "providing an efficient service," "high productivity," and "good employee morale" as sufficient criteria of effectiveness. What has undermined these as viable criteria has been (1) the discovery that seemingly rational organizations behave ineffectively if the sole criterion is profit or providing a good service, and (2) the discovery that organizations fulfill multiple functions and have multiple goals, some of which may be in conflict with each other. For example, if we think of organizations like universities, teaching hospitals, or prisons, we can immediately name several functions or goals, all of which are primary and essential. The university must teach and, at the same time, must create valid knowledge through research; the teaching hospital must take care of and cure patients, and must provide learning opportunities for interns and residents; the prison must keep criminals out of circulation, and must provide opportunities for rehabilitation. Is the effectiveness of the organization to be judged by its performance on one function, on both separately, or on some integration of the several functions?

One attempted resolution to these dilemmas has been to define effectiveness in terms of systems-level criteria. Acknowledging that every system has multiple functions and that it exists within an environment which provides unpredictable inputs, a system's effectiveness can be defined as its capacity to survive, adapt, maintain itself, and grow, regardless of the particular functions it fulfills. A number of students of organization, such as Argyris, Trist, Rice, and Bennis, have argued explicitly for this type of conception. Perhaps the clearest statement of effectiveness criteria in these terms has been given by Bennis (1962, p. 273). He introduces these ideas in reference to the traditional approaches of measuring output and satifaction at a given point in time:

> If we view organizations as adaptive, problem-solving, organic structures, then inferences about effectiveness have to be made, not from static measures of output, though these may be helpful, but on the basis of the processes through which the organization approaches problems. In other words, no single measurement of organizational efficiency or satisfaction—no single time slice of organizational performance—can provide valid indicators of organizational health.

Instead, Bennis proposes the following three criteria of health, criteria which, interestingly, closely mirror recent formulations about mental health proposed by Jahoda (1958):

1. *Adaptability*—the ability to solve problems and to react with flexibility to changing environmental demands.

2. *A sense of identity*—knowledge and insight on the part of the organization of what it is, what its goals are, and what it is to do. Pertinent questions are: To

"Organizational Effectiveness" from Edgar H. Schein, *Organizational Psychology* © 1956, pp. 96–106. Reprinted by permission of Prentice-Hall, Inc., Englewood Cliffs, New Jersey.

what extent are goals understood and shared widely by members of the organization, and to what extent is self-perception on the part of organization members in line with perceptions of the organization by others?

3. *Capacity to test reality*—the ability to search out, accurately perceive, and correctly interpret the real properties of the environment, particularly those which have relevance for the functioning of the organization.

A fourth criterion which is often mentioned, one which in effect underlies the others, is a state of "integration" among the subparts of the total organization, such that the parts are not working at cross-purposes. For Argyris, for example, this criterion is central, and he devotes most of his research and theorizing to finding those conditions which will permit an integration of individual needs and organizational goals (Argyris, 1964). What he regards as unhealthy or ineffective are restrictions on output, destructive competition, and apathy among employees in order to fulfill personal needs at the expense of organizational goals.

McGregor has argued in a similar vein for the integration of personal and organizational goals (McGregor, 1960). According to his theory, if management develops practices built on a more valid set of assumptions about man, it will produce this integration and hence greater effectiveness. Finally, Blake and Mouton (1964) argue for the integration of concern for production and concern for people. Organizational effectiveness, according to Blake and Mouton, is achieved when management succeeds in being both production- and people-centered. To support this theory, they have developed training programs which explicitly attempt to develop this managerial style. In summary, a systems-level criterion of organizational effectiveness must be a *multiple* criterion involving adaptability, sense of identity, capacity to test reality, and internal integration.

To the extent that effectiveness is a *multiple* criterion, we must be careful to avoid the trap of concluding that it depends on merely one thing. Thus, it would be a mistake to assume that if one selected the right people and trained them to do the job, effectiveness would be insured. It would be equally erroneous to assume that the establishment of a mutually satisfactory psychological contract with employees, or the reduction of intergroup competition, or leadership training, any of these alone, would guarantee effectiveness. Rather, the systems conception leads us to a different way of thinking about the problem: Viewed as a total system, how does an organization cope with its environment? How does it obtain information and process it validly? What mechanisms exist for translating information, particularly about alterations in the environment, into changed operations? Are the internal operations flexible enough to cope with changes?

MAINTAINING EFFECTIVENESS THROUGH AN ADAPTIVE-COPING CYCLE

The sequence of activities or processes which begin with some change in the internal or external environment and end with a more adaptive dynamic equilibrium for dealing with the change is the organization's *adaptive-coping cycle*. If we identify the various stages of processes of this cycle, we will also be able to identify the points where organizations typically may fail to cope adequately and where, therefore, consultants and researchers have been able in a variety of ways to help increase organizational effectiveness.

The stages of the adaptive-coping cycle are sixfold, as follows:

1. Sensing a change in the internal or external environment.
2. Importing the relevant information about the change into those parts of the organization which can act upon it.
3. Changing production or conversion processes inside the organization according to the information obtained.
4. Stabilizing internal changes while reducing or managing undesired by-products (undesired changes in related systems which have resulted from the desired changes).
5. Exporting new products, services, and so on, which are more in line with the originally perceived changes in the environment.
6. Obtaining feedback on the success of the change through further sensing of the state of the external environment and the degree of integration of the internal environment.

Let us illustrate this process with two simple examples. Suppose a manufacturing concern producing electronic equipment learns that the space program is going to increase the demand for this equipment a great deal (stage 1). The information about this change in demand must be imported into the organization in the sense of being taken seriously by those members who are in a position to do something about it. It is not sufficient for the market research department to have the information if it cannot convince the general management (stage 2). If management becomes convinced, it must change its production processes to enable the company to produce more of the equipment (stage 3). These changes must be accomplished without producing other undesirable internal changes (for example, a strike in response to unreasonable demands for increased production), and they must be stabilized (stage 4). The increased production must be marketed and sold (stage 5). And, finally sales figures and future-demand figures must then be analyzed to determine whether the organizational change has been "successful" in terms of increased marketability, and the internal environment must be assessed to determine whether unanticipated costs in the form of lowered morale or intergroup competition have been minimized (stage 6).

For a different example, let us take a college fraternity as the organization. The fraternity leadership might sense in the college administration a shift in policy toward shutting down fraternities unless scholastic standards increase (stage 1). Stage 2 would then be to get the membership to recognize the real danger to the survival of the fraternity. Stage 3 might be a program of changing norms by reducing emphasis on social activities and increasing emphasis on scholastic activities, without (stage 4) producing undesired changes, such as total loss of prestige among other fraternities. In connection with these stages, the fraternity leaders might also recognize the necessity of convincing *other* fraternities on the campus to develop similar programs in their own houses, because of the likelihood that university policy would respond only to changes in the whole fraternity system. Stage 5 would be the actual improvement in grades, test performance, and classroom behavior, while stage 6 would be a matter of checking with the administration about whether the fraternity's standing was improving, whether policy would again change, and what fraternity member attitudes now were.

Both examples cited start with some changes in the external environment. The coping cycle is no different, however, if the first step is the recognition that something is not right in the *internal* environment. Thus, an organization may sense that employee morale is too low, or that several departments are destructively competing with one another, or that a technologically sound process is not being used correctly in production, or that management attitudes and practices are failing to elicit adequate motivation and loyalty among the employees. Once the information of some change or problem is sensed by some part of the organization, it must then be imported and lead to changes in the manner described if organizational effectiveness is to be increased.

Problems and Pitfalls in the Adaptive-Coping Cycle

One advantage of considering the adaptive-coping cycle as a series of stages lies in its helping to identify areas of difficulty in maintaining and improving effectiveness in response to a changing environment. Certain problems and pitfalls characteristically are associated with each stage.

1. *Failure to sense changes in the environment or incorrectly sensing what is happening.* There are innumerable cases of organizations which have failed to survive because they did not sense either a decline in the demand for their product or an important internal problem. Many businesses can adjust to new conditions provided the organization can sense when the time is ripe to develop new products, or services, or procedures. If the organization has multiple functions, as does a university, it becomes especially important to accurately sense changing attitudes about education, the role of the university in the community, the feelings of alumni about contributions, the reputation it enjoys within the academic community, the morale of its faculty, and so on. Consulting and applied research specialities, like market research, consumer psychology, and public opinion polling, have developed partly in response to organizational needs for more accurate sensing of internal and external environmental changes.

2. *Failure to get the relevant information to those parts of the organization which can act upon it or use it.* One of the commonest problems of present-day large-scale organizations is that staff units within them obtain information which they are unable to impart to line management. For example, many personnel departments have become convinced that the management process would be more effective if line management would adopt different assumptions about the nature of man. . . . One could say that the personnel departments have correctly sensed a change in the state of research knowledge concerning the management process. But unless this knowledge can be imparted in a meaningful way to line managers, one cannot say that the information has really been imported into the system. This example illustrates another difficulty. To change assumptions about the nature of man involves a change of attitudes, self-images, and working procedures. Such a change will typically be strongly resisted because of its threatening nature. Any change implies that the former way of functioning has been erroneous. To get the information imported, therefore, might involve a major and lengthy program of influencing attitudes, self-images, and working procedures.

Often a research department or other unit of an organization comes upon information which argues for changes in technology, production methods, and the like, yet is unable to convince key management to consider the information seriously. Difficulties in introducing automatic data-processing equipment into various organizational departments often stem from a refusal of management to pay attention to information on how the equipment would really work because the implied change is too threatening to established ways of working, attitudes, and basic assumptions.

These difficulties of importing information into the relevant system have led to the use of external consultants or researchers as information transmitters. A staff group which already correctly senses a problem may find itself hiring a consultant to re-identify the problem and import it to other parts of the system. The consultant uses his prestige to help import the information into those parts of the system that have the power to do something about it.

3. *Failure to influence the conversion or production system to make the necessary changes.* Effecting internal changes in an organization requires more than the recognition that such changes are necessary. Organization planners or top managers often naïvely assume that simply announcing the need for a change and giving orders that the change should be made will produce the desired outcome. In practice, however, resistance to change is one of the most ubiquitous organizational phenomena. Whether it be an increase in production which is desired, or adaptation to a new technology, or a new method of doing the work, it is generally found that those workers and managers who are directly affected will resist the change or sabotage it if it is forced upon them. . . .

Probably the major reason for resistance to change is that the conversion or production parts of any organization are themselves systems—they generate ways of working, stable interpersonal relationships, common norms and values, and techniques of coping and surviving in their own environment. In other words, the subsystems of an organization operate by the same coping principles as the whole organization. In order to change, therefore, the subsystem must sense a change in management policy, be able to import this information into itself, manage its own change, stabilize it, export better results in terms of the desires of management, and obtain feedback on how it is doing. The line manager desiring the change can, from this point of view, accomplish more by viewing his own role as that of helping the system to change or cope, rather than giving orders or issuing directives. There is some evidence that one of the best ways of giving this help is to involve the system concerned in the decision making about *how* to produce the necessary changes. The more the system which must change participates in decisions about how to manage the change, the less likely it is to resist the change and the more stable the change is likely to be (Lewin, 1958, and Coch and French, 1948, pp. 512–32).

4. *Failure to consider the impact of changes on other systems and failure to achieve stable change.* There are some classic cases where attitudes changed during a program of training in human relations but reverted completely following a return to the job. Cases can also be cited where changes in administrative procedure in one department were so threatening to another department that they had to be abandoned to preserve the overall morale of the organization (Bavelas and Strauss, 1962). Because the various parts of an organization tend to be linked, a proposed change in one part must be carefully assessed in terms of its likely impact on other parts. Wherever possible, the linkage between systems should be used to positive advantage, in the sense that certain desired changes, if started in one part of the system, will tend to spread by themselves to other parts of the system.

A good example of this process would be in the changing of assumptions and attitudes toward people. If the top management of the organization can be helped to alter attitudes, then because of their strategic linkage to all parts of the organization, their resultant behavior change would automatically act as a force on all of their subordinates toward similar changes. The same change in attitudes in the middle or near the bottom of the hierarchy may fail to spread, or even to maintain itself, because of inadequate upward and lateral linkages to other systems.

5. *Failure to export the new product, service, or information.* Once changes have been made within the organization, there remains the problem of exporting the new results. In the case of business concerns, this is a problem of sales and marketing. In the case of other organizations, such as the fraternity cited above, it may be a problem of communicating as rapidly as possible to the relevant environmental systems the changes which have occurred. It does little good for the fraternity to change its norms of scholastic achievement if the time before grades improve is so long that the administration has already decided to close the fraternities.

If the organization wants to export information, the problem is one of advertising. But because advertising involves gaining a competitive advantage over another organization, forces that distort information are generated. Here, as in the above cases, one role the consultant has played has been to export *reliable* information about changes in the system. Thus, a neutral faculty member may be appointed jointly by the administration and the fraternity to evaluate changes in members' attitudes. Similarly, we send "political observers" to countries requesting foreign aid to evaluate the validity of their claims that they are changing toward democratic forms of government; government agencies send representatives to industrial firms that claim to have developed the capacity to provide a weapons system or some other product efficiently and cheaply. In all these cases, what is involved is accurate export of information about changes in the system which may not be immediately visible in such indexes as higher production rates or new products and services.

6. *Failure to obtain feedback on the success of the change.* The problems here are essentially the same as the problems of sensing changes in the environment in the first place. We need only add that many organizations have explicitly created systems to assess the impact of changes and thus to provide themselves the necessary feedback information. In the case of internal changes, there may be a research group in the employee relations department whose prime job is to survey employees periodically to determine how they are reacting to changes in management policy; political organizations will run polls immediately after a change in political platform to determine the public's reaction; production control units will assess whether a new process is producing the desired increase in efficiency; and so on.

In summary, for each stage in the adaptive-coping cycle one can identify characteristic pitfalls and problems. The important point is that the maintenance and increase of organizational effectiveness depend on successful coping, which means that *all* of the stages must be successfully negotiated. It does little good to have the best market research department in the world if the organization is unable to influence its own production systems; nor does it help to have a highly flexible production or conversion operation which cannot sense or digest information about environmental changes.

ORGANIZATIONAL CONDITIONS FOR EFFECTIVE COPING

We began this [essay] with some general criteria of organizational effectiveness or health. We then specified the coping processes which appear to be necessary in a rapidly changing environment for such effectiveness or health to be maintained or increased. In this final section, I would like to outline what internal organizational conditions appear to be necessary for effective coping to occur. To some extent the argument becomes circular here, in that some health must be present for health to maintain itself or increase. The organizational conditions I will identify will, therefore, somewhat resemble the ultimate criteria of health cited by Bennis.

1. Successful coping requires the ability to take in and communicate information reliably and validly.
2. Successful coping requires internal flexibility and creativity to make the changes which are demanded by the information obtained.
3. Successful coping requires integration and commitment to the goals of the organization, from which comes the willingness to change.
4. Successful coping requires an internal climate of support and freedom from threat, since being threatened undermines good communication, reduces flexibility, and stimulates self-protection rather than concern for the total system.

These four conditions are not easy to achieve in a complex system such as a large organization, but some guidelines for their achievement can be outlined. . . .

1. If we look first at the *recruitment, selection, induction, and training of human resources,* [we can ask the following questions]. Are many of the methods currently being used for the selection, testing, and training of employees likely to produce an image in the minds of employees that the organization is relatively indifferent to their personal needs and capacities? And is it possible, therefore, that employees learn early in their career to withhold involvement, to make their performance routine, and to respond to demands for changes by feeling threatened and anxious rather than helpful and committed?

If the organization is genuinely concerned about building long-range effectiveness, must it not develop a system for hiring employees which makes them feel wanted, secure, meaningfully engaged in their job, and positively committed to organizational goals, and must it not develop training and management development programs which stimulate genuine psychological growth in order to insure the flexibility and creativity that may be required at some future time? It would appear that one of the best guarantees of ability to cope with an unpredictable environment would be to develop everyone to a maximum degree, even at the expense of short-run efficiency.

2. Turning next to the *utilization of employees and the psychological contract,* it would appear evident that if the organization expects its members to be committed, flexible, and in good communication with one another for the sake of overall organizational effectiveness, it is in effect asking them to be *morally* involved in the enterprise, to be committed to organizational goals, and to value these. And if it expects them to be involved to this degree, the organization must for its part provide rewards and conditions consistent with such involvement. It cannot merely pay more money to obtain commitment, creativity, and flexibility; there must be the possibility of obtaining noneconomic rewards, such as autonomy, genuine responsibility, opportunities for challenge and for psychological growth.

Probably the most important thing the organization can do in this regard is to develop assumptions about people which fit reality. This, in turn, implies some willingness to find out what each man is like and what he truly wants. By making broad generalizations about people, the organization not only runs the risk of being wrong about the empirical realities, but, perhaps worse, it insults its employees by assuming they are all basically alike. If managerial assumptions begin to be exposed and tested, not only will this change provide a basis for learning what the facts are, but also the willingness to test assumptions will communicate a degree of concern for people which will reduce their feeling of being threatened or demeaned. As assumptions become increasingly realistic, management practices will begin to build the kind of climate which is needed for reliable and valid communication, creative effort, flexibility, and commitment.

3. Next, let us look at the *problem of groups and intergroup relations.* There is little question that groups are an integral part of any organization and that the basic choice is not whether to have them but, rather, how to create conditions under which group forces work toward organizational goals rather than counter to them. The first part of an answer is to be found in points 1 and 2 above, for the evidence seems quite clear that if employees feel threatened, demeaned, and unappreciated they will form together into *anti*-management groups. To prevent such groups from forming, therefore, requires management practices which are less threatening to the individual and more likely to enable him to integrate his own needs with organizational goals.

A second part of the answer lies in training for effective group membership and leadership. Though most of us have had much experience in groups, it is unlikely that we have had the opportunity to focus clearly on those factors which make groups more or less effective. If members of the organization come to understand better how groups work, they are less likely to form groups which are bound to fail. If groups are formed which can achieve some degree of psychological success, and if this success is perceived to be in part the result of good management, the group forces are more likely to be turned toward organizational goals. The point is, however, that it takes more than good intentions to make an effective group. It requires knowledge and training in how groups work.

When we turn to problems of intergroup competition, the answer seems clear that competition between the units or groups of a single organization or system must in the long run reduce effectiveness because competition leads to faulty communication, to greater pressures for conformity and hence less flexibility, and to commitment to subgroup rather than organizational goals. The dilemma is that competition also produces very high levels of motivation and productivity. As many case examples have shown, however, when organizational units are stimulated into competition, the short-run gains of increased production are greatly outweighed by the long-run losses of reduced internal communication and flexibility. What organizations must develop are programs which obtain motivation and commitment in an integrative manner, which keep communication channels between subparts open, and which maintain the focus on total, organizational performance rather than individual, subgroup performance.

4. Finally, let us look at a variable which has been implicit throughout, but has not been explicitly treated—the variable of *leadership*. Much has been written on leadership, and it is beyond the scope of this discussion to review even cursorily the mass of research findings and theoretical positions which have been published. Two points are worth noting, however.

First, leadership is a *function* in the organization, rather than the trait of an individual. It is *distributed among the members of a group or organization*, and is not automatically vested in the chairman or the person with the formal authority. Good leadership and good membership therefore blend into each other in an effective organization. It is just as much the task of a member to help the group reach its goals as it is the task of the formal leader.

Second, leadership has a unique obligation to manage the relationships between a system and its environment, particularly in reference to the key functions of setting goals for the organization and defining the values or norms in terms of which the organization must basically develop a sense of identity (Selznick, 1951). This function must be fulfilled by those members who are in contact with the organization-environment boundary and who have the power to set policy for organization. This leadership function, which usually falls to the top executives of organizations, is critical. If the organization does not have clear goals and cannot develop a sense of identity, there is nothing to be committed to and nothing to communicate. At the same time, no organization need have its goals and identity *imposed* by its top executives. There is no reason why the organization cannot develop its goals and identity collaboratively and participatively, engaging every member down to the lowest echelons. What the top executives must do is to insure that goals are somehow set, but they may choose a variety of ways of allowing this to occur.

CONCLUSION

I have tried to argue for an approach to organizational effectiveness which hinges upon good communication, flexibility, creativity, and genuine psychological commitment. These conditions are to be obtained by (1) recruitment, selection, and training practices which stimulate rather than demean people; (2) more realistic psychological relationships based on a more realistic psychological contract; (3) more effective group action; and (4) better leadership in the sense of goal setting and value definition. The argument is not based on the assumption that this would be nice for people or make them feel better. Rather, the argument is that systems *work better* if their parts are in good communication with each other, are committed, and are creative and flexible.

REFERENCES

Argyris, C. *Integrating the Individual and the Organization*. Wiley, 1964.

Bavelas, A., and G. Strauss. "Group Dynamics and Intergroup Relations." In *The Planning of Change*, ed. W. Bennis, K. Benne, and R. Chin. Holt, 1962.

Bennis, W. G. "Toward a 'Truly' Scientific Management: The Concept of Organizational Health." *General Systems Yearbook*, Vol. 7, 1962.

Blake, R. R., and Jane S. Mouton. *The Managerial Grid*. Gulf Publishing Co., 1964.

Coch, L., and J. R. P. French. "Overcoming Resistance to Change." *Human Relations*, Vol. 1, 1948.

Jahoda, M. *Current Concepts of Positive Mental Health*. Basic Books, 1958.

Lewin, K. "Group Decision and Social Change." In *Readings in Social Psychology*, ed. E. Maccoby, T. Newcomb, and E. Hartley. Holt, 1958.

McGregor, D. *The Human Side of Enterprise*. McGraw-Hill, 1960.

Selznick, P. *Leadership in Administration*. Harper & Row, 1957.

HENRY MINTZBERG

Managerial Work: Analysis from Observation

What do managers do? Ask this question and you will likely be told that managers plan, organize, coordinate, and control. Since Henri Fayol [9] first proposed these words in 1916, they have dominated the vocabulary of management. (See, for example, [8], [12], [17].) How valuable are they in describing managerial work? Consider one morning's work of the president of a large organization:

> As he enters his office at 8:23, the manager's secretary motions for him to pick up the telephone. "Jerry, there was a bad fire in the plant last night, about $30,000 damage. We should be back in operation by Wednesday. Thought you should know."
>
> At 8:45, a Mr. Jamison is ushered into the manager's office. They discuss Mr. Jamison's retirement plans and his cottage in New Hampshire. Then the manager presents a plaque to him commemorating his thirty-two years with the organization.
>
> Mail processing follows: An innocent-looking letter, signed by a Detroit lawyer, reads: "A group of us in Detroit has decided not to buy any of your products because you used that anti-flag, anti-American pinko, Bill Lindell, upon your Thursday night TV show." The manager dictates a restrained reply.
>
> The 10:00 meeting is scheduled by a professional staffer. He claims that his superior, a high-ranking vice-president of the organization, mistreats his staff, and that if the man is not fired, they will all walk out. As soon as the meeting ends, the manager rearranges his schedule to investigate the claim and to react to this crisis.

Which of these activities may be called planning, and which may be called organizing, coordinating, and controlling? Indeed, what do words such as "coordinating" and "planning" mean in the context of real activity? In fact, these four words do not describe the actual work of managers at all; they describe certain vague objectives of managerial work. ". . . they are just ways of indicating what we need to explain." [1, p. 537]

Other approaches to the study of managerial work have developed, one dealing with managerial decision-making and policy-making processes, another with the manager's interpersonal activities. (See, for example, [2] and [10].) And some empirical researchers, using the "diary" method, have studied, what might be called, managerial "media"—by what means, with whom, how long, and where managers spend their time.[1] But in no part of this literature is

"Managerial Work: Analysis from Observation" by Henry Mintzberg, *Management Science*, Vol. 18, No. 2, October 1971, pp. B97–B110. Reprinted by permission.

[1] Carlson [6] carried out the classic study just after World War II. He asked nine Swedish managing directors to record on diary pads details of each activity in which they engaged. His method was used by a group of other researchers, many of them working in the U.K. (See [4], [5], [15], [25]).

the actual content of managerial work systematically and meaningfully described.[2] Thus, the question posed at the start—what do managers do?—remains essentially unanswered in the literature of management.

This is indeed an odd situation. We claim to teach management in schools of both business and public administration; we undertake major research programs in management; we find a growing segment of the management science community concerned with the problems of senior management. Most of these people—the planners, information and control theorists, systems analysts, etc.—are attempting to analyze and change working habits that they themselves do not understand. Thus, at a conference called at MIT to assess the impact of the computer on the manager, and attended by a number of America's foremost management scientists, a participant found it necessary to comment after lengthy discussion [20, p. 198]:

> I'd like to return to an earlier point. It seems to me that until we get into the question of what the top manager does or what the functions are that define the top management job, we're not going to get out of the kind of difficulty that keeps cropping up. What I'm really doing is leading up to my earlier question which no one really answered. And that is: Is it possible to arrive at a specification of what constitutes the job of a top manager?

His question was not answered.

RESEARCH STUDY ON MANAGERIAL WORK

In late 1966, I began research on this question, seeking to replace Fayol's words by a set that would more accurately describe what managers do. In essence, I sought to develop by the process of induction a statement of managerial work that would have empirical validity. Using a method called "structured observation," I observed for one-week periods the chief executives of five medium to large organizations (a consulting firm, a school system, a technology firm, a consumer goods manufacturer, and a hospital).

Structured as well as unstructured (i.e., anecdotal) data were collected in three "records." In the *chronology record*, activity patterns throughout the working day were recorded. In the *mail record*, for each of 890 pieces of mail processed during the five weeks, were recorded its purpose, format and sender, the attention it received and the action it elicited. And, recorded in the *contact record*, for each of 368 verbal interactions, were the purpose, the medium (telephone call, scheduled or unscheduled meeting, tour), the participants, the form of initiation, and the location. It should be noted that all categorizing was done during and after observation so as to ensure that the categories reflected only the work under observation. [19] contains a fuller description of this methodology and a tabulation of the results of the study.

Two sets of conclusions are presented below. The first deals with certain characteristics of managerial work, as they appeared from analysis of the numerical data (e.g., How much time is spent with peers? What is the average

---

[2] One major project, involving numerous publications, took place at Ohio State University and spanned three decades. Some of the vocabulary used followed Fayol. The results have generated little interest in this area. (See, for example, [13].)

duration of meetings? What proportion of contacts are initiated by the manager himself?). The second describes the basic content of managerial work in terms of ten roles. This description derives from an analysis of the data on the recorded *purpose* of each contact and piece of mail.

The liberty is taken of referring to these findings as descriptive of managerial, as opposed to chief executive, work. This is done because many of the findings are supported by studies of other types of managers. Specifically, most of the conclusions on work characteristics are to be found in the combined results of a group of studies of foremen [11], [16], middle managers [4], [5], [15], [25], and chief executives [6]. And although there is little useful material on managerial roles, three studies do provide some evidence of the applicability of the role set. Most important, Sayles' empirical study of production managers [24] suggests that at least five of the ten roles are performed at the lower end of the managerial hierarchy. And some further evidence is provided by comments in Whyte's study of leadership in a street gang [26] and Neustadt's study of three U.S. presidents [21]. (Reference is made to these findings where appropriate.) Thus, although most of the illustrations are drawn from my study of chief executives, there is some justification in asking the reader to consider when he sees the terms "manager" and his "organization" not only "presidents" and their "companies," but also "foremen" and their "shops," "directors" and their "branches," "vice-presidents" and their "divisions." The term *manager* shall be used with reference to all those people in charge of formal organizations or their subunits.

SOME CHARACTERISTICS OF MANAGERIAL WORK

Six sets of characteristics of managerial work derive from analysis of the data of this study. Each has a significant bearing on the manager's ability to administer a complex organization.

Characteristic 1. The Manager Performs a Great Quantity of Work at an Unrelenting Pace

Despite a semblance of normal working hours, in truth managerial work appears to be very taxing. The five men in this study processed an average of thirty-six pieces of mail each day, participated in eight meetings (half of which were scheduled), engaged in five telephone calls, and took one tour. In his study of foremen, Guest [11] found that the number of activities per day averaged 583, with no real break in the pace.

Free time appears to be very rare. If by chance a manager has caught up with the mail, satisfied the callers, dealt with all the disturbances, and avoided scheduled meetings, a subordinate will likely show up to usurp the available time. It seems that the manager cannot expect to have much time for leisurely reflection during office hours. During "off" hours, our chief executives spent much time on work-related reading. High-level managers appear to be able to escape neither from an environment which recognizes the power and status of their positions nor from their own minds which have been trained to search continually for new information.

Characteristic 2. Managerial Activity Is Characterized by Variety, Fragmentation, and Brevity

There seems to be no pattern to managerial activity. Rather, variety and fragmentation appear to be characteristic, as successive activities deal with issues that differ greatly both in type and in content. In effect the manager must be prepared to shift moods quickly and frequently.

A typical chief executive day may begin with a telephone call from a director who asks a favor (a "status request"); then a subordinate calls to tell of a strike at one of the facilities (fast movement of information, termed "instant communication"); this is followed by a relaxed scheduled event at which the manager speaks to a group of visiting dignitaries (ceremony); the manager returns to find a message from a major customer who is demanding the renegotiation of a contract (pressure); and so on. Throughout the day, the managers of our study encountered this great variety of activity. Most surprisingly, the significant activities were interspersed with the trivial in no particular pattern.

Furthermore, these managerial activities were characterized by their brevity. Half of all the activities studied lasted less than nine minutes and only ten percent exceeded one hour's duration. Guest's foremen averaged 48 seconds per activity, and Carlson [6] stressed that his chief executives were unable to work without frequent interruption.

In my own study of chief executives, I felt that the managers demonstrated a preference for tasks of short duration and encouraged interruption. Perhaps the manager becomes accustomed to variety, or perhaps the flow of "instant communication" cannot be delayed. A more plausible explanation might be that the manager becomes conditioned by his workload. He develops a sensitive appreciation for the opportunity cost of his own time. Also, he is aware of the ever present assortment of obligations associated with his job—accumulations of mail that cannot be delayed, the callers that must be attended to, the meetings that require his participation. In other words, no matter what he is doing, the manager is plagued by what he must do and what he might do. Thus, the manager is forced to treat issues in an abrupt and superficial way.

Characteristic 3. Managers Prefer Issues That Are Current, Specific, and Ad Hoc

Ad hoc operating reports received more attention than did routine ones; current, uncertain information—gossip, speculation, hearsay—which flows quickly was preferred to historical, certain information; "instant communication" received first consideration; few contacts were held on a routine or "clocked" basis; almost all contacts concerned well-defined issues. The managerial environment is clearly one of stimulus-response. It breeds, not reflective planners, but adaptable information manipulators who prefer the live, concrete situation, men who demonstrate a marked action-orientation.

Characteristic 4. The Manager Sits Between His Organization and a Network of Contacts

In virtually every empirical study of managerial time allocation, it was reported that managers spent a surprisingly large amount of time in horizontal or lateral (nonline) communication. It is clear from this study and from that of Sayles [24] that the manager is surrounded by a diverse and complex web of contacts which serves as his self-designed external information system. Included in this web can be clients, associates and suppliers, outside staff experts, peers (managers of related or similar organizations), trade organizations, government officials, independents (those with no relevant organizational affiliation), and directors or superiors. (Among these, directors in this study and superiors in other studies did *not* stand out as particularly active individuals.)

The managers in this study received far more information than they emitted, much of it coming from contacts, and more from subordinates who acted as filters. Figuratively, the manager appears as the neck of an hourglass, sifting information into his own organization from its environment.

Characteristic 5. The Manager Demonstrates a Strong Preference for the Verbal Media

The manager has five media at his command—mail (documented), telephone (purely verbal), unscheduled meeting (informal face-to-face), scheduled meeting (formal face-to-face), and tour (observational). Along with all the other empirical studies of work characteristics, I found a strong predominance of verbal forms of communication.

Mail. By all indications, managers dislike the documented form of communication. In this study, they gave cursory attention to such items as operating reports and periodicals. It was estimated that only thirteen percent of the input mail was of specific and immediate use to the managers. Much of the rest dealt with formalities and provided general reference data. The managers studied initiated very little mail, only twenty-five pieces in the five weeks. The rest of the outgoing mail was sent in reaction to mail received—a reply to a request, an acknowledgment, some information forwarded to a part of the organization. The managers appeared to dislike this form of communication, perhaps because the mail is a relatively slow and tedious medium to use.

Telephone and unscheduled meetings. The less formal means of verbal communication—the telephone, a purely verbal form, and the unscheduled meeting, a face-to-face form—were used frequently (two-thirds of the contacts in the study) but for brief encounters (average duration of six and twelve minutes respectively). They were used primarily to deliver requests and to transmit pressing information to those outsiders and subordinates who had informal relationships with the manager.

Scheduled meetings. These tended to be of long duration, averaging sixty-eight minutes in this study, and absorbing over half the managers' time. Such meetings provided the managers with their main opportunities to interact with large groups and to leave the confines of their own offices. Scheduled meetings were used when the participants were unfamiliar to the manager (e.g., students who request that he speak at a university), when a large quantity of information had to be transmitted (e.g., presentation of a report), when ceremony had to take place, and when complex strategy-making or negotiation had to be undertaken. An important feature of the scheduled meeting was the incidental, but by no means irrelevant, information that flowed at the start and end of such meetings.

Tours. Although the walking tour would appear to be a powerful tool for gaining information in an informal way, in this study tours accounted for only three percent of the managers' time.

In general, it can be concluded that the manager uses each medium for particular purposes. Nevertheless, where possible, he appears to gravitate to verbal media since these provide greater flexibility, require less effort, and bring faster response. It should be noted here that the manager does not leave the telephone or the meeting to get back to work. Rather, communication is his work, and these media are his tools. The operating work of the organization—producing a product, doing research, purchasing a part—appears to be undertaken infrequently by the senior manager. The manager's productive output must be measured in terms of information, a great part of which is transmitted verbally.

Characteristic 6. Despite the Preponderance of Obligations, the Manager Appears to Be Able to Control His Own Affairs

Carlson suggested in his study of Swedish chief executives that these men were puppets, with little control over their own affairs. A cursory examination of our data indicates that this is true. Our managers were responsible for the initiation of only thirty-two percent of their verbal contacts and a smaller proportion of their mail. Activities were also classified as to the nature of the managers' participation, and the active ones were outnumbered by the passive ones (e.g., making requests vs. receiving requests). On the surface, the manager is indeed a puppet, answering requests in the mail, returning telephone calls, attending meetings initiated by others, yielding to subordinates' requests for time, reacting to crises.

However, such a view is misleading. There is evidence that the senior manager can exert control over his own affairs in two significant ways: (1) It is he who defines many of his own long-term commitments, by developing appropriate information channels which later feed him information, by initiating projects which later demand his time, by joining committees or outside boards which provide contacts in return for his services, and so on. (2) The manager can exploit situations that appear as obligations. He can lobby at ceremonial speeches; he can impose his values on his organization when his authorization is requested; he can motivate his subordinates whenever he interacts with them; he can use the crisis situation as an opportunity to innovate.

Perhaps these are two points that help distinguish successful and unsuccessful managers. All managers appear to be puppets. Some decide who will pull the strings and how, and they then take advantage of each move that they are forced to make. Others, unable to exploit this high-tension environment, are swallowed up by this most demanding of jobs.

THE MANAGER'S WORK ROLES

In describing the essential content of managerial work, one should aim to model managerial activity, that is, to describe it as a set of programs. But an undertaking as complex as this must be preceded by the development of a useful typological description of managerial work. In other words, we must first understand the distinct components of managerial work. At the present time we do not.

In this study, 890 pieces of mail and 368 verbal contacts were categorized as to purpose. The incoming mail was found to carry acknowledgements, requests and solicitations of various kinds, reference data, news, analytical reports, reports on events and on operations, advice on various situations, and statements of problems, pressures, and ideas. In reacting to mail, the managers acknowledged some, replied to the requests (e.g., by sending information), and forwarded much to subordinates (usually for their information). Verbal contacts involved a variety of purposes. In 15 percent of them activities were scheduled, in 6 percent ceremonial events took place, and a few involved external board work. About 34 percent involved requests of various kinds, some insignificant, some for information, some for authorization of proposed actions. Another 36 percent essentially involved the flow of information to and from the manager, while the remainder dealt specifically with issues of strategy and with negotiations. (For details, see [19].)

In this study, each piece of mail and verbal contact categorized in this way was subjected to one question: Why did the manager do this? The answers were collected and grouped and regrouped in various ways (over the course of three years) until a typology emerged that was felt to be satisfactory. While an example, presented below, will partially explain this process to the reader, it must be remembered that (in the words of Bronowski [3, p. 62]): "Every induction is a speculation and it guesses at a unity which the facts present but do not strictly imply."

Consider the following sequence of two episodes: A chief executive attends a meeting of an external board on which he sits. Upon his return to his organization, he immediately goes to the office of a subordinate, tells of a conversation he had with a fellow board member, and concludes with the statement: "It looks like we shall get the contract."

The purposes of these two contacts are clear—to attend an external board meeting, and to give current information (instant communication) to a subordinate. But why did the manager attend the meeting? Indeed, why does he belong to the board? And why did he give this particular information to his subordinate?

Basing analysis on this incident, one can argue as follows: The manager belongs to the board in part so that he can be exposed to special information which is of use to his organization. The subordinate needs the information but has not the status which would give him access to it. The chief executive does. Board memberships bring chief executives in contact with one another for the purpose of trading information.

Two aspects of managerial work emerge from this brief analysis. The manager serves in a "liaison" capacity because of the status of his office, and what he learns here enables him to act as "disseminator" of information into his organization. We refer to these as *roles*—organized sets of behaviors belonging to identifiable offices or positions [23]. Ten roles were chosen to capture all the activities observed during this study.

All activities were found to involve one or more of three basic behaviors—interpersonal contact, the processing of information, and the making of decisions. As a result, our ten roles are divided into three corresponding groups. Three roles—labelled *figurehead, liaison*, and *leader*—deal with behavior that is essentially interpersonal in nature. Three others—*nerve center, disseminator*, and *spokesman*—deal with information-processing activities performed by the manager. And the remaining four—*entrepreneur, disturbance handler, resource allocator*, and *negotiator*—cover the decision-making activities of the manager.

We describe each of these roles in turn, asking the reader to note that they form a *gestalt*, a unified whole whose parts cannot be considered in isolation.

The Interpersonal Roles

Three roles relate to the manager's behavior that focuses on interpersonal contact. These roles derive directly from the authority and status associated with holding managerial office.

Figurehead. As legal authority in his organization, the manager is a symbol, obliged to perform a number of duties. He must preside at ceremonial events, sign legal documents, receive visitors, make himself available to many of those who feel, in the words of one of the men studied, "that the only way to get something done is to get to the top." There is evidence that this role applies at other levels as well. Davis [7, pp. 43–44] cites the case of the field sales manager who must deal with those customers who believe that their accounts deserve his attention.

Leader. Leadership is the most widely recognized of managerial roles. It describes the manager's relationship with his subordinates—his attempts to motivate them and his development of the milieu in which they work. Leadership actions pervade all activity—in contrast to most roles, it is possible to designate only a few activities as dealing exclusively with leadership (these mostly related to staffing duties). Each time a manager encourages a subordinate, or meddles in his affairs, or replies to one of his requests, he is playing the *leader* role. Subordinates seek out and react to these leadership clues, and, as a result, they impart significant power to the manager.

Liaison. As noted earlier, the empirical studies have emphasized the importance of lateral or horizontal communication in the work of managers at all levels. It is clear from our study that this is explained largely in terms of the *liaison* role. The manager establishes his network of contacts essentially to bring information and favors to his organization. As Sayles notes in his study of production supervisors [24, p. 258], "The one enduring objective [of the manager] is the effort to build and maintain a predictable, reciprocating system of relationships. . . . "

Making use of his status, the manager interacts with a variety of peers and other people outside his organization. He provides time, information, and favors in return for the same from others. Foremen deal with staff groups and other foremen; chief executives join boards of directors, and maintain extensive networks of individual relationships. Neustadt notes this behavior in analyzing the work of President Roosevelt [21, p. 150]:

> His personal sources were the product of a sociability and curiosity that reached back to the other Roosevelt's time. He had an enormous acquaintance in various phases of national life and at various levels of government; he also had his wife and her variety of contacts. He extended his acquaintanceships abroad; in the war years Winston Churchill, among others, became a "personal source." Roosevelt quite deliberately exploited these relationships and mixed them up to widen his own range

> of information. He changed his sources as his interests changed, but no one who had ever interested him was quite forgotten or immune to sudden use.

The Informational Roles

A second set of managerial activities relate primarily to the processing of information. Together they suggest three significant managerial roles, one describing the manager as a focal point for a certain kind of organizational information, the other two describing relatively simple transmission of this information.

Nerve center. There is indication, both from this study and from those by Neustadt and Whyte, that the manager serves as the focal point in his organization for the movement of nonroutine information. Homans, who analyzed Whyte's study, draws the following conclusions [26, p. 187]:

> Since interaction flowed toward [the leaders], they were better informed about the problems and desires of group members than were any of the followers and therefore better able to decide on an appropriate course of action. Since they were in close touch with other gang leaders, they were also better informed than their followers about conditions in Cornerville at large. Moreover, in their positions at the focus of the chains of interaction, they were better able than any follower to pass on to the group decisions that had been reached.

The term *nerve center* is chosen to encompass those many activities in which the manager receives information.

Within his own organization, the manager has legal authority that formally connects him—and only him—to *every* member. Hence, the manager emerges as *nerve center* of internal information. He may not know as much about any one function as the subordinate who specializes in it, but he comes to know more about his total organization than any other member. He is the information generalist. Furthermore, because of the manager's status and its manifestation in the *liaison* role, the manager gains unique access to a variety of knowledgeable outsiders including peers who are themselves *nerve centers* of their own organizations. Hence, the manager emerges as his organization's *nerve center* of external information as well.

As noted earlier, the manager's nerve center information is of a special kind. He appears to find it most important to get his information quickly and informally. As a result, he will not hesitate to bypass formal information channels to get it, and he is prepared to deal with a large amount of gossip, hearsay, and opinion which has not yet become substantiated fact.

Disseminator. Much of the manager's information must be transmitted to subordinates. Some of this is of a *factual* nature, received from outside the organization or from other subordinates. And some is of a *value* nature. Here, the manager acts as the mechanism by which organizational influencers (owners, governments, employee groups, the general public, etc., or simply the "boss") make their preferences known to the organization. It is the manager's duty to integrate these value positions, and to express general organizational preferences as a guide to decisions made by subordinates. One of the men studied commented: "One of the principal functions of this position is to integrate the hospital interests with the public interests." Papandreou describes this duty in a paper published in 1952, referring to management as the "peak coordinator" [22].

Spokesman. In his *spokesman* role, the manager is obliged to transmit his information to outsiders. He informs influencers and other interested parties about his organization's performance, its policies, and its plans. Furthermore, he is expected to serve outside his organization as an expert in its industry. Hospital administrators are expected to spend some time serving outside as public experts on health, and corporation presidents, perhaps as chamber of commerce executives.

The Decisional Roles

The manager's legal authority requires that he assume responsibility for all of his organization's important actions. The *nerve center* role suggests that only he can fully understand complex decisions, particularly those involving difficult value tradeoffs. As a result, the manager emerges as the key figure in the making and interrelating of all significant decisions in his organization, a process that can be referred to as *strategy-making*. Four roles describe the manager's control over the strategy-making system in his organization.

Entrepreneur. The *entrepreneur* role describes the manager as initiator and designer of much of the controlled change in his organization. The manager looks for opportunities and potential problems which may cause him to initiate action. Action takes the form of *improvement projects*—the marketing of a new product, the strengthening of a weak department, the purchasing of new equipment, the reorganization of formal structure, and so on.

The manager can involve himself in each improvement project in one of three ways: (1) He may *delegate* all responsibility for its design and approval, implicitly retaining the right to replace that subordinate who takes charge of it. (2) He may delegate the design work to a subordinate, but retain the right to *approve* it before implementation. (3) He may actively *supervise* the design work himself.

Improvement projects exhibit a number of interesting characteristics. They appear to involve a number of subdecisions, consciously sequenced over long periods of time and separated by delays of various kinds. Furthermore, the manager appears to supervise a great many of these at any one time—perhaps fifty to one hundred in the case of chief executives. In fact, in his handling of improvement projects, the manager may be likened to a juggler. At any one point, he maintains a number of balls in the air. Periodically, one comes down, receives a short burst of energy, and goes up again. Meanwhile, an inventory of new balls waits on the sidelines and, at random intervals, old balls are discarded and new ones added. Both Lindblom [2] and Marples [18] touch on these aspects of strategy-making, the former stressing the disjointed and incremental nature of the decisions, and the latter depicting the sequential episodes in terms of a stranded rope made up of fibres of different lengths each of which surfaces periodically.

Disturbance handler. While the *entrepreneur* role focuses on voluntary change, the *disturbance handler* role deals with corrections which the manager is forced to make. We may describe this role as follows: The organization consists basically of specialist operating programs. From time to time, it experiences a stimulus that cannot be handled routinely, either because an operating program has broken down or because the stimulus is new and it is not clear which operating program should handle it. These situations constitute disturbances. As generalist, the manager is obliged to assume responsibility for dealing with the stimulus. Thus, the handling of disturbances is an essential duty of the manager.

There is clear evidence for this role both in our study of chief executives and in Sayles' study of production supervisors [24, p. 162]:

> The achievement of this stability, which is the manager's objective, is a never-to-be-attained ideal. He is like a symphony orchestra conductor, endeavoring to maintain a melodious performance in which contributions of the various instruments are coordinated and sequenced, patterned and paced, while the orchestra members are having various personal difficulties, stage hands are moving music stands, alternating excessive heat and cold are creating audience and instrument problems, and the sponsor of the concert is insisting on irrational changes in the program.

Sayles goes further to point out the very important balance that the manager must maintain between change and stability. To Sayles, the manager seeks "a dynamic type of stability" (p. 162). Most disturbances elicit short-term adjustments which bring back equilibrium; persistent ones require the introduction of long-term structural change.

Resource allocator. The manager maintains ultimate authority over his organization's strategy-making system by controlling the allocation of its resources. By deciding who will get what (and who will do what), the manager directs the course of his organization. He does this in three ways:

1. *In scheduling his own time*, the manager allocates his most precious resource and thereby determines organizational priorities. Issues that receive low priority do not reach the *nerve center* of the organization and are blocked for want of resources.
2. In designing the organizational structure and in carrying out many improvement projects, the manager *programs the work of his subordinates*. In other words, he allocates their time by deciding what will be done and who will do it.
3. Most significantly, the manager maintains control over resource allocation by the requirement that he *authorize all significant decisions* before they are implemented. By retaining this power, the manager ensures that different decisions are interrelated—that conflicts are avoided, that resource constraints are respected, and that decisons complement one another.

Decisions appear to be authorized in one of two ways. Where the costs and benefits of a proposal can be quantified, where it is competing for specified resources with other known proposals, and where it can wait for a certain time of year, approval for a proposal is sought in the context of a formal *budgeting* procedure. But these conditions are most often not met—timing may be crucial, nonmonetary costs may predominate, and so on. In these cases, approval is sought in terms of an *ad hoc request for authorization*. Subordinate and manager meet (perhaps informally) to discuss one proposal alone.

Authorization choices are enormously complex ones for the manager. A myriad of factors must be considered (resource constraints, influencer preferences, consistency with other decisions, feasibility, payoff, timing, subordinate feelings, etc.). But the fact that the manager is authorizing the decision rather than supervising its design suggests that he has little time to give to it. To alleviate this difficulty, it appears that managers use special kinds of *models* and *plans* in their decision-making. These exist only in their minds and are loose, but they serve to guide behavior. Models may answer questions such as, "Does this proposal make sense in terms of the trends that I see in tariff legislation?" or "Will the EDP department be able to get along with marketing on this?" Plans exist in the sense that, on questioning, managers reveal images (in terms of proposed improvement projects) of where they would like their organizations to go: "Well, once I get these foreign operations fully developed, I would like to begin to look into a reorganization," said one subject of this study.

Negotiator. The final role describes the manager as participant in negotiation activity. To some students of the management process [8, p. 343], this is not truly part of the job of managing. But such distinctions are arbitrary. Negotiation is an integral part of managerial work, as this study notes for chief executives and as that of Sayles made very clear for production supervisors [24, p. 131]: "Sophisticated managers place great stress on negotiations as a way of life. They negotiate with groups who are setting standards for their work, who are performing support activity for them, and to whom they wish to 'sell' their services."

The manager must participate in important negotiation sessions because he is his organization's legal authority, its *spokesman* and its *resource allocator*. Negotiation is resource trading in real time. If the resource commitments are to be large, the legal authority must be present.

These ten roles suggest that the manager of an organization bears a great burden of responsibility. He most oversee his organization's status system; he must serve as a crucial informational link between it and its environment; he must interpret and reflect its basic values; he must maintain the stability of its operations; and he must adapt it in a controlled and balanced way to a changing environment.

MANAGEMENT AS A PROFESSION AND AS A SCIENCE

Is management a profession? To the extent that different managers perform one set of basic roles, management satisfies one criterion for becoming a profession. But a profession must require, in the words of the Random House Dictionary, "knowledge of some department of learning or science." Which of the ten roles now requires specialized learning? Indeed, what school of business or public administration teaches its students how to disseminate information, allocate resources, perform as figurehead, make contacts, or handle disturbances? We simply know very little about teaching these things. The reason is that we have never tried to document and describe in a meaningful way the procedures (or programs) that managers use.

The evidence of this research suggests that there is as yet no science in managerial work—that managers do not work according to procedures that have been prescribed by scientific analysis. Indeed, except for his use of the telephone, the airplane, and the dictating machine, it would appear that the manager of today is indistinguishable from his predecessors. He may seek different information, but he gets much of it in the same way—from word-of-mouth. He may make decisions dealing with modern technology but he uses the same intuitive (that is, nonexplicit) procedures in making them. Even the computer, which has had such a great impact on other kinds of organizational work, has apparently done little to alter the working methods of the general manager.

How do we develop a scientific base to understand the work of the manager? The description of roles is a first and necessary step. But tighter forms of research are necessary. Specifically, we must attempt to model managerial work—to describe it as a system of programs. First, it will be necessary to decide what programs managers actually use. Among a great number of programs in the manager's repertoire, we might expect to find a time-scheduling program, an information-disseminating program, and a disturbance-handling program. Then, researchers will have to devote a considerable amount of effort to studying and accurately describing the content of each of these programs—the information and heuristics used. Finally, it will be necessary to describe the interrelationships among all of these programs so that they may be combined into an integrated descriptive model of managerial work.

When the management scientist begins to understand the programs that managers use, he can begin to design meaningful systems and provide help for the manager. He may ask: Which managerial activities can be fully reprogrammed (i.e., automated)? Which cannot be reprogrammed because they require human responses? Which can be partially reprogrammed to operate in a man-machine system? Perhaps scheduling, information collecting, and resource allocating activities lend themselves to varying degrees of reprogramming. Management will emerge as a science to the extent that such efforts are successful.

IMPROVING THE MANAGER'S EFFECTIVENESS

Fayol's fifty-year-old description of managerial work is no longer of use to us. And we shall not disentangle the complexity of managerial work if we insist on viewing the manager simply as a decision-maker or simply as a motivator of subordinates. In fact, we are unlikely to overestimate the complexity of the manager's work, and we shall make little headway if we take overly simple or narrow points of view in our research.

A major problem faces today's manager. Despite the growing size of modern organizations and the growing complexity of their problems (particularly those in the public sector), the manager can expect little help. He must design his own information system, and he must take full charge of his organization's strategy-making system. Furthermore, the manager faces what might be called the *dilemma of delegation*. He has unique access to much important information but he lacks a formal means of disseminating it. As much of it is verbal, he cannot spread it around in an efficient manner. How can he delegate a task with confidence when he has neither the time nor the means to send the necessary information along with it?

Thus, the manager is usually forced to carry a great burden of responsibility in his organization. As organizations become increasingly large and complex, this burden increases. Unfortunately, the man cannot significantly increase his available time or significantly improve his abilities to manage. Hence, in the large, complex bureaucracy, the top manager's time assumes an enormous opportunity cost and he faces the real danger of becoming a major obstruction in the flow of decisions and information.

Because of this, as we have seen, managerial work assumes a number of distinctive characteristics. The quantity of work is great; the pace is unrelenting; there is great variety, fragmentation, and brevity in the work activities; the manager must concentrate on issues that are current, specific, and ad hoc, and to do so, he finds that he must rely on verbal forms of communications. Yet it is on this man that the burden lies for designing and operating strategy-making and information-processing systems that are to solve his organization's (and society's) problems.

The manager can do something to alleviate these problems. He can learn more about his own roles in his organization, and he can use this information to schedule his time in a more efficient manner. He can recognize that only he has much of the information needed by his organization. Then, he can seek to find better means of disseminating it into the organization. Finally, he can turn to the skills of his management scientists to help reduce his workload and to improve his ability to make decisions.

The management scientist can learn to help the manager to the extent he can develop an understanding of the manager's work and the manager's information. To date, strategic planners, operations researchers, and information system designers have provided little help for the senior manager. They simply have had no framework available by which to understand the work of the men who employed them, and they have had poor access to the information which has never been documented. It is folly to believe that a man with poor access to the organization's true *nerve center* can design a formal management information system. Similarly, how can the long-range planner, a man usually uninformed about many of the *current* events that take place in and around his organization, design meaningful strategic plans? For good reason, the literature documents many manager complaints of naïve planning and many planner complaints of disinterested managers. In my view, our lack of understanding of managerial work has been the greatest block to the progress of management science.

The ultimate solution to the problem—to the overburdened manager seeking meaningful help—must derive from research. We must observe, describe, and understand the real work of managing; then and only then shall we significantly improve it.

REFERENCES

1. Braybrooke, David. "The Mystery of Executive Success Re-examined." *Administrative Science Quarterly*, Vol. 8 (1964), pp. 533–560.
2. ——, and Lindblom, Charles E. *A Strategy of Decision*. Free Press, 1963.
3. Bronowski, J. "The Creative Process." *Scientific American*, Vol. 199 (September 1958), pp. 59–65.
4. Burns, Tom. "The Directions of Activity and Communications in a Departmental Executive Group." *Human Relations*, Vol. 7 (1954), pp. 73–97.

5. ——. "Management in Action." *Operational Research Quarterly*, Vol. 8 (1957), pp. 45–60.
6. Carlson, Sune. *Executive Behavior*. Strömbergs, Stockholm, 1951.
7. Davis, Robert T. *Performance and Development of Field Sales Managers*. Division of Research, Graduate School of Business Administration, Harvard University, 1957.
8. Drucker, Peter F. *The Practice of Management*. Harper and Row, 1954.
9. Fayol, Henri. *Administration industrielle et générale*. Dunods, Paris, 1950 (first published 1916).
10. Gibb, Cecil A. "Leadership." Chapter 31 in Gardner Lindzey and Elliot A. Aronson (eds.), *The Handbook of Social Psychology*, Vol. 4, 2nd ed., Addison-Wesley, 1969.
11. Guest, Robert H. "Of Time and the Foreman." *Personnel*, Vol. 32 (1955–56) pp. 478–486.
12. Gulick, Luther H. "Notes on the Theory of Organization." In Luther Gulick and Lyndall Urwick (eds.), *Papers on the Science of Administration*. Columbia University Press, 1937.
13. Hemphill, John K. *Dimensions of Executive Positions*. Bureau of Business Research Monograph Number 98, The Ohio State University, 1960.
14. Homans, George C. *The Human Group*. Harcourt, 1950.
15. Horne, J. H., and Tom Lupton. "The Work Activities of Middle Managers—An Exploratory Study." *The Journal of Management Studies*, Vol. 2 (February 1965), pp. 14–33.
16. Kelly, Joe. "The Study of Executive Behavior by Activity Sampling." *Human Relations*, Vol. 17 (August 1964), pp. 277–287.
17. Mackenzie, R. Alex. "The Management Process in 3D." *Harvard Business Review* (November–December 1969), pp. 80–87.
18. Marples, D. L. "Studies of Managers—A Fresh Start?" *The Journal of Management Studies*, Vol. 4 (October 1967), pp. 282–299.
19. Mintzberg, Henry. "Structured Observation as a Method to Study Managerial Work." *The Journal of Management Studies*, Vol. 7 (February 1970), pp. 87–104.
20. Myers, Charles A. (ed.) *The Impact of Computers on Management*, MIT Press, Cambridge, Mass., 1967.
21. Neustadt, Richard E. *Presidential Power: The Politics of Leadership*. New American Library, 1964.
22. Papandreou, Andreas G. "Some Basic Problems in the Theory of the Firm." In Bernard F. Haley (ed.), *A Survey of Contemporary Economics*, Vol. II. Irwin, 1952, pp. 183–219.
23. Sarbin, T. R., and V. L. Allen. "Role Theory." In Gardner Lindzey and Elliot A. Aronson (eds.), *The Handbook of Social Psychology*, Vol. I, Addison-Wesley, 1968, pp. 488–567.
24. Sayles, Leonard R. *Managerial Behavior: Administration in Complex Enterprises*. McGraw-Hill, 1964.
25. Stewart, Rosemary. *Managers and Their Jobs*. Macmillan, London, 1967.
26. Whyte, William F. *Street Corner Society*, 2nd ed. University of Chicago Press, 1955.

Hengstler-Gleitzeit Case

The J. Hengstler KG is a well-known producer of a wide variety of mostly electronic counters and meters for industrial use, which it sells all over the world. The firm was founded in 1827 in Aldingen, a small south-German town, where it still has its headquarters and main facilities. Since its beginning, it has remained under the exclusive control of a single family. Two members of that family head its operations today, maintaining its rather rigid, conservative, puritan character.

In 1973, Hengstler employed close to 1700 people and totaled sales of approximately DM90 million, for profits of about DM7 million.

Late in 1969, a new affiliate was created under the name of Hengstler-Gleitzeit. Its purpose was—and still is—the production and marketing of time-recording equipment to be used by companies whose employees work on flexible or variable working hours. (The growth of this affiliate from 1970–73 is shown in Table 1.)

Table 1 Growth of Hengstler-Gleitzeit, 1970–73

	Number of Employees	Sales (in Million DM)	Profits (in Million DM)
1970	20	2.4	0.5
1971	50	5	1
1972	80	10	2
1973	200	25	5

"Hengstler-Gleitzeit Case" was prepared by Alexander Bergman, Professor at IMEDE.

The initiative for the creation of Hengstler-Gleitzeit came from Willi Haller, then 34, who was an assistant to Hengstler's marketing director. Ever since he had entered the firm as an apprentice, in 1951, he proved to be exceptional. His superiors appreciated his technical and managerial talents (he contributed several important inventions to the business; he discovered promising new markets; and he did a splendid job when sent to the United States to take over a newly purchased electronics firm). On the other hand, they were somewhat less enthusiastic about his spirit of independence and his leftist political convictions (he repeatedly had given them trouble as a member of the work council, and had once campaigned for the Social Democrats in front of the company's main building). He is at once an almost helplessly optimistic idealist and a very down-to-earth, hard-nosed businessman. He is a very inspiring person with an undeniable talent to stimulate others.

Initially, Willi Haller's suggestion to launch a new kind of device to measure and record working time was rejected by the owner/managers. Only when he insisted and began raising money from fellow employees to realize his plans on his own did the company change its posture. He was provided with DM500,000 (against the promise not to let any employees participate financially in the venture), and given the power to develop the subsidiary as an independent division along the lines he envisioned. The division would be geographically separated from the mother firm (it was actually established at Trossingen, 8 km away from Aldingen); and it would not be allowed to draw any personnel away from the mother firm. It could buy parts and technical services from Aldingen (at market prices), have new prototypes developed there according to its specifications, ask for administrative assistance, or use existing distribution channels. But it could also try to do everything itself or with the help of third parties. Of course, it would be fully responsible for profit and losses. Figure 1 presents the division's relationship to the mother firm.

As it turned out, the new division has most of its prototypes developed in Aldingen. It also gets the bulk of its parts produced there. It does, however, assemble these parts itself—in three different locations: two in Trossingen and one, 7 km away, in Zeitingen. In Germany, where Hengstler-Gleitzeit does about 50 percent of its business, and in a few other countries, it has created its own sales force and distribution system, while it uses existing Hengstler channels for sales in some eighteen other foreign countries, limiting its own efforts to promotion.

Promotion and sales efforts focus everywhere as much on the idea of flexible working hours (its advantages to the company, its employees, and society) as it does on the time-recording equipment. As a matter of fact, Willi Haller and his collaborators believe in a mission. They see themselves not as just selling some product at a profit, but as making a major contribution to the improvement of the condition of working people everywhere.

They themselves are, of course, on variable working hours. But this is only one dimension of a broad effort at Hengstler-Gleitzeit to accommodate the wants and needs of employees. Indeed, Willi Haller tries to provide an environment in which each individual can self-actualize, and in which work is not seen as a burden. He advocates teamwork, as much informality and flexibility as possible, self-direction and self-control, no hierarchy, profit sharing, and a better integration of the economic and noneconomic aspects of life at an individual as well as collective level.

Many of these ideas have been realized, to a greater or lesser extent, in Trossingen, and in particular for the employees there who are not involved in production.

Indeed, at headquarters, the heart of the whole enterprise, about ten men and twenty women work together in one big room on tables and cabinets that they chose and arranged themselves. Everybody can see everybody else and can talk to each other at any time. As a matter of fact, all communication is oral. The tone is frank. People call each other by their first names. They do not dress up for work. The atmosphere in the room is extremely relaxed. There is no sign of regimentation nor of superior/subordinate relationships.

Everybody is, as already mentioned, on variable working hours; they can come and go as they please. Moreover, they are frequently taking a break, mostly to play ping-pong in a back room—with the loser contributing a bottle of champagne into common stock (which at times totaled forty bottles). This stock is drawn on whenever there is a birthday, an anniversary, or some other memorable event to celebrate.

The average age in the office is about 30, with nobody older than 38. Many of the employees have come from distant places to Trossingen to work with Hengstler-Gleitzeit. To them, but not only to them, the firm has become something of a home. Indeed, there is a lot of socialization among them, on and off the job. On the job, much of the socializing evolves around the ping-pong matches, the occasional celebrations, and around a white kokadu that flies freely around the large room. (The bird was bought by a group of employees who formed a "stock company" for that purpose). Off work, the employees meet frequently for social events. Some of them play football together. There are regular outings. But most

Figure 1 J. Hengstler KG Organization Chart

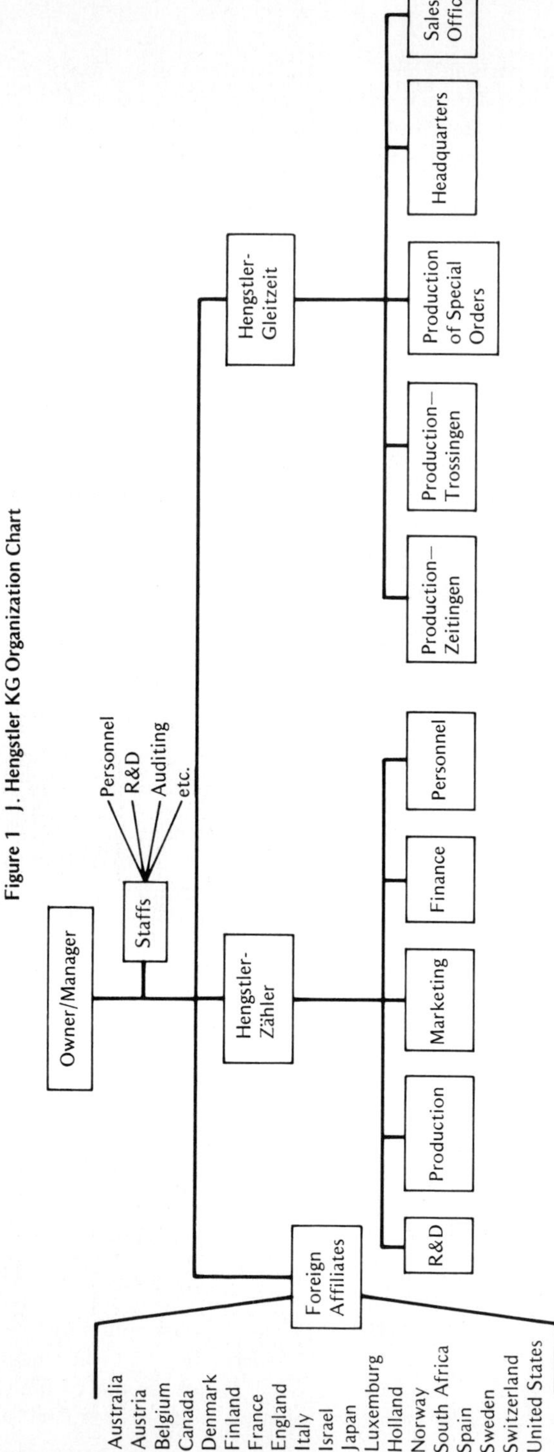

popular are small, informal gatherings at someone's home or in one of the numerous restaurants around.

The work itself is done in teams (see Figure 2). There are permanent and temporary teams, with the latter meeting either regularly or ad hoc (at the request of anybody and everybody). These teams were first introduced to solve the problem arising from individuals working on irregular schedules: in the absence of some of their members, the groups guaranteed continuity of operations. Over time, the teams have evolved into the major decision-making bodies. Willi Haller does not want to hear from anybody anything like "you ought to do"; he wants to hear instead "we ought to do" from someone who then goes ahead and tries his idea out on a group. The group decides on the proposal, if possible, by general consensus rather than through vote. But, whatever the decision, its execution still lies primarily with the individual, who is also responsible for the results.

To make the responsibility for results real for every employee, Willi Haller introduced a profit-sharing plan, according to which he distributes some of his own annual bonus to his collaborators on the basis of their performance. The performance of an individual is evaluated by all who interact frequently with her or him. Criteria are skill and knowledge, effort, quantity of work, quality of work, human relations, and impact on others. The final grade an individual gets is the sum of the averaged scores. For everybody the ideal overall score is the same, although the points one can get on each criterion vary with the type of job held. When this system was first introduced, the incumbents of more prestigious jobs tended to get higher overall scores than those in less prestigious ones, but in 1973 two typists got almost as high a score as did Willi Haller.

The members of permanent teams participate in the decision to include a new member. As of late 1973, there has been only one case when somebody was forced to leave a team and the company. The teams have no appointed—although often a natural—leader. It is understood that in any case the leader is more likely to be a servant to the team than its master. Thus, there should be no (and actually is little) competition for power within the group. Emphasis is on cooperation. The only competition encouraged in Trossingen is that between the Gleitzeit division and the mother firm in Aldingen. The latter is presented as the mean Big Brother who is all the time trying to bring the wild bunch in Trossingen back to order.

The organization and treatment of Hengstler-Gleitzeit employees not working at headquarters falls somewhat short of Willi Haller's ideals. Nevertheless, the attempt is made to come as close to these ideals as possible.

In principle, the sales offices should operate like headquarters. But control is not easy, and variations exist at different places mainly because of the personality and leadership style of each man in charge.

As to production, there is, first, a place adjacent to the headquarters room for the execution of special orders. It is run much like the office next door, except that there is no profit sharing. Then, there is a second workshop a few blocks down the road where some concessions had to be made owing to the fact that the work is done on a belt; moreover, the owner/managers imposed the application of a piece rate. Finally, there is a third production site in Zeitingen. Here, some sixty women (1970, twenty!) work totally on their own to produce small, rather cheap instrument components (in 1970, 30,000 pieces; in 1973, 300,000). Their workplaces have been arranged in a way (and with so-called bumper stocks between them) so that each of the women can work independently of the others. Moreover, every one of them was given her own key to the building so that she can come and work whenever it is convenient (including evenings and weekends).

Figure 2 Hengstler-Gleitzeit Permanent and Temporary Teams

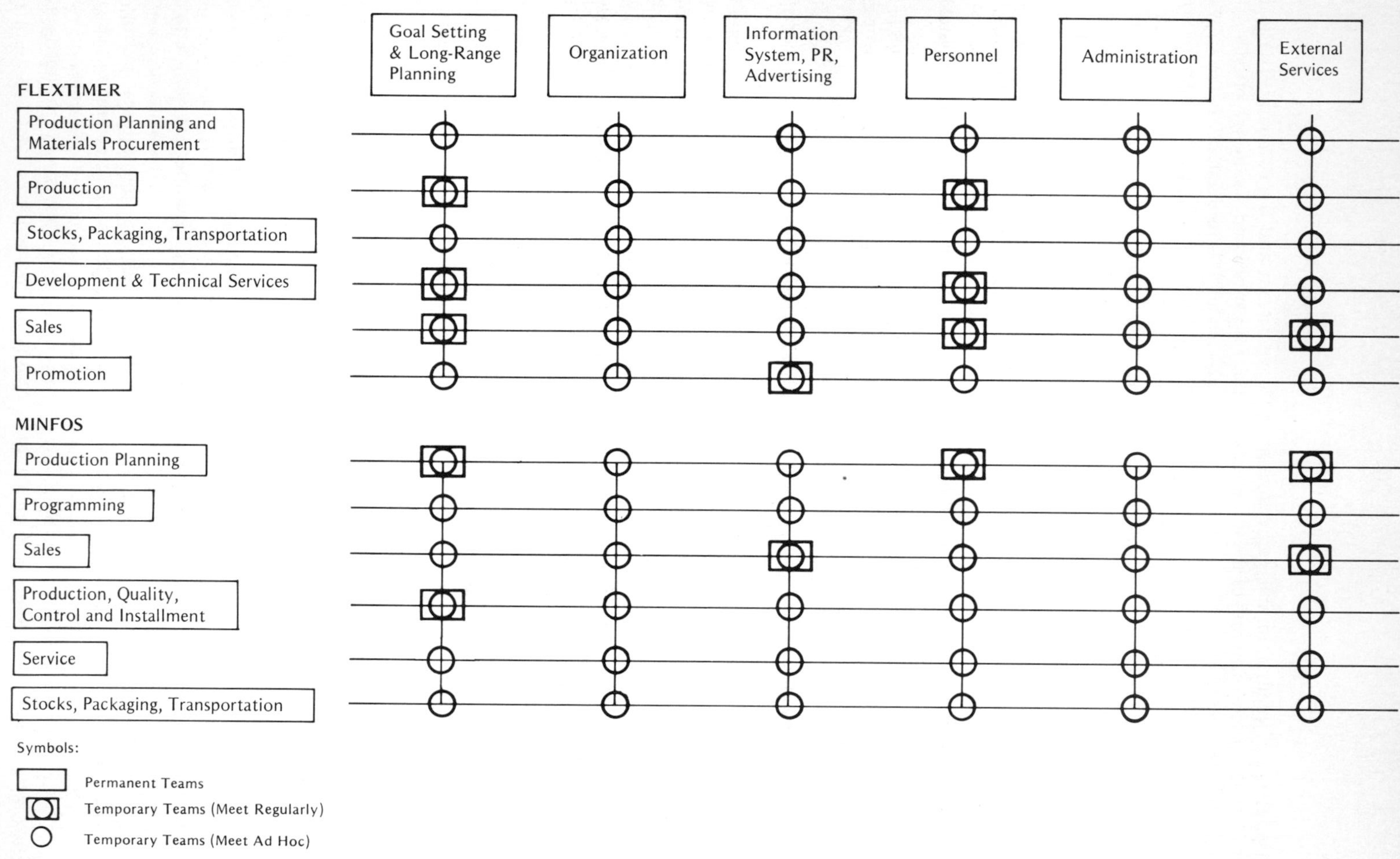

The Interflex Case

On July 1, 1974, in Durchausen, a village of 700 people in the Black Forest, Willi Haller started Interflex, GmbH & Co. KG.

Willi Haller was then 38, married, with four children. He had little formal education, but had read a lot and had a restless and very broad mind. He had made several successful technical inventions, had made an impressive managerial career with a medium-sized company (with which he had stayed for 20 years),[1] spoke fluent English, was politically and socially active, and taught some business courses at a night school.

Managerial Philosophy

The company Haller founded was conceived as a model organization, a social experiment, based on a philosophy which he described as follows:

"I believe that business, the way it operates today, no longer satisfies the individuals who operate it, nor the public for which it operates. The reason for this is that business has become an end in itself. This, in turn, is due to the fact that business has been depersonalized and segregated. What is needed, therefore, is to (re)introduce human dimensions into business and to (re)integrate the economic with noneconomic spheres on the individual as well as the societal level.

"More specifically, work should be humanized by giving it a meaning and by making it exciting; the worker's humanity should be better respected by accounting more for his psychological as well as material needs, and by adapting the organization to them rather than expecting them to adapt to the organization.

"Work can have a meaning only when it is perceived to contribute in a non-negligible way to a worthwhile purpose. Thus, the product of the business must be appreciable in other than only terms of profitability to the company. And the work organization must allow each employee to have a distinguishable impact on its performance.

"Work is exciting when the organizational constraints on it are reduced to a minimum and when it allows for enough variety to satisfy different interests one may have at different points in time. The basic organizing principles should be self-direction and self-control. Horizontal as well as vertical job rotation should be made possible on a large scale.

"People should work in organizations where everybody knows everybody, where everybody is more or less up to date on the others' activities; a community in which one can effectively participate and for which one can feel responsible.

"People's need for self-respect should be enhanced by reducing status symbols and by eliminating hierarchies. The rule of people over people must end. Superiors must become servants (who will offset their loss in power through gaining love) and subordinates must become respected collaborators (who will lose the comforts of followership but gain the rewards from re-

[1] At the end of 1973, Willi Haller resigned his position as Managing Director of Hengstler-Gleitzeit (see Hengstler-Gleitzeit case).

sponsible enterprising). Labor must be truly equal to capital by being rewarded the same way.

"People's needs for security must be responded to by guaranteeing greater equity and by replacing competition by cooperation. A man should be carried by the group with which he identifies and should feel secure through its support. Thus, the work group must in a way be like a family to its members.

"But the group should not be homogenous, for creativity and excitement will only come with diversity and tension. It should not be self-sufficient, for it should not become estranged from its environment. And it should not be all-embracing, for this might violate the integrity and curiosity of its members.

"Thus, the challenge is to create units which are closed and stable enough to provide a base for identification and empathy, but which at the same time are open enough to preserve individual freedom and multidimensionality. The openness of the unit should facilitate a better integration of the individual in it and of the unit into the environment. It should contribute to reduce worker alienation and to make business more socially responsible. Openness could be achieved through easy access to the group (especially for the members' friends and family), through the possibility for its members to be involved in other activities (especially family duties, continued education, or social work), and through the reduction of barriers (like regulations, traditions, or jargon) which inhibit contact with the outside."

Having verbalized his philosophy, Willi Haller thought that this was not enough. He was going to do something to implement it: he was going to create a company. The company would try to translate his philosophy into practice. If it was successful, it would hopefully serve as an example to others. For a successful demonstration is the best way to induce people to change: it does not hurt anybody, nor impose anything; it speaks for itself.

Business Practice

Willi Haller, by going into the business of producing and marketing time-recording equipment to be used by companies whose employees work on flexible or variable working hours, would compete with his former employer (see the Hengstler-Gleitzeit case). By turning down severance pay, he had obtained permission to go into a competitive business, although not to join an existing competitor.

The reason for going into the Flextime business was that this was the sector Willi Haller knew something about; but more importantly, he believed in a philosophy behind flexible working hours. He wanted to propagate that philosophy along with the sale of the time-recording equipment.

The idea to free himself from the organizational constraints of his job and to start his own business had, of course, been on Willi Haller's mind for some time. He actually quit his employment on December 31, 1973.

By that time, he had started tinkering with a new kind of electronic time-recording equipment, which he now took to two ex-NASA engineers. They developed it within record time to a marketable product. As a matter of fact, a prototype was ready for the Hannover Fair in June 1974.

Production of this model started immediately after the presentation to the public at the American engineers' Tronix Corp., New Jersey. Another smaller mechanical model is built in Durchhausen and the neighboring villages. At the same time, Interflex was set up to assure the marketing of the new products. It operates by buying its products from subcontractors and selling them in Germany through franchises and to foreign countries through general agents or directly from Durchhausen. The franchises

Figure 1 Interflex Organization

Legal Set-up

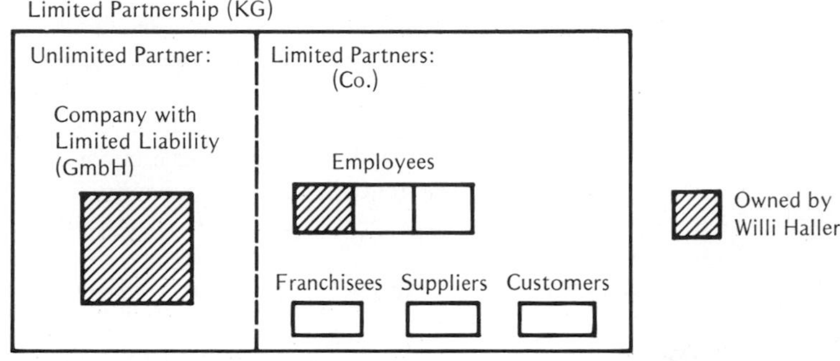

Financial Participation

Voting Rights

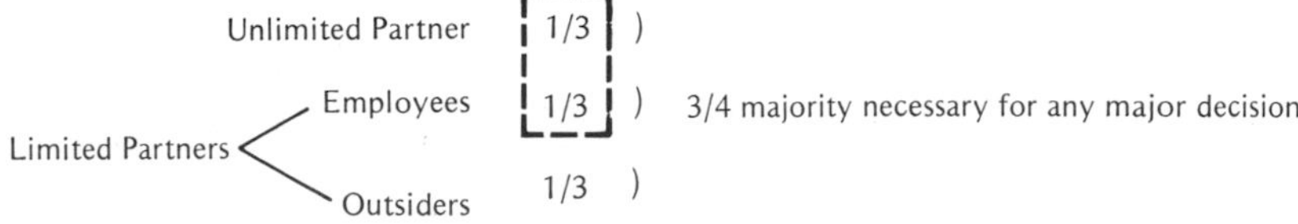

run five years and cost an amount that varies with the sales potential of the territory. They give the franchisee the right (and the duty) to the exclusive distribution, at a margin of 35 percent, of all Interflex products in his territory. All of the franchisees were well-introduced sales representatives who knew Willi Haller from the time he had been working with his former employer.

Company Organization

Interflex GmbH & Co. KG is a limited partnership consisting of:

- The unlimited (active) partner—the company with limited liability; and
- Limited (general) partners—a number of individual investors.

Willi Haller and his wife own all shares of the company with limited liability (GmbH). Their shares, worth DM20,000, amount to 1.6 percent of Interflex's total interests. The remaining 98.4 percent (DM1,180,000) of the company's interests are owned by the limited partners (Co.). Half of these shares belong to employees of the firm, including Haller; and half are owned by outsiders, most of whom have relationships with the firm. They are franchisees, suppliers, customers, consultants, auditors, etc. (see Figure 1). Since overall control of the company lies one third with the unlimited partner and two thirds with the limited partners, the company and its employees control two thirds of the shares, and outsiders control the other third. To avoid having the insiders impose their will on the outsiders, all major decisions must be made by a three-quarter majority of the shareholders.

As the owner/manager of the company with limited liability which is the active partner in the partnership, Willi Haller is by law the manager of the latter. However, he has agreed to share his power with his collaborators.

Indeed, he has plans to give first to the managerial and eventually to all employees the option to acquire shares of the GmbH which gives them the power to control and even fire him as managing director. Moreover, the franchise agreement stipulates that, with regard to marketing-related decisions, all seven managerial employees and the thirteen franchisees have a vote: A marketing conference is to be called quarterly to decide (formally through simple or qualified majority, but actually through consensus) on matters like product mix, sales targets, marketing and PR plans, attribution of vacant territories, etc.; it also arbitrates any conflict that may occur between the partners.

As to other decisions (financial, personnel, etc.), only the employees of Interflex (excluding therefore the franchisees), but all of them (including nonmanagerial employees) participate to the extent that they are concerned by them.

Working Conditions

Interflex is located in the old school building of Durchhausen, which the company has rented for DM150/month. There, ten employees work in one big former classroom that was repainted in orange, yellow, and blue, decorated with butterflies (which incidentally also adorn the company stationery), and furnished with second-hand desks. Everything is simple and gay.

In working conditions, Interflex closely resembles Hengstler-Gleitzeit, where Haller formerly was in charge: The average age is about 30. Everybody calls each other by first names. There are no status symbols of any kind, nor signs of regimentation and superior-subordinate relations. Nobody dresses up for work. Employees come and go as they please, and breaks are frequent. It is current practice to have members of the family of employees come for brief visits, or to see the employees go for a short meeting with the family member or with a friend. The whole atmosphere is very relaxed. There is a lot of socializing outside of work. There are no secrets. Everybody can hear and see everything happening, can participate in the success and difficulties of the others and the company. All communication is oral. Problems are often discussed among several or all employees. You never hear "you ought to do," but always "we ought to do." Everybody is encouraged to take the initiative to try new ideas out and to substitute for an absent colleague.

As to the organization of production, a number of women (some of them the wives of Interflex employees) assemble the mechanical models at home from parts supplied by Interflex. They work at their own rhythm and assemble the whole product. They are paid at a piece rate. There is no quality control. Instead, each woman marks the pieces she finishes with her name, thus becoming personally responsible for any reclamations.

In a year or two, Interflex plans to produce also the electronic model in a new factory to be built in Durchhausen. It is intended to run production as an independent unit which would sell its equipment to the marketing company the way Tronix does it. Of course, it will be set up and run internally on principles of self-determination, cooperation, flexibility, and integration.

Compensation

Not everybody earns the same amount, although an effort was made to reduce the distance between the lowest and the highest salaries (essentially by setting the top salaries at a relatively modest level). Willi Haller himself has a salary not higher than that of three other leading employees.

The way in which the salaries were set was as follows: First, the total wage bill to be distributed was assessed by the accountant and approved of in a meeting attended by all employees. Then, each employee, anonymously, prepared a plan for dividing the total pie among the members of the group. These plans were consolidated and discussed and a wage scheme derived which was acceptable to all. Finally, to check on the result, everybody was asked to rate his or her satisfaction with the conclusions—again anonymously—on a scale from 1 (very dissatisfied) to 10 (very satisfied). As the average level of satisfaction was almost 8 and no one had expressed dissatisfaction (lowest score was 6), the salary structure was definitely accepted as defined.

But salaries were to constitute only a part of the employees' income (and hopefully the smaller one), for all employees participate in a profit-sharing plan. As a matter of fact, Interflex has a complex system under which capital and labor are remunerated equally: First, the invested capital (whether it comes from owner or a creditor) is entitled to a fixed interest, like the other factors of production (labor and supplies) for which a fixed price has to be paid. Second, if the company realizes a profit, capital is not the only factor of production to benefit. Rather, profits are split three ways: one third for capital, one third for labor, and one third for the public. Of the first and second third, half is distributed among the owners (employees or outsiders) and employees respectively, while the other half is retained within the company either as a loan (at 12 percent) or as a silent participation (at minimally 10 percent, maximally 20 percent). The remaining third is remitted to a foundation which sponsors any kind of project that benefits not only the company or its constituents, but a wider public.

The third of the profit that goes to the employees is distributed among them on the basis of three criteria: function, performance, seniority.

According to the work done, every employee is classified in one of ten categories (which are based on work classifications developed through collective bargaining in the metal transforming industries in Baden-Würtemberg). This classification is done once a year by everyone, and for everyone, before being discussed and decided upon by all.

Performance evaluation is done for each individual by those who interact frequently with him (her). Criteria are skill, knowledge, effort, quantity of work, quality of work, human relations, and impact on others. Everybody can get up to 96 possible points, but depending on the type of work done, these points will be obtained on different criteria. The final grade an individual gets is the sum of average scores received on each of the criteria.

Finally, seniority is honored with 0.1 point per month worked with the company—up to three years (after 3 years, no additional premium is given).

The three elements are then combined (employment category × performance evaluation × months of service), to give each employee a certain number of points. The points of all employees, divided in the profit to be distributed, determine the amount attributed to each point. Every employee re-

Table 1 Interflex Profit-Sharing Plan

Example of Profit Sharing

Total profit: DM900,000 → to - Owners DM300,000
- Employees DM300,000 → for Distribution: DM150,000
- Foundation DM300,000

10 Employees:

	Monthly Salary	Category	Performance	Months of Service	Points	Bonus
A	DM2400	5	48	18	5 × 48 × 1.8 = 432.0	432.0 × 15.98 = 6903.36
B	DM3000	7	42	12	7 × 42 × 1.2 = 352.8	352.8 × 15.98 = 5637.74
C	DM2800	6	58	12	6 × 58 × 1.2 = 417.6	417.6 × 15.98 = 6673.25
D	DM1500	3	64	15	3 × 64 × 1.5 = 288.0	288.0 × 15.98 = 4602.24
E	DM3500	9	60	40	9 × 60 × 3.6 = 1944.0	1944.0 × 15.98 = 31065.12
F	DM3500	9	53	10	9 × 53 × 1.0 = 477.0	477.0 × 15.98 = 7622.46
G	DM2700	6	70	38	6 × 70 × 3.6 = 1512.0	1512.0 × 15.98 = 24161.76
H	DM3500	9	72	35	9 × 72 × 3.5 = 2268.0	2268.0 × 15.98 = 36242.64
I	DM2500	4	49	40	4 × 49 × 3.6 = 705.6	705.6 × 15.98 = 11275.49
J	DM3500	9	55	20	9 × 55 × 2.0 = 990.0	990.0 × 15.98 = 15820.20
					9387.0	DM150,000.00

$$\frac{DM150000}{9387} = DM15.98 \text{ per point}$$

ceives his or her total number of points times that amount (Table 1).

Public Interest

Willi Haller was most interested in the possible use of the third of profits dedicated to serve the public interest. He would like to see the funds used for projects like a kindergarten for Durchhausen (open to the children of employees and everybody else), a waste-recycling facility for the region, or a reforestry project in the Mediterranean. The latter idea should be realized by buying land in Southern France or Italy. Interflex employees who would be interested could then go, for anywhere between a week or a year, to plant trees.

PART FOUR

Behavioral Issues Confronting the Manager as Leader

Chapter

12 The Changing Meaning of Work

The primary task of management is to effectively utilize available resources—whether economic, technical, or human—in order to meet organizational goals and objectives. To use these resources effectively, managers need to understand the nature of the different resources, where they can be used, and how.

Among the available resources, the human resource is unique. It is the only resource that cares how you use it. The motivational force comes from within the resource itself, not from outside it. Economic and technical resources can be manipulated as one wishes, for whatever end one wishes. People, however, care about both how they are used and for what purpose. Unfortunately, therefore, the assumptions we have about the manipulation of economic and technical resources may not be appropriate in dealing with people in business.

To understand people and their work we need to understand not only how we would like the human resource to meet the needs of management, but also how the human resource is striving to meet its own needs, and what those needs are. It is the balance between the fulfilling of these two sets of needs which, in the end, results in organizational effectiveness. To complicate the problem, the balance has been changing over time. It is useful to look at this relationship in an historical perspective to better understand the situation we are facing today and will face in the future (see Table 1).

Table 1 People and Their Work in Historical Perspective

	Past	Present	Future
Dominant Needs of Human Resource*	Economic	Social	Self-Actualizing?
Management's Basic Approach to Human Resource	Design of Technical System; People Adapted to the System	Some Design of the Human System; Technology Is Adapted to Human Needs	Design of Organizations to Adapt to Human Needs

*See Maslow, "A Theory of Human Motivation," pp. 190–209 of this text.

THE HISTORIC VIEW OF PEOPLE AND THEIR WORK

It is easy to oversimplify a basic historical trend. Many changes have taken place, and not at the same time everywhere. There is evidence, however, that some major changes are occurring generally, and they help us understand the situation facing management today.

The Past

Prior to the Industrial Revolution and the accompanying increase in the factory system, people and their work were seen as essentially the same. If a man were a craftsman, he "was" that craft—carpenter, shoemaker, blacksmith, or candlemaker. Even the work of the peasant was his or her social identity. In that world, work was life.

The Industrial Revolution reduced the reliance on crafts—on personal skills—and, therefore, on the integration of work and life. Work was broken down into simplified, routine steps. People were hired not for their skills, but for their ability to fit into a technically designed job. The factory system also led to the grouping of large numbers of people around the factories in urban areas, each person becoming more and more dependent on money. The basic need being met by work was, indeed, economic. The work was no longer intrinsically satisfying. People no longer identified with the craft. They did a job. They worked. They did not produce anything. They just worked. Technology was constantly being redesigned to make the system more efficient, and people were asked to adapt to the ever changing technological system. The system produced.

The Present

The breakdown of the large independent family and the increased dependency of workers on industrial organizations in urban areas led, over the years, to an increase in social problems. To deal with these problems, governments gradually began to introduce various forms of welfare legislation. By the post-World-War II period in Western Europe and North America, the kind of economic insecurity that had existed in the first half of the twentieth century was generally reduced. An unemployed individual received unemployment benefits, a retired individual had a pension, a sick individual was cared for. Economic needs gradually reduced in importance.

As a result of the continued standardization, specialization, and routinization, however, work became less and less intrinsically satisfying. No longer was it enough to work just for money. The need for more than money led to demands for more social contact, groups, interaction on the job, and a more basic attempt to meet the social needs of workers. Management has responded to this in many places by reorganizing work in order for these needs to be met. It might be said that the needs of the human system are now in many large organizations identified first and then the technology is being adapted to meet those needs. Although there has not been a total revolution in work organization at the present, many examples of organizations changing their basic design to meet the social needs of the labor force are evident throughout the world.

The Future

What will happen next? Increasing levels of education, increasing amounts of freedom, and increasing concern for equality seem to be resulting in demands for more than economic and social rewards from work. Workers seem to be asking for work to have meaning in itself. Just working is not satisfying. People seem to want to make choices, make decisions, participate in the organizational process in a much more basic way. There seems to be a desire for some kind of self-actualization and self-realization through work. There seems to be a need for work to return to the role it once had, where work and life were more fully integrated.

From management's point of view, these new demands raise an interesting challenge. When the needs of the labor force were economic, it was possible to increase the efficiency of the system by increasing the economic rewards to workers. This did not necessarily take anything away from the manager. When the needs were social, it was possible to redesign the system so that social needs could be better met. These changes did not necessarily take anything away from the manager. However, when it is the self-actualizing or ego needs that are being met, workers seem to be asking to be part of management itself. They are asking not only to receive from the organization, but to be a part of it. To meet these needs, some people are asking others to give up part of their own organizational and social roles. This is a different kind of demand from those of the past.

CONCLUSION

In the past, the needs of the human resource did not require substantial changes in the hierarchy and status of the organization. The new demands seem to be for a more basic change in organizational relationships. This will not be as easy to give.

How we define our role as manager will determine how and whether these future needs are met. The task manager of the past is gradually becoming the coordinator of human activities in a much broader sense. It is useful to begin to articulate this changing role.

ALEXANDER BERGMANN

Worker Participation

Ideas of worker participation are almost as old as modern industry. Soon after the Industrial Revolution, and as a reaction to some of the practices by which it was brought about, various movements spread those ideas among the working class and some of them were, in fact, put to practice on a small scale.

HISTORICAL BACKGROUND

In Germany, for instance, the introduction of workers' committees had been discussed in the Constitutional Assembly of 1848, and a few companies actually introduced such committees, although the law making them mandatory was passed only some fifty years later. In France about at the same time, Fouriérism had a good number of followers, who established industrial communities along utopian cooperative principles. Later in the century, worker self-management was fought for, albeit with little success, by the French Commune of 1870 and by the Guedists. In England, it was Robert Owens who since 1834 inspired many to join industrial and social cooperatives. And in the United States, the Wobblies advocated worker control in and over industry well before the turn of the century.

After 1900, some form of worker participation was introduced in many European countries: it appeared during World War I (without much ideological discussion) to increase worker involvement in war production, and in the revolutionary period right after the war (with much ideological propaganda) to establish the rule of workers in industry as well as in government. However, where these attempts failed to bring about communism, worker control declined soon thereafter, and was not much of an issue again until after World War II.

But now, we have seen for several years in most Western European countries more or less heated discussions over worker participation. Occurring on an increasingly broad scale, these discussions involve not only unionized labor and employers and their associations, but also political parties and the public at large. And it does not look as if the question will go away again. Moreover, we have seen in North America the emergence of a very broad and no doubt irreversible movement toward a more participative management style.

Despite the rather long history of the idea and the number of theoretical discussions and practical applications exploring it, confusion still exists with regard to what is actually meant by worker participation.

Stretching the term to its broadest meaning, worker participation can be considered to be any limitation set by workers on managerial discretion to make and implement decisions. Thus, it covers all forms of worker participation in decision making. It even covers worker participation in results (profit sharing), insofar as profit sharing constrains management in the definition and use of the profits of the firm; and it covers worker participation in the capital of the company, insofar as partial ownership allows the workers to put pressure on management.

VARIATIONS IN FORMAL AND INFORMAL APPROACHES

Taking direct participation in decision making only, worker participation can be formal or informal. Formal, institutionalized approaches can vary according to:

- their basis: legal regulations, or collective agreements;
- the kind of managerial decisions to which they apply: setting of overall company goals and policies, or operating decisions on economic, technical, and personnel matters:
- the locus of influence or control: external (at a national, regional, or industry level), or internal (at top-management, middle-management, or shop-floor level);
- the amount of influence or control: information, consultation, co-decision, or self-management; and
- the agents of influence or control: blue-collar workers, white-collar workers, middle management, elected employees, or outside union officials.

Informal approaches comprise, on a supracompany level, concertations between unions and employers (with or without assistance of government representatives) and, within a company, job enrichment, management by objectives, democratic leadership, autonomous groups, flexible working hours, etc.

Whether the participation is formal or informal, another distinction is even more fundamental and critical: whether it means cooperation or negotiation. Some models are clearly based on cooperation, stressing the communality of interests of the social partners involved. Others, to the contrary, rest on competition. They emphasize the quality of the partners, the equal chance of both to defend their own interests, and the peaceful resolution of conflicts. But they continue to draw a clear line between workers, on the one side, and employers and managers on the other, and thus perpetuate a "we-they," rather than a "we," thinking.

The various forms of and approaches to worker participation often overlap. Thus, any particular case may contain various elements which are not always consistent with each other, and no particular case may exactly fit in any specific categorization. But it is possible to look at the general situation in some European countries, in terms of the categories established, and to distinguish different forms of worker participation. This may help reduce some of the confusion caused by indiscriminate use of the term *worker participation* for a very wide spectrum of developments that—taken together—reduce managerial discretion in decision making.

DIFFERENT APPROACHES IN VARIOUS COUNTRIES

Table 1 has been arranged to present the situation in various countries in an ideological order. It presents them on a continuum ranging from a communist to somewhat socialist and capitalist approaches. At one extreme, represented by Yugoslavia, the company is basically a collectivity of workers, who are its only

Table 1 Some Examples of Different Approaches to Worker Participation

				Yugoslavia	Germany	Denmark	France	Great Britain
Participation in Decision Making	Formal	Nation/Industry		Planning	Collective bargaining (broadening scope) "Investitionslenkung" (being discussed)	Collective bargaining (broad scope) Prospective planning Bipartite secretariate (for mediation, training)	Collective bargaining (narrow scope) "Plan"	Collective bargaining Productivity boards
Participation in Decision Making	Formal	Company	Supervisory board		Coal and steel industry: 5 owner representatives, 5 labor representatives, (2 from unions), 1 neutral Other big corporations: 10 owner representatives, 1 top management representative, 9 labor representatives (3 from unions), 1 neutral	Worker representatives -2 (from inside the company)	Nationalized companies: 1/3 government, 1/3 workers, 1/3 consumers Companies with supervisory board: 1/3 workers Other corporations: advisory delegation from works committee (2 workers, 1 foreman, 1 middle manager)	
Participation in Decision Making	Formal	Company	Management board	Appointed by workers	Coal and steel industry: labor director			
Participation in Decision Making	Formal	Company	Middle and upper management	Workers' council *Self-management*: all managerial matters	Works council (directly elected employees and workers) *Self-management*: social programs *Codetermination*: conditions, hours, safety, personnel policies, hiring, firing, transfers *Consultation*: mergers, shut-downs, major technical changes *Information*: final results, planning	Cooperative committee (management & union representatives): *Self-management*: welfare programs *Codetermination*: conditions, safety, personnel policies *Consultation*: production policies, product scheduling, major technical changes *Information*: final results, future prospects	Works committee (top manager & delegates proposed by unions); *Self-management*: social programs *Consultation*: conditions, training, mass lay-offs *Information*: product scheduling, economic results	
Participation in Decision Making	Formal	Shop floor		Workers' council	"Bill of rights of workers" (being discussed) Flexible working hours	Collective agreements on work design		Shop stewards Grievancy procedures
Participation in Decision Making	Informal	Nation/Industry			"Konzertierte Aktion"			
Participation in Decision Making	Informal	Company			Experiments with decentralization	Systematic decentralization		Participative management
Participation in Decision Making	Informal	Shop floor			Numerous experiments with team approaches for evaluation schemes, work design, organizational change	Teamwork		Job enrichment Organizational development
Participation in results/capital				Definition by and distribution of profits to workers Workers' own company	Voluntary profit sharing in 2000 companies	Compulsory profit sharing (being discussed): 50-50; reinvestment in company up to 50% of capital (1/3 union administered investment fund; 2/3 worker shares)	Mandatory profit sharing Nationalizations	Voluntary profit sharing Employee-shareholders

citizens: they elect and appoint its management. Capital plays a secondary role of a factor of production obtained from the outside. At the other extreme, represented by Great Britain (and the United States), the company is seen mainly as a creation of the capital owners: they are its citizens and have the right to appoint and control its management; labor plays merely the role of a factor of production purchased outside. Between these two extremes we find various dualist models—represented by Germany, Denmark, and France—in which a company is seen as the result of a joint effort of labor and capital. Here, both "social partners" have more or less say in management: in more paternalistic or human-relations-oriented firms, the preponderance is on the side of management (i.e., owner representatives), with labor being only consulted; in more democratic and human-resources-oriented firms, no stable pattern of preponderance of one of the partners is tolerated, and true co-decisions are possible.

Note that the three countries representing dualist approaches—Germany, France, and Denmark—do not only stand for more or less equal power sharing. They also differ with respect to the basis for that power sharing. In Germany and France it is mainly the law; in Denmark, collective bargaining. Looking at these three countries[1] a little more in detail (the two others are of less interest because the situations they represent seem to have little future—the pure capitalist model [England] being clearly on its way out, and the pure communist model [Yugoslavia] just as clearly not about to be widely copied in the Western world), it becomes apparent that different emphasis is given here and there to various forms of worker participation.

In Germany, France, and Denmark—all three—worker councils and some form of worker participation on the board are mandatory. However, in Germany the unions seek to extend worker participation within the company in an effort to get more representatives into decision-making positions. In France, the unions prefer to exert external pressures and are not interested in sharing managerial responsibilities. In Denmark, the unions have long been pushing for participation in the managerial decision-making process within companies (while also trying to strengthen the unions' collective bargaining position at the outside). But lately they seem to have some doubts about the compatibility of the two approaches: the question has been raised whether participation in managerial decisions does not lead to too close an identification of unions with management, and whether it reduces union credibility as defender of workers against managerial exploitation.

In France, unions and leftist parties propose to subject the management of a number of big companies to public control by nationalizing them; other companies have indeed already been nationalized (like Aérospatiale, Renault, Charbonnages de France, Société Générale, Crédit Lyonnais, and others). In Germany and Denmark no such movement exists. To the contrary, in Germany, certain nationalized companies (like VW or VEBA) were "reprivatized." As to ownership control by workers (and unions), not much progress has been made in any of the three countries, except for a few isolated cases in which owners turned their companies over to the workers, or in which the workers took over a bankrupt company. But while in Germany the unions have specifically stated that co-ownership was not on top of their priority list, in Denmark there is a rather far-reaching proposal to gradually associate workers (mainly via a union-managed investment fund) in 50 percent of the capital of the nation's larger firms.

Finally, in Germany, and to a lesser extent in Denmark, there seems to be considerable interest in shop-floor democratization and job redesign. In Germany about 40 percent of the total labor force is already on flexible working hours, job enrichment has been the subject of collective bargaining, and experiments with group decision making at the lowest levels are frequent. However, the unions have very recently decided not to push for more of this (apparently

[1] In the Netherlands and Austria the situation is in many respects comparable to that in Germany; in Italy, to that in France; and in Norway and Sweden, to that in Denmark.

fearing that workers having a very high degree of identification with their jobs and with their company's goals would eventually feel that union membership was unnecessary). The French unions and workers have always been more suspicious about efforts to involve them at the shop-floor level. Thus, they have done comparatively little to secure that involvement.

Looking for reasons behind these different approaches in the three countries, it seems as if union ideology, power, and structure, and the political climate and constellation are the major explanatory variables, while degree and pattern of industrialization or the standard of living have had indirect influence, at most. It does make a difference whether or not a union movement is militant, whether or not it is united and powerful (externally as well as with regard to the rank and file), whether it operates more on a plant than on a more aggregate level, and whether or not a strong socialist party exists and has strong relationships with the unions.

EVALUATION OF DIFFERENT APPROACHES

Whatever the approach, worker participation has been hailed by its advocates[2] as setting an end to the exploitation of man by man, as enhancing the dignity of workers, as eliminating the class struggle, as realizing freedom, equality, and fraternity,[3] as reconciling planning with individual freedom, as subordinating economic activity to social goals, or as providing economic democracy as a basis for and supplement to political democracy. On the other hand, its opponents claim that worker participation makes quick and efficient managerial decision making impossible; that it leads to dangerous leaks of information; that it is incompatible with free enterprise and private property; that it will put unbearable burdens on companies; that it discourages investors; that it does not enhance democracy, but syndicalism; and that it will lead to a syndicalist state.

So far, it seems as if worker participation has not borne out the hopes of its advocates nor the fears of its opponents. Neither has it brought about a major change in the condition of the workers, nor made business less efficient. Its various applications seem altogether to have had only a very modest impact.

The major reason for this modest impact is that, in general, the fundamental attitudes of the parties involved have not really changed. On the employer side, some may admit worker participation, but without really trusting workers' qualifications or motivations. Others may offer involvement, but deny the workers real influence. Managers continue to be afraid of losing their prerogatives[4] and of losing control to union officials who are foreign to the company. They also shy away from facing subordinates in situations where the latter can challenge their authority, and in which conflicts have to be met head-on. In short, there seems to be little in it for management but potential trouble. Similarly, on the labor side, it appears to many that there is as much to lose as to gain from participation. This is true for both union officials and workers. The

[2] They argue typically in the tradition of socialist thought or Christian social teaching, which is based on the writing of Marx and Leo XIII, but also on Proudhomme, Liebknecht, Kautzky, Kinsley, or the Webbs.

[3] In comparison, capitalism is said to favor freedom at the expense of equality, and communism to favor equality at the cost of freedom.

[4] Note that owner-managers are likely to be afraid of the erosion of their rights as owners, while professional managers (who like to think they perform a function for which they alone are qualified) are primarily worried about the erosion of their rights as experts.

former fear that they may be co-opted by management, and that participation, if successful, might make their role as intermediary between management and labor unnecessary. To many of the latter, participation spells manipulation. Moreover, they often feel that to let things happen and criticize management for it is so much easier than to make things happen and take the responsibility for it. And indeed, especially where participation has been introduced from the top down, it has often created more stress and feelings of frustration than of satisfaction.

The global judgment passed on worker participation, and the explanations given for its success (or lack of it) do not contribute very much to a better understanding of it. They only boil down to the fact that changes in attitudes cannot be decreed and that they come about very slowly. It may, therefore, be useful to take a second and closer look, and to make an assessment based on an analysis of the various forms of participation in the light of the problems they address.

We are, in this context, concerned with two kinds of problems: those concerning the inadequacies of decisions made by managers who are not best qualified or in a position to decide; and those concerning the frustrations suffered by those who are not involved in a decision which affects them. In the first case, the focus is on the decision; in the second case, it is on the decision maker. In the first case, participation may improve the quality of the decisions made; in the second, it may increase the satisfaction of those associated in the decision-making process.

As to the problem of improving the quality of decisions, we can distinguish technical and political decision; and as to the question of power distribution, we can distinguish between the control in and of a firm.

Participation and the Quality of Technical Decisions

The traditional "scientific" way of managing a business was to run it like a machine. So long as most of the work consisted of machine-tending, this made sense. So long as the production chain was the archetype of industrial operation, minute division of labor, simplification, standardization, and routinization meant maximum efficiency. Managers (who considered themselves, above all, as engineers applying laws of physics and principles of management) would define the "one best way" of organizing the business as a whole, as well as of each individual task. And the more discipline in carrying out their plans, the better.

Today, only a very small percentage of industrial operations correspond to an assembly-line model, and industry has been losing its importance as the main employer. Service jobs (as well as many industrial jobs) cannot any longer be rigidly structured. They are too complex and too unpredictable. Each worker has to cope with contingencies. He must meet them by making decisions, alone or as a member of a team or task force. Passive compliance to a set of rules is not sufficient. Efficiency depends on mobilizing the knowledge, initiative, and creativity of all human resources, and not only of a managing elite.

This mobilization and release of potential requires changes in organizational structure and management style: job enrichment instead of overspecialization, use of the pyramid instead of the circle as the basic organizational form, better communications, and supportive instead of authoritative leadership style. On the other hand, formal, institutional (nonspontaneous), and representative participation seems of little use unless it can be argued that it effectively forces managers to abandon inhibiting organization structures and their self-centered and self-serving leadership styles. But arguing the effectiveness of formal representative participation is, at least in the short run, unconvincing. Indeed, it seems quite likely (and is often the fact) that a worker representation has either no real influence or, when it has some, is perceived as using it to further the workers' rather than the company's interests, which does not encourage managers to give the workers any more rope anywhere.

Participation and "Political" Decisions

Managers are traditionally assumed to make only technical and economic decisions in the interest of the owners of the business—decisions for which objective criteria exist and which require their specific expertise. In reality they also make (especially in large corporations) more and more important "political" decisions—i.e., decisions in response to demands from all kinds of interest groups for which there are no other standards but personal values and preferences. These decisions require or imply a definition of the public interest.

It may be doubtful whether managers should make these decisions autonomously. Some critics have even gone so far as to suggest that, given their experiences and way of thinking and living, managers would seem to be among the least qualified. But even if that were not the case, one could argue that these political decisions could be improved (if not in each individual case, certainly on the average) if they reflected the priorities of a great number of interested parties, rather than those of managers only.

The question, then, is whether worker or union participation on the top management level would provide sufficient input and could confer legitimacy to those decisions. It seems as if worker participation could indeed be a step in the right direction, insofar as it brings a new and important group to the decision-making process. However, not much would be gained if one merely transferred decision-making power from one autonomous group to another, or if one combined two interest groups (employers and unions) who would, together, be strong enough to resist all public control. Thus, if one wants to make sure that the big companies act in the public interest, it is probably not enough to put union officials alongside managers in top positions of corporate decision making. It would be desirable that at that level of decision all those concerned are represented: owners, employees, consumers, suppliers, and different special-interest groups. For, if one denies managers the capacity or right to define the commonweal, one has to do so the same when it comes to employees or unions—even if the latter, by the mere number of their membership, can make a better claim to represent the general public.

Participation and Alienation

Today's workers know more and have more than ever before. Thus, they are less and less willing to make substantial sacrifices on the job in order to get the money that will provide satisfactions off the job. They want more meaningful jobs, more self-direction and self-control. They want more money and more dignity (instead of more money at the price of dignity). This means, above all, that they want to be treated not as children or as robots, but as responsible adults.

All this, in turn, means that workers want to have some say in what they do at work, how, and when; they want to get meaningful feedback on their efforts; they want to be coached, rather than bossed (to be better oriented, to feel greater security, and to get more recognition); they want to be informed about developments affecting their jobs and future—in short, they want to enjoy informal participation at every organizational level.[5]

It does not mean the presence of a few labor representatives in a workers' council or on some management committees, for these have little positive impact on the rank and file. For worker involvement and satisfaction depends on the treatment workers get from their immediate superiors, the composition and functioning of the groups in which they work, the control system, the job design, and working hours. And all these aspects are typically not, and often cannot be effectively handled by persons other than those directly concerned. Thus, the positive impact on the rank and file is minimal. Only those few who represent the rank and file would experience less powerlessness, meaninglessness, social isolation, and self-estrangement.

Participation and Power Distribution

Finally, participation must be seen in the light of the distribution of power within companies and society. The question here is whether participation is a means to achieve more power equalization, or whether it should or will lead to the replacement of one power elite by another.

Informal participation certainly does change the rapport between manager and the managed—in the direction away from giving and executing orders and toward a helping relationship between partners who are functionally, more than hierarchically, differentiated. This does, however, not have to mean a reversal of their roles. As a matter of fact, while the managed gain more influence over their jobs and work environment, the managers don't lose their right (and duty) to leadership. The power distribution is not one of a zero-sum game.

It is doubtful whether the same can be said about formal representative participation. First, the declared purpose of this form of participation is to curtail managerial decision-making power and to transfer some of it to the workers or unions. Moreover, the representative form implies that power is not really diluted, but remains concentrated in the hands of two small groups instead of one. Finally, so long as these groups see themselves, if not in outright opposition, at least in competition with each other, any gain of influence of one will mean a loss of influence of the other.

CONCLUSION

Without entering into a detailed analysis of particular modalities, we may conclude that formal representative participation of workers or unions in managerial decision making is a rather inadequate answer to the problems of reducing worker alienation and mobilizing all human resources of a firm operating in a complex and dynamic environment. It may be somewhat more

[5] Note that worker satisfaction with this kind of participation varies with the perceived quantity and quality of participation—i.e., the perceived amount of involvement and the perceived confidence of the superiors in their subordinates.

Table 2 A Normative Model for Different Forms of Worker Participation

Problems \ Solutions	What	Where	Who	How
Individual vs. organization: alienation	Job design working hours	Shop floor, department	Managers (immediate superiors), workers	Humanization of work
Management vs. workers: status, power, security	Working conditions, personnel and social policies	Plant, subsidiary	Managers (top level), workers' representatives	Codetermination
Company vs. competition: economic performance; mobilization of human resources	Organization structure, leadership style	Company	Managers (at all levels), workers	Matrix organization, Human resources management
Business vs. environment: poverty, social unrest, ecology	Plant locations; income distribution; consumer protection; nondiscrimination; support of education, health care, arts, sports, housing; control of waste, heat, noise, esthetic pollution	Company, industry, nation	Managers, owners, workers, unions, customers, government, interest groups	Industrial democracy

adequate when the problems consist of defining the social responsibilities of a firm or changing the power distribution in business.

We can summarize our argument in a normative model (Table 2).

Worker participation as a concept is here to stay. This follows, on the one hand, from the growing awareness that business firms are social and political institutions as well as economic ones, and, on the other hand, from the general development of our social and cultural environment. What specific forms of worker participation will be more prevalent than others is much less certain. Let us say only this: First, in trying to make predictions one should judge different approaches not only on their immediate merits or difficulties, but also on their potential as models for learning. The full acceptance of any model will take time. Second, one should encourage experimentation with various approaches rather than argue too quickly for a single model. The full acceptance of a model will depend on its appropriateness in a specific cultural and political environment and its adaptation to the peculiar economic and social reality of each company.

ALVAR O. ELBING, HERMAN GADON, and JOHN R. M. GORDON

Flexible Working Hours: The Missing Link

Control of working time has been one of the most universally cherished management prerogatives and has been viewed as a foundation of complex industrial organization. Indeed, the lack of respect for attendance and punctuality, as prescribed by management rules, is often cited as one critical problem facing today's management, both in highly developed countries where attitudes toward work appear to be changing and in developing countries attempting to adapt an unskilled labor force to modern production practices.

Presently, however, in thousands of companies throughout the world managements are relinquishing rigid control of working time by sharing control with workers through arrangements known as *flexible working hours*. In most of these cases fixed-working-hour systems seem to have been abandoned relatively easily for a variety of reasons: (1) there is no necessarily positive relationship between punctuality and performance; (2) time at work and productivity are not necessarily positively correlated; (3) rigid time-control systems have caused counterproductive systems of pegging; and (4) control systems imposed upon the individual do not appear to be universally applicable or effective.

Flexible-working-hour schemes are rapidly replacing traditional fixed-hour systems in many European companies. The practice was begun in Germany in the late 1960s. In 1970 ten companies were using flexible working hours; that number is about 6000 today. The results have been generally positive, transcending cultures and crossing national boundaries. Although data have been difficult to obtain—we are currently engaged in research projects in both Europe and North America to accumulate more information—the reactions of managers, supervisors, and employees have been universally favorable. In fact, in our three-year search in Europe we have found almost no negative reaction to the system, once it has been initiated. Since the switch to flexible working hours appears to be spreading rapidly, it is useful to attempt to explain its general acceptance and to place it within the appropriate theoretical framework for analysis.

Details of the design, operation, and experience with flexible-working-hour systems have been presented elsewhere.[1] Briefly, however, flexible working hours are an arrangement that gives employees some freedom in choosing the hours each day during which they will work. An employee may begin working at any time within specified limits in the morning (7:00 to 9:00, for instance); during a core period in the morning (such as 9:00 to 11:30) all employees in the organization are expected to be on the job.

---

[1] See J. R. M. Gordon and A. Elbing, "The Flexible Hours' Work Week—European Trend Is Growing," *The Business Quarterly* (Winter 1971); A. Elbing, H. Gadon, and J. R. M. Gordon, "Time for a Human Timetable," *European Business* (Autumn 1973), pp. 46–54; and A. Elbing, H. Gadon, and J. R. M. Gordon, "Flexible Working Hours: It's About Time," *Harvard Business Review* (January–February 1974), pp. 18–33.

Lunch may be taken within a band of time around noon, usually within a legally established minimum. After lunch all employees must be at work during another required core time (1:30 to 4:00). Following this core time an employee may leave work at any time during another flexible period (4:00 to 6:00). This means that the number of hours worked by an employee may vary from day to day. Usually over an accounting period such as a week or a month, an employee is required to maintain his total number of hours worked within a specified range.

PARTICIPATION

As a management system flexible working hours fall within the general area of theory known as participative management. Although participation in decision making has considerably different cultural connotations—from the worker councils of Germany and the group decision making of North America to the leaderless groups of Norway—it usually indicates management systems in which the employee has some say about some conditions or processes affecting his work.

Flexible working hours should be considered a participative system since when it is available, the employee has the opportunity to either contribute or to withhold his contributions toward meeting the organization's goals. Since work levels tend to vary, he has the ability to either work longer hours when there is more to do and then take off when things are slow, or vice versa. Since the potential availability of this "free" labor force, when needed during peak hours, is under the worker's control, flexible working hours can be considered as participative in nature.

Various plans to provide workers with satisfaction and the enterprise with increased performance have been proposed and tried. The Scanlon Plan, job enrichment, work teams, organization development, management by objectives, and other related programs are all attempts to apply the theory relating the source of human satisfaction to the organization of work. In general these plans have been based on some concept of worker participation in organizational decisions.

Systems of participative management have worked well in many instances, but some evidence suggests that participative systems have worked best in organizations where they were not needed—that is, in organizations that were already open, free, and involved—but have not worked as well in authoritarian, rigid, or highly structured organizations, where they may be most needed. There is no clear evidence that participative systems have fulfilled their theoretical potential, for several apparent reasons:

1. Participative systems tend to violate the traditional value systems of some managers and some organizations. If management is not convinced of the systems's real worth or feels threatened by its introduction, there may be participation in theory, but not in reality. This is quickly perceived by employees, who then resist real participation. In general, therefore, participative systems must fit with the value system of both management and organization.

2. A second consideration is that the benefits of participation tend to be in the long term. The results may be hardly visible in the short term, except in employee interest, if any. Long-term benefits, however, usually do not serve as short-term motivators unless they can be linked directly to the results of one's daily behavior. Therefore, the relationship between participation and its

benefits is not always clear in the short run, and this frequently interferes with its effectiveness.

3. When the participative system is imposed from above and employees are directed to use it, it becomes as authoritarian as a nonparticipative system. The common attitude is "if management requires it, is it really for me?" Unfortunately, in their fervor to "change," "be modern," or to "rescue a sinking ship," some managers impose participative systems as though they will work magically. A system that is imposed is by definition nonparticipative.

4. Participative systems are sometimes initiated on the presumption that employees have a participative spirit. But if employees have learned to function in a nonparticipative environment, there is no reason why a participative spirit should automatically exist. If no efforts have been made to produce such an environment, it may not exist at all. In some cultures, in fact, the employee has had no prior family, school, or social experience in participation and is not prepared for it. Most participative systems require some preparation.

5. Finally, many participative systems are actually carried out through representatives and therefore do not touch everyone. Although representative systems are participative from management's point of view, they are effectively participative only when the employees so perceive them. If distance develops between the representatives and the employees, no real participation may exist.

Hearing or reading that under the right conditions participation will stimulate improvement, increase commitment, and enlist the willing cooperation of employees is not sufficient justification for its implementation.

THE EXPERIENCE WITH FLEXIBLE WORKING HOURS

In our studies of the use of flexible working hours over the past three years, we have observed the following organizational, individual, and community effects.

Organizational Effects

Organizations using flexible working hours have reported a general increase in productivity resulting from reduced sick leave, turnover, absenteeism, and overtime. In addition, one large Swiss company attributes a 7-percent overall increase in productivity entirely to flexible working hours. These general effects have been similarly reported in every culture that we have been able to study so far. In addition, many of these same organizations have also reported positive changes in supervisory behavior, employee attitudes, and work cooperation. Our studies have turned up copious reports of satisfaction with the new system and no examples of organizations returning to fixed hours.

Individual Effects

Employees on flexible working hours overwhelmingly report increased personal satisfaction based on their ability to balance demands of their personal lives with demands of the organization. Surveys of individual satisfaction consistently indicate that about 90 percent of respondents wish to keep or extend the system.

Community Effects

The individual's ability to choose when to arrive and when to leave work has led to his ability to avoid the peak demand times for transportation, power, and recreation. Since flexible working hours are just beginning, there is not much data available about the cumulative effects of this change. The reduction in peak demand times for transportation, power, and recreation, however, suggest important hypotheses about the potential saving of energy and other community resources. In one community where about 60 percent of the population is on flexible working hours, such a change in resource consumption has been documented in terms of bus usage. With more people riding buses, the company can get by with 10 percent fewer buses because peak loads are reduced. One insurance company study shows a reduction in accidents by employees on flexible working hours.

WHY FLEXIBLE WORKING HOURS ARE EFFECTIVE

How can one account for the generally more effective response to flexible working hours than to other systems of participation in management? It appears that the assumptions of flexible hours differ from the assumptions of other participative systems. From our observations of flexible working hours in action, we can speculate why they have been received so well. Looking at the reasons for the general failure of other participative systems, we see that *none is applicable to flexible working hours.*

1. First, once the system of flexible working hours is established, it no longer violates or is necessarily in conflict with managerial and organizational value systems. When a system of flexible hours is initiated, management is not required to forego a significant part of its managerial philosophy. In fact, as long as organizational goals are met, the issue of value systems tends to be irrelevant. In general, there is little threat to management or to the organization by the introduction of flexible working hours, so resistance is generally minimal and acceptance universal.

2. The short-term benefits of flexible working hours are felt on a day-to-day basis. The individual can choose the relationship he wishes between his personal life and his organizational life, and he can realize the benefits immediately. The long-term or secondary benefits accrue at the same time, but the success of the system does not depend on the presence of those longer-term benefits. The availability and appearance of short-term benefits are in some ways unique to flexible working hours.

3. Flexible working hours are not imposed on employees since they are not required to change their work habits. The system is available and an employee can use it or not as he desires. It is not uncommon for employees to ignore the system at its inception and to continue to arrive and leave at the same times as before. There need be no pressure from management for any change. At the same time, the employee can test out the system gradually, if he wishes, with little risk to himself. This is a significant difference from most participative systems.

4. There is no presumption of any underlying participative spirit. Any spirit required will develop.

5. Finally, flexible working hours potentially involve the whole labor force.

Everyone can participate directly. If a man wishes to come late or leave early, he makes his own decision, and therefore participates in the organization. This is significantly different from other systems.

From our observations, a system of flexible working hours is unique among participative systems for these five reasons.

Although flexible working hours seem to be built on sound motivational theories, they have a biological foundation also. Studies of fatigue have shown that people have different personal rhythms. We tend to work at different speeds at different times, as functions of both physiology and mood. Performance suffers, concentration fails, mistakes occur, quality is irregular, and accidents are more frequent as a result of fatigue. We have only to look at our long expressways, with their warning signs, to note the effect of fatigue and boredom.

Most studies of fatigue show that performance improves following periods of rest and variety. Since personal rhythms vary, it is sensible to allow each person to decide for himself when he needs rest and change. One can also conclude that as a consequence of such an arrangement people approach work each time more ready for it. This proposition was made and recently confirmed by Wolfgang Hildebrandt at the University of Aachen.[2] Taking two variables, fixed hours and flexible hours, Hildebrandt found that under otherwise constant conditions, workers on a single repetitive task had a 17-percent greater physiological readiness for work when they controlled their own working time than when fixed hours were imposed.

WORKING HYPOTHESES ABOUT FLEXIBLE HOURS

As a result of our observations of flexible-working-hour systems, discussions with employers and workers using these systems, inquiries into organizational, personal, and societal consequences, and our own previous analysis, we have formulated several hypotheses to explain the success of the system and to place it in juxtaposition to other systems of participative management. If our current research—or the research of others—can substantiate these hypotheses, it is possible that flexible working hours may become a conceptual as well as a behavioral link between the theory and practice associated with participative management systems.

Hypothesis 1: Given the ability to allocate their time between demands of work and personal needs outside of work, employees find satisfactions not previously available to them that build a strong commitment to flexible working hours.

Observations: Although companies tend to approach flexible working hours experimentally at first, usually in a small department, the arrangement invariably has become permanent and has been extended to additional personnel. In data gathered from Europe, North America, and Japan covering a period from 1967 to the present, involving roughly 3 million persons in the private and public sectors in white- and blue-collar jobs, in manufacturing and service organizations, we have yet to learn of a company returning to fixed hours after experimenting with flexible hours.

---

[2] W. Hildebrandt, *Untersuchung zur Berücksichtigung der menschlichen Tagesrhythmik durch eine variable Arbeitszeitregelung* (Mainz, Aachen: Malteserstrasse 9, am Ponttor).

Assumptions: Flexible working hours appeal to man's requirement to be treated as a whole person with needs outside of work as well as at work. In general, the literature on job satisfaction and participation ignores factors outside of the organization and is concerned with satisfaction at the place of work. With flexible working hours, the individual has the freedom to consider all of his needs and to decide which work schedule suits him best.

Hypothesis 2: Persons in all cultures and countries will respond favorably to an opportunity to allocate their time between demands of work and personal life.

Observations: Flexible working hours have become a permanent arrangement in a large number of countries, including underdeveloped ones, and in diverse cultures. This system is common practice in northern Europe, it has been tried and accepted at an increasing rate in North America, and it has been successfully adopted by enterprises in Japan, Greece, Spain, and New Zealand. Hengstler-Gleitzeit, a manufacturer of time-keeping hardware, projects an increase to 5 million covered employees by the end of 1975. Regardless of the culture into which it is initiated, our observations of the response to the flexible-hour system seem to suggest that it follows a similar pattern.

Assumptions: People everywhere have the same need to be treated as whole persons. Perhaps because an operational concept that takes one's personal life into consideration has not been available before, his work life in industrial societies has taken precedence over his personal life. In our experience with international management-development programs, we have found that there are more similarities in reaction to work than there are differences based on culture. Flexible working hours provide an opportunity for individuals to satisfy basic needs common to all people with patterns of behavior that are acceptable within their own cultures, while also satisfying the organization's need for performance.

Hypothesis 3: Flexible working hours provide opportunities for self-control that act as a continual motivator for improved performance on the job.

Observations: We have a considerable amount of aggregate data that show a strong positive correlation between flexible working hours and effective on-the-job performance. Furthermore, improvements in performance, such as lower turnover, higher quality, fewer accidents, less absenteeism, reduction in overtime, and higher production have been sustained rather than rising and then declining, as often happens after the introduction of new programs.

Assumptions: We assume, as does much of the literature,[3-5] that self-control is generally a more effective and predictable motivator of high performance than external controls. Given the freedom, within limits, to decide when he will work and when he will not, a person will approach work more ready for it and with a stronger commitment to do it well than when he is told when to work.

Hypothesis 4: The time made available to first-line supervisors resulting from a decrease in policing activities under flexible working hours is likely to be devoted to more and better planning and organizing of work, which will result in improved performance of the work group.

---

[3] A. Maslow, "A Theory of Human Motivation," *Psychological Review*, Vol. 50 (1943), pp. 370–396.

[4] D. McGregor, "The Human Side of Enterprise," *Adventures in Thought and Actions*, Proceedings of the Fifth Anniversary Convocation of the School of Industrial Management. MIT Press, 1957.

[5] F. Hertzberg, B. Mausner, and B. B. Snyderman, *The Motivation of Work*. Wiley, 1957.

Observations: Many studies have identified the first-line supervisor as a critical factor in influencing the performance of his subordinates. We have seen that supervisors who are introduced to flexible working hours replace policing activities with planning and organizing ones. Since employees come and go at their own discretion during flexible periods, they must be trusted to do their work responsibly. Close supervision decreases, delegation increases, and supervisors provide more service.

Assumptions: The first-line supervisor is a key element in the motivation of his subordinates. Given an opportunity—rather than being told—to plan and organize, and the training to do it competently, he will welcome the chance to decrease his policing activities. A note of caution is necessary here, however. Though our data indicate that supervisors would generally prefer to increase time devoted to planning and organizing, management sometimes neglects to provide them with the necessary skills to do it. In the absence of the competence needed to implement flexible working hours successfully, supervisors may resist the change or may not be able to implement it satisfactorily.

Hypothesis 5: In an environment of trust, subordinates will respond by meeting the responsibilities they are given.

Observations: Case studies of organizations show that employees who have been seen as marginal, lazy, or ineffective have become productive workers under flexible working hours. While flexible working hours should not be seen as a cure for undesirable individual employees, they have sometimes responded dramatically, with improved performance, to the opportunity to increase control over their lives. More generally, the positive reaction of personnel is reinforced by the support received from supervisors with whom they must jointly develop and accept job and performance standards. Where goal setting is shared, supervisors as well as subordinates develop a mutual commitment to flexible scheduling arrangements and the confidence in their ability to take personal and organizational advantage of them.

Assumptions: We assume that interpersonal relations are strongly influenced by reciprocity. When a person is treated like an adult and given responsibility he will act responsibly. When a person is trusted he will respond by being trustworthy. The inclination of people to respond in kind has been widely reported and is sometimes identified by sociologists as "a universal norm of reciprocity."[6] Because employees are likely to respond positively to positive treatment, we also assume that the reverse is true. If employees are distrusted they will respond in kind. To some extent, therefore, employees are conditioned to behave as they do. Through a structural change, flexible working hours produce changes in behavior and attitude.

Hypothesis 6(A): When personnel are allowed to take responsibility for maintaining the flow of production by deciding among themselves how to overlap or interact with each other, many ways to coordinate become possible without loss of production or increased unit costs, which provide both individuals and organizations the benefits of flexibility.

Hypothesis 6(B): Arrangements that change the line or flow of work to take advantage of teams of workers, or increased in-process inventory that allows

---

[6] A. Gouldner, "The Norm of Reciprocity: A Preliminary Statement." *American Sociological Review* (April 1960), pp. 161–178.

self-regulation of work, will provide savings which may offset the increases in unit costs attributed to the additional investment.

Observations: Investigation of manufacturing firms using flexible working hours reveals that operations seen as so interdependent that flexibility was not possible without substantially increased costs have been successfully adapted to the new scheduling arrangements. Provisions for in-process inventory between operations, breakup of linear assembly lines into subassemblies produced by teams, allowance for employees to pace and space themselves as they see fit as long as they make the connections necessary to maintain work flow, have shown that interdependence can take many forms. Given the opportunity to take responsibility for maintenance of the production flow in an increasing number of instances, employees have been able to introduce flexibility without increasing unit costs despite some increase in total cost.

Assumptions: We assume that manufacturing operations heretofore seen as inflexible can in fact be changed, although the change would appear to raise costs. Our studies, and those of others, indicate that there is considerably more room for flexibility without unit-cost increase than had been supposed. We are not presently facing the issue of choosing between increased individual satisfaction and higher costs, though certainly this is something with which our society will be forced to contend more often as time passes.

Hypothesis 7: When employees have a stake in solving a problem and possess the competence to deal with it in an atmosphere of trust, they will find ingenious solutions that have eluded management.

Observations: We have observed many instances in which management has said "it can't be done," but has allowed employees to try, only to learn that the employees developed ingenious ways of overcoming objections to the introduction of flexible working hours. We have also seen that this has happened with organizational processes that presented problems management could not solve.

Assumptions: When an employee is given the opportunity to apply his skills to problems in which he has a stake, the added resources are likely to produce unusual and unforeseen solutions. The solution to the problem of traffic congestion at the Messerschmitt-Bölkow-Blohn plant at Ottobruhn, Germany, is a good example and illustrates as well the benefits of flexible working hours to organization and community. Each employee at Messerschmitt became his own search party. Individually, employees found new patterns of transportation, which evened out the traffic flow. With freedom to change in response to direct feedback ("Is the road congested or not?"), employees adjusted their arrival and departure times until they minimized their travel times. Each employee completed his own feedback loop.

Hypothesis 8: Systems of participation that do not meet the needs of the whole person contain an inherent contradiction which undermines their integrity and therefore leads to disappointment, limited involvement, and limited satisfaction.

Observations: Many participation programs fail to produce the expected involvement and results; among these are organization-development projects (OD) and management by objectives (MBO). We have observed that, in contrast to flexible working hours, those programs tend to focus on the needs of the organization rather than the needs of the individual even though they are intended to increase individual satisfaction.

Assumptions: Flexible working hours allow one to respond continually to his self-identified needs. Therefore, the system is consistent with the ideals and values professed by the concept of sharing influence through participation and allows a person to commit himself to it without risking being hurt or violated.

Hypothesis 9: New attitudes of trust will be acquired rapidly as experience with flexible working hours confirms the value of trust.

Observations: We have observed that many programs for participation first require a change in attitudes. Much time-consuming effort is expended on this objective, starting at the top of the organization, with uncertain results. Attitude changes that are supposed to lead to changes in behavior are achieved at an agonizingly slow pace and are extended only haltingly to lower levels of the hierarchy. Benefits sometimes never reach the wage earner.

Assumptions: It is easier for changes in attitudes to follow changes in behavior than vice versa. If attitudes are to change first, one must trust without first having the experience to reinforce it. Under these circumstances there is bound to be little risk taking and considerable withholding. The greater the stakes, the more reservations we can expect to encounter.

A system of flexible working hours is a structural change that allows people to behave differently and therefore to acquire new attitudes of trust as a consequence of the change rather than as a cause of it. Since trust is required for the success of participation, our studies suggest that a structural change such as flexible working hours, preceding attempts to introduce MBO or OD, will increase their rate and extent of acceptance and effectiveness.

CONCLUSION

Flexible working hours appear to be a readily acceptable, workable arrangement based on biological fact and sound motivational theory. The critical element is the choice a person is allowed to make as to when he works and for how long a time he works. Taking constraints established by agreement, an employee ought to be able to sort out his own needs and to arrange his time to satisfy them. No employer can program the commitment that an employee develops when he takes responsibility for himself.

Not only does self-regulation place more resources for problem solving at the disposal of the firm, but it seems also, in all developed, affluent societies, to be a basic source of satisfaction. When a society offers enough security to an individual to release him from preoccupation with making a living, he then becomes interested in living the "good life." And the good life is in part a function of a person's opportunities to decide for himself how he will live it. Autonomy seems to be in itself an enriching goodness.

Flexible working hours appeal to one's need for autonomy, and this is a common denominator that transcends culture. If the culture sets limits, the individual decides what they are and how he will respond to them, whether he is in West Germany, Japan, the United States, or France. A system of flexible working hours potentially places at an organization's disposal all the resources available to an individual, creatively applied, to solve problems it is facing. Thus, in flexible working hours we have an example of mutual commitment and reciprocity. Altruism is not an issue.

Flexible working hours illustrate dramatically the universal applicability of psychological theories that tell us that persons who mature in a healthy way move from childlike dependence in a process of growth toward a desire for autonomy and a need to participate responsibly with others in efforts to influence the environment in which they live.

Management by objectives, organization development, job enrichment, and self-governing work teams all are programs that organizations are using with mixed success to relieve the pressures at the work place which lead to anomie. These programs usually require substantial changes in the culture of the enterprise. One hopes for the best from them.

The reason the flexible-working-hour system has been generally more successful than other forms of participative management is that it gives the employee personal benefit. The flexible-hour system is a widely accepted, easily administered arrangement that can help organizations to acquire the values, attitudes, behavior, and habits that build the trust necessary to support attempts to extend the quantity and quality of participation at work. It is not a system that will overcome an existing bad environment, but it has the potential of helping an organization move toward becoming a more participative, totally involving entity.

REFERENCES

In addition to the works cited in footnotes, the authors suggest the following works for further information.

Baudraz, J. F. *Horaire Variable de Travail,* Paris: Editions d'Organisation, 1973.
Bolton, J. H. *Flexible Working Hours.* London: Anbar Publications, 1971.
De Chalendar, J. *L'Amenagement du Temps.* Paris: Desclee, de Brouwer, 1971.
Kapp, B., and O. Proust. *Les Horaires Libres.* Paris: Chotard, 1973.
"West Germany—Pick Your Own Hours." *Time* (July 19, 1971), p. 47.

Chapter

13 The Managerial Bank Account

So far, we have looked at the management of human resources by focusing primarily on the resource itself. Consideration of the individual and of various organizational relationships can create a feeling for human resources that are productive—that can make the organization work. But we must recognize that people in organizations give only what they "can" give: for the organization to get commitment, productivity, creativity, etc., *the employee must be able to give it.* As we have seen, part of the worker's ability to do so is in the worker and in the worker's primary relationships. But the other part—perhaps the most critical part—depends on the behavior of the manager. It has in fact been said, "There are no good or bad workers, only good or bad managers." The manager must behave in such a way that workers can be productive and creative. This is the challenge.

STYLES OF LEADERSHIP

The search for "the" management or leadership style has had a long history, never very successful. Probably the reason is that it has always been a search for "the one" style, the "right" approach. Given the variety of needs of employees, the different organizational stituations and goals, and the different frames of reference of managers, there may be no single "right" approach.

The literature on leadership tends to focus on two general styles: task-oriented (that is, more leader-centered) and participation-oriented (more relationship-centered). The task-oriented leader places primary focus on the job—the task—the goal. The participative leader is more concerned with the social process of the leadership situation.

Correlation Between Style and Performance

Fred Fiedler has researched the subject of leadership extensively and concludes that there are three basic conditions for leadership—the combination of which determines the appropriateness of leadership style.

> From our research, my associates and I have identified three major factors that can be used to classify group situations: (1) position power of the leader, (2) task structure, and (3) leader-member personal relationships. Basically, these classifications measure the kind of power and influence the group gives its leader.
>
> . . .
>
> In our search for the most effective leadership style, we went back to the studies that we had been conducting for more than a decade. These studies investigated a wide variety of groups and leadership situations, including basketball teams, business management, military units, boards of directors, creative groups, and scientists engaged in pure research. In all of these studies, we could determine the groups that had performed their tasks successfully or unsuccessfully and then correlate the effectiveness of group performance with leadership style.

Figure 1 The Effective Leader

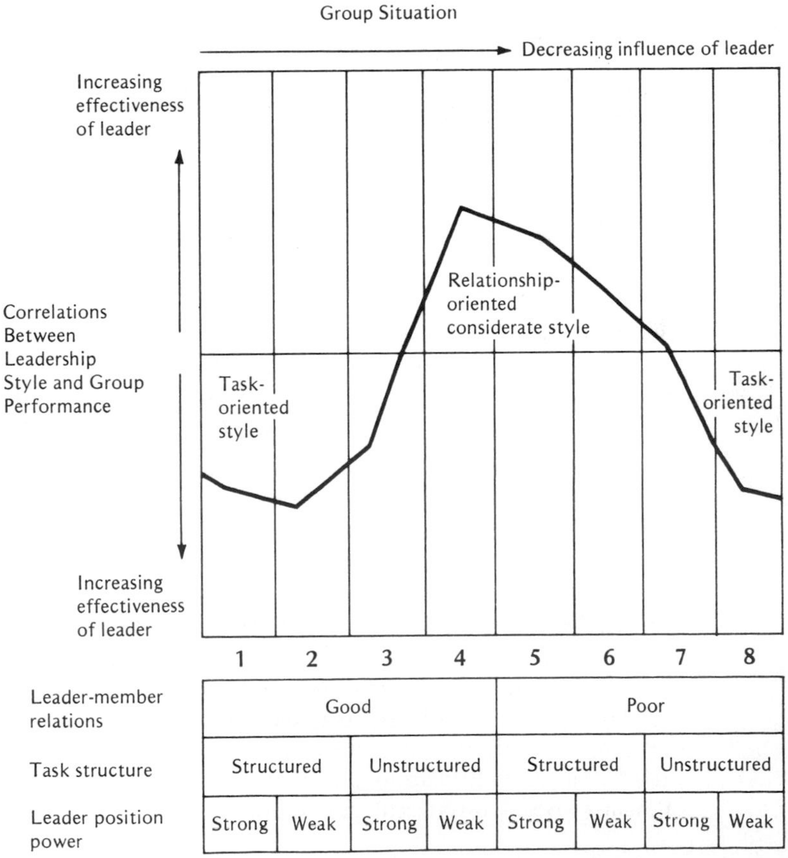

Group Situation

Decreasing influence of leader

Increasing effectiveness of leader

Correlations Between Leadership Style and Group Performance

Relationship-oriented considerate style

Task-oriented style

Task-oriented style

Increasing effectiveness of leader

	1	2	3	4	5	6	7	8
Leader-member relations	Good				Poor			
Task structure	Structured		Unstructured		Structured		Unstructured	
Leader position power	Strong	Weak	Strong	Weak	Strong	Weak	Strong	Weak

Directive leaders perform best in very favorable or in unfavorable situations. Permissive leaders are best in mixed situations. Graph is based on studies of over 800 groups.

Figure 2 Predicting Response to Leadership Approaches

	Task-Oriented/ Authoritarian Approach	Relationship-Oriented/ Participative Approach
Short-Run Response	Quick	Slow
Long-Run Response	Passive— "Waiting Behavior"	Creative— Commitment

Now by plotting these correlations of leadership style against our scale of group situations, we could, for the first time, find what leadership style works best in each situation. When we connected the median points on each column, the result was a bell-shaped curve.

The results show that a task-oriented leader performs best in situations at both extremes—those in which he has a great deal of influence and power, and also in situations where he has no influence and power over the group members.

Relationship-oriented leaders tend to perform best in mixed situations where they have only moderate influence over the group. A number of subsequent studies by us and others have confirmed these findings.

The results show that we cannot talk about simply good leaders or poor leaders. A leader who is effective in one situation may or may not be effective in another. Therefore, we must specify the situations in which a leader performs well or badly.[1]

As useful as Fiedler's model is, it is, however, not always possible to judge the leadership conditions in time to influence one's management approach. It is clear that different approaches fit different conditions, but the initiation of what turns out to be the wrong approach may not be discovered until too late. The damage is done, since the expectations are created. Once these expectations are created, they are difficult to change since a manager perceived as difficult to work with but who tries to behave differently may just be perceived as having a "good day." Likewise, a manager with whom we work well but who becomes more authoritarian may be perceived as having a "bad day."

Relating Managerial Approach to People's Perceptions

Since the needs, experiences, and expectations of subordinates vary, a new manager must behave in such a way that most people perceive that they can meet their needs and expectations within the manager's approach. To create this atmosphere, the manager has to develop a feeling of trust which we will call the "managerial bank account."

[1]From "Style or Circumstance: The Leadership Enigma" by Fred Fiedler, *Psychology Today,* March 1969. Copyright © 1969 Ziff-Davis Publishing Company. Reprinted by permission of *Psychology Today* Magazine.

Figure 3 Interplay Between the Leadership Approaches

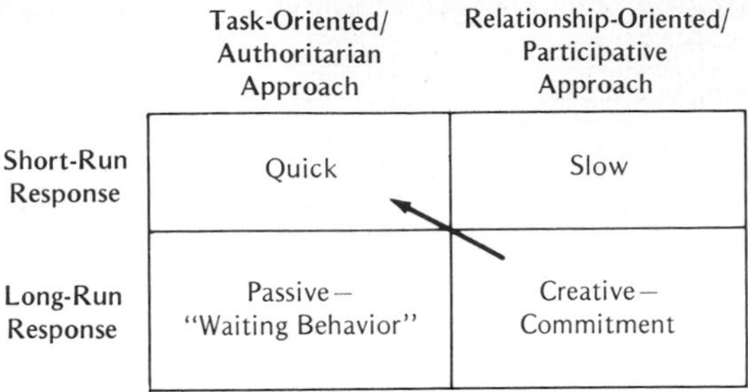

The conditions of a managerial bank account are not significantly different from those governing one's money reserves in a bank. The manager must work to build up reserves of trust and acceptance that can be drawn on in relationships with subordinates. When lacking a balance of trust, or when overdrawn in these relationships, the manager will constantly be challenged, resisted, or hindered, regardless of what the legal or organizational rules call for.

CHOICES IN BUILDING AND USING THE MANAGERIAL BANK ACCOUNT

It is useful to look at the continuum of leadership styles (Figure 2) in terms of building up a managerial bank account. We can predict, to a degree at least, how people will respond under different approaches. For example, some things need to happen immediately. We need to clear a building quickly in case of fire, to change the production run when it is outside of the tolerance limits, to take advantage of a market opportunity, etc. Task-oriented or authoritarian management approaches tend to be quick in the short run. They generate action, but action in the right direction only if the employees see that direction as meeting *their* needs as well.

Although potentially quick in the short run, what happens over time? The continued use of authoritarian methods in the long run will probably produce "waiting behavior"; that is, people will become *passive*. They will wait to be told what to do and when, and they will fail to introduce new or original ideas. When choosing such an approach, the manager may wish to have exactly that kind of behavior in the long run. The situation may be static, the options few, and the desirability of creativity low. Given these conditions, this managerial approach would be appropriate.

At the other extreme is some form of participative or relationship-oriented behavior. The possibilities are numerous. For our purposes we are interested only in the fact that in the short run these managerial styles tend to be slow. That is, some discussion, some checking out of other views, etc., takes time and delays decision making. But in the long run one would expect greater involvement, creativity, and commitment, especially in the processes of implementation. People more involved in decision making and planning tend to give more to them. Depending on what you want, you can choose your style. Or can you? Do the two styles have an effect on each other?

The concept of a managerial bank account is based on the premise that the only way you can benefit both from the speed of direct action in the short run, and creativity in the long run, is to first build a bank account of trust through participative means. Then, when you need something done quickly, you have an account to draw upon. Subordinates will be more apt to accept your orders because they know that they are and will be part of the broader picture (Figure 3).

A difficult time for all managers is at a point of change. If they take over a new unit, if there is a merger or a major reorganization, it is at these points that they may have little or no bank account at all. In fact, they may be overdrawn. Frequently, however, managers feel they must make changes immediately to establish their roles, their identities, their power in the organization. This may be necessary under some circumstances, but it has many risks. Negative reactions developed at this point may take superhuman managerial effort to overcome later—if, that is, one ever becomes aware that these negative reactions exist. Assuming that one has an overdrawn bank account at the time of change is generally a useful starting point.

CONCLUSION

When thinking about managerial style, it would serve the manager well to consider where his or her "bank account" is and what choices are available for maintaining and using it. A consideration of Fiedler's three conditions can expand the data base for choice. Through such considerations one can greatly improve one's overall managerial effectiveness.

ALVAR O. ELBING and HERMAN GADON

The Danger of Applying Packaged Solutions

Much has been said and written about such managerial techniques as T-Groups, sensitivity training, Blake's Grid, Likert's System 4, Kepner-Tregoe and Management by Objectives. Whenever we encounter one of these predetermined solutions to a difficult human problem, we are reminded of the story about the psychiatrist who met his new patient, an attractive young women with an eye-catching figure. The young lady proceeded to undress and quickly seduced the disarmed therapist. Later the patient said: "Well, doctor, that is my solution. What is my problem?"

Unhappily for many troubled companies, the world is full of salesmen with packaged solutions in search of a problem.

In the first place "packaged" programs are packaged by someone who expects to benefit from the sale of the package. Although some salesmen are deceptive, there is evidence to suggest that most packages are based on valid behavioral concepts, such as systematic thinking processes, motivation as a function of setting one's own goals, a good balance between human and product orientation, self-awareness, and clear job definitions.

What makes these programs "packaged" is that they are standardized, to be used in essentially the same way by everyone.

Firms which sell them often have names which sound academic or research oriented. "Scientific," "systems," "university" or words ending in "ictics" may appear in the title. Proof of value is supported by "evidence" of prior success available from any of the "approved" previous users.

Unfortunately the packaged program is usually not the panacea it portends to be, despite the validity of the underlying behavioral concepts. Success is often limited, and some results have been harmful.

Of course the same criticism could be levelled at almost any standardized product, including many business-school courses. There are valid reasons for packaging things, the main one being cost.

But packaged programs, by their very nature, tend to present themselves as ideal, ready-made solutions, straws for drowning managers to clutch at. Objective judgment as to their value is often suspended because, in many cases, the buyer finds himself unconsciously in league with the seller in selling the program to his organization.

The recent experience of a large European chemical company illustrates just what can happen.

For a long time the company had been faced with technical supervisors who failed to deal adequately with the human needs of their subordinates.

In spite of numerous interventions on his part, the personnel manager had

"The Perils of Packaged Solutions" by Alvar O. Elbing and Herman Gadon. Reprinted by special permission from the May 1974 issue of *International Management*.

been unable to overcome the technical orientation of these managers and to get them to function differently.

Morale declined, labor turnover increased, costs rose, and the personnel manager found himself on the defensive with top management.

While under pressure from his superiors to find a solution, an assistant introduced him to the salesman for a programmed organization-development package. In desperation, and encouraged by the assistant who had experienced the package in another company, the personnel manager became convinced that the package would solve his and the organization's problems.

He presented a proposal to the board of directors to expend the funds necessary to introduce the package and train several members of his staff to carry out the predetermined program. The board agreed and the package was introduced.

It turned out to be ineffective and gradually faded away. No concrete decision was made to terminate the arrangement but departments found reasons to postpone the implementation of the next steps.

Through procrastination and avoidance the program atrophied and was discontinued. By that time, however, the program seller was no longer on the scene. It was left to the personnel manager to defend the package in order to preserve confidence in his judgment.

When telephone calls came from other organizations, requesting information about the effectiveness of the package, the personnel manager gave it a very positive recommendation.

Problems associated with packaged programs generally do not appear early in their implementation. It is not until the program matures that its strengths or weaknesses begin to appear. If the program ultimately turns out to be an appropriate one for the organization, the personnel manager is reinforced in his good judgment. Because many packaged programs have a solid conceptual basis, good results do sometimes follow their introduction. However, often the improved performance may also be a function of other variables.

Measurement of results achieved through using a packaged program is critical to an evaluation of its worth. Yet many programs are only evaluated anecdotally, and sometimes only by the seller of the program himself.

If the program does not produce the results expected, the buyer and the seller will normally combine to defend its use. The buyer must justify his decision. The seller must make the program look successful so it can be sold again. Blame is placed on implementation.

And sometimes this is a valid excuse. Any basic change in an organization, short of revolution, needs support from top levels of management.

Since packaged programs tend to enter the organization through individual sponsors in lower levels of management, or through staff departments that have their own special interests, the support needed from the top is often missing.

The consequence is that changes in behavior are not rewarded and may even be punished. Since the new behavior leads to disappointment, old behavior patterns return rather quickly, generally with a considerable sense of disenchantment, lower morale, and cynicism resulting from expectations not met.

Although support from top management is vital to the success of a program, it alone is not enough.

Packaged programs invariably demand substantial change in values, attitudes, and behavior among individuals in the organization. But numerous studies indicate that substantial changes will take place in an organization only in response to a widely felt need.

Since packaged programs tend to proceed from the seller's needs, rather than the buyer's, the basic condition for significant change may never be met.

In some cases the program itself, rather than the company's problems, tends to become the center of attention. There is, therefore, a tendency to reward observation of the new rules of the game rather than changed performance.

How, then, can a company avoid the pitfalls of a packaged solution to its managerial ailments?

Obviously, the first and most important step is to determine the nature of its own problems and needs prior to even considering a solution.

The second cardinal rule is to distrust any salesman representing a packaged solution. If you accept his offer to help you define the organization's problems, you are already on the first step toward buying his solution. You can be certain that the problems he defines can be solved by the package he is selling.

You can avoid this if you simply separate the process of identifying your problems from the process of solving them. You can hire a consultant to help you define the organization's problems and make it clear to him that he will not be part of your solution.

Finally, it is useful to examine your own motivation when being quickly attracted to a readily available packaged program. Such attraction may represent a results orientation which places value on concrete, immediate behavior as contrasted to attempts to understand what is really necessary. "Doing something" is equated with results.

Top managers with this kind of orientation, combined with salesmen for ready-made answers, tend to foster approaches in organizations which leave the critical problems unsolved.

Chapter

14 The Value Issue of Business

Perhaps more than at any time in economic history, the Western world is faced with what can be called "the value issue of business." Questions are regularly raised in the public forum concerning business and its relationship to such problems as unemployment, racial discrimination, social conformity, automobile safety, air and water pollution, bribery, and collusion. The very raising of these questions brings with it some explicit or implicit theoretical concept of the nature of the relationship between people's values and their economic activity. To understand the value issue of business, it is necessary to understand what concepts the manager brings to these problems.

ECONOMICS AS A VALUE SYSTEM

The basic concepts which are commonly accepted today of the relationship between economic activity and values are a direct outgrowth of a formulation laid down by Adam Smith some 200 years ago. "Capitalism," "free enterprise," or, as it is commonly labeled, "the classical economic model," is the basic philosophical rationale to which most businessmen turn when faced with social value questions. To understand the businessman's approach to "the value issue," we need to understand the relationship between the classical economic rationale and social value questions.

From its inception, the classical economic model has combined a "scientific" theory—a descriptive-predictive theory about the exchange of economic units—and an ethical theory—a theory of social values. Moreover, from its inception, it has offered both its scientific and social value theories not only as theories of how economic activity and social values *ought* to be worked out, but as theories of how they *will*, more or less automatically, be worked out. The model presents the economic marketplace as a self-regulating device, at both the scientific and ethical levels.

Briefly, the important assumptions of this economic model are

This chapter was prepared with Carol J. Elbing. It is a summary of some of the major arguments which are fully developed in Elbing and Elbing (1967).

that the production of goods and services in the pursuit of self-interest are automatically regulated by the interactions of the marketplace. Those items which are "best," "most wanted," "least expensive," and so on, will prevail, driving the others from the market. The ultimate result of such competition is the economic good of the nation. This is the mechanism behind the descriptive-predictive aspect of the economic model. It is to this rationale that management tends to turn when confronted with questions about the relationship of business actions to social values.

Confusion about the two aspects of the economic model—the scientific and the ethical—underlies many of the difficulties facing business leaders as they attempt to deal with the value issue of business. Social value problems are frequently taken for granted, on the assumption that they are worked out automatically in the economic exchange of goods and services. But how sound are the social value theories that are offered by the economic model?

Economics as "Moral"

One rationale for dealing with the relationship between economic activity and social values is the notion that greater social good is directly concomitant with greater economic good. As Charles Wilson, former United States Secretary of Defense, is so often quoted as having said, "What is good for business is good for the country." The implicit social value theory here is that the value issue of business is dealt with automatically by the marketplace, in the same manner by which it works out the problems of economic exchange. This rationale thus posits economics as a moral system.

The difficulty with this argument is that, of course, the marketplace does not arbitrate all values optimally in the same sense that it optimally arbitrates the exchange of goods. The marketplace is not democratic, objective, scientific, or rational. Furthermore, it cannot be assumed that the marketplace even touches on all social value problems: many important business value issues are not affected by marketplace exchange. The quality of life in an organization, for example, is one value issue of business not directly arbitrated by the marketplace. The effects of multinational firms on the cultures of the world is another. Thus, whatever the usefulness of the marketplace as an optimum economic regulator, it is no guaranteed device for the automatic working out of social value problems. The assumption does not stand up to critical analysis that any economic system insures moral or social values by its very nature, so that value issues need not be of active and direct concern.

Thus, even if we could substantiate that the greatest profit to business brought about the greatest national wealth and the greatest *economic* well-being to the greatest number of individuals, the value issue is not thereby disposed. It is not justifiable to treat the entire value issue of business only by pointing to some standard of economic well-being. *Although the economic model is a useful explanation of the exchange of economic units, it must be concluded that it is inadequate if taken as a social or moral value rationale for business.* The surface of the value issue is barely scratched by application of the rationale of the nonobjective and nonrepresentative marketplace arbitrating the production of goods and services, or by reference to a broad general index of national economic level of activity.

Economics as "Amoral"

One way of attempting to dispose of the logical difficulties of the economic model as a social value rationale is to disengage it from all claims to its being a moral philosophy, and define it as amoral—having no reference to value issues. It is advised by some that the economic model should claim only technical or scientific utility and be judged in such terms only. Far from purporting to deal with behavior, values, or with the general relationship of economic activity to values, the economic model, conceived as amoral, claims to deal solely with economic man, economic events, and economic ends, and to take as given the relationship of economic activity to social values. The economist Frank Knight (1965), for example, has said: "The science (of economics) abstracts from *error* much as mechanics does from friction. . . . Analysis must begin with individual economic conduct, hence, with the man isolated from society. . . ."

Economic data of all kinds are thus declared to be separate from any value connotations. Whenever "man" is referred to in such a model, it is not social man or moral man or the total man, but an abstract "economic" man, who is presumed, for the purposes of economic discussion, to operate rationally in terms of purely economic factors. Similarly, in terms of this amoral model, economic activity is abstracted from the complex of human and social moral actions and viewed narrowly as a purely economic or technical pursuit. The implicit claim is merely that, *given* the economic system, the model serves a descriptive-predictive function.

It is commonly assumed that such a model of economic activity, claiming only technical or scientific utility and asking to be judged in such terms only, is entirely value free. But however much an amoral model of economic activity may be desired, such a model is as fraught with value assumptions as a broad social philosophy. At first it may seem that such an amoral model has narrowed itself to a strictly scientific theory, has avoided entanglements with value issues, and has placed value questions in a realm separate from economics and business, presumably to be dealt with by other disciplines. In actuality, it has not accomplished those feats at all. Inherent in such a model is the assumption that economic actions lead to consequences which are, if not positively good, at least socially or morally harmless. Thus, far from being value-free, the model fosters an assumption about the relationship between economic activities and values—the assumption that the two can, with impunity, be considered in isolation.

This value assumption is the most undermining of the value issue of business. While it is conceivable that we might generally isolate, with social and moral impunity, a concept of mechanics from a concept of friction, it is not conceivable that we could generally isolate economics from social value issues. Economic action does not in fact exist separately from social or moral action, any more than mechanical action exists separately from friction. Economic value is always a social value, always interacting with other values in the arena of human action, and strongly affected by and affecting other social values. Obviously it is legitimate to declare—in any field–that for certain technical problems it is useful to artifically set aside social value considerations as given. In a value context, however, any attempt to isolate economic and social considerations is not realistic.

The Shortcomings of Economics as a Value System

The economic model blocks active work on vital business value issues in that it fosters a groundless optimism. In the moral version of the model, the marketplace is imagined to be an automatic device for working out not only economic but social value questions and for insuring not only material but social progress. In the amoral model, the abstraction of social value issues from economic considerations fosters another sort of optimism, the optimism that somehow economic processes are of such nature that they can go on revolutionizing society without disrupting human values.

Both the moral and amoral economic models foster the attitide that the value issue of business is of merely peripheral concern. When business processes are broadly considered as automatically worked out in the marketplace or as inherently morally justifiable or legitimately amoral, value problems are seen as a mere side issue. Once social value is conceived as a side issue, an oversimplied formula may seem adequate to the magnitude of the social value problem. Values and business can then be discussed in terms of easy platitudes, or the entire issue can be reduced to a strictly legal matter, or it can be set aside as a matter for personal conscience.

BUSINESS AS A SOCIAL SYSTEM

The fundamental reason why the value issue cannot be satisfactorily formulated within a purely economic model is that the business institution is not merely an economic-technical system. It is a social system as well. Indeed, economic activity *is* social activity. Every business act, whether or not it has direct economic connotations and ramifications, is a social act in that it is a social response to other human beings. Even purely "technical" and "economic" acts have their social dimension. Business produces not only economic consequences—goods and services, profit and wealth (and the social ramifications of these economic consequences)—it also produces a great variety of important social consequences. Its moral nature derives from that fact. The value issue of business derives from the pervasive social (hence moral) nature of business, and cannot be extrapolated merely from its abstracted economic functions. Thus the full scope of the value issue of business can be understood and formulated adequately only when it is viewed within a social framework which includes all the social effects of business action.

Business and the Individual

Because the firm is a social system, its effect on individuals goes well beyond economics, influencing the individuals' sense of self and their functioning in the firm, family, and community. When the firm is recognized as a social system as well as a technical-economic system, the values of individuals are seen as growing, in part, out of social interaction within that system. The firm is thus recognized as a basic *source* of individuals' values as well as an arena for their enactment, affecting individuals' own evaluations of themselves, their value outlooks toward their world, and in turn, the sort of influence they will have on the values of their world.

Business and Other Groups

The relationships among various business groups—managers, workers, unions, stockholders, consumers, government agencies, schools of business, and so on—generate intergroup attitudes, social trends, and values far beyond those of merely economic import. Norms, goals, and values are formed within groups and solidified through intergroup action. Group action thus results not only in economic change but change in the social groups themselves. When business is viewed solely as an economic system in terms of the traditional economic model, it appears logical that its only responsibility is toward one group, its capital investors. However, when the various groups within the business institution are also recognized as claimants, all intergroup action, being social action, is seen to involve *reciprocal* social responsibility.

Business and the Society in Which It Operates

The influence of business on society as a whole extends so far beyond merely economic considerations that the Western world is often characterized as a distinctly business culture. The relationship between business and society is not primarily economic, nor is it primarily determined by the marketplace. When business is recognized as a vast social system, it is also recognized that a vast array of its social transactions, little affected by the marketplace, are as primary a function of business as its economic transactions. The social value implications of this cultural climate go far beyond what can be formulated in terms of the classical economic framework. The climate of this vast network of social transactions is a significant aspect of the characteristically Western culture.

Business and Foreign Societies

The relationship of business to foreign societies must also be viewed within a social framework. Business in foreign countries influences not only the economic life of the world, but the entire sociopolitical climate of a precarious international scene. Foreign trade today is often justified—as it was in the eighteenth century—in terms of national wealth and power, with the added boon of economic development for other nations. Now, as then, economic progress is equated with social progress. Yet the relationship between social values and economic forces should not be assumed *a priori*, but should be subjected to broad social analysis, in keeping with the fact that business does have critical social impact beyond its economic impact. Only by examining within a social framework our business relationships with other countries can we begin to assess how economic values relate to other crucial social values.

In summary, any attempt to deal with the *value* issue of business on any level—at the level of the individual, of groups, of domestic society, or at the level of the broad international scene—must begin by placing business in a social framework, rather than in the traditional economic framework. Whatever the utility may be of viewing the social relationships of business in narrowly economic terms for specified technical purposes, the traditional economic framework is useless for the purpose of formulating values. It merely distorts and reduces the value issue. The relationship between economic and other social values in society requires broad social analysis, rather than mere economic analysis, in keeping with the broad social influence of business.

A NEW SOCIAL VALUE THEORY FOR BUSINESS

We have concluded that the value issue of business is distorted and reduced when formulated in terms of the economic model. Let us now state explicitly the fundamentals of a *new social value theory* to replace the social value theory of the economic model. All of the foregoing discussion, of course, has been an implicit reformulation of theory, but a concise statement of basic principles is now possible on the basis of the foregoing discussion, and may serve as a useful reference point.

The first principle of a social value theory based on a recognition of business as a social system is that the moral nature of business inheres in all of its social acts, and is therefore pervasive. The social value rationale of the economic model is a claim that the moral nature of business inheres in its production of economic goods, services, and national wealth (and in directly resulting social goods). A value rationale derived from a social model is a recognition that the moral nature of business inheres in all of its social—not merely economic—acts and effects. The social influence of business is seen to be truly extensive when it is recognized that every act—even every "economic" act of business—is a social act. When it is recognized that every social act implies moral value, it can be seen that the value issue of business is pervasive.

The second principle of the theory is that business-social transactions at all levels are value arbitrations. The social value rationale of the economic model assumes the marketplace to be the arbiter of social values, but it has been demonstrated that the marketplace does not and cannot achieve such a role. It is clear that the social values of business are, in fact, worked out by all of the social actions and transactions of the entire business system, not merely those of the marketplace. All choices and acts regarding production, finance, advertising, marketing—all relationships with workers, stockholders, buyers, sellers, consumers, government—work out the value issue, not merely marketplace choices and acts.

The third principle of the theory is that because the social effects of business go beyond the economic, economic measures cannot be used as indexes for other social values. The social value rationale of the economic model makes the implicit claim that it is feasible to measure the social value of business in economic terms, and to take for granted all other social values as parallel; and it makes only economic factors explicit while all other social factors are implicit or taken as given. A value theory based on a social model recognizes that, in order to assess the social effects of business, it is essential to measure them explicitly.

The fourth principle of the theory is that the social value issue is as important as the economic issue of business. The social value rationale of the economic model assumes business to be an economic-technical system and the social model recognizes that business inescapably functions as a social system, and that social value issues cannot be subordinated. Recognized as a social system with pervasive social and moral influence, business cannot be written off as amoral, nor can economic considerations be said to be the main issue of business, and social and moral value concerns as side issues. While it is perfectly true that the economic profitability of the firm is essential to its ability to function at all, it is just as true that its overall "social" profitability is what justifies its existence in the first place.

CONCLUSIONS

Two hundred years after the first Industrial Revolution, business has become a continual revolutionizing force in Western society. The danger is that so long as the rationale of the economic model is the working social value theory, economic value will continue to be the driving revolutionary force, and technological means will determine social ends. If we are interested in social values, we are concerned that the growth and development of society and of the individuals within it be commensurate with technological revolution and business advance. Because business is a social system, a social value framework which includes criteria from all of the social sciences—not just economics—must be used to assess its social growth.

If we are concerned with the value issue of business, we are concerned that it be an active field of direct inquiry, and we are also concerned that the best methods available be used in the pursuit of such inquiry. Once freed from the assumptions of the economic model, which attempts to guarantee that values will be worked out automatically, the value issue of business is seen as a matter *requiring* investigation. Yet the concept of objective systematic investigation—of "method"—is not commonly accepted in the value realm. Certainly if by "method" we mean such popular concepts of method as those of the physical sciences, technology, mathematics, or computer programming, it may well be that the concept of method for social value inquiry is inappropriate. However, if by "method" we mean the most critical procedures available pertinent to the question of concern, the concept of method is not only appropriate but essential to value inquiry.

Some method is bound to be used in every inevitable encounter with the value issue of business. Insofar as our moral aspirations are high, our standards for methods of pursuing them must also be high. Certainly, business being a social system, methods from all of the social sciences, not just economics, must be used to deal with business value questions. They are essential if the value issue of business is to become an active field of study commensurate with its significance. If our most rigorous critical methods are merely harnessed to technological means and to the market, they will assuredly run away with ultimate ends.

Not only must interest in the social value issue of business be translated into direct critical inquiry, it must be translated into the very practical process of decision making. Values inhere in every stage of that process, so that the question is not whether we deal with value issues in decision making, but whether we deal with them by design or default. Viewed in a social framework, however, it is clear that the inherent value issue in decision making is by no means vital only to the business manager. It is through the decision making of all citizens that social values are made concrete in a business society.

REFERENCES

Elbing, Alvar O., Jr., and Carol J. Elbing. *The Value Issue of Business.* McGraw-Hill, 1967.
England, George W. "Personal Value Systems of American Managers." *Academy of Management Journal*, March 1967.
Freedman, Robert. "The Challenge of Business Ethics." *Atlanta Economic Review*, May 1962.
Galbraith, John K. *The Affluent Society*. Houghton Mifflin, 1958.
Heilbroner, Robert. "The Future of Capitalism." *Commentary*, April 1966.
Knight, Frank H. "Understanding Society through Economics." *American Behavioral Scientist*, September 1965.
Leighton, Dorothea, et al. *The Character of Danger.* Basic Books, 1963.
Parsons, Talcott, and Edward A. Shils, eds. *Toward a General Theory of Action.* Harvard University Press, 1951.
Schein, Edgar H. "Organizational Socialization and the Profession of Management." *Industrial Management Review*, Winter 1968.
Whyte, William H., Jr. *The Organization Man.* Doubleday, 1956.

ERICH FROMM

Personality and the Marketplace

The marketing orientation developed as a dominant one only in the modern era. In order to understand its nature one must consider the economic function of the market in modern society as being not only analogous to this character orientation but as the basis and the main condition for its development in modern man.

Barter is one of the oldest economic mechanisms. The traditional local market, however, is essentially different from the market as it has developed in modern capitalism. Bartering on a local market offered an opportunity to meet for the purpose of exchanging commodities. Producers and customers became acquainted; they were relatively small groups; the demand was more or less known; so the producer could produce for this specific demand.

The modern market[1] is no longer a meeting place but a mechanism characterized by abstract and impersonal demand. One produces for this market, not for a known circle of customers; its verdict is based on laws of supply and demand; and it determines whether the commodity can be sold and at what price. No matter what the *use value* of a pair of shoes may be, for instance, if the supply is greater than the demand, some shoes will be sentenced to economic

[1] For a study of the history and function of the modern market, see Polanyi (1945).

death; they might as well not have been produced at all. The market day is the "day of judgment" as far as the *exchange value* of commodities is concerned.

The reader may object that this description of the market is oversimplified. The producer does try to judge the demand in advance, and under monopoly conditions even obtains a certain degree of control over it. Nevertheless, the regulatory function of the market has been, and still is, predominant enough to have a profound influence on the character formation of the urban middle class and, through the latter's social and cultural influence, on the whole population. The market concept of value, the emphasis on exchange value rather than on use value, has led to a similar concept of value with regard to people and particularly to oneself. The character orientation which is rooted in the experience of oneself as a commodity and of one's value as exchange value I call the marketing orientation.

In our time the marketing orientation has been growing rapidly, together with the development of a new market that is a phenomenon of the last decades—the "personality market." Clerks and salesmen, business executives and doctors, lawyers and artists all appear on this market. It is true that their legal status and economic positions are different: some are independent, charging for their services; others are employed, receiving salaries. But all are dependent for their material success on a personal acceptance by those who need their services or who employ them.

The principle of evaluation is the same on both the personality and the commodity market: on the one, personalities are offered for sale; on the other, commodities. Value in both cases is their exchange value, for which use value is a necessary but not a sufficient condition. It is true, our economic system could not function if people were not skilled in the particular work they have to perform and were gifted only with a pleasant personality. Even the best bedside manner and the most beautifully equipped office on Park Avenue would not make a New York doctor successful if he did not have a minimum of medical knowledge and skill. Even the most winning personality would not prevent a secretary from losing her job unless she could type reasonably fast. However, if we ask what the respective weight of skill and personality as a condition for success is, we find that only in exceptional cases is success predominantly the result of skill and of certain other human qualities like honesty, decency, and integrity. Although the proportion between skill and human qualities on the one hand and "personality" on the other hand as prerequisites for success varies, the "personality factor" always plays a decisive role. Success depends largely on how well a person sells himself on the market, how well he gets his personality across, how nice a "package" he is; whether he is "cheerful," "sound," "aggressive," "reliable," "ambitious"; furthermore, what his family background is, what clubs he belongs to, and whether he knows the right people. The type of personality required depends to some degree on the special field in which a person works. A stockbroker, a salesman, a secretary, a railroad executive, a college professor, or a hotel manager must each offer different kinds of personality that, regardless of their differences, must fulfill one condition: to be in demand.

The fact that in order to have success it is not sufficient to have the skill and equipment for performing a given task but that one must be able to "put across" one's personality in competition with many others shapes the attitude toward oneself. If it were enough for the purpose of making a living to rely on what one knows and what one can do, one's self-esteem would be in proportion to one's capacities, that is, to one's use value; but since success depends largely on how one sells one's personality, one experiences oneself as a commodity, or rather simultaneously as the seller and the commodity to be sold. A person is not concerned with his life and happiness, but with becoming salable. This feeling might be compared to that of a commodity, of handbags on a counter, for instance, could they feel and think. Each handbag would try to make itself as "attractive" as possible in order to attract customers and to look as expensive as possible in order to obtain a higher price than its rivals. The handbag sold for the highest price would feel elated, since that would mean it was the most "valuable" one; the one which was not sold would feel sad and convinced of its own worthlessness. This fate might befall a bag which, though excellent in appearance and usefulness, had the bad luck to be out of date because of a change in fashion.

Like the handbag, one has to be in fashion on the personality market, and in order to be in fashion one has to know what kind of personality is most in demand. This knowledge is transmitted in a general way throughout the whole process of education, from kindergarten to college, and implemented by the family. The knowledge acquired at this early stage is not sufficient, however; it emphasizes only certain general qualities like adaptability, ambition, and sensitivity to the changing expectations of other people. The more specific picture of the models for success one gets elsewhere. The pictorial magazines, newspapers, and newsreels show the pictures and life stories of the successful in many variations. Pictorial advertising has a similar function. The successful executive who is pictured in a tailor's advertisement is the image of how one should look and be, if one is to draw down the "big money" on the contemporary personality market.

The most important means of transmitting the desired personality pattern to the average man is the motion picture. The young girl tries to emulate the facial expression, coiffure, gestures of a high-priced star as the most promising way to success. The young man tries to look and be like the model he sees on the screen. While the average citizen has little contact with the life of the most successful people, his relationship with the motion-picture stars is different. It is true that he has no real contact with them either, but he can see them on the screen again and again, can write them and receive their autographed pictures. In contrast to the time when the actor was socially despised but was nevertheless the transmitter of the works of great poets to his audience, our motion-picture stars have no great works or ideas to transmit, but their function is to serve as the link an average person has with the world of the "great." Even if he can not hope to become as successful as they are, he can try to emulate them; they are his saints, and because of their success they embody the norms for living.

Since modern man experiences himself both as the seller and as the commodity to be sold on the market, his self-esteem depends on conditions beyond his control. If he is "successful," he is valuable; if he is not, he is worthless. The degree of insecurity which results from this orientation can hardly be overestimated. If one feels that one's own value is not constituted primarily by the human qualities one possesses, but by one's success on a competitive market with ever-changing conditions, one's self-esteem is bound to be shaky and in constant need of confirmation by others. Hence one is driven to strive relentlessly for success, and any setback is a severe threat to one's self-esteem; helplessness, insecurity, and inferiority feelings are the result. If the vicissitudes of the market are the judges of one's value, the sense of dignity and pride is destroyed.

But the problem is not only that of self-evaluation and self-esteem but of one's experience of oneself as an independent entity, of one's *identity with oneself*. As we shall see later, the mature and productive individual derives his feeling of identity from the experience of himself as the agent who is one with his powers; this feeling of self can be briefly expressed as meaning *"I am what I do."* In the marketing orientation man encounters his own powers as commodities alienated from him. He is not one with them but they are masked from him because what matters is not his self-realization in the process of using them but his success in the process of selling them. Both his powers and what they create become estranged, something different from himself, something for others to judge and to use; thus his feeling of identity becomes as shaky as his self-esteem; it is constituted by the sum total of roles one can play: *"I am as you desire me."*

Ibsen has expressed this state of selfhood in Peer Gynt: Peer Gynt tries to discover his self and he finds that he is like an onion—one layer after the other can be peeled off and there is no core to be found. Since man cannot live doubting his identity, he must, in the marketing orientation, find the conviction of identity not in reference to himself and his powers but in the opinion of others about him. His prestige, status, success, the fact that he is known to others as being a certain person are a substitute for the genuine feeling of identity. This situation makes him utterly dependent on the way others look at him and forces him to keep up the role in which he once had become successful. If I and my powers are separated from each other, then, indeed, is my self constituted by the price I fetch.

The way one experiences others is not different from the way one experiences oneself. Others are experienced as commodities like oneself; they too do not present *themselves* but their salable part. The difference between people is reduced to a merely quantitative difference of being *more or less* successful, attractive, hence valuable. This process is not different from what happens to commodities on the market. A painting and a pair of shoes can both be expressed in, and reduced to, their exchange value, their price; so many pairs of shoes are "equal" to one painting. In the same way the difference between people is reduced to a common element, their price on the market. Their individuality, that which is peculiar and unique in them, is valueless and, in fact, a ballast. The meaning which the word *peculiar* has assumed is quite expressive of this attitude. Instead of denoting the greatest achievement of man—that of having developed his individuality—it has become almost synonymous with *queer*. The word *equality* has also changed its meaning. The idea that all men are created equal implied that all men have the same fundamental right to be considered as ends in themselves and not as means. Today, equality has become equivalent to *interchangeability*, and is the very negation of individuality. Equality, instead of being the condition for the development of each man's peculiarity, means the extinction of individuality, the "selflessness" characteristic of the marketing orientation. Equality was conjunctive with difference, but it has become synonymous with "in-difference," and, indeed, indifference is what characterizes modern man's relationship to himself and to others.

These conditions necessarily color all human relationships. When the individual self is neglected, the relationships between people must of necessity become superficial, because not they themselves but interchangeable commodities are related. People are not able and cannot afford to be concerned with that which is unique and "peculiar" in each other. However, the market creates a kind of comradeship of its own. Everybody is involved in the same battle of competition, shares the same striving for success; all meet under the same conditions of the market (or at least believe they do). Everyone knows how the others feel because each is in the same boat: alone, afraid to fail, eager to please; no quarter is given or expected in this battle.

The superficial character of human relationships leads many to hope that they can find depth and intensity of feeling in individual love. But love for one person and love for one's neighbor are indivisible; in any given culture, love relationships are only a more intense expression of the relatedness to man prevalent in that culture. Hence it is an illusion to expect that the loneliness of man, rooted in the marketing orientation, can be cured by individual love.

Thinking as well as feeling is determined by the marketing orientation. Thinking assumes the function of grasping things quickly so as to be able to manipulate them successfully. Furthered by widespread and efficient education, this leads to a high degree of intelligence, but not of reason. For manipulative purposes, all that is necessary to know is the surface features of things, the superficial. The truth, to be uncovered by penetrating to the essence of phenomena, becomes an obsolete concept—truth not only in the pre-scientific sense of "absolute" truth, dogmatically maintained without reference to empirical data, but also in the sense of truth attained by man's reason applied to his observations and open to revisions. Most intelligence tests are attuned to this kind of thinking; they measure not so much the capacity for reason and understanding as the capacity for quick mental adaptation to a given situation; "mental adjustment tests" would be the adequate name for them (see Schachtel, 1937, pp. 597–624). For this kind of thinking the application of the categories of comparison and of quantitative measurement—rather than a thorough analysis of a given phenomenon and its quality—is essential. All problems are equally "interesting" and there is little sense of the respective differences in their importance. Knowledge itself becomes a commodity. Here, too, man is alienated from his own power; thinking and knowing are experienced as a tool to produce results. Knowledge of man himself, psychology, which in the great tradition of Western thought was held to be the condition for virtue, for right living, for happiness, has degenerated into an instrument to be used for better manipulation of others and oneself, in market research, in political propaganda, in advertising, and so on.

Evidently this type of thinking has a profound effect on our educational system. From grade school to graduate school, the aim of learning is to gather as much information as possible that is mainly useful for the purposes of the market. Students are supposed to learn so many things that they have hardly time and energy left to *think*. Not the interest in the subjects taught or in knowledge and insight as such, but the enhanced exchange value knowledge gives, is the main incentive for wanting more and better education. We find today a tremendous enthusiasm for knowledge and education, but at the same time a skeptical or contemptuous attitude toward the allegedly impractical and useless thinking which is concerned "only" with the truth and which has no exchange value on the market.

Although I have presented the marketing orientation as one of the nonproductive orientations, it is in many ways so different that is belongs in a category of its own. The receptive, exploitative, and hoarding orientations have one thing in common: each is one form of human relatedness which, if dominant in a person, is specific of him and characterizes him. . . . The marketing orientation, however, does not develop something which is potentially in the person (unless we make the absurd assertion that "nothing" is also part of the human equipment); its very nature is that no specific and permanent kind of relatedness is developed, but that the very changeability of attitudes is the only permanent quality of such orientation. In this orientation, those qualities are developed which can best be sold. Not one particular attitude is predominant, but the emptiness which can be filled most quickly with the desired quality. This quality, however, ceases to be one in the proper sense of the word; it is only a role, the pretense of a quality, to be readily exchanged if another one is more desirable. Thus, for instance, respectability is sometimes desirable. The salesmen in certain branches of business ought to impress the public with those qualities of reliability, soberness, and respectability which were genuine in many a businessman of the nineteenth century. Now one looks for a man who instills confidence because he *looks* as if he had these qualities; what this man sells on the personality market is his ability to look the part; what kind of person is behind that role does not matter and is nobody's concern. He himself is not interested in his honesty, but in what it gets for him on the market. The premise of the marketing orientation is emptiness, the lack of any specific quality which could not be subject to change, since any persistent trait of character might conflict some day with the requirements of the market. Some roles would not fit in with the peculiarities of the person; therefore we must do away with them—not with the roles but with the peculiarities. The marketing personality must be free, free of all individuality.

The character orientations which have been described so far are by no means as separate from one another as it may appear from this sketch. The receptive orientation, for instance, may be dominant in a person but it is usually blended with any or all of the other orientations. While I shall discuss the various blendings later on, I want to stress at this point that all orientations are part of the human equipment, and the dominance of any specific orientation depends to a large extent on the peculiarity of the culture in which the individual lives. Although a more detailed analysis of the relationship between the various orientations and social patterns must be reserved for a study which deals primarily with problems of social psychology, I should like to suggest here a tentative hypothesis as to the social conditions making for the dominance of any of the four nonproductive types. It should be noted that the significance of the study of the correlation between character orientation and social structure lies not only in the fact that it helps us understand some of the most significant causes for the formation of character, but also in the fact that specific orientations—inasmuch as they are common to most members of a culture or social class—represent powerful emotional forces the operation of which we must know in order to understand the functioning of society. In view of the current emphasis on the impact of culture on personality, I should like to state that the relationship between society and the individual is not to be understood simply in the sense that cultural patterns and social institutions "influence" the individual. The interaction goes much deeper; the whole personality of the average individual is molded by the way people relate to each other, and it is determined by the socioeconomic and political structure of society to such an extent that, in principle, one can infer from the analysis of one individual the totality of the social structure in which he lives.

The receptive orientation is often to be found in societies in which the right of one group to exploit another is firmly established. Since the exploited group has no power to change, or any idea of changing, its situation, it will tend to look up to its masters as to its providers, as to those from whom one receives everything life can give. No matter how little the slave receives, he feels that by his own effort he could have acquired even less, since the structure of his society impresses him with the fact that he is unable to organize it and to rely on his own activity and reason. As far as contemporary American culture is concerned, it seems at first glance that the receptive attitude is entirely absent. Our whole culture, its ideas, and its practice discourage the receptive orientation and emphasize that each one has to look out, and be responsible, for himself and that he has to use his own initiative if he wants to "get anywhere." However, while the receptive orientation is discouraged, it is by no means absent. The need to conform and to please, which has been discussed in the foregoing pages, leads to the feeling of helplessness, which is the root of subtle receptiveness in modern man. It appears particularly in the attitude toward the "expert" and public opinion. People expect that in every field there is an expert who can tell them how things are and how they ought to be done, and that all they ought to do is listen to him and swallow his ideas. There are experts for science, experts for happiness, and writers become experts in the art of living by the very fact that they are authors of best sellers. This subtle but rather general receptiveness assumes somewhat grotesque forms in modern "folklore," fostered particularly by advertising. While everyone knows that realistically the "get-rich-quick" schemes do not work, there is a widespread daydream of the effortless life. It is partly expressed in connection with the use of gadgets; the car which needs no shifting, the fountain pen which saves the trouble of removing the cap are only random examples of this phantasy. It is particularly prevalent in those schemes which deal with happiness. A very characteristic quotation is the following: "This book," the author says, "tells you how to be twice the man or woman you ever were before—happy, well, brimming with energy, confident, capable and free of care. You are required to follow no laborious mental or physical program; it is much simpler than that. . . . As laid down here the route to that promised profit may appear strange, for few of us can imagine *getting without striving*. . . . Yet that is so, as you will see" (Falvey, 1946).

The exploitative character, with its motto "I take what I need," goes back to piratical and feudal ancestors and goes forward from there to the robber barons of the nineteenth century who exploited the natural resources of the continent. The "pariah" and "adventure" capitalists, to use Max Weber's terms, roaming the earth for profit, are men of this stamp, men whose aim was to buy cheap and sell dear and who ruthlessly pursued power and wealth. The free market, as it operated in the eighteenth and nineteenth centuries under competitive conditions, nurtured this type. Our own age has seen a revival of naked exploitativeness in the authoritarian systems which attempted to exploit the natural and human resources, not so much of their own country but of any other country they were powerful enough to invade. They proclaimed the right of might and rationalized it by pointing to the law of nature which makes the stronger survive; love and decency were signs of weakness; thinking was the occupation of cowards and degenerates.

The hoarding orientation existed side by side with the exploitative orientation in the eighteenth and nineteenth centuries. The hoarding type was conservative, less interested in ruthless acquisition than in methodical economic pursuits, based on sound principles and on the preservation of what had been acquired. To him property was a symbol of his self and its protection a supreme value. This orientation gave him a great deal of security; his possession of property and family, protected as they were by the relatively stable conditions of the nineteenth century, constituted a safe and manageable world. Puritan ethics, with the emphasis on work and success as evidence of goodness, supported the feeling of security and tended to give life meaning and a religious sense of fulfillment. This combination of a stable world, stable possessions, and a stable ethic gave the members of the middle class a feeling of belonging, self-confidence, and pride.

The marketing orientation does not come out of the eighteenth or nineteenth centuries; it is definitely a modern product. It is only recently that the package, the label, the brand name have become important, in people as well as in commodities. The gospel of working loses weight and the gospel of selling becomes paramount. In feudal times, social mobility was exceedingly limited and one could not use one's personality to get ahead. In the days of the competitive market, social mobility was relatively great, especially in the United States; if one "delivered the goods" one could get ahead. Today, the opportunities for the lone individual who can make a fortune all by himself are, in comparison with the previous period, greatly diminished. He who wants to "get ahead" has to fit into large organizations, and his ability to play the expected role is one of his main assets.

The depersonalization, the emptiness, the meaninglessness of life, the automatization of the individual result in a growing dissatisfaction and in a need to search for a more adequate way of living and for norms which could guide man to this end. . . .

REFERENCES

Falvey, Hal. *Ten Seconds That Will Change Your Life*. Wilcox & Follett, 1946.

Polanyi, K. *The Great Transformation*. Holt, 1945.

Schachtel, Ernest. "Zum Begriff und zur Diagnosis der Persönlichkeit in 'Personality Tests'" [On the Concept and Diagnosis of Personality Tests]. *Zeitschrift für Sozialforschung*, No. 6, 1937.

CARL ROGERS

The Place of the Individual in the New World of the Behavioral Sciences

Elsewhere I have endeavored to point out, in a very sketchy manner, the advances of the behavioral sciences in their ability to predict and control behavior. I have tried to suggest the new world into which we will be advancing at an ever more headlong pace. Here I want to consider the question of how we—as individuals, as groups, as a culture—will live in, will respond to, will adapt to this brave new world. What stance will we take in the face of these new developments?

I am going to describe two answers which have been given to this question, and then I wish to suggest some considerations which may lead to a third answer.

DENY AND IGNORE

One attitude which we can take is to deny that these scientific advances are taking place, and simply take the view that there can be no study of human behavior which is truly scientific. We can hold that the human animal cannot possibly take an objective attitude toward himself, and that therefore no real science of behavior can exist. We can say that man is always a free agent, in some sense that makes scientific study of his behavior impossible. Not long ago, at a conference on the social sciences, curiously enough, I heard a well-known economist take just this view. And one of this country's most noted theologians writes, "In any event, no scientific investigation of past behavior can become the basis of predictions of future behavior" (Niebuhr, 1955, p. 47).

The attitude of the general public is somewhat similar. Without necessarily denying the possibility of a behavioral science, the man in the street simply ignores the developments which are taking place. To be sure, he becomes excited for a time when he hears it said that the Communists have attempted to change the soldiers they have captured by means of "brainwashing." He may show a mild reaction of annoyance to the revelations of a book such as Whyte's *Organization Man* (1956), which shows how heavily, and in what manipulative fashion, the findings of the behavioral sciences are used by modern industrial corporations. But by and large he sees nothing in all this to be concerned about, any more than he did in the first theoretical statements that the atom could be split.

We may, if we wish, join him in ignoring the problem. We may go further, like the older intellectuals I have cited, and, looking at the behavioral sciences, may declare that "there ain't no such animal." But since these reactions do not seem particularly intelligent, I shall leave them to describe a much more sophisticated and much more prevalent point of view.

THE FORMULATION OF HUMAN LIFE IN TERMS OF SCIENCE

Among behavioral scientists, it seems to be largely taken for granted that the findings of such science will be used in the prediction and control of human behavior. Yet most psychologists and other scientists have given little thought to what this would mean. An exception to this general tendency is Dr. B. F. Skinner of Harvard, who has been quite explicit in urging psychologists to use the powers of control which they have in the interest of creating a better world. In an attempt to show what he means, Dr. Skinner wrote a book some years ago, entitled *Walden Two* (1948), in which he gives a fictional account of what he regards as a utopian community in which the learnings of the behavioral sciences are fully utilized in all aspects of life—marriage, child rearing, ethical conduct, work, play, and artistic endeavor. (I shall quote from his writings several times.)

There are also some writers of fiction who have seen the significance of the coming influence of the behavioral sciences. Aldous Huxley, in his *Brave New World* (1946), has given a horrifying picture of saccharine happiness in a scientifically managed world, against which man eventually revolts. George Orwell, in *1984* (1953), has drawn a picture of the world, created by dictatorial power, in which the behavioral sciences are used as instruments of absolute control of individuals so that not behavior alone but even thought is controlled.

The writers of science fiction have also played a role in visualizing for us some of the possible developments in a world where behavior and personality are as much the subject of science as chemical compounds or electrical impulses.

I should like to try to present, as well as I can, a simplified picture of the cultural pattern which emerges if we endeavor to shape human life in terms of the behavioral sciences.

There is first of all the recognition, almost the assumption, that scientific knowledge is the power to manipulate. Dr. Skinner says (1955/56, pp. 56–57):

> We must accept the fact that some kind of control of human affairs is inevitable. We cannot use good sense in human affairs unless someone engages in the design and construction of environmental conditions which affect the behavior of men. Environmental changes have always been the condition for the improvement of cultural patterns, and we can hardly use the more effective methods of science without making changes on a grander scale. . . . Science has turned up dangerous processes and materials before. To use the facts and techniques of a science of man to the fullest extent without making some monstrous mistake will be difficult and obviously perilous. It is no time for self-deception, emotional indulgence, or the assumption of attitudes which are no longer useful.

The next assumption is that such power to control is to be used. Skinner sees it as being used benevolently, though he recognized the danger of its being misused. Huxley sees it as being used with benevolent intent, but actually creating a nightmare. Orwell describes the results if such power is used malignantly, to enhance the degree of regulation exercised by a dictatorial government.

STEPS IN THE PROCESS

Let us look at some of the elements which are involved in the concept of the control of human behavior as mediated by the behavioral sciences. What would be the steps in the process by which a society might organize itself so as to formulate human life in terms of the science of man?

First would come the selection of goals. In a paper of his, Dr. Skinner suggests that one possible goal to be assigned to the behavioral technology is this: "Let man be happy, informed, skillful, well-behaved, and productive" (1955/56, p. 47). In his *Walden Two*, where he can use the guise of fiction to express his views, he becomes more expansive. His hero says:

> Well, what do you say to the design of personalities? Would that interest you? The control of temperament? Give me the specifications, and I'll give you the man! What do you say to the control of motivation, building the

> interests which will make men most productive and most successful? Does that seem to you fantastic? Yet some of the techniques are available, and more can be worked out experimentally. Think of the possibilities! . . . Let us control the lives of our children and see what we can make of them (p. 243).

What Skinner is essentially saying here is that the current knowledge in the behavioral sciences, plus that which the future will bring, will enable us to specify, to a degree which today would seem incredible, the kind of behavioral and personality results which we wish to achieve. This is obviously both an opportunity and a very heavy burden.

The second element in this process would be one which is familiar to every scientist who has worked in the field of applied science. Given the purpose, the goal, we proceed by the method of science—by controlled experimentation—to discover the means to these ends. If, for example, our present knowledge of the conditions which cause men to be productive is limited, further investigation and experimentation would surely lead us to new knowledge in this field. And still further work will provide us with the knowledge of even more effective means. The method of science is self-correcting in thus arriving at increasingly effective ways of achieving the purpose we have selected.

The third element in the control of human behavior through the behavioral sciences involves the question of power. As the conditions or methods are discovered by which to achieve our goal, some person or group obtains the power to establish those conditions or use those methods. There has been too little recognition of the problem involved in this. To hope that the power being made available by the behavioral sciences will be exercised by the scientists, or by a benevolent group, seems to me a hope little supported by either recent or distant history. It seems far more likely that behavioral scientists, holding their present attitudes, will be in the position of the German rocket scientists specializing in guided missiles. First, they worked devotedly for Hitler to destroy Russia and the United States. Now, depending on who captured them, they work devotedly for Russia in the interest of destroying the United States, or devotedly for the United States in the interest of destroying Russia. If behavioral scientists are concerned solely with advancing their science, it seems most probable that they will serve the purposes of whatever individual or group has the power.

But this is, in a sense, a digression. The main point of this view is that some person or group will have and use the power to put into effect the methods which have been discovered for achieving the desired goal.

The fourth step in this process whereby a society might formulate its life in terms of the behavioral sciences is the exposure of individuals to the methods and conditions mentioned. As individuals are exposed to the prescribed conditions, this leads, with a high degree of probability, to the behavior which has been desired. Men then become productive, if that has been the goal, or submissive, or whatever it has been decided to make them.

To give something of the flavor of this aspect of the process as seen by one of its advocates, let me again quote the hero of *Walden Two*:

> Now that we *know* how positive reinforcement works, and why negative doesn't [he says, commenting on the method he is advocating], we can be more deliberate, and hence more successful, in our cultural design. We can achieve a sort of control under which the controlled, though they are following a code much more scrupulously than was ever the case under

the old system, nevertheless *feel free*. They are doing what they want to do, not what they are forced to do. That's the source of the tremendous power of positive reinforcement—there's no restraint and no revolt. By a careful design, we control not the final behavior, but the *inclination* to behave—the motives, the desires, the wishes. The curious thing is that in that case *the question of freedom never arises* (p. 218).

THE PICTURE AND ITS IMPLICATIONS

Let me see if I can sum up very briefly the picture of the impact of the behavioral sciences upon the individual and upon society as this impact is explicitly seen by Dr. Skinner, and implied in the attitudes and work of many, perhaps most, behavioral scientists. Behavioral science is clearly moving forward; its increasing power for control will be held by some one or some group; such an individual or group will surely choose the purposes or goals to be achieved; and most of us will then be increasingly controlled by means so subtle we will not even be aware of them as controls. Thus, whether a council of wise psychologists (if this is not a contradiction in terms) or a Stalin or a Big Brother has the power, and whether the goal is happiness, or productivity, or resolution of the Oedipus complex, or submission, or love of Big Brother, we will inevitably find ourselves moving toward the chosen goal, and probably thinking that we ourselves desire it. Thus if this line of reasoning is correct, it appears that some form of completely controlled society—a *Walden Two* or a *1984*—is coming. The fact that it would surely arrive piecemeal, rather than all at once, does not greatly change the fundamental issues. Man and his behavior would become a planned product of a scientific society.

You may well ask, "But what about individual freedom? What about the democratic concepts of the rights of the individual?" Here, too, Dr. Skinner is quite specific. He says quite bluntly:

> The hypothesis that man is not free is essential to the application of scientific method to the study of human behavior. The free inner man who is held responsible for the behavior of the external biological organism is only a pre-scientific substitute for the kinds of causes which are discovered in the course of a scientific analysis. All these alternative causes lie *outside* the individual (1953, p. 447).

In another source, he explains this at somewhat more length:

> As the use of science increases, we are forced to accept the theoretical structure with which science represents its facts. The difficulty is that this structure is clearly at odds with the traditional democratic conception of man. Every discovery of an event which has a part in shaping a man's behavior seems to leave so much the less to be credited to the man himself; and as such explanations become more and more comprehensive, the contribution which may be claimed by the individual himself appears to approach zero. Man's vaunted creative powers, his original accomplishments in art, science and morals, his capacity to choose and our right to hold him responsible for the consequences of his choice—none of these is conspicuous in this new self-portrait. Man, we once believed, was free to express himself in art, music and literature, to inquire into nature, to seek salvation in his own way. He could initiate action and make spontaneous and capricious changes of course. Under

> the most extreme duress, some sort of choice remained to him. He could resist any effort to control him, though it might cost him his life. But science insists that action is initiated by forces impinging upon the individual, and that caprice is only another name for behavior for which we have not yet found a cause (1955/56, pp. 52–53).

The democratic philosophy of human nature and of government is seen by Skinner as having served a useful purpose at one time. "In rallying men against tyranny it was necessary that the individual be strengthened, that he be taught that he had rights and could govern himself. To give the common man a new conception of his worth, his dignity, and his power to save himself, both here and hereafter, was often the only resource of the revolutionist" (ibid., p. 53). He regards this philosophy as being now out of date, and indeed an obstacle "if it prevents us from applying to human affairs the science of man" (ibid., p. 54).

A PERSONAL REACTION

I have endeavored, up to this point, to give an objective picture of some of the developments in the behavioral sciences, and an objective picture of the kind of society which might emerge out of these developments. I do, however, have strong personal reactions to the kind of world I have been describing, a world which Skinner explicitly (and many other scientists implicitly) expect and hope for in the future. To me this kind of world would destroy the human person as I have come to know him in the deepest moments of psychotherapy. In such moments I am in relationship with a person who is spontaneous, who is responsibly free, that is, aware of his freedom to choose who he will be, and aware also of the consequences of his choice. To believe, as Skinner holds, that all this is an illusion, and that spontaneity, freedom, responsibility, and choice have no real existence, would be impossible for me.

I feel that to the limit of my ability I have played my part in advancing the behavioral sciences, but if the result of my efforts and those of others is that man becomes a robot, created and controlled by a science of his own making, then I am very unhappy indeed. If the good life of the future consists in so conditioning individuals through the control of their environment, and through the control of the rewards they receive, that they will be inexorably productive, well behaved, happy, or whatever, then I want none of it. To me this is a pseudo form of the good life which includes everything save that which makes it good.

And so, I ask myself, is there any flaw in the logic of this development? Is there any alternative view to what the behavioral sciences might mean to the individual and to society? It seems to me that I perceive such a flaw, and that I can conceive of an alternative view. These I would like to set before you.

ENDS AND VALUES IN RELATION TO SCIENCE

It seems to me that the view I have presented rests upon a faulty perception of the relationship of goals and values to the enterprise of science. The significance of the *purpose* of a scientific undertaking is, I believe, grossly underestimated. I would like to state a two-pronged thesis which in my estimation deserves consideration. Then I will elaborate the meaning of these two points.

1. In any scientific endeavor—whether "pure" or applied science—there is a prior personal subjective choice of the purpose or value which that scientific work is perceived as serving.
2. This subjective value choice which brings the scientific endeavor into being must always lie outside that endeavor, and can never become a part of the science involved in that endeavor.

Let me illustrate the first point from Dr. Skinner's writings. When he suggests that the task for the behavioral sciences is to make man "productive," "well-behaved," etc., it is obvious that he is making a choice. He might have chosen to make men submissive, dependent, and gregarious, for example. Yet, by his own statement in another context—man's "capacity to choose," his freedom to select his course and to initiate action—these powers do not exist in the scientific picture of man. Here is, I believe, the deep-seated contradiction, or paradox. Let me spell it out as clearly as I can.

Science, to be sure, rests on the assumption that behavior is caused—that a specified event is followed by a consequent event. Hence all is determined, nothing is free, choice is impossible. But we must recall that science itself, and each specific scientific endeavor, each change of course in a scientific research, each interpretation of the meaning of a scientific finding, and each decision as to how the finding shall be applied, rests upon a personal, subjective choice. Thus science in general exists in the same paradoxical situation as does Dr. Skinner. A personal, subjective choice made by man sets in motion the operations of science, which in time proclaims that there can be no such thing as a personal subjective choice. I shall make some comments about this continuing paradox at a later point.

I stressed the fact that each of these choices, initiating or furthering the scientific venture, is a value choice. The scientist investigates this rather than that because he feels the first investigation has more value for him. He chooses one method for his study rather than another because he values it more highly. He interprets his findings in one way rather than another because he believes the first way is closer to the truth, or more valid—in other words, that it is closer to a criterion which he values. Now these value choices are never a part of the scientific venture itself. The value choices connected with a particular scientific enterprise always and necessarily lie outside that enterprise.

I wish to make it clear that I am not saying that values cannot be included as a subject of science. It is not true that science deals only with certain classes of "facts" and that these classes do not include values. It is a bit more complex than that, as a simple illustration or two may make clear.

If I value knowledge of the "three Rs" as a goal of education, the methods of science can give me increasingly accurate information as to how this goal may be achieved. If I value problem-solving ability as a goal of education, the scientific method can give me the same kind of help.

Now if I wish to determine whether problem-solving ability is "better" than knowledge of the three Rs, then scientific method can also study those two values, but *only*—and this is very important—*only* in terms of some other value which I have subjectively chosen. I may value college success. Then I can determine whether problem-solving ability or knowledge of the three Rs is most closely associated with that value. I may value personal integration or vocational success or responsible citizenship. I can determine whether problem-solving ability or knowledge of the three Rs is "better" for achieving any one of these values. But the value or purpose which gives meaning to a particular scientific endeavor must always lie outside that endeavor.

What I have been saying seems equally true of applied and pure science. In pure science the usual prior subjective value choice is the discovery of truth. But this is a subjective choice, and science can never say whether it is the best choice, save in the light of some other value. Geneticists in Russia, for example, had to make a subjective choice of whether it was better to pursue truth or to discover facts which upheld a governmental dogma. Which choice is "better"? We could make a scientific investigation of those alternatives, but only in the light of some other subjectively chosen value. If, for example, we value the survival of a culture, then we could begin to investigate with the methods of science the question whether pursuit of truth or support of governmental dogma is most closely associated with cultural survival.

My point, then, is that any scientific endeavor, pure or applied, is carried on in the pursuit of a purpose or value which is subjectively chosen by persons. It is important that this choice be made explicit, since the particular value which is being sought can never be tested or evaluated, confirmed or denied, by the scientific endeavor to which it gives birth and meaning. The initial purpose or value always and necessarily lies outside the scope of the scientific effort which it sets in motion.

Among other things, this means that if we choose some particular goal or series of goals for human beings, and then set out on a large scale to control human behavior to the end of achieving those goals, we are locked in the rigidity of our initial choice, because such a scientific endeavor can never transcend itself to select new goals. Only subjective human persons can do that. Thus if we choose as our goal the state of happiness for human beings (a goal deservedly ridiculed by Aldous Huxley in *Brave New World*), and if we involved all of society in a successful scientific program by which people became happy, we would be locked in a colossal rigidity in which no one would be free to question this goal, because our scientific operations could not transcend themselves to question their guiding purposes. And, without laboring this point, I would remark that colossal rigidity, whether in dinosaurs or dictatorships, has a very poor record of evolutionary survival.

If, however, a part of our scheme is to set free some "planners" who do not have to be happy, who are not controlled, and who are therefore free to choose other values, this has several meanings. It means that the purpose we have chosen as our goal is not a sufficient and satisfying one for human beings, but must be supplemented. It also means that if it is necessary to set up an elite group which is free, then this shows all too clearly that the great majority are only the slaves—no matter by what high-sounding name we call them—of those who select the goals.

Perhaps, however, the thought is that a continuing scientific endeavor will evolve its own goals, that the initial findings will alter the directions, and subsequent findings will alter them still further, and that the science somehow develops its own purpose. This seems to be a view implicitly held by many scientists. It is surely a reasonable description, but it overlooks one element in this continuing development, which is that subjective, personal choice enters in at every point at which the direction changes. The findings of a science, the results of an experiment, do not and never can tell us what scientific purpose to pursue next. Even in the purest science, the scientist must decide what the findings mean, and must subjectively choose what next step will be most profitable in the pursuit of his purpose. And if we are speaking of the application of scientific knowledge, then it is distressingly clear that the increasing scientific knowledge of the structure of the atom carries with it no necessary choice as to the purpose to which this knowledge will be put. This is a subjective, personal choice which must be made by many individuals.

Thus I return to the proposition with which I began this section—and which I now repeat in different words. Science has its meaning as the objective pursuit of a purpose which has been subjectively chosen by a person or persons. This purpose or value can never be investigated by the particular scientific experiment or investigation to which it has given birth and meaning. Consequently, any discussion of the control of human beings by the behavioral sciences must first and most deeply concern itself with the subjectively chosen purposes which such an application of science is intended to implement.

AN ALTERNATIVE SET OF VALUES

If the line of reasoning I have been presenting is valid, then it opens new doors to us. If we frankly face the fact that science takes off from a subjectively chosen set of values, then we are free to select the values we wish to pursue. We are not limited to such stultifying goals as producing a controlled state of happiness, productivity, and the like. I would like to suggest a radically different alternative.

Suppose we start with a set of ends, values, purposes, quite different from the type of goals we have been considering. Suppose we do this quite openly, setting them forth as a possible value choice to be accepted or rejected. Suppose we select a set of values which focuses on fluid elements of process, rather than static attributes. We might then value:

1. Man as a process of becoming, as a process of achieving worth and dignity through the development of his potentialities.
2. The individual human being as a self-actualizing process, moving on to more challenging and enriching experiences.
3. The process by which the individual creatively adapts to an ever new and changing world.
4. The process by which knowledge transcends itself; for example, the theory of relativity transcended Newtonian physics, and will itself be transcended in some future day by a new perception.

If we select values such as these, we turn to our science and technology of behavior with a very different set of questions. We will want to know such things as these:

1. Can science aid us in the discovery of new modes of richly rewarding living? More meaningful and satisfying modes of interpersonal relationships?
2. Can science inform us as to how the human race can become a more intelligent participant in its own evolution—its physical, psychological, and social evolution?
3. Can science inform us as to ways of releasing the creative capacity of individuals, which seem so necessary if we are to survive in this fantastically expanding atomic age? Dr. Oppenheimer has pointed out (1956) that knowledge, which used to double in millennia or centuries, now doubles in a generation or a decade. It appears that we will need to discover the utmost in the release of creativity if we are to be able to adapt effectively.
4. In short, can science discover the methods by which man can most readily become a continually developing and self-transcending process, in his be-

havior, his thinking, his knowledge? Can science predict and release an essentially "unpredictable" freedom?

It is one of the virtues of science as a method that it is as able to advance and implement goals and purposes of this sort as it is to serve static values, such as states of being well informed, happy, obedient. Indeed, we have some evidence of this.

A SMALL EXAMPLE

I will perhaps be forgiven if I document some of the possibilities along this line by turning to psychotherapy, the field I know best.

Psychotherapy, as Meerloo (1955, pp. 353–60) and others have pointed out, can be one of the most subtle tools for the control of one person by another. The therapist can subtly mold individuals in imitation of himself. He can cause an individual to become a submissive and conforming being. When certain therapeutic principles are used in extreme fashion, we call it brainwashing—an instance of the disintegration of the personality and a reformulation of the person along lines desired by the controlling individual. So the principles of therapy can be used as a most effective means of external control of human personality and behavior. Can psychotherapy be anything else?

I find the developments in client-centered psychotherapy (Rogers, 1951) an exciting hint of what a behavioral science can do in achieving the kinds of values I have stated. Quite aside from being a somewhat new orientation in psychotherapy, this development has important implications regarding the relation of a behavioral science to the control of human behavior. Let me describe our experience as it relates to the issues of the present discussion.

In client-centered therapy, we are deeply engaged in the prediction and influencing of behavior. As therapists, we institute certain attitudinal conditions, and the client has relatively little voice in the establishment of these conditions. To put it very briefly, we have found that the therapist is most effective if he is (*a*) genuine, integrated, transparently real in the relationship; (*b*) acceptant of the client as a separate, different person, and acceptant of each fluctuating aspect of the client as it comes to expression; and (*c*) sensitively empathic in his understanding, or seeing the world through the client's eyes. Our research permits us to predict that if these attitudinal conditions are instituted or established, certain behavioral consequences will ensue. Putting it this way sounds as if we are again back in the familiar groove of being able to predict behavior, and hence able to control it. But it is precisely here that we find a sharp difference.

The conditions we have chosen to establish predict such behavioral consequences as these: the client will become more self-directing, less rigid, more open to the evidence of his senses, better organized and integrated, more similar to the ideal which he has chosen for himself. In other words, by external control we have established conditions which we predict will be followed by internal control by the individual, in pursuit of internally chosen goals. We have set the conditions which predict various classes of behavior—self-directing behaviors, sensitivity to realities within and without, flexible adaptiveness—which are by their very nature *unpredictable* in their specifics. The conditions we have established predict behavior which is essentially "free." Our recent research (Rogers and Dymond, 1954), indicates that our predictions are to a significant degree corroborated, and our commitment to the scientific method causes us to believe that more effective means of achieving these goals may be realized.

Research exists in other fields—industry, education, group dynamics—which seems to support our own findings. I believe it may be conservatively stated that scientific progress has been made in identifying those conditions in an interpersonal relationship which, if they exist in B, are followed in A by greater maturity in behavior, less dependence upon others, an increase in expressiveness as a person, an increase in variability, flexibility and effectiveness of adaptation, an increase in self-responsibility and self-direction. And quite in contrast to the concern expressed by some, we do not find that the creatively adaptive behavior which results from such self-directed variability of expression is too chaotic or too fluid. Rather, the individual who is open to his experience, and self-directing, is harmonious, not chaotic, and ingenious rather than random as he orders his responses imaginatively toward the achievement of his own purposes. His creative actions are no more a chaotic accident than was Einstein's development of the theory of relativity.

Thus we find ourselves in fundamental agreement with John Dewey's statement: "Science has made its way by releasing, not by suppressing, the elements of variation, of invention and innovation, of novel creation in individuals" (in Ratner, 1939, p. 359). We have come to believe that progress in personal life and in group living is made in the same way, by releasing variation, freedom, creativity.

A POSSIBLE CONCEPT OF THE CONTROL OF HUMAN BEHAVIOR

It is quite clear that the point of view I am expressing is in sharp contrast to the usual conception of the relationship of the behavioral sciences to the control of human behavior, previously mentioned. In order to make this contrast even more blunt, I will state this possibility in a form parallel to the steps which I described before:

1. It is possible for us to choose to value man as a self-actualizing process of becoming; to value creativity, and the process by which knowledge becomes self-transcending.
2. We can proceed, by the methods of science, to discover the conditions which necessarily precede these processes, and, through continuing experimentation, to discover better means of achieving these purposes.
3. It is possible for individuals or groups to set these conditions, with a minimum of power or control. According to present knowledge, the only authority necessary is the authority to establish certain qualities of interpersonal relationship.
4. Present knowledge suggests that, exposed to these conditions, individuals become more self-responsible, make progress in self-actualization, become more flexible, more unique and varied, more creatively adaptive.
5. Thus such an initial choice would inaugurate the beginnings of a social system or subsystem in which values, knowledge, adaptive skills, and even the concept of science would be continually changing and self-transcending. The emphasis would be upon man as a process of becoming.

I believe it is clear that such a view as I have been describing does not lead to any definable Utopia. It would be impossible to predict its final outcome. It involves a step-by-step development, based upon a continuing subjective choice of purposes, which are implemented by the behavioral sciences. It is in the direction of the "open society," as that term has been defined by Popper (1945), where individuals carry responsibility for personal decisions. It is at the opposite pole from his concept of the closed society, of which *Walden Two* would be an example.

I trust it is also evident that the whole emphasis is upon process, not upon end states of being. I am suggesting that it is by choosing to value certain qualitative elements of the process of becoming that we can find a pathway toward the open society.

THE CHOICE

It is my hope that I have helped to clarify the range of choice which will lie before us and our children in regard to the behavioral sciences. We can choose to use our growing knowledge to enslave people in ways never dreamed of before, depersonalizing them, controlling them by means so carefully selected that they will perhaps never be aware of their loss of personhood. We can choose to utilize our scientific knowledge to make men necessarily happy, well behaved, and productive, as Dr. Skinner suggests. We can, if we wish, choose to make men submissive, conforming, docile. Or, at the other end of the spectrum of choice, we can choose to use the behavioral sciences in ways which will free, not control; which will bring about constructive variability, not conformity; which will develop creativity, not contentment; which will facilitate each person in his self-directed process of becoming; which will aid individuals, groups, and even the concept of science to become self-transcending in freshly adaptive ways of meeting life and its problems. The choice is up to us, and because the human race is what it is, we are likely to stumble about, making at times some nearly disastrous value choices, and at other times highly constructive ones.

If we choose to utilize our scientific knowledge to free men, then it will demand that we live openly and frankly with the great paradox of the behavioral sciences. We will recognize that behavior, when examined scientifically, is surely best understood as determined by prior causation. This is the great fact of science. But responsible personal choice, which is the most essential element in being a person, which is the core experience in psychotherapy, which exists prior to any scientific endeavor, is an equally prominent fact in our lives. We will have to live with the realization that to deny the reality of the experience of responsible personal choice is as stultifying, as closed minded, as to deny the possibility of a behavioral science. That these two important elements of our experience appear to be in contradiction has perhaps the same significance as the contradiction between the wave theory and the corpuscular theory of light, both of which can be shown to be true, even though incompatible. We cannot profitably deny our subjective life, any more than we can deny the objective description of that life.

In conclusion, then, it is my contention that science cannot come into being without a personal choice of the values we wish to achieve. And the values we choose to implement will forever lie outside the science which implements them; the goals we select, the purposes we wish to follow, must always be outside the science which achieves them. To me this has the encouraging meaning that the human person, with his capacity of subjective choice, can and will always exist separate from and prior to any of his scientific undertakings.

Unless, as individuals and groups, we choose to relinquish our capacity of subjective choice, we will always remain free persons, not simply pawns of a self-created behavioral science.

REFERENCES

Huxley, Aldous. *Brave New World.* Harper & Row, 1946.

Meerloo, J. A. M. "Medication into Submission: The Danger of Therapeutic Coercion." *Journal of Nervous and Mental Disorders,* Vol. 122, 1955.

Niebuhr, Reinhold. *The Self and the Dramas of History*. Scribner, 1955.

Oppenheimer, J. Robert. "Science and Our Times." *Roosevelt University Occasional Papers,* Vol. 2, 1956.

Orwell, George. *1984*. Harcourt, 1948.

Popper, K. R. *The Open Society and Its Enemies.* Routledge and Kegan Paul, 1945.

Ratner, J., ed. *Intelligence in the Modern World: John Dewey's Philosophy*. 1939.

Rogers, C. R. *Client-Centered Therapy*. Houghton Mifflin, 1951.

——, and Rosalind Dymond, eds. *Psychotherapy and Personality Change*. University of Chicago Press, 1954.

Skinner, B. F. "Freedom and the Control of Men." *American Scholar,* Vol. 25, Winter 1955/56.

——. *Science and Human Behavior*. Macmillan, 1953.

——. *Walden Two*. Macmillan, 1948.

Whyte, William H., Jr. *The Organization Man*. Simon & Schuster, 1956.

Chapter 15

Self-Management in the Flexible Organization

ALVAR ELBING and JOHN GORDON

Worker participation in management had been discussed long before its experimentation in organizations, and these experiments significantly predated its success as a system. Success, in fact, has not always resulted from participative systems of management. The record is at best ambiguous. However, at the present time in Europe, systems of flexibility in working hours, job design, and organizational structure—all participative in nature—are producing individual, organizational, and community consequences in keeping with early participative theories.

Although participation in management has many different connotations—from the worker councils of Germany, the group decision making in the United States, to the leaderless groups of Norway—our reference is to what can be labelled "self-management" systems in which the employee can participate in the management of his own life on and off the job. The successful emergence of these self-management systems raises numerous questions for the future, especially for planning and forecasting of organizational changes. If the current trends continue, the organization model of today—the status quo–will have to yield to new forms, still only vaguely definable with present data.

The "manager" of these self-managing systems—an apparent contradiction in terms—will require a new style, focusing more on the needs of the self-managing employee than on the leadership style of the formal manager. Managers of the future will be—as they should be now—servants of the people who produce, rather than pied pipers to followers, often hypothesized as mindless, lazy, disinterested, and irresponsible.

This shifting focus is already evident in many organizations

"Self-Management in the Flexible Organization" by Alvar Elbing and John Gordon, *Futures*, August 1974, pp. 319–328. Reprinted by permission of IPC Science and Technology Press Ltd.

where managers trained in the traditional way struggle with the changes frequently emerging from the bottom of the organization, in conflict with management tradition. In one French factory, for example, a well-trained engineer given "responsibility" for a manufacturing unit was told: "Your job is to be available when needed. Don't interfere. How and when the work is done is the responsibility of the workers. They will come to you if needed." Despite the doubling of productivity in "his" unit, the frustrated manager was forced to search for things to do to placate his traditional assumptions about his role.

The key word in the changes taking place all over Europe is *flexibility*. It has appeared in the organizational parameters which formerly bound the worker to the regimen of the job and subordinated his needs to those of the system. Flexibility has also allowed workers to make decisions about their own jobs—their own lives—that are anathema to the principles of management diligently learned by a former generation. Organizational blinds to this emerging flexibility will result in plans and forecasts based on a static model of the present.

TRENDS AND CONSEQUENCES OF FLEXIBILITY

Flexibility in organizations now exists, at least in terms of working hours, job design, and organizational structure. Although these changes are only beginning, they are visible in many different kinds of organizations in different cultures.

Working Hour Arrangements

Since its inception about 1967, the system known as flexible working hours has emerged rapidly in Western Europe and spread worldwide. To date, at least 6000 organizations are known to be using the system. The actual number is probably more. Details of the system have been presented elsewhere (Elbing, Gadon, and Gordon, 1973, 1974; Gordon and Elbing, 1971), but briefly it is one in which employees may choose the hours each day that they will work. Systems of flexible working hours generally include some limitations on the choice, but in general the employee does not have to ask permission to arrive any time within roughly a 2-hour time span, or to leave in the evening within an equally long period. He can accumulate time and in many cases is allowed to take off half or full days in return.

A different version of the system is known as variable working hours, where the employee can come and go whenever he wishes. He must still work a certain number of hours per accounting period, but there is no core time specified. He is not required to be at the job at any particular time. This has been observed in some organizations on a 24-hour basis—especially in computer centers where the computers are in heavy use—and in others during extended daytime hours. The essential feature of both flexible and variable hours is that the employee is in a position to make choices about the relationship between his personal life and his work life without asking permission from management.

Data related to observable consequences are still being gathered, but early results appear to be the same in different countries, and the system seems to be received universally well. The behavioral effects currently reported are reductions in turnover, absenteeism, sick leave, and overtime costs. In addition, changes in satisfaction and productivity have been reported, as have changes in the behavior of first-line supervisors.

While the observable behavioral consequences of flexible hours appear at the moment to be positive in terms of motivation, satisfaction, and productivity, perhaps the most significant feature is the rapid manner in which the system is being accepted. Control of working time has long been a tightly held management prerogative. Tremendous emphasis has been placed on punctuality and attendance and, therefore, the ability of management to control employee performance. Flexible and variable working hours significantly shift the basis of control from the manager to the employee himself and take away punctuality and attendance as items directly under managerial control. The relatively rapid and successful introduction of this system seems to violate the general resistance to organizational changes frequently reported. In Europe, management seems as willing to introduce the system as are the workers. It is only the unions, who sometimes see this as a loss of control, who have resisted its introduction.

Job Design

Changes in this area have been steadily emerging since the advent of scientific management, but their nature itself seems to have been changing in recent years. In earlier systems, management relied heavily on the industrial engineer to determine the most efficient system, which was then imposed on the work force. It was therefore necessary for the labor force to adapt to a predesigned system.

In recent years many experiments have taken place, giving workers greater control, or flexibility, in respect to their jobs. In essence the design is focused on the needs of the workers and adapted to them, making possible adjustments and variations to suit his or the work group's needs. Examples of these experiments can be seen at General Foods, Volvo, SAAB, IBM, Philips, etc. The labels used to describe many of these changes are *job rotation, job enlargement*, and *job enrichment*.

Job rotation means that the worker moves from one job to another during the day, week, or month, in some pattern designed to reduce the sameness of work. In the motor industry, e.g., the worker would move perhaps every hour from installing hubcaps to installing mufflers and then to working on interior trim. At higher organizational levels, job rotation may mean moving from one section of the accounting or finance department to another every six months. This would help the individual to build a total work experience.

The difference between job enlargement and job enrichment may best be visualized as the difference between a horizontal and a vertical expansion of the job. The concept of increasing the cycle time of work is an example of job enlargement, whereas increasing the job responsibility and decision-making input is an example of job enrichment. Frequently both kinds of changes take place at the same time. In the European motor industry, for example, the cycle time on the assembly line is being increased so that the individual can do several different tasks on each car. At the same time, jobs may be enriched by, e.g., extending the worker's responsibility beyond installing the window and the hardware on a door, to inspecting and approving the door for quality. He may then be required to place his signature on a paper attesting to this quality.

In other industries such as typewriter production at IBM or television sets at Philips, the traditional assembly line is being broken down into movable parts over which the worker exerts some control. Instead of doing only one part of the job, the team completes the whole typewriter or television set and certifies its quality. In some situations in the United States, workers hire, evaluate, and fire their peers, and in extreme cases determine the future of their supervisors (*Work in America*, 1973). These rapidly emerging job designs are a dramatic change from the industrial-engineered workplaces of the past.

Reported results have included 10–40 percent reductions in labor and maintenance costs at General Foods, reduced turnover at Volvo, and increased satisfaction at most organizations which have made such experiments. However, controversy still exists over whether job enrichment is really an effective technique, but at the moment much of the controversy seems to be semantic. Writers favorable to job enrichment can classify successful experiences as job enrichment, and thus demonstrate its effectiveness. Writers less favorable to job enrichment can take examples that have not succeeded and define them as job enrichment and thus support their hypotheses. In both cases the motives may be good, but the results seem to be considerable confusion about the exact reason for the consequences one sees when these job changes are initiated.

What is it that motivates the worker? In many cases it is the method of installation or implementation rather than the system itself–the Hawthorne Effect. On the other hand, if a new system is introduced by management directive, even if the system is quite participative in nature, it may not be perceived that way. Whether the good effects observed now will persist will be carefully monitored. It would be unwise to make extrapolations based totally on the present experience, but the accumulated data are, in general, so consistent that it is equally unwise to fail to take these changes into consideration. It also seems unwise to disregard changes that promise to deal with the problem of alienation.

Organization Structure

Several kinds of structural changes seem to be taking place in organizations, but one which tends to increase managerial flexibility is the movement toward matrix or project organizations. Our experiences at Sandoz, Dow-Corning, Philips, and many others indicate the spreading of responsibility for various projects or sub-units to numerous members of the organization who might otherwise not have such an opportunity. Other organizations are experimenting with less vertically structured hierarchies, sabbatical leaves for managers, and early retirement for managing directors.

The rapidly increasing introduction of groups into organizations is also changing relationships dramatically. Whereas in the past the hierarchy tended to start from managing director and end with worker through individual levels of managers, today there are groups in the executive committees at the top, project teams in the middle, and the work groups on the assembly lines. This tends to change not only the traditional concept of authority, or reporting, but also requires that employees change some of their attitudes towards the job. Changes in job design which have resulted in formation of teams that can evaluate their own performance, organize their own work, recruit their own members, and evaluate management significantly modify the nature of organizational structures.

With this internal change comes the increased ability of employees to alter their career opportunities. Leave of absence for education or for social service work is now common in many large organizations. The idea that a person may wish to retrain at middle life and have a second career is being discussed readily. Although not every experiment is carried through, or is effective, it is inconceivable that the formal hierarchy of the past should continue. The major consequence of matrix or project forms of organization seems to be the tapping of additional managerial skills and the initiation of increased responsibility for members who might not otherwise have such an opportunity. In one organization where there may not be enough promotion opportunities for everyone, the matrix organization provides an opportunity for managerial responsibility. Although complicated to initiate, the systems tend to increase communication horizontally as well as vertically and produce a revitalization of management.

WHAT ARE THE EFFECTS?

The Individual Worker

The specific effects may vary under the different systems described but, in general, these systems appear to be giving the employee an increase in power by offering him additional choices in life and work. He acquires opportunities in areas of behavior not previously available to him, and these can amount to an increased feeling of power over those aspects of his life that may be most important to him. In flexible systems of working, the individual has the opportunity to balance his personal and organizational lives in a way that could increase his self-respect.

In addition to satisfaction, growth, and development for employees, the emerging flexible system also changes dramatically the traditional stability within organizations. Managers who once made decisions now consult with colleagues. Plans that used to be implemented by directive are now discussed with the people affected. Organizational goals which were determined by representatives of shareholders are now influenced by all who have a "stake" in the organization.

The Organization

The behavior of individuals determines the organization's design. Intra-organizational communication will change as people are more flexible in their working times and places. Inter-company relations will develop in different ways since the former predictable rigidities will not be existing between them. New boundary relationships between organizations may emerge when individuals at the interface between groups, divisions, and organizations can now relate to one another more in terms of their own needs.

Earlier we indicated that organizations benefited in terms of reductions of overtime, turnover, absenteeism, etc; they also benefit in terms of style of supervision and other intra-organizational relationships. However, there is the possibility of breakdowns in communication because people are not there at the same time, difficulty in control since people have responsibility for their own work, and an increased amount of independence on the part of the labor force.

The Community

Perhaps the most interesting social effect of the flexible working hours is the change in patterns of transport, recreation, and energy consumption. Figures 1 and 2 show the effect on transportation in a Swiss city

Figure 1 Comparison of Occupancy, in a Medium-Sized Swiss Industrial City, of Public Transportation

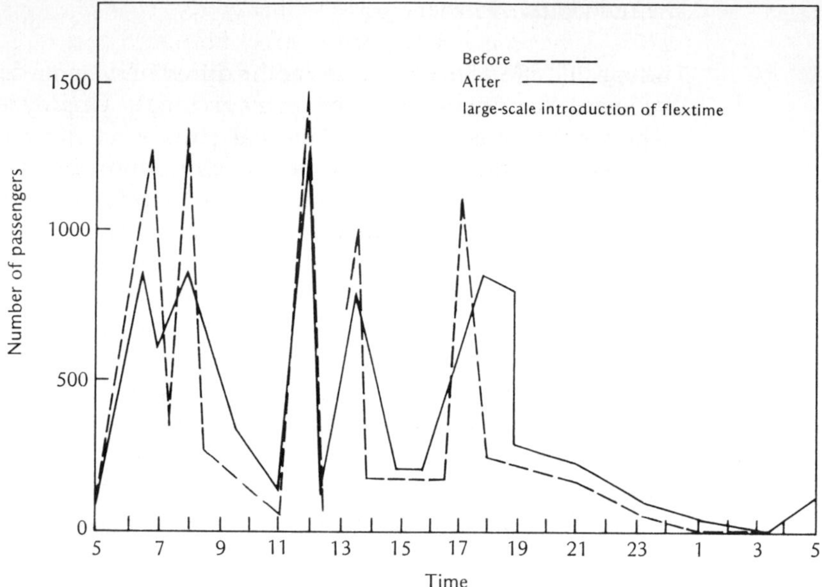

Figure 2 Arrival Times of Citizens Attending a Registration Agency in a Medium-Sized Swiss Industrial City

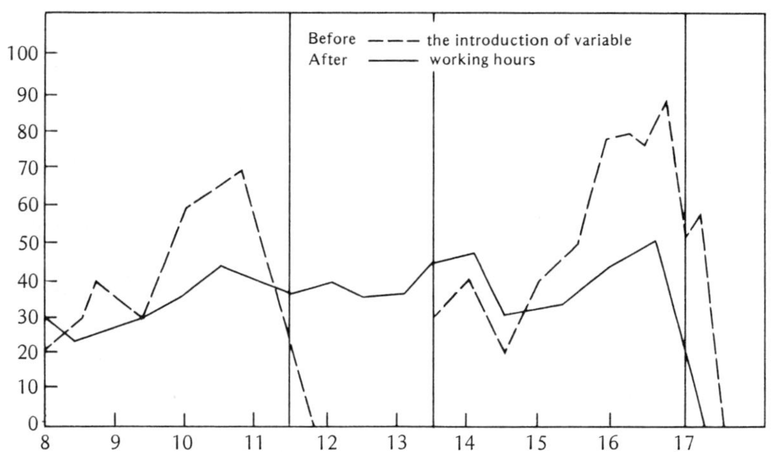

where 60 percent of the population is on such a system. From 1970 to 1973, the amount of people using the buses in this city increased but the number of buses necessary was reduced by 10 percent since the peak operating periods were significantly reduced. In a government office where variable hours were introduced, the waiting times of citizens were dramatically reduced, thus wasting less aggregate employee time.

In Ottawa, Ontario, Canada, where 42,000 governmental employees are on flexible working hours, similar traffic effects have been noted. John Bonsell, Director of Planning for the Ottawa-Carleton Regional Transit Company, said about flexible hours: "The scheme has been the biggest thing that's happened to transit and transport." An increase in public transportation usage together with a reduction in waiting times has had a marked effect on traffic flow in Ottawa. Even parking lot utilization has changed. Although so far the experience is short-run, the effects are quite similar to those in Switzerland (List, 1974).

The potential effects on society are numerous, but at the moment only hypothetical. To our knowledge, there is only one city with such a large percentage of its population on flexible hours, but over time, the Ottawa experience could tell us what would happen in a large metropolitan area. We might see changes in shopping and transportation patterns, increased use of recreational facilities, etc. The Chamber of Commerce of the City of London suggested, in December 1973, that by introducing flexible hours peak loads on transportation and energy could be reduced by 25 percent (*Financial Times*, 1973).

WHAT'S IN IT FOR WOMEN?

Women are likely to be the group most affected. There are three aspects of this: the individual woman and her ability to interact in the community; the organization facing a labor shortage; the community which must solve the problem of lack of opportunity for women. The woman at 40 finds herself free of children, interested in the world at large, freer to travel and meet people, but unable to obtain positions in industry or in society in general. The mother with children at school may not want the constraints of fixed organizational relationships. The introduction of flexible organizations dramatically increases the possibility of women participating in society.

Flexible working hours can allow women to come and go from work so that they can fulfill the needs of their families. Flexible working hours have also led to variable amounts of time worked in a day or week. Therefore women are now, in some companies, able to work between 20 and 40 hours—whatever meets their needs. Flexible job design increases the kinds of jobs available and the amount of satisfaction that can be derived.

The consequences for women will, of course, have effects for men. The traditional assumptions about male employees will have to change (e.g., some men will be supervised by women), and the biological and family needs of women will become more important to planning and organizing in business.

CONSEQUENCES ON MANAGEMENT

The individual's greater sense of self-identity and freedom of choice surrounding his own life will affect both organization and society. The

Table 1 Functions of the Manager in Nonflexible and Flexible Organizations

Traditional Assumptions About Management	Future Assumptions About Management
Planning	
An executive function moving down the organization.	A function for everyone, essentially moving up the organization.
Organizing	
The manager determines how and when work is to be done, assigns it to employees.	The employee determines how and when his work is done within jointly determined deadlines.
Authority and Responsibility	
Rests with the manager. He delegates authority commensurate with responsibility. Each employee has one boss.	Authority and responsibility rest with employees who exercise it over their own work. They seek help from managers when it is needed. In matrix organizations employees will have to report to 2 or 3 people.
Staffing	
Management determines the staffing needs and selects employees based on industrial-engineered work systems.	The working group determines the staffing requirements, hires employees, and designates and evaluates managers.
Hierarchy	
There was some limit to the number of people whom one could control. Extent of control was discussed in terms of quantity of workers per manager.	Hierarchy will be significantly flatter since people will be left to manage themselves.
Directing	
The manager directs and motivates the work of subordinates.	Employees are self-directed and self-motivated and turn to management when they need help.
Controlling	
Uses external control systems for management.	Will rely on employee self-control.

adjustment of traditional organizational and societal boundaries to new expectations of freedom on the part of the employee can only reinforce the desires and satisfaction attained from this increasing control.

The evidence to date is not extensive, since we are talking only about thousands of organizations out of many millions in the world. However, two factors make these data of considerable importance: (1) the effects of these systems have mainly been favorable, and (2) the effects appear to be the same in different cultures. This means that the introduction of flexible working arrangements is meeting both individual and organizational needs. It also means that the motivation behind this satisfaction must be even more fundamental than culture.

What in fact would it mean for the manager of the future? A look at the traditional aspects of management in terms of coping with potential changes indicates that quite a different style will be necessary in the future (Table 1). The foreseeable shift, then, is from the concept of manager as boss to manager as servant. For the traditionally trained manager, this may be perceived as virtually a role reversal; from parent he may see himself becoming child. In fact, the emerging flexible systems require greater maturity than the old directive managements. The manager will be held responsible to his "subordinates" as well as to his superiors. Success will emerge in relation to his ability to influence rather than to overpower. Power will exist in the individual over his own life situation and over others *only* when the system broadly defined fails to function.

The initial reaction to the emergence of this changing role will certainly be resistance on the part of traditionally trained managers. It is interesting to note, however, that although the concept of participating in managerial decisions has been discussed for at least a generation, it is only now that organizations are experimenting with and fully accepting this concept as a reality. To explain this, we suggest that the organizational changes are subject to a generation lag, i.e., an individual learns his concept of reality during the formative years—school and early work relationships—and it remains throughout his lifetime. The effect of this is that ideas which do not fit his views of reality may not even be viewed as legitimate for consideration.

The ideas associated with participation in the running of organizations have essentially matured with the current generation. Having studied, discussed and experienced participation during the post World War II period, managers in the United States and Western Europe confronted with such a style have a greater receptivity to it. One could therefore expect that the managers of the next generation who grew up in organizations with the beginnings of involvement, due to organizational flexibility, would gradually be able to adapt to the demands of a more flexible managerial system.

Finally, the nature of the organization in which the manager operates will change. The concepts of specialization, standardization and economy of scale which evolved from scientific management in the past no longer seem appropriate. The Lordstown, Ohio, plant of General Motors was the epitome of industrial organization which led to a simplification and routinization of work, the interchangeability of parts and equipment. This giant system seems to become overpowered by its inherent alienation. It is very likely, therefore, that organizations will reduce in size to gain psychological economies of scale. Smaller organizations are also more suited to flexible organizational structures and design than giant ones. The emergence of smaller organizations may also suit the de-urbanization of society where large cities have become difficult places to live in.

Perhaps the biggest problem exists for schools of management, business administration, public administration, and management development. Although these institutions tend to perceive themselves at the forefront, they can frequently teach only what is acceptable to the current generation of top management. It is not uncommon to have organizations resist hiring the most far-out, creative, and talented of these graduates since they do not fit in traditional organizations.

How, then, do schools prepare people more rapidly for the ever changing flexible organization of the future? Perhaps in the short run it must be a balance between the two. At some point, however, training methods which truly develop the tolerance for constantly changing work situations must be evolved.

FINAL NOTE

If indeed work is important to man and necessary for society, the satisfactions that can be obtained from it are an important societal goal. The emerging flexible organization should help man meet these needs. The desire for a more meaningful position or role in society, rather than just being a cog in a machine, may tend to foster these changes in organizational design and behavior. Smaller organizations may appear, reducing problems of communication and frustration. The availability of such systems has emerged and the needs of people may well push these systems farther than we may be able to hypothesize today.

REFERENCES

Elbing, Alvar, Herman Gadon, and John Gordon. "Flexible Working Hours: It's About Time." *Harvard Business Review*, January–February 1974.

——. "Time for a Human Time-Table." *European Business*, Autumn 1973.

Gordon, John, and Alvar Elbing. "The 'Flexible Hours' Work Week—European Trend Is Growing." *The Business Quarterly*, Winter 1971.

Financial Times, December 12, 1973.

List, Wilfred. "Flexible Hours Experiment in Ottawa Called Successful." *Toronto Globe and Mail*, May 31, 1974.

Work in America. Report of a Special Task Force to the Secretary of Health, Education, and Welfare. MIT Press, 1973.

ALAN N. SCHOONMAKER

Individualism in Management

The traditional American dream is dead for most of us. The traditional American dream has always centered on independence and individualism. A man could open his own business, buy a small business, get his own farm, move

"Individualism in Management" by Alan N. Schoonmaker. © 1968 by the Regents of the University of California. Reprinted from *California Management Review*, Vol. 11, No. 2, pp. 9–22, by permission of the Regents.

West, etc. These opportunities no longer exist for most of us, especially for the professional manager. We are employees and *will always be employees.* Furthermore, an increasing percentage of us will always be employees of large organizations.

Being an employee, especially an employee of a large organization, necessarily leads to the loss of a great deal of independence. Instead of making his own decisions, an employee (whether he is a manager or a worker) responds to the decisions of other people. Instead of acting independently to control his own life and career, an employee gives up this control and becomes dependent upon his superiors and his organization. This loss of control is especially noticeable for decisions related to his own career. Instead of acting for his own interests, an employee is expected to work for the good of his organization and leave the decisions about his career to other people. . . .

As Professor C. Argyris and many others have observed, some conflict between the individual's needs and desires and the demands of his organization is inevitable, regardless of the level the individual occupies in the organization: "There are some basic incongruencies between the growth trends of a healthy personality and the requirements of a formal organization."[1] These conflicts and incongruencies can be reduced, but some conflict is *inevitable.*

Some of the more important conflicts are between the organization's need for control and predictability and the individual's desire for freedom and independence; between the organization's need for standardization and the individual's desire for variety and enjoyable work; between the organization's demand for loyalty (even unquestioning loyalty) and the individual's belief that his primary loyalties should be to himself, his ideals, his career, and his family.

Although the conflict between individuals and organizations is a general one, occurring between each individual and every organization to which he belongs, I will direct attention to conflicts between the needs and aspirations of middle managers and the organizations which employ them.

REASONS FOR DEPENDENCE

I am focusing upon middle managers because these conflicts are more important for them than for other managers. Top managers have greater control over their organizations and are more able to act independently than middle managers. The problem is more acute for middle managers than it is for workers for several reasons:

- There is much less awareness of these conflicts among managers than there is among workers. Workers generally recognize the conflicts between their interests and the organization's, but many managers and writers about management assume (or act as if they assume) that the interests of managers and their organizations are identical[2] —a fiction top management is very eager to preserve. Obviously, until these conflicts of interest are recognized, no effective action can be taken.
- Workers have unions (or can acquire them) to represent their interests against the interests of the corporation, but managers have no such organizations. Since they must bargain with the organization as individuals and the organi-

[1] C. Argyris, *Personality and Organization.* New York: Harper & Row, 1957, p. 67.
[2] C. W. Mills, *White Collar.* New York: Oxford University Press, 1953, pp. 100–106.

zation is so much more powerful than they are, they have very limited power to influence it.

- The idea of company loyalty is much stronger for managers than it is for workers, further increasing the powerlessness and dependency of individual managers.
- Managers are generally more concerned about their jobs and careers than workers. Their jobs and careers greatly influence their beliefs about themselves and their personal satisfaction, while workers are more likely to regard their jobs as simply a source of income. The psychological and social effects of powerlessness, etc., are therefore greater.
- The organization interferes much more with the family and home life of managers than it does with workers. Managers spend much more time away from home, have to relocate their families if the organization transfers them, are often required to involve their wives in business socializing, and may even have their careers affected by their superiors' opinions of their wives or home life.
- Many managers are "locked into" their organizations by deferred compensation and pension plans. These plans greatly increase the organization's control over their lives since they can't afford to quit and may even be afraid to act independently in any way.
- Many professional managers do not possess the skills (or the capital) to start their own business. Their skills and backgrounds are suitable only for work in large organizations.

Because of these factors, most middle managers are quite powerless and dependent upon their organizations. They are well paid and well treated, but they know that they have lost control over their own lives and become dependent upon their organizations. And, because a basic part of their nature is a desire for independence and the self-respect and inner security that only independence can provide, this knowledge is painful. They may attempt to avoid thinking about their dependency and powerlessness by concentrating upon their homes, cars, and other material evidence of the organization's generosity, they may dull their senses with too many cocktails, but they can never really escape the knowledge that the organization controls them, nor can they escape the anxiety and resentment this knowledge causes. Managers, who are often regarded as "exploiters," are today one of the most exploited groups in our society. They have money, prestige, and comfort, but they have paid dearly for them—with their independence and self-respect.

> Our aspiring executives (while the most fussed-over segment of our society) are the most manipulated and exploited steady jobholders in the land. A new kind of gruff paternalism has developed in our large enterprises, an exploitation of leaders rather than laborers.[3]
>
> In the movement from authority to manipulation, power shifts from the visible to the invisible, from the known to the anonymous, and with rising material standards, exploitation becomes less material and more psychological.[4]. . .

---

[3] Vance Packard, *The Pyramid Climbers*. New York: McGraw-Hill, 1962, p. 18.
[4] Mills, op. cit., p. 110.

CAREER DECISIONS

The task, then, is not to beat our breasts and call for a return to the American tradition of individualism, but to present a comprehensive program for *successfully exerting independence in large organizations*. Such a program must specify the areas in which an individual can most legitimately and effectively exert his independence and provide methods for increasing his ability to resist the organization.

Although there are other areas in which he can and should exert his independence, we believe that the area in which independence is most legitimate and necessary is his own career development—his compensation, promotions, duties, responsibilities, transfers, etc. This area is the most legitimate one because the conflicts between his interests and the organization's are greatest here and because decisions about his career have such a great impact upon his life, happiness, and family. Independence can most effectively be exerted here because there are ways to counter the power of his organization which can greatly increase his satisfaction, independence, and self-respect.

However, even though there are clear conflicts between his interests and the organization's, and decisions about his career are more important for him than for the organization, attempts to advance his own interests are usually regarded as illegitimate (or even antisocial). He is not supposed to think about his career; he is expected to be loyal to the organization, work for its interests, and leave the decisions about his career to his superiors.

> The organization communicates to the manager that he is not expected to take responsibility for his own career at the same time that it is trying to teach him to be able to take responsibility for important decisions![5]

This ethic is communicated to him in many ways—in derogatory comments about "company politicians," in satirical works such as "How to Succeed in Business Without Really Trying," in constant reminders of the need for "company loyalty," and in a variety of much more subtle ways.

If, despite these pressures, a man still wanted to learn how to advance his career, he would find that the publishers and educators have generally ignored the topic. They, too, have assumed that men should work for the good of their organizations and ignore their own interests. They have focused on ways for men to help their organizations and have ignored ways for them to help themselves. A man seeking advice on how to advance his career would find that there are hundreds of books and articles which tell him how to improve his work, but almost none which tell him how to get rewarded for it. He is bombarded with advice on how to manipulate his subordinates (and doing so is regarded as legitimate), but can't get advice on how to manipulate his superiors (and his superiors have much more effect upon his career than his subordinates do). He can take courses on almost every aspect of his job—leadership, communication, cost accounting, decision making, etc.—but no school offers courses in company politics, techniques for negotiating raises or promotions, or any other aspect of executive career planning. He is simply not supposed to think about these things. Doing so is regarded as illegitimate, unethical, or antisocial.

I challenge this ethic. I regard it as another clever psychological trick for

---

[5] E. Schein, "Management Development as a Process of Influence," *Industrial Management Review*, May 1961, pp. 59–77.

manipulating individuals for the benefit of organizations and feel that it is a perversion of the American tradition to regard a man's attempts to control his own career as unethical. It is not regarded as unethical for him to control his own capital or to strive for the maximum return on it. Why, then, is it unethical for him to try to control his career and strive for the maximum return on his time and earning ability? His time and earning capacity are his primary capital; they are worth far more than any other asset he has. Why should he be more restricted in the way he invests his life than in the way he invests his money? I believe that lives are more important than money, and people more important than organizations. I therefore feel that it is legitimate, proper, and ethical for a man to try to control his own career, increase his independence of his organization, and work for his own interests.

NEED FOR INFORMATION

Even if a man agreed with my position about *where* he should fight the organization, he would still face the problem of *how* to fight it successfully, how to control his own career.

An important related problem is the lack of good information and advice on executive career problems. This issue merits discussion because a man who decides to resist the vast power of his own and other organizations and ignore the pressures against trying to control his own career needs good information and advice, but can't get it today. Without this information and advice his chances for successfully exerting his independence are very limited; therefore, if individualism is to survive, adequate sources of information and advice must be developed.

There can be no doubt whatsoever that there is a serious lack of information related to executive career problems. Counseling and clinical psychologists, who are usually the major source of information about individual problems, have devoted nearly all of their attention to children and people who are abnormal or deficient in some way—physically handicapped, mentally retarded, emotionally disturbed, etc. Far more work has been done with children and abnormal adults than with normal, intelligent, reasonably successful adults.[6] We know much more about the career problems of blind people or amputees or ex-mental patients than we do about the career problems of executives.

Executives and executive careers have been studied many times by industrial social scientists, but, as we noted earlier, nearly all of their work has focused on ways to increase organizational effectiveness rather than on the career problems and ambitions of the executives themselves.

Many of the people who have studied executives have intended to work solely or primarily for the benefit of organizations and have been indifferent to the executives themselves. Although I don't care for their emphasis, I have no real quarrel with them; helping organizations and our industrial and social system to work better is certainly a reasonable and legitimate goal. My quarrel is with the social scientists and other serious students of management who have refused to make a choice between working for individuals or organizations, or who have acted as if no choice were necessary because they saw no fundamental

[6] M. Hahn, *Psychoevaluation*. New York: McGraw-Hill, 1963.

and irreconcilable conflicts between them. Unfortunately, many people fall into this category.

> There seems to be a certain amount of confusion as to whether prescriptions for power-equalization (i.e., modern leadership techniques) are written from the point of view of organizational efficiency or that of mental health. . . . There are those who claim that what is good for the individual will, in the long run, be good for the organization and vice versa. Regardless, it is useful to keep one's criteria explicit.[7] . . .

SPECIFIC ADVICE

Until now, my remarks have been impersonal; I have commented upon certain developments and their consequences. Now I am going to make specific recommendations for the manager who wants to control his own career. In other words, I am no longer referring to people or careers in general, but making direct recommendations to a manager that can be used to increase his independence and control over his own career.

1. *Accept the fact that there are some inescapable and irreconcilable conflicts between you and your organization.* There are many areas in which your interest and your organization's are nearly identical, others in which they are unrelated to each other, and others in which they are opposed. This rather obvious fact is hard for some men to accept. They prefer to believe that there are no real conflicts, that all problems and frictions are caused by poor communication, misunderstandings, etc. They do not want to believe that, even if communication were perfect and there were no misunderstandings, there would still be conflicts, problems, and friction because there are opposed interests. What is good for the organization is not always good for you or vice versa. If you do not accept this simple fact, if you assume, or act as if you assume, that there are no conflicts between your interests and your organization's, you can never become truly independent of your organization.

On the other hand, seeing conflicts where none exist, or unduly emphasizing the conflicts which do exist, can be self-destructive because your superiors will regard you as disloyal, a troublemaker, or a nuisance. You therefore need to strike a balance, recognizing common interests as well as conflicts of interests, working for the organization's interests when possible, your own when necessary; being loyal, but not blindly loyal; creating the impression that you are loyal, but also letting your superiors know that you are aware of your own interests.

2. *Accept the fact that your superiors are essentially indifferent to your career ambitions.* You are a means to an end for them, not an end in yourself. They are primarily concerned with their own careers and ambitions and the survival, growth, and functioning of their units and the organization. Their jobs and their responsibilities are to look out for their units' and the organization's welfare, not yours. They are therefore indifferent to your career ambitions (except, of course, for the effects these ambitions have upon them, their units, or the organization).

---

[7] G. Strauss, "Some Notes on Power-Equalization," *The Social Science of Organizations*, ed. H. Leavitt. Englewood Cliffs, N.J.: Prentice-Hall, 1963, p. 47.

They are not opposed to your ambitions; they are simply indifferent to them.[8] Furthermore, since they are responsible for their units and the organizations, not your career, it would be irresponsible for them to be anything but indifferent to your career. These obvious facts are also hard for some men to accept. They want to believe that their superiors care for them, that they are not alone. Personnel men and their superiors work very hard to create and sustain this impression since it helps them acquire and control people. They communicate in a variety of ways that "the sky is the limit" or "We have great things planned for you." But thousands of you have already discovered that they don't mean it, and many more of you will discover it when you are passed over for promotion, get fired, don't get a raise, or are transferred to some unpleasant place or job "for the good of the organization."

It may be hard for you to accept the facts of conflict and indifference. It requires courage and realistic thinking. It requires accepting the frightening knowledge that you are alone, that your organization and superiors don't really care about you, that beneath the friendly, benevolent surface are inescapable conflicts, and that you are the only one who is really concerned about your career. It may be unpleasant to face these facts, but doing so is absolutely necessary if you are to be truly independent. Until you accept them, you can be manipulated, dominated, and controlled; after you accept them, you can resist. You can see through the false promises and vague hints about "the great things we have planned for your future" and avoid the dead end that comes to so many people who believe them. You can turn down the transfer to the Oshkosh office if you don't want to live in Oshkosh. You can listen without feeling guilty to the executive recruiters. You can bluntly ask your boss for a raise, based not on your needs (because he doesn't really care about your financial problems), but on your value, including your value to other firms. You can insist that your superiors spell out their future plans for you instead of making vague promises and hints. In other words, you can act freely and in good conscience for your own interests.

3. *Analyze your own goals.* An intelligent career strategy obviously requires a clear understanding of your own goals. If you don't know what you want, you obviously can't get it. If you don't understand your own goals, you can't work toward them. Unfortunately, relatively few people ever carefully analyze their own goals; they simply accept the goals that other people say they *should want* instead of determining what they *do want*. Then, if they do succeed in reaching these goals, they may find that their success is meaningless and empty because it does not provide the satisfaction they anticipated.

The American emphasis upon material success creates many such problems. We are told that we *should want to get ahead*, that we *should want a lot of money*, that we *should try for the top*. For some people these are meaningful goals, but not for everyone. Many of you would be a lot happier if you would honestly face up to the fact that you are not the most ambitious person in the world, that you really don't like a lot of pressure, that you want a lot of time for yourself, that money is not that important to you, that your family means more to you than your job, etc. I am not saying here that the traditional goals of a business career are incorrect; I am simply saying that they are not correct for everyone.

---

[8] W. R. Dill, T. L. Hilton, and W. R. Reitman, "How Aspiring Managers Promote Their Own Careers," *California Management Review*, Vol. 2, No. 4 (1960), 9–15.

If, in fact, you are primarily concerned with material success, with reaching the top of the pyramid, I have no objection whatsoever. A major purpose of this article is to help you get there. But, if you want something else from your career, it is best that you not kid yourself. If you really want to spend a lot of time with your family, if you are attracted to your present neighborhood and advancement would require that you change it, if you don't like playing politics or business socializing, it is best that you realize it now and take a job which will satisfy the goals that you really have. Otherwise, you may waste your life seeking things that cannot satisfy you.

ANALYZE YOUR GOALS

A complete analysis of your goals is probably not possible without professional assistance, but you can greatly increase your understanding of them by asking yourself a series of fairly specific questions, writing down the answers, and looking for patterns in these answers. Talking over your answers with your wife, a friend, or a minister can be very helpful. Ask yourself this kind of question and don't be embarrassed or discouraged if you can't give a complete or logical answer. Acquiring self-knowledge is always a slow process.

- If you could have any job that you wanted, what job would you take?
- How important is making a lot of money to you?
- How much income do you want?
- How much income does your wife want?

. . . .

- Do you really want to do executive work (not lead an executive's life)? That is, do you want to do things by motivating, directing, and controlling other people, or would you prefer a job in which you worked on your own or advised people?
- In what size firm would you prefer to work?
- For what company would you like to work?
- Would you rather work in a company where most decisions are made by individuals or by committees?
- Would you rather have a secure job or one in which you could "sink or swim"?
- Would you rather work independently in an unstructured situation or have clear guidelines from above?

. . . .

- Where do you want to work and live?
- What price are you willing to pay to get ahead?
- What price is your wife willing to pay?
- Are you willing to drop old friends as you go upward?
- How many hours a week do you want to work?
- Are you willing to spend a lot of time away from home on company travel?
- Are you willing to play politics?

TWO KEY QUESTIONS

These and many other specific questions should cover enough areas so that you can ultimately answer the two key questions related to overall career goals; again, I suggest that you write out your answers.

- There are many factors to be considered for any career choice (e.g., duties, titles, income, superiors, location, firm, travel, etc.). Which factors are important to you, and how important is each factor?
- What do you really want to do with your career?

4. *Analyze your assets and liabilities.* It is not enough to understand your goals; you must also understand the assets which will help you reach them and the liabilities which will hold you back. You wouldn't even try to make a company's future plans without a clear understanding of its assets and liabilities, and you obviously can't plan your own career without a similar understanding. Unfortunately, analyzing your personal assets and liabilities is much more difficult than analyzing a company's. A business generally has standardized accounting procedures for measuring its assets and liabilities, and they can be made directly comparable to each other by converting them into dollars. A person's assets and liabilities are usually very hard to measure and cannot be compared directly with each other. For example, it is nearly impossible to say how much intelligence compensates for the lack of a college degree or how much a proved record of success compensates for the fact that a man is over fifty.

Even though you can't make a completely accurate estimate of your personal assets and liabilities, you can greatly increase your understanding of them by using the same general technique that is used to analyze personal goals: ask yourself a large number of specific questions and look for patterns in the answers. Since most of us have rather biased opinions of ourselves, the help of another person (particularly a trained specialist[9]) can be invaluable but is not absolutely necessary.

Ask yourself this kind of question and, again, don't be embarrassed or discouraged if you can't give a complete or logical answer. Even an incomplete or somewhat illogical answer can improve your self-understanding.

- How intelligent are you? (The important comparison for intelligence and all other assets and liabilities is not with the general population, but with the people with whom you are competing for jobs, promotions, and raises. You are probably not competing with average men and must therefore compare yourself with your competitors rather than with the general public.)
- How does your income progress compare with the progress of other people in your firm?
- How does it compare with other people your age in other firms?
- Do you have favorable contacts in your firm?
- Do you have favorable contacts in other firms?
- How do your social skills compare with your competitors'?

. . . .

- Do you have all of the necessary credentials for the jobs you want (degrees,

---

[9] Many of the people and organizations which offer this assistance are unqualified, overpriced, or unethical. The best way to get this assistance is to contact a university testing service or psychology department.

certificates, proper experience, the right social and religious background, etc.)?

- If not, can you acquire these credentials?
- How valuable is your experience to your firm?
- How valuable is your experience to another firm?
- How valuable will it be in the future?

Answering these and similar questions should help you decide how realistic your ambitions are and what steps you must take to make the best use of your assets and minimize the effects of your liabilities.

5. *Analyze your opportunities.* Normally, the word "opportunity" refers primarily or entirely to the chances for advancement, but here it is used to refer to your chances of reaching your goals, regardless of what these goals may be. If you want to move into top management, the word "opportunity" refers to your chances of doing so; if you want a lower-pressure job, or one with more satisfying work, more regular hours, less company travel, etc., the word "opportunity" refers to your chances of reaching these goals.

Make as cold-blooded an analysis of your real opportunities as possible. Determine as carefully, systematically, and unemotionally as you can the opportunities you really have to reach your goals in your own or another firm. It is usually very hard to make this analysis, because most firms are quite dishonest about the opportunities which they really offer; they try to create the impression of a much better situation than really exists. Fortunately, there are other sources of information than interviews with recruiters, personnel managers, and your superiors (published data, stock analysts, friends, management consultants, personal observations, etc.). Using these other sources of information in a systematic way can result in a much clearer understanding of your real opportunities than you have now. You can use the same general technique here as in the other analyses, answering many specific questions and then looking for patterns to answer the key questions. You need to know the answers to such questions as:

- How rapidly is your industry growing?
- How profitable is your industry compared to other industries?
- How well does your industry pay compared to other industries?
- What would be the effect upon your industry of a great decrease in military or governmental spending?
- How does the growth of your firm compare to the growth of the rest of the industry?
- How profitable is your company compared to the rest of the industry?
- How well does your company pay?
- How many new products has your firm introduced in the past ten years?

. . . .

- How much agreement is there between your goals and values and official and unofficial company policy and practices?
- How many people have moved upward from your unit or present job to higher management?
- Is your boss promotable?
- Does your boss want to help you get ahead?
- Do your superiors want to help you get ahead?
- How many people who are important to your future do you normally contact on your job?

- How much has your income increased since you joined the firm?
- How many real promotions have you had?
- How high do you think you have a reasonable chance of going in your firm?

YOUR OPPORTUNITIES

Answering these and many similar questions should help you answer the four key questions:

- Should you stay in your present job?
- Should you look for another job with your current firm?
- Should you look for a job in another firm?
- Which firms or industries should you consider?

6. *Learn the rules of company politics.* For centuries political scientists have recognized the distinction between techniques for acquiring power (the art of politics) and techniques for using it wisely (the art of government) and, as even the most casual examination of any government clearly reveals, the masters of politics, not the masters of government, have most of the power. Unfortunately, this distinction is rarely made in the business world, despite the abundant evidence that many executives got their jobs for reasons other than their competence and performance.

Of course, doing your job well will probably help your career, but it will not guarantee that you will get the job that you want or that you will be properly rewarded for your work. In fact, good performance may not have much effect on your career at all because it is usually very difficult or impossible to say how good a job a manager is doing. A worker's performance can often be rated on several fairly objective criteria such as number of units produced per hour or amount of scrap, but a manager's performance can very rarely be judged as accurately or objectively.[10]

Therefore, a manager's pay, performance ratings, advancement, and all other aspects of his career are very dependent upon his superiors' opinion of him and his work, opinions which are influenced by many factors besides performance. In a word, a manager's career depends upon politics.

You may dislike the fact that your career depends upon politics, but you cannot escape it. Politics exist in every department and in every organization, particularly at the managerial and executive levels. The only way you can completely avoid politics is to leave executive life.

The question, then, is not *whether* you get involved in politics, but *how you get involved and what kind of politics you get involved in*. Here again there is no substitute for a thorough analysis, both of yourself and your situation. You have to decide what kind of political role you are willing and able to play and what effect your particular style of politics will have on your career in your current or another job. To do so you have to understand yourself and the rules of the political games in your own or any organization you are considering joining. There are really several sets of rules in each organization or department, rules for getting ahead quickly, rules for surviving quietly, etc. After you understand these rules, you have to decide whether you want to play according to them or

[10] *Performance Appraisal: Research and Practice*, eds. T. L. Whisler and S. F. Harper. New York: Holt, 1962. Many of the articles in this book discuss this problem.

whether you should go elsewhere to find a game more to your liking. And, once you understand the games and have selected one, you can play it more effectively. You can obviously do better if you know what the rules are, how points are really scored, how evaluations are really made, how people really get ahead, etc.

POWER POLITICS

To understand the politics in any department or organization, you must determine two things:

- Who has the real power (especially the power to influence your career)?
- How do they make their decisions (especially decisions related to your career)?

Once you know who has the power to influence your career and how they decide to use that power, you can evaluate your own situation and take steps to improve it. You can leave, "play it cool," try to build good relationships with the right people, etc.

7. *Plan your career*. Although these analyses can be time-consuming and even annoying, they make it possible for you to do something that very few men ever do—to plan your career—to decide where you are going and how you are going to get there. Successful businessmen nearly always plan for the future of their firms, but very few men plan their careers. They take a job and then let inertia and their emotions take over. They may stay at that job long after they should have quit or change jobs prematurely or for irrational reasons. They rarely have an overall concept of where they are going and how they are going to get there. They are, therefore, rarely successful (defining success in terms of reaching all of their goals rather than just their monetary and advancement goals). . . .

Index